· Bartholomew ·
MINI ATLAS
WORLD

· Bartholomew ·

MINI ATLAS
WORLD

Bartholomew

An Imprint of HarperCollins*Publishers*

Bartholomew Mini Atlas World

Bartholomew
An Imprint of HarperCollins*Publishers*
77-85 Fulham Palace Road, Hammersmith, London W6 8JB

First published 1991
Revised 1992, 1993, 1995

The contents of this edition of the Bartholomew Mini Atlas World are believed
correct at the time of printing. Nevertheless the publisher can accept no responsibility
for errors or omissions, changes in the detail given or for any expense or loss thereby
caused.

Printed in Great Britain by The Edinburgh Press Limited.

ISBN 0 7028 2966 8 (Paperback)
ISBN 0 7028 2965 X (Deluxe hardback)

HH8013

CONTENTS

ix–xxiii	World Factfile
xxiv–xxv	World Physical
xxvi–xxvii	World Political
xxviii–xxix	World Time Zones
xxx–xxxi	World Environment
xxxii	Key to Symbols
1	Arctic Ocean
2–3	North America
4–5	Canada, West
6–7	Canada, East
8–9	USA, West
10–11	USA, East
12	USA, Alaska
13	Canada Pacific
14–15	Lower Canada, USA North-East
16	Washington – New York – Boston
17	USA, South-East
18–19	USA, South-Central
20	USA, Pacific NW
21	USA, Pacific S
22	San Francisco & Los Angeles
23	Central Mexico
24–25	Mexico & Central America
26–27	Caribbean
28	South America
29	South America, South
30	South America, Central
31	South America, NE

32-33	South America, North
34	Central Argentina
35	South-East Brazil
36-37	Europe
38-39	Scandinavia
40-41	British Isles
42-43	England & Wales
44	Scotland, North
45	Ireland
46	Paris - Brussels - Ruhr
47	Alps
48-49	France
50-51	Spain & Portugal
52-53	Italy
54-55	The Balkans
56-57	Germany & Austria
58-59	East-Central Europe
60-61	European Russia, Ukraine & Baltic States
62	North Asia
63	Russian Federation, East
64-65	Russian Federation, West
66-67	South Asia
68-69	East Asia
70-71	South-East Asia
72-73	Central China
74	Japan & Korea
75	Central Japan
76-77	Indo-China & Singapore

Index

WORLD FACTFILE

Abbreviations List

Fr. Franc	French Franc
Fr.	French
Eng.	English
Ger.	German
Ital.	Italian
EC Dollar	Eastern Caribbean Dollar

Fed. Const. Mon.	Federal Constitutional Monarchy
Fed. of Emirates	Federation of Emirates
Fed. Islamic Rep.	Federal Islamic Republic
Soc. People's Rep.	Socialist People's Republic
People's Soc. Rep.	People's Socialist Republic
Const. Monarchy	Constitutional Monarchy
Parl. State	Parliamentary State

The statistics on the following pages are from the latest available sources including UN data.

The Factfile shows capital city names in their English form. In the Atlas, capital city names are in the local form.

Flag	COUNTRY	Status	Area (sq km)	Population ('000)	Capital City
	Afghanistan	Republic	652 225	20 547	Kabul
	Albania	Republic	28 750	3 338	Tirana
	Algeria	Republic	2 381 745	27 070	Algiers
	Andorra	Principality	465	62	Andorra la Vell
	Angola	Republic	1 246 700	10 276	Luanda
	Antigua & Barbuda	Const. Monarchy	442	62	St John's
	Argentina	Federal Republic	2 777 815	33 778	Buenos Aires
	Armenia	Republic	29 800	3 732	Yerevan
	Australia	Federal State	7 682 300	17 662	Canberra
	Austria	Federal Republic	83 855	7 988	Vienna
	Azerbaijan	Republic	86 600	7 392	Baku
	The Bahamas	Const. Monarchy	13 865	269	Nassau
	Bahrain	Monarchy	661	539	Manama
	Bangladesh	Republic	144 000	122 210	Dhaka
	Barbados	Const. Monarchy	430	260	Bridgetown
	Belarus (Belorussia)	Republic	208 000	10 353	Minsk
	Belgium	Const. Monarchy	30 520	10 068	Brussels
	Belize	Const. Monarchy	22 965	205	Belmopan
	Benin	Republic	112 620	5 215	Porto-Novo (de fa
	Bhutan	Const. Monarchy	46 620	1 650	Thimphu
	Bolivia	Republic	1 098 575	7 065	La Paz
	Bosnia-Herzegovina	Republic	51 130	4 422	Sarajevo
	Botswana	Republic	600 372	1 443	Gaborone
	Brazil	Federal Republic	8 511 965	151 534	Brasília
	Brunei	Monarchy	5 765	276	Bandar Seri Bega
	Bulgaria	Republic	110 910	8 469	Sofia
	Burkina	Republic	274 200	9 682	Ouagadougou

Main Languages	Main Religions	Currency	GNP (US$)
...shtu, Dari	Sunni Muslim	Afghani	250
...banian	Muslim	Lek	1200
...abic	Sunni Muslim	Dinar	2170
...talan	Roman Catholic	Fr. Franc , Span. Peseta	16600
...rtuguese	Roman Catholic	Kwanza	620
...glish	Protestant	EC Dollar	2800
...anish	Roman Catholic	Austral	2160
...menian	Orthodox	Dram	9211
...glish	Protestant, Roman Catholic	Dollar	14440
...rman	Roman Catholic	Schilling	17360
...erbaijani	Shi'a Muslim	Manat	9211
...glish	Protestant	Dollar	10570
...abic	Muslim	Dinar	6360
...ngali	Muslim	Taka	180
...glish	Protestant	Dollar	6370
...lorussian	Orthodox	Belo. Rouble (Rubel)	9211
...nch, Dutch	Roman Catholic	Franc	16390
...glish	Roman Catholic	Dollar	1600
...nch	Traditional	CFA Franc	380
...ongkha	Buddhist	Indian Rupee, Ngultrum	190
...anish	Roman Catholic	Boliviano	600
...rbo-Croat	Muslim, Orthodox, Rom.Cath.	Dinar	2490
...glish, Tswana	Traditional	Pula	940
...rtuguese	Roman Catholic	Real	2550
...lay	Muslim	Dollar	14120
...garian	Orthodox	Lev	2320
...nch	Traditional, Muslim	CFA Franc	310

Flag	COUNTRY	Status	Area (sq km)	Population ('000)	Capital City
	Burundi	Republic	27 834	5 958	Bujumbura
	Cambodia	Kingdom	181 000	9 308	Phnom Penh
	Cameroon	Republic	475 500	12 547	Yaoundé
	Canada	Federal State	9 970 610	28 436	Ottawa
	Cape Verde	Republic	4 035	395	Praia
	Central African Rep.	Republic	624 975	3 258	Bangui
	Chad	Republic	1 284 000	6 098	Ndjamena
	Chile	Republic	751 625	13 813	Santiago
	China	People's Republic	9 579 000	1 205 181	Beijing
	Colombia	Republic	1 138 915	33 951	Bogotá
	Comoros	Fed. Islamic Rep.	1 860	607	Moroni
	Congo	Republic	342 000	2 441	Brazzaville
	Costa Rica	Republic	50 900	3 199	San José
	Côte d'Ivoire (Ivory Coast)	Republic	322 465	13 397	Yamoussoukro
	Croatia	Republic	56 540	4 821	Zagreb
	Cuba	Soc. People's Rep.	114 525	10 905	Havana
	Cyprus	Republic	9 250	723	Nicosia
	Czech Republic	Republic	78 863	10 328	Prague
	Denmark	Const. Monarchy	43 075	5 189	Copenhagen
	Djibouti	Republic	23 000	481	Djibouti
	Dominica	Republic	751	72	Roseau
	Dominican Rep.	Republic	48 440	7 608	Santo Domingo
	Ecuador	Republic	461 475	10 981	Quito
	Egypt	Republic	1 000 250	56 488	Cairo
	El Salvador	Republic	21 395	5 517	San Salvador
	Equatorial Guinea	Republic	28 050	379	Malabo
	Eritrea	Republic	93 679	3 421	Asmara

Main Languages	Main Religions	Currency	GNP (US$)
ench, Kirundi	Roman Catholic	Franc	220
mer	Buddhist	Riel	130
ench, English	Roman Catholic	CFA Franc	1010
glish, French	Rom.Cath.,Prot.,East.Orthodox	Dollar	19020
rtuguese	Roman Catholic	Escudo	760
nch, Sango	Traditional	CFA Franc	390
nch, Arabic	Muslim	CFA Franc	190
anish	Roman Catholic	Peso	1770
andarin	Confucion, Buddhist	Yuan	360
anish	Roman Catholic	Peso	1190
abic, French	Muslim	CFA Franc	460
nch	Traditional	CFA Franc	930
anish	Roman Catholic	Colón	1790
nch	Muslim, Roman Catholic	CFA Franc	790
rbo-Croat	Roman Catholic	Kuna	2490
anish	Roman Catholic	Peso	2000
eek	Greek Orthodox, Muslim	Pound	7050
ech	Roman Catholic	Koruna	3140
nish	Protestant	Krone	20510
nch, Somali	Muslim	Franc	1070
glish, French	Roman Catholic	EC Dollar	1650
anish	Roman Catholic	Peso	790
anish	Roman Catholic	Sucre	1040
abic	Muslim	Pound	630
anish	Roman Catholic	Colón	1040
anish	Roman Catholic	CFA Franc	430
., Arabic, Tigrinya	Christian, Muslim	Ethiopian Birr	120

Flag	COUNTRY	Status	Area (sq km)	Population ('000)	Capital City
	Estonia	Republic	45 100	1 517	Tallinn
	Ethiopia	Republic	1 128 221	56 900	Addis Ababa
	Fiji	Republic	18 330	747	Suva
	Finland	Republic	337 030	5 067	Helsinki
	France	Republic	543 965	57 660	Paris
	Gabon	Republic	267 665	1 012	Libreville
	The Gambia	Republic	10 690	1 026	Banjul
	Georgia	Republic	69 700	5 493	Tbilisi
	Germany	Federal Republic	357 868	81 187	Berlin (de jure)
	Ghana	Military Regime	238 305	16 446	Accra
	Greece	Republic	131 985	10 350	Athens
	Grenada	Const. Monarchy	345	92	St. George's
	Guatemala	Republic	108 890	10 029	Guatemala City
	Guinea	Military Regime	254 855	6 306	Conakry
	Guinea-Bissau	Republic	36 125	1 028	Bissau
	Guyana	Republic	214 970	816	Georgetown
	Haiti	Republic	27 750	6 903	Port-au-Prince
	Honduras	Republic	112 085	5 595	Tegucigalpa
	Hungary	Republic	93 030	10 294	Budapest
	Iceland	Republic	102 820	263	Reykjavik
	India	Federal Republic	3 166 830	896 567	New Delhi
	Indonesia	Republic	1 919 445	189 136	Jakarta
	Iran	Islamic Republic	1 684 000	63 180	Tehran
	Iraq	Republic	438 445	19 918	Baghdad
	Republic of Ireland	Republic	68 895	3 563	Dublin
	Israel	Republic	20 770	5 256	Jerusalem
	Italy	Republic	301 245	57 057	Rome

ain nguages	Main Religions	Currency	GNP (US$)
⸱nian	Protestant	Kroon	9211
⸱haric	Orthodox	Birr	120
⸱lish, Fiji, Hindi	Christian, Hindu	Dollar	1640
⸱ish, Swedish	Protestant	Markka	22060
⸱nch	Roman Catholic	Franc	17830
⸱nch	Roman Catholic	CFA Franc	2770
⸱lish	Muslim	Dalasi	230
⸱rgian	Orthodox	Rouble	9211
⸱man	Protestant, Roman Catholic	Mark	20750
⸱ish	Christian	Cedi	380
⸱ek, Turkish	Orthodox	Drachma	5340
⸱lish	Roman Catholic	EC Dollar	1265
⸱nish	Roman Catholic	Quetzal	920
⸱nch	Muslim	Franc	430
⸱tuguese	Traditional, Muslim	Peso	180
⸱lish	Protestant, Hindu	Dollar	340
⸱nch, Creole	Roman Catholic	Gourde	400
⸱nish	Roman Catholic	Lempira	900
⸱garian	Roman Catholic	Forint	2560
⸱andic	Protestant	Króna	21240
⸱di, English	Hindu	Rupee	350
⸱asa Indonesia	Muslim	Rupiah	490
⸱sian	Shi'a Muslim	Rial	1800
⸱bic, Kurdish	Muslim	Dinar	1940
⸱lish, Irish	Roman Catholic	Punt	8500
⸱rew	Jewish	Shekel	9750
⸱an	Roman Catholic	Lira	15150

Flag	COUNTRY	Status	Area (sq km)	Population ('000)	Capital City
	Jamaica	Const. Monarchy	11 425	2 495	Kingston
	Japan	Const. Monarchy	369 700	124 959	Tokyo
	Jordan	Const. Monarchy	96 000	4 440	Amman
	Kazakhstan	Republic	2 717 300	16 956	Almaty
	Kenya	Republic	582 645	28 113	Nairobi
	Kiribati	Republic	684	75	Bairiki
	Kuwait	Const. Monarchy	24 280	1 433	Kuwait City
	Kyrgyzstan (Kirghizia)	Republic	198 500	4 528	Bishkek
	Laos	Republic	236 725	4 605	Vientiane
	Latvia	Republic	63 700	2 586	Riga
	Lebanon	Republic	10 400	2 901	Beirut
	Lesotho	Military Regime	30 345	1 882	Maseru
	Liberia	Republic	111 370	2 640	Monrovia
	Libya	Socialist State	1 759 540	4 700	Tripoli
	Liechtenstein	Const. Monarchy	160	28	Vaduz
	Lithuania	Republic	65 200	3 730	Vilnius
	Luxembourg	Const. Monarchy	2 585	380	Luxembourg
	Macedonia	Republic	25 713	2 060	Skopje
	Madagascar	Republic	594 180	13 259	Antananarivo
	Malawi	Republic	94 080	9 135	Lilongwe
	Malaysia	Fed. Const. Mon.	332 965	19 239	Kuala Lumpur
	Maldives	Republic	298	238	Male
	Mali	Republic	1 240 140	10 137	Bamako
	Malta	Republic	316	361	Valletta
	Marshall Islands	Republic	181	52	Dalap-Uliga-D
	Mauritania	Republic	1 030 700	2 206	Nouakchott
	Mauritius	Const. Monarchy	1 865	1 098	Port Louis

Main Languages	Main Religions	Currency	GNP (US$)
...glish	Protestant	Dollar	1260
...panese	Shintoist, Buddhist	Yen	23730
...abic	Sunni Muslim	Dinar	1730
...zakh	Sunni Muslim	Tanga	9211
...ahili, English	Roman Catholic, Protestant	Shilling	380
...glish	Protestant, Roman Catholic	Australian Dollar	650
...abic	Sunni Muslim	Dinar	16380
...ghiz	Sunni Muslim	Som	9211
...o	Buddhist	Kip	170
...vian	Protestant	Lat	9211
...abic	Muslim, Christian	Pound	690
...glish, Sesotho	Roman Catholic, Protestant	Loti	470
...glish	Christian	Dollar	450
...abic	Sunni Muslim	Dinar	5410
...rman	Roman Catholic	Swiss Franc	21000
...uanian	Roman Catholic	Litas	9211
...embourgian, Fr., Ger.	Roman Catholic	Franc	24860
...cedonian	Orthodox	Denar	2490
...lagasy, French	Christian, Traditional	Franc	230
...glish, Chichewa	Christian	Kwacha	180
...hasa Malay	Muslim	Ringgit	2130
...ehi	Sunni Muslim	Rufiyaa	410
...nch, Bambara	Sunni Muslim	CFA Franc	260
...ltese, English	Roman Catholic	Lira	5820
...rshallese, Eng.	Protestant	US Dollar	1500
...bic, French	Sunni Muslim	Ouguiya	490
...lish	Hindu	Rupee	1950

Flag	COUNTRY	Status	Area (sq km)	Population ('000)	Capital City
	Mexico	Federal Republic	1 972 545	91 261	Mexico City
	Micronesia	Republic	702	114	Palikir on Pohr
	Moldova (Moldavia)	Republic	33 700	4 356	Kishinev
	Monaco	Const. Monarchy	2	28	Monaco-Ville
	Mongolia	Republic	1 565 000	2 371	Ulan Bator
	Morocco	Const. Monarchy	446 550	26 069	Rabat
	Mozambique	Republic	784 755	15 322	Maputo
	Myanmar (Burma)	Military Regime	678 030	44 613	Rangoon
	Namibia	Republic	824 295	1 584	Windhoek
	Nauru	Republic	21	10	Yaren
	Nepal	Const. Monarchy	141 415	21 086	Kathmandu
	Netherlands	Const. Monarchy	41 160	15 287	Amsterdam (off
	New Zealand	Const. Monarchy	265 150	3 451	Wellington
	Nicaragua	Republic	148 000	4 265	Managua
	Niger	Republic	1 186 410	8 361	Niamey
	Nigeria	Federal Republic	923 850	119 328	Abuja
	North Korea	Socialist Republic	122 310	23 054	Pyongyang
	Norway	Const. Monarchy	323 895	4 312	Oslo
	Oman	Monarchy	271 950	1 697	Muscat
	Pakistan	Fed. Islamic Rep.	803 940	122 802	Islamabad
	Panama	Republic	78 515	2 535	Panama City
	Papua New Guinea	Const. Monarchy	462 840	3 922	Port Moresby
	Paraguay	Republic	406 750	4 643	Asunción
	Peru	Republic	1 285 215	22 454	Lima
	Philippines	Republic	300 000	65 649	Manila
	Poland	Republic	312 685	38 459	Warsaw
	Portugal	Parl. State	88 940	9 860	Lisbon

...ain ...nguages	Main Religions	Currency	GNP (US$)
...nish	Roman Catholic	Peso	1990
...lish	Christian	US$	1500
...manian	Orthodox	Leu	9211
...nch	Roman Catholic	French Franc	11350
...alka Mongol	Shamanist	Tugrik	470
...bic	Sunni Muslim	Dirham	900
...tuguese	Roman Catholic	Metical	80
...mese	Buddhist	Kyat	200
...ikaans, English	Protestant	Namibian Dollar	1245
...uruan, English	Christian	Australian Dollar	9091
...pali	Hindu	Rupee	170
...tch	Roman Catholic, Protestant	Guilder	16010
...lish, Maori	Protestant, Roman Catholic	Dollar	11800
...anish	Roman Catholic	Córdoba	800
...nch	Sunni Muslim	CFA Franc	290
...lish	Muslim, Christian	Naira	250
...ean	Shamanist	Won	1240
...rwegian	Protestant	Krone	21850
...bic	Muslim	Rial	5220
...du	Muslim	Rupee	370
...anish	Roman Catholic	Balboa	1780
...lish	Protestant, Roman Catholic	Kina	900
...anish, Guarani	Roman Catholic	Guaraní	1030
...anish, Quechua	Roman Catholic	Sol	1090
...ino, English	Roman Catholic	Peso	700
...ish	Roman Catholic	Złoty	1760
...rtuguese	Roman Catholic	Escudo	4260

Flag	COUNTRY	Status	Area (sq km)	Population ('000)	Capital City
	Qatar	Monarchy	11 435	559	Doha
	Romania	Republic	237 500	22 755	Bucharest
	Russian Federation	Republic	17 078 000	148 000	Moscow
	Rwanda	Republic	26 330	7 789	Kigali
	St Kitts-Nevis	Const. Monarchy	261	42	Basseterre
	St Lucia	Const. Monarchy	616	139	Castries
	St Vincent	Const. Monarchy	389	111	Kingstown
	Sao Tome & Principe	Republic	964	122	São Tomé
	Saudi Arabia	Monarchy	2 400 900	16 472	Riyadh
	Senegal	Republic	196 720	7 736	Dakar
	Seychelles	Republic	404	72	Victoria
	Sierra Leone	Republic	72 325	4 494	Freetown
	Singapore	Republic	616	2 874	Singapore
	Slovakia	Republic	49 036	5 318	Bratislava
	Slovenia	Republic	20 250	1 990	Ljubljana
	Solomon Islands	Const. Monarchy	29 790	354	Honiara
	Somalia	Republic	630 000	9 517	Mogadishu
	South Africa	Republic	1 184 825	40 774	Pretoria/Cape To
	South Korea	Republic	98 445	44 056	Seoul
	Spain	Const. Monarchy	504 880	39 143	Madrid
	Sri Lanka	Republic	65 610	17 619	Colombo
	Sudan	Military Regime	2 505 815	28 129	Khartoum
	Surinam	Republic	163 820	446	Paramaribo
	Swaziland	Monarchy	17 365	814	Mbabane
	Sweden	Const. Monarchy	449 790	8 716	Stockholm
	Switzerland	Federal State	41 285	6 938	Berne
	Syria	Republic	185 680	13 393	Damascus

ain nguages	Main Religions	Currency	GNP (US$)
bic	Muslim	Riyal	9920
nanian	Orthodox	Leu	3445
sian	Orthodox	Rouble	9211
yarwanda, Fr.	Roman Catholic	Franc	310
lish	Protestant	EC Dollar	2770
lish	Roman Catholic	EC Dollar	1540
lish	Protestant	EC Dollar	1100
tuguese	Roman Catholic	Dobra	280
bic	Sunni Muslim	Riyal	6230
nch	Sunni Muslim	CRA Franc	650
nch Creole	Roman Catholic	Rupee	3590
lish	Traditional, Sunni Muslim	Leone	200
hasa Malay	Taoist, Buddhist, Christian	Dollar	10450
vak	Roman Catholic	Koruna	3140
vene	Roman Catholic	Tólar	2490
lish	Protestant	Dollar	570
bic, Somali	Sunni Muslim	Shilling	170
kaans, English, tribal	Christian	Rand	2460
ean	Buddhist, Christian	Won	4400
nish	Roman Catholic	Peseta	9150
halese, Tamil	Buddhist, Hindu	Rupee	430
bic	Sunni Muslim	Pound	540
ch, English	Hindu, Roman Catholic	Guilder	3020
lish, SiSwati	Christian	Emalangeni (sing. Lilangeni)	900
edish	Protestant	Krona	21710
., Fr., Ital.	Roman Catholic, Protestant	Franc	30270
bic	Sunni Muslim	Pound	1100

Flag	COUNTRY	Status	Area (sq km)	Population ('000)	Capital City
	Taiwan	Republic	35 990	20 926	Taipei
	Tajikistan	Republic	143 100	5 705	Dushanbe
	Tanzania	Republic	939 760	28 783	Dodoma
	Thailand	Const. Monarchy	514 000	58 584	Bangkok
	Togo	Republic	56 785	3 885	Lomé
	Tonga	Const. Monarchy	699	98	Nuku'alofa
	Trinidad & Tobago	Republic	5 130	1 260	Port of Spain
	Tunisia	Republic	164 150	8 579	Tunis
	Turkey	Republic	779 450	60 227	Ankara
	Turkmenistan	Republic	488 100	4 294	Ashkhabad
	Tuvalu	Const. Monarchy	25	13	Funafuti
	Uganda	Republic	236 580	19 246	Kampala
	Ukraine	Republic	603 700	52 179	Kiev
	United Arab Emirates	Fed. of Emirates	75 150	1 206	Abu Dhabi
	United Kingdom	Const. Monarchy	244 755	57 826	London
	United States	Federal Republic	9 363 130	258 233	Washington
	Uruguay	Republic	186 925	3 149	Montevideo
	Uzbekistan	Republic	447 400	21 901	Tashkent
	Vanuatu	Republic	14 765	156	Port-Vila
	Venezuela	Federal Republic	912 045	20 712	Caracas
	Vietnam	People's Soc. Rep.	329 565	70 902	Hanoi
	Western Samoa	Const. Monarchy	2 840	158	Apia
	Yemen	Republic	481 155	12 302	Sana
	Yugoslavia	Federal Republic	127 885	10 485	Belgrade
	Zaire	Republic	2 345 410	41 166	Kinshasa
	Zambia	Republic	752 615	8 885	Lusaka
	Zimbabwe	Republic	390 310	10 898	Harare

ain nguages	Main Religions	Currency	GNP (US$)
ndarin	Buddhist, Taoist	Dollar	7990
ik	Sunni Muslim	Rouble	9211
ahili, English	Christian, Muslim	Shilling	120
ai	Buddhist	Baht	1170
nch	Traditional	CFA Franc	390
glish, Tongan	Protestant	Pa'anga	800
glish	Roman Catholic, Hindu	Dollar	3160
abic	Sunni Muslim	Dinar	1260
rkish	Sunni Muslim	Lira	1360
rkmenian	Sunni Muslim	Manat	9211
glish, Tuvaluan	Protestant	Dollar	500
ahili, English	Roman Catholic	Shilling	250
rainian, Russian	Orthodox	Karbovanets	9211
abic	Sunni Muslim	Dirham	18430
glish	Protestant, Roman Catholic	Pound	14570
glish	Protestant, Roman Catholic	Dollar	21100
anish	Roman Catholic	Uruguayan Peso	2620
bek	Sunni Muslim	Som	9211
g., Fr., Bislama	Christian	Vatu	820
anish	Roman Catholic	Bolívar	2450
etnamese	Buddhist	Dong	215
moan, English	Protestant	Tala	580
abic	Muslim	Rial, Dinar	745
rbo-Croat	Orthodox, Rom. Cath., Muslim	Dinar	2490
nch, Lingala	Roman Catholic	New Zaïre	260
glish	Christian	Kwacha	390
glish	Christian, Traditional	Dollar	640

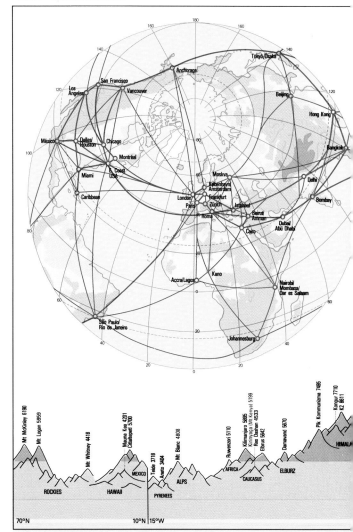

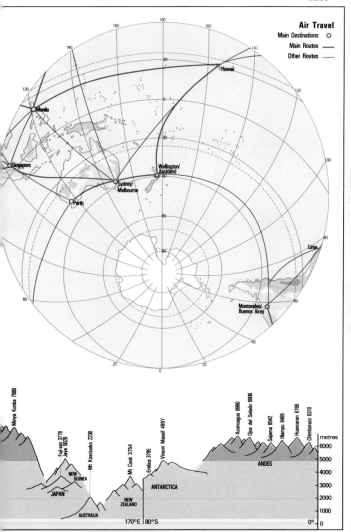

Air Travel

Main Destinations ○
Main Routes ━━━
Other Routes ───

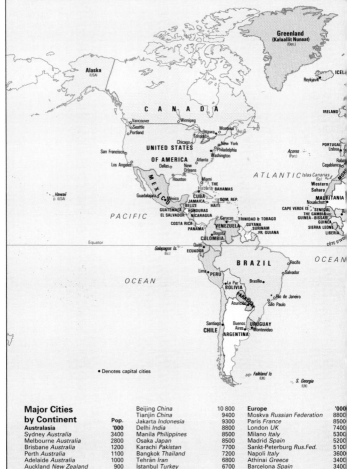

• Denotes capital cities

Major Cities by Continent

Australasia	Pop. '000
Sydney *Australia*	3400
Melbourne *Australia*	2800
Brisbane *Australia*	1200
Perth *Australia*	1100
Adelaide *Australia*	1000
Auckland *New Zealand*	900

Asia	'000
Tōkyō *Japan*	18 100
Shanghai *China*	13 400
Calcutta *India*	11 800
Bombay *India*	11 200
Sŏul *South Korea*	11 000
Beijing *China*	10 800
Tianjin *China*	9400
Jakarta *Indonesia*	9300
Delhi *India*	8800
Manila *Philippines*	8500
Osaka *Japan*	8500
Karachi *Pakistan*	7700
Bangkok *Thailand*	7200
Tehrān *Iran*	6800
Istanbul *Turkey*	6700
Dhākā *Bangladesh*	6600
Madras *India*	5700
Hong Kong *Hong Kong*	5400
Bangalore *India*	5000
Shenyang *China*	4800
Lahore *Pakistan*	4100

Europe	'000
Moskva *Russian Federation*	8800
Paris *France*	8500
London *UK*	7400
Milano *Italy*	5300
Madrid *Spain*	5200
Sankt-Peterburg *Rus.Fed.*	5100
Napoli *Italy*	3600
Athinai *Greece*	3400
Barcelona *Spain*	3400
Berlin *Germany*	3200
Roma *Italy*	3100
Kiyev *Ukraine*	2600
Birmingham *UK*	2300
Manchester *UK*	2300
Bucureşti *Romania*	2200

North and Central America	'000	South America	'000	Africa	'000
México *Mexico*	20 200	São Paulo *Brazil*	17 400	Cairo *Egypt*	9000
New York *USA*	16 200	Buenos Aires *Argentina*	11 500	Lagos *Nigeria*	7700
Los Angeles *USA*	11 900	Rio de Janeiro *Brazil*	10 700	Alexandria *Egypt*	3700
Chicago *USA*	7000	Lima *Peru*	6200	Kinshasa *Zaire*	3500
Philadelphia *USA*	4300	Santiago *Chile*	5000	Casablanca *Morocco*	3200
Detroit *USA*	3700	Bogotá *Colombia*	4900	Alger *Algeria*	3000
San Francisco *USA*	3700	Caracas *Venezuela*	4100	Cape Town *South Africa*	2300
Toronto *Canada*	3500	Belo Horizonte *Brazil*	3600	Abidjan *Côte d'Ivoire*	2200
Dallas *USA*	3400	Pôrto Alegre *Brazil*	3100	Tarābulus *Libya*	2100
Guadalajara *Mexico*	3200	Recife *Brazil*	2500	Adis Abeba *Ethiopia*	1900
Houston *USA*	3000	Brasília *Brazil*	2400	Khartoum *Sudan*	1900
Monterrey *Mexico*	3000	Salvador *Brazil*	2400	Dar es Salaam *Tanzania*	1700
Montréal *Canada*	3000	Fortaleza *Brazil*	2100	Johannesburg *South Africa*	1700
Washington *USA*	2900	Curitiba *Brazil*	2000	Luanda *Angola*	1700
Boston *USA*	2800	Guayaquil *Ecuador*	1700	Maputo *Mozambique*	1600

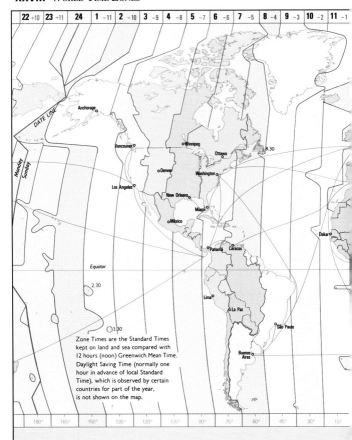

22 +10	23 +11	24	1 −11	2 −10	3 −9	4 −8	5 −7	6 −6	7 −5	8 −4	9 −3	10 −2	11 −1

DATE LINE

Monday
Sunday

Anchorage

Vancouver
Winnipeg
Ottawa
8.30

Denver
Washington

Los Angeles

New Orleans

Miami

México

Dakar

Panama
Caracas

Equator

2.30

Lima

La Paz

São Paulo

3.30

Zone Times are the Standard Times
kept on land and sea compared with
12 hours (noon) Greenwich Mean Time.
Daylight Saving Time (normally one
hour in advance of local Standard
Time), which is observed by certain
countries for part of the year,
is not shown on the map.

Buenos
Aires

180°	165°	150°	135°	120°	105°	90°	75°	60°	45°	30°	15°

Journey Times

Sail (via Cape)
164 days

Steam (via Cape)
43 days

Steam (via Suez)
30 days

Supertanker
(via Cape)
28 days

Singapore ⟵

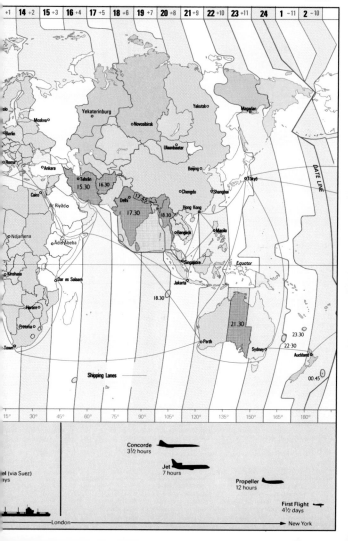

+1	**14** +2	**15** +3	**16** +4	**17** +5	**18** +6	**19** +7	**20** +8	**21** +9	**22** +10	**23** +11	**24**	**1** −11	**2** −10

Moskva
Berlin
Roma
Ankara
Cairo
Ar Riyād
Ndjamena
Adis Abeba
Kinshasa
Dar es Salaam
Harare
Pretoria
Town

Yekaterinburg
Novosibirsk
Ulaanbaatar
Tehrān 15.30
16.30
Delhi 17.45
17.30
18.30
Bangkok
Singapore
Jakarta 18.30
Perth

Yakutsk
Magadan
Beijing
Chengdu
Shanghai
Hong Kong
Manila
Tōkyō

Equator

21.30
Sydney 22.30
Auckland
23.30
00.45

DATE LINE

Shipping Lanes ——

| 15° | 30° | 45° | 60° | 75° | 90° | 105° | 120° | 135° | 150° | 165° | 180° |

Concorde
3½ hours

Jet
7 hours

Propeller
12 hours

First Flight
4½ days

el (via Suez)
ays

——London——
New York →

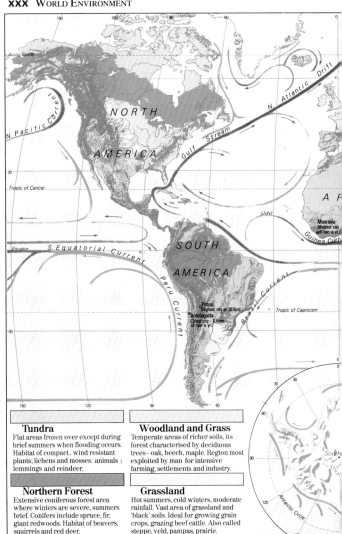

Tundra
Flat areas frozen over except during brief summers when flooding occurs. Habitat of compact, wind resistant plants; lichens and mosses: animals : lemmings and reindeer.

Northern Forest
Extensive coniferous forest area where winters are severe, summers brief. Conifers include spruce, fir, giant redwoods. Habitat of beavers, squirrels and red deer.

Woodland and Grass
Temperate areas of richer soils, its forest characterised by deciduous trees - oak, beech, maple. Region most exploited by man for intensive farming, settlements and industry.

Grassland
Hot summers, cold winters, moderate rainfall. Vast area of grassland and 'black' soils. Ideal for growing grain crops, grazing beef cattle. Also called steppe, veld, pampas, prairie.

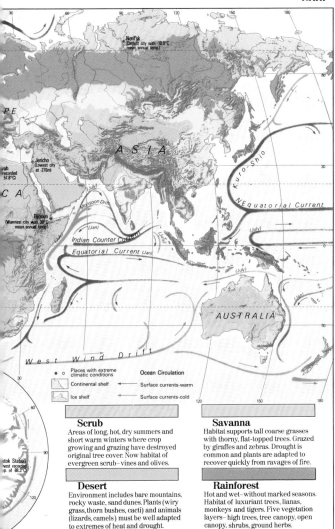

Norilsk
(Coldest city with -10.9°C
mean annual temp.)

ASIA

Jericho
(Lowest city
at -270m)

...rah
...corded
57.8°C

Djibouti
(Warmest city with 30°C
mean annual temp.)

Kuro-Shio

N Equatorial Current

(July)

(July)

Monsoon Drift

(Jan)

(July)

Indian Counter Current

(Jan)

Equatorial Current (Jan)

(Jan)

(July)

(July)

AUSTRALIA

(Jan)

West Wind Drift

...stok Station
...west recorded
...p. of 88.3°C)

Places with extreme
climatic conditions

Continental shelf

Ice shelf

Ocean Circulation

→ Surface currents-warm

→ Surface currents-cold

Scrub

Areas of long, hot, dry summers and
short warm winters where crop
growing and grazing have destroyed
original tree cover. Now habitat of
evergreen scrub – vines and olives.

Savanna

Habitat supports tall coarse grasses
with thorny, flat-topped trees. Grazed
by giraffes and zebras. Drought is
common and plants are adapted to
recover quickly from ravages of fire.

Desert

Environment includes bare mountains,
rocky waste, sand dunes. Plants (wiry
grass, thorn bushes, cacti) and animals
(lizards, camels) must be well adapted
to extremes of heat and drought.

Rainforest

Hot and wet – without marked seasons.
Habitat of luxuriant trees, lianas,
monkeys and tigers. Five vegetation
layers – high trees, tree canopy, open
canopy, shrubs, ground herbs.

BOUNDARIES

	International
	International under Dispute
	Cease Fire Line
	Autonomous or State
	Administrative
	Maritime (National)

LETTERING STYLES

CANADA	Independent Nation
FLORIDA	State, Province or Autonomous Region
Gibraltar (U.K.)	Sovereignty of Dependent Territory
Lothian	Administrative Area
LANGUEDOC	Historic Region
Loire **Vosges**	Physical Feature or Physical Region

TOWNS AND CITIES

Square Symbols denote capital cities. Each settlement is given a symbol according to its relative importance, with type size to match.

■	●	**New York**	Major City
■	●	**Montréal**	City
□	○	Ottawa	Small City
■	●	**Québec**	Large Town
□	○	St John's	Town
□	○	Yorkton	Small Town
□	○	Jasper	Village
			Built-up-area

LAKE FEATURES

	Permanent
	Seasonal

OTHER FEATURES

	River
	Seasonal River
=	Pass, Gorge
	Dam, Barrage
	Waterfall, Rapid
	Aqueduct
	Reef
▲ 4237	Summit, Peak
.217	Spot Height, Depth
⌣	Well
⌂	Oil Field
▲	Gas Field
Gas / Oil	Oil/Natural Gas Pipeline
Gemsbok Nat Pk	National Park
∴ UR	Historic Site
	Main Railway
	Other Railway
--------	Under Construction
⊢----⊣	Rail Tunnel
---------	Rail Ferry
	Canal
⊕	International Airport
↑	Other Airport

For pages 102-103, 104-105 only:

0	Sea Level
200m	
2000m	
4000m	
6000m	
	Depth

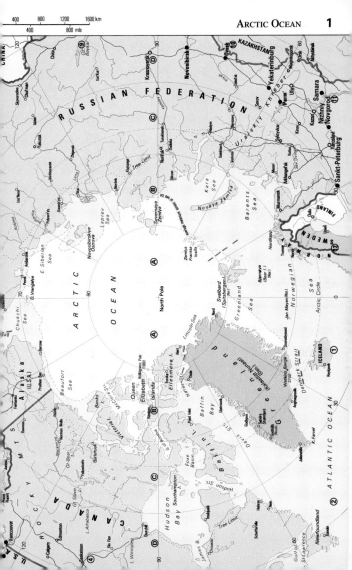

Sverdrup Islands

ARCTIC OCEAN

Prince of Wales Island

Peel Sound

Bathurst Island

Melville Island

Viscount Melville Sound

McClintock Channel

King William

Gjoahaven

Adelaide Pen.

Pelly Bay

BAFFIN ISLAND

PARRY ISLANDS

Prince Patrick I.

McClure Strait

Banks Island

Victoria Island

Kitikmeot

Cambridge Bay

Queen Maud Gulf

Bathurst Inlet

NORTHWEST TERRITORIES

Prince Albert Pen.

Amundsen Gulf

Prince Albert

Holman Island

Coronation Gulf

Dolphin and Union Str.

Great Bear Lake

Fort Smith

BEAUFORT SEA

Mackenzie

Franklin Mts

Mackenzie Mountains

Richardson Mts

Selwyn Mountains

British Mts

YUKON TERRITORY

Ogilvie Mts

Pelly Mts

Cassiar

Brooks Range

Endicott Mts

Davidson Mts

Klondike

Whitehorse

CANADA

St. Elias Mts

Wrangell Mts

ALASKA

U.S.A.

Alaska Range

Mt. McKinley

Chugach Mts

Kenai Pen.

Cook Inlet

Gulf of Alaska

Kodiak Island

Seward Peninsula

Norton Sound

Bering Strait

RUS. FED.

St. Lawrence I.

Nome

Bethel

Kuskokwim

Yukon

Naknek

Point Barrow

Barrow

Wainwright

Prudhoe Bay

North Slope

Point Lay

C. Lisburne

Pt Hope

Kivalina

Kotzebue

Kotzebue Sound

Kobuk

Noatak

Fairbanks

Tanana

Delta

Kenai

Homer

Valdez

Cordova

Yakutat

Haines

Skagway

Juneau

100

ICELAND

Keflavik · Reykjavík
Borðeyri
Stykkishólmur
Varmur · Blönduós
Ísafjörður
Akureyri
Horn

DENMARK STRAIT

Kap Brewster
Kronprins Frederik Bjerge
Angmagssalik · Ammassalik
Kong Frederik VI Kyst
Kap Christian

Scoresbysund

Kong Christian IX Land

Knud Rasmussens Land

GREENLAND
(KALAALLIT NUNAAT)
(Denmark)

Arctic Circle

Nanortalik
Frederikshåb
Narssaq
Julianehåb

DAVIS STRAIT

Godthåb

Holsteinsborg

Egedesminde

Disko

Upernavik

BAFFIN BAY

Melville Bay

Smith Sound

Kane Basin

Washington Land

Ellesmere Island

QUEEN ELIZABETH ISLANDS

Axel Heiberg Island
Eureka
Sverdrup
Amund Ringnes Island
Ellef Ringnes Island
Grinnell Pen.
Graham I.
Bathurst Island
Cornwallis Island
Devon Island
PARRY ISLANDS
Melville Island
Prince Patrick Island
Byam Martin I.
Lancaster Sound
Barrow Strait
Prince of Wales Island
Somerset Island
Peel Sound
Boothia Peninsula

Jones Sound

Baffin Island

Bylot I.
Pond Inlet

Foxe Basin

Foxe Channel

Cumberland Sound

Cumberland Peninsula

Frobisher Bay

Hall Peninsula

Resolution I.

HUDSON STRAIT

Hall Beach
Igloolik

Prince Charles I.

Southampton Island

Coral Harbour

Roes Welcome Sound

Chesterfield Inlet

Baker Lake

Gulf of Boothia

King William Island

Gjoa Haven

Labrador Sea

Labrador

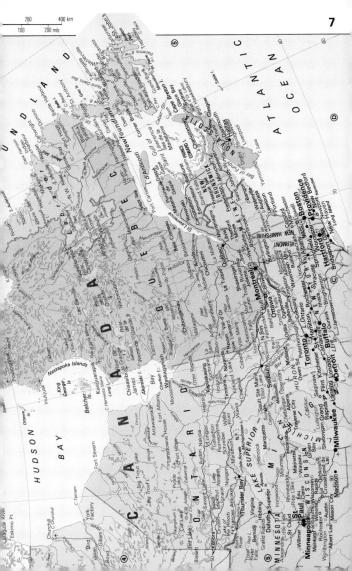

MANITOBA

SASKATCHEWAN

ALBERTA

BRITISH COLUMBIA

ROCKY MOUNTAINS

MONTANA

NORTH DAKOTA

SOUTH DAKOTA

MINNESOTA

IOWA

NEBRASKA

WYOMING

IDAHO

UTAH

NEVADA

OREGON

WASHINGTON

CALIFORNIA

Vancouver Island

Edmonton · Calgary · Regina · Saskatoon

Winnipeg

Bismarck · Fargo · Grand Forks · Aberdeen

Pierre · Rapid City · Sioux Falls

Billings · Great Falls · Helena · Missoula · Butte

Boise · Twin Falls · Pocatello · Idaho Falls

Salt Lake City · Provo · Ogden

Denver · Cheyenne · Boulder · Laramie

Omaha · Lincoln

Spokane · Seattle · Tacoma · Yakima · Olympia

Portland · Salem · Eugene · Medford

Sacramento · San Francisco · Berkeley · Oakland · San Jose · Stockton

Reno · Carson City · Winnemucca · Elko

Vancouver · Victoria

Lewis Range · Bitterroot Range · Absaroka Ra. · Salmon River Mts. · Blue Mts. · Selkirk Mountains · Monashee Mts.

Columbia River · Snake River · Missouri · Yellowstone · Great Salt Lake

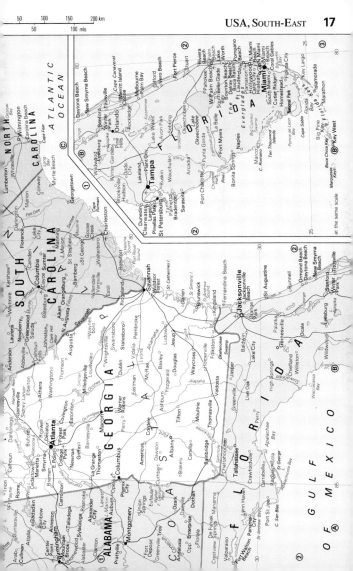

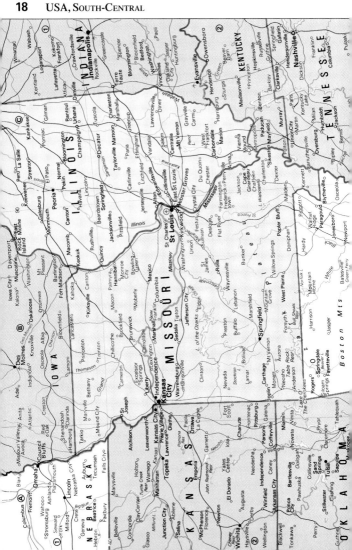

50   100   150   200 km
50   100 mls

ALABAMA ③

④

Cullman · Lewis Smith L.
Birmingham
Jasper · Winfield · Bessemer · Centreville
Hamilton · Fayette · Columbus · Tuscaloosa · Grove Hill
New Albany · Aberdeen · West Point · Starkville · Eutaw · Demopolis
Tupelo · Houston · Louisville · Philadelphia · Meridian · Thomasville · Waynesboro · Jackson · Mt. Vernon · Mobile · Bay Minette · Warrington
Pontotoc · Oxford · Chickasawhay · Citronelle · Prichard · Pascagoula · Ocean Springs · Biloxi · Gulfport · Bayou La Batre

ⓒ Chandeleur Is · Mississippi Delta · Breton Sound · East Bay · West Bay

MISSISSIPPI

Batesville · Grenada · Kosciusko · Newton · Laurel · Hattiesburg · Wiggins · Poplarville · Picayune
Clarksdale · Winona · Eupora · Collins · Columbia · Purvis · Bogalusa · Slidell
Helena · Cleveland · Greenwood · Indianola · Yazoo City · Canton · Hazlehurst · Brookhaven · McComb · Magnolia · Kentwood · Hammond · Covington · New Orleans · Kenner · Metairie · Gretna · Marrero · Port Sulphur · Grand Isle · Pilottown
Greenville · Jackson · Clinton · Vicksburg · Port Gibson · Natchez · Baton Rouge · Laplace

LOUISIANA

Stuttgart · De Witt · Monticello · Lake Village · Hamburg · Crossett · Tallulah · St. Joseph · Plaquemine · Morgan City · Houma · Thibodaux · Terre Bonne Bay · Timbalier Bay
Dumas · McGehee · Providence · Port Allen · Patterson · Franklin · New Iberia · Jeanerette
Bastrop · Monroe · Ferriday · Marksville · Opelousas · Lafayette · Abbeville · Kaplan · Crowley · Marsh I. · White L. · Pecan Island · Grand L. · Marsh L.

Arkansas · Little Rock · Hot Springs · Benton · Bryant · Sheridan · Warren · Fordyce · Hampton · El Dorado
Malvern · Pine Bluff · Ruston · Homer · Jonesboro · Winnfield · Pineville · Alexandria · Ville Platte · Eunice · Jennings · Kinder · Lake Charles · Sulphur · Cameron · Sabine L.
Arkadelphia · Prescott · Camden · Magnolia · Minden · Bossier City · Shreveport · Natchitoches · Colfax · Leesville · De Ridder · Jasper · Kirbyville
Nashville · Hope · Lewisville · L. Erling · Mansfield · Toledo Bend Resr. · Merryville · Sulphur · Orange · Port Arthur · High Island

TEXAS

De Queen · Glenwood · Texarkana · Marshall · Many · Pineland · Woodville · Slidell · Beaumont · Orange · Galveston Bay
Mena · Broken Bow · Idabel · Naples · Jefferson · Longview · Kilgore · Center · Logansport · Nacogdoches · Lufkin · Livingston · Cleveland · Dayton · Baytown · Texas City · Galveston
Broken Bow · Little · Mt. Pleasant · Henderson · Carthage · Rusk · Corrigan · Liberty · Houston · Pasadena · La Marque
De Kalb · Paris · Sulphur Springs · Tyler · Jacksonville · Crockett · Livingston · Conroe · Bellaire · La Porte · Alvin · Angleton · Lake Jackson · Freeport
Antlers · Hugo · Bonham · Greenville · Mineola · Athens · Palestine · Trinity · Huntsville · Magnolia · Navasota · Hempstead
Atoka · Durant · McKinney · Terrell · Cedar Creek L. · Sabine · Madisonville · College Sta. · Bryan
Tishomingo · Denison · Sherman · Plano · Garland · Ennis · Corsicana · Buffalo · Hearne
Ardmore · Marietta · Gainesville · Denton · Lewisville · Richardson · Irving · Dallas · Arlington · Grand Prairie · Waxahachie · Mexia · Navasota · Brenham · La Grange
Pauls Valley · Ada · Nocona · Bridgeport · Fort Worth · Weatherford · Cleburne · Alvarado · Hillsboro · Cameron · Columbus
Bowie · Eagle Mtn. L. · Granbury · Glen Rose · Waco · Gatesville · Temple · Taylor · Georgetown · Sommerville Resr. · Yoakum · Cuero · Edna · Bay City · Wharton · Rosenberg
Killeen · Belton · Luling · Gonzales · Austin · Bastrop

Rivers and lakes: L. Ouachita · Arkansas · Saline · Ouachita · L. Texoma · Red · Sulphur · Cypress Creek L. · Sabine · Neches · Angelina · Sam Rayburn Resr. · Trinity · Navasota · Brazos · Colorado · Lake Buchanan · Big Black · Yazoo · Pearl · Leaf · Chickasawhay · Tombigbee · Black Warrior · L. Pontchartrain · L. Maurepas · Atchafalaya Bay · Vermilion Bay

CANADA

WASHINGTON

OREGON

NEVADA

CALIFORNIA

Vancouver, Victoria, Seattle, Tacoma, Olympia, Spokane, Portland, Salem, Eugene, Bend, Medford, Klamath Falls, Mount Rainier Nat. Park, Mt Rainier 4392, Mt St Helens 2950, Mt Adams 3751, Mt Hood 3427, Mt Jefferson 3199, Three Sisters 3156, Mt Shasta 4317, Columbia R., Snake R., Coast Range, Cascade Range, Columbia Plateau, Harney Basin, High Desert, Klamath Mts, Blue Mountains, Wallowa Mts, Santa Rosa Ra.

Map labels

50 100 150 200 km
50 100 mls

Dunsmuir
Adin
120
Winnemucca
Golconda
B
Emigrant Pass
Arcata
Eureka
Fortuna
Weaverville
Shasta
Burney
Project City
Redding
Lassen Pk.
Nat. Pk. 3187
Eagle L.
Rye Patch Resr
Imlay
Battle Mountain
Mt Tobin 2979
Chester
Almanor
Susanville
Lovelock
40
rville
Red Bluff
Quincy
Honey L.
Pyramid L.
Humboldt L.
Stillwater Ra.
Bragg
Paradise
Chico
Oroville
Feather
N. Fork
Reno
Sparks
Fernley
Fallon
Eastgate
Austin
Summit Mtn 3188
Shoshone Mts
Willows
Sacramento
Grass Valley
Donner Pass
Virginia City
Silver City
Carson City
Yerington
Schurz
Gabbs
Wildcat Pk 3203
Ukiah
Lakeport
Clear L.
Yuba City
Marysville
Roseville
Colfax
Auburn
Tahoe City
Lake Tahoe
S. Lake Tahoe
Walker L.
Mt Jefferson 3642
Monitor Ra.
Arena
Woodland
Davis
Carmichael
Sacramento
Placerville
Hawthorne
Mt Grant 3426
Healdsburg
Santa Rosa
Napa
Vacaville
Fairfield
Vallejo
Sutter Creek
San Andreas
Bridgeport
Mono L.
Coaldale
Warm Springs
Bodega Head
Petaluma
San Rafael
Berkeley
Oakland
Antioch
Concord
Lodi
Stockton
Sonora
Oakdale
Yosemite Nat. Park
Boundary Peak 4005
Piper Pk 2880
Tonopah
Goldfield
2
San Francisco
Daly City
San Mateo
Alameda
Hayward
Livermore
Modesto
Turlock
El Portal
White Mtn Peak 4342
Redwood City
Sunnyvale
Santa Clara
San Jose
Los Gatos
Gustine
Merced
Mariposa
Bishop
Big Pine
Pine Flat Resr
Kings Canyon Nat. Park
Owens L.
Beatty
Santa Cruz
Watsonville
Monterey Bay
Pt Pinos
Monterey
Salinas
Gonzales
Los Banos
San Joaquin Valley
Madera
Pinedale
Fresno
Sequoia Nat. Park
Mt Whitney 4418
Independence
Lone Pine
Death Valley
Panamint Range
King City
Coalinga
Hanford
Lemoore
Tulare
Visalia
Exeter
Keeler
Telescope Peak 3368
Paso Robles
Wasco
Oildale
Porterville
Delano
Inyokern
Morro Bay
San Luis Obispo
Bakersfield
Arvin
Johannesburg
Grover City
Santa Maria
Tehachapi Pass
Mojave
Mojave Desert
35
Lompoc
Tehachapi Mts
Barstow
Yermo
A
Pt Conception
Santa Barbara Chan.
Santa Barbara
Santa Paula
Fillmore
Ventura
Oxnard
Lancaster
Victorville
Mt San Antonio 3069
San Bernardino
Redlands
Beaumont
Burbank
Glendale
Pasadena
Beverly
Santa Monica
Los Angeles
Torrance
Long Beach
Huntington Beach
Anaheim
Santa Ana
Riverside
Pomona
San Jacinto Peak 3301
Palm Springs
3
Laguna Beach
San Clemente
Santa Catalina
Gulf of Santa Catalina
San Clemente
Oceanside
Carlsbad
Palomar Mtn 1871
Vista
Escondido
Ramona
El Cajon
San Diego
National City
Chula Vista
Tijuana
Tecate
Descanso
B

PACIFIC OCEAN

NEVADA

C A L I F O R N I A

Sacramento Valley

Coast Ranges

Diablo Range

Santa Lucia Range

Santa Cruz

Channel Islands

San Miguel
Santa Rosa
Santa Cruz

120

USA, Hawaii inset

50
A
Hanalei
Kauai 1544
Lihue
Mana
Kauai Channel
Kaena Pt
Kahuku Pt
Wahiawa
Kailua
Oahu
Pearl City
Honolulu
Kaunakakai
Lanai City
Lanai
Molokai
Palolo Chan.
Wailuku
Hana
Maui
Kahoolawe
Kealaikahiki Chan.
Alenuihaha Channel
Upolu Pt
Kapaau
Waimea
Mauna Kea 4201
Kailua
Hakalau
Hilo
Hawaii
Mauna Loa 4169
Kilauea Crater 1243
Hawaii Volcanoes Nat. Park
Pahoa
Milolii
Ka Lae (South Cape)
Naalehu
20 N
155
C
B

PACIFIC
OCEAN

USA, Hawaii
0 100 200 km
0 100 mls
60

CEAN
60

0 25 50 75 100
0 25 50 mls

Lytton Calistoga
Healdsburg St Berryessa
Forestville
Sebastopol
Santa Rosa Sonoma Napa Vacaville Elmira
Petaluma
Fairfield
Novato Vallejo
San Rafael Concord
Mill Valley Berkeley Richmond Mt Diablo 1173 Antioch Oakley Brentwood
San Francisco Oakland
Daly City Alameda San Leandro Byron Tracy
S. San Francisco Hayward
San Mateo Pleasanton Livermore Vernalis
Redwood City Mountain View
Palo Alto Sunnyvale Mt Hamilton 1284 Newman
San Gregorio Santa Clara San Jose Coyote Gustine Volta
Pescadero
Boulder Creek Los Gatos Morgan Hill
Davenport Soquel Gilroy
Santa Cruz Watsonville San Juan Bautista
Monterey Castroville Hollister Tres Pinos
Bay Salinas Alisal
Pacific Grove Seaside Mendota
Monterey
Carmel Pinnacles N.M.
Carmel Valley Gonzales

Woodland
Folsom Placerville Camino
Davis Carmichael Folsom Diamond Springs
Winters Sacramento Markleeville Topaz
Plymouth Highland Pk 3333 Coleville
Elk Grove Sutter Ck West Pt Bear Valley Devils Gate
Galt Jackson Arnold Dardanelle Sonora Pass 2933 Bridgeport
Lodi San Andreas Murphys Pinecrest
Isleton Angels Camp Sonora Groveland Mather Tioga Mt Dana 3790
Stockton Bellota Hetch Hetchy Tuolumne Mdws
Manteca Farmington Resr Oakdale Yosemite Mt Lyell 3997
Ripon Riverbank Modesto El Portal National Mt Ritt 4016
Patterson Ceres Turlock Park Fish Camp
Turlock Resr Mariposa Wawona Bass Lake
Merced Yosemite Lakeshore
Atwater Planada Raymond Huntington L
Chowchilla Berenda Madera Friant Dam Humphreys
Dos Palos Firebaugh Pinedale Friant Piedra
Kerman Clovis Minkler
Helm Fresno Sanger Reedley
Selma Kingsburg Dinuba

Gorman Lake Hughes Rosamond Helendale
Sisquoc Los Alamos San Rafael Mtn 2081 Castaic Lancaster Mirage L Adelanto Victorville
Lompoc Buellton Los Olivos La Cachuma Acton Palmdale Littlerock Hesperia
Pt Arguello Solvang Santa Ynez Mts Santa Ynez Resr Wrightwood
Pt Conception Gaviota Goleta Santa Barbara Ojai Fillmore Newhall San Fernando Mt San Antonio San Bernardino
Santa Barbara Carpinteria Santa Paula Moorpark Burbank Mt Wilson Pasadena Upland Colton
Ventura Oxnard Camarillo Glendale Hollywood Monrovia Ontario Riverside
Santa Barbara Channel Port Hueneme Los Angeles Beverly Hills Redlands
San Miguel Santa Rosa Santa Cruz Anacapa Is Santa Monica Inglewood Whittier Fullerton Corona Perris
Channel Islands Santa Monica Bay Torrance Redondo Beach Garden Grove Anaheim Santa Ana Santiago Pk 1736
Long Beach Costa Mesa Elsinore L
Huntington Beach Newport Beach Laguna Beach
Santa Barbara San Clemente
Avalon San Pedro Channel Oceanside
Santa Catalina Gulf of Santa Catalina Carlsbad
San Nicolas Outer Santa Barbara Channel Encinitas
Del Mar
San Clemente La Jolla San Diego

PACIFIC OCEAN

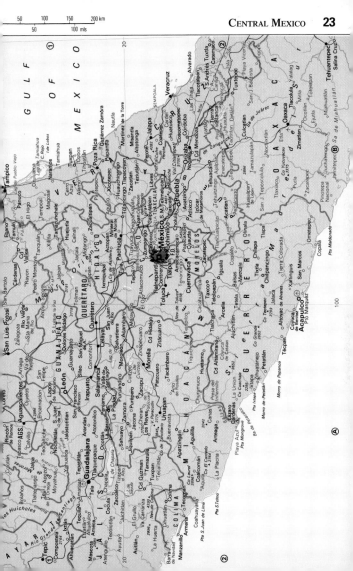

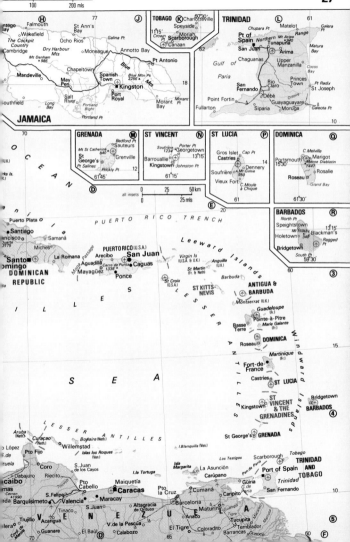

JAMAICA (inset H, J)

100 200 300 400 km
100 200 mls

77

Falmouth
St Ann's Bay
Ocho Rios
Galina Pt

The Cockit Country
Cambridge
Moneague
Annotto Bay

Mandeville
Mt Denham 986
Dry Harbour Mts
Chapelton
Blue Mtn Pk 2256
Blue Mtns
Pt Antonio

May Pen
Spanish Town
Kingston
Port Royal
18

Southfield
Salt River
Morant Pt
Morant Bay

Long Bay
Portland Bight
Portland Pt

JAMAICA

TOBAGO / TRINIDAD (inset K, L)

TOBAGO
Charlotteville
115°
Speyside
Crown Pt
Moriah
Scarborough
Canaan

TRINIDAD
Chupara Pt
Matelot
Galera Pt
Pt of Spain
Northern Range
Mt Aripo 940
San Juan
Tunapuna
Arima

Chaguanas
Upper Manzanilla
Matura Bay

Gulf of Paria
San Fernando
Rio Claro
Princes Town
Cocos Bay
Pt Radix
St Joseph

Point Fortin
Débé
Guayaguayare
Siparia
Moruga
Galeota Pt

Fullarton
10

GRENADA (inset M)

70

Bedford Pt
Sauteurs
St Catherine 840

St George's
St Salines
Grenville
Prickly Pt
12

61°45'

ST VINCENT (inset N)

Soufrière 1234
Porter Pt
Georgetown
13°15'

Barrouaillie
Johnston Pt
Kingstown

61°15'

ST LUCIA (inset P)

Gros Islet
Cap Pt
14

Castries
Dennery
Mt Gimie 950
Soufrière
Vieux Fort
Pt Moule à Chique

61

DOMINICA (inset Q)

C.Melville
Portsmouth
Marigot
Marine Diablotin 1447

Roseau
Rosalie

Grand Bay
61°30'

all insets
0 25 50km
0 25 mls

E
20

BARBADOS (inset R)

North Pt
Speightstown
13°15'
Mt Hillaby 340
Holetown
Blackman's
Ragged Pt

Bridgetown
South Pt
59°30'

3

Main map

O C E A N

rks Is.

P U E R T O   R I C O   T R E N C H

Puerto Plata
Santiago
Samaná
L e e w a r d   I s l a n d s
60

ancisco
Miches
La Romana
Mona Passage
Aguadilla
Arecibo
Virgin Is
(U.S.A. & U.K.)
Anguilla
(U.K.)

Santo Domingo
Pico Duarte 3175
PUERTO RICO (U.S.A.)
San Juan
Cerro de Punta 1336
Caguas
St Martin
(Fr. & Neth)

DOMINICAN REPUBLIC
Mayagüez
Ponce
St Croix
(U.S.A.)
Barbuda

A N T I L L E S
ANTIGUA & BARBUDA

L E S S E R
Montserrat (U.K.)
Guadeloupe (Fr.)
Pointe-à-Pitre

Basse-Terre
Marie Galante (Fr.)

Roseau
DOMINICA
15

S E A
Martinique (Fr.)
Fort-de-France
W i n d w a r d   I s l a n d s

Castries
ST LUCIA

Kingstown
ST VINCENT & THE GRENADINES
Bridgetown
BARBADOS
4

L E S S E R
St George's
GRENADA

A N T I L L E S
Aruba (Neth.)
Curaçao (Neth.)
Bonaire (Neth.)
I.Blanquilla (Ven.)

o López
Willemstad
Islas los Roques (Ven.)
Los Testigos
Scarborough
Tobago

Pto Fijo
Isla Margarita
La Asunción
Pen.de Paria
TRINIDAD AND TOBAGO

eruela
Coro
I.la Tortuga
Carúpano
Güiria
Port of Spain

Dabajuro
Riecito
S.Juan de los Cayos
Maiquetía
G.de Paria
San Fernando

caibo
Pto Cabello
Cerrón 1990
Maturín
10

mas
S.Felipe
CARACAS
Pto.Cruz
Cumaná
Carúpano
Carúpano

Barquisimeto
Valencia
S.Juan
Maracay
Barcelona
Anaco
Tucupita
Orinoco

Trujillo
Acarigua
Tinaco
Altagracia de
V E N E Z U E L A

Cord.de
Guanare
El Baúl
V.de la Pascua
El Tigre
Coloradito
Barrancas
5

Trujillo 1990
70
Calabozo
60
F

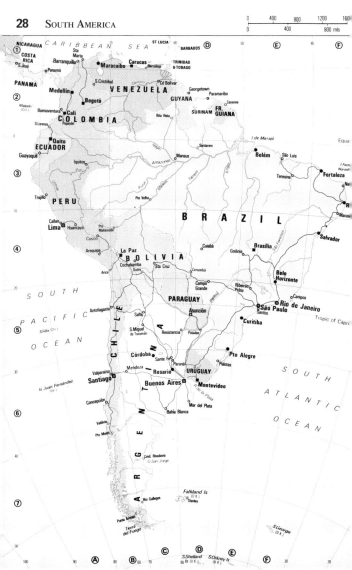

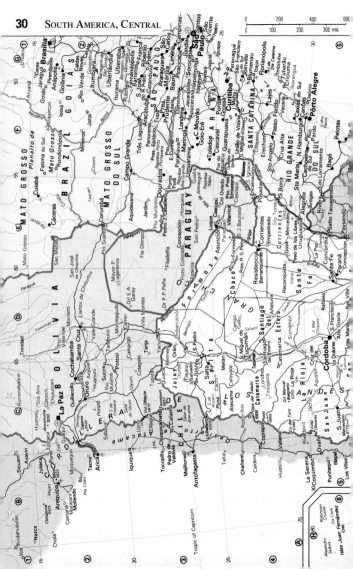

200   400   600 km
100   200   300 mils

Equator

B   45   **C**   40   **D**   35   **E**

①
0

C. Maguarinho
B. de Marajó
Salinópolis
Bragança
Marajó   Capanema
Pa-   Belém   Alcântara   B. de São Marcos
eta   Abaetetuba   Pinheiro   São Luís
Monção   Rosário   Parnaíba
Bacabal   Chapadinha
A R A   M A R A N H Ã O   Coroatá   Codó   Caxias
Marabá   Imperatriz   Castelo
Grajaú   Teresina
Pto Franco
Araguaína   Carolina
Balsas   Floriano
P I A U Í   Oeiras
raguaia   Picos
T O C A N T I N S   S.Raimundo
Nonato
Palmas   B R A Z I L
Ilha do Bananal   Barra   Paulistana
Barreiras   B A H I A   Jacobina
Ibotirama
Bom Jesus   R.de Jacuípe
da Lapa
Caetité
G O I Á S   Uruaçu   Vitória da
Ceres   Conquista   Itabuna
Formosa
Pirenópolis   Brasília
Anápolis   São Francisco   Itapetinga
Goiânia   Januária   Porteirinha
Caldas   Paracatu   Salinas
Novas   Piraporaо
io Verde   Pirapora   Araçuaí
Itumbiara   João   Corinto
Goiandira   Pinheiro   Diamantina
Catalão   Patos   Curvelo   Gov.
Barragem de   Araguari   de Minas   Teófilo Otôni   Valadares
São Simão   M I N A S   G E R A I S
Uberlândia   Uberaba   Sete Lagoas
urama   Araxá   Itabira   Cnl
Barragem Agua   Belo
binéia   Vermelha   Franca   Horizonte   Marabá   Fabriciano   Colatina
Ferlandópolis   Barretos   Passos   Divinópolis   Carangola   Cariacica
tuba   R.Preto   Ribeirão Prêto   S.João del Rei   Cafaleite   Ponte Nova
A O   P A U L O   Poços de   Lavras   Barbacena   Itaperuna
Araraquara   Caldas   Juiz
Bauru   São Carlos   de Fora   Nova
Marília   Limeira   Sta de Mantiqueira   Redonda   Friburgo
nte   Piracicaba   Campinas   Barra   Petrópolis
a Itapeva   Sorocaba   São Paulo   Mansa   Niterói
Itapetininga   Jundiaí   Santos
Itararé   Juquiá   São Vicente
apuava   Itanhaém   Rio de Janeiro
São   Iguape
Mafra   São Francisco do Sul   Curitiba
Paranaguá

B   45   **C**   40   **D**   35   **E**

São Marcos
Camocim   Acaraú
Itapipoca
Sobral   Sta   Caucaia   **Fortaleza** (Ceará)
Piripiri   Quitéria   Canindé   Aracati
Campo   Maior   Russas
Caxias   Crateús   Quixadá
C E A R Á   Areia Branca
Mombaça   Acopiara   Macau   Pta do Calcanhar
Tauá   Iguatu   Patu   Mossoró   Natal
RIO GRANDE DO NORTE
J.do Norte   Sousa   Patos   Caicó
Crato   Salgueiro   P A R A Í B A   Cabedelo
Ouricuri   Sa   Limoeiro   Campina Grande   João Pessoa
P E R N A M B U C O   Caruaru   Olinda
Petrolina   Juazeiro   Garanhuns   (Pernambuco)   **Recife**
Palmeira dos   Palmares   Vitória   Barreiros
Sen do Bonfim   A L A G O A S   Maceió
Propriá   Arapiraca   Penedo
Serrinha   S E R G I P E   Lagarto
Feira de S.   Alagoinhas   Aracaju
Iaçu   Cachoeira   Estância
Castro   Salvador (Bahia)
Alves
Valença   Ipiaú   os Santos
Jequié   B. de T. os Santos
Ilhéus
A T L A N T I C
O C E A N
Canavieiras
Belmonte
Pôrto Seguro
Itamaraju
Nanuque
São Mateus
E S P Í R I T O
Linhares
S A N T O   Vitória
Vila Velha
Cachoeiro de Itapemirim
São João da Barra
Campos
Magé

Tropic of Capricorn

Rocas
J. Fernando
de Noronha

②

5

③

10

④

15

⑤

20

⑥

25

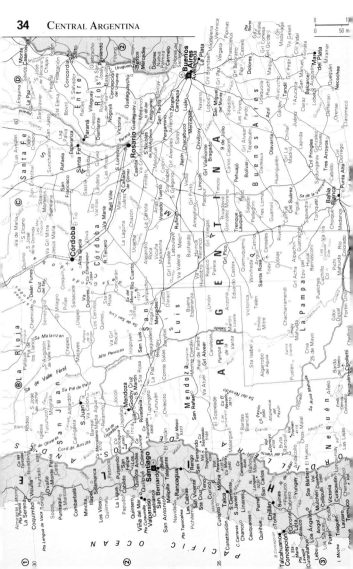

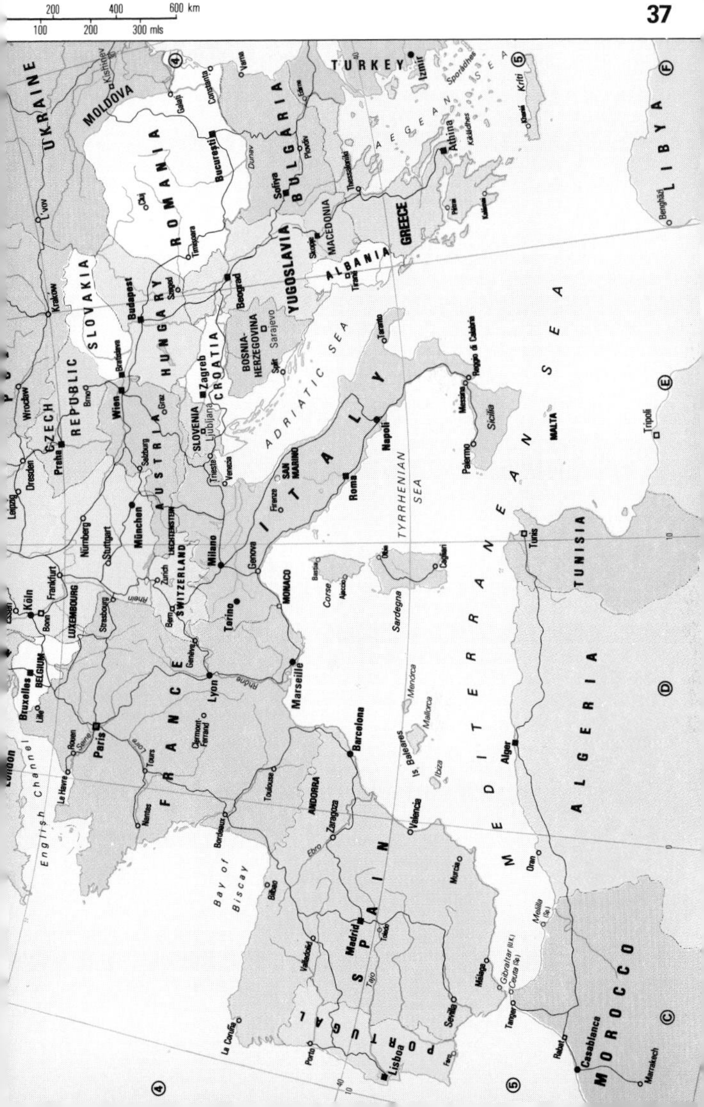
200 400 600 km
100 200 300 mls
UKRAINE
MOLDOVA
Kishinev
ROMANIA
Cluj
Timişoara
Bucureşti
Galaţi
Constanţa
Varna
BULGARIA
Sofiya
Plovdiv
Edirne
Dunav
TURKEY
İzmir
AEGEAN SEA
Sporádhes
Kikládhes
Kriti
Khaniá
Athína
Pátra
Kalamai
GREECE
Thessaloníki
MACEDONIA
Skopje
ALBANIA
Tiranë
YUGOSLAVIA
Beograd
Szeged
HUNGARY
Budapest
SLOVAKIA
Kraków
L'vov
Wrocław
CZECH REPUBLIC
Praha
Brno
Bratislava
Wien
Graz
AUSTRIA
Salzburg
München
Nürnberg
Stuttgart
Dresden
Leipzig
Frankfurt
Köln
Bonn
Essen
LUXEMBOURG
BELGIUM
Bruxelles
Lille
London
English Channel
Rouen
Seine
Le Havre
Paris
Tours
Loire
Nantes
FRANCE
Clermont-Ferrand
Lyon
Rhône
Genève
Bern
Zürich
SWITZERLAND
LIECHTENSTEIN
Strasbourg
Rhein
Marseille
MONACO
Torino
Milano
Genova
Venezia
Trieste
SLOVENIA
Ljubljana
Zagreb
CROATIA
BOSNIA-HERZEGOVINA
Sarajevo
Split
ADRIATIC SEA
ITALY
Firenze
SAN MARINO
Roma
Napoli
Taranto
Reggio di Calabria
Messina
Palermo
Sicilia
MALTA
TYRRHENIAN SEA
Corse
Bastia
Ajaccio
Sardegna
Olbia
Cagliari
MEDITERRANEAN SEA
Tunis
TUNISIA
Tripoli
LIBYA
Benghāzī
Bordeaux
Bay of Biscay
Toulouse
ANDORRA
Barcelona
Zaragoza
Ebro
Valencia
Is. Baleares
Menorca
Mallorca
Ibiza
Bilbao
SPAIN
Madrid
Toledo
Tajo
Valladolid
Murcia
Sevilla
Málaga
Gibraltar (U.K.)
Ceuta (Sp.)
Melilla (Sp.)
Tanger
La Coruña
Porto
PORTUGAL
Lisboa
Faro
Alger
Oran
ALGERIA
Rabat
Casablanca
Marrakech
MOROCCO
4
5
C
D
E
F
10
40

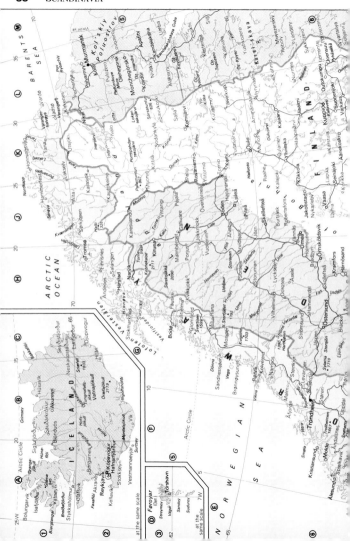

E ① Nordhordland Dalsfj

Bergen 60

Sotra

NORWAY

Sunnhordland Stord

Bømlo

Skjold

Leirvik

Karmøy

Haugesund

②

N O R T H

S E A

55

D

C

Hermä Ness

Unst

Isbister

Yell Feðar

Whalsay

St Magnus B.

Shetland

Lerwick

Foula

Sumburgh Hd

Fair Isle

Westray

Sanday

Rousay Stronsay

Stromness Kirkwall

Orkney

Sule Skerry Hoy Scapa Flow Duncansby Hd

Stack Skerry

Thurso Wick

C. Wrath Helmsdale

Ben Hope Halladale

N. Rona Altnaharra

Ben More Dornoch Firth

Ullapool 998 Moray Firth

Dingwall L. Ness Elgin Banff Fraserhead

SCOTLAND Buchan Ness

Sule Sgeir Inverness Peterhead

Butt of Lewis Don

Stornoway Fort Augustus Ben Macdui Aberdeen

Lewis Mallaig Ben Nevis 1309 Stonehaven

Flannan Is Harris 1344 Braemar

Portree Fort William Dee Montrose

Skye L. Oich Pitlochry Arbroath

Outer Hebrides Rum Oban L. Tay St Andrews

N. Uist Eigg Perth F. of Tay

St Kilda S. Uist Coll L. Lomond Stirling Kirkcaldy

Tiree Mull Grampians F. of Forth

Barra Loch Edinburgh St Abbs Hd

Colonsay Jura F. of Lorn Greenock Motherwell Berwick-upon-Tweed

Islay Glasgow Galashiels Holy I.

Campbeltown Paisley White Hawick Morpeth Blyth

Coldstr. 862 Newbiggin

Arran Irvine Kilmarnock Moffat Cheviot Newcastle upon Tyne

Rathlin I. Kintyre Ayr Nith Morpeth S. Shields

N. IRELAND Giralt Dumfries

Coleraine Stranraer

Tory I. Malin Hd

L. Foyle

Errigal Londonderry

752 Atlan L.

A

① 60   ② 55

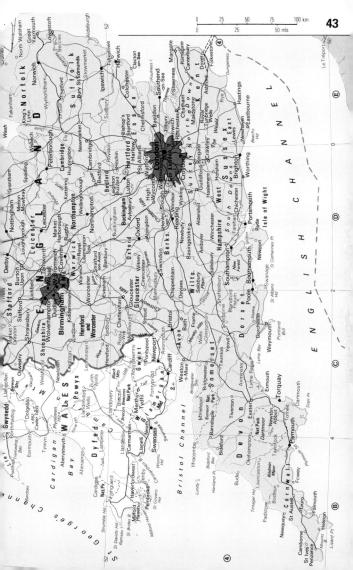

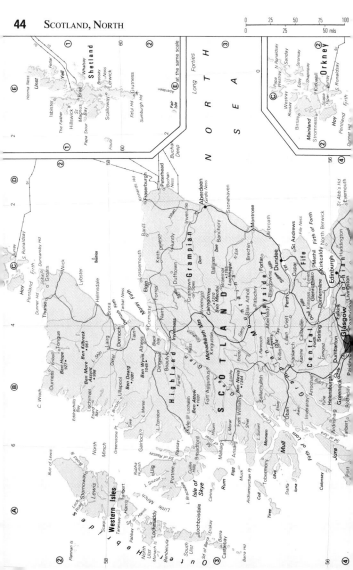

0   25   50   75   100
0   25   50 mils

① Fetlar
Whalsay
Unst
Herma Ness
The Faither
Yell
Shetland
Istbister
Hillswick
St Magnus Bay
Bressay
Lerwick
Scalloway Head
Papa Stour
Foula
Fitful Hd
Sumburgh Hd
Fair Isle
② (at the same scale)

Long   Forties
N   O   R   T   H

Orkney
② Papa Westray
N Ronaldsay
Westray   Sanday
Rousay   Stronsay
Eday
Mainland
Kirkwall
Stromness
Hoy   Scapa Flow
S Ronaldsay
Pentland Firth   Duncansby Hd

③ Aberdeen
Girdle Ness
Fair Head
Buchan Deep

S   E   A

Kinnairds Hd
④ Fraserburgh
Peterhead
Buchan Ness
56

Banff
Inverurie
Aberdeen
Girdle Ness
Stonehaven
Montrose
Arbroath
St Andrews
Fife Ness
Dundee
Firth of Forth
North Berwick
Haddington
St Abb's Hd
Eyemouth

Elgin
Lossiemouth
Keith
Huntly
Don
Grampian
Dufftown
Ballater
Banchory
Brechin
Forfar
Tayside
Blairgowrie
Perth
Crieff
Dunfermline
Glenrothes
Kirkcaldy
Edinburgh
Lothian
Queensferry
Falkirk

Nairn
Forres
Cromdale-on-Spey
Cairngorms
Ben Macdui 1310
Braemar
Lochnagar 1155
Blair Atholl
Pitlochry
Aberfeldy
G   r   a   m   p   i   a   n

Thurso
Durness
John o' Groats
Duncansby Hd
Wick
Lybster
Helmsdale
Brora
Dornoch
Tain
Golspie
Lairg
Cromarty Firth
Invergordon
Dingwall
Inverness
Loch Ness
Fort Augustus
S   C   O   T   L   A   N   D
H   i   g   h   l   a   n   d
Ben Wyvis 1046
Ben Dearg 1084
Strathpeffer
Beauly

Ben Hope 927
Tongue
Ben Kilbreck 961
Ben More 998
Loch Shin
Oykel
Loy
Altnaharra

C. Wrath
Durness
Eriboll
Scourie
Edrachillis Bay
Lochinver
Enard
Ullapool
Loch Broom
L. Maree
Gairloch
Greenstone Pt
Poolewe
Kyle of Lochalsh
Loch Torridon
Applecross
Raasay
Sd of Raasay
Broadford
Isle of Skye
Portree

Ben Attow 1037
Glen Affric
Kintail
Ben Nevis 1344
Fort William
Ballachulish
L. Linnhe
Oban
L. Etive
Connel
Callander
Stirling
Doune
Central
Loch Lomond
Dumbarton
Greenock
Paisley
Glasgow
Helensburgh
Gare Loch
Arrochar

Mallaig
Arisaig
L. Shiel
Moidart
Morvern
Mull
Tobermory
Staffa
Iona
Colonsay
Jura
L. Awe
Loch Fyne
Inveraray
Lochgilphead
Ardrishaig
Tarbert
Rothesay

Butt of Lewis
Stornoway
Lewis
North Minch
Shiant Is
Rubha Réidh
Rona
L. Snizort
Raasay
Rum
Eigg
Muck
Canna
Coll
Tiree
Ardnamurchan Pt

Flannan Is
Western Isles
Tarbert
Harris
Pabbay
Monach Is
North Uist
Lochmaddy
Benbecula
South Uist
Sd of Barra
Barra
Eriskay
Castlebay
Barra Hd
56

25 50 75 100 km
25 50 mls

Mull of
Oa
Campbeltown

Malin
Hd
Inishowen Mull of
Slieve Hua Mhuish Carndonagh Kintyre
Tory I. L. Swilly Portrush
Bloody Foreland Carndonagh Ballycastle North
Buncrana L. Foyle Portrush Fair Channel
Rathlin I.
Errigal ▲762 Limavady Coleraine Hd
Aran I. Londonderry Ballymoney
Donegal Lifford Strabane Sperrin Mts Maghera felt Ballymena **Antrim** Larne
Gweebarra B. Dee Blue Stack ▲676 Newtown Belfast L.
Rossan Pt. Glenties Stewart **NORTHERN IRELAND** Bangor
Killybegs Donegal **Tyrone** Omagh L. Belfast Newtownards
Donegal Neagh Lisburn Strangford
Donegal Bay Ballyshannon Fintona **ULSTER** Portadown Lurgan **Down** Lough
Inishmurray Bundoran Melvin **Fermanagh** Armagh Banbridge Downpatrick
Benwee Hd Sligo Enniskillen **Armagh** Newcastle
Erris Hd Ballycastle Sligo Monaghan Clones Newry Mourne Dundrum B.
Belmullet Bay **Leitrim** Upper **Monaghan** Mts Warrenpoint
Inishkea Blacksod Mts of L. Conn Erne Oughter Cootehill Carrickmacross Dundalk 54
Achill Mayo Nephin Allen **Cavan** Kells **Louth** Dundalk Bay
Clare ▲807 Carrick on Boderg Ardee Dunary Hd
Inishturk **Mayo** Shannon **Cavan** Carrickmacross Drogheda
Clew Castlebar Ballaghaderreen Sheelin An Uaimh Balbriggan
Inishbofin Bay Westport Claremorris **Roscommon** Bowna Derravaragh **Meath** Trim Swords
Inishshark **CONNAUGHT** Castlerea **Longford** L. Ree Royal Can. Dublin
Mask Ballinrobe Roscommon Longford Mullingar (Baile Átha Cliath)
Mts of Corrib Tuam **Westmeath** Ennell Dún Laoghaire
Connemara **Galway** Athenry Ballinasloe **REPUBLIC** Clara Kildare Liffey Bray
Slyne Hd Clifden Galway **OF** **Offaly** Naas Kippure Greystones
Bertraghboy B. Loughrea Gort Shannon Birr Portarlington ▲754
Kilkieran B. Aran Inishmaan Gort Lough **LEINSTER** Port **Wicklow**
Is. Hags Hd Derg L. Brown Laoise Athy **Mts** Wicklow
Inishmore Liscannor B. **Clare** Scarriff Roscrea **Laois** Carlow
Mutton I. Milltown Ennis Killaloe **IRELAND** Tullow
Kilkee Malbay **Tipperary** Templemore **Kilkenny** Muine Bheag Gorey
Loop Hd Kilrush Thurles Kilkenny Carlow Enniscorthy
Mouth of the Shannon Foynes Limerick Cashel Thomastown **Wexford**
Tralee Bay Rathkeale **Limerick** Tipperary Carrick-on-Suir New Rosslare
Listowel Abbeyfeale **MUNSTER** Cahir Clonmel Ross Wexford
Dingle Castleisland Newmarket Mitchelstown Comeragh Waterford
Blasket Tralee **Kerry** Mallow Fermoy Mts **Waterford** Tramore
Dingle B. Killarney Boggeragh Mts Blackwater Dungarvan Hook
▲1041 Macroom Lee **Cork** Youghal Hd Waterford Hd
encia MacGillycuddys Bandon Passage Youghal Harb. Harb.
Cahersiveen Reeks **Cork** West Mine Hd
Sneem Kenmare River Dunmanway Cobh Kinsale
Dursey Caha Mts Bantry Clonakilty Old Head
Bantry Bay of Kinsale St George's Channel
Mizen Hd Skibbereen Baltimore
Roaringwater B. I. Clear
Fastnet Kinsale
Rock

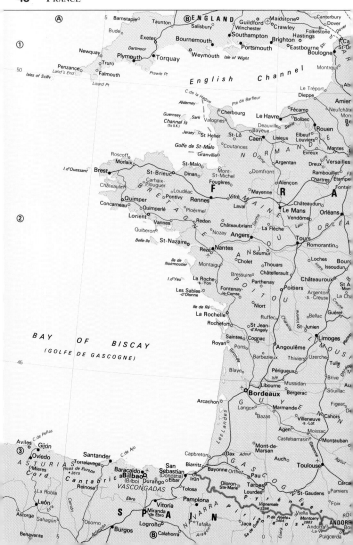

① ②

Budapest
Vác
Esztergom
Székesfehérvár
Siófok
Nové Zámky
Komárno
Talabánya
Győr
Mór
Pápa
Veszprém
Dombóvár
Szekszárd
Baja
Apatin
Vukovar
Osijek
Vác
Nitra
Trnava
Bratislava
Sopron
Szombathely
Zalaegerszeg
Nagykanizsa
Kaposvár
Pécs
Vinkovci
Dakovo
Našice
Bosanski Brod
Doboj
Dervta
Vrbas
Banja Luka
Zenica
Sarajevo
Goražde
Nikšić
Budva
Kotor

HUNGARY

Wien
Mödling
Hainfeld
Wr. Neustadt
Bruck an der Mur
Neunkirchen
St. Pölten
Eisenerz
Leoben
Mürzzuschlag
Judenburg
Graz
Leibnitz
Maribor
Varaždin
Koprivnica
Bjelovar
Virovitica
Sisak
Kutina
Pakrac
Daruvar
Požega

CROATIA

Zagreb
Karlovac
Novo Mesto
Celje
Velenje
Klagenfurt
Kranj
Ljubljana
Postojna
Rijeka (Fiume)
Vrbovsko
Ogulin

SLOVENIA

BOSNIA i HERZEGOVINA

Kljuc
Knin
Sibenik
Split (Spalato)
Brač
Hvar
Korčula
Makarska
Ploče
Metković
Dubrovnik
Mostar
Konjic
Livno
Jajce

Zadar
Biograd
Dugi O.
Kornat
Vis
Lastovo
Palagruža
Pianosa

A D R I A T I C

Linz
Wels
Steyr
Gmunden
Bad Ischl
Salzburg
Radstad
Badgastein
Spittal
Villach
Lienz
Kufstein
Garmisch-P.
Innsbruck
Landeck
Brenner
Bolzano
Merano
Brunico
Cortina d'A.
Belluno
Vittorio V.
Udine
Gorizia
Trieste
Koper
Monfalcone
Gemona
Conegliano
Treviso
Venezia (Venice)
Chioggia
Mestre
Pordenone

München
Dachau
Rosenheim
Freilassing
Berchtesgaden
Bad Tölz
Starnberg

G E R.

A U S T R I A

Memmingen
Kempten
Füssen
Reutte
Imst
Oberstdorf

Bregenz
Feldkirch
Vaduz
Buchs
Davos
St. Moritz
Chur
Sondrio
Tirano
Edolo
Lovere
Trento
Rovereto
Bassano
Vicenza
Padova
Rovigo
Ferrara
Argenta
Imola
Faenza
Ravenna
Cesena
Forlì
Rimini
Pesaro
Fano
Senigallia
Ancona
Jesi
Fabriano
Macerata
Ascoli Piceno
Teramo
Pescara
Chieti
L'Aquila
Terni
Rieti
Viterbo

ADR.

Biberach
Tuttlingen
Friedrichshafen
Lindau
Ravensburg
Dornbirn

Schaffhausen
Konstanz
Winterthur
St. Gallen
Zürich
Zug
Luzern
Altdorf
Schwyz
Glarus
Einsiedeln

Bern
Interlaken
Thun
Brig
Locarno
Bellinzona
Domodossola
Lugano
Como
Varese
Lecco
Bergamo
Brescia
Verona
Mantova
Cremona
Lodi
Pavia
Milano (Milan)
Monza
Piacenza
Parma
Reggio
Modena
Carpi
Bologna
Prato
Firenze (Florence)
Pistoia
Lucca
Empoli
Siena
Arezzo
Perugia
Foligno
Città di Castello
Urbino
Gubbio
Orvieto

APPENNINO TOSCO-EMILIANO

Massa
Carrara
La Spezia
Viareggio
Pisa
Livorno
Pontedera
Cecina
Grosseto
Orbetello
Elba
Piombino
Portoferraio
Gigilio
Pianosa
Follonica

Colmar
Freiburg
Mulhouse
Belfort
Basel
Montbéliard
Olten
Delémont
Besançon
Biel
Neuchâtel
Lausanne
Montreux
Genève

SWITZERLAND

Martigny
Aosta
Ivrea
Biella
Vercelli
Novara
Alessandria
Asti
Alba
Mondovì
Cuneo
Torino (Turin)
Susa
Albertville
Briançon
Gap

Savona
Genova (Genoa)
Rapallo
Novi Ligure
Ovada

APPENNINO LIGURE

L I G U R I A N   S e a

Alassio
San Remo
Monte Carlo
Nice
Cannes
St Raphaël
St Tropez
Grasse
Castellane
Monte Cinto
C. Rosso
Calvi
Bastia
Île Rousse
Cap Corse
Ponte Leccia
Montecristo

F R A N C E

Côte d'Azur

S A V O I E

Mont Blanc

①②

50 100 150 200 km
50 100 mls

③

I O N I A N   S E A

S E A

A D R I A T I C S E A (implied)

Lecce
Maglie
Gallipolo
C. Sta Maria di Leuca
Brindisi
Manduria
Monopoli
Bari
Molfetta
Barletta
Andria
Le Murge
Altamura
Matera
Taranto
Golfo di Taranto
Metaponto
Pta Alice
Crotone
Corigliano Calabro
Rossano
C. Rizzuto
G. di Squillace
Catanzaro
Nicastro
La Sila
Paola
Cosenza
Castrovillari
Potenza
Appno Lucano
Monte Pollino 2248
Appno Napoletano
Campobasso
Cerignola
Foggia
Benevento
Avellino
Cassino
Mte Miletto 2050
Caserta
Napoli (Naples)
Pozzuoli
Torre del Greco
Sorrento
Salerno
Eboli
Agropoli
Sapri
Ischia
Capri
Gaeta
Formia
Terracina
Latina
Anzio
I. Ponzane

T Y R R H E N I A N   S E A

Stromboli
Lipari
Isole Lipari (Eolie)
Alicudi
Filicudi
Salina
Vulcano
Ustica
Cefalù
Palermo
Partinico
Alcamo
Castelvetrano
Trapani
I. Egadi
Marsala
Mazara del Vallo
Sciacca
C. San Vito
SICILIA (SICILY)
Mti Nebrodi
Etna 3323
Bronte
Paterno
Caltanissetta
Enna
Canicatti
Agrigento
Gela
Licata
Vittoria
Modica
Ragusa
Lentini
Catania
Acireale
Giarre
Messina
Str. de Messina
Reggio di Calabria
Palmi
Vibo Valentia
Pecoraro 1423
Montalto 1955
Locri
C. Spartivento
Siracusa (Syracuse)
Noto
C.I. Scicli (?)
C. di Correnti
Pantelleria (It.)
Sicilian Channel

MALTA
Gozo
Mdina
Valletta
Malta Channel

M E D I T E R R A N E A N   S E A

③

S A R D E G N A (SARDINIA)
Asinara
Sta Teresa
Strait of Bonifacio
Olbia
Porto Torres
Sassari
Alghero
Macomer
Mti del Gennargentu 1836
Nuoro
Oristano
G. di Oristano
Arbatax
Muravera
S. Pietro
S. Antioco
Iglesias
Carbonia
Cagliari
G. di Cagliari
C. Teulada
C. Carbonara

SEA

Kelibia
C. Bon
Nabeul
Hammamet
Golfe de Hammamet
Sousse
M'saken
Monastir
Moknine
Kairouan
Nabeul
Enfida
Tunis
Bizerte
Menzel
G. de Tunis
C. Blanc
Mateur
C. Serrat
Tabarka
Béja
Medjerda
Mts de la Medjerda
Jendouba
Le Kef
El Kala
Annaba (Bône)
Souk Ahras
Guelma
Tébessa
Mts de Tébessa
Kalaat Khasba
Makthar
Kasserine
TUNISIA

Dj. Zaghouan 1295

15

10

Ⓐ

Ⓑ

Ⓒ

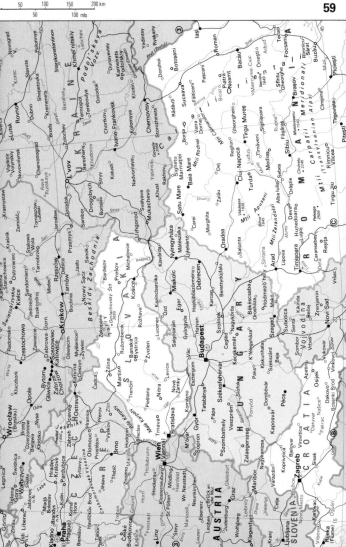

100 200 300 400 km
100 200 mils

F G H J K

RUSSIAN FEDERATION

Vel'sk · Krasavino · Solikamsk · Serov · Sos'va
Velikiy Ustyug · Griva · Kazhim · Gayny · Kizel · Nov. Lyalya · Turinsk
nosha · Tot'ma · Brusenets · Pinyug · Lesnoy · Kudymkar · Kachkanar · Kushva · Nizhniy Tagil · Alapayevsk · Irbit
arovsk · Roslyatino · Murashi · Omutninsk · Kirs · Kirovskiy · Krasnokamsk · Chusovoy · Lys'va · Nev'yansk · Artemovskiy
ogda · Nikol'sk · Khalturin · Ino-Vyatsk · Zuyevka · Vereshchagino · Ocher · **Perm** · Kungur · Kirovgrad · **Yekaterinburg** · Sverdlovsk
Buy · Manturovo · Neya · Sharya · Kotel'nich · Glazov · Igra · Osa · Shamary · Pervoural'sk · Revda · Sysert · Kamensk-Ural'skiy
Galich · Kostroma · Kineshma · Vichuga · Uren · Sanchursk · Nolinsk · Urzhum · Mozhga · Chaykovskiy · Krasnoufimsk · Chernushka · Nyazepetrovsk · Kasli · Kyshtym
Shuya · Gorodets · Semenov · Yoshkar-Ola · Malmyzh · Agryz · Sarapul · Kambarka · Asha · Zlatoust · **Chelyabinsk** · Kopeysk
rov · Dzerzhinsk · **Nizhniy Novgorod (Gor'kiy)** · Koz'modemyansk · Cheboksary · Zelenodolsk · Naberezhnyye Chelny · Menzelinsk · Birsk · Katav · Miass · Korkino · Plast
Vyazniki · Pavlovo · Chuvashskaya R. · **Kazan'** · Mamadysh · **Ufa** · Beloretsk
Khrustalnyy · Murom · Arzamas · Sergach · Alatyr · Tetyushi · **Tatarstan** · Zainsk · Nurlat · Al'met'yevsk · Bugul'ma · **Bashkortostan** · Tiryanskiy · Verkhneural'sk
simov · Pervomaysk · Saransk · Simbirsk · Chistopol · Leninogorsk · Belebey · Davlekanovo · Krasnousol'-skiy · Magnitogorsk
an · Sasovo · **Mordovskaya R.** · Kovylkino · Dimitrovgrad · Sernovodsk · Bugulma · Buguruslan · Abdulino · Sterlitamak · Salavat · Baymak · Kartaly
Shilova · Morshansk · Nizhniy Lomov · **Privolzhskaya** · Barysh · Syzran · Kuznetsk · Kinel · **Samara (Kuybyshev)** · Sorochinsk · Meleuz · Kumertau · Baymak Bredy
plygin · Michurinsk · **Vozvyshennost** · Penza · Khvalynsk · Buzuluk · Sol'-Iletsk
mbov · Rasskazovo · Serdobsk · Vol'sk · Balakovo · Pugachev · **Obshchiy** · Orenburg · Saraktash · Mednogorsk · Orsk
azi · Rtishchevo · Petrovsk · Ural'sk · **Syrt** · Sol'-Iletsk · Kuvandyk · Novotroitsk · Dombarovskiy
ardevka · Arkadak · Atkarsk · **Saratov** · Yershov · Aksay · Aktyubinsk · Alga · Mugodzhary
orisoglebsk · Balashov · Povorino · **Pokrovsk** · Krasnyy Kut · Novoalekseyevka
urlinovka · Uryupinsk · Krasnoarmeysk · Novo Uzensk · Chapayevo · Oktyabr
vlovsk · Novoanninnskiy · **Mednvezhitsa** · Kamyshin · Pallasovka · Mei-Una · Uil · Uilo · Emba
Kalach · Mikhaylovka · Frolovo · Don · Nikolayevsk · **Caspian** · Masteksay · Shubar-Kuduk
Perelazovskiy · **Depression** · Inderborskiy · **KAZAKHSTAN** · Zharkamys · Emba
Millerovo · Kalach-na-Donu · Saykhin · Makat · Kulakshi · Aktumsyk
shakhty · Morozovsk · **Volzhskiy** · Akhtubinsk · Ryn · Peski · Gur'yev · Kul'sary · Sarykamys
vgodonsk · Kotel'nikovo · **Volgograd (Stalingrad)** · Kharabali · Balykshi · Say-Utes · Plateau
tov · **Kalmytskaya** · Krasnyy Yar · **R.** · Sarymgas · Ova Tyuleni · Say-Utes
Sal'sk · Proletarskaya · Yashkul · **Astrakhan'** · Mumra · Burynshik · Ser. Mertvyy · Kultuk Beyneu · Ustyurt · **UZBEKISTAN**
Kropotkin · Ipatovo · Elista · Chernyye Zemli · Lagan (Kaspiyskiy) · M. Tyub-Karagan · Ft Shevchenko · Mangyshlak · Aktau (Shevchenko) · Novyy Uzen
sk · Armavir · Budennovsk · **Kuma R.** · Prokhladnyy · Georgiyevsk · Pyatigorsk · Ova (Kaspiyskiy) · Fetisovo
o Labinsk · Cherkessk · Kislovodsk · Nal'chik · Grozny · **CASPIAN**
khazskaya · Elbrus 5645 · Kazbek 5203 · Alagir · Vladikavkaz · **Makhachkala** · **SEA**

2

3

4

45

RUSSIAN FEDERATION
1 Chuvashskaya R.
2 Checheno-Ingushskaya R.
3 Severo-Osetinskaya R.
4 Kabardino-Balkarskaya R.
GEORGIA
5 Abkhazskaya R.
6 Adzharskaya R.
AZERBAIJAN
7 Nakhichevanskaya R.

400 800 1200 1600 km
400 800 mls

RUSSIAN FEDERATION

Krasnoyarsk
Irkutsk
Ulaanbaatar
MONGOLIA
Ürümqi
Lhasa
BHUTAN
BANGLADESH
Dhaka
Chittagong
Calcutta
Imphal
MYANMAR (BURMA)
Mandalay
Chiang Mai
THAILAND
Yangon (Rangoon)
Moulmein
Bangkok
Bay of Bengal
Andaman Is (Ind.)
Nicobar Is (Ind.)
Surat Thani
George Town
Kuala Lumpur
SINGAPORE
Padang
SUMATERA
INDONESIA
Palembang
Jakarta
JAWA
Surabaya
Christmas I. (Aust.)
Cocos Is (Aust.)

XINJIANG
Lanzhou
CHINA
Chengdu
Chongqing
Kunming
Guiyang
Changsha
Wuhan
Xi'an
Zhengzhou
Taiyuan
Beijing
Tianjin
INNER MONGOLIA
Qiqihar
Harbin
Changchun
Shenyang
Dalian
Qingdao
Yellow Sea
Huang He
Chang Jiang
Nanjing
Shanghai
Hangzhou
Nanchang
Fuzhou
T'ai-pei
TAIWAN
Guangzhou
Hong Kong (U.K.)
Macao (Port.)
Hainan
Hanoi
Haiphong
LAOS
VIETNAM
Vientiane
Da Nang
CAMBODIA
Phnom Penh
Ho Chi Minh (Saigon)
SOUTH CHINA SEA
MALAYSIA
BRUNEI
Sabah
Sarawak
BORNEO
Kuching
Sulawesi
Seram
Irian Jaya
Halmahera
Manado
Mindanao
PHILIPPINES
Manila
Luzon
Palawan
Davao
Samboanga

Sea of Japan
N. KOREA
Pyongyang
S. KOREA
Seoul
Pusan
Kita-Kyushu
Kyushu
Shikoku
JAPAN
Osaka
Nagoya
Tokyo
Sapporo
Hokkaido
Sakhalin
Khabarovsk
Vladivostok
Ostrov Sakhalin

PACIFIC OCEAN
Tropic of Cancer
Flores
Timor
Sumba
Kupang
Darwin
AUSTRALIA

200 400 600 800 km
200 400 mls

WAN (FORMOSA) Ⓓ
tung (China Nat. Rep.)
ung

Batan Is

a Strait
abuyan Is
C. Engaño
Aparri
uguegarao

Ilagan
LUZON
anatuan
zon City

PHILIPPINES
anila
Daet ○Catanduanes
Naga ●Polillo Is
Boac Bulan Legazpi
on Catarman
Masbate ○Masbate Oras
●Roxas Catbalogan Samar
colod ●Cebu Guiuan ○Leyte 10497
ros Bohol ○Dinaget ○10265
aton Bohol ○Siargao
Ozamiz ○Surigao
anukan Marawi ●Butuan
Larso ○Malanbang
boanga Cotabato ○Davao
Moro General Santos Digos
Gulf Arch ○Tinaca Pt.

MINDANAO

P A C I F I C   O C E A N

Ⓔ   140   Ⓕ
Farallon de Pajaros
Maug Is   20
Parece Vela
Asuncion
Agrihan

Northern   Pagan
Mariana   Alamagan
Islands   Guguan
                 Sarigan
                 Anatahan
                 Farallon
                 de Medinilla
                 ○Saipan   Ⓐ2
                 ○Tinian
                 Rota
            (A) Guam North Deep
                (U.S.A.)   9637

Mansyu Deep ·Challenger Deep
9818   ·11033

Ulithi Fais   ·Gafer Jt

Yap·   Faraulep
Ngulu   Sorol
         Fed.States of Micronesia
Palau   Woleai Ifalik
Islands ○Koror   Eauripik
                              Lamotrek

C A R O L I N E   I S L A N D S Ⓐ3

Sonsorol
Pulo Anna
Merir

Tobi· Helen Reef

Equator

BES

Kepulauan
Talaud Karakelong
Tahuna
Sangine

Kepulauan
Sanghie   Morotai
         ○Tobelo
Manado● Ternate ○Halmahera
Kuandang· Belang
Gorontalo Teluk
Kep. Togian Weda   Waigeo
Luwuk   Bacan Selat Dampier Kwoka
Peleng Taliabu Mangole Sorong Peg.Arfak 3000▲
Kep. Banggai Misool   2935
Kendari Wowoni   Teluk Berau
olaka Butung Namlea Bula Fakfak
one Kep.   Piru ▲3019
una Baubau Buru Seram Ambon
                Kep.Banda
B A N D A   S E A Kep.Kai
                    Dobo○
                 Kep.
                 Aru
S I A   Nila   Trangan
                 Wokam
S E A   Damar· Teun Yamdena
     Wetar Romang Kepulauan
Lomblen· Alor Selat Wetar Kep.Leti Tanimbar
  Selat Babar Saumlaki
s Endeh Dili   Sermata Selaru
          Atambua
vu Sea Kupang TIMOR
   Roti   A R A F U R A   S E A

MOLUCCAS

Manokwari Supiori
         Biak
Cendrawasih Numfoor Tg.d'Urville
         Yapen   Sarmi
Teluk
Cendrawasih   Jayapura
      ·Dom   Aitape
      1340
IRIAN Angemuk Mamberamo
      3741
Pegunungan Maoke ▲Pk.Mandala
  Pk.Jaya▲5029   4702
JAYA   N
Kaimana   E
         Kokonau W
Adi   Tk Flamingo
     Kokonau   Tanahmerah
              G
P.Kolepom U
         I Merauke
Wokam   N
Kobroör E Daru
         A
         P.Kolepom
              Saibai

Schouten Is
         Wewak Ⓐ4
              Karkar
P A P U A
N E W   G U I N E A
    Mt
  Hagen Goroka
5029   4359 Lae
Mendi   Bulolo
  Central   Wau
  PAPUA
Kikori Kerema
     Gulf of
     Papua
         Port Moresby Ⓐ5

Ninigo Group
         Wuvulu
         Long I
              Umbol

Mulgrave· Banks I.
Thursday I. C.Arnhem
Pr.of Wales C.York
         Somerset

C.Grenville
Banks I.

C O R A L
     Great Barrier Rf Ⓕ5

C.V.Diemen Croker I.
Melville   Cobourg Pen
Bathurst   C.Arnhem
Clarence   Wessel Is
   Darwin   Arnhem Land Ⓔ
                Nhulunbuy
A U S T R A L I A
         Weipa Iron
              Range
Albatross B.   Ⓕ

T I M O R   S E A   140

100 200 300 400 km
100 200 mls

SOUTH CHINA SEA

Zhoushan Qundao
Dinghai

Ningbo
Shaoxing
Hangzhou
Wuxing
Huzhou
Linhai
Huangyan
Wenling
Wenzhou
Zhejiang
Huangshan
Quxian
Jinhua
Shangrao
Jiande
Pucheng
Jianyang
Ningde
Fuding
Fuzhou (Foochow)
Fujian
Fuqing
Putian
Quanzhou (Amoy)
Xiamen (Amoy)
Zhangzhou
Longyan
Meizhou
Shantou (Swatow)
Chaozhou
Huilai

TAIWAN
Chi-lung
Tai-pei (Taipei)
Su-ao
Hsin-chu
Chang-hua
Tai-chung
Chia-i
Tai-nan
Kao-hsiung
Ping-tung
Tai-tung
Heng ch'un
FORMOSA (TAIWAN) STRAIT

Nanchang
Jiangxi
Fuzhou
Nancheng
Shaowu
Sanming
Yong'an
Ganzhou
Ruijin
Xingguo
Xinfeng
Longchuan
Heyuan
Huizhou
Kowloon
HONG KONG (U.K.)
Guangzhou (Canton)
Foshan
Zhaoqing

Wuhan
Hubei
Huangshi
Xianning
Jiujiang
Jingdezhen
Fengcheng
Changsha
Hunan
Zhuzhou
Xiangtan
Hengyang
Shaoyang
Lingling
Guilin
Liuzhou
Guangxi
Nanning
Wuzhou
Yulin
Guiping
Beihai
Zhanjiang
Maoming
Yangjiang

Hainan
Haikou
Qionghai

GULF OF TONGKIN

VIETNAM
Hanoi
Haiphong
Nam Dinh

LAOS

Sichuan
Chengdu
Chongqing (Chungking)
Neijiang
Luzhou
Yibin
Zigong
Leshan
Xichang
Panzhihua
Dukou

Guizhou
Guiyang
Zunyi
Anshun
Duyun
Kaili

Yunnan
Kunming
Qujing
Gejiu
Mengzi
Kaiyuan
Lijiang

50 100 150 200km
50 100 mils

① ② ©

N

J A P A N

S E A   O F   J A P A N

P A C I F I C   O C E A N

SHIKOKU

KYŪSHŪ

35

140

135

B

A

Ullŭng-do
Todong

Tok-to (Take-shima / Liancourt Rocks)

Sado-shima
Ryōtsu
Hajiki-zaki

Hegura-jima

Noto hantō
Wajima
Nanao
Suzu
Suzu-misaki

Oki-shotō Dōgo
Dōzen

Mi-shima

Hime-shima

Hachijō-jima
Aoga-shima

Mikura-jima
Miyake-jima
Kōzu-shima
Nii-jima
To-shima
Ō-shima

Izu-shotō

Inamba-jima

Shiogama
Shinemaki
Higashimatsushima
Ishinomaki
Sendai
Murayama
Natori
Shiroishi
Fukushima
Kakuda
Iwaki
Hitachi
Hitachi-Ōta
Nakaminato
Mito
Tsuchiura
Chōshi
Inubō-zaki
Katsuura
Bōsō-hantō
Mobara
Narita
Chiba
Kawasaki
Yokosuka
Uraga
Tokyo
Yokohama

Kōriyama
Sukagawa
Tanagura
Nagai
Yonezawa
Aizu-Wakamatsu
Kitakata
Kaminoyama
Nikkō
Utsunomiya
Kiryū
Ōta
Kumagaya
Ōmiya
Hachiōji
Fuji
Odawara
Atami
Itō
Shimoda

Nagaoka
Shibata
Niigata
Sanjō
Nagano
Ueda
Matsumoto
Suwa
Kōfu
Fujinomiya
Shimizu
Shizuoka
Hamamatsu

Naoetsu
Takada
Itoigawa
Ōmachi
Takayama

Kanazawa
Komatsu
Kaga
Fukui
Sabae
Tsuruga

Maizuru
Obama
Miyazu
Fukuchiyama

KYŌTO
ŌSAKA
Sakai
Kōbe
Nara
Tsu
Suzuka
Yokkaichi
Nagoya
Okazaki
Toyota
Gifu
Ichinomiya
Seto
Handa
Toyohashi

Kasumi
Toyooka
Tottori
Yonago
Matsue
Sakaiminato

Okayama
Kurashiki
Fukuyama
Hiroshima
Kure
Mihara
Onomichi
Imabari
Matsuyama
Takamatsu
Tokushima
Kōchi

Kita-Kyūshū
Shimonoseki
Ube
Yamaguchi
Ōita
Beppu
Usuki
Nobeoka

PACIFIC OCEAN

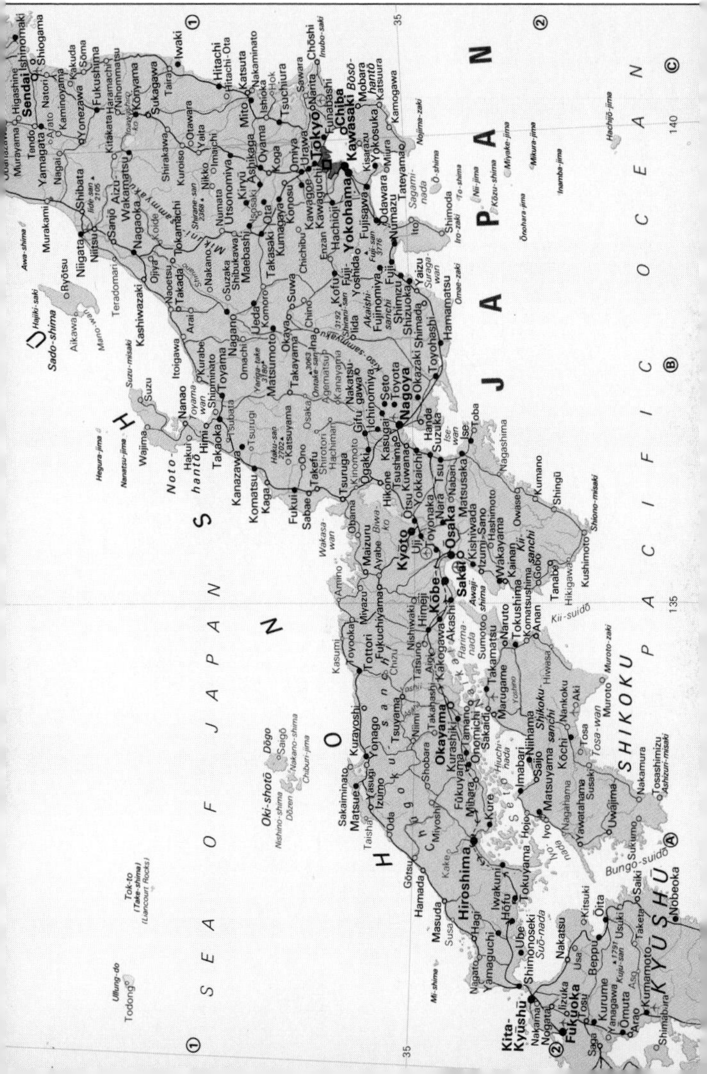

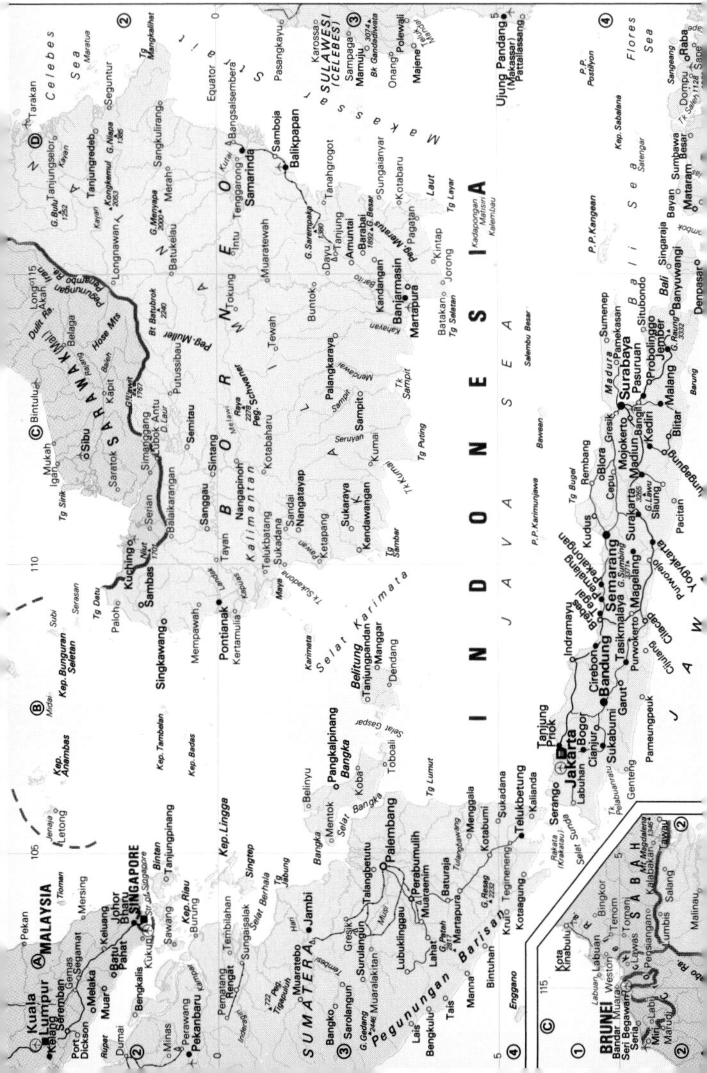

0	100	200	300	400

200 mls

Celebes Sea

Makassar Strait

Flores Sea

Java Sea

Selat Karimata

EQUATOR

MALAYSIA

SARAWAK

KALIMANTAN (BORNEO)

SUMATERA

JAVA

SULAWESI (CELEBES)

INDONESIA

BRUNEI

SABAH

SINGAPORE

Kuala Lumpur
Johor Baharu
Melaka
Pekanbaru
Jambi
Palembang
Pangkalpinang
Bangka
Pontianak
Singkawang
Kuching
Sambas
Sibu
Balikpapan
Samarinda
Tarakan
Banjarmasin
Martapura
Palangkaraya
Ujung Pandang (Makassar)
Pattallassang
Mamuju
Majene
Polewali

Jakarta
Tanjung Priok
Serang
Bogor
Bandung
Cirebon
Semarang
Yogyakarta
Surakarta
Magelang
Purwokerto
Tasikmalaya
Sukabumi
Indramayu
Tegal
Pekalongan
Kudus
Rembang
Blora
Cepu
Madiun
Kediri
Madura
Surabaya
Gresik
Mojokerto
Malang
Blitar
Probolinggo
Pasuruan
Jember
Banyuwangi
Bali
Denpasar
Singaraja
Mataram
Sumbawa
Bima
Raba
Dompu
Sumbawa

Kota Kinabalu
Labuan
Bandar Seri Begawan
Tenom
Keningau

100 200 300 400 km
100 200 mls

PACIFIC

①

*Dongsha
Qundao*

Luzon Batan
Strait Islands
Basco

Balintang Channel

②

Babuyan Islands

Cape Bojeador *Babuyan Channel* *Cape Engaño*

Laoag Aparri

Bangued Tuguegarao
Vigan

San Santiago
Fernando Solano
La Trinidad Ilagan
Baguio Bayombang
Lingayen Dagupan
San Carlos San Baler
Camiling Jose
Tarlac Cabanatuan
Gapan
San Antonio San Fernando Polillo
Angeles Malolos Islands
Olongapo Quezon City 15
Corregidor Manila
Cavite Laguna Calaguas Islands
Lubang San Pablo Santa Cruz Jose Panganiban
Islands Lipao Lucban Daet
Batangas Sipocot Catanduanes
Calapan Boac Naga Virac
Iriga Legazpi
MINDORO Mt Halcon Sorsogon Gubat
Sablayan Mt Baco *Sibuyan* Bulan

③

Busuanga San Jose *Tablas* Romblon Masbate Catarman
Calamian *Sibuyan* Calbayog Oras
Group Kalibo *Sea* SAMAR
Culion *Semirara* Masbate Catbalogan
Linapacan *Islands* Roxas *Visayan* Isidro
PANAY *Sea* Carigara Tacloban
Taytay *Cuyo* Cadiz Bogo Ormoc Guiuan
Dalanganem *Islands* Iloilo Silay Escalante Burauen
Islands Bacolod Danao *Leyte* *Gulf*
Roxas La Carlota Lapu-Lapu •10497
Dumaran Binalbagan Cebu Maasin •10265
NEGROS Dinagat
Puerto Sipalay Bohol Surigao Siarao
Princesa Bais Tagbilaran
Aborlan Dumaguete Tanjay *BOHOL* Butuan
Siaton Siquijor *Bohol Sea*
Tubbataha Dapitan Camiguin Gingoog
Brooke's *Reefs* Dipolog Oroquieta Cagayan
Point Manukan de Oro Lianga

④

Mt Balabac
Mantalingahan Liloy Iligan Bislig
Ozamiz Marawi
Tangub Malaybalay
Pagadian *Lanao* Taqum
Zamboanga Malabang
Pen. Illana Tagum
Bay MINDANAO
Cotabato Davao
Zamboanga *Moro* Datu Mt Apo Mati
Isabela *Gulf* Piang Digos
General Lais
Santos *Cape San Agustin*

SULU SEA *Jolo* Jolo
Parang *Samales*
Group Tinaca Point *Sarangani*
Jolo *Islands*

⑤

CELEBES 5
SEA

Tawitawi *Kepulauan*
Group Kawio
Kepulauan
Nenusa
Karakelong

Ⓑ 125 Ⓒ ⑤

KAZAKHSTAN

Kzyl-Orda
Aral'sk
Chelkar
Aral Sea (Aral'skoye More)
Kazakhstan
Novokazalinsk

UZBEKISTAN
Chimbay
Nukus
Tashauz
Urgench
Bukhara
Turtkul
Amu Darya

TURKMENISTAN
Mary
Chardzhou
Meymaneh
AFGHANISTAN
Herat
Shindand
Farah
Dilaram
Zaranj
Qala-y
Karakum Canal
Kyzyl-Arvat
Nebit-Dag
Kara-Bogaz
Tedzhen
Mashhad
Sabzevar
Kashmar
Kopet Dag
Baluchistan

Gur'yev
Kul'sary
Ustyurt Plateau
Pt Shevchenko
Shevchenko
Fort-Shevchenko

CASPIAN SEA
Makhachkala
Groznyy
Astrakhan'
Volgograd
Elista

Bandar 'Abbas
Makran
IRAN
Yazd
Esfahan
Dasht-e Lut
Kerman
Dasht-e Kavir
Tehran
Qom
Bandar-e 'Abbas
Shiraz
Bushehr

Baku (Baky)
AZERBAIJAN
Sumqayit
Tabriz
Ardabil
Rasht
Qazvin
Hamadan
Kermanshah
Zanjan
GEORGIA
Tbilisi
ARMENIA
Yerevan
Kumayri
Batumi
Sukhumi
Kutaisi

Baghdad
IRAQ
Mawsil
Kirkuk
Karbala'
An Najaf
Basra
KUWAIT
Ad Dahna
An Nafud
SAUDI ARABIA
Buraydah
Ha'il
Medina

BAHRAIN
Al Manamah
QATAR
Dubai
Dhahran
Dammam
The Gulf
Al Hufuf
AL-'ARABIYA

Donetsk
Zaporozh'ye
Rostov-na-Donu
Nikolayev
Mariupol'
Melitopol'
Kerch
Simferopol'
Sevastopol'
Novorossiysk
Krasnodar
Stavropol'
Sochi
Trabzon

ROMANIA
Bucuresti
Constanta
Pitesti
Ploiesti
Galati
Braila
Odessa
BLACK SEA
Varna
Burgas
BULGARIA
Sofia
Plovdiv
Ruse

TURKEY
Ankara
Istanbul
Bursa
Izmir
Konya
Kayseri
Adana
Gaziantep
Malatya
Sivas
Samsun
Erzurum
Diyarbakir
Van

Halab
SYRIA
Damascus
Hims
Hamah
Al Ladhiqiyah
LEBANON
Beirut
Tadmur
Dayr az Zawr
Al Hasakah
Mardin
Al Qamishli
Ar Raqqah
Tigris
Euphrates

ISRAEL
Tel Aviv
Jerusalem
Haifa
JORDAN
Amman
Dar'a
'Aqaba
Tabuk
Al Wajh
HIJAZ

CYPRUS
Nicosia
Famagusta

MEDITERRANEAN SEA

Alexandria
Cairo
EGYPT
Port Said
Damietta
Tanta
Suez
Ismailiya
El Faiyum
Beni Suef
El Minya
Asyut
Luxor
Aswan
Nile
El Kharga Oasis
Farafra Oasis
Siwa
Qattara Depression
Libyan Desert

Tobruk
Derna
LIBYA

GREECE
Athina
Thessaloniki
Larisa
Patrai
Kalamai
Aegean Sea
Peloponnesos
Kriti

ALBANIA
Tirane
MACEDONIA
Skopje
YUGOSLAVIA
Beograd
BOSNA I HERCEGOVINA
Dubrovnik
Split
Nis

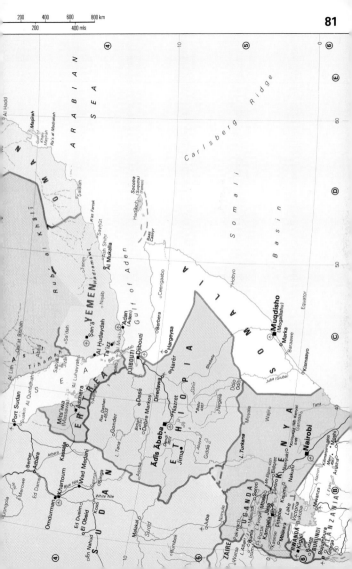

200   400   600   800 km
200   400 mils

④   ⑤   ⑥

Ⓔ

A R A B I A N   S E A

○Al Hadd

Masīrah

Gulf of
Masīrah

Ra's al Madrakah

Ⓓ

Carlsberg   Ridge

60

O M A N

al   Khālī

Rub'

○Ṣalālah

Ra's Fartak

Socotra
(Soqotra)
(Yemen)

Hadbo○

Ra's
Ḥāsiq

Ⓓ

S o m a l i

B a s i n

50

○Sayhūt

Ash Shihr

Al Mukalla

Ḥaḍramawt

Ra's Faruq

Ⓒ

Muqdisho
(Mogadishu)

Equator

Hobyo○

Ceerigaabo○

Marka

Baraawe

S O M A L I A

Berbera○

Kismaayo○

Juba (Guba)

○Najrān

Ṣan'ā'

YEMEN

Ta'izz

Al Ḥudaydah

'Adan
(Aden)

Gulf of Aden

DJIBOUTI

Djibouti

Harēr○

Hargeysa○

Shabeelle

Giriir○

Dolo Odo○

Negēlē○

Moyale○

Waiiir○

Tana○

K E N Y A

Nairobi

Ⓑ

Laascaanood○

Garoowe○

Laasqoray

Ra's Ḥāfun

○Najab

Sabyā○
Jazan○

Abhā○
○Khamīs Mushayt

A S I R

Al Luhayyah○

Tihama

Zabīd○

Ṣa'dah○

Al Lith○
Qal'at Bishah○

○Baljurshī

Sa'dah

Mandeb Bāb el

Aseb

Mitsiwa
(Massawa)

Asmera

ERITREA

Desē○

Dirēdawa○

Nazrēt○

Ras Dashen
△4533

Gonder○

Debre Markos○

L. Tana

Bahir○
Dar

Āksum○

Ādīs Ābeba

E T H I O P I A

Jīma○

Dendī
3672

Gīdolē○

○L. Ābaya

Batu
4307

L. Turkana

Port Sudan○

Suakin Al Qunfudhah○

Karima○

Berber○
Atbara○

Kassala○

Omdurman○
Khartoum

Wad Madani○

Singa○
Ed Damer○

El Obeid○

En Nahud○

Dongola○
○Merowe

Atbara

Blue Nile

White Nile

S U D A N

Kosti○

El Dueim○

Malakal○

Sudd

○Rumbek

○Juba

Nimule○

○Marsabit

Mt. Kenya
(Kirinyaga)
5199 △

L. Victoria

Lake

U G A N D A

Kampala○

Entebbe○

Mbarara○

Jinja○

Z A I R E

R W A N D A

Kigali

BURUNDI

Bujumbura

Butare○

T A N Z A N I A

Ⓑ

Nakuru○

Nyahururu○

Narok○

Eldoret○

Meru○

Embu○

Thika○

Arusha○

Kilimanjaro
(Mt. Kilimanjaro)
5895 △

Mt. Elgon 4321

Kitale○

Kisumu○

Tororo○

Soroti○

Lira○

Gulu○

L. Albert

L. Kyoga

Bukoba○

Musoma○

Watsa○

Pakwach○

Mwanza○

⑥

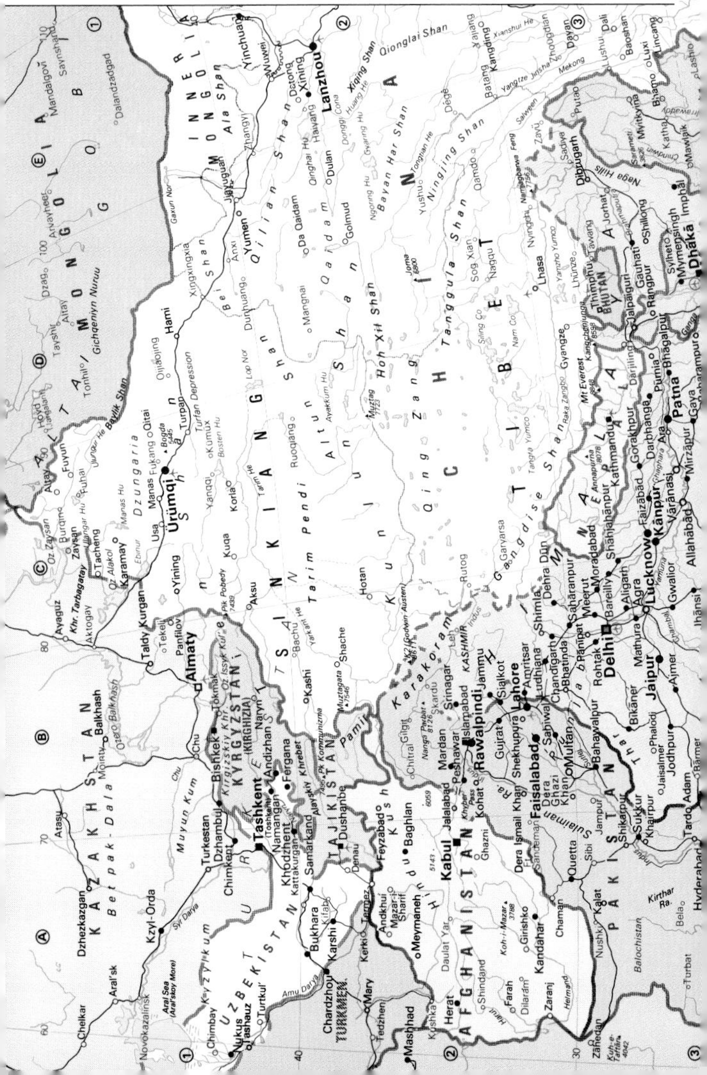

INNER MONGOLIA

KAZAKHSTAN

UZBEKISTAN

TURKMEN

AFGHANISTAN

KYRGYZSTAN (KIRGHIZIA)

TAJIKISTAN

SINKIANG

PAKISTAN

KASHMIR

BHUTAN

Lanzhou

Ürümqi

Almaty

Tashkent

Bishkek

Kabul

Delhi

Jaipur

Lucknow

Kanpur

Patna

Dhaka

Qilian Shan

Qinghai Zang Gaoyuan

Kunlun Shan

Karakoram

Himalaya

Hindu Kush

Pamir

Tarim Pendi

Dzungaria

Betpak-Dala

Aral Sea

Baikhash

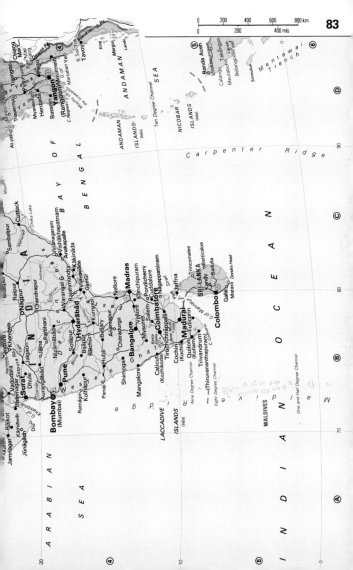

0 200 400 600 800 km
0 200 400 mils

A R A B I A N   S E A

Jamnagar
Rajkot
Kathiawar
Junagadh
Diu
Bhavnagar
Gulf of Khambhat
Vadodara
Surat

Bhilwara
Indore
Khandwa
Nagpur
Raipur
Bilaspur
Sambalpur
Cuttack
Chilka Lake

Narmada
Satpura Ra.
Damoh
Jalgaon
Ujjain
Chandrapur

Dhule
Aurangabad
Nizamabad
Warangal
Rajahmundry
Kakinada
Vijayawada
Gumur

Pune
Solapur
Raichur
Hyderabad
Kurnool
Nellore

Ramagundam
Parbhani
Bidar
Bellary
Chitradurga

Kolhapur
Hubli
Bangalore
Vellore
Kanchipuram
Madras
Pondicherry
Cuddalore

Panaji
Shimoga
Mysore
Salem
Nagapattinam

LACCADIVE
ISLANDS (India)

Mangalore
Coimbatore
Tiruchirappalli
Thanjavur

Calicut
(Kozhikode)
Madurai
Tuticorin

Cochin
(Kochi)
Quilon
(Kollam)
Trivandrum
(Thiruvananthapuram)
C. Comorin

I N D I A

D e c c a n

B O M B A Y
(Mumbai)

I N D I A N   O C E A N

Nine Degree Channel

Eight Degree Channel

MALDIVES

One and Half Degree Channel

B A Y   O F   B E N G A L

Vizianagaram
Vishakhapatnam
Anakapalle

Carpenter   Ridge

ANDAMAN   SEA

Chiang
Mai

Toungoo
Pegu (Bago)
Prome (Pyè)
Yenangyaung
Magwe

Yangon
(Rangoon)
Bassein
Henzada

Mandalay
Meiktila
Thazi

Alyabo

Mouths of the Irrawaddy
Gulf of Martaban

Moulmein
Martaban

Thaton
Tavoy

Mergui

ANDAMAN
ISLANDS (India)

Ten Degree Channel

NICOBAR
ISLANDS (India)

Banda Aceh
Lhokseumawe
Takéngon
Calang
Meulaboh
Belangpidie
Tapaktuan

Mentawai
Trench

Simeulue

SRI LANKA
Trincomalee
Batticaloa
Anuradhapura
Kandy
Colombo
Galle
Matara
Dondra Head

Gulf of Mannar
C. Pedro
Jaffna

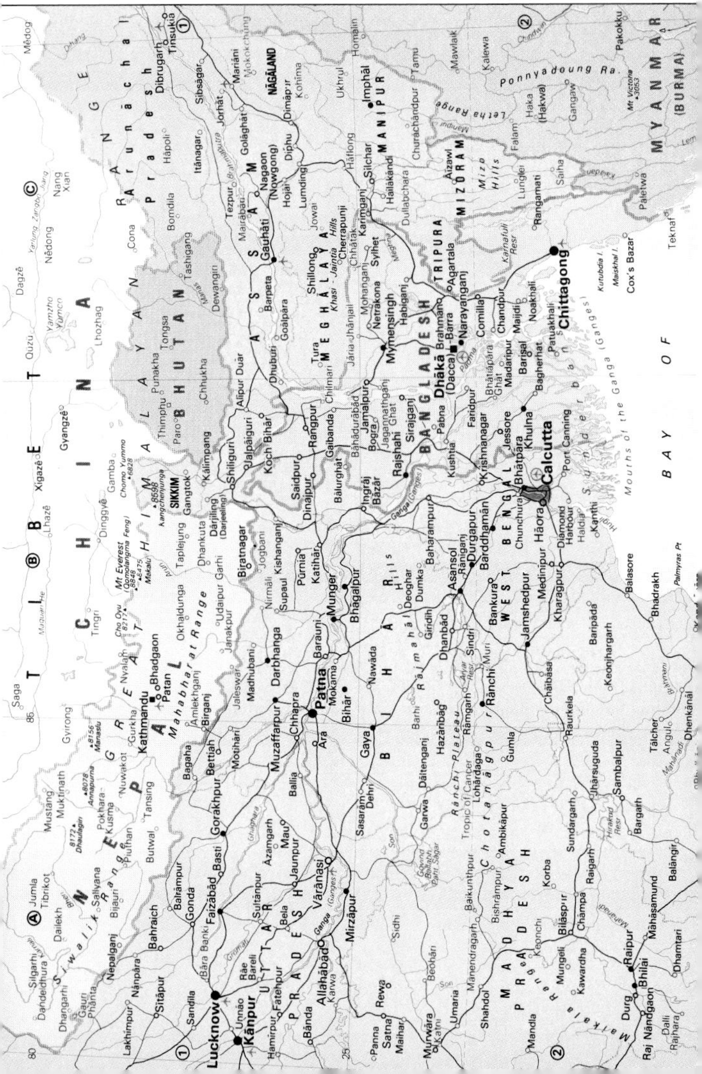

0 100 200 300
0 50 100 150 mls

CHINA

TIBET

HIMALAYA

BHUTAN

NEPAL

SIKKIM

Mt Everest

Kathmandu

ARUNACHAL PRADESH

NAGALAND

ASSAM

MEGHALAYA

MANIPUR

MIZORAM

TRIPURA

BANGLADESH

MYANMAR (BURMA)

Ponnyadoung Ra.

Letha Range

Dibrugarh
Tinsukia
Sibsagar
Jorhat
Mariani
Golaghat
Nowgong (Nowong)
Kohima
Dimapur
Imphal
Silchar
Haflong
Lumding
Tezpur
Gauhati
Shillong
Cherrapunji
Sylhet
Agartala
Aizawl

Dhaka (Dacca)
Narayanganj
Comilla
Chittagong
Cox's Bazar

Calcutta
Haora
Khulna
Jessore

WEST BENGAL

BIHAR

Patna
Gaya
Ranchi
Jamshedpur
Asansol
Bardhaman

Lucknow
Kanpur
Allahabad
Varanasi
Faizabad

UTTAR PRADESH

MADHYA PRADESH

ORISSA

Raipur
Bhilai
Durg

Chota Nagpur

BAY OF

Mouths of the Ganga (Ganges)

Sundarbans

100   200   300 km
50   100   150 mls

Bombay Ⓐ
Mumbai
Lonavale
Pune MAHARASHTRA
Mahād
Wai
Bārāmati
Chiplūn
Satāra
Phaltan
Vite
Sāngli
Miraj
Kolhāpur
Ichalkaranji
Belgaum
Panaji Goa
Madgaon
Kārwār
Sirsi
Kumta
Bhatkal
Shimoga
Kundāpura
Udupi
Mangalore
Kāsaragod
Cannanore
Tellicherry Mahe
Badagara
Calicut Ōtacamund
(Kozhikode) Nīlgiri Hills
Beypore
Coimbatore
Trichūr Shoranur
(Thrissur) Pālghāt
Ponnāni (Palakhat)
Pollāchi
Cochin Palani
(Kochi)
Ernākulam
Kottayam
Alleppey
Kāyankulam
Quilon
(Kollam)
Trivandrum
(Thiruvananthapuram)
Nāgercoil
Kanniyakumari C. Comorin

Ahmadnajar
Parbhani Purna Nānded
Bīr
Parli
Nirmal
Udgir
Daund
Bodhan
Nizāmābād
Mancherāl
Latūr
Bidar
Siddipet
Barsi
Homnābād
Gulbarga
Sangāreddi
Shāhābād
Tāndūr
Hyderābād
Bijāpur
Yādgir
Shorāpur
Narāyanpet
Mahbūbnagar
Bāgalkot
Guledagudda
Gajendragarh
Gadag
Koppal
Rāichur
Kurnool
Adoni
Nandyāl
Hubli
Hospet Bellary
Guntakal
Gooty
Dhone
Gadwāl
Haveri Kottūru Swāmihalli
Rānibennur Hirihar Rāyadurg
Dāvangere Kalyandurg
Chitradurga
Dhamavaram
Bhadrāvati
Tarikere
Kādūr Sira
Chikmagalūr
Tumkūr
Dod Ballāpur
Dharmapuri
Hassan
Madikeri
Nanjangūd
Chāmrājnagar

Warangal
Belampalli Sironcha
Jagtial
Karimnagar
Bhadrāchalam
Kottagūdem
Khammam
Nalgonda Surāpet
Vijayawāda
Guntūr
Tenāli
Macherla
Narasarāopet
Chilakalūripet
Bāpatla
Chirāla
Ongole
Kani
Kondukūr
Kavali
Nellore
Gudūr
Venkatagiri
Sri Kālahasti Pulicat L.
Tirupati
Chittoor
Arakkonam
Madras
Vellore
Kānchipuram
Āmbūr
Javadi Hills
Tiruvannāmalai
Tindivanam
Pondicherry
Cuddalore
Chidambaram
Vriddháchalam
Kumbakonam
Kāraikāl
Nāgappattinam
Thanjāvūr
Mannārgudi
Pudukkottai
Pt Calimere
Kodiyakkari
Paramakkudi
Rāmanāthapuram
Jaffna
Mullaittvu
Talaimannar
Mannar
Vavuniya
Trincomalee
Anurādhapura

ANDHRA
PRADESH
KARNATAKA
TAMIL NĀDU

Bangalore
Kolār
Gold Fields
Kolār
Krishnagiri
Tiruppattūr
Salem
Erode
Vellore
Villupuram
Tiruchchirāppalli
Dindigul
Madurai
Virudunagar
Aruppukkottai
Rājapālaiyam
Tenkāsi
Tirunelveli
Tuticorin
Palayankottai
Tiruchchendūr

Gulf of
Mannār

SRI LANKA
CEYLON
Colombo
Dehiwala-Mt Lavinia
Moratuwa
Negombo
Chilaw
Kurunegala
Gampola Kandy
Nuwara-Eliya
Ratnapura
Badulla
Opanake
Ambalangoda
Galle
Matara Dondra Hd
Hambantota
Batticaloa
Matale
Dambulla
Puttalam
Havankulam

Coromandel Coast

Malabar Coast

Palk Strait
Adam's
Bridge
Pt Pedro

Androth

Kalpeni

e Degree Channel

ht Degree Channel

ALDIVES

Ⓐ   75   Ⓑ   Ⓒ

① ② ③
15
10

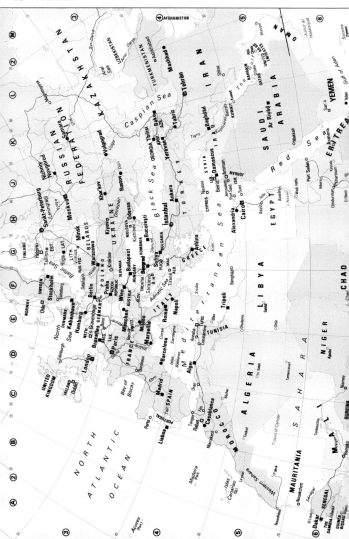

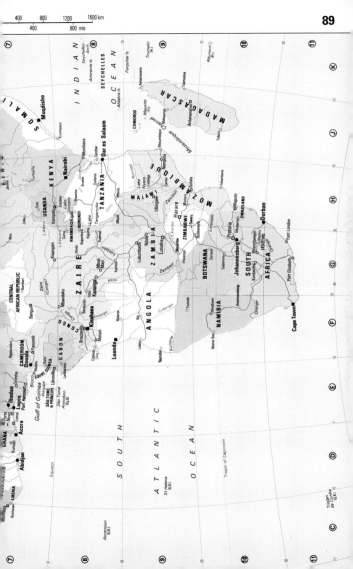

400 800 1200 1600 km
400 800 mls

I N D I A N

O C E A N

Seychelles Is

SEYCHELLES

⑧

Trompelin (Fr)

Ⓚ

Amirante Is

Farquhar Is

Aldabra Is

Providence

Mayotte (Fr)

Cosmoledo

Assumption

COMOROS

Moroni

Juan de Nova (Fr)

M A D A G A S C A R

Antananarivo

Ⓙ

Réunion (Fr)

⑩

SOMALI

Muqdisho

Kismaayo

Mombasa

Zanzibar

Dar es Salaam

Mozambique

Channel

Toliary

Morondava

Tolañaro

SOMALIA

Juba

Turkana

KENYA

Nairobi

Tana

UGANDA

Kampala

L.Albert

L.Kyoga

L.Edward

L.Victoria

RWANDA

Kigali

BURUNDI

Bujumbura

Arusha

Dodoma

TANZANIA

L.Tanganyika

Mbeya

L.Nyasa

MALAWI

Lilongwe

Blantyre

MOZAMBIQUE

Beira

Sofala

Ⓗ

⑨

Gulu

Mbale

Kisangani

ZAIRE

Kananga

Kananga

Mbuji-Mayi

Kamina

Lubumbashi

ZAMBIA

Kitwe

Ndola

Lusaka

Kabwe

Kafue

Zambezi

Luangwa

Kariba

ZIMBABWE

Harare

Mutare

Gweru

Bulawayo

Hwange

Kwekwe

Limpopo

BOTSWANA

Gaborone

Francistown

Serowe

Mazoe

SWAZILAND

Mbabane

Maputo

SOUTH

Pretoria

Johannesburg

AFRICA

LESOTHO

Maseru

Durban

East London

Ⓖ

⑩

CENTRAL

AFRICAN REPUBLIC

Bangui

Zaire (Congo)

Congo

CONGO

Brazzaville

Kinshasa

Matadi

Kikwit

Cabinda (Ang)

Kasai

Kwango

ANGOLA

Luanda

Malanje

Lobito

Benguela

Kwanza

Cuango

Cuanza

Bié

Cubango

Huambo

Lubango

Menongue

Okavango

L.Ngami

NAMIBIA

Windhoek

Walvis Bay (SA)

Keetmanshoop

Orange

Kimberley

Bloemfontein

Mafikeng

Cape Town

Port Elizabeth

Ⓕ

CAMEROON

Douala

Yaoundé

Ngaoundéré

GABON

Libreville

Port-Gentil

Lambaréné

Oyem

EQUAT. GUINEA

Bioko

São Tomé

& PRÍNCIPE

Príncipe

São Tomé

Annobón (EqG)

Gulf of Guinea

Ⓔ

⑧

Ibadan

Lagos

Porto-Novo

Cotonou

GHANA

Accra

Kumasi

Abidjan

Port Harcourt

Calabar

Warri

Benin

Ouidah

LIBERIA

Monrovia

Ⓓ

⑦

Equator

S O U T H

A T L A N T I C

O C E A N

St Helena (UK)

Tropic of Capricorn

Ascension (UK)

Tristan da Cunha (UK)

Ⓒ

⑦

⑧

⑨

⑩

⑪

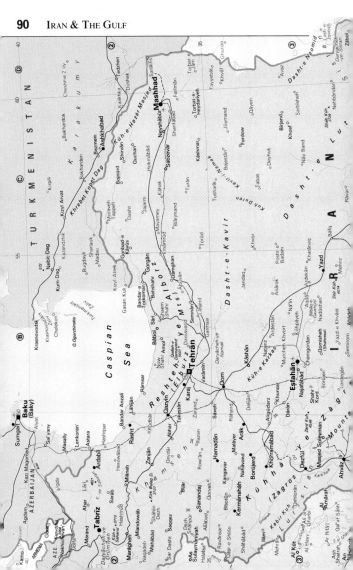

Edirne Kırklareli
Babaeski
Uzunköprü İğneada (A)
Çorlu
Tekirdağ **İstanbul**
Üsküdar
Gelibolu Adapazarı
Gemlik İzmit
Eceabat Biga Bandırma
Çanakkale Gönen Bursa
İznik
Edremit
Ayvalık Balıkesir
Mitilíni Bergama Akhisar
Lésvos Manisa Turgutlu
Khíos Çeşme Alaşehir
İzmir
Sámos Aydın Nazilli
Ikaria Söke Saraykoy
Mílas Denizli
Muğla Burdur
Kás Köyceğiz Korkuteli
Ródhos Fethiye
GREECE Ródhos Finike
Kárpathos Kastellorizon

İnebolu Sinop
Zonguldak Bartın Kastamonu Boyabat Bafra Br.
Ereğli Karabük Ilgaz Dağları Tosya İskilip
Düzce Bolu Çankırı Kalecik
Köroğlu Tepesi ▲2378 **Ankara** Delice
Eskişehir Polatlı Balâ Kırıkkale
Kütahya Sivrihisar Yozgat Sorgun
Emirdağ Kulu Kırşehir
Afyon Bolvadin Tuz Gölü Nevşehir
Sandıklı Cihanbeyli Aksaray Eroıas D.
Akşehir Kadınhanı Konya Karapınar
Eğridir G. İsparta Beyşehir Ereğli Pozantı
Beyşehir Karaman Tarsus
Akseki Toros Dağları Adana
Antalya Alanya Silifke Mersin Ceyhan
Manavgat Caga Tepe 2294 Karataş
Antalya Gelidonya Br. İnce kum Br. Samandağ
Körfezi Anamur

C. Arnauti **Nicosia** Famagusta
Mt Troodos ▲1951 **CYPRUS** Larnaca C. Greco
Limassol

M e d i t e r r a n e a n

S e a

Samsun Ter
Merzifon Amasya Yeşi Tasova
Çorum Turhal
Boğazlıyan Şarkışla
Kızıl Gemerek
Kayseri Gür
Elbistan Göksu
Niğde Bor Feke Kahramanm
Ala D. Kozan Ceyhan Ga
İskenderun Osmaniye
Antakya Idlib
Jisr esh Shughūr
Al Lādhiqiyah Masyâf Ha
Bāniyās Hi
Tartūs Al
Tall Kalakh Qa
Tripoli
(Tarabulus esh Sharqi) Al Qu
Ba'albek
Beirut
(Beyrouth) Zahle **Dāma**
LEBANON (Dimash
Saida Al Qunaytirah As S
Tyre Dar'a Salkh
'Akko Zefat Mafraq
Haifa Nazareth Irbid
Netanya Dar'a
Tel Aviv Yafo Nablus Zarqa
Ashdod **ISRAEL** **Amman**
Gaza **Jerusalem**
Hebron Dead Sea Qatrâna
Beersheba Kârak
El 'Arîsh Safi Bâvi
Negev Ma'ân
Shaubak El Tîh
Birket Qârûn Nakhl Naqb Ishtar

Matrûh Râs el Kenâyis
Alexandria
(El Iskandariya) Rashîd Dumyât Baltîm Port Said (Bûr Sa'îd)
Damanhûr El Mahalla el Kubra El Mansûra
El 'Alamein Tanta Benha Ismâ'îliya Suez Canal Bitter Lakes
Libyan Wâdi el Natrûn Zagâzig Suez (El Suweis)
Plateau **El Gîza** Helwân 'Ain Sukhna
Qattâra Depression -133 **Cairo** (El Qâhira)
Qara Birkat Qârûn S I N A I El 'Igma
El Faiyûm El Kuntilla
El Fashn Beni Suef Râs Ghârib Dahab G. Katharîna ▲2637 El Tûr
Bawiti El Harra Maghâgha Biba **E G Y P T** Sharqiya Ras esh J. al Lawz ▲2578 Tabûk
Bahâriya Oasis Beni Mazâr Nile Sahra Qâbâ Mudawwara At T
El Minya Mallawi (B) Aqaba Al Bi't Haql

L i b y a n
P l a t e a u El 'Alamein

J O R
Wâ
Ardh
'Il
Ard e
Bâyir

0 25 50 75 100
0 25 50 mls

Paleokhóri Larnaca C Greco
Lefkara Larnaca Bay
Zyyi 34
Limassol **CYPRUS**
Akrotiri Bay
C. Gata

B

Tartūs Kafrūn Bashūr
Arwad An Nāṣirah Tall Bīsā
Duraykīsh Shafta Qal'at al Hiṣ
KRAK-DES-CHEVALIERS
Hamīdīyah Tall Kalākh
Kleiat Kebīr Qoubayāt Shayr
El Mīna El Hermel Ūy
Tripoli Zghorta Halba H
(Tarābulus esh Shām) Qornet es Saouda 3086 Laboue
Batroun Amioune Deir el Ahmar Day A
Jubail Kartaba El Haï An N
BYBLOS Yabrūd
Rhazīr Ba'albek 2559
LEBANON An N
Jounieh Bikfaya 2628 Yabrūd
Beirut Ba'abda Zahle Rayak
(Beyrouth) Aley Zabdāni Al Mazūra
Damour Zabdāni 1970 Qutayfa
Beit ed Dine 'Ayn al Fījah
Machgharah Barada **Damas**
Saida Jezzine Rachaya Qatana (Dimashq)
(Sidon) Hāsbaiya Jash Shaykh
Litāni (Mt Hermon) A'way Al Hijar
Tyr Marjayoun Al Kiswah
(Tyre, Sour) Banyas Dayr 'Alī
Q.Shemona Mas'adah
Enn Nāqoūra Jouai'ya CEASE FIRE Ghabāghib Qutayfa
LINES 1974 Al Qunayṭirah Mismiye
Bennt Yesud Aş Şanamayn
Nahariya Jbail Hamadia Khushnīyah Khabāb
Ma'alot 1208 Har Meron Nawā Al Lajāh Izra'
Akko Tarshiha Zefat 863
(Acre) Rama (Safad) Tiberias Tasīl Shahb
Q.Yam Shefar'am (Yam Kinneret/ Shaykh
Haifa B.of Haifa Sea of Galilee) Miskīn Jai
(Hefa) Q. Ata Tiberias
'Atlit Nazareth Fīq As Suwaydā'
Mt Carmel Ma'agan Irbid
Afula Dar'ā Ramtha
Zikhron Ya'aqov MEGIDDO Deir Abu ash
CAESAREA ARMAGEDDON Beyt o Husn Buṣr
Pardes Hanna Jenin Shean Ajlūn Mafraq
Hadera Jabatiya Um el 1247 Jarash
Netanya Tubas Daraj Er Rumman Sabha
ISRAEL Sabastiya Zarqa
Herzliyya Nablus Suweilih Marka Zarqa
Ramat Gan Kefar Sava Ba'al Hazor Salt Amman
Tel Aviv Petah Tiqwa 1016 Karama Sahāb
Yafo (Jaffa) Holon Ramallah Wadi es Sir
Rishon le Zion Lod Jericho Naur Qasr el Kharana
Rehovot Rama (Ariha) Jabal
Ashdod Jerusalem (El Quds) Mādaba Mudeissat
(Yerushalayim) Dhibān Khan ez Zabib
Ashqelon Beit Jala Bethlehem
Qiryat (El Khalil) Qatrāna
Gat Bet Hebron
Gaza Guvrin En Gedi
Sederot LACHISH Dura Yatta Karak
Gaza Strip Gerar Edh Mazra el Meise
Khan Yunis Dhahiriya MEZADA Mazār Manzil
Rafah Ofaqim Be'er Sheva' El Lisān Rabba Qatrāna
Ras Burūn Zeelim Arad Qā'el Ḥafīra
Sabkhet HALUZA Sedom
el Bardawil Revivim MAMSHIT **JORDA**
El 'Arīsh Qeziot Dimona 1305
SHIVTA Yeroham Sal J. Ed Daba Tafila
Bir Lahfān NIZANA Sede Oron 1365 Ḥasā Qal'el Jinz
Abu 'Aweigila AVEDAT Boqer Hazeva Qasr ed Dalāwīsh Jebel
G. Maghāra El Quseima **N** e g e v Mizpe 1641 1082
735 Ramon Dana Al 'Atā'ita
G. Libni 463 892 Ramon Ein 1654
G. Hasana G.Halal Yahav Shaubak Uneisa
Bir Gifgāfa **E G Y P T** Har Nafha Nijil
1006 Har Hakippa Umm Suwwāna
A 34 Har Saggi PETRA 36 C

(A) (B) (C)

MEDITERRANEAN

SEA

SYRIA

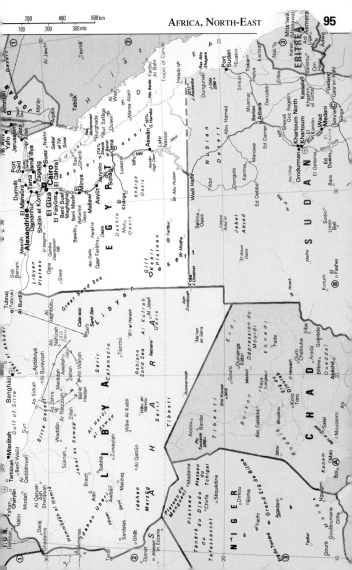

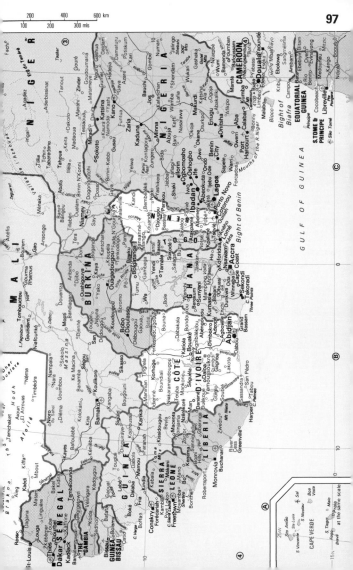

200   400   600 km
100   200   300 mls

Rukwa
Nat.Pk.   Ruaha   Mikumi   Kisiju
mbawanga   Chunya   Iringa   Ifakara   Kilindoni   Mafia I.
Mbeya   Rungwe   Sao   Mahenge   Kilwa Kivinje   SEYCHELLES
2969   Hill   Njombe   Kilwa Kisiwani   Aldabra Is   Providence
Tukuyu   Karonga   Luwegu   Liwale   Lindi   Assumption   Cosmoledo   Is
Iloska   Manda   Nachingwea   Masasi   Mtwara   Is   Farquhar
Chilumba   Rumphi   Mbamba Bay   Tunduru   Newala   C.Delgado   Is Glorieuses   Is
Mzuzu   Lupilichi   Mueda   Mocimboa   da Praia   Grande   COMOROS   Tj. Babaomby
Mzimba   Metangula   Macaloge   Quissanga   Ilbo   Moroni   Comore   Anjouan   Antseranana
Lundazi   Lichinga   Marrupa   Montepuez   de Pemba   Mutsamudu   Mahéli   C.   St Sébastien   1478
Kasungu   Mandimba   Namuno   Pemba   Mayotte   Dzaoudzi   Ambilobe   Mrgne
Mchinji   Salima   Maúa   Meconta   Mecufi   (Fr.)   Nosy Bé   Massif   Vohimarina
Lilongwe   Dedza   Mangoche   Cuamba   Namapa   Memba   Ambanja   du   2876
Furancungo   Malema   Ribáuè   Nacala   Analalava   Saratanana   Sambava
Cabora   Zomba   Chiwa   Molócuas   Nampula   B. de Mahajamba   Antsohihy   Befandriana   Antalaha
Bassa   Blantyre   Limbe   Erego   Moçambique   B.de Bombetoka   Mandritsara   Marantsetra   C.Masoala
Teto   Chikwawa   Milange   Gilé   Mogincual   Mahajanga   Marovoay   Mampikony   Antongila   Nosy Boraha
Changara   Mocuba   Angoche   (Majunga)   Ambato   Andilamena   Ivongo   Ambodifototra
Chemba   Mutarara   Pebane   Moma   Tsaratanana   Boeny   Soanierana   Atsinanana
Mutoko   Caia   Vila da Magania   Juan   Maevatanana   Morafenobe   Ambatondrazaka   Fenoarivo
yanga   Catandica   Quelimane   de Nova   Ambatolampy   Anjozorobe   Toamasina
Rusape   Mopeia   (Fr.)   Maintirano   Morarano   (Tamatave)
Mutare   Gorongosa   Marromeu   Nosy Barren   Tsiroanomandidy   Moramanga   Vohibinany
Chimoio   Chinde   Ambatolampy   Antananarivo
Va Machado   Dondo   Miandrivazo   340   (Tananarive)   Mahanoro
Binga   Sofala (Beira)   Betafo   Antsirabe
Machaze   MADAGASCAR   Morondava   Manabo   Atofinandrahana   Nosy Varika
Save   Nova Mambone   (MALAGASY REP.)   Malaimbandy   Ambositra   Ifanadiana   Mananjary
acuala   Bartolomeu Dias   Manja   Ambohimahasoa   Manakara
Mabote   Vilanculos   Morombe   Fianarantsoa   Ambalavao
Machalla   Pta de   Tanjona   Ihosy   Ivohibe   Manakara
Funhalouro   Barra Falsa   Ankaboa   Ankazoabo   Vangaindrano   Farafangana
Massingir   Massinga   Bassas   Sakaraha   Betroka   Midongy   Tropic of Capricorn
Mabalane   Homoine   da India   Toliara   Betioky   Atsimo
Maça   Morrumbene   (Fr.)   B.de St Augustin   Onilahy   Bekily   Ampanihy   Amboasary   Tôlañaro
Manhica   Inhambane   Europa   Beloha   Tsihombe   Ambovombe
Moamba   Quissico   (Fr.)   Ampanihy   Vohimena
Maputo   Xai Xai   Tanjona
(Lourenço Marques)   Bela   Vohimena
Bela Vista

Swartruggens   Rustenburg   Brits   Middelburg   Waterval   Maputo
goma   Mafikeng   Koster   Rustenburg   Pretoria   Witbank   Belfast   Boven   Barberton
Mtubatuba   Zeerust   Lichtenburg   Randburg   Johannesburg   Carolina   Komati   Namaacha   Matola   Bela
C.St Lucia   Delareyville   Sanrieshof   Randfontein   Soweto   Germiston   Leslie   Breyten   Mbabane   Vista
mpangeni   Ottosdal   Carletonville   Evaton   Springs   Bethal   Ermelo   Amsterdam   SWAZILAND   Stegi
burg   Quaggablat   Viljoenskroon   Potchefstroom   Parys   Sasolburg   Heidelberg   Morgenzon   Piet Retief   Usutu   Luvumisa
an   Taung   Schweizer   Wolmaransstad   Vereeniging   Standerton   Villiers   Amersfoort   Nhlangano   Sibayi
oti   Reneke   Bloemhof   Frankfort   Volksrust   Paulpietersburg   Mkuzi   L.St Lucia   30
Warrenton   Bothaville   Kroonstad   Retz   Vrede   Utrecht   Vryheid   Nongoma   Mtubatuba
Christiana   Hoopstad   Odendaalsrus   Lindley   Warden   Newcastle   Dundee   Melmoth   Empangeni
Bultfontein   Welkom   Ventersburg   Bethlehem   Glencoe   Wasbank   Richard's Bay
Kimberley   Dealesville   Virginia   Winburg   Senekal   Harrismith   Ladysmith   Eshowe   Gingindlovu
Boshof   Theunissen   Ladybrand   Colenso   Weenen   Stanger
Bloemfontein   Brandfort   Ficksburg   Champagne Castle   Estcourt   Tugela   Greytown   Tongaat
Petrusburg   Thaba   Escourt   Mooi   New Hanover   Verulam
Hopetown   Teyateyaneng   Nkosi   Weenen   River   Howick   Durban
Luckhoff   Edenburg   Wepener   Thabana   Ntlenyana   Pietermaritzburg   Richmond
Trompsburg   Mafeteng   LESOTHO   Donnybrook

100 km
50 mls

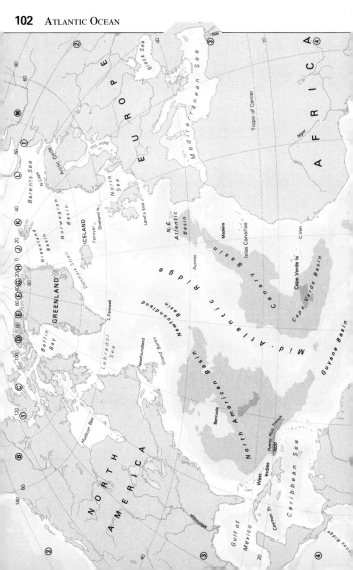

600   1200   1800   2400 km
600   1200 mls

⑤   ⑥   ⑦   Ⓜ   ⑧   Ⓛ   Ⓚ   Ⓙ   Ⓘ   Ⓗ   Ⓖ   Ⓕ   Ⓔ   Ⓓ   Ⓒ   Ⓑ

Tropic of Capricorn

Crozet Plateau

Agulhas Plateau

C. Agulhas

Prince Edward Is.

Angola Basin

St Helena

Walvis Ridge

Cape Basin

Discovery Tablemount ·411

Atlantic-Indian Ridge

Bouvet I.

Atlantic-Indian Antarctic Basin

Maud Seamount ·1798

A N T A R C T I C A

Ascension

Tristan da Cunha

Gough I.

Mid-Atlantic Ridge

Brazil Basin

Martin Vaz

Trindade

Rio Grande Rise ·637

Argentine Basin

S. Georgia

S. Sandwich Tr. 8264

S. Sandwich Is.

Scotia Sea

N. Scotia Ridge

Falkland Is.

S. Orkney Is.

Weddell Sea

S O U T H   A M E R I C A

Cabo de Hornos

Drake Passage

Antarctic Penin.

Peter I I.

Antarctic Circle

South Pacific Basin

South Pacific Basin

Peru-Chile Trench

·6066 ·7635

·6081

I. San Ambrosio
I. San Felix

Is. Juan Fernandez

S.W. Peru K.M.S.

Pacific-Antarctic Ridge

40   60   80   60   40   20   80   60   40   20   0   20   40   60   80   100   120   140   20   40   60

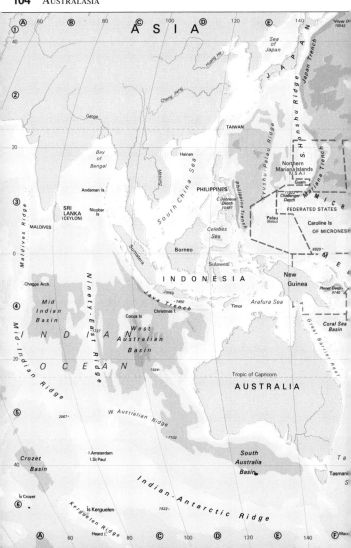

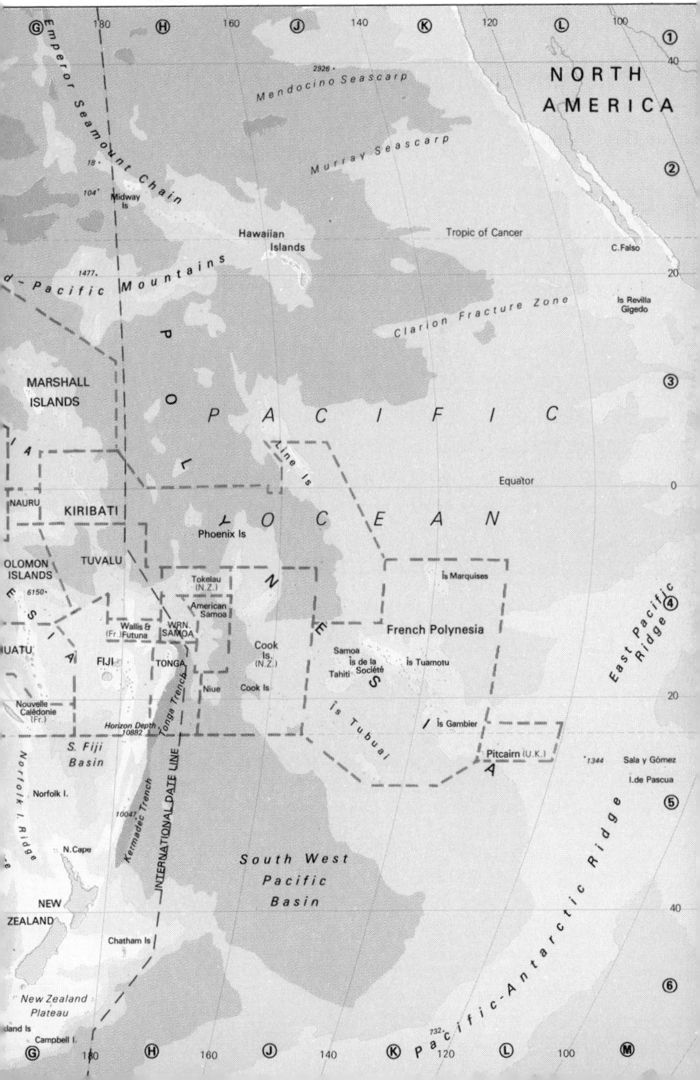

Scale bar: 600 1200 1800 2400 km / 600 1200 mils

NORTH AMERICA

40

2926 · Mendocino Seascarp

Murray Seascarp

Emperor Seamount Chain

18·

104·

Midway Is

1477·

Hawaiian Islands

Tropic of Cancer

20

C. Falso

d - Pacific Mountains

Mid-Pacific Mountains

Clarion Fracture Zone

Is Revilla Gigedo

MARSHALL ISLANDS

P A C I F I C

3

NAURU

KIRIBATI

Line Is

Equator

0

OLOMON ISLANDS

TUVALU

6150·

Phoenix Is

L O C E A N

is Marquises

4

UATU

Tokelau (N.Z.)

WRN. SAMOA

Walis & (Fr) Futuna

American Samoa

French Polynesia

East Pacific Ridge

FIJI

TONGA

Cook Is. (N.Z.)

Samoa Tahiti is de la Société

is Tuamotu

20

Nouvelle Calédonie (Fr.)

Niue

Cook Is.

N

is Tubuai

is Gambier

Horizon Depth 10882·

Pitcairn (U.K.)

·1344

Sala y Gómez

S. Fiji Basin

Kermadec Trench

INTERNATIONAL DATE LINE

A

i. de Pascua

Norfolk I. Ridge

Norfolk I.

10047·

N. Cape

South West Pacific Basin

5

40

NEW ZEALAND

New Zealand Plateau

Chatham Is

island Is

Campbell I.

Pacific-Antarctic Ridge

732·

6

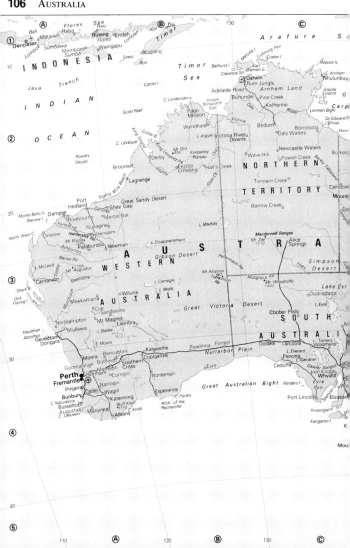

200   400   600   800 km

200   400 mls

Darwu   Gulf of Papua   Popondetta **PAPUA**   Ⓔ   New   Santa Isabel   **SOLOMON**
Sabai   Port Moresby   Okoka   Etirecasteaux   Wigodlark   Georgia   **ISLANDS**   Stewart Is   Ⓕ
rres Strait   C York   **NEW   GUINEA**   Alotau   Florida Is   Malaita   ①
Vales   Somerset   Kupiano   Samarai   Misima   Guadalcanal   Honiara   Maramasike
C York   Misima**Louisiade   Arch**   10   San Cristobal
Cape   C Grenville   Taguta   Rossel
York   Iron   Range   Bennell
Coen   Princess   Charlotte B   ②
Peninsula   C   o   r   a   l
Mitchell River   Laura   Cooktown   **Coral Sea**
Gilbert   Mt Barrie Frere   Cairns   **Island Territories**   Récifs
Normanton   Ravenshoe   Innisfail   d'Entrecasteaux
lydon   Forsayth   Palm Is   S   Conina Is   ②
Ingham   e   a   Marion Reef   Îles   Îles Belep
Townsville   Chesterfield   Mueo   Lifu
curry   Richmond   Charters Towers   Ayr   Brit   Boutali   Uvéa
Hughenden   Bowen   Collinsville   Mackay   Bellona   **Nouvelle**   Nouméa
wyn   **QUEENSLAND**   Sarina   Northumberland   Reefs   **Calédonie**   Île des Pins
Winton   Clermont   Swan   Cato   Tropic of Capricorn
Longreach   Emerald   Reefs   **Rockhampton**   Mount Morgan
Barcaldine   Mount Morgan   **Gladstone**
Blackall   Theodore   **Bundaberg**   Fraser or   **P   A   C   I   F   I   C**
Windorah   Taroom   Gt Sandy I   ③
Charleville   Roma   Miles   **Maryborough**
Quilpie   Range   Dalby   Gympie   **O   C   E   A   N**
Mitparinka   St George   **Toowoomba**   **Brisbane**
Cunnamulla   Goondiwindi   **Ipswich**
Bourke   Warwick   Lismore
Wilcannia   Moree   Glen   Casino   Norfolk I   ④
ken Hill   Darling   Narrabri   Inness   Grafton   (Aust.)
Menindee   Cobar   Armidale   Rocky Mtn
Ivanhoe   Nyngan   Tamworth   Port Macquarie   Lord Howe I   30
NEW   SOUTH   Taree   (Aust.)
ura   Balranald   Gunnedah   Nyngan   **Maitland**
Idge   **WALES**   Gongolgon   Dubbo   Cessnock
Riverina   Bathurst   **Newcastle**   170
Wagga Wagga   Orange   Lithgow
Denliquin   Griffith   **Sydney**
VICTORIA   Cootamundra   Junee   **Wollongong**   ④
Amstel   Bendigo   Shepparton   Albury   **Canberra**   Goulburn
Ballarat   Echuca   Kosciusko   Bombala
Geelong   **Melbourne**   Bairnsdale   Howe
mbool   Colac   Morwell   Sale   **T   A   S   M   A   N**
Wonthaggi   Wilson's Prom.
King I   **Bass Strait**   Flinders
C Grim   Furneaux   Barren   **S   E   A**
Smithton   Group
Devonport   Burnie   **NEW**   C Farewell   Ⓖ
Queenstown   Launceston   St Mary's   **ZEALAND**   Nelson   Westport
TASMANIA   **South Island**   Greymouth
Geeveston   40
Hobart
South West C   South East C   Ⓔ   150   Ⓕ   160   Ⓖ

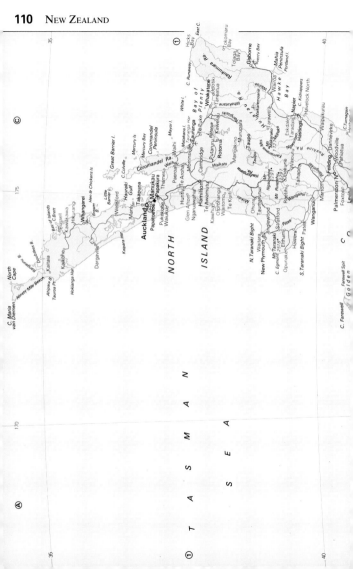

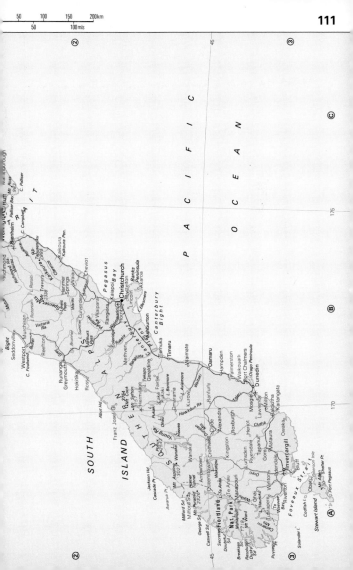

50 100 150 200km
50 100mis

②

③

ⓒ

ⓑ

ⓐ

③

②

P A C I F I C

O C E A N

45

175

170

45

SOUTH

ISLAND

S O U T H E R N   A L P S

Fiordland Nat. Park

Wellington
Hutt
Blenheim
Richmond
Seddonville
Westport
Greymouth
Hokitika
Ross
Franz Josef Gl.
Murchison
Reefton
Runanga
Kaikoura
Hanmer Springs
Culverden
Rangiora
Christchurch
Lincoln
Lyttelton
Akaroa
Banks Peninsula
Ashburton
Methven
Geraldine
Temuka
Timaru
Waimate
Oamaru
Hampden
Palmerston
Dunedin
Mosgiel
Milton
Balclutha
Kaitangata
Owaka
Gore
Mataura
Invercargill
Bluff
Riverton
Winton
Lumsden
Kingston
Queenstown
Arrowtown
Wanaka
Cromwell
Alexandra
Roxburgh
Tapanui
Ranfurly
Mt Cook
C. Campbell
C. Palliser
Palliser Bay
Mt Ross
Kaikoura Pen.
Pegasus Bay
Canterbury Bight
Otago Peninsula
Port Chalmers
Foveaux Strait
Stewart Island
Te Anau
Manapouri
Milford Sd.
Caswell Sd.
George Sd.
Doubtful Sd.
Breaksea Sd.
Dusky Sd.
Resolution I.
Solander I.
Preservation Inlet
Port Pegasus

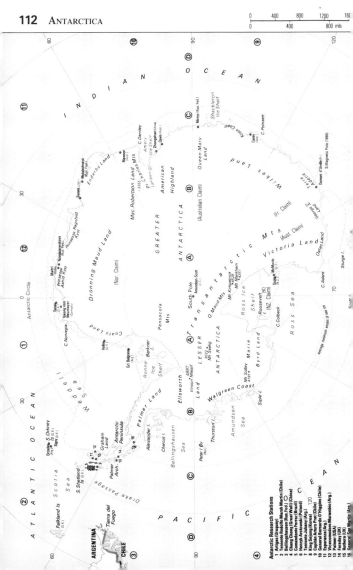

120

Antarctic Research Stations
1 Artigas (Uruguay)
2 Teniente Rodolfo Marsh Martin (Chile)
3 Bellingshausen (Rus. Fed.)
4 Chang Cheng (Great Wall) (China)
5 Comandante Ferraz (Brazil)
6 Henryk Arctowski (Poland)
7 Teniente Jubany (Arg.)
8 King Sejong (Korea)
9 Capitán Arturo Prat (Chile)
10 General Bernardo O'Higgins (Chile)
11 Esperanza (Arg.)
12 Vicecomodoro Marambio (Arg.)
13 Palmer (USA)
14 Faraday (UK)
15 Rothera (UK)
16 General San Martin (Arg.)

Index

In the index, the first number refers to the page, and the following letter and number to the section of the map in which the index entry can be found. For example, 48C2 **Paris** means that Paris can be found on page 48 where column C and row 2 meet.

Abbreviations used in the index

Afghan	Afghanistan	Hung	Hungary	Phil	Philippines	Arch	Archipelago
Alb	Albania	Ind	Indonesia	Pol	Poland	B	Bay
Alg	Algeria	Irish Rep	Ireland	Port	Portugal	C	Cape
Ant	Antarctica	Leb	Lebanon	Rom	Romania	Chan	Channel
Arg	Argentina	Lib	Liberia	Russian Fed	Russian	Gl	Glacier
Aust	Australia	Liech	Liechtenstein		Federation	I(s)	Island(s)
Bang	Bangladesh	Lux	Luxembourg	S Arabia	Saudi Arabia	Lg	Lagoon
Belg	Belgium	Madag	Madagascar	Scot	Scotland	L	Lake
Bol	Bolivia	Malay	Malaysia	Sen	Senegal	Mt(s)	Mountain(s)
Bulg	Bulgaria	Maur	Mauritania	S Africa	South Africa	O	Ocean
Burk	Burkina	Mor	Morocco	Switz	Switzerland	P	Pass
Camb	Cambodia	Mozam	Mozambique	Tanz	Tanzania	Pen	Peninsula
Can	Canada	Myan	Myanmar	Thai	Thailand	Plat	Plateau
CAR	Central African Republic	Neth	Netherlands	Turk	Turkey	Pt	Point
Den	Denmark	NZ	New Zealand	USA	United States	Res	Reservoir
Dom Rep	Dominican Republic	Nic	Nicaragua		of America	R	River
El Sal	El Salvador	N Ire	Northern Ireland	Urug	Uruguay	S	Sea
Eng	England	Nig	Nigeria	Ven	Venezuela	Sd	Sound
Equ Guinea	Equatorial Guinea	Nor	Norway	Viet	Vietnam	Str	Strait
Eth	Ethiopia	Pak	Pakistan	Yugos	Yugoslavia	V	Valley
Fin	Finland	PNG	Papua New Guinea	Zim	Zimbabwe		
Germ	Germany	Par	Paraguay				

A

57B2 **Aachen** Germany
46C1 **Aalst** Belg
38K6 **Äänekoski** Fin
47C1 **Aarau** Switz
47B1 **Aare** R Switz
72A3 **Aba** China
97C4 **Aba** Nig
99D2 **Aba** Zaïre
91A3 **Abadan** Iran
90B3 **Abadeh** Iran
35B1 **Abaeté** Brazil
35B1 **Abaeté** R Brazil
31B2 **Abaetetuba** Brazil
72D1 **Abagnar Qi** China
72D1 **Abakaliki** Nig
63B2 **Abakan**
Russian Fed
97C3 **Abala** Niger
96C2 **Abalessa** Alg
90B3 **Abarqu** Iran
74E2 **Abashiri** Japan
74E2 **Abashiri-wan** B
Japan
71F4 **Abau** PNG
99D2 **Abaya** L Eth
99D1 **Abbai** R Eth
99E1 **Abbe** L Eth
48C1 **Abbeville** France
19A3 **Abbeville** Louisiana,
USA
17B1 **Abbeville** S Carolina,
USA
45B2 **Abbeyfeale** Irish Rep
47C2 **Abbiategrasso** Italy
20B1 **Abbotsford** Can
84C2 **Abbottabad** Pak
61H3 **Abdulino**
Russian Fed
98C6 **Abéché** Chad
39F7 **Åbenrå** Den
97C4 **Abeokuta** Nig
99D2 **Abera** Eth
43B3 **Aberaeron** Wales

15C3 **Aberdeen** Maryland,
USA
100B4 **Aberdeen** S Africa
44C3 **Aberdeen** Scot
8D2 **Aberdeen** S Dakota,
USA
8A2 **Aberdeen**
Washington, USA
4J3 **Aberdeen L** Can
44C3 **Aberfeldy** Scot
43C4 **Abergavenny** Wales
43B3 **Aberystwyth** Wales
81C4 **Abha** S Arabia
90A2 **Abhar** Iran
97B4 **Abidjan** Ivory Coast
18A2 **Abilene** Kansas, USA
9D3 **Abilene** Texas, USA
43D4 **Abingdon** Eng
7B4 **Abitibi** R Can
7C5 **Abitibi,L** Can
61F5 **Abkhazskaya**
Respublika, Georgia
84C2 **Abohar** India
97C4 **Abomey** Benin
98B2 **Abong Mbang** Cam
79A4 **Aborlan** Phil
98B1 **Abou Deïa** Chad
91A4 **Abqaiq** S Arabia
50A2 **Abrantes** Port
95C2 **Abri** Sudan
106A3 **Abrolhos** Is Aust
8B2 **Absaroka Range** Mts
USA
91B5 **Abū al Abyad** I UAE
91A4 **Abū 'Alī** I S Arabia
91B5 **Abū Dhabi** UAE
95C3 **Abu Hamed** Sudan
97C4 **Abuja** Nig
33C6 **Abunã** Brazil
32D6 **Abuná** R Bol
93D3 **Abut Head** C NZ
111B2 **Abū 'Uruq** Well
Sudan
99D1 **Abuye Meda** Mt Eth
99C1 **Abu Zabad** Sudan
99D2 **Abwong** Sudan

56B1 **Åby** Den
94B3 **Aby 'Aweigila** Well
Egypt
99C2 **Abyei** Sudan
24B2 **Acámbaro** Mexico
24B2 **Acaponeta** Mexico
24B3 **Acapulco** Mexico
31D2 **Acaraú** Brazil
32D2 **Acarigua** Ven
24C3 **Acatlán** Mexico
23B2 **Acatzingo** Mexico
97B4 **Accra** Ghana
85D4 **Achalpur** India
29B4 **Achao** Chile
17C1 **Achensee** L Austria
46E2 **Achern** Germany
41A3 **Achill I** Irish Rep
63B2 **Achinsk** Russian Fed
53C3 **Acireale** Italy
26C2 **Acklins I**
Caribbean S
32C6 **Acobamba** Peru
29B2 **Aconcagua** Mt Chile
31B3 **Acopiara** Brazil
88B4 **Açores** Is Atlantic O
A Coruña = La Coruña
47C2 **Acqui** Italy
108A2 **Acraman,L** Aust
Acre = 'Akko
32C5 **Acre** State, Brazil
22C3 **Acton** USA
23B1 **Actopan** Mexico
19A3 **Ada** USA
50B1 **Adaja** R Spain
91C5 **Adam** Oman
35A2 **Adamantina** Brazil
98B2 **Adamaoua** Region,
Nig/Cam
47D1 **Adamello** Mt Italy
16C1 **Adams** USA
87B3 **Adam's Bridge** India/
Sri Lanka
13D2 **Adams L** Can
8A2 **Adams,Mt** USA
87C3 **Adam's Peak** Mt
Sri Lanka
81C4 **'Adan** Yemen

92C2 **Adana** Turk
60D5 **Adapazari** Turk
112B7 **Adare,C** Ant
108B1 **Adavale** Aust
47C2 **Adda** R Italy
91A4 **Ad Dahna'** Region,
S Arabia
96A2 **Ad Dakhla** Mor
81C4 **Ad Dālī'** Yemen
91B4 **Ad Damman**
S Arabia
91A4 **Ad Dibdibah** Region,
S Arabia
91A5 **Ad Dilam** S Arabia
91A5 **Ad Dir'iyah** S Arabia
93D3 **Ad Diwaniyah** Iraq
93D3 **Ad Duwayd** S Arabia
106C4 **Adelaide** Aust
4J3 **Adelaide Pen** Can
22D3 **Adelanto** USA
Aden = 'Adan
81C4 **Aden,G of** Yemen/
Somalia
97C3 **Aderbissinat** Niger
94C2 **Adhra** Syria
71E4 **Adi** I Indon
52B1 **Adige** R Italy
99D1 **Adigrat** Eth
85D5 **Adilabad** India
20B2 **Adin** USA
15D2 **Adirondack Mts** USA
99D2 **Adīs Abeba** Eth
99D1 **Adi Ugai** Eritrea
93C2 **Adıyaman** Turk
54C1 **Adjud** Rom
4E4 **Admiralty I** USA
6B2 **Admiralty Inlet** B
Can
87B1 **Adoni** India
48B3 **Adour** R France
96A2 **Adrar** Region, Maur
96C2 **Adrar** Mts Alg
96A2 **Adrar Souttouf**
Region, Mor
98C1 **Adré** Chad
95A2 **Adri** Libya
47E2 **Adria** Italy

Adrian

14B2 **Adrian** Michigan, USA
52B2 **Adriatic S** S Europe
99D1 **Adwa** Eth
97B4 **Adzopé** Ivory Coast
55B3 **Aegean S** Greece
80E2 **Afghanistan** Republic, Asia
99E2 **Afgooye** Somalia
97C4 **Afikpo** Nig
38G6 **Afjord** Nor
96C1 **Aflou** Alg
99D2 **Afmadu** Somalia
97A3 **Afolle** Region, Maur
94B2 **Afula** Israel
92B2 **Afyon** Turk
94A3 **Agadem** Niger
97C3 **Agadez** Niger
96B1 **Agadir** Mor
85D4 **Agar** India
86C2 **Agartala** India
97B4 **Agboville** Ivory Coast
93E1 **Agdam** Azerbaijan
75B1 **Agematsu** Japan
48C3 **Agen** France
90A3 **Agha Jari** Iran
96A2 **Aghwinit** *Well* Mor
47D2 **Agno** *R* Italy
47E1 **Agordo** Italy
48C3 **Agout** *R* France
85D3 **Agra** India
93D2 **Ağri** Turk
53C2 **Agri** *R* Italy
53B3 **Agrigento** Italy
55B3 **Agrinion** Greece
34A3 **Agrio** *R* Chile
53B2 **Agropoli** Italy
61H2 **Agryz** Russian Fed
6E3 **Agto** Greenland
27D3 **Aguadilla** Puerto Rico
24B1 **Agua Prieta** Mexico
24B2 **Aguascalientes** Mexico
23A1 **Aguascalientes** State, Mexico
35C1 **Aguas Formosas** Brazil
50A1 **Agueda** Port
96C3 **Aguelhok** Mali
50B2 **Aguilas** Spain
22A2 **Aguililla** Mexico
100B4 **Agulhas,C** S Africa
79C4 **Agusan** *R* Phil
Ahaggar = Hoggar
93E2 **Ahar** Iran
110B1 **Ahipara B** NZ
85C4 **Ahmadābād** India
87A1 **Ahmadnagar** India
99E2 **Ahmar** *Mts* Eth
46D1 **Ahrgebirge** Region, Germany
23A1 **Ahuacatlán** Mexico
23A1 **Ahualulco** Mexico
39G7 **Åhus** Sweden
90B2 **Ahuvān** Iran
90A3 **Ahvāz** Iran
26A4 **Aiajuela** Costa Rica
47B1 **Aigle** Switz
47B2 **Aiguille d'Arves** *Mt* France
47B2 **Aiguille de la Grand Sassière** *Mt* France
75B1 **Aikawa** Japan
17B1 **Aiken** USA
73A5 **Ailao Shan** *Upland* China
35C1 **Aimorés** Brazil
96B1 **Ain Beni Mathar** Mor
95B2 **Ain Dalla** *Well* Egypt
51C2 **Ain el Hadjel** Alg
95A3 **Ain Galakka** Chad
96B1 **Ain Sefra** Alg
92B4 **'Ain Sukhna** Egypt
75A2 **Aioi** Japan
96B2 **Aïoun el Abd el Malek** *Well* Maur
97B3 **Aïoun El Atrouss** Maur
30C2 **Aiquile** Bol
97C3 **Aïr** *Desert Region* Niger

13E2 **Airdrie** Can
46B1 **Aire** France
42D3 **Aire** *R* Eng
46C2 **Aire** *R* France
6C3 **Airforce I** Can
47C1 **Airolo** Switz
4E3 **Aishihik** Can
12G2 **Aishihik L** Can
46B2 **Aisne** Department, France
49C2 **Aisne** *R* France
71F4 **Aitape** PNG
58D1 **Aivekste** *R* Latvia
72B2 **Aixa Zuogi** China
49D1 **Aix-en-Provence**
47A2 **Aix-les-Bains** France
86B2 **Aiyar Res** India
55B3 **Aíyion** Greece
55B3 **Aíyna** / Greece
86C2 **Aizawl** India
100A3 **Aizeb** *R* Namibia
74E3 **Aizu-Wakamatsu** Japan
52A2 **Ajaccio** Corse
22A2 **Ajalpan** Mexico
95B1 **Ajdābiyā** Libya
74E2 **Ajigasawa** Japan
94B2 **Ajlūn** Jordan
91C4 **Ajman** UAE
85C3 **Ajmer** India
983 **Ajo** USA
23A2 **Ajuchitan** Mexico
55C3 **Ak** *R* Turk
75B1 **Akaishi-sanchi** *Mts* Japan
87B1 **Akalkot** India
111B2 **Akaroa** NZ
75A2 **Akashi** Japan
61J3 **Akbulak** Russian Fed
93C2 **Akçakale** Turk
96A2 **Akchar** *Watercourse* Maur
55C3 **Akdağ** *Mt* Turk
98C2 **Aketi** Zaïre
93D1 **Akhalkalaki** Georgia
93D1 **Akhalsikhe** Georgia
55B3 **Akharnaí** Greece
1203 **Akhiok** USA
92A2 **Akhisar** Turk
58D1 **Akhiste** Latvia
95C2 **Akhmim** Egypt
61G4 **Aktiubinsk** Russian Fed
60D4 **Akhtyrka** Ukraine
75A2 **Aki** Japan
7B4 **Akimiski I** Can
74E3 **Akita** Japan
96A3 **Akjoujt** Maur
94B2 **'Akko** Israel
4E3 **Aklavik** Can
97B3 **Aklé Aouana** *Desert Region* Maur
99D2 **Akobo** Sudan
99D2 **Akobo** *R* Sudan
84B1 **Akoha** Afghan
85D4 **Akola** India
85D4 **Akot** India
6D3 **Akpatok I** Can
55B3 **Åkra Kafirévs** *C* Greece
55B3 **Åkra Maléa** *C* Greece
38A2 **Akranes** Iceland
55C3 **Åkra Sidheros** *C* Greece
55B3 **Åkra Spátha** *C* Greece
55B3 **Åkra Taínaron** *C* Greece
10B2 **Akron** USA
94A1 **Akrotiri B** Cyprus
84D1 **Aksai Chin** *Mts* China
93C2 **Aksaray** Turk
61H3 **Aksay** Kazakhstan
84D1 **Aksayquin Hu** *L* China
92B2 **Akşehir** Turk
92B2 **Akseki** Turk
63D2 **Aksenovo Zilovskoye** Russian Fed
68D1 **Aksha** Russian Fed
82C1 **Aksu** China
61H5 **Aktau** Kazakhstan

65J5 **Aktogay** Kazakhstan
61J4 **Aktumsyk** Kazakhstan
65G4 **Aktyubinsk** Kazakhstan
38B1 **Akureyri** Iceland
Akyab = Sittwe
65K5 **Akzhal** Kazakhstan
11B3 **Alabama** State, USA
11B3 **Alabama** *R* USA
17A1 **Alabaster** USA
92C2 **Ala Dağlari** *Mts* Turk
61F5 **Alagir** Russian Fed
47B2 **Alagna** Italy
31D3 **Alagoas** State, Brazil
31D4 **Alagoinhas** Brazil
51B1 **Alagón** Spain
93E4 **Al Ahmadi** Kuwait
25D3 **Alajuela** Costa Rica
12B2 **Alakanuk** USA
38L5 **Alakurtti** Russian Fed
91A4 **Al Amārah** Iraq
21A2 **Alameda** USA
23B1 **Alamo** Mexico
9C3 **Alamogordo** USA
9C3 **Alamosa** USA
39H6 **Åland** / Fin
92B2 **Alanya** Turk
17B1 **Alapaha** *R* USA
65H4 **Alapayevsk** Russian Fed
92A2 **Alaşehir** Turk
68C3 **Ala Shan** *Mts* China
4C3 **Alaska** State, USA
4C3 **Alaska,G of** USA
12C3 **Alaska Pen** USA
4C3 **Alaska Range** *Mts* USA
52A2 **Alassio** Italy
12D1 **Alatna** *R* USA
61G3 **Alatyr'** Russian Fed
108B2 **Alawoona** Aust
91C5 **Al'Ayn** UAE
82A1 **Alayskiy Khrebet** *Mts* Tajikistan
49D3 **Alba** Italy
92C2 **Al Bāb** Syria
51B2 **Albacete** Spain
50A1 **Alba de Tormes** Spain
93D2 **Al Badi** Iraq
54B1 **Alba Iulia** Rom
54A2 **Albania** Republic, Europe
106A4 **Albany** Aust
17B1 **Albany** Georgia, USA
15D2 **Albany** New York, USA
8A2 **Albany** Oregon, USA
7B4 **Albany** *R* Can
34B2 **Albardón** Arg
91C5 **Al Bātinah** Region, Oman
71F5 **Albatross B** Aust
95B1 **Al Baydā** Libya
11C3 **Albemarle Sd** USA
50B1 **Alberche** *R* Spain
108A1 **Alberga** *R* Aust
46B1 **Albert** France
5G4 **Alberta** Province, Can
99D2 **Albert,L** Uganda/Zaïre
10A2 **Albert Lea** USA
99D2 **Albert Nile** *R* Uganda
49D2 **Albertville** France
48C3 **Albi** France
18B1 **Albia** USA
34D3 **Albina** Suriname
14B2 **Albion** Michigan, USA
15C2 **Albion** New York, USA
92C4 **Al'Biyah** S Arabia
91A5 **Al Biyadh** Region, S Arabia
50B2 **Alborán I** Spain
39H7 **Alborg** Den
93D3 **Al Bū Kamāl** Syria
47C1 **Albula** *R* Switz
9C3 **Albuquerque** USA
91C5 **Al Buraymi** Oman
95A1 **Al Burayqah** Libya

95B1 **Al Burdi** Libya
107D4 **Albury** Aust
93E3 **Al Buşayyah** Iraq
50B1 **Alcalá de Henares** Spain
53B3 **Alcamo** Italy
51B3 **Alcaniz** Spain
31C2 **Alcântara** Brazil
50B2 **Alcaraz** Spain
50B2 **Alcazar de San Juan** Spain
51B2 **Alcira** Spain
35D1 **Alcobaça** Brazil
51B2 **Alcolea de Pinar** Spain
51B2 **Alcoy** Spain
51C2 **Alcudia** Spain
89J8 **Aldabra Is** Indian O
63E2 **Aldan** Russian Fed
63E2 **Aldanskoye Nagor'y** *Upland* Russian Fed
43E3 **Aldeburgh** Eng
48B2 **Alderney** / UK
43D4 **Aldershot** Eng
97A3 **Aleg** Maur
34D3 **Alegrete** Brazil
34C2 **Alejandro Roca** Arg
30H6 **Alejandro Selkirk** / Chile
63G2 **Aleksandrovsk Sakhalinskiy** Russian Fed
65J4 **Alekseyevka** Kazakhstan
60E3 **Aleksin** Russian Fed
58C1 **Alem** Sweden
35C1 **Além Paraíba** Brazil
49C2 **Alençon** France
21C4 **Alenuihaha Chan** Hawaiian Is
Aleppo = Halab
6D1 **Alert** Can
47C2 **Alès** France
52A2 **Alessandria** Italy
64B3 **Alesund** Nor
12C3 **Aleutian Range** *Mts* USA
4E4 **Alexander Arch** USA
100A3 **Alexander Bay** S Africa
17A1 **Alexander City** USA
112C3 **Alexander I** Ant
111A3 **Alexandra** NZ
29G8 **Alexandra,C** South Georgia
6C2 **Alexandra Fjord** Can
95B1 **Alexandria** Egypt
11A3 **Alexandria** Louisiana, USA
10A2 **Alexandria** Minnesota, USA
10C3 **Alexandria** Virginia, USA
55C2 **Alexandroúpolis** Greece
13C2 **Alexis Creek** Can
94B2 **Aley** Leb
65K4 **Aleysk** Russian Fed
93D3 **Al Falūjah** Iraq
51B1 **Alfaro** Spain
54C2 **Alfatar** Bulg
93E3 **Al Fāw** Iraq
35B2 **Alfenas** Brazil
55B3 **Alfiós** *R* Greece
47D2 **Alfonsine** Italy
35C2 **Alfredo Chaves** Brazil
65H4 **Alga** Kazakhstan
34B3 **Algarrobo del Águila** Arg
50A2 **Algeciras** Spain
96C1 **Alger** Alg
96B2 **Algeria** Republic, Africa
53A2 **Alghero** Sardegna
96C1 **Algiers = Alger**
15C1 **Algonquin Park** Can
91C5 **Al Hadd** Oman
93D3 **Al Hadīthah** Iraq
92C3 **Al Hadīthah** S Arabia
93D2 **Al Hadr** Iraq

91C5 Al Hajar al Gharbī Mts Oman
91C5 Al Hajar ash Sharqi Mts Oman
93C3 Al Hamad Desert Region Jordan/ S Arabia
91H4 Al Hanīyah Desert Region Iraq
91A5 Al Harīq S Arabia
93C3 Al Harrah Desert Region S Arabia
95A2 Al Harūj al Aswad Upland Libya
91A4 Al Hasa Region, S Arabia
93D2 Al Hasakah Syria
91A5 Al Hawījā' S Arabia
93E3 Al Hayy Iraq
94C2 Al Hijānah Syria
93D3 Al Hillah Iraq
91A4 Al Hillah S Arabia
96B1 Al Hoceima Mor
91A4 Al Hufūf S Arabia
91A4 Al Humrah Region, UAE
91C5 Al Huwatsat Oman
90A2 Aliabad Iran
91C4 Aliabad Iran
55B2 Aliákmon R Greece
93E3 Ali al Gharbi Iraq
87A1 Alibāg India
51B2 Alicante Spain
9D4 Alice USA
106C3 Alice Springs Aust
53B3 Alicudi I Italy
84D3 Aligarh India
90A3 Aligūdarz Iran
84B2 Ali-Khel Afghan
55A1 Alimniá I Greece
86B1 Alipur Duar India
14B2 Aliquippa USA
23C2 Alisal USA
47B2 Al' Isawiyah S Arabia
100B4 Alival North S Africa
95B2 Al Jaghbūb Libya
93D3 Al Jalāmīd S Arabia
93C3 Al Jawf S Arabia
91A4 Al Jawf S Arabia
93D2 Al Jazirah Desert Region Syria/Iraq
50A2 Aljezur Port
91A4 Al Jubayl S Arabia
91C5 Al Kāmil Oman
93D2 Al Khābūr R Syria
91C5 Al Khābūrah Oman
93D3 Al Khāls Iraq
91C4 Al Khasab Oman
91B4 Al Khawr Qatar
95A1 Al Khums Libya
91B5 Al Kidan Region, S Arabia
94C2 Al Kiswah Syria
56A2 Alkmaar Neth
95B2 Al Kufrah Oasis Libya
93E3 Al Kūt Iraq
92C2 Al Lādhiqīyah Syria
86A1 Allahābād India
94C2 Al Lajāh Syria
12D1 Allakaket USA
76B2 Allanmyo Myan
95C2 'Allaqi Watercourse Egypt
17B1 Allatoona L USA
15C2 Allegheny R USA
10C3 Allegheny Mts USA
17B1 Allendale USA
111A3 Allen,Mt NZ
15C2 Allentown USA
49C2 Aller R France
47B1 Allgäu Mts Germany
8C2 Alliance USA
91A4 Al Lith S Arabia
91B5 Al Liwā Region, UAE
109D1 Allora Aust
14B2 Alma Michigan, USA
50A2 Almada Port
Al Madīnah = Medina
71F2 Almagan I Pacific O
91B4 Al Manāmah Bahrain
93D3 Al Ma'niyah Iraq
21A1 Almanor,L USA
51B2 Almansa Spain

13B1 Alma Peak Mt Can
91B5 Al Māriyyah UAE
95B1 Al Marj Libya
82B1 Almaty Kazakhstan
93D2 Al Mawsil Iraq
50B1 Almazán Spain
35C1 Almenara Brazil
50B2 Almeria Spain
61H3 Al'met'yevsk Russian Fed
56C1 Älmhult Sweden
93E3 Al Miqdādīyah Iraq
112C3 Almirante Brown Base Ant
34A1 Almirante Latorre Chile
55B3 Almirós Greece
91A4 Al Mish'āb S Arabia
50A2 Almodôvar Port
84D3 Almora India
91A4 Al Mubarraz S Arabia
92C4 Al Mudawwara Jordan
91C5 Al Mudaybi Oman
91C5 Al Muharraq Bahrain
81C4 Al Mukallā Yemen
81C4 Al Mukha Yemen
93D3 Al Musayyib Iraq
44B3 Alness Scot
93E3 Al Nu'mānīyah Iraq
42D2 Alnwick Eng
71D4 Alor I Indon
77C4 Alor Setar Malay
Alost = Aalst
107E2 Alotau PNG
106B3 Aloysius,Mt Aust
34C3 Alpachiri Arg
14B1 Alpena USA
47B2 Alpes du Valais Mts Switz
Alpi Dolomitiche Mts Italy
47B2 Alpi Graie Mts Italy
9C3 Alpine Texas, USA
47C1 Alpi Orobie Mts Italy
47B2 Alpi Pennine Mts Italy
47C1 Alpi Retiche Mts Switz
47D1 Alpi Venoste Mts Italy
52A1 Alps Mts Europe
95A1 Al Qaddāhīyah Libya
92C3 Al Qadmūs Syria
93D3 Al Qā'im Iraq
93C4 Al Qalībah S Arabia
93D2 Al Qāmishlī Syria
91A4 Al Qaryah ash Sharqiyah Libya
92C3 Al Qaryatayn Syria
91A4 Al Qātif S Arabia
95A2 Al Qaţrūn Libya
94C2 Al Qaysāmah S Arabia
94C2 Al Quatayfah Syria
93A2 Alqueva R Port
92C3 Al Qunaytirah Syria
81C4 Al Qunfidhah S Arabia
93E3 Al Qurnah Iraq
94C1 Al Qusayr Syria
92C3 Al Qutayfah Syria
56B1 Als I Den
49D2 Alsace Region, France
57B2 Alsfeld Germany
42C2 Alston Eng
29D2 Alta Nor
29D2 Alta Gracia Arg
27D5 Altagracia de Orituco Ven
68A2 Altai Mts Mongolia
7E1 Altamaha R USA
33G4 Altamira Brazil
23B1 Altamira Mexico
53C2 Altamura Italy
68C1 Altanbulag Mongolia
71F4 Altape PNG
24B2 Altata Mexico
63A3 Altay China
63B3 Altay Mongolia
63A2 Altay Russian Fed

47C1 Altdorf Switz
46D1 Altenkirchen Germany
34B3 Altiplanicie del Payún Plat Arg
47B1 Altkirch France
101C2 Alto Molócue Mozam
10A3 Alton USA
15C2 Altoona USA
93E4 Alto Pencoso Mts Arg
35A1 Alto Sucuriú Brazil
23B2 Altotonga Mexico
23A2 Altoyac de Alvarez Mexico
82C2 Altun Shan Mts China
20B2 Alturas USA
9D3 Altus USA
91B5 Al'Ubaylah S Arabia
93C4 Al Urayq Desert Region S Arabia
91B5 Al'Uruq al Mu'taridah Region, S Arabia
9D2 Alva USA
23B2 Alvarado Mexico
9D3 Alvarado USA
39C6 Älvdalen Sweden
19A4 Alvin USA
38J5 Älvsbyn Sweden
80B3 Al Wajh S Arabia
85D3 Alwar India
93D3 Al Widyān Desert Region Iraq/S Arabia
72A2 Alxa Yougi China
93E2 Alyat Azerbaijan
39J8 Alytus Lithuania
46E2 Alzey Germany
23B2 Amacuzac R Mexico
98D1 Amadi Sudan
6C3 Amadjuak L Can
74B4 Amakusa-shotō I Japan
39G7 Åmål Sweden
63D2 Amalat R Russian Fed
55B3 Amaliás Greece
85D4 Amalner India
69E4 Amami I Japan
69E4 Amami gunto Arch Japan
100C4 Amanzimtoti S Africa
33G3 Amapá Brazil
33G3 Amapá State, Brazil
9C3 Amarillo USA
60E5 Amasya Turk
23A1 Amatitan Mexico
Amazonas = Solimões
32D4 Amazonas State, Brazil
28C3 Amazonas R Brazil
87D3 Ambala India
87D3 Ambalangoda Sri Lanka
101D3 Ambalavao Madag
101D2 Ambam Cam
101D2 Ambanja Madag
1C7 Ambarchik Russian Fed
32B4 Ambato Ecuador
101D2 Ambato-Boeny Madag
101D2 Ambatolampy Madag
101D2 Ambatondrazaka Madag
57C3 Amberg Germany
25D3 Ambergris Cay I Belize
86A2 Ambikāpur India
101D2 Ambilobe Madag
101D3 Ambinany Madag
101D3 Ambodifototra Madag
101D2 Ambohimahasoa Madag
71D4 Ambon Indon
101D3 Ambositra Madag
101D3 Ambovombe Madag
98B3 Ambriz Angola
98B3 Am Dam Chad

64H3 Amderma Russian Fed
24B2 Ameca Mexico
23B2 Amecacameca Mexico
34C2 Ameghino Arg
56B2 Ameland I Neth
16C2 Amenia USA
112B10 American Highland Upland Ant
105H4 American Samoa Is Pacific O
17B1 Americus USA
101G1 Amersfoort S Africa
112C10 Amery Ice Shelf Ant
55B3 Amfilokhia Greece
55B3 Amfissa Greece
63F1 Amga Russian Fed
75B1 Amino Japan
63F1 Amgal R Russian Fed
69F2 Amgu Russian Fed
69F1 Amguema' R Russian Fed
99D1 Amhara Region Eth
7D5 Amherst Can
16C1 Amherst Massachusetts, USA
Amherst = Kyaikkami
87B2 Amhūr India
48C2 Amiens France
75B1 Amino Japan
94B1 Amioûn Leb
89K8 Amirante Is Indian O
86B1 Amlekhgan Nepal
92C3 Amman Jordan
38K6 Ämmänsaari Fin
56B2 Amersfoort Neth
90B2 Amol Iran
55C3 Amorgós I Greece
7C5 Amos Can
Amoy = Xiamen
101D3 Ampanihy Madag
35B2 Amparo Brazil
51C1 Amposta Spain
85D4 Amravati India
85C4 Amreli India
84C2 Amritsar India
10H1 Amsterdam Neth
101H1 Amsterdam S Africa
15D2 Amsterdam USA
98C1 Am Timan Chad
88L3 Amu Darya R Uzbekistan
6A2 Amund Ringes I Can
4F2 Amundsen G Can
112B4 Amundsen S Ant
80E Amundsen-Scott Base Ant
78D3 Amuntai Indon
63E2 Amur R Russian Fed
33E2 Anaco Ven
20B1 Anacortes USA
55C3 Anáfi I Greece
93D3 'Anah Iraq
21B3 Anaheim USA
21B3 Anaimalai Hills India
83C4 Anakapalle India
12E1 Anaktuvuk P USA
101D2 Analalava Madag
75A2 Anan Japan
87B2 Anantapur India
84D2 Anantnag India
31B5 Anápolis Brazil
90C3 Anar Iran
90B3 Anārak Iran
71F2 Anatahan I Pacific O
47B3 Añatuya Arg
74B3 Anbyon N Korea
22C4 Ancapa Is USA
4D3 Anchorage USA
30C2 Ancohuma Mt Bol
32B6 Ancón Peru
52B2 Ancona Italy
16C1 Ancram USA
29B4 Ancud Chile
34A3 Andacollo Chile
108A1 Andado Aust
32C6 Andahuaylas Peru
38F6 Åndalsnes Nor
50A2 Andalucia Region, Spain
17A1 Andalusia USA

Andaman Is

83D4 **Andaman I** Myan
83D4 **Andaman S** Myan
108A2 **Andamooka** Aust
38H5 **Andenes** Nor
17J1 **Andermatt** Switz
57B2 **Andernach** Germany
14A2 **Anderson** Indiana, USA
18B2 **Anderson** Missouri, USA
17B1 **Anderson** S Carolina, USA
4F3 **Anderson** R Can
87B1 **Andhra Pradesh** State, India
55B3 **Andikithira** I Greece
65J5 **Andizhan** Uzbekistan
65H6 **Andkhui** Afghan
74B3 **Andong** S Korea
51C1 **Andorra** Principality, SW Europe
51C1 **Andorra-La-Vella** Andorra
43D4 **Andover** Eng
35A2 **Andradina** Brazil
12B2 **Andreafsky** USA
92B2 **Andreas,C** Cyprus
53C2 **Andria** Italy
11C4 **Andros** I The Bahamas
55B3 **Andros** I Greece
87A2 **Androth** I India
50B2 **Andújar** Spain
100A2 **Andulo** Angola
47C4 **Anécho** Togo
97C3 **Anéfis** Mali
34B3 **Añelo** Arg
63C2 **Angarsk** Russian Fed
38H6 **Ånge** Sweden
24A2 **Angel de la Guarda** I Mexico
79B2 **Angeles** Phil
39G7 **Ängelholm** Sweden
109C1 **Angellala Creek** R Aust
22B1 **Angels Camp** USA
71E4 **Angemuk** Mt Indon
48B2 **Angers** France
76C3 **Angkor** Hist Site Camb
41C3 **Anglesey** I Wales
19A4 **Angleton** USA
6G3 **Angmagssalik** Greenland
101D2 **Angoche** Mozam
29B3 **Angol** Chile
14B2 **Angola** Indiana, USA
100A2 **Angola** Republic, Africa
103H6 **Angola Basin** Atlantic O
12H3 **Angoram** PNG
48C2 **Angoulême** France
96A1 **Angra do Heroísmo** Açores
35C2 **Angra dos Reis** Brazil
34C3 **Anguil** Arg
27E3 **Anguilla** I Caribbean S
26B2 **Anguilla Cays** Is Caribbean S
86B2 **Angul** India
99C3 **Angumu** Zaïre
56C1 **Anholt** I Den
73C4 **Anhua** China
72D3 **Anhui** Province, China
12C2 **Aniak** USA
35B1 **Anicuns** Brazil
46B2 **Anizy-le-Château** France
4C3 **Anjak** USA
48B2 **Anjou** Region, France
101D2 **Anjouan** I Comoros
101D2 **Anjozorobe** Madag
74B3 **Anju** N Korea
72B3 **Ankang** China
92B2 **Ankara** Turk
101D2 **Ankaratra** Mt Madag
101D3 **Ankazoabo** Madag
101D2 **Ankazobe** Madag
56C2 **Anklam** Germany
76D3 **An Loc** Viet

73B4 **Anlong** China
73C3 **Anlu** China
18C2 **Anna** USA
96C1 **'Annaba** Alg
92C3 **An Nabk** S Arabia
92C3 **An Nabk** Syria
108A1 **Anna Creek** Aust
80C3 **An Nafud** Desert S Arabia
93D3 **An Najaf** Iraq
42C2 **Annan** Scot
15C3 **Annapolis** USA
86A1 **Annapurna** Mt Nepal
14B2 **Ann Arbor** USA
94C1 **An Nāsirah** Syria
93E3 **An Nāsiriyah** Iraq
47B2 **Annecy** France
47B1 **Annemasse** France
76D3 **An Nhon** Viet
73A5 **Anning** China
17A1 **Anniston** USA
89E8 **Annobon** I Eq Guinea
49C2 **Annonay** France
27J1 **Annotto Bay** Jamaica
73D3 **Anqing** China
72B2 **Ansai** China
57C3 **Ansbach** Germany
26C3 **Anse d'Hainault** Haiti
72E1 **Anshan** China
73B4 **Anshun** China
97C3 **Ansongo** Mali
14B3 **Ansted** USA
92C2 **Antakya** Turk
101E2 **Antalaha** Madag
92B2 **Antalya** Turk
92B2 **Antalya Körfezi** B Turk
101D2 **Antananarivo** Madag
112C1 **Antarctic Circle** Ant
112C3 **Antarctic Pen** Ant
50B2 **Antequera** Spain
96B2 **Anti-Atlas** Mts Mor
7D5 **Anticosti, I. d'** Can
27E3 **Antigua** I Caribbean S
Anti-Lebanon = Jebel esh Sharqi (Leb)
21A2 **Antioch** USA
19A3 **Antlers** USA
30B3 **Antofagasta** Chile
45C1 **Antrim** County, N Ire
45C1 **Antrim** N Ire
45C1 **Antrim Hills** N Ire
101D2 **Antseranana** Madag
101D2 **Antsirabe** Madag
101D2 **Antsohiny** Madag
76D3 **An Tuc** Viet
46C1 **Antwerpen** Belg
45C2 **An Uaimh** Irish Rep
87C3 **Anuradhapura** Sri Lanka
Anvers = Antwerpen
4B3 **Anvik** USA
63B3 **Anxi** China
72C2 **Anyang** China
72A3 **A'nyêmaqên Shan** Upland China
47C2 **Anza** R Italy
13E1 **Anzac** Can
65K4 **Anzhero-Sudzhensk** Russian Fed
53B2 **Anzio** Italy
74E2 **Aomori** Japan
52A1 **Aosta** Italy
97B3 **Aoukar** Desert Region Maur
96C2 **Aoulef** Alg
95A2 **Aozou** Chad
30E3 **Apa** R Brazil/Par
11B4 **Apalachee B** USA
17B2 **Apalachicola** USA
17A2 **Apalachicola B** USA
23B2 **Apan** Mexico
64E3 **Apatity** Russian Fed
32C3 **Apaporis** R Colombia
35A2 **Aparecida do Taboado** Brazil
79B2 **Aparri** Phil
54A1 **Apatin** Croatia

64E3 **Apatity** Russian Fed
24B3 **Apatzingan** Mexico
56B2 **Apeldoorn** Neth
53B2 **Apiai** Brazil
33F2 **Apoera** Surinam
108B3 **Apollo Bay** Aust
79C4 **Apo,Mt** Mt Phil
17B2 **Apopka,L** USA
30E2 **Aporé** R Brazil
10A2 **Apostle Is** USA
10A2 **Apostle L** USA
23A1 **Apozol** Mexico
11B3 **Appalachian Mts** USA
52B2 **Appennino Abruzzese** Mts Italy
52A2 **Appennino Ligure** Mts Italy
53C2 **Appennino Lucano** Mts Italy
53B2 **Appennino Napoletano** Mts Italy
52B2 **Appennino Tosco-Emilliano** Mts Italy
52B2 **Appennino Umbro-Marchigiano** Mts Italy
47C1 **Appenzell** Switz
42C2 **Appleby** Eng
14A2 **Appleton** Wisconsin, USA
30F3 **Apucarana** Brazil
23B1 **Apuloco** Mexico
32D2 **Apure** R Ven
32C6 **Apurimac** R Peru
92C4 **'Aqaba** Jordan
92B4 **'Aqaba,G of** Egypt/S Arabia
90B3 **'Aqdā** Iran
30E3 **Aquidauana** Brazil
23A2 **Aquila** Mexico
86A1 **Ara** India
17A1 **Arab** USA
81D4 **Arabian S** Asia/Arabian Pen
31D4 **Aracaju** Brazil
30E3 **Aracanguy, Mts de de**
31D2 **Aracati** Brazil
30F3 **Araçatuba** Brazil
50A2 **Aracena** Spain
31C5 **Araçuai** Brazil
94B3 **Arad** Israel
60B4 **Arad** Rom
98C1 **Arada** Chad
91B5 **'Arādah** UAE
106C1 **Arafura S** Indon/Aust
30F2 **Aragarças** Brazil
51B1 **Aragón** Region, Spain
50B1 **Aragón** R Spain
33G6 **Araguaia** R Brazil
31B3 **Araguaina** Brazil
31B5 **Araguari** Brazil
35B1 **Araguari** R Brazil
75B1 **Arai** Japan
90A3 **Arāk** Iran
76A2 **Arakan Yoma** Mts Myan
87B2 **Arakkonam** India
65G5 **Aral Sea** Kazakhstan/Uzbekistan
80E1 **Aral'sk** Kazakhstan
Aral'skoye More = Aral S
40B2 **Aran** I Irish Rep
50B1 **Aranda de Duero** Spain
23A1 **Arandas** Mexico
50B1 **Aranjuez** Spain
75A2 **Arao** Japan
97B3 **Araouane** Mali
29E2 **Arapey** R Urug
31D4 **Arapiraca** Brazil
35A2 **Araporgas** Brazil
30G4 **Ararangua** Brazil
31B6 **Araraquara** Brazil
35B2 **Araras** Brazil
107D4 **Ararat** Aust
93D2 **Ararat** Armenia
93E2 **Aras** R Azerbaijan
75C1 **Arato** Japan
32D2 **Arauca** R Ven

34A3 **Arauco** Chile
32C2 **Arauea** Colombia
85C4 **Arāvalli Range** Mts India
25A3 **Araxá** Brazil
99D2 **Arba Minch** Eth
53A3 **Arbatax** Sardegna
93D2 **Arbil** Iraq
47A1 **Arbois** France
39H6 **Arbrå** Sweden
44C3 **Arbroath** Scot
47A1 **Arc** France
47B2 **Arc** R France
48B3 **Arcachon** France
17B2 **Arcadia** USA
20B2 **Arcata** USA
23A1 **Arcelia** Mexico
26B2 **Archipiélago de Camaguey** Arch Cuba
29B6 **Archipiélago de la Reina Adelaida** Arch Chile
29B4 **Archipiélago de las Chones** Arch Chile
32B2 **Archipiélago de las Perlas** Arch Panama
35B2 **Arcos** Brazil
50A2 **Arcos de la Frontera** Spain
6B2 **Arctic Bay** Can
1C1 **Arctic Circle**
4E3 **Arctic Red** R Can
4E3 **Arctic Red** R Can
4D3 **Arctic Village** USA
54C2 **Arda** R Bulg
65F6 **Ardabil** Iran
93D1 **Ardahan** Turk
39F6 **Ardal** Nor
96C2 **Ardar des Iforas** Upland Alg/Mali
45C2 **Ardee** Irish Rep
91B4 **Ardekān** Iran
46C2 **Ardennes** Department, France
57A2 **Ardennes** Region, Belg
90B3 **Ardestan** Iran
92C3 **Ardh es Suwwan** Desert Region Jordan
50A2 **Ardila** R Port
109C2 **Ardlethan** Aust
9D3 **Ardmore** USA
44A3 **Ardnamurchan** Pt Scot
46A1 **Ardres** France
44B3 **Ardrishaig** Scot
42B2 **Ardrossan** Scot
27D3 **Arecibo** Puerto Rico
31D2 **Areia Branca** Brazil
21A2 **Arena,Pt** USA
39F7 **Arendal** Nor
30B2 **Arequipa** Peru
52B2 **Arezzo** Italy
52B2 **Argenta** Italy
49C2 **Argentan** France
46B2 **Argenteuil** France
28C7 **Argentina** Republic, S America
103F7 **Argentine Basin** Atlantic O
48C2 **Argenton-sur-Creuse** France
54C2 **Argeş** R Rom
84B2 **Arghardab** R Afgha
55B3 **Argolikós Kólpos** G Greece
46C2 **Argonne** Region, France
55B3 **Argos** Greece
55B3 **Argostólion** Greece
22B2 **Arguello,Pt** USA
106B2 **Argyle,L** Aust
100A3 **Ariamsvlei** Namibia
50B1 **Arián zón** R Spain
34C2 **Arias** Arg
97B3 **Aribinda** Burkina
30B2 **Arica** Chile
84C2 **Arifwala** Pak
Arihã = Jericho
27L1 **Arima** Trinidad
35B1 **Arinos** Brazil

33F6 Arinos *R* Brazil
23A2 Ario de Rosales Mexico
27L1 Aripo,Mt Trinidad
33E5 Aripuana Brazil
33E5 Aripuanã *R* Brazil
44B3 Arisaig Scot
87B2 Ariskere India
33A2 Aristazabal *I* Can
34B3 Arizona Arg
9B3 Arizona State, USA
39G7 Ärjäng Sweden
61F3 Arkadak Russian Fed
19B3 Arkadelphia USA
65H4 Arkalyk Kazakhstan
11A3 Arkansas State, USA
11A3 Arkansas *R* USA
18A2 Arkansas City USA
64F3 Arkhangel'sk Russian Fed
41B3 Arklow Irish Rep
47D1 Arlberg *P* Austria
49C3 Arles France
19A3 Arlington Texas, USA
15C3 Arlington Virginia, USA
20B1 Arlington Washington, USA
97C3 Arlit Niger
57B3 Arlon Belg
Armageddon = Megiddo
45C1 Armagh County, N Ire
45C1 Armagh N Ire
61F5 Armavir Russian Fed
23A2 Armenia Mexico
32B3 Armenia Colombia
65F5 Armenia Republic, Europe
107E4 Armidale Aust
13D2 Armstrong Can
7C3 Arnaud *R* Can
82B2 Arnauti *C* Cyprus
56B2 Arnhem Neth
106C2 Arnhem,C Aust
106C2 Arnhem Land Aust
52B2 Arnold USA
15C1 Arnprior Can
46E1 Arnsberg Germany
100A3 Aroab Namibia
47C2 Arona Italy
12B2 Aropuk L USA
52A1 Arosa Switz
97A3 Arquipélago dos Bijagós *Arch* Guinea-Bissau
93D3 Ar Ramādī Iraq
42B2 Arran *I* Scot
92C2 Ar Raqqah Syria
95A2 Ar Rāqubah Libya
49C1 Arras France
96A2 Arrecife Canary Is
34C2 Arrecifes Arg
23A1 Arriaga Mexico
93E3 Ar Rifā'ī Iraq
93E3 Ar Rihāb *Desert Region* Iraq
91A5 Ar Riyāḍ S Arabia
44B3 Arrochar Scot
111A2 Arrowtown NZ
23B1 Arroyo Seco Mexico
91B4 Ar Ru'ays Qatar
91C5 Ar Rustaq Oman
93D3 Ar Ruṭbah Iraq
47D2 Arsiero Italy
49D2 Arsizio Italy
61G2 Arsk Russian Fed
55B3 Árta Greece
23A2 Arteaga Mexico
63D2 Artemovsk Russian Fed
63D2 Artemovskiy Russian Fed
9C3 Artesia USA
111B2 Arthurs P NZ
112C2 Artigas *Base* Ant
29E2 Artigas Urug
4H3 Artillery L Can
48C1 Artois Region, France
112C2 Arturo Prat *Base* Ant
93D1 Artvin Turk

99D2 Aru Zaïre
33G6 Aruanã Brazil
27C4 Aruba *I* Caribbean S
86B1 Arun *R* Nepal
86C1 Arunachal Pradesh Union Territory, India
99D3 Arusha Tanz
99C2 Aruwimi *R* Zaïre
68C2 Arvayheer Mongolia
47B2 Arve *R* France
7C5 Arvida Can
38H5 Arvidsjaur Sweden
39G7 Arvika Sweden
21B2 Arvin USA
94B1 Arwad *I* Syria
61G2 Arzamas Russian Fed
84C2 Asadabad Afghan
75A2 Asahi *R* Japan
74E2 Asahi dake *Mt* Japan
74E2 Asahikawa Japan
86B2 Asansol India
95A2 Asawanwah *Well* Libya
61K2 Asbest Russian Fed
15D2 Asbury Park USA
103H5 Ascension *I* Atlantic O
57B3 Aschaffenburg Germany
56C2 Aschersleben Germany
47D2 Ascoli Piceno Italy
47C1 Ascona Switz
99E1 Aseb Eritrea
99D2 Asela Eth
38H6 Åsele Sweden
54B2 Asenovgrad Bulg
46E1 Asfeld France
61J2 Asha Russian Fed
17B1 Ashburn USA
111B2 Ashburton NZ
106A3 Ashburton *R* Aust
92B3 Ashdod Israel
19B3 Ashdown USA
15D2 Asheville USA
109D1 Ashford Aust
43E4 Ashford Eng
Ashgabat = Ashkhabad
74D3 Ashikaga Japan
75A2 Ashizuri-misaki *Pt* Japan
65G6 Ashkhabad Turkmenistan
10B3 Ashland Kentucky, USA
18A1 Ashland Nebraska, USA
14B2 Ashland Ohio, USA
8A2 Ashland Oregon, USA
109C1 Ashley Aust
16B2 Ashokan *Res* USA
94B3 Ashqelon Israel
93D3 Ash Shabakh Iraq
91C4 Ash Sha'm UAE
93D2 Ash Sharqāt Iraq
93D3 Ash Shaţrah Iraq
81C4 Ash Shiḥr Yemen
91A4 Ash Shumlul S Arabia
14B2 Ashtabula USA
7D4 Ashuanipi L Can
92C3 'Aşi *R* Syria
47D2 Asiago Italy
53A2 Asinara *I* Medit S
65K4 Asino Russian Fed
93D2 Aşkale Turk
39G7 Askersund Sweden
84C1 Asmar Afghan
99D1 Asmera Eritrea
75A2 Aso Japan
99D1 Asosa Eth
111A2 Aspiring,Mt NZ
93C2 As Sabkhah Syria
91A5 As Salamiyah S Arabia
92C2 As Salamiyah Syria
93D3 As Salmān Iraq
86C1 Assam State, India

93E3 As Samāwah Iraq
91B5 As Şanām Region, S Arabia
94C2 As Sanamayn Syria
56B2 Assen Neth
56B1 Assens Den
95A1 As Sidrah Libya
5G4 Assiniboia Can
5G4 Assiniboine,Mt Can
30F3 Assis Brazil
93C3 As Sukhnah Syria
93E2 As Sulaymānīyah Iraq
91A5 As Summan Region, S Arabia
99E3 Assumption *I* Seychelles
93C3 As Suwaydā' Syria
93D3 As Suwayrah Iraq
93E2 Astara Azerbaijan
52A2 Asti Italy
55C3 Astipálaia *I* Greece
50A1 Astorga Spain
8A2 Astoria USA
61G4 Astrakhan' Russian Fed
50A1 Asturias Region, Spain
30E4 Asunción Par
99D2 Aswa *R* Uganda
80B3 Aswân Egypt
80B3 Aswân High Dam Egypt
95C2 Asyûṭ Egypt
92C3 As Zilaf Syria
97C4 Atakpamé Togo
71D4 Atambua Indon
6E3 Atangmik Greenland
96A2 Atar Maur
65J5 Atasu Kazakhstan
95C3 Atbara Sudan
65H4 Atbasar Kazakhstan
11A4 Atchafalaya B USA
10A3 Atchison USA
16B3 Atco USA
23A1 Atenguillo Mexico
52B2 Atessa Italy
46B1 Ath Belg
13E2 Athabasca Can
5G4 Athabasca *R* Can
5H4 Athabasca L Can
41B3 Athenry Irish Rep
Athens = Athína
11B3 Athens Georgia, USA
14B3 Athens Ohio, USA
19A3 Athens Texas, USA
55B3 Athína Greece
41B3 Athlone Irish Rep
16C1 Athol USA
55B2 Áthos *Mt* Greece
41B3 Athy Irish Rep
98B1 Ati Chad
7A5 Atikokan Can
61F3 Atkarsk Russian Fed
18A1 Atkinson USA
23B2 Atlacomulco Mexico
11B3 Atlanta Georgia, USA
14B2 Atlanta Michigan, USA
18A1 Atlantic USA
10C3 Atlantic City USA
16B2 Atlantic Highlands USA
103H8 Atlantic Indian Basin Atlantic O
103H7 Atlantic Indian Ridge Atlantic O
96C1 Atlas Saharien *Mts* Alg
4E4 Atlin Can
4E4 Atlin L Can
94B1 Atlit Israel
23B2 Atlixco Mexico
11B3 Atmore USA
101D3 Atofinandrahana Madag
12D3 Atognak *I* USA
19A3 Atoka USA
23A1 Atotonilco Mexico
23B2 Atoyac *R* Mexico
32B2 Atrato *R* Colombia

91B5 Attaf Region, UAE
81C3 At Tā'if S Arabia
94C2 At Tall Syria
17A1 Attala USA
7B4 Attawapiskat Can
7B4 Attawapiskat *R* Can
93D3 At Taysīyah *Desert Region* S Arabia
14A2 Attica Indiana, USA
46C2 Attigny France
15D2 Attleboro Massachusetts, USA
76D3 Attopeu Laos
92C4 At Tubayq *Upland* S Arabia
34B3 Atuel *R* Arg
39H7 Ätvidaberg Sweden
22B2 Atwater USA
49D3 Aubagne France
46C2 Aube Department, France
49C3 Aubenas France
17A1 Auburn Alabama, USA
14A2 Auburn Indiana, USA
18A1 Auburn Nebraska, USA
15C2 Auburn New York, USA
20B1 Auburn Washington, USA
48C3 Auch France
110B1 Auckland NZ
105G6 Auckland Is NZ
48C3 Aude *R* France
7B4 Auden Can
48B1 Audincourt France
109C1 Aughathella Aust
57C3 Augsburg Germany
106A4 Augusta Aust
11B3 Augusta Georgia, USA
18A2 Augusta Kansas, USA
10D2 Augusta Maine, USA
12D3 Augustine I Can
58C2 Augustów Pol
106A3 Augustus,Mt Aust
46A2 Aumale France
85D3 Auraiya India
85D5 Aurangābād India
96C1 Aurès *Mts* Alg
48C3 Aurillac France
8C3 Aurora Colorado, USA
10B2 Aurora Illinois, USA
14B3 Aurora Indiana, USA
18B2 Aurora Missouri, USA
100A3 Aus Namibia
14B2 Au Sable USA
10A2 Austin Minnesota, USA
21B2 Austin Nevada, USA
19A3 Austin Texas, USA
106C3 Australia Fed. State/ Monarchy
107D4 Australian Alps *Mts* Aust
37E4 Austria Federal Republic, Europe
46A1 Authie *R* France
24B3 Autlán Mexico
49C2 Autun France
49C2 Auvergne Region, France
49C2 Auxerre France
46B1 Auxi-le-Châteaus France
49C2 Avallon France
22C4 Avalon USA
7E5 Avalon Pen Can
35B2 Avaré Brazil
90D3 Avaz Iran
94B3 Avedat *Hist Site* Israel
33F4 Aveiro Brazil
50A1 Aveiro Port
29E2 Avellaneda Arg
53B2 Avellino Italy
46B1 Avesnes-sur-Helpe France

Avesta

39H6 Avesta Sweden
52B2 Avezzano Italy
44C3 Aviemore Scot
111B2 Aviemore,L NZ
47B2 Avigliana Italy
49C3 Avignon France
50B1 Avila Spain
50A1 Aviles Spain
47D1 Avisio R Italy
108B3 Avoca R Aust
43C4 Avon County, Eng
43D4 Avon R Dorset, Eng
43D3 Avon R Warwick, Eng
43C4 Avonmouth Wales
17B2 Avon Park USA
46B2 Avre R France
54A2 ac Avtovac Bosnia-Herzegovina
94C2 A'waj R Syria
74D4 Awaji-shima B Japan
99E2 Aware Eth
111A2 Awarua Pt NZ
99E2 Awash Eth
99E2 Awash R Eth
75B1 Awa-shima / Japan
11B2 Awatere R NZ
95A2 Awbārī Libya
98C2 Aweil Sudan
95B2 Awjilah Libya
96A2 Awserd Well Mor
6A2 Axel Heiburg I Can
43C4 Axminster Eng
75B1 Ayabe Japan
29E2 Ayacucho Arg
32C6 Ayacucho Peru
65K5 Ayaguz Kazakhstan
82C2 Ayakkum Hu L China
50A2 Ayamonte Spain
63F2 Ayan Russian Fed
32C6 Ayauiri Peru
92A2 Aydin Turk
55C3 Áyios Evstrátios / Greece
43D4 Aylesbury Eng
13D2 Aylmer,Mt Can
94C2 'Ayn al Fijah Syria
93D2 Ayn Zālah Iraq
95B2 Ayn Zuwayyah Well Libya
99D2 Ayod Sudan
107D2 Ayr Aust
42B2 Ayr Scot
42B2 Ayr R Scot
42B2 Ayre,Pt of Eng
54C2 Aytos Bulg
76C3 Ayutthaya Thai
23A1 Ayutla Mexico
55C3 Ayvacik Turk
55C3 Ayvalik Turk
84A1 Azamgarh India
97B3 Azaouad Desert Region Mali
97D3 Azare Nig
92C2 A'Zāz Syria
Azbine = Air
65F5 Azerbaijan Republic, Russian Fed
32B4 Azogues Ecuador
Azores = Açores
98C1 Azoum R Chad
60E4 Azov, Sea of Russian Fed/Ukraine
Azovskoye More = Azov, Sea of
96B1 Azrou Mor
34D3 Azucena Arg
32A2 Azuero,Pen de Panama
29E3 Azúl Arg
94C2 Az-Zabdani Syria
91C5 Az Zāhirah Mts Oman
95A2 Aj Zāhra R Maur
96A2 Azzeffal R Maur
93E3 Az Zubayr Iraq

B

94B2 Ba'abda Leb
92C3 Ba'albek Leb
94B3 Ba'al Hazor Mt Israel

99E2 Baardheere Somalia
54C2 Babadag Rom
92A1 Babaeski Turk
32B4 Babahoyo Ecuador
81C4 Bāb al Mandab Str Djibouti/Yemen
71D4 Babar / Indon
99D3 Babati Tanz
60E2 Babayevo Russian Fed
14B2 Baberton USA
13B1 Babine R Can
5F4 Babine L Can
90B2 Bābol Iran
79B2 Babuyan Chan Phil
79B2 Babuyan Is Phil
31C2 Bacabal Brazil
71D4 Bacan / Indon
60C4 Bačau Rom
76D1 Bac Can Viet
108B3 Bacchus Marsh Aust
82B2 Bachu China
4J3 Back R Can
12J2 Backbone Ranges Mts Can
76D1 Bac Ninh Viet
79B3 Bacolod Phil
79B3 Baco,Mt Phil
87B2 Badagara India
72A1 Badain Jaran Shamo Desert China
50A2 Badajoz Spain
51C1 Badalona Spain
93D3 Badanah S Arabia
46D2 Bad Bergzabern Germany
46D1 Bad Ems Germany
47C1 Baden Switz
57B3 Baden-Baden Germany
57B3 Baden-Württemberg State, Germany
57C3 Badgastein Austria
22C2 Badger USA
57B2 Bad-Godesberg Germany
57B2 Bad Hersfeld Germany
46D1 Bad Honnef Germany
85B4 Badin Pak
52B1 Bad Ischl Austria
93C3 Badiyat ash Sham Desert Region Jordan/Iraq
57B3 Bad-Kreuznach Germany
46D1 Bad Nevenahr-Ahrweiler Germany
47C1 Bad Ragaz Switz
57C3 Bad Tolz Germany
87C3 Badulla Sri Lanka
50D2 Baena Spain
97A3 Bafatá Guinea-Bissau
4H2 Baffin Region Can
6C2 Baffin B Greenland/Can
6C2 Baffin I Can
98B2 Bafia Cam
97A3 Bafing R Mali
97A3 Bafoulabé Mali
98B2 Bafoussam Cam
90C3 Bāfq Iran
60E5 Bafra Burun Pt Turk
91C4 Bāft Iran
98C2 Bafwasende Zaire
86A1 Bagaha India
87B1 Bāgalkot India
99D3 Bagamoyo Tanz
29F2 Bagé Brazil
93D3 Baghdād Iraq
86B2 Bagherhat Bang
91C3 Bāghin Iran
84B1 Baghlan Afghan
49C3 Bagnols-sur-Cèze France
97B3 Bagoé R Mali
79B2 Baguio Phil
86B1 Bahadurābād India
11C4 Bahamas,The Is Caribbean S
86B2 Baharampur India
92A4 Bahariya Oasis Egypt

84C3 Bahawalpur Pak
84C3 Bahawalpur Province, Pak
85C3 Bahawalnagar Pak
31C4 Bahia State, Brazil
29D3 Bahia Blanca Arg
29D3 Bahía Blanca Arg
34A3 Bahía Concepción B Chile
35C2 Bahia da Ilha Grande B Brazil
24B2 Bahia de Banderas B Mexico
24C2 Bahia de Campeche B Mexico
25D3 Bahia de la Ascension B Mexico
24B3 Bahía de Petacalco B Mexico
96A2 Bahia de Rio de Oro B Mor
35C2 Bahia de Sepetiba B Brazil
29C6 Bahía Grande B Arg
9B4 Bahia Kino Mexico
24A2 Bahía Magdalena B Mexico
24A2 Bahía Sebastia Vizcaino B Mexico
99D1 Bahar Dar Eth
86D1 Bahraich India
80D3 Bahrain Sheikdom, Arabian Pen
93D3 Bahr al Milh L Iraq
98C2 Bahr Aouk R Chad/CAR
Bahrat Lut = Dead S
98C2 Bahr el Arab Watercourse Sudan
99D2 Bahr el Ghazal R Sudan
98B1 Bahr el Ghazal Watercourse Chad
101H1 Baia de Maputo B Mozam
31B2 Baia de Marajó B Brazil
101D2 Baia de Pemba B Mozam
31C2 Baia de São Marcos B Brazil
50A2 Baia de Setúbal B Brazil
31D4 Baia de Todos os Santos B Brazil
100A2 Baia dos Tigres Angola
60B4 Baia Mare Rom
98B2 Baïbokoum Chad
69E2 Baicheng China
101E2 Baie Antongila B Madag
7D5 Baie-Comeau Can
101D2 Baie de Bombetoka B Madag
101D2 Baie de Mahajamba B Madag
101D3 Baie de St Augustin B Madag
94B2 Baie de St Georges B Leb
10D2 Baie des Chaleurs B Can
7C4 Baie-du-Poste Can
72B3 Baihe China
72C3 Bai He R China
93D3 Ba'iji Iraq
86A2 Baikunthpur India
Baile Atha Cliath = Dublin
54B2 Băilesti Rom
46H1 Bailleul France
72A3 Baima China
15C3 Bainbridge USA
12B2 Baird Inlet USA
4B3 Baird Mts USA
72D1 Bairin Youqi China
72D1 Bairin Zuoqi China
108C3 Bairnsdale Aust
79B4 Bais Phil
54A1 Baja Hung
9B3 Baja California State, Mexico

24A1 Baja California Pen Mexico
61J2 Bakal Russian Fed
98C2 Bakala CAR
97A3 Bakel Sen
8C2 Baker Montana, USA
8B2 Baker Oregon, USA
6A3 Baker Foreland Pt Can
4J3 Baker L Can
4J3 Baker Lake Can
9B3 Bakersfield USA
90C2 Bakharden Turkmenistan
60D3 Bakhmach Ukraine
38C1 Bakkafloi R Iceland
99D2 Bako Eth
98C2 Bakouma CAR
65F5 Baku Azerbaijan
Baky = Baku
92B2 Balâ Turk
79A4 Balabac / Phil
70C3 Balabac Str Malay
78C2 Balaikarangan Indon
108A2 Balaklava Aust
61G3 Balakovo Russian Fed
86A2 Balāngir India
61F3 Balashov Russian Fed
86B2 Balasore India
80A3 Balât Egypt
52C1 Balaton L Hung
45C2 Balbriggan Irish Rep
29E3 Balcarce Arg
54C2 Balchik Bulg
111B3 Balclutha NZ
18B2 Bald Knob USA
17B1 Baldwin USA
9D3 Baldy Peak Mt USA
Balearic Is = Islas Baleares
78C2 Balen R Malay
79D2 Baler Phil
61H2 Balezino Russian Fed
106A1 Bali / Indon
92A2 Balikesir Turk
93C2 Balikh R Syria
78D3 Balikpapan Indon
79B2 Balintang Chan Phil
78C4 Bali S Indon
35A1 Baliza Brazil
84B1 Balkh Afghan
65J5 Balkhash Kazakhstan
44B3 Ballachulish Scot
45C2 Ballaghaderreen Irish Rep
42B2 Ballantrae Scot
4G2 Ballantyne Str Can
87B2 Ballapur India
107D4 Ballarat Aust
44C3 Ballater Scot
112C7 Balleny Is Antarctica
86A1 Ballia India
109D1 Ballina Aust
41B3 Ballina Irish Rep
45B2 Ballinasloe Irish Rep
45B2 Ballinrobe Irish Rep
55A2 Ballsh Alb
45B1 Ballycastle Irish Rep
45M1 Ballycastle N Ire
45C1 Ballymena N Ire
45C1 Ballymoney N Ire
45B1 Ballyshannon Irish Rep
45B2 Ballyvaghan Irish Rep
108B3 Balmoral Aust
34C2 Balnearia Arg
84B3 Balochistān Region, Pak
100A2 Balombo Angola
100A2 Balonn R Aust
85C3 Balotra India
86A1 Balrāmpur India
107D4 Balranald Aust
31B3 Balsas Brazil
23B2 Balsas Mexico
24B3 Balsas R Mexico
60C4 Balta Ukraine
39H7 Baltic S N Europe

92B3 Baltim Egypt
45B3 Baltimore Irish Rep
10C3 Baltimore USA
86B1 Bālurghāt India
81A4 Balykshi Kazakhstan
91C4 Bam Iran
98B1 Bama Nig
97B3 Bamako Mali
98C2 Bambari CAR
17B1 Bamberg USA
57C3 Bamberg Germany
98C2 Bambili Zaire
35B2 Bamboi Ghana
98B2 Bamenda Cam
13C3 Bamfield Can
98B2 Bamingui R CAR
98B2 Bamingui Bangoran National Park CAR
84B2 Bamyan Afghan
91D4 Bampūr Iran
91D4 Bampūr R Iran
98C2 Banalia Zaire
97B3 Banamba Mali
76C3 Ban Aranyaprathet Thai
76C2 Ban Ban Laos
77C4 Ban Betong Thai
45C1 Banbridge N Ire
43D3 Banbury Eng
44C3 Banchory Scot
25D3 Banco Chinchorro Is Mexico
15C1 Bancroft Can
86A1 Bānda India
70A3 Banda Aceh Indon
97B4 Bandama R Ivory Coast
91C4 Bandar Abbās Iran
90A2 Bandar Anzalī Iran
99F2 Bandarbeyla Somalia
91B4 Bandar-e Daylam Iran
91B4 Bandar-e Lengheh Iran
91B4 Bandar-e Māqām Iran
91B4 Bandar-e Rīg Iran
90B2 Bandar-e Torkoman Iran
91A3 Bandar Khomeyni Iran
78C2 Bandar Seri Begawan Brunei
71D4 Banda S Indon
91C4 Band Boni Iran
35C2 Bandeira Mt Brazil
97B3 Bandiagara Mali
60C5 Bandirma Turk
45B3 Bandon Irish Rep
98B3 Bandundu Zaire
78B4 Bandung Indon
25E2 Banes Cuba
13D2 Banff Can
44C3 Banff Scot
5C4 Banff Nat Pk Can
13D2 Banff Nat Pk Can
87B2 Bangalore India
98C2 Bangassou CAR
70C3 Banggi I Malay
95B1 Banghāzī Libya
76D2 Bang Hieng R Laos
78B3 Bangka I Indon
78A3 Bangko Indon
76C3 Bangkok Thai
82C3 Bangladesh Republic, Asia
84D2 Bangong Co L China
10D2 Bangor Maine, USA
45D1 Bangor N Ire
16B2 Bangor Pennsylvania, USA
42B3 Bangor Wales
78D3 Bangsalsembera Indon
76B3 Ban Saphan Yai Thai
79B2 Bangued Phil
98B2 Bangui CAR
100C2 Bangweulu L Zambia
77C4 Ban Hat Yai Thai
76C2 Ban Hin Heup Laos
76B1 Ban Houei Sai Laos
76B1 Ban Hua Hin Thai

97B3 Bani R Mali
97C3 Bani Bangou Niger
95A1 Bani Walīd Libya
92C2 Bāniyās Syria
94B2 Baniyas Syria
52C2 Banja Luka Bosnia-Herzegovina
78C3 Banjarmasin Indon
97A3 Banjul The Gambia
77B4 Ban Kantang Thai
76D2 Ban Khemmarat Laos
77B4 Ban Khok Kloi Thai
71F5 Banks I Aust
76B1 Banks I British Columbia, Can
4F2 Banks I Northwest Territories, Can
20C1 Banks I USA
111B2 Banks Pen NZ
109C4 Banks Str Aust
86B2 Bankura India
76B2 Ban Itae Sariang Thai
76B2 Ban Mae Sot Thai
76D3 Ban Me Thuot Viet
45C1 Bann R N Ire
77B4 Ban Na San Thai
84C2 Bannu Pak
44A3 Baños Maule Chile
76C2 Ban Pak Neun Laos
77C4 Ban Pak Phanang Thai
76D3 Ban Ru Kroy Camb
76B3 Ban Sai Yok Thai
76B3 Ban Sattahip Thai
59B3 Banská Bystrica Slovakia
85C4 Bānswāra India
77B4 Ban Tha Kham Thai
76C2 Ban Thateng Laos
76C2 Ban Tha Tum Thai
41B3 Bantry Irish Rep
41A3 Bantry B Irish Rep
76D3 Ban Ya Soop Viet
77C4 Banyuwangi Indon
72C3 Baofeng China
76C1 Bao Ha Viet
72B3 Baoji China
76D3 Bao Loc Viet
68B4 Baoshan China
72C1 Baotou China
87C1 Bāpatla India
81B3 Bapaume France
93D3 Ba'Qūbah Iraq
32J7 Baquerizo Moreno Ecuador
54A2 Bar Montenegro, Yugos
99D1 Bara Sudan
99E2 Baraawe Somalia
78D3 Barabai Indon
86A1 Bara Banki India
65J4 Barabinsk Russian Fed
65J4 Barabinskaya Step Steppe Kazakhstan/Russian Fed
50B1 Baracaldo Spain
26C2 Baracoa Cuba
94C2 Baradá R Syria
72C3 Baradine Aust
87A1 Bāramati India
84C2 Baramula Pak
85D3 Bārān India
79B3 Barangas Phil
4E4 Baranof I USA
60C3 Baranovichi Belarus
108A2 Baratta Aust
86B1 Barauni India
31C6 Barbacena Brazil
27F4 Barbados I Caribbean S
51C1 Barbastro Spain
101H1 Barberton S Africa
48B2 Barbezieux France
32C2 Barbosa Colombia
27E3 Barbuda I Caribbean S
33E8 Barcaldine Aust
53A2 Barce = Al Marj
53C3 Barcellona Italy
51C1 Barcelona Spain
33E1 Barcelona Ven

107D3 Barcoo R Aust
34B3 Barda del Medio Arg
95A2 Bardai Chad
29C3 Bardas Blancas Arg
86B2 Barddhaman India
59C3 Bardejov Slovakia
47C2 Bardi Italy
47B2 Bardonecchia Italy
43B3 Bardsey I Wales
84D3 Bareilly India
64D2 Barentsøya I Barents S
64E2 Barents S Russian Fed
95C3 Barentu Eritrea
86A2 Bargarh India
47B2 Barge Italy
63D2 Barguzin Russian Fed
63D2 Barguzin R Russian Fed
86B2 Barhi India
53C2 Bari Italy
51D2 Barika Alg
32C2 Barinas Ven
85C4 Bari Sādri India
86C2 Barisal Bang
78C3 Barito R Indon
95A2 Barjuj Watercourse Libya
73A3 Barkam China
18C2 Barkley,L USA
13B3 Barkley Sd Can
100B4 Barkly East S Africa
106C2 Barkly Tableland Mts Aust
46C2 Bar-le-Duc France
106A3 Barlee,L Aust
106A3 Barlee Range Mts Aust
53C2 Barletta Italy
85C3 Barmer India
108B2 Barmera Aust
43B3 Barmouth Wales
42D2 Barnard Castle Eng
65K4 Barnaul Russian Fed
16B3 Barnegat USA
16B3 Barnegat B USA
6C2 Barnes Icecap Can
18C2 Barnesville Georgia, USA
14B3 Barnesville Ohio, USA
42D3 Barnsley Eng
43B4 Barnstaple Eng
97C4 Baro Nig
86C1 Barpeta India
32D1 Barquisimeto Ven
31C4 Barra Brazil
44A3 Barra I Scot
109D2 Barraba Aust
23A2 Barra de Navidad Mexico
35C2 Barra de Pirai Brazil
35A1 Barragem de São Simão Res Brazil
35A1 Barra do Garças Brazil
35B1 Barragem Agua Vermelha Res Brazil
50A2 Barragem do Castelo do Bode Res Port
50A2 Barragem do Maranhão Res Port
35A2 Barragem Três Irmãos Res Brazil
44A3 Barra Head Pt Scot
31C6 Barra Mansa Brazil
32B6 Barranca Peru
32C2 Barrancabermeja Colombia
33E2 Barrancas Ven
30E4 Barranqueras Arg
32C1 Barranquilla Colombia
44A3 Barra,Sound of Chan Scot
16C1 Barre USA
34B2 Barreal Arg
31C4 Barreiras Brazil
50A2 Barreiro Port
31D3 Barreiros Brazil

107D5 Barren,C Aust
12D3 Barren Is USA
31B6 Barretos Brazil
14C2 Barrhead Can
13C2 Barrie Can
13C2 Barrière Can
108B2 Barrier Range Mts Aust
107E4 Barrington,Mt Aust
27N2 Barrouaillie St Vincent and the Grenadines
45C2 Barrow R Irish Rep
4C2 Barrow USA
106C3 Barrow Creek Aust
106A3 Barrow I Aust
42C2 Barrow-in-Furness Eng
4C2 Barrow,Pt USA
6A2 Barrow Str Can
15C1 Barry's Bay Can
87B1 Barsi India
9B3 Barstow USA
49C2 Bar-sur-Aube France
33F2 Bartica Guyana
92B1 Bartin Turk
107D2 Bartle Frere,Mt Aust
9D3 Bartlesville USA
101C3 Bartolomeu Dias Mozam
58C2 Bartoszyce Pol
78C4 Barung I Indon
85D4 Barwāh India
85C4 Barwāni India
109C1 Barwon R Aust
61G3 Barysh Russian Fed
98B2 Basankusu Zaire
34D2 Basavilbas Arg
79B1 Basco Phil
52A1 Basel Switz
53C2 Basento R Italy
13E2 Bashaw Can
79B1 Bashi Chan Phil
61H3 Bashkortostan Russian Fed
79B4 Basilan Phil
79B4 Basilan I Phil
43E4 Basildon Eng
43D4 Basingstoke Eng
8B2 Basin Region USA
93E3 Basra Iraq
46D2 Bas-Rhin Department, France
76D3 Bassac R Camb
13E2 Bassano Can
52B1 Bassano del Grappa Italy
97A4 Bassari Togo
101C3 Bassas da India I Mozam Chan
76A2 Bassein Myan
27E3 Basse Terre Guadeloupe
97C4 Bassila Benin
22C2 Bass Lake USA
107D4 Bass Str Aust
39G7 Båstad Sweden
9184 Bastak Iran
86A1 Basti India
52A2 Bastia Corse
57B3 Bastogne Belg
19B3 Bastrop Louisiana, USA
19A3 Bastrop Texas, USA
98A2 Bata Eq Guinea
78C3 Batakan Indon
84D2 Batala India
68B3 Bātang China
98B2 Batangafo CAR
79B1 Batan Is Phil
78B3 Batanta I Indon
15C2 Batavia USA
109D3 Batemans Bay Aust
17B1 Batesburg USA
18B2 Batesville Arkansas, USA
19C3 Batesville Mississippi, USA
43C4 Bath Eng
15C2 Bath New York, USA
98B1 Batha R Chad
107D4 Bathurst Aust
7D5 Bathurst Can

Bathurst,C

4F2 **Bathurst,** C Can
106C2 **Bathurst I** Aust
4H2 **Bathurst I** Can
4H3 **Bathurst Inlet** B Can
97B3 **Batié** Burkina
90B3 **Bätlaq-e Gavkhüni** Salt Flat Iran
109C3 **Batlow** Aust
92D3 **Batman** Turk
96C1 **Batna** Nig
11A3 **Baton Rouge** USA
94B1 **Batroun** Leb
76C3 **Battambang** Camb
87C3 **Batticaloa** Sri Lanka
13F2 **Battle** R Can
10B2 **Battle Creek** USA
7E4 **Battle Harbour** Can
20C2 **Battle Mountain** USA
78D2 **Batukelau** Indon
65F5 **Batumi** Georgia
77C5 **Batu Pahat** Malay
78A3 **Baturaja** Indon
94B2 **Bat Yam** Israel
71D4 **Baubau** Indon
97C3 **Bauchi** Nig
47B2 **Bauges** Mts France
7E4 **Bauld,C** Can
47B1 **Baumes-les-Dames** France
63D2 **Baunt** Russian Fed
31B6 **Bauru** Brazil
35A1 **Baus** Brazil
57C2 **Bautzen** Germany
78C4 **Baween** I Indon
95B2 **Bawiti** Egypt
76B2 **Bawlake** Myan
108A2 **Bawlen** Aust
17B1 **Baxley** USA
25E2 **Bayamo** Cuba
77C4 **Bayan** Indon
68C2 **Bayandzürh** Mongolia
68B3 **Bayan Har Shan** Mts China
72A1 **Bayan Mod** China
72B1 **Bayan Obo** China
47A2 **Bayard** P France
12J3 **Bayard,Mt** Can
63D3 **Bayasgalant** Mongolia
79B3 **Baybay** Phil
93D1 **Bayburt** Turk
10B2 **Bay City** Michigan, USA
19A4 **Bay City** Texas, USA
92B2 **Bay Dağlari** Turk
64H3 **Baydaratskaya Guba** B Russian Fed
99E2 **Baydhabo** Somalia
48B2 **Bayeux** France
47D1 **Bayerische Alpen** Mts Germany
57C3 **Bayern** State, Germany
92C3 **Bāyir** Jordan
63C2 **Baykalskiy Khrebet** Mts Russian Fed
63B1 **Baykit** Russian Fed
63B3 **Baylik Shan** Mts China/Mongolia
61J3 **Baymak** Russian Fed
79B2 **Bayombong** Phil
48B3 **Bayonne** France
57C3 **Bayreuth** Germany
16B3 **Bay St Louis** USA
15D2 **Bay Shore** USA
15C1 **Bays,L of** Can
68A2 **Baytik Shan** Mts China
Bayt Lahm = Bethlehem
19B4 **Baytown** USA
50B2 **Baza** Spain
59D3 **Bazaliya** Ukraine
48B3 **Bazas** France
73B3 **Bazhong** China
91D4 **Bazmān** Iran
94C1 **Bcharre** Leb
18C3 **Beach Haven** USA
43E4 **Beachy Head** Eng
16C2 **Beacon** USA
101D2 **Bealanana** Madag
18B1 **Beardstown** USA

Bear I = Bjørnøya
22B1 **Bear Valley** USA
8D2 **Beatrice** USA
44C2 **Beatrice** Oilfield N Sea
13C1 **Beatton** R Can
5F4 **Beatton River** Can
29E6 **Beauchene Is** Falkland Is
109D1 **Beaudesert** Aust
1B5 **Beaufort S** Can
100B4 **Beaufort West** S Africa
15D1 **Beauharnois** Can
44B3 **Beauly** Scot
21B3 **Beaumont** California, USA
11A3 **Beaumont** Texas, USA
49C2 **Beaune** France
48C2 **Beauvais** France
13F1 **Beauval** Can
12E1 **Beaver** Alaska, USA
13F2 **Beaver** R Saskatchewan, Can
4D3 **Beaver Creek** Can
12E1 **Beaver Creek** USA
18C2 **Beaver Dam** Kentucky, USA
13E2 **Beaverhill L** Can
14A1 **Beaver I** USA
18B2 **Beaver L** USA
13D1 **Beaverlodge** Can
85C3 **Beawar** India
34B2 **Beazley** Arg
35B2 **Bebedouro** Brazil
43E3 **Beccles** Eng
54B1 **Bečej** Serbia, Yugos
96B1 **Béchar** Alg
12C3 **Becharof L** USA
11B3 **Beckley** USA
43D3 **Bedford** County, Eng
43D3 **Bedford** Eng
14A3 **Bedford** Indiana, USA
27M2 **Bedford Pt** Grenada
4D2 **Beechey** Pt USA
109C3 **Beechworth** Aust
109D1 **Beenleigh** Aust
92B3 **Beersheba** Israel
Beer Sheva = Beersheba
94B3 **Beér Sheva** R Israel
90A4 **Beeville** USA
98C2 **Befale** Zaire
101D2 **Befandriana** Madag
109C3 **Bega** Aust
91B3 **Behbehān** Iran
90B2 **Behshahr** Iran
84B2 **Behsud** Afghan
69E2 **Bei'an** China
73B5 **Beihai** China
72D2 **Beijing** China
76E1 **Beiliu** China
73B4 **Beipan Jiang** R China
72E1 **Beipiao** China
Beira = Sofala
92C3 **Beirut** Leb
68B2 **Bei Shan** Mts China
12H3 **Behm Canal** Sd USA
84B3 **Beit Jala** Israel
50A2 **Beja** Port
96C1 **Beja** Tunisia
96C1 **Bejaia** Alg
50A1 **Bejar** Spain
90C3 **Bejestān** Iran
59C3 **Békéscsaba** Hung
101D3 **Bekily** Madag
86A1 **Bela** India
85B3 **Bela** Pak
78C2 **Belaga** Malay
16A3 **Bel Air** USA
87B1 **Belamoalli** India
71D3 **Belang** Indon
70A3 **Belangpidie** Indon
60C3 **Belarus** Republic, Europe
Belau = Palau Is.
101C3 **Bela Vista** Mozam
70A3 **Belawan** Indon
61J2 **Belaya** R Ukraine
6A2 **Belcher Chan** Can

7C4 **Belcher Is** Can
84B1 **Belchiragh** Afghan
61H3 **Belebey** Russian Fed
99E2 **Beled Weyne** Somalia
31B2 **Belém** Brazil
32B3 **Belén** Colombia
34D2 **Belén** Urug
9C3 **Belen** USA
45D1 **Belfast** N Ire
101H1 **Belfast** S Africa
45D1 **Belfast Lough** Estuary N Ire
99D1 **Bēlfodiyo** Eth
42D2 **Belford** Eng
49D2 **Belfort** France
87A1 **Belgaum** India
56A2 **Belgium** Kingdom, N W Europe
60E3 **Belgorod** Russian Fed
60D4 **Belgorod Dnestrovskiy** Ukraine
Belgrade = Beograd
95A2 **Bel Hedan** Libya
78B3 **Belinyu** Indon
78B3 **Belitung** I Indon
25D3 **Belize** Belize
25D3 **Belize** Republic, Cent America
48C2 **Bellac** France
5F4 **Bella Coola** Can
47C2 **Bellagio** Italy
19A4 **Bellaire** USA
47C1 **Bellano** Italy
87B2 **Bellary** India
109C1 **Bellata** Aust
47B2 **Belledonne** Mts France
20C2 **Belle Fourche** USA
49D2 **Bellegarde** France
17B2 **Belle Glade** USA
7E4 **Belle I** Can
48B2 **Belle-Ile** I France
7E4 **Belle Isle,Str of** Can
7C5 **Belleville** Can
18A2 **Belleville** Kansas, USA
20B1 **Bellevue** Washington, USA
109D2 **Bellingen** Aust
8A2 **Bellingham** USA
112C2 **Bellingshausen** Base Ant
112C3 **Bellingshausen S** Ant
52A1 **Bellinzona** Switz
32B2 **Bello** Colombia
107E3 **Bellona Reefs** Nouvelle Calédonie
22B1 **Bellota** USA
15D2 **Bellows Falls** USA
6B3 **Bell Pen** Can
52B1 **Belluno** Italy
29D2 **Bell Ville** Arg
31D5 **Belmonte** Brazil
25D3 **Belmopan** Belize
45B1 **Belmullet** Irish Rep
69E1 **Belogorsk** Russian Fed
101D3 **Beloha** Madag
31C5 **Belo Horizonte** Brazil
10B2 **Beloit** Wisconsin, USA
64E3 **Belomorsk** Russian Fed
61J3 **Beloretsk** Russian Fed
Belorussia = Belarus
101D2 **Belo-Tsiribihina** Madag
64E3 **Beloye More** S Russian Fed
60E1 **Beloye Ozero** L Russian Fed
60E1 **Belozersk** Russian Fed
14B3 **Belpre** USA
108A2 **Beltana** Aust
19A3 **Belton** USA
59D3 **Bel'tsy** Moldova
16B2 **Belvidere** New Jersey, USA
98B3 **Bembe** Angola

97C3 **Bembéréke** Benin
10A2 **Bemidji** USA
39G6 **Bena** Nor
98C3 **Bena Dibele** Zaire
108C3 **Benalla** Aust
44B3 **Ben Attow** Mt Scot
50A1 **Benavente** Spain
44A3 **Benbecula** I Scot
106B4 **Bencubbin** Aust
8A2 **Bend** USA
44B3 **Ben Dearg** Mt Scot
60C4 **Bendery** Moldova
107D4 **Bendigo** Aust
57C3 **Benešov** Czech Republic
53C2 **Benevento** Italy
83C4 **Bengal,B of** Asia
96D1 **Ben Gardane** Tunisia
72D3 **Bengbu** China
78A2 **Bengkalis** Indon
78A3 **Bengkulu** Indon
100A2 **Benguela** Angola
92B3 **Benha** Egypt
44B3 **Ben Hope** Mt Scot
99C2 **Beni** Zaire
32D6 **Béni** R Bol
96B1 **Beni Abbes** Alg
51C1 **Benicarló** Spain
7A5 **Benidji** USA
51B2 **Benidorm** Spain
51C2 **Beni Mansour** Alg
95C2 **Beni Mazar** Egypt
96B1 **Beni Mellal** Mor
97C4 **Benin** Republic, Africa
97C4 **Benin City** Nig
95C2 **Beni Suef** Egypt
44B2 **Ben Kilbreck** Mt Scot
44B3 **Ben Lawers** Mt UK
109C4 **Ben Lomond** Mt Aust
44B2 **Ben Macdui** Mt Scot
44C3 **Ben More Assynt** Mt Scot
111B2 **Benmore,L** NZ
44B3 **Ben Nevis** Mt Scot
15D2 **Bennington** USA
94B2 **Bennt Jbail** Leb
98B2 **Bénoué** R Cam
98C2 **Bentiu** Sudan
19B3 **Benton** Arkansas, USA
18C2 **Benton** Kentucky, USA
14A2 **Benton Harbor** USA
97C4 **Benue** R Nig
45B1 **Benwee Hd** C Irish Rep
44B3 **Ben Wyvis** Mt Scot
72E1 **Benxi** China
54B2 **Beograd** Serbia, Yugos
86A2 **Beohari** India
74C4 **Beppu** Japan
55A2 **Berat** Alb
95C3 **Berber** Sudan
99E1 **Berbera** Somalia
98B2 **Berbérati** CAR
46A1 **Berck** France
60C4 **Berdichev** Ukraine
60E4 **Berdyansk** Ukraine
97B4 **Berekum** Ghana
22B2 **Berenda** USA
5J4 **Berens** R Can
5J4 **Berens River** Can
108A1 **Beresford** Aust
59C3 **Berettyóújfalu** Hung
58D2 **Bereza** Belarus
59C3 **Berezhany** Ukraine
65G4 **Bereznik** Russian Fed
60D4 **Berezovka** Ukraine
64H3 **Berezovo** Russian Fed
92A2 **Bergama** Turk
52A1 **Bergamo** Italy
39F6 **Bergen** Nor
46C1 **Bergen op Zoom** Neth
48C3 **Bergerac** France
46D1 **Bergisch-Gladbach** Germany
12F2 **Bering GI** USA

1C6	Bering Str USA/Russian Fed
91C4	Berizak Iran
50B2	Berja Spain
8A3	Berkeley USA
112B2	Berkner I Ant
54B2	Berkovitsa Bulg
43D4	Berkshire County, Eng
16C1	Berkshire Hills USA
13D2	Berland R Can
56C2	Berlin Germany
56C2	Berlin State, Germany
15D2	Berlin New Hampshire, USA
30D3	Bermejo Bol
30D4	Bermejo R Arg
3M5	Bermuda I / Atlantic O
52A1	Bern Switz
16B2	Bernardsville USA
34C3	Bernasconi Arg
56C2	Bernburg Germany
47B1	Berner Oberland Mts Switz
6B2	Bernier B Can
57C3	Berounka R Czech Republic
108B2	Berri Aust
96C1	Berriane Alg
48C2	Berry Region, France
22A1	Berryessa,L USA
11C4	Berry Is The Bahamas
98B2	Bertoua Cam
45B2	Bertraghboy B Irish Rep
55C1	Berwick USA
42C2	Berwick-upon-Tweed Eng
43C3	Berwyn Mts Wales
101D2	Besalampy Madag
49D2	Besançon France
59C3	Beskydy Zachodnie Mts Pol
93C2	Besni Turk
94B3	Besor R Israel
11B3	Bessemer USA
101D2	Betafo Madag
50A1	Betanzos Spain
94B3	Bet Guvrin Israel
101G1	Bethal S Africa
100A3	Bethanie Namibia
18B1	Bethany Missouri, USA
18B2	Bethany Oklahoma, USA
4B3	Bethel Alaska, USA
16C2	Bethel Connecticut, USA
14B2	Bethel Park USA
15C3	Bethesda USA
14B3	Bethlehem Israel
101G1	Bethlehem S Africa
15C2	Bethlehem USA
48C1	Bethune France
101D3	Betioky Madag
98B2	Betou Cam
82A1	Betpak Dala Steppe Kazakhstan
101D3	Betroka Madag
7D5	Betsiamites Can
86A1	Bettiah India
12D1	Bettles USA
47C2	Béttola Italy
85B3	Betul India
46D1	Betzdorf Germany
12C3	Beverley,L USA
16C1	Beverly USA
21B3	Beverly Hills USA
97B4	Beyla Guinea
87B2	Beypore India
92B2	Beyşehir Turk
92B2	Beyşehir Gölü L Turk
94B2	Beyt Shean Israel
47C1	Bezau Austria
60E2	Bezhetsk Russian Fed
49C3	Béziers France
90C2	Bezmein Turkmenistan
63C2	Beznosova Russian Fed
86B1	Bhadgaon Nepal
87C1	Bhadráchalam India
86B2	Bhadrakh India
87B2	Bhadra Res India
87B2	Bhadrávati India
84B3	Bhag Pak
86B1	Bhágalpur India
84C2	Bhakkar Pak
82D3	Bhamo Myan
85D4	Bhandára India
85D3	Bharatpur India
85C4	Bharuch India
86B2	Bhátiápára Ghat Bang
84C2	Bhatinda India
87A2	Bhatkal India
86B2	Bhátpára India
85C4	Bhávnagar India
86A1	Bheri R Nepal
85B3	Bhilai India
85C3	Bhilwara India
87C1	Bhimavaram India
85D3	Bhind India
84D3	Bhiwani India
87B1	Bhongir India
85D4	Bhopal India
86B2	Bhubaneshwar India
85B4	Bhuj India
85D4	Bhusawal India
82C3	Bhutan Kingdom, Asia
71E4	Biak I Indon
58C2	Biala Podlaska Pol
58B2	Bialograd Pol
58B2	Bialystok Pol
38A1	Biargtangar C Iceland
90C2	Biarjmand Iran
48B3	Biarritz France
47C1	Biasca Switz
92B4	Biba Egypt
74E2	Bibai Japan
100A2	Bibala Angola
57B3	Biberach Germany
97B4	Bibiani Ghana
54C1	Bicaz Rom
83B3	Bida Nig
87B1	Bidar India
91C5	Biddid Oman
43B4	Bideford Eng
43B4	Bideford B Eng
96C2	Bidon 5 Alg
58C2	Biebrza Pol
52A1	Biel Switz
59B2	Bielawa Pol
56B2	Bielefeld Germany
47B1	Bieler See L Switz
52A1	Biella Italy
58C2	Bielsk Podlaski Pol
58B2	Bien Hoa Viet
53B2	Biferno R Italy
92A1	Biga Turk
55C3	Bigadiç Turk
19C3	Big Black R USA
18A1	Big Blue R USA
17B2	Big Cypress Swamp USA
4D3	Big Delta USA
49D2	Bigent Germany
13F2	Bigger Can
5H4	Biggar Kindersley Can
109D1	Biggenden Aust
12G3	Bigger,Mt Can
8C2	Bighorn R USA
76C3	Bight of Bangkok B Thai
97C4	Bight of Benin B W Africa
97C4	Bight of Biafra B Cam
6C3	Big I Can
47C1	Bignasco Switz
97A3	Bignona Sen
21B2	Big Pine Mt USA
17B2	Big Pine Key USA
22C3	Big Pine Mt USA
14A2	Big Rapids USA
5H4	Big River Can
9C3	Big Spring USA
7A4	Big Trout L Can
7B4	Big Trout Lake Can
52C2	Bihać Bosnia-Herzegovina
86B1	Bihar India
86B2	Bihar State, India
99D3	Biharamulo Tanz
60B4	Bihor Mt Rom
87B1	Bijapur India
87C1	Bijapur India
90A2	Bijar Iran
86A1	Bijauri Nepal
54A2	Bijeljina Bosnia-Herzegovina
73B4	Bijie China
84D3	Bijnor India
84C3	Bijnot Pak
85D3	Bikaner India
16B1	Bikfaya Leb
69F2	Bikin Russian Fed
98B3	Bikoro Zaire
85C3	Bilara India
84D2	Bilaspur India
84D2	Bilaspur India
76B3	Bilauktaung Range Mts Thai
50B1	Bilbao Spain
	Bilbo = Bilbao
59B3	Bílé R Czech Republic
54A2	Bileća Bosnia-Herzegovina
92B1	Bilecik Turk
98C2	Bili R Zaire
79B3	Biliran I Phil
8C2	Billings USA
95A3	Bilma Niger
11B3	Biloxi USA
98C1	Biltine Chad
85D4	Bina-Etawa India
79B3	Binalbagan Phil
101C2	Bindura Zim
100B2	Binga Zim
101C2	Binga Mt Zim
109D1	Bingara Aust
56B2	Bingen Germany
10C2	Binghamton USA
78D1	Bingkor Malay
93D2	Bingöl Turk
72D3	Binhai China
78A2	Bintan I Indon
78A3	Bintuhan Indon
78D2	Bintulu Malay
29B3	Bió Bió R Chile
102J4	Bioco I Atlantic O
87B1	Bir India
95B2	Bir Abu Husein Well Egypt
95B2	Bi'r al Harash Well Libya
98C1	Birao CAR
86B1	Biratnagar Nepal
12E1	Birch Creek USA
108B3	Birchip Aust
5C4	Birch Mts Can
7A4	Bird Can
106C3	Birdsville Aust
106A3	Birdum Aust
86A1	Birganj Nepal
94A3	Bir Gifgâfa Well Egypt
94A3	Bir Hasana Well Egypt
35A2	Birigui Brazil
90C3	Birjand Iran
92B4	Birkat Qarun L Egypt
46D2	Birkenfeld Germany
42C3	Birkenhead Eng
60C4	Birlad Rom
94A3	Bir Lahfân Well Egypt
43C3	Birmingham Eng
11B3	Birmingham USA
95B2	Bir Misâha Well Egypt
96A2	Bir Moghrein Maur
97C3	Birnin Kebbi Nig
97C3	Birni N'Konni Nig
69F2	Birobidzhan Russian Fed
45C2	Birr Irish Rep
51C2	Bir Rabalou Alg
109C1	Birrie R Aust
44C2	Birsay Scot
61J2	Birsk Russian Fed
95B2	Bir Tarfâwi Well Egypt
63B2	Biryusa Russian Fed
39J7	Biržai Lithuania
96B2	Bir Zreigat Well Maur
48A2	Biscay,B of France/Spain
17B2	Biscayne B USA
46D2	Bischwiller France
73B4	Bishan China
82B1	Bishkek Kirghizia
8B3	Bishop USA
42D2	Bishop Auckland Eng
43E4	Bishop's Stortford Eng
86A2	Bishrámpur India
96C1	Biskra Alg
79C4	Bislig Phil
97A3	Bismarck USA
90A3	Bisotún Iran
97A3	Bissau Guinea-Bissau
10A1	Bissett Can
5G4	Bistcho L Can
54C1	Bistrita R Rom
99B2	Bitam Gabon
57B3	Bitburg Germany
46D2	Bitche France
93D2	Bitlis Turk
55B2	Bitola Macedonia
56C2	Bitterfeld Germany
100A4	Bitterfontein S Africa
92B3	Bitter Lakes Egypt
8B2	Bitteroot Range Mts USA
74D3	Biwa-ko L Japan
99E1	Biyo Kaboba Eth
65K4	Biysk Russian Fed
96B1	Bizerte Tunisia
51C2	Bj bou Arréridj Alg
52C1	Bjelovar Croatia
96B2	Bj Flye Ste Marie Alg
64C2	Bjørnøya I Barents S
12F1	Black R USA
18B2	Black R USA
107D3	Blackall Aust
42C3	Blackburn Eng
4D3	Blackburn,Mt USA
13E2	Black Diamond Can
5H5	Black Hills USA
44B3	Black Isle Pen Scot
27R3	Blackman's Barbados
43C4	Black Mts Wales
43C3	Blackpool Eng
27H1	Black River Jamaica
8B2	Black Rock Desert USA
65E5	Black S Asia/Europe
45A1	Blacksod B Irish Rep
109D2	Black Sugarloaf Mt Aust
97B3	Black Volta R Ghana
41B3	Blackwater R Irish Rep
18A2	Blackwell USA
54B2	Blagoevgrad Bulg
63E2	Blagoveshchensk Russian Fed
20B1	Blaine USA
44C3	Blair Atholl Scot
44C3	Blairgowrie Scot
17B1	Blakely USA
108A1	Blanche,L Aust
34A2	Blanco R Arg
34B1	Blanco R Arg
8A2	Blanco,C USA
7E4	Blanc Sablon Can
14D2	Blandford Forum Eng
46A2	Blangy-sur-Bresle France
46B1	Blankenberge Belg
101C2	Blantyre Malawi
48B2	Blaye France
109C2	Blayney Aust
111B2	Blenheim NZ
56C2	Blida Alg
14B1	Blind River Can
108A2	Blinman Aust
78C4	Blitar Indon
15D2	Block I USA
16D2	Block Island Sd USA

Bloemfontein

101G1	Bloemfontein S Africa
101G1	Bloemhof S Africa
101G1	Bloemhof Dam Res S Africa
33F3	Blommesteinmeer L Surinam
38A1	Blonduós Iceland
45B1	Bloody Foreland C Irish Rep
14A3	Bloomfield Indiana, USA
18B1	Bloomfield Iowa, USA
10B2	Bloomington Illinois, USA
14A3	Bloomington Indiana, USA
16A2	Bloomsburg USA
78C4	Blora Indon
6H3	Blosseville Kyst Mts Greenland
57B3	Bludenz Austria
11B3	Bluefield USA
32A1	Bluefields Nic
26B3	Blue Mountain Peak Mt Jamaica
16A2	Blue Mts USA
109D2	Blue Mts Aust
27J1	Blue Mts Jamaica
8A2	Blue Mts USA
Blue Nile = Bahr el Azraq
99D1	Blue Nile R Sudan
4G3	Bluenose L Can
11B3	Blue Ridge Mts USA
13D2	Blue River Can
45B1	Blue Stack Mt Irish Rep
111A3	Bluff NZ
106A4	Bluff Knoll Mt Aust
30G4	Blumenau Brazil
49D2	Blundez Austria
20B2	Bly USA
12E3	Blying Sd USA
42D2	Blyth Eng
9B3	Blythe USA
11B3	Blytheville USA
97A4	Bo Sierra Leone
79B3	Boac Phil
72D2	Boading China
14B2	Boardman USA
63C3	Boatou China
33E3	Boa Vista Brazil
97A4	Boa Vista / Cape Verde
76E1	Bobai China
47C2	Bóbbio Italy
97B3	Bobo Dioulasso Burkina
60C3	Bobruysk Belarus
17B2	Boca Chica Key / USA
32D5	Bôca do Acre Brazil
35C1	Bocaiúva Brazil
98B2	Bocaranga CAR
17B2	Boca Raton USA
59C3	Bochnia Pol
56B2	Bocholt Germany
46D1	Bochum Germany
100A2	Bocoio Angola
98B2	Boda CAR
63D2	Bodaybo Russian Fed
21A2	Bodega Head Pt USA
95A3	Bodélé Region Chad
38J5	Boden Sweden
47C1	Bodensee L Switz/Germany
87B1	Bodhan India
87B2	Bodinäyakkanür India
43B4	Bodmin Eng
43B4	Bodmin Moor Upland Eng
38G5	Bodø Nor
55C3	Bodrum Turk
98C3	Boende Zaire
97A4	Boffa Guinea
76B2	Bogale Myan
19C3	Bogalusa USA
109C2	Bogan R Aust
97B3	Bogandé Burkina
6H3	Bogarnes Iceland
92C2	Boğazliyan Turk
61K2	Bogdanovich Russian Fed
68A2	Bogda Shan Mt China
100A3	Bogenfels Namibia
109D1	Boggabilla Aust
109C2	Boggabri Aust
45B2	Boggeragh Mts Irish Rep
79B3	Bogo Phil
109C3	Bogong,Mt Aust
78B4	Bogor Indon
61H2	Bogorodskoye Russian Fed
32C3	Bogotá Colombia
63A2	Bogotol Russian Fed
86B2	Bogra Bang
72D2	Bo Hai B China
46B2	Bohain-en-Vermandois France
72D2	Bohai Wan B China
57C3	Bohmer Wald Upland Germany
79B4	Bohol / Phil
79B4	Bohol S Phil
35A1	Bois R Brazil
14B1	Bois Blanc I USA
8B2	Boise USA
9C4	Bojador,C Mor
79B2	Bojeador,C Phil
90C2	Bojnürd Iran
97A3	Boké Guinea
109C1	Bokhara R Aust
39F7	Boknafjord Inlet Nor
98B3	Boko Congo
76C3	Bokor Camb
98C3	Bokungu Zaire
98C2	Bol Chad
23A1	Bolaanos Mexico
97A3	Bolama Guinea-Bissau
23A1	Bolanos R Mexico
48C2	Bolbec France
97B4	Bole Ghana
59B2	Boleslawiec Pol
97B3	Bolgatanga Ghana
60C4	Bolgrad Ukraine
43C3	Bolivar Arg
18B2	Bolivar Missouri, USA
18C2	Bolivar Tennessee, USA
30C2	Bolivia Republic, S America
38H5	Bollnas Sweden
109C1	Bollon Aust
32C2	Bolivar Mt Ven
52B2	Bologna Italy
60D2	Bologoye Russian Fed
69F2	Bolon' Russian Fed
61G3	Bol'shoy Irgiz R Russian Fed
74C2	Bol'shoy Kamen Russian Fed
Bol'shoy Kavkaz =Caucasus
61G4	Bol'shoy Uzen R Kazakhstan
9C4	Bolson de Mapimi Desert Mexico
43C3	Bolton Eng
92B1	Bolu Turk
38A1	Bolungarvik Iceland
92B2	Bolvadin Turk
52B1	Bolzano Italy
98B3	Boma Zaire
107D4	Bombala Aust
87A1	Bombay India
99D2	Bombo Uganda
35B1	Bom Despacho Brazil
86C1	Bomdila India
97A4	Bomi Hills Lib
31C4	Bom Jesus da Lapa Brazil
63E2	Bomnak Russian Fed
99C2	Bomokandi R Zaire
98C2	Bomu R CAR/Zaire
27D4	Bonaire I Caribbean S
12F2	Bona,Mt USA
25D3	Bonanza Nic
7E5	Bonavista Can
108A2	Bon Bon Aust
98C2	Bondo Zaire
97B4	Bondoukou Ivory Coast
Bóne = 'Annaba
33E3	Bonfim Guyana
98C2	Bongandanga Zaire
98B1	Bongor Chad
19A3	Bonham USA
53A2	Bonifacio Corse
52A2	Bonifacio,Str of Chan Medit S
Bonin Is = Ogasawara Gunto
17B2	Bonita Springs USA
57B2	Bonn Germany
20C1	Bonners Ferry USA
12H1	Bonnet Plume R Can
13E2	Bonnyville Can
97A4	Bonthe Sierra Leone
11E1	Booaaso Somalia
108B2	Booligal Aust
109D1	Boonah Aust
15C2	Boonville USA
109C2	Boorowa Aust
6A2	Boothia,G of Can
6A2	Boothia Pen Can
98B3	Bouké Gabon
108A1	Bopeechee Aust
99C2	Bor Sudan
92B2	Bor Turk
54B2	Bor Serbia, Yugos
8B2	Borah Peak Mt USA
39G7	Boräs Sweden
91B4	Borãzjan Iran
108A3	Borda,C Aust
48B3	Bordeaux France
4G2	Borden I Can
62B2	Borden Pen Can
16B2	Bordentown USA
42C2	Borders Region, Scot
108B3	Bordertown Aust
96C2	Bordi Omar Dris Alg
8D1	Borkens River Can
38A2	Borgarnes Iceland
9C3	Borger USA
39H7	Borgholm Sweden
54C2	Borgosia Italy
47D1	Borgo Valsugana Italy
59C3	Borislav Ukraine
61F3	Borisoglebsk Russian Fed
60C3	Borisov Belarus
60E3	Borisovka Russian Fed
95A3	Borkou Region Chad
39H6	Borlänge Sweden
47C2	Bormida Italy
47D1	Bormio Italy
67F5	Borneo / Malay/ Indon
39H7	Bornholm I Den
55C3	Bornova Turk
98C2	Boro R Sudan
97B3	Boromo Burkina
60D2	Borovichi Russian Fed
106C2	Borroloola Aust
54B1	Borsa Iran
90A3	Borüjed Iran
90B3	Borüjen Iran
58B2	Bory Tucholskie Region, Pol
63D2	Borzya Russian Fed
73B5	Bose China
101G1	Boshof S Africa
54A2	Bosna R Bosnia-Herzegovina
37E4	Bosnia-Herzegovina Republic, Europe
75C1	Bósó-hantó B Japan
Bosporus = Karadeniz Boğazi
5C1	Bosquet Alg
98B2	Bossangoa CAR
98B2	Bossèmbélé CAR
19B3	Bossier City USA
65K5	Bosten Hu L China
43D3	Boston Eng
10C2	Boston USA
11A3	Boston Mts USA
85C4	Botad India
54B2	Botevgrad Bulg
101G1	Bothaville S Africa
64C3	Bothnia,G of Sweden/Fin
100B3	Botletli R Botswana
60C4	Botosani Rom
100B3	Botswana Republic, Africa
53C3	Botte Donato Mt Italy
46D1	Bottrop Germany
35B2	Botucatu Brazil
7E5	Botwood Can
89D7	Bouaké Ivory Coast
98B2	Bouar CAR
96B1	Bouârfa Mor
98B2	Bouca CAR
51C2	Boufarik Alg
Bougie = Bejaia
97B3	Bougouni Mali
46C2	Bouillon France
96B2	Bou Izakarn Mor
46D2	Boulay-Moselle France
8C2	Boulder Colorado, USA
9B3	Boulder City USA
22A2	Boulder Creek USA
48C1	Boulogne France
98B2	Boumba R CAR
97B4	Bouna Ivory Coast
8B3	Boundary Peak Mt USA
97B4	Boundiali Ivory Coast
107F3	Bourail Nouvelle Calédonie
97B3	Bourem Mali
49D2	Bourg France
49D2	Bourg de Péage France
48C2	Bourges France
48C3	Bourg-Madame France
49C2	Bourgogne Region, France
47B2	Bourg-St-Maurice France
108C2	Bourke Aust
43D4	Bournemouth Eng
96C1	Bou Saâda Alg
98B1	Bousso Chad
97A3	Boutilmit Maur
103J7	Bouvet I Atlantic O
46C2	Bovril Arg
13E2	Bow R Can
107D2	Bowen Aust
19A3	Bowie Texas, USA
13E2	Bow Island Can
11B3	Bowling Green Kentucky, USA
18B2	Bowling Green Missouri, USA
14B2	Bowling Green Ohio, USA
15C3	Bowling Green Virginia, USA
15C2	Bowmanville Can
109D2	Bowral Aust
13C2	Bowron R Can
72D3	Bo Xian China
72D2	Boxing China
92B1	Boyabat Turk
98B2	Boyali CAR
5J4	Boyd Can
16B2	Boyertown USA
13E2	Boyle USA
45B3	Boyle Irish Rep
45C2	Boyne R Irish Rep
17B2	Boynton Beach USA
98C2	Boyoma Falls Zaire
55C3	Bozca Ada / Turk
92E2	Boz Dağlari Mts Turk
8B2	Bozeman USA
Bozen = Bolzano
98B2 | Bozene Zaire
98B2 | Bozoum CAR
47B2 | Bra Italy
52C2 | Brač / Croatia
15C1 | Bracebridge Can
95A2 | Brach Libya
38H6 | Bräcke Sweden
17B2 | Bradenton USA

42D3	Bradford Eng
44E1	Brae Scot
44C3	Braemar Scot
50A1	Braga Port
34C3	Bragado Arg
50A1	Bragança Port
31B2	Bragança Brazil
35B2	Bragança Paulista Brazil
86C2	Brahman-Baria Bang
86B2	Brahmani R India
86C1	Brahmaputra R India
7E5	Braie Verte Can
60C4	Bráila Rom
104Z	Brainerd Can
97A3	Brakna Region, Maur
5F4	Bralorne Can
14C2	Brampton Can
33E3	Branco R Brazil
100A3	Brandberg Mt Namibia
56C2	Brandenburg Germany
56C2	Brandenburg State, Germany
101G1	Brandfort S Africa
8D2	Brandon Can
100B4	Brandvlei S Africa
57C2	Brandys nad Lebem Czech Republic
58B2	Braniewo Pol
10B2	Brantford Can
108B3	Branxholme Aust
7D5	Bras D'Or L Can
35C1	Brasila de Minas Brazil
32D6	Brasiléia Brazil
31B5	Brasília Brazil
54C1	Brasov Rom
78D1	Brassay Range Mts Malay
59B3	Bratislava Slovakia
63C2	Bratsk Russian Fed
15D2	Brattleboro USA
56C2	Braunschweig Germany
97A4	Brava I Cape Verde
9B3	Brawley USA
45C2	Bray Irish Rep
6C3	Bray I Can
13D2	Brazeau R Can
13D2	Brazeau,Mt Can
28D4	Brazil Republic, S America
103G5	Brazil Basin Atlantic O
9D3	Brazos R USA
98B3	Brazzaville Congo
57C3	Brdy Upland Czech Republic
111A3	Breaksea Sd NZ
110B1	Bream B NZ
78B4	Brebes Indon
44C3	Brechin Scot
46C1	Brecht Belg
59B3	Břeclav Czech Republic
43C4	Brecon Wales
43C4	Brecon Beacons Mts Wales
43B3	Brecon Beacons Nat Pk Wales
56B2	Breda Neth
100B4	Bredasdorp S Africa
38H6	Bredbyn Sweden
61J3	Bredy Russian Fed
15C2	Breezewood USA
47C1	Bregenz Austria
47C1	Bregenzer Ache R Austria
38A1	Breiðafjörður B Iceland
47C2	Brembo R Italy
17A1	Bremen USA
56B2	Bremen Germany
56B2	Bremerhaven Germany
20B1	Bremerton USA
19A3	Brenham USA
57C3	Brenner P Austria/Italy
47D2	Breno Italy
47D1	Brenta R Italy
22B2	Brentwood USA

52B1	Brescia Italy
	Breslau = Wrocław
47D1	Bressanone Italy
44E1	Bressay I Scot
48B2	Bressuire France
58C2	Brest Belarus
48B2	Brest France
48B2	Bretagne Region, France
46B2	Breteuil France
16B1	Breton Woods USA
110B1	Brett,C NZ
109C1	Brewarrina Aust
16C2	Brewster New York, USA
20C1	Brewster Washington, USA
101G1	Breyten S Africa
52C1	Brežice Slovenia
98C2	Bria CAR
49D3	Briançon France
49C2	Briare France
21B2	Bridgeport California, USA
16B3	Bridgeport Connecticut, USA
19A3	Bridgeport Texas, USA
22C1	Bridgeport Res USA
16B3	Bridgeton USA
27F4	Bridgetown Barbados
7D5	Bridgewater Can
16D2	Bridgewater USA
43C4	Bridgwater Eng
43C4	Bridgwater B Eng
42D2	Bridlington Eng
109C4	Bridport Aust
47B1	Brienzer See L Switz
46C2	Briey France
52A1	Brig Switz
8B2	Brigham City USA
109C3	Bright Aust
43D4	Brighton Eng
46E1	Brilon Germany
55A2	Brindisi Italy
19B3	Brinkley USA
107E3	Brisbane Aust
15D2	Bristol Connecticut, USA
43C4	Bristol Eng
15D2	Bristol Pennsylvania, USA
16D2	Bristol Rhode Island, USA
11B3	Bristol Tennessee, USA
12B3	Bristol B USA
43B4	Bristol Chan Eng/Wales
10D3	British Mts USA
5F4	British Columbia Province, Can
6B1	British Empire Range Mts Can
101G1	Brits S Africa
100B4	Brittstown S Africa
48C2	Brive France
59B3	Brno Czech Republic
17B1	Broad R USA
44A2	Broad Bay Inlet Scot
44B3	Broadford Scot
5H4	Brochet Can
4G2	Brock I Can
15C2	Brockport USA
16D1	Brockton USA
15C2	Brockville Can
6B2	Brodeur Pen Can
42B2	Brodick Scot
60C3	Brodnica Pol
19B3	Broken Bow Oklahoma, USA
19B3	Broken Bow L USA
107D4	Broken Hill Aust
47C2	Broni Italy
38G5	Brønnøysund Nor
16C2	Bronx Borough, New York, USA
79A4	Brooke's Point Phil
22B2	Brookfield Missouri, USA
11A3	Brookhaven USA

20B2	Brookings Oregon, USA
20D2	Brookings South Dakota, USA
16D1	Brookline USA
16C2	Brooklyn Borough, New York, USA
5G4	Brooks Can
12C3	Brooks,L USA
12A1	Brooks Mt USA
4C3	Brooks Range Mts USA
17B2	Brooksville USA
109D1	Brooloo Aust
106B2	Broome Aust
44C2	Brora Scot
20B2	Brothers USA
95A3	Broulkou Chad
13E3	Browning USA
9D4	Brownsville USA
9D3	Brownwood USA
46B1	Bruay-en-Artois France
106A3	Bruce,Mt Aust
14B1	Bruce Pen Can
59B3	Brück an der Mur Austria
	Bruges = Brugge
46B1	Brugge Belg
46D1	Brühl Germany
91C5	Brunei Sultanate, S E Asia
52B1	Brunico Italy
111B2	Brunner,L NZ
11B3	Brunswick Georgia, USA
18B2	Brunswick Mississippi, USA
29B6	Brunswick,Pen de Chile
109C4	Bruny I Aust
61F1	Brusenets Russian Fed
26A3	Brus Laguna Honduras
	Brüssel = Bruxelles
56A2	Bruxelles Belg
9D3	Bryan Ohio USA
9D4	Bryan,Mt Aust
60D3	Bryansk Russian Fed
19B3	Bryant USA
59B2	Brzeg Pol
93E4	Būbiyan I Kuwait/Iraq
99D3	Bubu R Tanz
32C2	Bucaramanga Colombia
44D3	Buchan Oilfield N Sea
97A4	Buchanan Lib
44D3	Buchan Deep N Sea
6C2	Buchan G Can
40C2	Buchan Ness Pen Scot
34C2	Buchardo Arg
	Bucharest = Bucureşti
47C1	Buchs Switz
43D3	Buckingham Eng
12B1	Buckland USA
12B1	Buckland R USA
108A2	Buckleboo Aust
98B3	Buco Zau Congo
54C2	Bucureşti Rom
59B3	Budapest Hung
84D3	Badaun India
43B4	Bude Eng
19B3	Bude USA
61F5	Budennovsk Russian Fed
54A2	Budva Montenegro, Yugos
98A2	Buéa Cam
34C2	Buena Arg
53B2	Bucharest = Bucureşti
53B2	Buena Esperanza Arg
32B3	Buenaventura Colombia
23A2	Buenavista Mexico
29E2	Buenos Aires Arg
29D3	Buenos Aires State, Arg
18B2	Buffalo Mississipi, USA

10C2	Buffalo New York, USA
20D2	Buffalo South Dakota, USA
19A3	Buffalo Texas, USA
8C2	Buffalo Wyoming, USA
101H1	Buffalo R S Africa
13E2	Buffalo L Alberta, Can
5G3	Buffalo L Northwest Territories, Can
5H4	Buffalo Narrows Can
17B1	Buford USA
54C2	Buftea Rom
59C2	Bug R Pol/Ukraine
32B3	Buga Colombia
90B2	Bugdaylı Turkmenistan
61H3	Bugulma Russian Fed
61H3	Buguruslan Russian Fed
93C2	Buhayrat al Asad Res Syria
41C3	Builth Wells Wales
34A2	Buin Chile
99C3	Bujumbura Burundi
98C3	Bukama Zaïre
99C3	Bukavu Zaïre
80E2	Bukhara Uzbekistan
78C2	Bukit Batubrok Mt Indon
70B4	Bukittinggi Indon
99D3	Bukoba Tanz
78D3	Buku Gandadiwata Mt Indon
71E4	Bula Indon
79B3	Bulan Phil
84D3	Bulandshahr India
100B3	Bulawayo Zim
55C3	Buldan Turk
85D4	Buldana India
68C2	Bulgan Mongolia
54B2	Bulgaria Republic, Europe
47B1	Bulle Switz
111B2	Buller R NZ
106A4	Buller,Mt Aust
108B1	Bulloo R Aust
108B1	Bulloo Downs Aust
108B1	Bulloo L Aust
18B2	Bull Shoals Res USA
34A3	Bulnes Chile
71F4	Bulolo PNG
101G1	Bultfontein S Africa
98C2	Bumba Zaïre
76B2	Bumphal Dam Thai
99D2	Buna Kenya
106A4	Bunbury Aust
45C1	Buncrana Irish Rep
107E3	Bundaberg Aust
109D2	Bundarra Aust
85D3	Bündi India
45B1	Bundoran Irish Rep
109C1	Bungil R Aust
99B3	Bungo Angola
75A2	Bungo-suidō Str Japan
70B3	Bunguran I Ind
99D2	Bunia Zaïre
18B2	Bunker USA
78C3	Buntok Indon
71D3	Buol Indon
94C2	Buráq Syria
98C1	Buram Sudan
79A3	Buranen Phil
79B3	Burauen Phil
80C3	Buraydah S Arabia
21B3	Burbank USA
109C2	Burcher Aust
92B2	Burdur Turk
63F3	Bureinskiy Khrebet Mts Russian Fed
56C2	Burg Germany
54C2	Burgas Bulg
17C1	Burgaw USA
47B1	Burgdorf Switz
100B4	Burgersdorp S Africa
50B1	Burgos Spain
58B1	Burgsvik Sweden

Burhaniye

55C3 **Burhaniye** Turk
85D4 **Burhānpur** India
79B3 **Burias** I Phil
76C2 **Buriram** Thai
35B1 **Buritis** Brazil
13B2 **Burke** Chan Can
106C2 **Burketown** Aust
97B3 **Burkina** Republic, Africa
15C1 **Burks Falls** Can
8B2 **Burley** USA
10A2 **Burlington** Iowa, USA
16B2 **Burlington** New Jersey, USA
10C2 **Burlington** Vermont, USA
20B1 **Burlington** Washington, USA
Burma = Myanmar
20B2 **Burney** USA
16A2 **Burnham** USA
107D5 **Burnie** Aust
42C3 **Burnley** Eng
20C2 **Burns** USA
5F4 **Burns Lake** Can
82C1 **Burqin** China
108A2 **Burra** Aust
109D2 **Burragorang,L** Aust
44C2 **Burray** I Scot
109C2 **Burren Junction** Aust
109C2 **Burrinjuck Res** Aust
60C5 **Bursa** Turk
80B3 **Bur Safâga** Egypt
 Bûr Sa'îd = Port Said
14B2 **Burton** USA
43D3 **Burton upon Trent** Eng
38J6 **Burtrask** Sweden
108B2 **Burtundy** Aust
71D4 **Buru** Indon
99C3 **Burundi** Republic, Africa
78A2 **Burung** Indon
63D2 **Buryatskaya Respublika,** Russian Fed
99D1 **Burye** Eth
61H4 **Burynshik** Kazakhstan
43E3 **Bury St Edmunds** Eng
91B4 **Bushehr** Iran
98B3 **Busira** R Zaire
58C2 **Buskozdroj** Pol
94C2 **Busrá ash Shām** Syria
106A4 **Busselton** Aust
49D2 **Busto** Italy
52A1 **Busto Arsizio** Italy
79A3 **Busuanga** I Phil
98C2 **Buta** Zaire
34B3 **Buta Ranquil** Arg
99C3 **Butare** Rwanda
42B2 **Bute** I Scot
67B2 **Butha Qi** China
14C2 **Butler** USA
8B2 **Butte** USA
77C4 **Butterworth** Malay
40B2 **Butt of Lewis** C Scot
6D3 **Button Is** Can
79C4 **Butuan** Phil
71D4 **Butung** I Indon
61F3 **Buturlinovka** Russian Fed
86A1 **Butwal** Nepal
99E2 **Buulo Barde** Somalia
99E2 **Buur Hakaba** Somalia
61F2 **Buy** Russian Fed
72B1 **Buyant Ovvo** Mongolia
61G5 **Buynaksk** Russian Fed
63D3 **Buyr Nuur** L Mongolia
93D2 **Büyük Ağri** Mt Turk
92A2 **Büyük Menderes** R Turk
54C1 **Buzău** Rom
54C1 **Buzau** R Rom
61H3 **Buzuluk** Russian Fed

16D2 **Buzzards B** USA
54C2 **Byala** Bulg
54B2 **Byala Slatina** Bulg
4H2 **Byam Martin** Chan Can
4H2 **Byam Martin I** Can
 Byblos = Jubail
94B1 **Byblos** Hist Site, Leb
58B2 **Bydgoszcz** Pol
39F7 **Bygland** Nor
6C2 **Bylot I** Can
109C2 **Byrock** Aust
22B2 **Byron** USA
109D1 **Byron,C** Aust
59B2 **Bytom** Pol

C

30E4 **Caacupé** Par
100A2 **Caála** Angola
13B2 **Caamano Sd** Can
30E4 **Caazapá** Par
16A2 **Cabanatuan** Phil
31E3 **Cabedelo** Brazil
50A2 **Cabeza del Buey** Spain
34C3 **Cabildo** Arg
34A2 **Cabildo** Chile
32C1 **Cabimas** Ven
98B3 **Cabinda** Angola
98B3 **Cabinda** Province, Angola
27C3 **Cabo Beata** Dom Rep
51C2 **Cabo Binibeca** C Spain
53A3 **Cabo Carbonara** C Sardegna
34A3 **Cabo Carranza** C Chile
50A2 **Cabo Carvoeiro** C Port
9B3 **Cabo Colnett** C Mexico
32B2 **Cabo Corrientes** C Colombia
24B2 **Cabo Corrientes** C Mexico
26B3 **Cabo Cruz** C Cuba
50B1 **Cabo de Ajo** C Spain
51C1 **Cabo de Caballeria** C Spain
51C1 **Cabo de Creus** C Spain
50B2 **Cabo de Gata** C Spain
29C7 **Cabo de Hornos** C Chile
50B2 **Cabo de la Nao** C Spain
50A1 **Cabo de Peñas** C Spain
50A2 **Cabo de Roca** C Port
51C2 **Cabo de Salinas** C Spain
35C2 **Cabo de São Tomé** C Brazil
50A2 **Cabo de São Vicente** C Port
50A2 **Cabo de Sines** C Port
51C1 **Cabo de Tortosa** C Spain
29C4 **Cabo Dos Bahias** C Arg
50A2 **Cabo Espichel** C Port
9B4 **Cabo Falso** C Mexico
51B2 **Cabo Ferrat** C Alg
50A1 **Cabo Finisterre** C Spain
51C1 **Cabo Formentor** C Spain
35C2 **Cabo Frio** Brazil
35C2 **Cabo Frio** C Brazil
26A4 **Cabo Gracias à Dios** Honduras
31B2 **Cabo Maguarinho** C Brazil
50A2 **Cabo Negro** C Mor
109D1 **Caboolture** Aust
33G3 **Cabo Orange** C Brazil
21B3 **Cabo Punta Banda** C Mexico
101C2 **Cabora Bassa Dam** Mozam

24A1 **Caborca** Mexico
24C2 **Cabo Rojo** C Mexico
23B1 **Cabos** Mexico
29C6 **Cabo San Diego** C Arg
32A4 **Cabo San Lorenzo** C Ecuador
53A3 **Cabo Teulada** C Sardegna
50A2 **Cabo Trafalgar** C Spain
50B2 **Cabo Tres Forcas** C Spain
29C5 **Cabo Tres Puntas** C Arg
7D5 **Cabot Str** Can
50B2 **Cabra** Spain
50A1 **Cabreira** Mt Port
51C2 **Cabrera** I Spain
34A3 **Cabrero** Chile
51B2 **Cabriel** R Spain
23B2 **Cacahuamilpa** Mexico
54B2 **Čačak** Serbia, Yugos
23B2 **C A Carillo** Mexico
50A2 **Caceres** Spain
50A2 **Cáceres** Spain
18B2 **Cache** R USA
13C2 **Cache Creek** Can
30C4 **Cachi** Arg
33E5 **Cachimbo** Brazil
31D4 **Cachoeira** Brazil
35A1 **Cachoeira Alta** Brazil
31D3 **Cachoeira de Paulo Alfonso** Waterfall Brazil
29F2 **Cachoeira do Sul** Brazil
31C6 **Cachoeiro de Itapemirim** Brazil
22C3 **Cachuma,L** USA
100A2 **Cacolo** Angola
100A2 **Caconda** Angola
35A1 **Caçu** Brazil
100A2 **Çaculuvar** R Angola
59B3 **Čadca** Slovakia
43C3 **Cader Idris** Mts Wales
10B2 **Cadillac** USA
79B3 **Cadiz** Phil
50A2 **Cadiz** Spain
48B2 **Caen** France
43C3 **Caernarfon** Wales
43B3 **Caernarfon B** Wales
94B2 **Caesarea** Hist Site, Israel
31C4 **Caetité** Brazil
30C4 **Cafayate** Arg
92B2 **Caga Tepe** Turk
79B2 **Cagayan** R Phil
79B4 **Cagayan de Oro** Phil
79B2 **Cagayan Is** Phil
53A3 **Cagliari** Sardegna
27D3 **Caguas** Puerto Rico
45B3 **Caha Mts** Irish Rep
45A3 **Cahersiveen** Irish Rep
45C2 **Cahir** Irish Rep
45C2 **Cahone Pt** Irish Rep
48C3 **Cahors** France
101C2 **Caia** Mozam
100B2 **Caianda** Angola
35A1 **Caiapó** R Brazil
35A1 **Caiapônia** Brazil
31D3 **Caicó** Brazil
26C2 **Caicos Is** Caribbean S
11C4 **Caicos Pass** The Bahamas
12C2 **Cairn Mt** USA
44C3 **Cairngorms** Mts Scot
107D2 **Cairns** Aust
92B3 **Cairo** Egypt
11B3 **Cairo** USA
108B1 **Caiwarro** Aust
32B5 **Cajabamba** Peru
32B5 **Cajamarca** Peru
27D5 **Calabozo** Ven
54B2 **Calafat** Rom
29B6 **Calafate** Arg
79B3 **Calagua Is** Phil
51B1 **Calahorra** Spain
48C1 **Calais** France

30E4 **Calama** Chile
32C3 **Calamar** Colombia
79A3 **Calamian Group** Is Phil
98B3 **Calandula** Angola
70A3 **Calang** Indon
95B2 **Calanscio Sand Sea** Libya
79B3 **Calapan** Phil
54C2 **Calarasi** Rom
51B1 **Calatayud** Spain
22B2 **Calaveras Res** USA
79B3 **Calbayog** Phil
19B4 **Calcasieu L** USA
86B2 **Calcutta** India
50A2 **Caldas da Rainha** Port
31B5 **Caldas Novas** Brazil
30B4 **Caldera** Chile
8B2 **Caldwell** USA
29C5 **Caleta Olivia** Arg
5G4 **Calgary** Can
17B1 **Calhoun** USA
17B1 **Calhoun Falls** USA
32B3 **Cali** Colombia
87B2 **Calicut** India
8B3 **Caliente** Nevada, USA
8A3 **California** State, USA
22C3 **California Aqueduct** USA
87B2 **Calimera,Pt** India
34B2 **Calingasta** Arg
22A1 **Calistoga** USA
108B1 **Callabonna** R Aust
108A1 **Callabonna,L** Aust
15C1 **Callander** Can
44B3 **Callander** Scot
108A1 **Callanna** Aust
32B6 **Callao** Peru
13E1 **Calling L** Can
23B1 **Calnali** Mexico
17B2 **Caloosahatchee** R USA
109D1 **Caloundra** Aust
23B2 **Calpulalpan** Mexico
53B3 **Caltanissetta** Italy
100A2 **Caluango** Angola
100A2 **Calulo** Angola
100A2 **Caluquembe** Angola
99F1 **Caluula** Somalia
13B2 **Calvert I** Can
52A2 **Calvi** France
23A1 **Calvillo** Mexico
100A4 **Calvinia** S Africa
25E2 **Camagüey** Cuba
25E2 **Camagüey,Arch de** I. Cuba
30B2 **Camaná** Peru
30C3 **Camargo** Bol
22C3 **Camarillo** USA
29C4 **Camarones** Arg
20B1 **Camas** USA
98B3 **Camaxilo** Angola
98B3 **Camabatela** Angola
76C3 **Cambodia** Republic, S E Asia
43B4 **Camborne** Eng
49C1 **Cambrai** France
43C3 **Cambrian** Mts Wales
14B2 **Cambridge** County, Eng
43D3 **Cambridge** County, Eng
43E3 **Cambridge** Eng
27H1 **Cambridge** Jamaica
15C3 **Cambridge** Maryland, USA
15D2 **Cambridge** Massachussets, USA
110C1 **Cambridge** NZ
14B2 **Cambridge** Ohio, USA
4H3 **Cambridge Bay** Can
60E5 **Cam Burun** Pt Turk
10A3 **Camden** Arkansas, USA
109D2 **Camden** Aust
15D3 **Camden** New Jersey, USA
17B1 **Camden** South Carolina, USA
18B2 **Cameron** Missouri, USA

19A3 Cameron Texas, USA
4H2 Cameron I Can
111A3 Cameron Mts NZ
98A2 Cameroun Federal Republic, Africa
98A2 Cameroun Mt Cam
31B2 Cametá Brazil
7A1 Camiguin I Phil
79B2 Camiling Phil
17B1 Camilla USA
22B1 Camino USA
30D3 Camiri Bol
31C2 Camocim Brazil
98C3 Camissombo Angola
106C2 Camooweal Aust
34D2 Campana USA
29A5 Campana I Chile
11B2 Campania I Can
13B2 Campbell I NZ
105G6 Campbell I NZ
4E3 Campbell,Mt Can
84C2 Campbellpore Pak
5F5 Campbell River Can
7D5 Campbellton Can
109D2 Campbelltown Aust
42B2 Campbeltown Scot
25C3 Campeche Mexico
108B3 Camperdown Can
31D3 Campina Grande Brazil
31B6 Campinas Brazil
35B1 Campina Verde Brazil
98A2 Campo Cam
53B2 Campobasso Italy
35B2 Campo Belo Brazil
35B1 Campo Florido Brazil
30D4 Campo Gallo Arg
35B2 Campo Grande Brazil
31C2 Campo Maior Brazil
30F3 Campo Mourão Brazil
35C2 Campos Brazil
35B1 Campos Altos Brazil
47D1 Campo Tures Italy
76D3 Cam Ranh Viet
5G4 Camrose Can
100A2 Camucuio Angola
27K1 Canaan Tobago
16C1 Canaan USA
100A2 Canacupa Angola
29D2 Cañada de Gomez Arg
9C3 Canadian R USA
60C5 Canakkale Turk
34B3 Canalejas Arg
13D2 Canal Flats Can
24A1 Cananea Mexico
100A2 Canangá Angola
7C3 Canada Dominion, N America
Canary Is = Islas Canarias
23A2 Canas Mexico
25D3 Canatlán Mexico
11B4 Canaveral,C USA
31D5 Canavieiras Brazil
107D4 Canberra Aust
22B2 Canby California, USA
55C3 Çandarlı Körfezi B Turk
16C2 Candlewood,L USA
29E2 Canelones Urug
18A2 Caney USA
100A2 Cangamba Angola
100B2 Cangombe Angola
72D2 Cangzhou China
7D4 Caniapiscau R Can
53B3 Canicatti Italy
31D2 Canindé Brazil
92B1 Çankırı Turk
13D2 Canmore Can
44A3 Canna I Scot
87B2 Cannanore India
49D3 Cannes France
43C4 Cann River Aust
30F4 Canoas Brazil
13F1 Canoe L Can
9C3 Canon City USA
108B2 Canopus Aust

5H4 Canora Can
109C2 Canowindra Aust
45C2 Cansore Pt Irish Rep
43E4 Canterbury Eng
111B2 Canterbury Bight B NZ
111B2 Canterbury Plains NZ
77D4 Can Tho Viet
Canton = Guangzhou
19C3 Canton Mississippi, USA
18B1 Canton Missouri, USA
10B2 Canton Ohio, USA
12E2 Cantwell USA
21A2 Canyon City USA
12J2 Canyon Range Mts Can
21A2 Canyonville USA
98C3 Canzar Angola
76D1 Cao Bang Viet
31B2 Capanema Brazil
35B2 Capão Bonito Brazil
48B3 Capbreton France
24B2 Cap Corrientes C Mexico
52A2 Cap Corse C Corse
48B2 Cap de la Hague C France
15D1 Cap-de-la-Madeleine Can
6C3 Cap de Nouvelle-France C Can
51C2 Capdepera Spain
23A2 Cap de Tancitiario C Mexico
109C4 Cape Barren I Aust
103J6 Cape Basin Atlantic O
7E5 Cape Breton I Can
97B4 Cape Coast Ghana
15D2 Cape Cod B USA
6C3 Cape Dorset Can
17C1 Cape Fear R USA
18C2 Cape Girardeau USA
6B3 Cape Henrietta Maria Can
Cape Horn = Cabo de Hornos
104E3 Cape Johnston Depth Pacific O
35C1 Capelinha Brazil
98B3 Cape Lisburne USA
100A2 Capelongo Angola
15D3 Cape May USA
5F5 Cape Mendocino USA
98B3 Capenda Camulemba Angola
4F2 Cape Perry Can
7A4 Cape Tatnam Can
100A4 Cape Town S Africa
102G4 Cape Verde Is Atlantic O
102G4 Cape Verde Basin Atlantic O
12F3 Cape Yakataga USA
107D2 Cape York Pen Aust
46A1 Cap Gris Nez C France
26C3 Cap-Haitien Haiti
31B2 Capim R Brazil
112C2 Capitán Arturo Prat Base Ant
27P2 Cap Moule à Chique C St Lucia
53C3 Capo Isola di Correnti C Italy
53C3 Capo Rizzuto C Italy
55A3 Capo Santa Maria di Leuca C Italy
53B3 Capo San Vito Italy
53B3 Capo Spartivento C Italy
27P2 Cap Pt St Lucia
53B2 Capri I Italy
100B2 Caprivi Strip Region, Namibia
52A2 Cap Rosso C Corse
102H4 Cap Vert C Sen
32C4 Caquetá R Colombia
54B2 Caracal Rom

33E3 Caracaraí Brazil
32D1 Caracas Ven
35B2 Caraguatatuba Brazil
29B3 Carahue Chile
35C1 Caraí Brazil
35C2 Carandaí Brazil
31C6 Carangola Brazil
54B1 Caransebeş Rom
108A2 Carappee Hill Mt Aust
26A3 Caratasca Honduras
35C1 Caratinga Brazil
51B2 Caravaca Spain
35D1 Caravelas Brazil
18C2 Carbondale Illinois, USA
53A3 Carbonia Sardegna
5F4 Carborear Can
5G4 Carcaion Can
99E1 Carcar Mts Somalia
48C3 Carcassonne France
48C3 Carcross Can
23B2 Cardel Mexico
25D2 Cárdenas Cuba
23B1 Cárdenas Mexico
43C4 Cardiff Wales
43B3 Cardigan Wales
43B3 Cardigan B Wales
13E2 Cardston Can
54B1 Carei Rom
33F4 Careiro Brazil
34A2 Carén Chile
14B2 Carey USA
48B2 Carhaix-Plouguer France
29D3 Carhué Arg
31C6 Cariacica Brazil
5J4 Caribou Can
5G4 Caribou Mts Alberta, Can
5F4 Caribou Mts British Columbia, Can
79B3 Carigara Phil
46C2 Carignan France
33E1 Caripito Ven
15C1 Carleton Place Can
101G1 Carletonville S Africa
18C2 Carlinville USA
42C2 Carlisle Eng
15C2 Carlisle USA
34C3 Carlos Arg
35C1 Carlos Chagas Brazil
42C2 Carlow County, Irish Rep
45C2 Carlow Irish Rep
21B3 Carlsbad California, USA
9C3 Carlsbad New Mexico, USA
5H5 Carlyle Can
12G2 Carmacks Can
47B2 Carmagnola Italy
43B4 Carmarthen Wales
43B4 Carmarthen B Wales
22B2 Carmel California, USA
16C2 Carmel New York, USA
94B2 Carmel,Mt Israel
34D2 Carmelo Urug
22B2 Carmel Valley USA
23B1 Carmen I Mexico
29D4 Carmen de Patagones Arg
18C2 Carmi USA
21A2 Carmichael USA
35B2 Carmo do Paranaiba Brazil
50A2 Carmona Spain
106A3 Carnarvon Aust
100A4 Carnarvon S Africa
35D1 Carncacá Brazil
45C1 Carndonagh Irish Rep
106B3 Carnegie,L Aust
98B2 Carnot CAR
34D3 Carnot,C Aust
17B2 Carol City USA
31B3 Carolina Brazil
101H1 Carolina S Africa
17C1 Carolina Beach USA
104F3 Caroline Is Pacific O
60B4 Carpathians Mts E Europe

59D3 Carpatii Orientali Mts Rom
106C2 Carpentaria,G of Aust
83C5 Carpenter Ridge Indian O
49D3 Carpentras France
52B2 Carpi Italy
22C3 Carpinteria USA
17B2 Carrabelle USA
52B2 Carrara Italy
41B3 Carrauntoohill Mt Irish Rep
108A2 Carrieton Aust
8D2 Carrington USA
50B1 Carrión R Spain
10A2 Carroll USA
17A1 Carrollton Georgia, USA
14A3 Carrollton Kentucky, USA
18B2 Carrollton Missouri, USA
18C2 Carruthersville USA
60E5 Carsamba Turk
92B2 Carşamba Turk
8B3 Carson City USA
14B2 Carsonville USA
26B4 Cartagena Colombia
51B2 Cartagena Spain
32B3 Cartago Colombia
25D4 Cartago Costa Rica
111C2 Carterton NZ
18B2 Carthage Missouri, USA
15C2 Carthage New York, USA
19B3 Carthage Texas, USA
106B2 Cartier I Timor S
7E4 Cartwright Can
31D3 Caruaru Brazil
33E1 Carúpano Ven
46B1 Carvin France
34A2 Casablanca Chile
96B1 Casablanca Mor
35B2 Casa Branca Brazil
9B3 Casa Grande USA
52A1 Casale Monferrato Italy
47D2 Casalmaggiore Italy
34C3 Casares Arg
13C3 Cascade Mts Can/USA
111A2 Cascade Pt NZ
8A2 Cascade Range Mts USA
30F3 Cascavel Brazil
53B2 Caserta Italy
112C9 Casey Base Ant
45C2 Cashel Irish Rep
34C2 Casilda Arg
107D3 Casino Aust
32B5 Casma Peru
51B1 Caspe Spain
8C2 Casper USA
61G4 Caspian Depression Region Kazakhstan
65G6 Caspian S Asia/Europe
14C3 Cass USA
100B2 Cassamba Angola
46B1 Cassel France
12J3 Cassiar Can
4E3 Cassiar Mts Can
35A1 Cassilândia Brazil
53B2 Cassino Italy
22C3 Castaic USA
34B2 Castaño R Arg
47D2 Castelfranco Italy
49D3 Castellane France
34D3 Castelli Arg
51B2 Castellón de la Plana Spain
31C3 Castelo Brazil
50A2 Castelo Branco Port
48C3 Castelsarrasin France
53B3 Castelvetrano Italy
108B3 Casterton Aust

Castilla La Nueva

50B2 **Castilla La Nueva** Region, Spain
50B1 **Castilla La Vieja** Region, Spain
41B3 **Castlebar** Irish Rep
44A3 **Castlebay** Scot
42C2 **Castle Douglas** Scot
20C1 **Castlegar** Can
42C2 **Castleisland** Irish Rep
108B3 **Castlemain** Aust
45B2 **Castlerea** Irish Rep
109C2 **Castlereagh** Aust
48C3 **Castres-sur-l'Agout** France
27E4 **Castries** St Lucia
29B4 **Castro** Arg
30F3 **Castro** Brazil
31D4 **Castro Alves** Brazil
53C3 **Castrovillari** Italy
22B2 **Castroville** USA
111A2 **Caswell Sd** NZ
25C2 **Cat** / The Bahamas
79B3 **Catabalogan** Phil
32A5 **Catacaos** Peru
35C2 **Cataguases** Brazil
19B3 **Catahoula L** USA
35B1 **Catalão** Brazil
51C1 **Cataluña** Region, Spain
30C4 **Catamarca** Arg
30C4 **Catamarca** State, Arg
101C2 **Catandica** Mozam
79B3 **Catanduanes** / Phil
3186 **Catanduva** Brazil
53C3 **Catania** Italy
53C3 **Catanzaro** Italy
79B3 **Catarman** Phil
108A2 **Catastrophe,C** Aust
26C5 **Catatumbo** R Ven
74A2 **Catawissa** USA
23B2 **Catemaco** Mexico
49D3 **Cater** Corse
52A2 **Cateraggio** Corse
98B3 **Catete** Angola
97A3 **Catio** Guinea-Bissau
7A4 **Cat Lake** Can
13D3 **Catlegar** Can
107E3 **Cato** / Aust
25D2 **Catoche,C** Mexico
16A3 **Catoctin Mt** USA
15C3 **Catonsville** USA
34C3 **Catrilo** Arg
15D2 **Catskill** USA
15D2 **Catskill Mts** USA
32C2 **Cauca** R Colombia
31D2 **Caucaia** Brazil
32B2 **Caucasia** Colombia
65F5 **Caucasus Mts** Georgia
46B1 **Caudry** France
98B3 **Caungula** Angola
29B3 **Cauquenes** Chile
97A4 **Cauvery** R India
49D3 **Cavaillon** France
97B4 **Cavally** R Lib
45C2 **Cavan** County, Irish Rep
45C2 **Cavan** Irish Rep
79B3 **Cavite** Phil
31C2 **Caxias** Brazil
32C4 **Caxias** Brazil
30F4 **Caxias do Sul** Brazil
98B3 **Caxito** Angola
17B1 **Cayce** USA
93D1 **Çayeli** Turk
33G3 **Cayenne** French Guiana
46A1 **Cayeux-sur-Mer** France
25E3 **Cayman Brac** / Caribbean S
26A3 **Cayman Is** Caribbean S
26A3 **Cayman Trench** Caribbean S
99E2 **Caynabo** Somalia
25E2 **Cayo Romana** / Cuba
25D3 **Cayos Miskitos** Is Nic
24A2 **Cay Sal** / Caribbean S
100B2 **Cazombo** Angola
Ceará = Fortaleza

31C3 **Ceara** State, Brazil
79B3 **Cebu** Phil
79B3 **Cebu** / Phil
16B3 **Cecilton** USA
52B2 **Cecina** Italy
8B3 **Cedar City** USA
19A3 **Cedar Creek Res** USA
5J4 **Cedar L** Can
10A2 **Cedar Rapids** USA
17A1 **Cedartown** USA
24A2 **Cedros** / Mexico
106C4 **Ceduna** Aust
99E2 **Ceelbuur** Somalia
99E1 **Ceerigaabo** Somalia
53B3 **Cefalù** Italy
59B3 **Cegléd** Hung
100A2 **Cela** Angola
24B2 **Celaya** Mexico
70C3 **Celebes S** S E Asia
14B2 **Celina** USA
52C1 **Celje** Slovenia
56C2 **Celle** Germany
71E4 **Cendrawasih** Pen Indon
47C2 **Ceno** R Italy
19B3 **Center** USA
16C2 **Center Moriches** USA
17A1 **Center Point** USA
47D2 **Cento** Italy
44B3 **Central** Region, Scot
98B2 **Central African Republic** Africa
16D2 **Central Falls** USA
18C2 **Centralia** Illinois, USA
8A2 **Centralia** Washington, USA
20B2 **Central Point** USA
71F4 **Central Range Mts** PNG
16A3 **Centreville** Maryland, USA
78C4 **Cepu** Indon
70D4 **Ceram = Seram** Indon
70D4 **Ceram Sea** Indon
34C3 **Cereales** Arg
31B5 **Ceres** Brazil
100A4 **Ceres** S Africa
22B2 **Ceres** USA
48C2 **Cergy-Pontoise** France
53C2 **Cerignola** Italy
60C5 **Cernavodă** Rom
9C4 **Cerralvo** / Mexico
23A1 **Cerritos** Mexico
34B2 **Cerro Aconcagua** Mt Arg
23B1 **Cerro Azul** Mexico
34A3 **Cerro Campanario** Mt Chile
34C2 **Cerro Champaqui** Mt Arg
23A2 **Cerro Cuachaia** Mt Mexico
23B1 **Cerro de Astillero** Mexico
34B2 **Cerro de Olivares** Mt Arg
32B6 **Cerro de Pasco** Peru
27D3 **Cerro de Punta** Mt Puerto Rico
23A2 **Cerro El Cantado** Mt Mexico
34B3 **Cerro El Nevado** Mt Arg
23A2 **Cerro Grande** Mts Mexico
34A2 **Cerro Juncal** Mt Arg/Chile
23A1 **Cerro la Ardilla** Mts Mexico
34B1 **Cerro las Tortolas** Mt Chile
23A2 **Cerro Laurel** Mt Mexico
34A2 **Cerro Mercedario** Mt Arg
34A3 **Cerro Mora** Mt Chile
27C4 **Cerron** Mt Ven
34B3 **Cerro Payún** Mt Arg

23B2 **Cerro Penón del Rosario** Mt Mexico
34B2 **Cerro Sosneado** Mt Arg
23A2 **Cero Teotepec** Mt Mexico
34B2 **Cerro Tupungato** Mt Arg
23B2 **Cerro Yucuyacau** Mt Mexico
47C2 **Cervo** R Italy
52B2 **Cesena** Italy
60B2 **Cēsis** Latvia
57C3 **České Budějovice** Czech Republic
59B3 **Českomoravská Vysocina** Mts Czech Republic
55C3 **Çeşme** Turk
107E4 **Cessnock** Aust
52C2 **Cetina** R Croatia
96B1 **Ceuta** N W Africa
92C2 **Ceyhan** Turk
93C2 **Ceylanpınar** Turk
Ceylon = Sri Lanka
63B2 **Chaa-Khol** Russian Fed
48C2 **Chaâteaudun** France
47B1 **Chablais** Region, France
34C2 **Chacabuco** Arg
32B5 **Chachapoyas** Peru
84B3 **Chacharramendi** Arg
84C3 **Chachran** Pak
30A2 **Chaco** State, Arg
98B1 **Chad** Republic, Africa
98B1 **Chad** L C Africa
84B3 **Chadileuvu** R Arg
8C2 **Chadron** USA
18C2 **Chaffee** USA
85A3 **Chagai** Pak
63F2 **Chagda** Russian Fed
84B2 **Chaghcharan** Afghan
104B4 **Chagos Arch** Indian O
27L1 **Chaguanas** Trinidad
91B4 **Chāh Bahār** Iran
76C2 **Chai Badan** Thai
76C2 **Chaine des Cardamomes** Mts Camb
98C4 **Chaine de Mitumba** Mts Zaire
76C2 **Chaiyaphum** Thai
34D2 **Chajari** Arg
84C2 **Chakwal** Pak
32B6 **Chala** Peru
100C2 **Chalabesa** Zambia
84A2 **Chalap Dalam** Mts Afghan
73C4 **Chaling** China
85C4 **Chalisgaon** India
12F1 **Chalkyitsik** USA
46C2 **Challerange** France
46C2 **Chalons sur Marne** France
49C2 **Chalon sur Saône** France
57C3 **Cham** Germany
8C2 **Chama** USA
84D2 **Chaman** Pak
85D3 **Chamba** India
15C3 **Chambersburg** USA
49C2 **Chambéry** France
46B2 **Chambly** France
85A3 **Chambor Kalat** Pak
90B3 **Chamgordan** Iran
34B2 **Chamical** Arg
49C2 **Chamonix** France
86A2 **Champa** India
49C2 **Champagne** Region, France
101G1 **Champagne Castle** Mt Lesotho
47A1 **Champagnole** France
10B2 **Champaign** USA
76D3 **Champassak** Laos
15C2 **Champlain,L** USA
87B2 **Chamrajnagar** India
30B4 **Chañaral** Chile
34A3 **Chanco** Chile
4D3 **Chandalar** USA

4D3 **Chandalar** R USA
84D2 **Chandigarh** India
86C2 **Chandpur** Bang
85D5 **Chandrapur** India
9104 **Chanf** Iran
101C2 **Changara** Mozam
74B2 **Changbai** China
69E2 **Changchun** China
73C4 **Changde** China
68E4 **Changhua** Taiwan
76D2 **Changjiang** China
73D3 **Chang Jiang** R China
73C4 **Changjin** N Korea
73C4 **Changsha** China
72E3 **Changshu** China
74A2 **Changtu** China
73C4 **Changwu** China
74B3 **Changyôn** N Korea
72C2 **Changzhi** China
73E3 **Changzhou** China
44B2 **Channel Is** Europe
9B3 **Channel Is, US**
7E5 **Channel Port-aux-Basques** Can
76C3 **Chanthaburi** Thai
48B2 **Chantilly** France
18A2 **Chanute** USA
73D5 **Chao'an** China
73D5 **Chao'an** China
73D3 **Chao Hu** L China
76C3 **Chao Phraya** R Thai
72E1 **Chaoyang** China
31C4 **Chapada Diamantina** Mts Brazil
31C2 **Chapadinha** Brazil
23A1 **Chapala** Mexico
23A1 **Chapala,Lac de** L Mexico
61H3 **Chapayevo** Kazakhstan
30F4 **Chapecó** Brazil
27H1 **Chapelton** Jamaica
7B5 **Chapleau** Can
61E3 **Chaplygin** Russian Fed
112C3 **Charcot I** Ant
80E2 **Chardzhou** Turkmenistan
47C2 **Charente** R France
98B1 **Chari** R Chad
98B1 **Chari Baguirmi** Region, Chad
84B1 **Charikar** Afghan
18B1 **Chariton** R USA
33F2 **Charity** Guyana
85D3 **Charkhāri** India
46C1 **Charleroi** Belg
10C2 **Charleston** Illinois, USA
18C2 **Charleston** Missouri, USA
11C3 **Charleston** S Carolina, USA
10B3 **Charleston** W Virginia, USA
98C3 **Charlesville** Zaire
107D3 **Charleville** Aust
49C2 **Charleville-Mézières** France
14A1 **Charlevoix** USA
14B2 **Charlotte** Michigan, USA
11B3 **Charlotte** N Carolina, USA
17B2 **Charlotte Harbor** B USA
10C3 **Charlottesville** USA
7D5 **Charlottetown** Can
27K1 **Charlotteville** Tobago
108B3 **Charlton** Aust
10C1 **Charlton I** Can
84C2 **Charsadda** Pak
107D3 **Charters Towers** Aust
48C2 **Chartres** France
29E3 **Chascomús** Arg
13D2 **Chase** Can
48C2 **Châteaubriant** France
48C2 **Château-du-Loir** France
48C2 **Châteaudun** France
48B2 **Châteaulin** France
48C2 **Châteauroux** France

46D2 **Château-Salins** France
49C2 **Château-Thierry** France
46C1 **Châtelet** Belg
47E2 **Châtellerault** France
43E4 **Chatham** France
7D5 **Chatham** New Brunswick, Can
16C1 **Chatham** New York, USA
14B2 **Chatham** Ontario, Can
13A2 **Chatham** Sd Can
12H3 **Chatham Str** USA
49C2 **Châtillon** France
43D3 **Châtillon** Italy
16B3 **Chatsworth** USA
17B1 **Chattahoochee** USA
17A1 **Chattahoochee** *R* USA
11B3 **Chattanooga** USA
76A1 **Chauk** Myan
49D2 **Chaumont** France
46B2 **Chauny** France
77D3 **Chau Phu** Viet
50A1 **Chaves** Port
61H2 **Chaykovskiy** Russian Fed
50B2 **Chazaouet** Alg
34C2 **Chazón** Arg
52C2 **Chcontá** Colombia
57C2 **Cheb** Czech Republic
65F4 **Cheboksary** Russian Fed
10B2 **Cheboygan** USA
74B3 **Chech'on** S Korea
85C3 **Chechro** Pak
74B3 **Checotah** USA
76A2 **Cheduba** *I* Myan
108B1 **Cheepie** Aust
96B2 **Chegga** Maur
100C2 **Chegutu** Zim
20B1 **Chehalis** USA
74B4 **Cheju** S Korea
74B4 **Cheju do** *I* S Korea
74B4 **Cheju-haehyop** *Str* S Korea
63F2 **Chekunda** Russian Fed
20B1 **Chelan,L** USA
90B2 **Cheleken** Turkmenistan
34B3 **Chelforo** Arg
80D1 **Chelkar** Kazakhstan
59C2 **Chelm** Pol
58B2 **Chelmno** Pol
43C4 **Chelmsford** Eng
43C4 **Cheltenham** Eng
65H4 **Chelyabinsk** Russian Fed
101C2 **Chemba** Mozam
57C2 **Chemnitz** Germany
84D2 **Chenab** *R* India/Pak
96B2 **Chenachane** Alg
20C1 **Cheney** USA
14A2 **Cheney Res** USA
18A2 **Cheney Res** USA
72D1 **Chengde** China
73A3 **Chengdu** China
72E2 **Chengshan Jiao** *C* China
73C4 **Chenxi** China
73C4 **Chen Xian** China
73D3 **Cheo Xian** China
73D3 **Chepén** Peru
34B2 **Chepes** Arg
48C2 **Cher** *R* France
23A2 **Cheran** Mexico
17C1 **Cheraw** USA
48B2 **Cherbourg** France
50B2 **Cherchell** Alg
63C2 **Cheremkhovo** Russian Fed
60E2 **Cherepovets** Russian Fed
60D4 **Cherkassy** Ukraine
61F5 **Cherkessk** Russian Fed
60D3 **Chernigov** Ukraine
60D3 **Chernobyl** Ukraine
60C4 **Chernovtsy** Ukraine
61J2 **Chernushka** Russian Fed

60B3 **Chernyakhovsk** Russian Fed
61G4 **Chernyye Zemli** Region, Russian Fed
18A2 **Cherokees,L o'the** USA
34A3 **Cherquenco** Chile
86C1 **Cherrapunji** India
60C3 **Cherven'** Belarus
59C2 **Chervonograd** Ukraine
42C3 **Chesapeake** *B* USA
42C3 **Cheshire** County, Eng
16C1 **Cheshire** Eng
64F3 **Chëshskaya Guba** *B* Russian Fed
21A1 **Chester** California, USA
42C3 **Chester** Eng
18C2 **Chester** Illinois, USA
16C1 **Chester** Massachusets, USA
15C3 **Chester** Pennsylvania, USA
17B1 **Chester** S Carolina, USA
16A3 **Chester** *R* USA
42D3 **Chesterfield** Eng
4H3 **Chesterfield Inlet** Can
13D3 **Chewelah** USA
8C2 **Cheyenne** USA
86A1 **Chhapra** India
86C1 **Chhatak** Bang
85D4 **Chhatarpur** India
85D4 **Chhindwära** India
86B1 **Chhuka** Bhutan
73E5 **Chia'i** Taiwan
100A2 **Chiange** Angola
76D2 **Chiang Khan** Thai
76B2 **Chiang Mai** Thai
47C1 **Chiavenna** Italy
74E3 **Chiba** Japan
86B2 **Chibása** India
100A2 **Chibia** Angola
7C4 **Chibougamau** Can
75A1 **Chiburi-jima** *I* Japan
101C3 **Chibuto** Mozam
10B2 **Chicago** USA
14A2 **Chicago Heights** USA
12G3 **Chichagof I** USA
43D4 **Chichester** Eng
74C3 **Chichibu** Japan
69G4 **Chichi-jima** *I* Japan
11B3 **Chickamauga L** USA
19C3 **Chickasawhay** *R* USA
9D3 **Chickasha** USA
6C2 **Chicken** USA
32A5 **Chiclayo** Peru
8A3 **Chico** USA
29C4 **Chico** *R* Arg
101C2 **Chicoa** Mozam
15D2 **Chicopee** USA
15D1 **Chicoutimi** Can
101C3 **Chicualacuala** Mozam
87B2 **Chidambaram** India
6D3 **Chidley,C** Can
17B2 **Chiefland** USA
99C3 **Chiengi** Zambia
47B2 **Chieri** Italy
46C2 **Chiers** *R* France
47C1 **Chiese** *R* Italy
52B2 **Chieti** Italy
72D1 **Chifeng** China
12C3 **Chigignik,Mt** USA
4C3 **Chigmit Mts** USA
23B2 **Chignahuapán** Mexico
12C3 **Chigu** China
24B2 **Chihuahua** Mexico
87B2 **Chik Ballápur** India
87B2 **Chikmagalúr** India
12C2 **Chikuminuk L** USA

101C2 **Chikwawa** Malawi
76A1 **Chi-kyaw** Myan
87C1 **Chilakalúrupet** India
23B2 **Chilapa** Mexico
87B3 **Chilaw** Sri Lanka
28B6 **Chile** Republic
34B2 **Chilecito** Mendoza, Arg
100B2 **Chililabombwe** Zambia
86B2 **Chilka** *L* India
13C2 **Chilko** *R* Can
5F4 **Chilko L** Can
13C2 **Chilkotin** *R* Can
34A3 **Chillán** Chile
34D3 **Chillar** Arg
18B2 **Chillicothe** Missouri, USA
14B3 **Chillicothe** Ohio, USA
13C3 **Chilliwack** Can
86B1 **Chilmari** India
101C2 **Chilongozi** Zambia
20B2 **Chiloquin** USA
24C3 **Chilpancingo** Mexico
43D4 **Chiltern Hills** *Upland* Eng
14A2 **Chilton** USA
101C2 **Chilumba** Malawi
69E4 **Chi-lung** Taiwan
101C2 **Chilwa** *L* Malawi
100C2 **Chimanimani** Zim
46C1 **Chimay** Belg
52C2 **Chimbay** Uzbekistan
32A4 **Chimborazo** *Mt* Ecuador
32B5 **Chimbote** Peru
65H5 **Chimkent** Kazakhstan
101C2 **Chimoio** Mozam
67E3 **China** Republic, Asia
China National Republic = Taiwan
25D3 **Chinandega** Nic
32B6 **Chincha Alta** Peru
109D1 **Chinchilla** Aust
101C2 **Chinde** Mozam
86C2 **Chindwin** *R* Myan
100B2 **Chingola** Zambia
100A2 **Chinguar** Angola
96A2 **Chinguetti** Maur
74B3 **Chinhae** S Korea
100C2 **Chinhoyi** Zim
42D3 **Chiniak,C** USA
84C2 **Chiniot** Pak
74B3 **Chinju** S Korea
98C2 **Chinko** *R* CAR
75B1 **Chino** Japan
101C2 **Chinsali** Zambia
52B1 **Chioggia** Italy
101C2 **Chipata** Zambia
101C3 **Chipinge** Zim
87A1 **Chiplún** India
43C4 **Chippenham** Eng
10A2 **Chippewa Falls** USA
32A4 **Chira** *R* Peru
87C1 **Chirála** India
101C3 **Chiredzi** Zim
95A2 **Chirfa** Niger
32A2 **Chiriquí** *Mt* Panama
54C2 **Chirpan** Bulg
25D3 **Chirripó Grande** *Mt* Costa Rica
100B2 **Chirundu** Zim
100B2 **Chisamba** Zambia
7C4 **Chisasibi** Can
73B4 **Chishui He** *R* China
Chişinău = Kishinev
47B2 **Chisone** *R* Italy
61H2 **Chistopol'** Russian Fed
68D1 **Chita** Russian Fed
100A2 **Chitado** Angola
100A2 **Chitembo** Angola
74E2 **Chitose** Japan
87B2 **Chitradurga** India
84C1 **Chitral** Pak
32J7 **Chitré** Panama
86C2 **Chittagong** Bang
85C4 **Chittaurgarh** India
87B2 **Chittoor** India
100B2 **Chiume** Angola
47D1 **Chiusa** Italy

47B2 **Chivasso** Italy
100C2 **Chivhu** Zim
29D2 **Chivilcoy** Arg
100C2 **Chivu** Zim
75A1 **Chizu** Japan
29C3 **Choele Choel** Arg
34C3 **Choique** Arg
24B2 **Choix** Mexico
58B2 **Chojnice** Pol
99D1 **Choke** *Mts* Eth
48B2 **Cholet** France
23A2 **Cholula** Mexico
100B2 **Choma** Zambia
86B1 **Chomo Yummo** *Mt* China/India
57C2 **Chomutov** Czech Republic
63C1 **Chona** *R* Russian Fed
74B3 **Ch'ŏnan** S Korea
76C3 **Chon Buri** Thai
32A4 **Chone** Ecuador
74B2 **Ch'ŏngjin** N Korea
74B3 **Chongju** N Korea
74B3 **Ch'ŏngju** S Korea
100A2 **Chongoroi** Angola
73B4 **Chongqing** China
74B3 **Chŏngŭp** S Korea
74B3 **Chŏnju** S Korea
86B1 **Chooyu** *Mt* China/Nepal
59D3 **Chortkov** Ukraine
74B3 **Ch'ŏrwŏn** N Korea
59B2 **Chorzow** Pol
74E2 **Choshi** Japan
34A3 **Choshuenco** Chile
58B2 **Choszczno** Pol
86A2 **Chotanãgpur** Region, India
96C1 **Chott Melrhir** Alg
22B2 **Chowchilla** USA
63D3 **Choybalsan** Mongolia
6A3 **Chrantrey Inlet** *B* Can
111B2 **Christchurch** NZ
101G1 **Christiana** S Africa
6D2 **Christian,C** Can
12H3 **Christian Sd** USA
6E3 **Christianshab** Greenland
104D4 **Christmas I** Indian O
65J5 **Chu** Kazakhstan
65J5 **Chu** *R* Kazakhstan
29C4 **Chubut** State, Arg
29C4 **Chubut** *R* Arg
60D2 **Chudovo** Russian Fed
Chudskoye Ozero = Peipus, Lake
4D3 **Chugach Mts** USA
12E2 **Chugiak** USA
75A1 **Chūgoku-sanchi** *Mts* Japan
29F2 **Chui** Brazil
29B3 **Chuillán** Chile
77C5 **Chukai** Malay
76D2 **Chu Lai** Viet
21B3 **Chula Vista** USA
12E2 **Chulitna** USA
63C2 **Chulman** Russian Fed
32A5 **Chulucanas** Peru
30C2 **Chulumani** Bol
65K4 **Chulym** Russian Fed
63A2 **Chulym** *R* Russian Fed
63B2 **Chuma** *R* Russian Fed
84D2 **Chumar** India
63F2 **Chumikan** Russian Fed
77B3 **Chumphon** Thai
74B3 **Ch'unch'ŏn** S Korea
86B2 **Chunchura** India
74B3 **Ch'ungju** S Korea
Chungking = Chongqing
99D3 **Chunya** Tanz
63A1 **Chunya** *R* Russian Fed
27L1 **Chupara Pt** Trinidad
30C3 **Chuquicamata** Chile
52A1 **Chur** Switz

Churāchāndpur

16

86C2 **Churāchāndpur** India
7A4 **Churchill** Can
7D4 **Churchill** *R* Labrador, Can
7A4 **Churchill** *R* Manitoba, Can
7A4 **Churchill,C** Can
7D4 **Churchill Falls** Can
5H4 **Churchill L** Can
84C3 **Chūru** India
23A2 **Churumuco** Mexico
61J2 **Chusovoy** Russian Fed
61G2 **Chuvashskaya Respublika,** Russian Fed
68B4 **Chuxiong** China
76D3 **Chu Yang Sin** *Mt* Viet
78B4 **Cianjur** Indon
47D2 **Ciano d'Enza** Italy
35A2 **Cianorte** Brazil
58C2 **Ciechanów** Pol
25E2 **Ciego de Avila** Cuba
32C1 **Ciénaga** Colombia
72C2 **Cienfuegos** Cuba
59B3 **Cieszyn** Pol
51B2 **Cieza** Spain
92B2 **Cihanbeyli** Turk
23A2 **Cihuatlán** Mexico
50B2 **Cijulang** Indon
78B4 **Cilacap** Indon
54C1 **Cîmpina** Rom
51C1 **Cinca** *R* Spain
52C2 **Cinčer** *Mt* Bosnia-Herzegovina
10B3 **Cincinnati** USA
54B1 **Cindrelu** *Mt* Rom
55C3 **Cine** *R* Turk
51A2 **Ciney** Belg
34B3 **Cipolletti** Arg
4D3 **Circle** Alaska, USA
14B3 **Circleville** USA
78B4 **Cirebon** Indon
43D4 **Cirencester** Eng
47D2 **Citadella** Italy
24C3 **Citlaltepetl** *Mt* Mexico
100A4 **Citrusdal** S Africa
52B2 **Citta del Vaticano** Italy
52B2 **Città di Castello** Italy
24B2 **Ciudad Acuña** Mexico
23A2 **Ciudad Altamirano** Mexico
33E2 **Ciudad Bolívar** Ven
24B2 **Ciudad Camargo** Mexico
25C3 **Ciudad del Carmen** Mexico
23B1 **Ciudad del Maíz** Mexico
51C1 **Ciudadela** Spain
33E2 **Ciudad Guayana** Ven
24B3 **Ciudad Guzman** Mexico
23A2 **Ciudad Hidalgo** Mexico
24B1 **Ciudad Juárez** Mexico
9C4 **Ciudad Lerdo** Mexico
24C2 **Ciudad Madero** Mexico
23B2 **Ciudad Mendoza** Mexico
24B2 **Ciudad Obregon** Mexico
27C4 **Ciudad Ojeda** Ven
33E2 **Ciudad Piar** Ven
50B2 **Ciudad Real** Spain
50A1 **Ciudad Rodrigo** Spain
24C2 **Ciudad Valles** Mexico
24C2 **Ciudad Victoria** Mexico
52B2 **Civitavecchia** Italy
93D2 **Cizre** Turk
43E4 **Clacton-on-Sea** Eng
5G4 **Claire,L** Can
14C2 **Clairton** USA
47A1 **Clairvaux** France

17A1 **Clanton** USA
100A4 **Clanwilliam** S Africa
45C2 **Clara** Irish Rep
34D3 **Claraz** Arg
45B2 **Clare** County, Irish Rep
14B2 **Clare** Irish Rep
45C2 **Clare** *I* Irish Rep
15D2 **Claremont** USA
18A2 **Claremore** USA
45B2 **Claremorris** Irish Rep
109D1 **Clarence** *R* Aust
111B2 **Clarence** *R* NZ
106C2 **Clarence Str** Aust
12H3 **Clarence Str** USA
19B3 **Clarendon** USA
7E5 **Clarenville** Can
5G4 **Claresholm** Can
18A1 **Clarinda** USA
15C2 **Clarion** Pennsylvania, USA
24A3 **Clarión** *I* Mexico
15C2 **Clarion** *R* USA
105J3 **Clarion Fracture Zone** Pacific O
11B3 **Clark Hill Res** USA
14B2 **Clark,Pt** Can
14B3 **Clarksburg** USA
11A3 **Clarksdale** USA
12C3 **Clarks Point** USA
20C1 **Clarkston** USA
18D1 **Clarksville** Arkansas, USA
35A1 **Claro** *R* Brazil
29A2 **Claromecó** Arg
18A2 **Clay Center** USA
44D2 **Claymore** *Oilfield* N Sea
13B3 **Clayoquot Sd** Can
9C3 **Clayton** New Mexico, USA
15C2 **Clayton** New York, USA
41B3 **Clear** *C* Irish Rep
12E3 **Cleare,C** USA
13D1 **Clear Hills** *Mts* Can
21A2 **Clear L** USA
20B2 **Clear Lake Res** USA
13C2 **Clearwater** USA
11B4 **Clearwater** USA
13E1 **Clearwater** *R* Can
13C2 **Clearwater L** Can
9D3 **Cleburne** USA
22E2 **Cleeton** *Oilfield* North Sea
3S **Clements** USA
79A3 **Cleopatra Needle** *Mt* Phil
107D3 **Clermont** Aust
46B2 **Clermont** France
46C2 **Clermont-en-Argonne** France
47C2 **Clermont-Ferrand** France
46D1 **Clervaux** Germany
25C **Clés** Italy
24C **Cleve** Aust
42D2 **Cleveland** County, Eng
19B3 **Cleveland** Mississippi, USA
10B2 **Cleveland** Ohio, USA
11B3 **Cleveland** Tennessee, USA
19A3 **Cleveland** Texas, USA
41B3 **Clew** *R* Irish Rep
45A2 **Clifden** Irish Rep
109D1 **Clifton** Aust
16B2 **Clifton** New Jersey, USA
108A1 **Clifton Hills** Aust
13F3 **Climax** Can
18B2 **Clinton** Arkansas, USA
5F4 **Clinton** Can
16C2 **Clinton** Connecticut, USA
16D1 **Clinton** Massachusetts, USA
19B3 **Clinton** Mississippi, USA
18B2 **Clinton** Missouri, USA

16B2 **Clinton** New Jersey, USA
4H3 **Clinton-Colden L** Can
29D1 **Clipperton I** Pacific O
30C2 **Cliza** Bol
45B3 **Clonakilty** Irish Rep
107D3 **Cloncurry** Aust
45C1 **Clones** Irish Rep
45C1 **Clonmel** Irish Rep
10A2 **Cloquet** USA
12C2 **Cloudy Mt** Can
22C2 **Clovis** California, USA
9C3 **Clovis** New Mexico, USA
60B4 **Cluj** Rom
54C1 **Cluj-Napoca** Rom
47B1 **Cluses** France
47C2 **Cluson** *R* Italy
111A3 **Clutha** *R* NZ
43C3 **Clwyd** County, Wales
6D2 **Clyde** Can
42B2 **Clyde** *R* NZ
111A3 **Clyde** NZ
23A2 **Coahuayana** Mexico
23A2 **Coalcomán** Mexico
13C2 **Coaldale** Can
21B2 **Coaldale** USA
21A2 **Coalinga** USA
33E5 **Coari** *R* Brazil
17A1 **Coastal Plain** USA
4E4 **Coast Mts** Can
17A1 **Coast Ranges** *Mts* USA
42B2 **Coatbridge** Scot
23B2 **Coatepec** Mexico
16B3 **Coatesville** USA
15D1 **Coaticook** Can
6B3 **Coats I** Can
112B1 **Coats Land** Region, Ant
25C3 **Coatzacoalcos** Mexico
7C5 **Cobalt** Can
25C3 **Cobán** Guatemala
107D4 **Cobar** Aust
109C3 **Cobargo** Aust
45B3 **Cobh** Irish Rep
32C6 **Cobija** Bol
16B1 **Cobleskill** USA
51B2 **Cobo de Palos** *C* Spain
7C5 **Cobourg** Can
106C2 **Cobourg Pen** Aust
57C2 **Coburg** Germany
32B4 **Coca** Ecuador
17B2 **Coca** USA
32C6 **Cochabamba** Bol
46D1 **Cochem** Germany
87B3 **Cochin** India
13E2 **Cochrane** Alberta, Can
7B5 **Cochrane** Ontario, Can
108B2 **Cockburn** Aust
16A3 **Cockeysville** USA
27H1 **Cockpit Country,The** Jamaica
25D3 **Coco** *R* Honduras/Nic
98A2 **Cocobeach** Gabon
27L1 **Cocos B** Trinidad
104C4 **Cocos Is** Indian O
23A1 **Cocula** Mexico
10C2 **Cod,C** USA
111A3 **Codfish I** NZ
7D4 **Cod I** Can
47E2 **Codigoro** Italy
31C2 **Codó** Brazil
9D3 **Cody** USA
56B2 **Coesfeld** Germany
8B2 **Coeur d'Alene** USA
9D3 **Coffeyville** USA
109D2 **Coff's Harbour** Aust
23B2 **Cofre de Perote** *Mt* Mexico
48B2 **Cognac** France
15D2 **Cohoes** USA
108B3 **Cohuna** Aust
29B5 **Coihaique** Chile
87B2 **Coimbatore** India
50A1 **Coimbra** Port

32A3 **Cojimies** Ecuador
107D4 **Colac** Aust
31C5 **Colatina** Brazil
112B6 **Colbeck,C** Ant
43E4 **Colchester** Eng
16C2 **Colchester** USA
47B1 **Col de la Faucille** France
13E2 **Cold L** Can
52A1 **Col du Grand St Bernard** *P* Italy/Switz
47B2 **Col du Lautaret** *P* France
52A1 **Col du Mont Cenis** *P* France/Italy
14B2 **Coldwater** USA
12F1 **Coleen** *R* USA
14B2 **Coleman** Michigan, USA
101G1 **Colenso** S Africa
45C1 **Coleraine** N Ire
111B2 **Coleridge,L** NZ
100B4 **Colesberg** S Africa
22C1 **Coleville** USA
21A2 **Colfax** California, USA
19B3 **Colfax** Louisiana, USA
20C1 **Colfax** Washington, USA
24B3 **Colima** Mexico
23A2 **Colima** State, Mexic
34A2 **Colina** Chile
44A3 **Coll** *I* Scot
109C1 **Collarenebri** Aust
47B2 **Colle de Tende** *P* France/Italy
12E2 **College** USA
17B1 **College Park** Georgia, USA
16A3 **College Park** Washington, USA
19A3 **College Station** USA
106A4 **Collie** Aust
106B2 **Collier B** Aust
46A1 **Collines de L'Artois** France
46B2 **Collines De Thiérach** France
14B2 **Collingwood** Can
110B2 **Collingwood** NZ
19C3 **Collins** Mississippi, USA
4H2 **Collinson Pen** Can
107D3 **Collinsville** Aust
18C2 **Collinsville** Illinois, USA
18A2 **Collinsville** Oklahoma, USA
34A3 **Collipulli** Chile
49D2 **Colmar** France
Cologne = Köln
35B2 **Colômbia** Brazil
32B3 **Colombia** Republic, S America
15C3 **Colombia** USA
87B3 **Colombo** Sri Lanka
25D2 **Colon** Cuba
72C2 **Colón** Panama
29E2 **Colonia** Urug
34D2 **Colonia del Sacramento** Urug
34B3 **Colonia 25 de Mayo** Arg
29C5 **Colonia Las Heras** Arg
44A3 **Colonsay** *I* Scot
23A1 **Colotlán** Mexico
27E5 **Colorádito** Ven
8C3 **Colorado** State, USA
9B3 **Colorado** *R* Arizona, USA
29D3 **Colorado** *R* Buenos Aires, Arg
8C3 **Colorado** *R* Texas, USA
9B3 **Colorado Plat** USA
8C3 **Colorado Springs** USA
22D3 **Colton** USA
16A3 **Columbia** Maryland, USA

19C3 Columbia
　　Mississippi, USA
10A3 Columbia Missouri,
　　USA
15C2 Columbia
　　Pennsylvania, USA
11B3 Columbia S Carolina,
　　USA
11B3 Columbia Tennessee,
　　USA
13D2 Columbia R Can
8A2 Columbia R USA
5G4 Columbia,Mt Can
20C1 Columbia Plat USA
11B3 Columbus Georgia,
　　USA
14A3 Columbus Indiana,
　　USA
11B3 Columbus
　　Mississippi, USA
8D2 Columbus Nebraska,
　　USA
10B2 Columbus Ohio,
　　USA
19A4 Columbus Texas,
　　USA
20C1 Colville USA
4C3 Colville R USA
110C1 Colville,C NZ
4C3 Colville L Can
42C3 Colwyn Bay Wales
47E2 Comacchio Italy
22B1 Comanche Res USA
112C2 Comandante Ferraz
　　Base Ant
34A2 Combarbalá Chile
25D3 Comayagua
　　Honduras
86C2 Comilla Bang
25C3 Comitán Mexico
46C2 Commercy France
6B3 Committees B Can
52A1 Como Italy
29C5 Comodoro Rivadavia
　　Arg
23A1 Comonfort Mexico
87B3 Comorin,C India
101D2 Comoros Is Indian O
49C2 Compiègne France
23A1 Compostela Mexico
34B2 Comte Salas Arg
86C1 Cona China
97A4 Conakry Guinea
34B2 Concarán Arg
48B2 Concarneau France
35D1 Conceição da Barra
　　Brazil
31B3 Conceição do
　　Araguaia Brazil
35C1 Conceição do Mato
　　Dentro Brazil
30E3 Concepción Chile
29E2 Concepción R Arg
23A2 Concepción del Oro
　　Mexico
34D2 Concepcion del
　　Uruguay R Arg
9A3 Concepción,Pt Can
35B2 Conchas Brazil
9C4 Conchos R Mexico
21A2 Concord California,
　　USA
10C2 Concord New
　　Hampshire, USA
29E2 Concordia Arg
8D3 Concordia USA
20B1 Concrete USA
109D1 Condamine Aust
47D4 Condobolin Aust
20B1 Condon USA
14A1 Condroz Mts Belg
47E2 Conegliano Italy
99F8 Congo Republic,
　　Africa
89F8 Congo R Zaire
　　Congo,R = Zaire
14B1 Coniston Can
45B2 Connaught Region,
　　Irish Rep
14B2 Conneaut USA

10C2 Connecticut State,
　　USA
15D2 Connecticut R USA
14C2 Connellsville USA
45B2 Connemara,Mts of
　　Irish Rep
14A3 Connersville USA
108B2 Conoble Aust
19A3 Conroe USA
35C2 Conselheiro Lafaiete
　　Brazil
77D4 Con Son Is Viet
　　Constance,L =
　　Bodensee
60C5 Constanta Rom
96C1 Constantine Alg
12C3 Constantine,C USA
29B3 Constitución Chile
13F3 Consul Can
47E2 Contarina Italy
31C4 Contas R Brazil
23B2 Contreras Mexico
4H3 Contuyoto L Can
11A3 Conway Arkansas,
　　USA
15D2 Conway New
　　Hampshire, USA
17C1 Conway South
　　Carolina, USA
108A1 Conway,L Aust
42C3 Conwy Wales
106C3 Coober Pedy Aust
110B2 Cook Str NZ
13B2 Cook,C Can
110C1 Cook Inlet B USA
105H4 Cook Is Pacific O
111B2 Cook,Mt NZ
107D2 Cooktown Aust
109C2 Coolabah Aust
108C2 Cooladdi Aust
109C2 Coolah Aust
109C2 Coolamon Aust
106B4 Coolgardie Aust
109C2 Cooma Aust
109C2 Coonabarabran Aust
109C2 Coonamble Aust
108B2 Coonbah Aust
108A2 Coondambo Aust
109C2 Coongoola Aust
87B2 Coonoor India
108B1 Cooper Basin Aust
108B1 Cooper Creek Aust
108B1 Cooper Creek R
　　Aust
108A3 Coorong,The Aust
109D1 Cooroy Aust
20B2 Coos B USA
2092 Coos Bay USA
107D4 Cootamundra Aust
45C1 Cootehill Irish Rep
23B2 Copala Mexico
23B2 Copalillo Mexico
　　Copenhagen =
　　København
30B4 Copiapó Chile
47D2 Copparo Italy
12F2 Copper R USA
14B1 Copper Centre USA
14B1 Copper Cliff Can
　　Coppermine =
　　Qurlurtuak
4G3 Coppermine R Can
　　Coquilhatville =
　　Mbandaka
30B4 Coquimbo Chile
54B2 Corabia Rom
17B2 Coral Gables USA
6B3 Coral Harbour Can
107D2 Coral S Aust/PNG
104F4 Coral Sea Basin
　　Pacific O
107E2 Coral Sea Island
　　Territories Aust
108B3 Corangamite,L Aust
33F3 Corantijn R
　　Surinam/Guyana
46B2 Corbeil-Essonnes
　　France
50A1 Corcubion Spain
11B3 Cordele USA
50A1 Cordillera Cantabrica
　　Mts Spain
26C3 Cordillera Central
　　Mts Dom Rep

79B2 Cordillera Central
　　Mts Phil
34B2 Cordillera de Ansita
　　Mts Arg
32B5 Cordillera de los
　　Andes Mts Peru
30C4 Cordillera del Toro
　　Mt Arg
32C2 Cordillera de Mérida
　　Ven
34A3 Cordillera de Viento
　　Mts Arg
25D3 Cordillera Isabella
　　Mts Nic
32B3 Cordillera Occidental
　　Mts Colombia
32B3 Cordillera Oriental
　　Mts Colombia
108I1 Cordillo Downs Aust
29D2 Córdoba Arg
24C3 Córdoba Mexico
50B2 Córdoba Spain
29D2 Córdoba State, Arg
4D3 Cordova USA
　　Corfu = Kérkira
109D2 Coricudgy,Mt Aust
53C3 Corigliano Calabro
　　Italy
11B3 Corinth Mississippi,
　　USA
31C5 Corinto Brazil
45B2 Cork County,
　　Irish Rep
41B3 Cork Irish Rep
92A1 Çorlu Turk
31C5 Cornel Fabriciano
　　Brazil
35A2 Cornelio Procópio
　　Brazil
7E5 Corner Brook Can
109C3 Corner Inlet B Aust
15C2 Corning USA
7C5 Cornwall USA
43B4 Cornwall County,
　　Eng
44H2 Cornwall,C Eng
6A2 Cornwallis I Can
32D1 Coro Ven
31C2 Coroatá Brazil
32C2 Coroico Bol
35B1 Coromandel Coast
　　India
110C1 Coromandel Pen NZ
110C1 Coromandel Range
　　Mts NZ
22D4 Corona California,
　　USA
13E2 Coronation Can
4G3 Coronation G Can
29B3 Coronel Arg
34D3 Coronel Brandsen
　　Arg
34C3 Coronel Dorrego Arg
29D3 Coronel Pringles Arg
34C3 Coronel Suárez Arg
34C3 Coronel Vidal Arg
30B2 Coropuna Mt Peru
109C3 Corowa Aust
49D3 Corps France
9D4 Corpus Christi USA
9D4 Corpus Christi,L USA
79B3 Corregidor I Phil
35A1 Corrente R Mato
　　Grosso, Brazil
30E4 Corrientes Arg
29D3 Corrientes State, Arg
19B3 Corrigan USA
106A4 Corrigin Aust
107E2 Corringe Is Aust
109C3 Corryong Aust
52A2 Corse I Medit S
42B2 Corsewall Pt Scot
　　Corsica = Corse
9D3 Corsicana USA
52A2 Corte Corse
9C3 Cortez USA
52B1 Cortina d'Ampezzo
　　Italy

15C2 Cortland USA
23A2 Coruca de Catalan
　　Mexico
93D1 Çoruh R Turk
60E5 Çorum Turk
30E2 Corumbá Brazil
35B1 Corumba R Brazil
35B1 Corumbaíba Brazil
29D2 Corumbá Brazil
96A1 Corvo I Açores
43C3 Corwen Wales
23B2 Coscomatopec
　　Mexico
53C3 Cosenza Italy
101D1 Cosmoledo Is
　　Seychelles
34C2 Cosquin Arg
51C1 Costa Blanca Region,
　　Spain
50B2 Costa Brava Region,
　　Spain
50B2 Costa de la Luz
　　Region, Spain
50B2 Costa del Sol Region,
　　Spain
22D4 Costa Mesa USA
25D3 Costa Rica Republic,
　　Cent America
79B4 Cotabato Phil
30C3 Cotagaita Bol
46C2 Côte d'Azur Region,
　　France
46C2 Côtes de Meuse Mts
　　France
97B4 Côte d'Ivoire Africa
97C4 Cotonou Benin
32B4 Cotopaxi Mt Ecuador
43E4 Cotswold Hills
　　Upland Eng
20B2 Cottage Grove USA
56C2 Cottbus Germany
108A3 Couedic,C du Aust
20C1 Couer d'Alene L USA
48B2 Coulommiers France
15C1 Coulonge R Can
22B2 Coulterville USA
4B3 Council USA
8D2 Council Bluffs USA
60B2 Courland Lagoon Lg
　　Lithuania/Russian Fed
47B2 Courmayeur Italy
13B3 Courtenay Can
　　Courtrai = Kortrijk
48B2 Coutances France
43D3 Coventry Eng
50A1 Covilhã Spain
17B1 Covington Georgia,
　　USA
19B3 Covington Louisiana,
　　USA
109C2 Cowal,L Aust
108B3 Cowangie Aust
15D1 Cowansville Can
108A3 Coward Springs Aust
108A2 Cowell Aust
108C3 Cowes Aust
20B1 Cowichan L Can
20C1 Cowlitz R USA
109C2 Cowra Aust
30F2 Coxim Brazil
16C1 Cox'sackie USA
86C2 Cox's Bazar Bang
22B2 Coyote USA
23A2 Coyuca de Benitez
　　Mexico
58B2 Cracow Pol
100B4 Cradock S Africa
8C2 Craig USA
57C3 Crailsheim Germany
54B2 Craiova Rom
15D2 Cranberry L USA
5G5 Cranbrook Can
20C2 Crane Oregon, USA
16D2 Cranston USA
20B2 Crater L USA
20B2 Crater Lake Nat Pk
　　USA
31C3 Crateus Brazil
31D3 Crato Brazil
14A2 Crawfordsville USA
17B1 Crawfordville USA
43D4 Crawley Eng
5H4 Cree L Can
46B2 Creil France

Crema

47C2 **Crema** Italy
52B1 **Cremona** Italy
46B2 **Crépy-en-Valois** France
52B2 **Cres** / Yugos
20B2 **Crescent City** USA
34C2 **Crespo** Arg
13C0 **Creston** Can
18B1 **Creston** USA
17A1 **Crestview** USA
108B3 **Creswick** Aust
47A1 **Crêt de la Neige** Mt France
 Crête = Kríti
18A1 **Crete** USA
55B3 **Crete,S of** Greece
48C2 **Creuse** R France
43C3 **Crewe** Eng
44B3 **Crianlarich** Scot
30G4 **Criciúma** Brazil
44C3 **Crieff** Scot
12G3 **Crillon,Mt** USA
35B1 **Cristalina** Brazil
52C1 **Croatia** Republic, Europe
78D1 **Crocker Range** Mts Malay
19A3 **Crockett** USA
106C2 **Croker I** Aust
44C3 **Cromarty** Scot
43E3 **Cromer** Eng
111A3 **Cromwell** NZ
11C4 **Crooked** R Can
 Crooked I The Bahamas
13C2 **Crooked** R Can
8D2 **Crookston** USA
109C2 **Crookwell** Aust
109D1 **Croppa Creek** Aust
11A3 **Crossett** USA
12G3 **Cross Sd** USA
53C3 **Crotone** Italy
19B3 **Crowley** USA
17C1 **Crown Pt** Tobago
109D1 **Crows Nest** Aust
107D2 **Croydon** Aust
43D4 **Croydon** Eng
104B5 **Crozet Basin** Indian O
4F2 **Crozier Chan** Can
30F4 **Cruz Alta** Brazil
25E3 **Cruz,C** Cuba
35C2 **Cruzeiro** Arg
32C6 **Cruzeiro do Sul** Brazil
13C1 **Crysdale,Mt** Can
108A2 **Crystal Brook** Aust
18B2 **Crystal City** Missouri, USA
14A1 **Crystal Falls** USA
101C2 **Cuamba** Mozam
100B2 **Cuando** R Angola
100A2 **Cuangar** Angola
 Cuango,R = Kwango,R
34C2 **Cuarto** R Arg
24B2 **Cuauhtémoc** Mexico
23B2 **Cuautla** Mexico
25D2 **Cuba** Republic, Caribbean S
100A2 **Cubango** R Angola
100A2 **Cuchi** Angola
100A2 **Cuchi** R Angola
34C3 **Cuchillo Có** Arg
32D3 **Cucuí** Brazil
32C3 **Cúcuta** Colombia
87B2 **Cuddalore** India
87B2 **Cuddapah** India
106A3 **Cue** Aust
32B4 **Cuenca** Ecuador
51B1 **Cuenca** Spain
24C3 **Cuernavaca** Mexico
19A4 **Cuero** USA
30E2 **Cuiabá** Brazil
30E2 **Cuiabá** R Brazil
23B2 **Cuicatlan** Mexico
35C1 **Cuieté** R Brazil
44A3 **Cuillin Hills** Mts Scot
98B3 **Cuilo** R Angola
100A2 **Cuito** R Angola
100A2 **Cuito Cunavale** Angola
23A2 **Cuitzeo** Mexico
77D3 **Cu Lao Hon** / Viet
109C3 **Culcairn** Aust

109C1 **Culgoa** R Aust
24B2 **Culiacán** Mexico
62D1 **Culion** / Phil
17A1 **Cullman** USA
47A2 **Culoz** France
15C3 **Culpeper** USA
32J7 **Culpepper** / Ecuador
111B2 **Culverden** NZ
33E1 **Cumaná** Ven
10C3 **Cumberland** Maryland, USA
11B3 **Cumberland** R USA
6D3 **Cumberland Pen** Can
6D3 **Cumberland Sd** Can
42C2 **Cumbria** Eng
108A2 **Cummings** USA
42B2 **Cumnock** Scot
34A3 **Cunco** Chile
100A2 **Cunene** R Angola/ Namibia
52A2 **Cuneo** Italy
107D3 **Cunnamulla** Aust
44C3 **Cupar** Scot
54B2 **Ćuprija** Serbia, Yugos
27D4 **Curaçao** / Caribbean S
34A3 **Curacautín** Chile
34B3 **Curacó** R Arg
34A3 **Curanilahue** Chile
34A3 **Curepto** Chile
29B2 **Curicó** Chile
30G4 **Curitiba** Brazil
108A2 **Curnamona** Aust
100A2 **Curoca** R Angola
31C5 **Curvelo** Brazil
32C6 **Cusco** Peru
18A2 **Cushing** USA
13D2 **Cutbank** R Can
17B1 **Cuthbert** USA
34B3 **Cutral-Có** Arg
86B2 **Cuttack** India
100A2 **Cuvelai** Angola
56B2 **Cuxhaven** Germany
14B2 **Cuyahoga Falls** USA
79B3 **Cuyo Is** Phil
99C3 **Cyangugu** Zaire
 Cyclades = Kikládhes
13F3 **Cypress Hills** Mts Can
92B3 **Cyprus** Republic, Medit S
6D3 **Cyrus Field B** Can
59B3 **Czech Republic** Republic, Europe
59B2 **Częstochowa** Pol

D

76C1 **Da** Viet
69E2 **Da'an** China
44C3 **Dab'a** Jordan
27C4 **Dabajuro** Ven
99E2 **Dabaro** Somalia
73B3 **Daba Shan** Mts China
99D1 **Dabat** Eth
85C4 **Dabhoi** India
73C3 **Dabie Shan** Mts China
97A3 **Dabola** Guinea
97B4 **Dabou** Ivory Coast
59B2 **Dabrowa Gorn** Pol
59C3 **Dachau** Germany
52B1 **Dachstein** Mt Austria
73A3 **Dada He** R China
17B2 **Dade City** USA
84B3 **Dadhar** Pak
85B3 **Dadu** Pak
68C3 **Dadu He** R China
79B3 **Daet** Phil
73B4 **Dafang** China
76B2 **Daga** R Myan
99E2 **Dagabur** Eth
97A3 **Dagana** Sen
65F5 **Dagestanskaya Respublic,** Russian Fed
79B2 **Dagupan** Phil
92B4 **Dahab** Egypt
63E3 **Da Hinggan Ling** Mts China
17B1 **Dahlonega** USA

85C4 **Dāhod** India
86A1 **Dailekh** Nepal
34C3 **Daireaux** Arg
86A1 **Daitō Is** Pacific O
106C3 **Dajarra** Aust
97A3 **Dakar** Sen
95B2 **Dakhla Oasis** Egypt
97C3 **Dakoro** Niger
54B2 **Dakovica** Serbia, Yugos
54A1 **Dakovo** Croatia
100B2 **Dala** Angola
23B3 **Dalaba** Guinea
21D1 **Dalai Nur** L China
68C2 **Dalandzadgad** Mongolia
79B3 **Dalanggaern Is** Phil
76D3 **Da Lat** Viet
72A1 **Dalay** Mongolia
107E3 **Dalby** Aust
39F7 **Dalen** Nor
42C2 **Dales,The** Upland Eng
17A1 **Daleville** USA
9C3 **Dalhart** USA
7D5 **Dalhousie,C** Can
72E2 **Dalian** China
9D3 **Dallas** USA
20B1 **Dalles,The** USA
58C4 **Dall I** USA
86A2 **Dalli Rajhara** India
97C3 **Dallol** / Niger
97C3 **Dallol Bosso** R Niger
52C2 **Dalmatia** Region Bosnia-Herzegovina
69F2 **Dal'nerechensk** Russian Fed
97B4 **Daloa** Ivory Coast
73B4 **Dalou Shan** Mts China
86A2 **Dāltenganj** India
17B1 **Dalton** Georgia, USA
16C1 **Dalton** Massachusetts, USA
106C2 **Daly** R Aust
21A2 **Daly City** USA
106C2 **Daly Waters** Aust
79B4 **Damaguete** Phil
85C4 **Damān** India
92B3 **Damanhûr** Egypt
71D4 **Damar** / Indon
98B2 **Damara** CAR
92C3 **Damascus** Syria
14B3 **Damascus** USA
97D3 **Damaturu** Nig
90B2 **Damavand** Iran
99B3 **Damba** Angola
87C3 **Dambulla** Sri Lanka
90B2 **Damghan** Iran
85D4 **Damoh** India
99D2 **Damot** Eth
108A2 **Damour** Leb
106A3 **Dampier** Aust
94B3 **Dana** Jordan
22C2 **Dana,Mt** USA
76D2 **Da Nang** Viet
79B3 **Danao** Viet
70A3 **Danau Tobo** L Indon
71D4 **Danau Tuwuti** L Indon
73A3 **Danbu** China
15D2 **Danbury** USA
86A1 **Dandeldhura** Nepal
87A1 **Dandeli** India
108C3 **Dandenong** Aust
74A2 **Dandong** China
100A4 **Danger Pt** S Africa
99D1 **Dangila** Eth
6D1 **Danguard Jenson Land** Region Can
7E4 **Daniels Harbour** Can
6G3 **Dannebrogs Øy** / Greenland
110C2 **Dannevirke** NZ
87C1 **Dantewara** India
 Danube = Donau
10B2 **Danville** Illinois, USA
11B3 **Danville** Kentucky, USA
16A2 **Danville** Pennsylvania, USA

11C3 **Danville** Virginia, USA
 Danzig = Gdansk
73C4 **Dao Xian** China
73B4 **Daozhen** China
79B4 **Dapiak,Mt** Phil
79B4 **Dapitan** Phil
68B3 **Da Qaidam** China
69C2 **Daqing** China
94C2 **Dar'a** Syria
90B3 **Dārāb** Iran
95A1 **Daraj** Libya
92C3 **Dar'a Salkhad** Syria
86B1 **Darbhanga** India
22C1 **Dardanelle** USA
18B2 **Dardanelle,L** USA
 Dar-al-Beida = Casablanca
99D3 **Dar es Salaam** Tanz
110B1 **Dargaville** NZ
17B1 **Darien** USA
 Darjeeling = Dārjiling
86B1 **Dārjiling** India
107D4 **Darling** R Aust
109C1 **Darling Downs** Aust
6C1 **Darling Pen** Can
108B2 **Darlington** Aust
42D2 **Darlington** Eng
17C1 **Darlington** USA
57B3 **Darmstadt** Germany
95B1 **Darnah** Libya
108B2 **Darnick** Aust
47B3 **Darnley B** Can
112C10 **Darnley,C** Ant
51B1 **Daroca** Spain
98C2 **Dar Rounga** Region, CAR
43C4 **Dart** R Eng
41C3 **Dartmoor** Moorland Eng
43C4 **Dartmoor Nat Pk** Eng
7D5 **Dartmouth** Can
43C4 **Dartmouth** Eng
107D1 **Daru** PNG
52C1 **Daruvar** Croatia
106C2 **Darwin** Aust
91B4 **Daryacheh-ye Bakhtegan** L Iran
91B4 **Daryacheh-ye Mahārlū** L Iran
90B3 **Daryacheh-ye Namak** Salt Flat Iran
90D3 **Daryacheh-ye-Sistan** Salt L Iran/Afghan
91B4 **Daryacheh-ye Tashk** L Iran
80C2 **Daryacheh-ye Orümiyeh** L Iran
91C4 **Dārzin** Iran
91B4 **Das** / UAE
73C3 **Dashennonglia** Mt China
90C2 **Dasht** Iran
90B3 **Dasht-e-Kavir** Salt Desert Iran
90C3 **Dasht-e-Lut** Salt Desert Iran
90D3 **Dasht-e Naomid** Desert Region Iran
83D2 **Datia** India
72A2 **Datong** China
72C1 **Datong** China
72C1 **Datong He** R China
79B4 **Datu Piang** Phil
39K7 **Daugava** R Latvia
60C2 **Daugavpils** Latvia
6D1 **Dauguard Jensen Land** Greenland
84A1 **Daulatabad** Afghan
85B3 **Daulpur** India
46D1 **Daun** Germany
87A1 **Daund** India
5H4 **Dauphin** Can
16A2 **Dauphin** USA
49D2 **Dauphiné** Region, France
97C3 **Daura** Nig
85D3 **Dausa** India
87B2 **Dāvangere** India
79C4 **Davao** Phil
79C4 **Davao G** Phil
22A2 **Davenport** California, USA

10A2 Davenport Iowa, USA
32A2 David Panama
4D3 Davidson Mts USA
21A2 Davis USA
12C10 Davis *Base* Ant
7D4 Davis Inlet Can
6E3 Davis Str Greenland/Can
61J3 Davlekanovo Russian Fed
47C1 Davos Switz
99E2 Dawa R Eth
73A4 Dawan China
84B2 Dawat Yar Afghan
Dawei = Tavoy
91B4 Dawhat Salwah B Qatar/S Arabia
76B2 Dawna Range Mts Myan
4E3 Dawson Can
17B1 Dawson Georgia, USA
107D3 Dawson R Aust
5F4 Dawson Creek Can
12G2 Dawson Range Mts Can
73A3 Dawu China
73C3 Dawu China
83A2 Dawu China
84F4 Dax France
73B3 Daxian China
73B5 Daxin China
73A3 Daxue Shan Mts China
73A4 Dayong China
94C2 Dayr 'Ali Syria
94C1 Dayr 'Atiyah Syria
93D2 Dayr az Zawr Syria
10B3 Dayton Ohio, USA
19B4 Dayton Texas, USA
20C1 Dayton Washington, USA
14B3 Daytona Beach USA
73C4 Dayu China
73A3 Dazhu China
72D2 Da Yunhe R China
20C2 Dayville USA
73B3 Dazhu China
100B4 De Aar S Africa
26C2 Deadman's Cay The Bahamas
92C3 Dead S Israel/Jordan
46A1 Deal Eng
101G1 Dealesville S Africa
13B2 Dean R Can
13B2 Dean Chan Can
34C2 Dean Funes Arg
4F3 Dease Arm B Can
4E4 Dease Lake Can
8E4 Death V USA
48C2 Deauville France
97B4 Debakala Ivory Coast
12B2 Debauch Mt USA
27L1 Débé Trinidad
59C2 Debica Pol
58C2 Deblin Pol
97B3 Débo,L Mali
59C3 Debrecen Hung
99D2 Debre Birhan Eth
99D1 Debre Markos Eth
99D1 Debre Tabor Eth
11B3 Decatur Alabama, USA
17B1 Decatur Georgia, USA
10B3 Decatur Illinois, USA
14B2 Decatur Indiana, USA
48C3 Decazeville France
73A4 Dechang China
87B3 Dédougou Burkina
101C2 Dedza Malawi
42B2 Dee R Dumfries and Galloway, Scot
42C3 Dee R Eng/Wales
44C3 Dee R Grampian, Scot
15C1 Deep River Can
16C2 Deep River USA
109D1 Deepwater Aust
7E5 Deer Lake Can
8B2 Deer Lodge USA

34D3 Defferrari Arg
17A1 De Funiak Springs USA
68B3 Dégé China
99E1 Degeh Bur Eth
106A3 De Grey R Aust
91B3 Deh Bid Iran
84B1 Dehi Afghan
96D1 Dehibat Tunisia
87B3 Dehiwala-Mt Lavinia Sri Lanka
90A3 Dehlorán Iran
84D2 Dehra Dún India
86A2 Dehri India
98C2 Deim Zubeir Sudan
94B2 Deir Abu Sa'id Jordan
94C1 Deir el Ahmar Leb
60B4 Dej Rom
19B3 De Kalb Texas, USA
63G2 De Kastri Russian Fed
98C3 Dekese Zaire
98B2 Dekoa CAR
106B1 Dekusi Indon
5J3 Delano USA
10C3 Delaware State, USA
14B2 Delaware R USA
15C2 Delaware R USA
109C3 Delegate Aust
47B1 Delemont Switz
101D2 Delgado C Mozam
84D3 Delhi India
15D2 Delhi New York, USA
92B2 Delice Turk
24B2 Delicias Mexico
90B3 Delijan Iran
47B1 Delle France
22D4 Del Mar USA
39F8 Delmenhorst Germany
4B3 De Long Mts USA
109C4 Deloraine Aust
5H5 Deloraine Can
13C3 Delray Beach USA
9C4 Del Rio USA
8D2 Delta USA
12E2 Delta R USA
12E2 Delta Junction USA
99D2 Dembi Dolo Eth
46C1 Demer R Belg
9C3 Deming USA
92A2 Demirköy Turk
49C1 Denain France
82A2 Denau Uzbekistan
42C3 Denbigh Wales
12B2 Denbigh,C USA
78B3 Dendang Indon
46C1 Dendermond Belg
99D2 Dendi Mt Eth
46B1 Dendre R Belg
72B1 Dengkou China
72C3 Deng Xian China
Den Haag = 's-Gravenhage
27H1 Denham,Mt Jamaica
56A2 Den Helder Neth
51C2 Denia Spain
107D4 Deniliquin Aust
20C2 Denio USA
9D3 Denison Texas, USA
12D3 Denison,Mt USA
92A2 Denizli Turk
Denmark Kingdom, Europe
1C1 Denmark Str Greenland/Iceland
27P2 Dennery St Lucia
78D4 Denpasar Indon
16B3 Denton Maryland, USA
9D3 Denton Texas, USA
107E1 D'Entrecasteaux Is PNG
47B1 Dents du Midi Mt Switz
8C3 Denver USA
98B2 Déo R Cam
86B2 Deoghar India
85B4 Deolali India
84D1 Deosai Plain India

95B3 Dépression du Mourdi Chad
19B3 De Queen USA
84C3 Dera Pak
84B3 Dera Bugti Pak
84C2 Dera Ismail Khan Pak
106B2 Derby Aust
16C2 Derby Connecticut, USA
43D3 Derby County, Eng
43D3 Derby Eng
18A2 Derby Kansas, USA
60E3 Dergachi Ukraine
19B3 De Ridder USA
Derna = Darnah
95C3 Derudeb Sudan
109C4 Derwent Bridge Aust
34B2 Desaguadero R Arg
34B2 Desaguadero R Arg
30C2 Desaguadero R Bol
21B3 Descanso Mexico
20B2 Deschutes R USA
99D1 Desê Eth
29C5 Deseado Arg
29C5 Deseado R Arg
96A1 Deserta Grande I Medeira
34C3 Desierto de Atacama Desert Chile
18B2 Desloge USA
10A2 Des Moines Iowa, USA
60D3 Desna R Russian Fed
29B6 Desolación I Chile
14A2 Des Plaines USA
56C2 Dessau Germany
12G2 Destruction Bay Can
46A1 Desvres France
64A1 Deta Rom
100B2 Dete Zim
10D2 Detroit USA
76D3 Det Udom Thai
54B4 Deva Rom
56B2 Deventer Neth
44C3 Deveron R Scot
85C3 Devikot India
22C2 Devil Postpile Nat Mon USA
22C1 Devils Gate P USA
Devil's Island = Isla du Diable
8D2 Devils Lake USA
12H3 Devils Paw Mt Can
85C4 Devizes Eng
85D3 Devli India
85B2 Devoll R Alb
43B4 Devon County, Eng
6A2 Devon I Can
107D5 Devonport Aust
86C1 Dewangiri Bhutan
101C1 Dewetsdorp S Africa
11B3 Dewey Res USA
19B3 De Witt USA
18C2 Dexter Missouri, USA
73A3 Deyang China
90C3 Deyhuk Iran
90C2 Dezfül Iran
72D2 Dezhou China
90A2 Deh Shāhpūr Iran
91B4 Dhahran S Arabia
86C2 Dhākā Bang
85B4 Dhamavaram India
84B2 Dhamtari India
85D4 Dhanbād India
86A1 Dhangarhi Nepal
86B1 Dhankuta Nepal
85D4 Dharmapuri India
84D2 Dharmsala India
91B4 Dhar Oualata Desert Region Maur
86A1 Dhaulagiri Mt Nepal
86B2 Dhenkānāi India
94B3 Dhibah Jordan
85C3 Dhidhi Ori Mt Greece
55C3 Dhodhekánisos Is Greece
55B3 Dhomokós Greece
87B1 Dhone India

85C4 Dhoraji India
85C4 Dhrāngadhra India
86B1 Dhuburi India
85C4 Dhule India
2282 Diablo,Mt USA
21A2 Diablo Range Mts USA
34B2 Diamante Arg
34B2 Diamante R Arg
31C5 Diamantina Brazil
107D3 Diamantina R Aust
86B2 Diamond Harbours India
22B1 Diamond Springs USA
91C4 Dibā UAE
98C3 Dibaya Zaire
86C1 Dibrugarh India
8C2 Dickinson USA
13E3 Dickson City USA
13E2 Didsbury Can
85C3 Didwāna India
97B3 Diebougou Burkina
46D2 Diekirch Lux
91B3 Diema Mali
76C1 Dien Bien Phu Viet
56B2 Diepholz Germany
48C2 Dieppe France
46C1 Diest Belg
46D2 Dieuze France
7D5 Digby Can
49D3 Digne-les-Bains France
49C2 Digoin France
79C4 Digos Phil
71E4 Digul R Indon
86C1 Dihang R India
Dijlah = Tigris
49C2 Dijon France
98A2 Dik Chad
99E1 Dikhil Djibouti
46B1 Diksmuide Belg
1BI0 Dikson Russian Fed
82A2 Dilaram Afghan
71E4 Dili Indon
76D3 Di Linh Viet
46E1 Dillenburg Germany
99C1 Dilling Sudan
12C3 Dillingham USA
8B2 Dillon USA
16A2 Dillsburg USA
98C3 Dilolo Zaire
Dimashq = Damascus
98C3 Dimbelenge Zaire
97B4 Dimbokro Ivory Coast
54C2 Dimitrovgrad Bulg
61G3 Dimitrovgrad Russian Fed
33A6 Dimona Israel
86C1 Dinajpur India
76D3 Dinagat I Phil
86B1 Dinajpur India
48B2 Dinan France
46C1 Dinant Belg
92B2 Dinar Turk
99D1 Dinder R Sudan
87B2 Dindigul India
72B2 Dingbian China
86B1 Dinggyê China
41A3 Dingle Irish Rep
41A3 Dingle B Irish Rep
97A3 Dinguiraye Guinea
44B3 Dingwall Scot
72A2 Dingxi China
72D2 Ding Xian China
76C1 Dinh Lap Viet
22C2 Dinuba USA
97A3 Dioulouloulou Sen
86C1 Diphu India
99E2 Diré Dawa Eth
106A3 Dirk Hartog I Aust
95A3 Dirkou Niger
109C1 Dirranbandi Aust
96B2 Dirri Somalia
29G8 Disappointment,C South Georgia
20B1 Disappointment,C USA
106B3 Disappointment,L Aust
108B3 Discovery B Aust

Discovery Tablemount

103J7 Discovery
Tablemount
Atlantic O
47C1 Disentis Muster
Switz
6E3 Disko Greenland
6E3 Disko Bugt B
Greenland
6E3 Diskojord Greenland
58D1 Disna R Belarus
35B1 Distrito Federal
Federal District, Brazil
85C4 Diu India
79C4 Diuat Mts Phil
31C6 Divinópolis Brazil
61F4 Divnoye Russian Fed
93C2 Divriği Turk
22B1 Dixon California,
USA
5E4 Dixon Entrance Sd
Can/USA
13D1 Dixonville Can
93E3 Diyālá R Iraq
65F6 Diyarbakir Turk
9A3 Diz R Iran
98B2 Dja R Cam
96C1 Djadi R Alg
95A2 Djado,Plat du Niger
98B3 Djambala Congo
96C2 Djanet Alg
50A2 Djebel Bouhalla Mt
Mor
96C1 Djelfa Alg
29B3 Djéma CAR
97B3 Djenné Mali
97B3 Djibo Burkina
99E1 Djibouti Djibouti
99E1 Djibouti Republic, E
Africa
98C2 Djolu Zaire
97C4 Djougou Benin
99D2 Djugu Zaire
38C2 Djúpivogur Iceland
51C2 Djurdjura Mts Alg
60E2 Dmitrov Russian Fed
Dnepr = Dnieper
60D4 Dneprodzerzhinsk
Ukraine
60E4 Dnepropetrovsk
Ukraine
60C3 Dneprovskaya
Nizmennost' Region,
Belarus
Dnestr = Dniester
60D4 Dnieper R Ukraine
60B4 Dniester R Ukraine
60D2 Dno Russian Fed
98B2 Doba Chad
58C1 Dobele Latvia
34C3 Doblas Arg
71E4 Dobo Indon
54A2 Doboj Bosnia-
Herzegovina
54B2 Dobreta-Turnu-
Severin Rom
54C2 Dobrich Bulg
60D3 Dobrush Belarus
31C5 Doce R Brazil
30D3 Doctor R P Peña Arg
87B2 Dod India
87B2 Doda Betta Mt India
Dodecanese =
Sporádhes
9C3 Dodge City USA
95C3 Dodoma Tanz
75A1 Dōgo I Japan
97C3 Dogondoutchi Niger
93D2 Doğubayazit Turk
91B4 Doha Qatar
7C5 Dolbeau Can
49D2 Dôle France
43C3 Dolgellau Wales
47D1 Dolomitiche Mts Italy
99E2 Dolo Odo Eth
29E3 Dolores Arg
34D2 Dolores Urug
23A1 Dolores Hidalgo
Mexico
4G3 Dolphin and Union
Str Can
29E6 Dolphin,C Falkland Is
71E4 Dom Mt Indon
65G4 Dombarovskiy
Russian Fed

38F6 Dombas Nor
46D2 Dombasle-sur-
Meurthe France
54A1 Dombóvár Hung
48B2 Domfront France
27E3 Dominica I,
Caribbean S
27C3 Dominican Republic
Caribbean S
6C3 Dominion,C Can
7E4 Domino Can
68D1 Domna Russian Fed
52A1 Domodossola Italy
78D4 Dompu Indon
29B3 Domuyo Mt Arg
109D1 Domville,Mt Aust
9C4 Don R Scot
61F4 Don R Russian Fed
45C1 Donaghadee N Ire
57C3 Donau R Germany
57C3 Donauwörth
Germany
50A2 Don Benito Spain
42D3 Doncaster Eng
98B3 Dondo Angola
101C2 Dondo Mozam
87C3 Dondra Head C
Sri Lanka
45B1 Donegal County,
Irish Rep
40B3 Donegal Irish Rep
40B3 Donegal B Irish Rep
45B1 Donegal Mts
Irish Rep
60E4 Donetsk Ukraine
73C4 Dong'an China
106A3 Dongara Aust
73A4 Dongchuan China
72D2 Dongfang China
74B2 Dongfeng China
70C4 Donggala Indon
68B3 Donggi Cona L
China
74A3 Donggou China
73C5 Donghai Dao I China
72A1 Dong He R China
76D2 Dong Hoi Viet
73C5 Dong Jiang R China
95C3 Dongola Sudan
73D5 Dongshan China
68D4 Dongsha Qundao I
China
72C2 Dongsheng China
72E3 Dongtai China
73C4 Dongting Hu L China
73B5 Dongxing China
73D3 Dongzhi China
18B2 Doniphan USA
52C2 Donji Vakuf Bosnia-
Herzegovina
38G5 Dönna I Nor
21A2 Donner P USA
46D2 Donnersberg Mt
Germany
101G1 Donnybrook S Africa
Donostia = San
Sebastian
22B2 Don Pedro Res USA
12D1 Doonerak,Mt USA
79B4 Dopolong Phil
73A3 Do Qu R China
47B2 Dora Baltea R Italy
49D2 Dorbirn Austria
43C4 Dorchester Eng
6C3 Dorchester,C Can
48C2 Dordogne R France
56A2 Dordrecht Neth
13F2 Dore L Can
13F2 Dore Lake Can
97B3 Dori Burkina
46B2 Dormans France
57B3 Dornbirn Austria
44B3 Dornoch Scot
44B3 Dornoch Firth
Estuary Scot
38H6 Dorotea Sweden
109D2 Dorrigo Aust
20D2 Dorris USA
43C4 Dorset County, Eng
46D1 Dorsten Germany
56B2 Dortmund Germany
98C2 Doruma Zaire
63D2 Dosatuy Russian Fed
84B1 Doshi Afghan

22B2 Dos Palos USA
97C3 Dosso Niger
65G5 Dossor Kazakhstan
11B3 Dothan USA
49C1 Douai France
98A2 Douala Cam
109D1 Double Island Pt
Aust
49D2 Doubs R France
111A3 Doubtful Sd NZ
97B3 Douentza Mali
9C3 Douglas Arizona,
USA
42B2 Douglas Eng
17B1 Douglas Georgia,
USA
8C2 Douglas Wyoming,
USA
12A1 Douglas,C USA
13B2 Douglas Chan Can
12D3 Douglas,Mt USA
45C1 Doullens France
45C1 Doun County, N Ire
30F3 Dourados Brazil
50A1 Douro R Port
50C2 Dover Delaware,
USA
43E4 Dover Eng
16B2 Dover New
Hampshire, USA
16B2 Dover New Jersey,
USA
14B2 Dover Ohio, USA
43D3 Dover R Eng
41D3 Dover,Str of UK/
France
16B3 Downington USA
42B2 Downpatrick N Ire
16B2 Doylestown USA
75A1 Dōzen I Japan
96A2 Dr'aa R Mor
35A2 Dracena Brazil
16D1 Dracut USA
49D3 Draguignan France
101C3 Drakensberg Mts
S Africa
101G1 Drakensberg Mt
S Africa
103E7 Drake Pass Pacific/
Atlantic O
55B2 Dráma Greece
39G7 Drammen Nor
38A1 Drangajökull Iceland
52C1 Drava R Slovenia
13D2 Drayton Valley Can
49D2 Dreaux France
57C2 Dresden Germany
48C2 Dreux France
20C2 Drewsey USA
54B2 Drin R Alb
54A2 Drina R Bosnia-
Herzegovina/Serbia
58D1 Drissa R Belarus
45C2 Drogheda Irish Rep
59C3 Drogobych Ukraine
112B12 Dronning Maud Land
Region, Ant
30D3 Dr P.P. Pená Par
50A4 Drumheller Can
14B1 Drummond I USA
15D1 Drummondville Can
58C2 Druskininksi
Lithuania
12G3 Dry B USA
7A5 Dryden Can
27H1 Dry Harbour Mts
Jamaica
91C4 Dubai UAE
5H3 Dubawnt R Can
4H3 Dubawnt L Can
107D4 Dubbo Aust
45C2 Dublin County,
Irish Rep
45C2 Dublin Irish Rep
17B1 Dublin USA
60E2 Dubna Russian Fed
60D3 Dubno Ukraine
15C2 Du Bois USA
13B2 Dubose,Mt Can
58D2 Dubrovica Ukraine
54A2 Dubrovnik Croatia
10A2 Dubuque USA

46D2 Dudelange Lux
1C10 Dudinka Russian Fed
93C2 Düğ Turk
97B4 Duekoue Ivory Coast
50B1 Duero R Spain
44C3 Dufftown Scot
52B2 Dugi Otok I Croatia
56B2 Duisburg Germany
93E3 Dukan Iraq
99D2 Duk Faiwil Sudan
91B4 Dukhān Qatar
73A4 Dukou China
68B3 Dulan China
34C2 Dulce R Arg
78C2 Dulit Range Mts
Malay
62C2 Dullabchara India
10A2 Duluth USA
79A3 Dumaran I Phil
9C3 Dumas USA
94C2 Dumayr Syria
42B2 Dumbarton Scot
42C2 Dumfries Scot
42B2 Dumfries and
Galloway Region,
Scot
86B2 Dumka India
15C1 Dumoine,L Can
112C8 Dumont d'Urville
Base Ant
55C3 Dumyat Egypt
54C2 Dunărea R Rom
45C2 Dunany Head Pt
Irish Rep
58B2 Dunav R Bulg
59D3 Dunayevtsy Ukraine
14C3 Duncan Can
64C2 Duncannon USA
44C2 Duncansby Head Pt
Scot
45C1 Dundalk Irish Rep
16A3 Dundalk USA
45C2 Dundalk B Irish Rep
6D2 Dundas Greenland
4G2 Dundas Pen Can
71E5 Dundas Str Aust
101H1 Dundee S Africa
44C3 Dundee Scot
108B1 Dundoo Aust
42C2 Dundrum B N Ire
86B1 Dunedin NZ
17B2 Dunedin USA
110B3 Dunedoo Aust
44C3 Dunfermline Scot
45C2 Dungarvan Irish Rep
45C2 Dungarvan Irish Rep
43E4 Dungeness Eng
109D2 Dungog Aust
99C2 Dungu Zaire
99C2 Dungunab Sudan
68B2 Dunhuang China
46B1 Dunkerque France
10C2 Dunkirk USA
99D1 Dunkur Eth
97B4 Dunkwa Ghana
41B3 Dun Laoghaire
Irish Rep
26B1 Dunmore Town
The Bahamas
44C2 Dunnet Head Pt Scot
11C2 Dunn USA
20B2 Dunsmuir USA
111A2 Dunstan Mts NZ
46C2 Dun-sur-Meuse
France
72D1 Duolun China
18C2 Du Quoin USA
94B3 Dura Israel
49D3 Durance R France
23B2 Durango Mexico
50B1 Durango Spain
9C3 Durango USA
29E2 Durano Urug
101H1 Durban S Africa
94C1 Duraykīsh Syria
101H1 Durban S Africa
86A2 Durg India
88B2 Durgapur India
42D2 Durham County, Eng

42D2 Durham Eng
11C3 Durham N Carolina, USA
16D1 Durham New Hampshire, USA
43B3 Durham Downs Aust
54A2 Durmitor Mt Montenegro, Yugos
44B2 Durness Scot
55A2 Durrës Alb
108B1 Durrow Irish Rep
45A3 Dursey I Irish Rep
55C3 Dursunbey Turk
110B2 D'Urville I NZ
90D2 Dushak Turkmenistan
73A4 Dushan China
82A2 Dushanbe Tajikistan
111A3 Dusky Sd NZ
56B2 Düsseldorf Germany
73A4 Duyun China
92B1 Düzce Turk
60C2 Dvina R Latvia
85B4 Dwärka India
6D3 Dyer,C Can
11B3 Dyersburg USA
43B3 Dyfed County, Wales
61F5 Dykh Tau Mt Russian Fed
108B1 Dynevor Downs Aust
62B2 Dzag Mongolia
63C3 Dzamin Uüd Mongolia
101D2 Dzaoudzi Mayotte
68C2 Dzarnin Uüd Mongolia
62B2 Dzavhan Gol R Mongolia
80E1 Dzhezkazgan Kazakhstan
61F2 Dzerzhinsk Russian Fed
63E2 Dzhalinda Russian Fed
65J5 Dzhambul Kazakhstan
60D4 Dzhankov Ukraine
65H4 Dzhezkazgan Kazakhstan
84B1 Dzhilikul' Tajikistan
63J3 Dzhungarskiy Alatau Mts Kazakhstan
59B2 Dzierzoniow Pol
63B3 Dzüyl Mongolia
82C1 Dzungaria Basin, China

E

7B4 Eabamet L Can
12F2 Eagle Alaska, USA
20B2 Eagle L California, USA
19A3 Eagle Mountain L USA
9C4 Eagle Pass USA
4E3 Eagle Plain Can
8B3 Eagle River USA
21B2 Earlimart USA
17B1 Easley USA
15C2 East Aurora USA
43E4 Eastbourne Eng
14A2 East Chicago USA
69E3 East China Sea China/Japan
100B4 Eastern Cape Province, S Africa
87B2 Eastern Ghats Mts India
100B3 Eastern Transvaal Province, S Africa
29E6 East Falkland I Falkland Is
12E1 East Fork R USA
21B2 Eastgate USA
16C1 Easthampton USA
16C2 East Hampton USA
14A2 East Lake USA
108B2 East Liverpool USA
100B4 East London S Africa
7C4 Eastmain Can
7C4 Eastmain R Can
17B1 Eastman USA
15C3 Easton Maryland, USA

15C2 Easton Pennsylvania, USA
16B2 East Orange USA
105L4 East Pacific Ridge Pacific O
17B1 East Point USA
11A3 East St Louis USA
1B7 East Siberian S Russian Fed
43E4 East Sussex County, Eng
17B1 Eatonton USA
10A2 Eau Claire USA
71F3 Eauripik I Pacific O
23B1 Ebano Mexico
98B2 Ebebiyin Eq Guinea
56C2 Eberswalde Germ
73A4 Ebian China
65K5 Ebinur L China
53C2 Eboli Italy
98B2 Ebolowa Cam
51B1 Ebro R Spain
92A1 Eceabat Turk
96C1 Ech Cheliff Alg
53C2 Eching China
20C1 Echo USA
4G3 Echo Bay Can
46D2 Echternach Lux
50A2 Écija Spain
68Z Eclipse Sd Can
32B4 Ecuador Republic, S America
99E1 Ed Eritrea
44C2 Eday I Scot
98C1 Ed Da'ein Sudan
99D1 Ed Damer Sudan
99D1 Ed Debba Sudan
44B2 Eddrachillis B Scot
99D1 Ed Dueim Sudan
109C4 Eddystone Pt Aust
98A2 Edea Cam
109C3 Eden Aust
42C2 Eden R Eng
101G1 Edenburg S Africa
111A3 Edendale NZ
46E2 Edenkoben Germany
46E1 Eder R Germany
6D3 Edgell I Can
62A1 Edgeeya I Barents S
16A3 Edgewood USA
94B3 Edh Dhahiriya Israel
56C2 Edhessa Greece
44C3 Edinburgh Scot
60C5 Edirne Turk
17B1 Edisto R USA
13D2 Edith Cavell,Mt Can
20B1 Edmonds USA
5G4 Edmonton Can
7D5 Edmundston Can
19A4 Edna USA
12H3 Edna Bay USA
52B1 Edolo Italy
94B3 Edom Region, Jordan
92A2 Edremit Turk
92A2 Edremit Körfezi B Turk
68B2 Edrengiyn Nuruu Mts Mongolia
5G4 Edson Can
34C3 Eduardo Castex Arg
12J2 Eduni,Mt Can
108B3 Edward R Aust
99C3 Edward,L Uganda/Zaire
108A1 Edwards Creek Aust
9C3 Edwards Plat USA
18C2 Edwardsville USA
12H3 Edziza,Mt Can
12B2 Eek USA
46B1 Eeklo Belg
10B3 Effingham USA
6E3 Egedesminde Greenland
22C3 Egegik USA
59C3 Eger Hung
39F7 Egersund Nor
16B3 Egg Harbor City USA
4G2 Eglinton I Can
110B1 Egmont,C NZ
92B2 Egridir Gölü L Turk

95B2 Egypt Republic, Africa
51B1 Eibar Spain
49C2 Eibeuf France
46D1 Eifel Region, Germ
44A3 Eigg I Scot
83B5 Eight Degree Chan Indian O
106B2 Eighty Mile Beach Aust
108C3 Eildon,L Aust
56B2 Eindhoven Neth
47C1 Einsiedeln Switz
94B3 Ein Yahav Israel
57C2 Eisenach Germany
57C3 Eisenerz Austria
46D1 Eitorf Germany
72A1 Ejin qi China
23B2 Ejutla Mexico
110C2 Eketahuna NZ
65J4 Ekibastuz Kazakhstan
63F2 Ekimchan Russian Fed
95A3 Ek Mahalla el Kubra Egypt
39H7 Eksjo Sweden
10B1 Ekwen R Can
92A3 El'Alamein Egypt
92B3 El'Arish Egypt
94B3 Elat Israel
94C1 El Bega'a R Leb
14A2 Elberta USA
8C3 Elbert,Mt USA
17B1 Elberton USA
92C2 Elbistan Turk
58B2 Elblag Pol
29B4 El Bolson Arg
61F5 Elbrus Mt Russian Fed
Elburz Mts = Reshteh-ye Alborz
21B3 El Cajon USA
19A4 El Campo USA
51B2 Elche Spain
51B2 Elda Spain
32B3 El Diviso Colombia
96B2 El Djouf Desert Region Maur
7B5 Eldon USA
18B1 El Dorado Arkansas, USA
35B2 Eldorado Brazil
9D3 El Dorado Kansas, USA
24B2 El Dorado Mexico
33E2 El Dorado Ven
99D2 Eldoret Kenya
22C1 Eleanor,L USA
96B2 El Eglab Region, Alg
50B1 El Escorial Spain
99D3 Eleskirt Turk
11C4 Eleuthera I The Bahamas
95A3 El Faiyûm Egypt
96B2 El Farsia Well Mor
98C1 El Fasher Sudan
92B4 El Fashn Egypt
50A1 El Ferrol del Caudillo Spain
99C1 El Fula Sudan
96C1 El Gassi Alg
99D1 El Geteina Sudan
99D1 El Gezira Region, Sudan
94B3 El Ghor V Israel/Jordan
10B2 Elgin Illinois, USA
44C3 Elgin Scot
92B3 El Giza Egypt
96C1 El Golea Alg
99D2 Elgon,Mt Uganda/Kenya
99E2 El Goran Eth
23B2 El Grullo Mexico

96B2 El Guettara Well Mali
96B1 El Haricha Desert Region Mali
92A4 El Harra Egypt
51C2 El Harrach Alg
99D1 El Hawata Sudan
23B1 El Higo Mexico
34A3 El Huecu Arg
92B4 El Igma Desert Region Egypt
12B2 Elim USA
4H2 Elira,C Can
Elisabethville = Lubumbashi
39K6 Elisenvaara Fin
El Iskandariya = Alexandria
61F4 Elista Russian Fed
106C4 Elizabeth Aust
15D2 Elizabeth USA
11C3 Elizabeth City USA
17C1 Elizabethtown N Carolina, USA
16A2 Elizabethtown Pennsylvania,USA
96B1 El Jadida Mor
92C3 El Jafr Jordan
99D1 El Jebelein Sudan
96D1 El Jem Tunisia
58C2 Elk Pol
16B3 Elk R Maryland, USA
14B3 Elk R W Virginia, USA
95C3 El Kamlin Sudan
22B1 Elk Grove USA
El Khalil = Hebron
80B3 El Khárga Egypt
80B3 El-Khârga Oasis Egypt
14A2 Elkhart USA
96B2 El Khenachich Desert Region Mali
54C2 Elkhovo Bulg
14C3 Elkins USA
8B2 Elko USA
16B3 Elkton USA
92B3 El Kuntilla Egypt
99C1 El Lagowa Sudan
4H2 Ellef Ringnes I Can
8A2 Ellensburg USA
110B1 Ellenville USA
6B2 Ellesmere I Can
111B2 Ellesmere,L NZ
16A3 Ellicott City USA
100B4 Elliot S Africa
7B5 Elliot Lake Can
94B3 El Lisan Pen Jordan
112B3 Ellsworth Land Region Ant
95B1 El Maghra L Egypt
92B3 El Mansûra Egypt
16B3 Elmer USA
96B3 El Merelé Desert Region Maur
34B2 El Milagro Arg
94B1 El Mina Leb
92B4 El Minya Egypt
22B1 Elmira California, USA
10C2 Elmira New York, USA
96B2 El Mreitl Well Maur
56B2 Elmshorn Germany
98B2 El Muglad Sudan
96B2 El Mzereb Well Mali
79A3 El Nido Phil
99D1 El Obeid Sudan
23B2 El Oro Mexico
96C1 El Oued Alg
21A2 El Palmito Mexico
22C2 El Portal USA
50A2 El Puerto del Sta Maria Spain
El Qâhira = Cairo
El Quds = Jerusalem
94B3 El Quseima Egypt
9D3 El Reno USA
4E3 Elsa Can
25D3 El Salvador Republic, Cent America
22D4 Elsinore L USA
34B3 El Sosneade Arg

Elsterwerde

57C2 Elsterwerde Germany
El Suweis = Suez
50A1 El Teleno Mt Spain
110B1 Eltham NZ
33E2 El Tigre Ven
92B4 El Tih Desert Region Egypt
34C2 El Tio Arg
20C1 Eltopia USA
92B4 El Tûr Egypt
109C1 Eluru India
50A2 Elvas Port
32C5 Elvira Brazil
34A2 El Volcán Chile
14A2 Elwood USA
43E3 Ely Eng
10A2 Ely Minnesota, USA
8B3 Ely Nevada, USA
14B2 Elyria USA
90B2 Emāmrūd Iran
84B1 Emām Sāheb Afghan
58B1 Eman R Sweden
61J4 Emba Kazakhstan
61A4 Emba R Kazakhstan
29C3 Embalse Cerros Colorados L Arg
51B2 Embalse de Alarcón Res Spain
50A2 Embalse de Alcántara Res Spain
50A1 Embalse de Almendra Res Spain
50A2 Embalse de Garcia de Sola Res Spain
33E2 Embalse de Guri L Ven
51B1 Embalse de Mequinenza Res Spain
50A1 Embalse de Ricobayo Res Spain
29E2 Embalse de Rio Negro Res Urug
29C3 Embalse El Chocón L Arg
29C4 Embalse Florentine Ameghino L Arg
50A1 Embalse Gabriel y Galan Res Spain
30D3 Embarcación Arg
5G4 Embarras Portage Can
47B2 Embrun France
99D3 Embu Kenya
56B2 Emden Germany
73A4 Emei China
107D3 Emerald Aust
7D4 Emeri Can
5J5 Emerson Can
21B1 Emigrant P USA
95A3 Emi Koussi Mt Chad
34B3 Emilo Mitre Arg
92B2 Emirdağ Turk
16B2 Emmaus USA
56B2 Emmen Neth
20C2 Emmett USA
16A3 Emmitsburg USA
12C2 Emmonak USA
9C4 Emory Peak Mt USA
24A2 Empalme Mexico
101H1 Empangeni S Africa
30E4 Empedrado Arg
105G1 Emperor Seamount Chain Pacific O
18A2 Emporia Kansas, USA
56B2 Ems R Germany
44B2 Enard B Scot
23A1 Encarnacion Mexico
30E4 Encarnación Par
97B4 Enchi Ghana
22D4 Encinitas USA
35C1 Encruzilhada Brazil
106B1 Endeh Indon
13D2 Enderby Can
112C11 Enderby Land Ant
15C2 Endicott USA
12D1 Endicott Mts USA
47D1 Engadin Mts Switz
79B2 Engaño,C Phil
94B3 En Gedi Israel

47C1 Engelberg Switz
78A4 Enggano I Indon
41C3 England Country, UK
7E4 Englee Can
41C3 English Channel Eng/France
97B3 Enji Well Maur
39H7 Enköping Sweden
53B3 Enna Italy
99C1 En Nahud Sudan
95B3 Ennedi Region Chad
109C1 Enngonia Aust
41B3 Ennis Irish Rep
19A3 Ennis Texas, USA
45C2 Enniscorthy Irish Rep
45C1 Enniskillen N Ire
45B2 Ennistimon Irish Rep
94B2 Enn Nâqoûra Leb
57C3 Enns R Austria
39F8 Enschede Neth
24A1 Ensenada Mexico
73B3 Enshi China
99D2 Entebbe Uganda
17A1 Enterprise Alabama, USA
20C1 Enterprise Oregon, USA
97C4 Enugu Nig
51B2 Enzan Japan
49C2 Epernay France
14B1 Ephrata Pennsylvania, USA
20C1 Ephrata Washington, USA
49D2 Epinal France
46A2 Epte R France
100A3 Epukiro Namibia
91B4 Epu pel Arg
90B3 Eqlid Iran
89D7 Equator
98A2 Equatorial Guinea Republic, Africa
47C2 Erba Italy
46D2 Erbeskopf Mt Germany
34A3 Ercilla Chile
93D2 Erciş Turk
92C2 Erciyas Daglari Mt Turk
74B2 Erdaobaihe China
72C1 Erdene Mongolia
62C1 Erdenet Mongolia
95B3 Erdi Region Chad
30F4 Erechim Brazil
92B1 Ereğli Turk
92B2 Ereğli Turk
68D2 Erenhot China
50B1 Eresma R Spain
46D1 Erft R Germany
57C2 Erfurt Germany
92B2 Ergani Turk
96B2 Erg Chech Desert Region Alg
95A3 Erg du Djourab Desert Chad
97D3 Erg Du Ténéré Desert Region Niger
92A1 Ergene R Turk
96B2 Erg Iguidi Region Alg
58D1 Ēgli Latvia
98B1 Erguig R Chad
68D1 Ergun' R China/Russian Fed
63E2 Erguo Zuoqi China
95C3 Eriba Sudan
10C2 Erie USA
10B2 Erie,L Can/USA
44A3 Eriskay I Scot
99D1 Eritrea Republic,Africa
46D1 Erkelenz Germany
57C3 Erlangen Germany
1983 Erling,L USA
101G1 Ermelo S Africa
87B3 Ernakulam India
87B2 Erode India
108B1 Eromanga Aust
96B1 Er Rachidia Mor
99D1 Er Rahad Sudan
101C2 Errego Mozam
40B2 Errigal Mt Irish Rep
41A3 Erris Head Pt Irish Rep

99D1 Er Roseires Sudan
94B2 Er Rummân Jordan
57C2 Erzgebirge Upland Germany
93C2 Erzincan Turk
65F6 Erzurum Turk
48C3 Esara R Spain
56B1 Esbjerg Den
21D3 Escalante USA
10B2 Escanaba USA
25C3 Escárcega Mexico
46C2 Esch Lux
21B3 Escondido USA
25C2 Escuinapa Mexico
25C3 Escuintla Guatemala
98B2 Eséka Cam
51C1 Esera R Spain
90B3 Eşfahān Iran
101H1 Eshowe S Africa
110C1 Eskdale NZ
38C1 Eskifjörður Iceland
39H7 Eskilstuna Sweden
4E3 Eskimo L Can
7A3 Eskimo Point Can
92D2 Eskişehir Turk
50A1 Esla R Spain
29A5 Esmeralda I Chile
32B3 Esmeraldas Ecuador
26B2 Esmeralda Cuba
14B1 Espanola USA
32J7 Española I Ecuador
106B4 Esperance Aust
9B2 Esperanza Arg
112C2 Esperanza Base Ant
35C1 Espírito Santo State, Brazil
101C3 Espungabera Mozam
29B4 Esquel Arg
20B1 Esquimalt Can
34D2 Esquina Arg
94C2 Es Samra Jordan
96B1 Essaouira Mor
96A2 Es Semara Mor
56B2 Essen Germany
33F3 Essequibo R Guyana
43E4 Essex County, Eng
14B2 Essexville USA
57B3 Esslingen Germany
46B2 Essonne France
31D4 Estância Brazil
100A4 Estcourt S Africa
47D2 Este Italy
46B2 Esternay France
30D3 Esteros Par
17B1 Estill USA
60B2 Estonia Republic, Europe
29B6 Estrecho de Magallanes Str Chile
50A2 Estremoz Port
59B3 Esztergom Hung
108A1 Etadunna Aust
47C2 Etam France
48C2 Etampes France
108A1 Etamunbame,L Aust
46A1 Etaples France
85D3 Etāwah India
99D2 Ethiopia Republic, Africa
23B2 Etla Mexico
53B3 Etna Mt Italy
21C3 Etolin I USA
12A2 Etolin Str Can
6C2 Eton Can
100A2 Etosha Nat Pk Namibia
100A2 Etosha Pan Salt L Namibia
17B1 Etowah R USA
46D2 Ettelbruck Lux
100C2 Euabalong Aust
14B2 Euclid USA
109C3 Eucumbene,L Aust
108A2 Eudunda Aust
19A2 Eufala L USA
17A1 Eufaula USA
8A2 Eugene USA
108C1 Eulo Aust
19B3 Eunice Louisiana, USA
46D1 Eupen Germany
93D3 Euphrates R Iraq

19C3 Eupora USA
48C2 Eure R France
20B2 Eureka California, USA
6B1 Eureka Can
8B3 Eureka Nevada, USA
6B2 Eureka Sd Can
108C3 Euroa Aust
109C1 Eurombah R Aust
101D3 Europa I Mozam Chan
Euskirchen Germany
13B2 Eutsuk L Can
13D2 Evansburg Can
6B1 Evans,C Can
6C3 Evans,L Can
6E3 Evans Str Can
14A2 Evanston Illinois, USA
8B2 Evanston Wyoming, USA
11B3 Evansville Indiana, USA
101G1 Evaton S Africa
106C4 Everard,L Aust
82C3 Everest,Mt China/Nepal
8A2 Everett Washington, USA
16C1 Everett,Mt USA
11B4 Everglades,The Swamp USA
43D5 Evesham Eng
98B2 Evinayong Eq Guinea
39F7 Evje Nor
47B1 Evolène Switz
50A2 Evora Port
48C2 Evreux France
10A1 Evvoia I Greece
98B3 Ewo Congo
22C1 Excelsior Mt USA
18B2 Excelsior Springs USA
21B2 Exeter California, USA
43C4 Exeter Eng
15D2 Exeter New Hampshire, USA
43C4 Exmoor Nat Pk Eng
43C4 Exmouth Eng
50A2 Extremadura Region Spain
25E2 Exuma Sd The Bahamas
99D3 Eyasi L Tanz
42C2 Eyemouth Scot
99E2 Eyl Somalia
106B4 Eyre Aust
106C3 Eyre Creek R Aust
106C3 Eyre,L Aust
106C4 Eyre Pen Aust
79B3 Eyte I Phil
23A1 Ezatlan Mexico
55C3 Ezine Turk

F

4G3 Faber L Can
39G7 Fåborg Den
52B2 Fabriano Italy
97B3 Fachi Niger
95B3 Fada Chad
97C3 Fada N'Gourma Burkina
52B2 Faenza Italy
6E3 Faeringehavn Greenland
98B2 Fafa R CAR
99E2 Fafan R Eth
54B1 Făgăraş Rom
46C1 Fagnes Region, Belg
97B3 Faguibine,L I Mali
91C5 Fahud Oman
96A1 Faial I Açores
4D3 Fairbanks USA
14B3 Fairborn USA
8D2 Fairbury USA
16A3 Fairfax USA
21A2 Fairfield California, USA
16C2 Fairfield Connecticut, USA
14B3 Fairfield Ohio, USA
45C1 Fair Head Pt N Ire
40C2 Fair Isle I Scot

111B2 Fairlie NZ
14B3 Fairmont W Virginia, USA
13D1 Fairview Can
4E4 Fairweather,Mt USA
71F3 Fais I Pacific O
84C2 Faisalabad Pak
8C2 Faith USA
44E1 Faither,The Pen Scot
86A1 Faizābād India
43E3 Fakenham Eng
39G7 Fåköping Sweden
86C2 Falam Myan
24C2 Falcon Res Mexico/ USA
97A3 Falémé R Mali/Sen
39G7 Falkenberg Sweden
42C2 Falkirk Scot
29D6 Falkland Is
24A2 Falkland Is Dependency, S Atlantic
29E6 Falkland Sd Falkland Is
22D4 Fallbrook USA
8B3 Fallon USA
15D2 Fall River USA
18A1 Falls City USA
43B4 Falmouth Eng
27H1 Falmouth Jamaica
15D2 Falmouth Massachusetts, USA
100A4 False B S Africa
24A2 Falso,C Mexico
56C2 Fălticeni Rom
54C1 Fălticeni Rom
39H6 Falun Sweden
92B2 Famagusta Cyprus
46C1 Famenne Region, Belg
76B2 Fang Thai
99D2 Fangak Sudan
73E5 Fang liao Taiwan
52B2 Fano Italy
112C3 Faraday Base Ant
99C2 Faradje Zaire
101D3 Farafangana Madag
95A2 Farafra Oasis Egypt
80E2 Farah Afghan
71F2 Farallon de Medinilla I Pacific O
97A3 Faranah Guinea
71F3 Fararulep I Pacific O
43D4 Fareham Eng
Farewell,C = Kap Farvel
107G5 Farewell,C NZ
110B2 Farewell Spit Pt NZ
8D2 Fargo USA
94B2 Far'a R Israel
10A2 Faribault USA
86B2 Faridpur Bang
90C2 Farīmān Iran
18B2 Farmington Missouri, USA
9C3 Farmington New Mexico, USA
22B2 Farmington Res USA
42D2 Farne Deep N Sea
32C2 Farnham,Mt Can
12H2 Faro Can
50A2 Faro Port
39H7 Fårø I Sweden
89K9 Farquhar Is Indian O
44B3 Farrar R Scot
14B2 Farrell USA
55B3 Fársala Greece
91B4 Fasā Iran
45B3 Fastnet Rock Irish Rep
60C3 Fastov Ukraine
86A1 Fatehpur India
13D1 Father Can
30F2 Fatima do Sul Brazil
101G1 Fauresmith S Africa
47B2 Faverges France
7B4 Fawn R Can
38H6 Fax R Sweden
38A2 Faxaflói B Iceland
95A3 Faya Chad
11A3 Fayetteville Arkansas, USA
11C2 Fayetteville N Carolina, USA

93E4 Faylakah I Kuwait
84C2 Fāzilka India
96A2 Fdérik Maur
11C3 Fear,C USA
21A2 Feather Middle Fork R USA
48C2 Fécamp France
34D2 Federación Arg
34D2 Federal Arg
71F3 Federated States of Micronesia I, Pacific O
56C2 Fehmarn I Germany
32C5 Feijó Brazil
73C5 Feilai Xai Bei Jiang R China
110C2 Feilding NZ
100C2 Feira Zambia
31D4 Feira de Santan Brazil
92C2 Feke Turk
57B3 Feldkirch Austria
34D2 Feliciano R Arg
41D3 Felixstowe Eng
47D1 Feltre Italy
38G6 Femund L Nor
74A2 Fengcheng China
73B4 Fengdu China
72D1 Fengning China
73B3 Fengjie China
72B3 Feng Xian China
72C1 Fengzhen China
72C2 Fen He R China
101D2 Fenoarivo Atsinanana Madag
60E5 Feodosiya Ukraine
90C3 Ferdow Iran
46B2 Fère-Champenoise France
82B2 Fergana Uzbekistan
45C1 Fermanagh County, N Ire
45B2 Fermoy Irish Rep
47D1 Fermo Mt Austria
32J7 Fernandina I Ecuador
Fernandina Beach
103G5 Fernando de Noronha I Atlantic O
35A2 Fernandópolis Brazil
20D1 Ferndale USA
21B2 Fernley USA
52B2 Ferrara Italy
32B5 Ferreñafe Peru
19B3 Ferriday USA
96B1 Fès Mor
18B2 Festus USA
54C2 Feteşti Rom
92A2 Fethiye Turk
61H5 Fetisovo Kazakhstan
44E1 Fetlar I Scot
80B2 Feyzābād Afghan
101D3 Fianarantsoa Madag
99D2 Fichē Eth
101G1 Ficksburg S Africa
47D2 Fidenza Italy
55A2 Fier Alb
11C1 Fiera Di Primeiro Italy
17A1 Fife Region, Scot
44C3 Fife Ness Pen Scot
48C3 Figeac France
50A1 Figueira da Foz Port
51C1 Figueras Spain
Figueres = Figueras
89J1 Figuig Mor
105G4 Fiji Is Pacific O
30D3 Filadélfia Brazil
54B2 Filiaşi Rom
55B3 Filiátra Greece
53B3 Filicudi I Italy
21B3 Fillmore California, USA
44B3 Findhorn R Scot
10B2 Findlay USA
13D2 Findlay,Mt Can
15C2 Finger Lakes I USA
101C2 Fingoè Mozam
92B2 Finike Turk
106C2 Finke R Aust
108A1 Finke Flood Flats Aust
64D3 Finland Republic, N Europe

39J7 Finland,G of N Europe
5F4 Finlay R Can
5F4 Finlay Forks Can
108C3 Finley Aust
38H5 Finnsnes Nor
71F4 Finschhafen PNG
47C1 Finsteraarhorn Mt Switz
56C2 Finsterwalde Germany
45C1 Fintona N Ire
111A3 Fiordland Nat Pk NZ
94B2 Fiq Syria
93C2 Firat R Turk
52B2 Firenze Italy
52B2 Firenze Italy
34C2 Firmat Arg
85D3 Firozābād India
84C2 Firozpur India
39H7 Firspang Sweden
42B2 Firth of Clyde Estuary Scot
44C3 Firth of Forth Estuary Scot
44A3 Firth of Lorn Estuary Scot
40C2 Firth of Tay Estuary Scot
91B4 Fīrūzābād Iran
100A3 Firth R Namibia
22C2 Fish Camp USA
16C2 Fishers I USA
43B4 Fishguard Wales
6E3 Fiskenaesset Greenland
99C3 Fizi Zaire
9B3 Flagstaff USA
42D2 Flamborough Head C Eng
8C2 Flaming Gorge Res USA
44A2 Flannan Isles Is Scot
12J2 Flat R Can
13E3 Flathead R USA
8B2 Flathead L USA
4B4 Flat River USA
8A2 Flattery,C USA
42C3 Fleetwood Eng
39H7 Flekkefjord Nor
69G4 Fleming Deep Pacific O
16B2 Flemington USA
56B2 Flensburg Germany
47B1 Fleurier Switz
106C4 Flinders I Aust
107D4 Flinders I Aust
107D2 Flinders R Aust
106C4 Flinders Range Mts Aust
5H4 Flin Flon Can
10B2 Flint USA
42C3 Flint Wales
11B3 Flint R USA
46B1 Flixecourt France
17A1 Florala USA
11B3 Florence Alabama, USA
18A2 Florence Kansas, USA
20B2 Florence Oregon, USA
11C3 Florence S Carolina, USA
32B3 Florencia Colombia
46C2 Florennville Belg
25D3 Flores Guatemala
96A1 Flores I Açores
106B1 Flores I Indon
34D3 Flores R Arg
70C4 Flores S Indon
31C3 Floriano Brazil
30G4 Florianópolis Brazil
25D2 Florida State, USA

29E2 Florida Urug
17B2 Florida B USA
17B2 Florida City USA
107E1 Florida Is Solomon Is
11B4 Florida Keys Is USA
11B4 Florida,Strs of USA
17B4 Florina Greece
38F6 Florø Nor
47D1 Fluchthorn Mt Austria
54C1 Focsani Rom
53C2 Foggia Italy
97A4 Fogo I Cape Verde
48C3 Foix France
6C3 Foley I Can
52B2 Foligno Italy
43E4 Folkestone Eng
17B1 Folkston USA
52B2 Follonica Italy
22B1 Folsom USA
22B1 Folsom L L USA
5H4 Fond-du-Lac Can
10B2 Fond du Lac USA
48C2 Fontainebleau France
18B2 Fontenac USA
48B2 Fontenay-le-Comte France
52C1 Fonyód Hung
Foochow = Fuzhou
12D2 Forbes,Mt USA
46D2 Forbach France
109C2 Forbes Aust
26C5 Forcados Nig
38F6 Forde Nor
108C1 Fords Bridge Aust
19B3 Fordyce USA
97A4 Forécariah Guinea
6G3 Forel,Mt Greenland
14B2 Forest Can
17B1 Forest Park USA
22A1 Forestville USA
44C3 Forfar Scot
46A2 Forges-les-Eaux France
10B2 Forks USA
51C2 Formentera I Spain
52B2 Formia Italy
96A1 Formigas I Açores
Formosa = Taiwan
30E4 Formosa Arg
31B5 Formosa Brazil
30D3 Formosa State, Arg
73D5 Formosa Str Taiwan/China
47D2 Fornovo di Taro Italy
38D3 Føroyar Is N Atlantic O
44C3 Forres Scot
106B4 Forrest Aust
11A3 Forrest City USA
107D2 Forsayth Aust
39J6 Forssa Fin
109D2 Forster Aust
18B2 Forsyth Missouri, USA
84C3 Fort Abbas Pak
7B4 Fort Albany Can
31D4 Fortaleza Brazil
44B3 Fort Augustus Scot
100B4 Fort Beaufort S Africa
21A2 Fort Bragg USA
8C2 Fort Collins USA
15C1 Fort Coulogne Can
27E4 Fort de France Martinique
17A1 Fort Deposit USA
10A2 Fort Dodge USA
106A3 Fortescue R Aust
7A5 Fort Frances Can
4F3 Fort Franklin Can
4F3 Fort Good Hope Can
108B1 Fort Grey Aust
44B3 Forth R Scot
7B4 Fort Hope Can
10B Umo Arg
4F3 Fort Laird
96C1 Fort Lallemand Alg
Fort Lamy = Ndjamena
11B4 Fort Lauderdale USA
4F3 Fort Liard Can

Fort Mackay

5G4 **Fort Mackay** Can
5G5 **Fort Macleod** Can
5G4 **Fort McMurray** Can
4E3 **Fort McPherson** Can
18B2 **Fort Madison** USA
8C2 **Fort Morgan** USA
11B4 **Fort Myers** USA
5F4 **Fort Nelson** Can
4F3 **Fort Norman** Can
17A1 **Fort Payne** USA
8C2 **Fort Peck Res** USA
11A4 **Fort Pierce** USA
4G3 **Fort Providence** Can
5G3 **Fort Resolution** Can
98B3 **Fort Rousset** Congo
5F4 **Fort St James** Can
13C1 **Fort St John** Can
13E2 **Fort Saskatchewan** Can
18B2 **Fort Scott** USA
4E3 **Fort Selkirk** Can
7B4 **Fort Severn** Can
61H5 **Fort Shevchenko** Kazakhstan
4F3 **Fort Simpson** Can
6G3 **Fort Smith** Can
6G3 **Fort Smith** Region, Can
11A3 **Fort Smith** USA
9C3 **Fort Stockton** USA
20B2 **Fortuna** California, USA
5G4 **Fort Vermillion** Can
17A1 **Fort Walton Beach** USA
10B2 **Fort Wayne** USA
44B3 **Fort William** Scot
9D3 **Fort Worth** USA
12F2 **Fortymile** R Can
12E1 **Fort Yukon** USA
73C5 **Foshan** China
47B2 **Fossano** Italy
12G3 **Foster,Mt** USA
98B3 **Fougamou** Gabon
48B2 **Fougeres** France
44D1 **Foula** I Scot
43E4 **Foulness** I Eng
11B2 **Foulwind,C** NZ
98B2 **Foumban** Cam
49C1 **Fourmies** France
55C3 **Fournoí** I Greece
97A3 **Fouta Djallon** Mts Guinea
111B3 **Foveaux** Str NZ
43B4 **Fowey** Eng
13D2 **Fox Creek** Can
6B3 **Foxe Basin** G Can
6B3 **Foxe Chan** Can
6C3 **Foxe Pen** Can
110C2 **Foxton** NZ
13F2 **Fox Valley** Can
43E3 **Foynes** Irish Rep
100A2 **Foz do Cuene** Angola
30F4 **Foz do Iguaçu** Brazil
16A2 **Frackville** USA
43A2 **Fraga** Arg
16D1 **Framingham** USA
31B6 **Franca** Brazil
49C2 **France**
  Republic, Europe
10A2 **Frances** Can
12J2 **Frances** R Can
98B3 **Franceville** Gabon
49D2 **Franche Comté** Region, France
100B3 **Francistown** Botswana
13B2 **François** L Can
14A2 **Frankfort** Indiana, USA
11B3 **Frankfort** Kentucky, USA
101G1 **Frankfort** S Africa
57B2 **Frankfurt** Germany
46E1 **Frankfurt am Main** Germany
56C2 **Frankfurt-an-der-Oder** Germany
57C3 **Fränkischer Alb** Upland Germany
14A3 **Franklin** Indiana, USA
19B4 **Franklin** Louisiana, USA

16D1 **Franklin** Massachusetts, USA
16B2 **Franklin** New Jersey, USA
14C2 **Franklin** Pennsylvania, USA
4F2 **Franklin B** Can
20C1 **Franklin D Roosevelt** L USA
4F3 **Franklin Mts** Can
4J2 **Franklin Str** Can
111B2 **Franz Josef Glacier** NZ
 Franz-Joseph-Land =
 Zemlya Frantsa Iosifa
5F5 **Fraser** R Can
44C3 **Fraserburgh** Scot
107E3 **Fraser** I Aust
13B2 **Fraser L** Can
47B1 **Frasne** France
47C1 **Frauenfeld** Switz
34D2 **Fray Bentos** Urug
40C2 **Frazerburgh** Scot
16B3 **Frederica** Italy
56B1 **Fredericia** Den
15C3 **Frederick** Maryland, USA
15C3 **Fredericksburg** Virginia, USA
12H3 **Frederick Sd** Can
18B2 **Fredericktown** USA
7D5 **Fredericton** Can
6E3 **Frederikshab** Greenland
39G7 **Frederikshavn** Den
15C2 **Fredonia** USA
39G7 **Fredrikstad** Nor
16B2 **Freehold** USA
26B1 **Freeport** The Bahamas
19A4 **Freeport** Texas, USA
97A4 **Freetown** Sierra Leone
57B3 **Freiburg** Germany
57C3 **Freistadt** Austria
106A4 **Fremantle** Aust
22B2 **Fremont** California, USA
18A1 **Fremont** Nebraska, USA
14B2 **Fremont** Ohio, USA
33G3 **French Guiana** Dependency, S America
109C4 **Frenchmans Cap** Mt Aust
105A4 **French Polynesia** Is Pacific O
24B2 **Fresnillo** Mexico
8B3 **Fresno** USA
22C2 **Fresno** R USA
47C1 **Fretigney** France
46B1 **Frévent** France
109C4 **Freycinet Pen** Aust
97A3 **Fria** Guinea
22C2 **Friant** USA
22C2 **Friant Dam** USA
52A1 **Fribourg** Switz
57B3 **Friedrichshafen** Germany
6D3 **Frobisher B** Can
6D3 **Frobisher Bay** Can
5H4 **Frobisher L** Can
61F4 **Frolovo** Russian Fed
43C4 **Frome** Eng
108A1 **Frome** R Aust
43C4 **Frome** R Eng
106C4 **Frome,L** Aust
25C3 **Frontera** Mexico
15C3 **Front Royal** USA
53B2 **Frosinone** Italy
73C5 **Fuchuan** China
73E4 **Fuding** China
24B2 **Fuerte** R Mexico
30E3 **Fuerte Olimpo** Par
96A2 **Fuerteventura** I Canary Is
72C2 **Fugu** China
68A2 **Fuhai** China
91C4 **Fujairah** UAE
75B1 **Fuji** Japan
73D4 **Fujian** Province, China
69F2 **Fujin** China

75B1 **Fujinomiya** Japan
74D3 **Fuji-san** Mt Japan
75B1 **Fuji-Yoshida** Japan
63A3 **Fukang** China
74C3 **Fukuchiyima** Japan
74D3 **Fukui** Japan
74C4 **Fukuoka** Japan
74E3 **Fukushima** Japan
74C4 **Fukuyama** Japan
57B2 **Fulda** Germany
57B2 **Fulda** R Germany
73B4 **Fuling** China
27L1 **Fullarton** Trinidad
22D4 **Fullerton** USA
18C2 **Fulton** Kentucky, USA
15C2 **Fulton** New York, USA
46C1 **Fumay** France
75C1 **Funabashi** Japan
96A1 **Funchal** Medeira
35C1 **Fundão** Brazil
7D5 **Fundy,B of** Can
101C3 **Funhalouro** Mozam
72D3 **Funing** China
73B5 **Funing** China
97C3 **Funtua** Nig
73D4 **Fuqing** China
101C2 **Furancungo** Mozam
91C4 **Furg** Iran
47C1 **Furka P** Switz
107D5 **Furneaux Group** Is Aust
56C2 **Fürstenwalde** Germany
57C3 **Fürth** Germany
74D3 **Furukawa** Japan
6B3 **Fury and Hecla St** Can
74A2 **Fushun** Liaoning, China
73A4 **Fushun** Sichuan, China
74B2 **Fusong** China
57C3 **Füssen** Germany
72E2 **Fu Xian** China
72E1 **Fuxin** China
72D3 **Fuyang** China
72E1 **Fuyang** Liaoning, China
73A4 **Fuyuan** Yunnan, China
68A2 **Fuyun** China
73D4 **Fuzhou** China
56C1 **Fyn** I Den

G

99E2 **Gaalkacyo** Somalia
21B2 **Gabbs** USA
100A2 **Gabela** Angola
96A1 **Gabe's** Tunisia
22B2 **Gabilan Range** Mts USA
98B3 **Gabon** Republic, Africa
100B3 **Gaborone** Botswana
54C2 **Gabrovo** Bulg
91B3 **Gach Sārān** Iran
17A1 **Gadsden** Alabama, USA
10A1 **Gads L** Can
53B2 **Gaeta** Italy
71F3 **Gaferut** I Pacific O
96C1 **Gafsa** Tunisia
60D2 **Gagarin** Russian Fed
97B4 **Gagnoa** Ivory Coast
7D4 **Gagnon** Can
61G5 **Gagra** Georgia
86B1 **Gaibanda** India
29C4 **Gaimán** Arg
17B2 **Gainesville** Florida, USA
17B1 **Gainesville** Georgia, USA
19A3 **Gainesville** USA
42D3 **Gainsborough** Eng
108A2 **Gairdner,L** Aust
44B3 **Gairloch** Scot
16A3 **Gaithersburg** USA
87B1 **Gajendragarh** India
73D4 **Ga Jiang** R China
99D3 **Galana** R Kenya

103D5 **Galapagos** Is Pacific O
42C2 **Galashiels** Scot
54C1 **Galați** Rom
4C3 **Galena** Alaska, USA
18B2 **Galena** Kansas, USA
27L1 **Galeota Pt** Trinidad
27L1 **Galera Pt** Trinidad
10A2 **Galesburg** USA
15C2 **Galeton** USA
61F2 **Galich** Russian Fed
50A1 **Galicia** Region, Spain
  Galilee,S of =
  Tiberias,L
21J1 **Galina Pt** Jamaica
99D1 **Gallabat** Sudan
47C2 **Gallarate** Italy
87C3 **Galle** Sri Lanka
51B1 **Gállego** R Spain
  Gallipoli = Gelibolu
55A2 **Gallipoli** Italy
38J5 **Gällivare** Sweden
42B2 **Galloway** District
42B2 **Galloway,Mull of** C Scot
8C3 **Gallup** USA
22B1 **Galt** USA
96A2 **Galtat Zemmour** Mor
25C2 **Galveston** USA
11A4 **Galveston B** USA
34C2 **Gálvez** Arg
49D3 **Galvi** Corse
45B2 **Galway** County, Irish Rep
41B3 **Galway** Irish Rep
41B3 **Galway B** Irish Rep
86B1 **Gamba** China
97B3 **Gambaga** Ghana
4A3 **Gambell** USA
97A3 **Gambia** R The Gambia/Sen
97A3 **Gambia,The** Republic, Africa
98B3 **Gamboma** Congo
100A2 **Gambos** Angola
87C3 **Gampola** Sri Lanka
99E2 **Ganale Dorya** R Eth
15C2 **Gananoque** Can
  Gand = Gent
100A2 **Ganda** Angola
98C3 **Gandajika** Zaire
84B3 **Gandava** Pak
7E5 **Gander** Can
85C4 **Gändhidham** India
85C4 **Gändhinagar** India
85D4 **Gändhi Sägar** L India
51B2 **Gandia** Spain
86B2 **Ganga** R India
85C3 **Ganganar** India
86C2 **Gangaw** Myan
72A2 **Gangca** China
  Gangdise Shan Mts China
  Ganges = Ganga
86B1 **Gangtok** India
72B3 **Gangu** China
8C2 **Gannett Peak** Mt USA
72B2 **Ganquan** China
108A3 **Gantheaume C** Aust
39K8 **Gantsevichi** Belarus
72D4 **Ganzhou** China
97C3 **Gao** Mali
72A2 **Gaolan** China
72C2 **Gaoping** China
97B3 **Gaoua** Burkina
97A3 **Gaoual** Guinea
72D3 **Gaoyou Hu** L China
73C5 **Gaozhou** China
49D3 **Gap** France
79B2 **Gapan** Phil
84D2 **Gar** China
109C1 **Garah** Aust
31D3 **Garanhuns** Brazil
21A1 **Garberville** USA
35B2 **Garça** Brazil
35A2 **Garcias** Brazil
47D2 **Garda** Italy
9C3 **Garden City** USA
14A1 **Garden Pen** USA
34D3 **Gardey** Arg
84B2 **Gardez** Afghan
16C2 **Gardiners I** USA

16D1 Gardner USA
47D2 Gardone Italy
47D2 Gargano Italy
85D4 Garhākota India
61X2 Gari Russian Fed
100A4 Garies S Africa
57C3 Garissa Kenya
19A3 Garland USA
57C3 Garmisch-Partenkirchen Germany
90B2 Garmsar Iran
18A2 Garnett USA
8B2 Garnett Peak Mt USA
48C3 Garonne R France
44B3 Garry R Scot
78B4 Garut Indon
16A2 Garwa India
82C2 Garyarsa China
4H3 Gary L Can
19A3 Garza-Little Elm Res USA
90B2 Gasan Kuli Turkmenistan
48B3 Gascogne Region, France
18B2 Gasconade R USA
96A3 Gascoyne R Aust
98B2 Gashaka Nig
97D3 Gashua Nig
10D2 Gaspé Can
10D2 Gaspé,C. de Can
94A1 Gata,C Cyprus
60C2 Gatchina Russian Fed
42D2 Gateshead Eng
19A3 Gatesville USA
15C1 Gatineau Can
15C1 Gatineau R Can
109D1 Gatton Aust
86C1 Gauhāti India
58C1 Gauja R Latvia
86A1 Gauri Phanta India
22B3 Gaviota USA
39H6 Gävle Sweden
108A2 Gawler Ranges Mts Aust
72A1 Gaxun Nur L China
86A2 Gaya India
97C3 Gaya Niger
14B1 Gaylord USA
109D1 Gayndah Aust
61H1 Gayny Russian Fed
60C4 Gaysin Ukraine
92B3 Gaza Israel
92C2 Gaziantep Turk
97B4 Gbaringa Lib
58B2 Gdańsk Pol
39K7 Gdov Russian Fed
58B2 Gdynia Pol
94A3 Gebel Halâl Mt Egypt
95C2 Gebel Hamata Mt Egypt
92B4 Gebel Katherina Mt Egypt
94A3 Gebel Libni Mt Egypt
94A3 Gebel Maghâra Mt Egypt
99D1 Gedaref Sudan
55C3 Gediz R Turk
56C2 Gedser Den
46C1 Geel Belg
108B3 Geelong Aust
109C4 Geeveston Aust
97D3 Geidam Nig
57C2 Geilenkirchen Germany
99D3 Geita Tanz
73A5 Gejiu China
99E2 Geladī Eth
53B3 Gela Italy
57C3 Geldern Germany
55C2 Gelibolu Turk
92A2 Gelidonya Burun Turk
57C2 Gelsenkirchen Germany
39F8 Gelting Germany
77C5 Gemas Malay

46C1 Gembloux Belg
98B2 Gemena Zaïre
92C2 Gemerek Turk
92A1 Gemlik Turk
52B1 Gemona Italy
100B3 Gemsbok Nat Pk Botswana
98C1 Geneina Sudan
34C3 General Acha Arg
34C3 General Alvear Buenos Aires, Arg
34B2 General Alvear Mendoza, Arg
34C2 General Arenales Arg
34D3 General Belgrano Arg
112B2 General Belgrano Base Ant
112C2 General Bernardo O'Higgins Base Ant
34D3 General Conesa Buenos Aires, Arg
30D3 General Eugenio A Garay Par
34D3 General Guido Arg
34D3 General La Madrid Arg
34C2 General Levalle Arg
30C4 General Manuel Belgrano Mt Arg
34D3 General Paz Buenos Aires, Arg
34C3 General Pico Arg
34C2 General Pinto Arg
34D3 General Pirán Arg
29C3 General Roca Arg
112C3 General San Martin Base Ant
79C4 General Santos Phil
34C3 General Viamonte Arg
34C3 General Villegas Arg
15C2 Genesee R USA
15C2 Genesee USA
46B1 Geneva = Genève
18A1 Geneva Nebraska, USA
15C2 Geneva New York, USA
Geneva,L = LacLéman
52A1 Genève Switz
50B2 Genil R Spain
Genoa = Genova
109C3 Genoa Aust
52A2 Genova Italy
32J7 Genovesa I Ecuador
46B1 Gent Belg
78B4 Genteng Indon
56C2 Genthin Germany
93E1 Geokchay Azerbaijan
100B4 George S Africa
7D4 George R Can
109C2 George R Aust
17B2 George,L Florida, USA
15C2 George,L New York, USA
111A2 George Sd NZ
109C4 George Town Aust
15C3 Georgetown Delaware, USA
33F2 Georgetown Guyana
14A3 Georgetown Kentucky, USA
77C4 George Town Malay
27N2 Georgetown St Vincent and the Grenadines
17C1 Georgetown S Carolina, USA
19A3 Georgetown Texas, USA
97A3 Georgetown The Gambia
112C8 George V Land Region, Ant
65F5 George Forster Base Ant
112C2 Georg Forster Base Ant
17B1 Georgia State, USA
14B1 Georgian B Can

13C3 Georgia,Str of Can
106C3 Georgina R Aust
61F5 Georgiyevsk Russian Fed
57C2 Gera Germany
46B1 Geraardsbergen Belg
111B2 Geraldine NZ
106A3 Geraldton Aust
10B2 Geraldton Can
94B3 Gerar R Israel
4C3 Gerdine,Mt USA
12E2 Gerdova Peak Mt USA
77C4 Gerik Malay
68B2 Gerlachovský Štít Mt Pol
13C1 Germanson Lodge Can
56C2 Germany Republic, Europe
101G1 Germiston S Africa
46D1 Gerolstein Germany
51C1 Gerona Spain
46E1 Geseke Germany
57E3 Gestro R Eth
50B1 Getafe Spain
16A3 Gettysburg Pennsylvania, USA
93D2 Gevaş Turk
55B2 Gevgelija Macedonia
47B1 Gex France
96C1 Ghabāghib Syria
96C1 Ghadames Libya
90B2 Ghaem Shahr Iran
86A1 Ghāghara R India
97B4 Ghana Republic, Africa
100B3 Ghanzi Botswana
96C1 Ghardaia Alg
95A1 Gharyan Libya
95A2 Ghāt Libya
84B3 Ghāziābād India
84C3 Ghazi Khan Pak
84B2 Ghazni Afghan
54C1 Gheorgheni Rom
88E4 Ghudamis Alg
90D3 Ghurian Afghan
95B2 Gialo Libya
99E2 Giamame Somalia
53C3 Giarre Italy
100A3 Gibeon Namibia
50A2 Gibraltar Colony, SW Europe
50A2 Gibraltar,Str of Spain/Africa
106B3 Gibson Desert Aust
20B1 Gibsons Can
87B1 Giddalūr India
99D2 Gidolē Eth
57B2 Giessen Germany
17B2 Gifford USA
74D3 Gifu Japan
42B2 Gigha I Scot
52B2 Giglio I Italy
50A1 Gijón Spain
107D2 Gilbert R Aust
13C2 Gilbert,Mt USA
101C2 Gilé Mozam
94B3 Gilead Region, Jordan
95B2 Gilf Kebir Plat Egypt
84C2 Gilgandra Aust
84C1 Gilgit Pak
84C1 Gilgit R Pak
109C2 Gilgunnia Aust
7A4 Gillam Can
108A2 Gilles L Aust
13B2 Gill I Can
14A1 Gills Rock USA
14A2 Gilman USA
22B2 Gilroy USA
8D1 Gimli Can
101H1 Gingindlovu S Africa
79C4 Gingoog Phil
99E2 Ginir Eth
55B3 Gióna Mt Greece
109C3 Gippsland Mts Aust
14E2 Girard USA
32C3 Girardot Colombia
44C3 Girdle Ness Pen Scot
93C1 Giresun Turk
85C4 Gir Hills India
98C3 Giri R Zaire

86B2 Giridih India
Girona = Gerona
48B2 Gironde R France
44B3 Girvan Scot
111C2 Gisborne NZ
46A2 Gisors France
99C3 Gitega Burundi
Giuba,R = Juba,R
54C2 Giurgiu Rom
46C1 Givet Belg
58C2 Gizycko Pol
55B2 Gjirokastër Alb
4J3 Gjoatlaven Can
39G6 Gjøvik Nor
7D5 Glace Bay Can
12G3 Glacier Bay Nat Mon USA
13E3 Glacier Nat Pk USA/Can
20B1 Glacier Peak Mt USA
6B2 Glacier Str Can
107E3 Gladstone Queensland, Aust
108A2 Gladstone S Aust, Aust
109C4 Gladstone Tasmania, Aust
14A1 Gladstone USA
38A1 Gláma R Iceland
39G6 Gláma R Nor
46D2 Glan R Germany
47C1 Glarner Mts Switz
47C1 Glarus Switz
18A2 Glasco USA
8C2 Glasgow Montana, USA
42B2 Glasgow Scot
16B3 Glassboro USA
43C4 Glastonbury Eng
61H2 Glazov Russian Fed
59B3 Gleisdorf Austria
110C1 Glen Afton NZ
16A3 Glen Burnie USA
101H1 Glencoe S Africa
9B3 Glendale Arizona, USA
22C3 Glendale California, USA
12E2 Glenhallen USA
109D1 Glen Innes Aust
109C1 Glenmorgan Aust
110C2 Glenreagh Aust
16A3 Glen Rock USA
19A3 Glen Rose USA
43C4 Glenrothes UK
15D2 Glens Falls USA
45B1 Glenties Irish Rep
19B3 Glenwood Arkansas, USA
8C3 Glenwood Springs USA
39F6 Glittertind Mt Nor
58B2 Gliwice Pol
9B3 Globe USA
58B2 Głogów Pol
38C5 Glomfjord Nor
109D2 Gloucester Aust
43C4 Gloucester Eng
16D1 Gloucester USA
58D1 Glubokoye Belarus
60D3 Glukhov Russian Fed
59B3 Gmünd Austria
58B2 Gniezno Pol
100A3 Goabeg Namibia
87A1 Goa, Daman and Diu Union Territory, India
86C1 Goalpara India
99D2 Goba Eth
100A3 Gobabis Namibia
34C2 Gobernador Crespo Arg
34B3 Gobernador Duval Arg
72B1 Gobi Desert China/Mongolia
87B1 Gobo Japan
87B1 Godag India
87B1 Godāvari R India
14B2 Goderich Can
6E3 Godhavn Greenland
85C4 Godhra India
34B2 Godoy Cruz Arg

Gods L

7A4 **Gods L** Can
6E3 **Godthab** Greenland
**Godwin Austen =
K2**
35B1 **Goianápolis** Brazil
35B1 **Goianésia** Brazil
35B1 **Goiânia** Brazil
35A1 **Goiás** Brazil
31B4 **Goiás** State, Brazil
35A2 **Goio-Erê** Brazil
99D2 **Gojab** *R* Eth
55C2 **Gökçeada** *I* Turk
55C2 **Gökova Körfezi** *B*
Turk
92C2 **Göksun** Turk
63C3 **Gol** *R* Mongolia
86C1 **Golaghat** India
93C2 **Gölbaşi** Turk
20C2 **Golconda** USA
20B2 **Gold Beach** USA
21B2 **Gold Coast** Aust
13D2 **Golden** Can
110B2 **Golden B** NZ
20B1 **Goldendale** USA
22A2 **Golden Gate** *Chan*
USA
19B4 **Golden Meadow**
USA
21B2 **Goldfield** USA
13B3 **Gold River** Can
56C2 **Goleniów** Pol
22C3 **Goleta** USA
52A2 **Golfe d'Ajaccio** *G*
Corse
96D1 **Golfe de Gabes** *G*
Tunisia
**Golfe de Gascogne =
Biscay,Bay Of**
52A2 **Golfe de St Florent** *G*
Corse
48B2 **Golfe de St-Malo** *B*
France
49C3 **Golfe du Lion** *G*
France
29B4 **Golfo Corcovado** *G*
Chile
50B2 **Golfo de Almeria** *G*
Spain
29B4 **Golfo de Ancud** *G*
Chile
25D2 **Golfo de Batabano** *G*
Cuba
50A2 **Golfo de Cadiz** *G*
Spain
53A3 **Golfo de Cagliari** *G*
Sardegna
24A1 **Golfo de California** *G*
Mexico
25D4 **Golfo de Chiriqui** *G*
Panama
25D3 **Golfo de Fonseca**
Honduras
26B2 **Golfo de
Guacanayabo** *G*
Cuba
32A4 **Golfo de Guayaquil**
G Ecuador
26B5 **Golfo del Darien** *G*
Colombia/Panama
32A4 **Golfo de los
Mosquitos** *G*
Panama
25D3 **Golfo del Papagaya**
G Nic
51B2 **Golfo de Mazarrón** *G*
Spain
25D4 **Golfo de Nicoya** *G*
Costa Rica
53A3 **Golfo de Oristano** *G*
Sardegna
25E4 **Golfo de Panamá** *G*
Panama
25D3 **Golfo de Papagayo** *G*
Costa Rica
27E4 **Golfo de Paria** *G* Ven
29B5 **Golfo de Penas** *G*
Chile
49D3 **Golfe de St Florent**
Corse
51C1 **Golfo de San Jorge** *G*
Spain
24C3 **Golfo de
Tehuantepec** *G*
Mexico

32B3 **Golfo de Torugas** *G*
Colombia
32B2 **Golfo de Uraba** *G*
Colombia
51C2 **Golfo de Valencia** *G*
Spain
27C4 **Golfo de Venezuela**
G Ven
52A2 **Golfo di Genova** *G*
Italy
53C3 **Golfo di Policastro** *G*
Italy
53C3 **Golfo di Squillace** *G*
Italy
52B1 **Golfo di Taranto** *G*
Italy
52B1 **Golfo di Venezia** *G*
Italy
25D4 **Golfo Dulce** *G*
Costa Rica
29C5 **Golfo San Jorge** *G*
Arg
29D4 **Golfo San Matias** *G*
Arg
68B3 **Golmud** China
99E2 **Golocha** Eth
12B2 **Golovin B** USA
74F2 **Golovnino**
Russian Fed
99C3 **Goma** Zaire
97D3 **Gombe** Nig
60D3 **Gomel** Belarus
96A2 **Gomera** *I* Canary Is
24B2 **Gómez Palacio**
Mexico
63E2 **Gonam** *R*
Russian Fed
90C2 **Gonbad-e Kãvús**
Iran
86A1 **Gonda** India
85C4 **Gondal** India
99D1 **Gonder** Eth
92A1 **Gönen** Turk
55C3 **Gönen** *R* Turk
73A4 **Gongga Shan** *Mt*
China
72A2 **Gonghe** China
97D3 **Gongola** *R* Nig
22B2 **Gonzales** California,
USA
19A4 **Gonzales** Texas, USA
34C3 **Gonzalez Chaves** Arg
13C2 **Good Hope Mt** Can
8C2 **Goodland** USA
12B3 **Goodnews Bay** USA
109C1 **Goodooga** *R* Aust
42D3 **Goole** Eng
108C2 **Goolgowi** Aust
108A3 **Goolwa** Aust
106A4 **Goomalling** Aust
108C2 **Goombalie** Aust
109D1 **Goomeri** Aust
109D1 **Goondiwindi** Aust
109D1 **Goomeri** Aust
7E4 **Goose Bay** Can
17C1 **Goose Creek** USA
20B2 **Goose L** USA
87B1 **Gooty** India
63C2 **Gora Munku Sardyk**
Mts Mongolia/
Russian Fed
64H3 **Gora Narodnaya** *Mt*
Russian Fed
64G3 **Gora Tel'pos-iz**
Russian Fed
54A2 **Goražde** Bosnia-
Herzegovina
4D3 **Gordan** USA
13E1 **Gordon L** Can
15C3 **Gordonsville** USA
98B2 **Goré** Chad
99D2 **Goré** Eth
111A3 **Gore** NZ
63F2 **Gore Topko** *Mt*
Russian Fed
45C2 **Gorey** Irish Rep
90B2 **Gorgãn** Iran
93E2 **Goris** Armenia
52B1 **Gorizia** Italy
**Gor'kiy = Nizniy
Novgorod**
61F2 **Gor'kovskoye
Vodokhranilishche**
Res Russian Fed

57C2 **Görlitz** Germany
60E4 **Gorlovka** Ukraine
22C3 **Gorman** USA
54C2 **Gorna Orjahovica**
Bulg
68A1 **Gorno-Altaysk**
Russian Fed
69G2 **Gornozavodsk**
Russian Fed
61F2 **Gorodets**
Russian Fed
59C3 **Gorodok** Ukraine
59D3 **Gorodok** Ukraine
71F4 **Goroka** PNG
86A1 **Gorokhpur** India
101C2 **Gorongosa** Mozam
71D3 **Gorontalo** Indon
61K2 **Goro Yurma** *Mt*
Russian Fed
45B2 **Gort** Irish Rep
63C2 **Goryachinsk**
Russian Fed
59D3 **Goryn'** *R* Ukraine
59C2 **Góry Świetokrzyskie**
Upland Pol
64G3 **Gory Tel'pos-iz'** *Mt*
Russian Fed
39H8 **Gorzów Wielkopolski**
Pol
74E2 **Goshogawara**
Japan
52C2 **Gospić** Croatia
54B2 **Gostivar** Macedonia
58B2 **Gostynin** Pol
39G7 **Göteborg** Sweden
98B2 **Gotel** *Mts* Nig
39H7 **Gotland** *I* Sweden
74B4 **Gotō-retto** *I* Japan
39H7 **Gotska Sandön** *I*
Sweden
74C3 **Gōtsu** Japan
98B3 **Goudoumaria** Niger
103H7 **Gough I** Atlantic O
109C2 **Goulburn** Aust
97B3 **Goumbou** Mali
97B3 **Goundam** Mali
98B1 **Gouré** Niger
97B3 **Gourma Rharous**
Mali
46A2 **Gournay-en-Bray**
France
98A2 **Gouro** Chad
71E5 **Gove Pen** Aust
60B4 **Goverla** *Mt* Ukraine
35C1 **Governador
Valadares** Brazil
86A2 **Govind Ballabh Paht
Sägar** *L* India
15C2 **Gowanda** USA
84B3 **Gowärän** Afghan
30E4 **Goya** Arg
98C1 **Goz-Beida** Chad
53B3 **Gozo** *I* Medit S
95C3 **Goz Regeb** Sudan
100B4 **Graaff-Reinet**
S Africa
15C1 **Gracefield** Can
109D1 **Grafton** USA
8D2 **Grafton** N Dakota,
USA
14B3 **Grafton** W Virginia,
USA
5E4 **Graham I** Can
13C1 **Graham** *R* Can
13E1 **Graham L** Can
100B4 **Grahamstown**
S Africa
31B3 **Grajaú** Brazil
58C2 **Grajewo** Pol
55B2 **Grammos** *Mt*
Greece/Alb
44C3 **Grampian** Region,
Scot
44B3 **Grampian Mts** Scot
32C3 **Granada** Colombia
25D3 **Granada** Nic
50B2 **Granada** Spain
15D1 **Granby** Can
96A2 **Gran Canaria** *I*
Canary Is
30D4 **Gran Chaco** *Region*
Arg
14A2 **Grand** *R* Michigan,
USA

18B1 **Grand** *R* Missouri,
USA
27Q2 **Grand B** Dominica
11C4 **Grand Bahama** *I*
The Bahamas
7E5 **Grand Bank** Can
102F2 **Grand Banks**
Atlantic O
97B4 **Grand Bassam** Ivory
Coast
9B3 **Grand Canyon** USA
26A3 **Grand Cayman** USA
Caribbean S
13E2 **Grand Centre** Can
20C1 **Grand Coulee** USA
34B3 **Grande** *R* Arg
31C4 **Grande** *R* Bahia,
Brazil
35B1 **Grande** *R* Minas
Gerais/São Paulo,
Brazil
13D2 **Grande Cache** Can
47A2 **Grande Chartreuse**
Region, France
101D2 **Grande Comore** *I*
Comoros
13D1 **Grande Prairie** Can
19A3 **Grande Prairie** USA
95A3 **Grand Erg de Bilma**
Desert Niger
96B2 **Grand erg Occidental**
Mts Alg
96C2 **Grand erg Oriental**
Mts Alg
7C4 **Grande Rivière de la
Baleine** *R* Can
20C1 **Grande Ronde** *R*
USA
7D5 **Grand Falls** New
Brunswick, Can
7E5 **Grand Falls**
Newfoundland, Can
20C1 **Grand Forks** Can
8D2 **Grand Forks** USA
16B1 **Grand Gorge** USA
14A2 **Grand Haven** USA
19C3 **Grand Isle** USA
1984 **Grand L** USA
15D1 **Grand Mère** Can
50A2 **Grândola** Port
5J4 **Grand Rapids** Can
14A2 **Grand Rapids**
Michigan, USA
10A2 **Grand Rapids**
Minnesota, USA
47B2 **Grand St Bernard** *P*
Italy/Switz
8B2 **Grand Teton** *Mt*
USA
8B2 **Grand Teton Nat Pk**
USA
46A2 **Grandvilliers** France
25D1 **Grangeburg** USA
51C1 **Granollers** Spain
52A1 **Gran Paradiso** *Mt*
Italy
47D1 **Gran Pilastro** *Mt*
Austria/Italy
43D3 **Grantham** Eng
21B2 **Grant,Mt** USA
44C3 **Grantown-on-Spey**
Scot
9C3 **Grants** USA
20B2 **Grants Pass** USA
48B2 **Granville** France
5H4 **Granville L** Can
35C1 **Grão Mogol** Brazil
49D3 **Grasse** France
21A2 **Grass Valley** USA
5H5 **Gravelbourg** Can
46B1 **Gravelines** France
100C3 **Gravelotte** S Africa
15C2 **Gravenhurst** Can
109D1 **Gravesend** Aust
12H3 **Gravina I** USA
12B2 **Grayling** USA
20B1 **Grays Harbor** USA
14B3 **Grayson** USA
18C2 **Grayville** USA
59B3 **Graz** Austria
27H1 **Great** *R* Jamaica
11C4 **Great Abaco** *I*
The Bahamas

106B4 Great Australian
Bight *G* Aust
16B3 Great B New Jersey,
USA
25E2 **Great Bahama Bank**
The Bahamas
110C1 Great Barrier I NZ
107D2 Great Barrier Reef *Is*
Aust
16C1 Great Barrington
USA
4F3 Great Bear L Can
9D2 Great Bend USA
107D3 Great Dividing Range
Mts Aust
42D2 Great Driffield Eng
16B3 Great Egg Harbor *B*
USA
12B10 Greater Antarctic
Region, Ant
26B2 **Greater Antilles** *Is*
Caribbean S
43D4 **Greater London**
Metropolitan County,
Eng
43C3 **Greater Manchester**
County, Eng
25E2 **Great Exuma** *I*
The Bahamas
8B2 Great Falls USA
44B3 Great Glen *V* Scot
86B1 **Great Himalayan
Range** *Mts* Asia
11C4 Great Inagua *I*
The Bahamas
100B4 Great Karroo *Mts*
S Africa
109C4 Great L Aust
100A3 **Great Namaland**
Region, Namibia
42A3 Great Ormes Head *C*
Wales
11C4 Great Ragged *I*
The Bahamas
99D3 Great Ruaha *R* Tanz
15D2 Great Sacandaga L
USA
8B2 Great Salt L USA
95B2 Great Sand Sea
Libya/Egypt
107D3 Great Sandy Desert
Aust
8A2 Great Sandy Desert
USA
Great Sandy I =
Fraser I
4G3 Great Slave L Can
16C2 Great South B USA
106B3 Great Victoria Desert
Aust
112C2 Great Wall *Base* Ant
72B2 Great Wall China
43E3 Great Yarmouth Eng
94B1 Greco,C Cyprus
55B3 **Greece**
Republic, Europe
15C2 Greece USA
8C2 Greeley USA
6B1 Greely Fjord Can
14A1 Green B USA
14A2 Green Bay USA
16C1 Greencastle Indiana,
USA
16C1 Greenfield
Massachusetts, USA
14A2 Greenfield
Wisconsin, USA
13F2 Green Lake Can
6F2 **Greenland**
Dependency,
N Atlantic O
102H1 Greenland Basin
Greenland S
1B1 **Greenland S**
Greenland
42B2 Greenock Scot
16C2 Greenport USA
16B3 Greensboro
Maryland, USA
11C3 Greensboro N
Carolina, USA
15C2 Greensburg
Pennsylvania, USA
44B3 Greenstone *Pt* Scot

18C2 Greenup USA
17A1 Greenville Alabama,
USA
97B4 Greenville Lib
19B3 Greenville
Mississippi, USA
16D1 Greenville
N Hampshire, USA
14B2 Greenville Ohio, USA
17B1 Greenville S
Carolina, USA
19A3 Greenville Texas,
USA
43E4 Greenwich Eng
16C2 Greenwich USA
16B3 Greenwood
Delaware, USA
19B3 Greenwood
Mississippi, USA
17B1 Greenwood S
Carolina, USA
18B2 Greers Ferry L USA
108A1 Gregory,L Aust
107D2 Gregory Range *Mts*
Aust
56C2 Greifswald Germany
64F3 Gremikha
Russian Fed
56C1 Grenå Den
19C3 Grenada USA
27E4 **Grenada** *I*
Caribbean S
109C2 Grenfell Aust
49D2 Grenoble France
27M2 Grenville Grenada
107D2 Grenville,C Aust
20B1 Gresham USA
78C4 Gresik Jawa, Indon
78A3 Gresik Sumatera,
Indon
42E3 Gretna Eng
111B2 Grey *R* NZ
12G2 Grey Hunter Pk *Mt*
Can
7E4 Grey Is Can
16C1 Greylock,Mt USA
111B2 Greymouth NZ
107D3 Grey Range *Mts*
Aust
45C2 Greystones Irish Rep
101H1 Greytown S Africa
101F1 Griekwastad
S Africa
17B1 Griffin USA
108C2 Griffith Aust
16C1 Grim,C Aust
15C2 Grimsby Can
42D3 Grimsby Eng
38B1 Grimsey *I* Iceland
13D1 Grimshaw Can
39F7 Grimstad Nor
47C1 Grindelwald Switz
6A2 Grinnell Pen Can
6B2 Grise Fjord Can
61H1 Griva Russian Fed
39J7 Grobina Latvia
58C2 Grodno Belarus
86A1 Gromati *R* India
56B2 Groningen Neth
100A2 Grootfontein
Namibia
100B3 Grootvloer *Salt L*
S Africa
27P2 Gros Islet St Lucia
46E1 Grosser Feldberg *Mt*
Germany
52B2 Grosseto Italy
46E2 Gross-Gerau
Germany
57C3 Grossglockner *Mt*
Austria
47E1 Gross Venediger *Mt*
Austria
12C3 Grosvenor,L USA
22B2 Groveland USA
21A2 Grover City USA
15D2 Groveton USA
61G5 Groznyy Russian Fed
58B2 Grudziądz Pol
100A3 Grünau Namibia
44E2 Grutness Scot
61F3 Gryazi Russian Fed

61E2 Gryazovets
Russian Fed
29G8 Grytviken South
Georgia
45A2 Gt Blasket *I*
Irish Rep
35C2 Guaçui Brazil
23A1 Guadalajara Mexico
50B1 Guadalajara Spain
107E1 Guadalcanal *I*
Solomon Is
50B2 Guadalimar *R* Spain
51B1 Guadalope *R* Spain
50B2 Guadalqivir *R* Spain
24B2 Guadalupe Mexico
3G6 Guadalupe *I* Mexico
27E3 Guadeloupe *I*
Caribbean S
50B2 Guadian *R* Spain
50A2 Guadiana *R* Port
50B2 Guadix Spain
32D6 Guajará Mirim Brazil
32C1 Guajira,Pen de
Colombia
32B4 Gualaceo Ecuador
34D2 Gualeguay Arg
34D2 Gualeguaychú Arg
71F2 Guam *I* Pacific O
34C3 Guamini Arg
77C5 Gua Musang Malay
23A1 Guanajuato Mexico
23A1 Guanajuato State,
Mexico
32D2 Guanare Ven
25D2 Guane Cuba
73C5 **Guangdong**
Province, China
73A3 Guanghan China
72C3 Guanghua China
73A4 Guangmao Shan *Mt*
China
73B5 Guangnan China
72B3 Guangyuan China
73D4 Guangze China
67F3 Guangzhou China
35C1 Guanhães Brazil
32D3 Guania *R* Colombia
27E5 Guanipa *R* Ven
26B2 Guantánamo Cuba
72D1 Guanting Shuiku *Res*
China
73B5 Guanxi Province,
China
73A3 Guan Xian China
32B2 Guapa Colombia
33C6 Guaporé *R* Brazil/Bol
30C2 Guaqui Bol
32B4 Guaranda Ecuador
30F4 Guarapuava Brazil
35B2 Guaratinguetá Brazil
50A1 Guarda Port
35B1 Guarda Mor Brazil
9C4 Guasave Mexico
47D2 Guastalla Italy
25C3 Guatemala
Guatemala
25C3 Guatemala Republic,
Cent America
34C3 Guatraché Arg
32C3 Guaviare *R*
Colombia
35B2 Guaxupé Brazil
27L1 Guayaguayare
Trinidad
32A4 Guayaquil Ecuador
24A2 Guaymas Mexico
34D2 Guayquiraró *R* Arg
100B2 Guba *R* Zaïre
99E2 **Guban** Region
Somalia
79B3 Gubat Phil
56C2 Gubin Pol
87B2 Gūdūr India
11J2 Guelpho Can
26A2 Guenabacoa Cuba
98C1 Guéréda Chad
48C2 Guéret France
48B2 Guernsey *I* UK
23A2 Guerrero State,
Mexico
99D2 Gughe *Mt* Eth
63E2 Gugigu China
71F2 Guguan *I* Pacific O
109C2 Guiargambone Aust

73C4 Guidong China
97B4 Guiglo Ivory Coast
73C5 Gui Jiang *R* China
43D4 Guildford Eng
73C4 Guilin China
47B2 Guillestre France
72A2 Guinan China
97A3 **Guinea** Republic,
Africa
102H4 Guinea Basin
Atlantic O
97A3 **Guinea-Bissau**
Republic, Africa
97C4 Guinea,G of
W Africa
26A2 Güines Cuba
97B3 Guir *Well* Mali
84C2 Guiranwala Pak
33E1 Güiria Ven
46B2 Guise France
79C3 Guiuan Phil
73B5 Gui Xian China
73B4 Guiyang China
73B4 **Guizhou** Province,
China
85C4 **Gujarat** State, India
84C2 Gujrat Pak
87B1 Gulbarga India
58D1 Gulbene Latvia
87B1 Guledagudda India
80D3 Gulf,The S W Asia
109C2 Gulgong Aust
73B4 Gulin China
12E2 Gulkana USA
12E2 Gulkana *R* USA
13C2 Gull L Can
13F2 Gull Lake Can
55C3 Güllük Körfezi *B*
Turk
99D2 Gulu Uganda
109C1 Guluguba Aust
97C3 Gumel Nig
46D1 Gummersbach
Germany
86A2 Gumpla India
93C1 Gümüşhane Turk
86A2 Guna India
99D1 Guna Mt Eth
109C3 Gundagai Aust
98B3 Gungu Zaïre
6H3 Gunnbjørn Fjeld *Mt*
Greenland
109D2 Gunnedah Aust
87B1 Guntakal India
17A1 Guntersville USA
17A1 Guntersville L USA
87C1 Guntúr India
77C5 Gunung Batu Putch
Mt Malay
78D3 Gunung Besar *Mt*
Indon
78D2 Gunung Bulu *Mt*
Indon
78A3 Gunung Gedang *Mt*
Indon
78A3 Gunung Lawit *Mt*
Malay
78C4 Gunung Lawu *Mt*
Indon
78D2 Gunung Menyapa *Mt*
Indon
78A3 Gunung Niapa *Mt*
Indon
78A3 Gunung Patah *Mt*
Indon
78C4 Gunung Raung *Mt*
Indon
78A3 Gunung Resag *Mt*
Indon
78D3 Gunung Sarempaka
Mt Indon
77C5 Gunung Sumbing *Mt*
Indon
77C5 Gunung Tahan *Mt*
Malay
78A2 Gunung Talakmau
Mt Indon
100A2 Gunza Angola
72D3 Guoyang China
84D2 Gurdaspur India
84D3 Gurgaon India
86A1 Gurkha Nepal
92C2 Gürün Turk
31B2 Gurupi *R* Brazil

Guruve

100C2 **Guruve** Zim
72A1 **Gurvan Sayhan Uul** *Upland* Mongolia
61H4 **Gur'yev** Kazakhstan
97C3 **Gusau** Nig
58C2 **Gusev** Russian Fed
74A3 **Gushan** China
61F2 **Gus'khrustalnyy** Russian Fed
12G3 **Gustavus** USA
22B2 **Gustine** USA
11B3 **Guston** USA
56B2 **Gütersloh** Germany
18C2 **Guthrie** Kentucky, USA
18A2 **Guthrie** Oklahoma, USA
23B1 **Gutiérrez Zamora** Mexico
33F3 **Guyana** Republic, S America
102F4 **Guyana Basin** Atlantic O
72C1 **Guyang** China
48B3 **Guyenne** Region, France
9C3 **Guymon** USA
109D2 **Guyra** Aust
72B2 **Guyuan** China
109C2 **Gwabegar** Aust
85D3 **Gwalior** India
100B3 **Gwanda** Zim
98C2 **Gwane** Zaire
82A3 **Gwardar** Pak
45B1 **Gweebarra B** Irish Rep
89G9 **Gwelo** Zim
43C4 **Gwent** County, Wales
100B2 **Gweru** Zim
109C1 **Gwydir** *R* Aust
43C3 **Gwynedd** Wales
65F5 **Gyandzha** Azerbaijan
86B1 **Gyangzê** China
68B3 **Gyaring Hu** *L* China
64J2 **Gydanskiy Poluostrov** *Pen* Russian Fed
86B1 **Gyirong** China
6F3 **Gyldenløves** Greenland
109D1 **Gympie** Aust
59B3 **Gyöngyös** Hung
59B3 **Györ** Hung

H

38K6 **Haapajärvi** Fin
60B2 **Haapsalu** Estonia
56A2 **Haarlem** Neth
46D1 **Haarstrang** Region, Germany
25D2 **Habana** Cuba
86C2 **Habiganj** Bang
74D4 **Hachijo-jima** *I* Japan
75B1 **Hachiman** Japan
74C3 **Hachinohe** Japan
75B1 **Hachioji** Japan
16B2 **Hackettstown** USA
108A2 **Hack,Mt** *Mt* Aust
42C2 **Haddington** Scot
108B1 **Haddon Corner** Aust
108B1 **Haddon Downs** Aust
97D3 **Hadejia** Nig
97C3 **Hadejia** *R* Nig
94B2 **Hadera** Israel
56B1 **Haderslev** Den
81D4 **Hadiboh** Socotra
4H2 **Hadley B** Can
73B5 **Hadong** Vietnam
81C4 **Hadramawt** Region, Yemen
56C1 **Hadsund** Den
74B3 **Haeju** N Korea
91A4 **Hafar al Batin** S Arabia
6D2 **Haffners Bjerg** *Mt* Greenland
84C2 **Hafizabad** Pak
86C1 **Haflong** India
38A2 **Hafnafjörður** Iceland
12B3 **Hagemeister** *I* USA
56B2 **Hagen** Germany
15C3 **Hagerstown** USA
75A2 **Hagi** Japan

73A5 **Ha Giang** Vietnam
46D2 **Hagondange** France
46B2 **Hags Hd** *C* Irish Rep
46D2 **Haguenan** France
96A2 **Hagunia** *Well* Mor
69G4 **Haha-jima** *I* Japan
68B3 **Hah Xil Hu** *L* China
74A2 **Haicheng** China
76D1 **Hai Duong** Viet
94B2 **Haifa** Israel
94B2 **Haifa,B of** Israel
72A2 **Hai He** *R* China
73C5 **Haikang** China
76E1 **Haikou** China
80C3 **Ha'il** S Arabia
86C2 **Hailakandi** India
63D3 **Hailar** China
74B2 **Hailong** China
69E2 **Hailun** China
38J5 **Hailuoto** / Fin
76D2 **Hainan** / China
12G3 **Haines** USA
12G2 **Haines Junction** Can
59B3 **Hainfeld** Austria
73B5 **Haiphong** Vietnam
26C3 **Haiti** Republic, Caribbean S
95C3 **Haiya** Sudan
72C2 **Haiyan** China
72B2 **Haiyuan** China
72D3 **Haizhou Wan** *B* China
59C3 **Hajdúböszörmény** Hung
75B1 **Hajiki-saki** *Pt* Japan
86C2 **Haka** Myan
21C4 **Hakalau** Hawaiian Is
74E3 **Hanamaki** Japan
93O2 **Hakkârî** Turk
74E2 **Hakodate** Japan
Hakwa = Haka
75B1 **Hakui** Japan
75B1 **Haku-san** *Mt* Japan
92C2 **Halab** Syria
93E3 **Halabja** Iraq
95C2 **Halaib** Sudan
94C1 **Halba** Leb
68B2 **Halban** Mongolia
56C2 **Halberstadt** Germany
79B3 **Halcon,Mt** Phil
39G7 **Halden** Nor
86B2 **Haldia** India
84D3 **Haldwäni** India
13C1 **Halfway** *R* Can
7D5 **Halifax** Can
42D3 **Halifax** Eng
6D1 **Hall Basin** *Sd* Can
6B3 **Hall Beach** Can
46C1 **Halle** Belg
56C2 **Halle** Germany
112B1 **Halley** Base Ant
39F6 **Hallingdal** *R* Nor
6D3 **Hall Pen** Can
106B2 **Hall's Creek** Aust
71D3 **Halmahera** *I* Indon
39G7 **Halmstad** Sweden
56B2 **Haltern** Germany
38J5 **Halti** *Mt* Nor
42C2 **Haltwhistle** Eng
91B4 **Halul** / Qatar
94B3 **Haluza** *Hist Site* Israel
75A2 **Hamada** Japan
96C2 **Hamada de Tinrhert** *Desert* Region Alg
96B2 **Hamada du Dra** *Upland* Alg
90A3 **Hamadan** Iran
96B2 **Hamada Tounassine** Region, Alg
92C2 **Hamäh** Syria
75B2 **Hamamatsu** Japan
39G6 **Hamar** Nor
87C3 **Hambantota** Sri Lanka
19B3 **Hamburg** Arkansas, USA
18A1 **Hamburg** Iowa, USA
16B2 **Hamburg** Pennsylvania, USA
56B2 **Hamburg** Germany
16C2 **Hamden** USA
39J6 **Hämeenlinna** Fin

106B2 **Hamersley Range** *Mts* Aust
74B2 **Hamgyong Sanmaek** *Mts* N Korea
74B2 **Hamhüng** N Korea
68B2 **Hami** China
94B1 **Hamidiyah** Syria
108B3 **Hamilton** Aust
14C2 **Hamilton** Can
110C1 **Hamilton** NZ
14B3 **Hamilton** Ohio, USA
42B2 **Hamilton** Scot
22B2 **Hamilton,Mt** USA
38K6 **Hamina** Fin
86A1 **Hamirpur** India
56B2 **Hamm** Germany
95A2 **Hammādāh al Hamra** *Upland* Libya
38H6 **Hammerdal** Sweden
38J4 **Hammerfest** Nor
14A2 **Hammond** Illinois, USA
19B3 **Hammond** Louisiana, USA
16B3 **Hammonton** USA
111B3 **Hampden** NZ
43D4 **Hampshire** County, Eng
19B3 **Hampton** Arkansas, USA
91C4 **Hamün-e Jaz Mürian** *L* Iran
84B3 **Hamun-i-Lora** *Salt L* Pak
21C4 **Hana** Hawaiian Is
21C4 **Hanalei** Hawaiian Is
74E3 **Hanamaki** Japan
72C2 **Hancheng** China
73C3 **Hanchuan** China
15C3 **Hancock** Maryland, USA
10B2 **Hancock** Michigan, USA
75B2 **Handa** Japan
72C2 **Handan** China
99D3 **Handeni** Tanz
72B2 **Hanggin Qi** China
39J7 **Hango** Fin
73E3 **Hangzhou** China
73E3 **Hangzhou Wan** *B* China
111B2 **Hanmer Springs** NZ
13E2 **Hanna** Can
18B2 **Hannibal** USA
56B2 **Hannover** Germany
39G7 **Hanöbukten** *B* Sweden
76D1 **Hanoi** Viet
16A3 **Hanover** USA
29B6 **Hanover** / Chile
73C3 **Han Shui** China
73C3 **Han Shui** *R* China
85D3 **Hänsi** India
72A3 **Hantay** Mongolia
72B3 **Hanzhong** China
86B2 **Häora** India
38J5 **Haparanda** Sweden
86C1 **Häpoli** India
92C4 **Haql** S Arabia
99E2 **Hara Fanna** Eth
75C1 **Haramachi** Japan
101C2 **Harare** Zim
98C1 **Harazé** Chad
14B2 **Harbor Beach** USA
85D4 **Harda** India
39F6 **Hardangerfjord** *Inlet* Nor
46D2 **Hardt** Region, Germany
108A2 **Hardwicke B** Aust
18B2 **Hardy** USA
91B4 **Harey** Eth
99E2 **Hargeysa** Somalia
94B3 **Har Hakippa** *Mt* Israel
68B3 **Harhu** *L* China
78A3 **Hari** *R* Indon
74D3 **Harima-nada** *B* Japan
56B2 **Harlingen** Neth
9D4 **Harlingen** USA
43E4 **Harlow** Eng
94B2 **Har Meron** *Mt* Israel

20C2 **Harney Basin** USA
20C2 **Harney L** USA
38H6 **Härnösand** Sweden
63B3 **Har Nuur** *L* Mongolia
97B4 **Harper** Lib
12F2 **Harper,Mt** USA
15C3 **Harpers Ferry** USA
94B3 **Har Ramon** *Mt* Israel
7C4 **Harricanaw** *R* Can
16B3 **Harrington** USA
110C1 **Harrington Harbour** Can
44A3 **Harris** *District* Scot
18C2 **Harrisburg** Illinois, USA
16A2 **Harrisburg** Pennsylvania, USA
101G1 **Harrismith** S Africa
18B2 **Harrison** USA
15C3 **Harrisonburg** USA
12C3 **Harrison,C** Can
13C3 **Harrison L** Can
18B2 **Harrisonville** USA
44A3 **Harris,Sound of** *Chan* Scot
14B2 **Harrisville** USA
42D3 **Harrogate** Eng
94B3 **Har Saggi** *Mt* Israel
38H5 **Harstad** Nor
12G2 **Hart** *R* Can
39F6 **Hårteigen** *Mt* Nor
16C2 **Hartford** Connecticut, USA
14A2 **Hartford** Michigan, USA
38G6 **Hartkjølen** *Mt* Nor
44B2 **Hart,L** Aust
43D4 **Hartland** Eng
42D2 **Hartlepool** Eng
19A3 **Hartshorne** USA
17B1 **Hartwell Res** USA
101F1 **Hartz** *R* S Africa
68B2 **Har Us Nuur** *L* Mongolia
43E4 **Harwich** Eng
84D3 **Haryana** State, India
94B3 **Häsä** Jordan
94B2 **Häsbaiya** Leb
43D4 **Haselmere** Eng
75B2 **Hashimoto** Japan
90A2 **Hashtpar** Iran
90A2 **Hashtrüd** Iran
87B2 **Hassan** India
56B2 **Hasselt** Belg
96C2 **Hassi Inifel** Alg
96B2 **Hassi Mdakane** *Well* Alg
96C1 **Hassi Messaoud** Alg
108C3 **Hastings** Aust
43E4 **Hastings** Eng
8D2 **Hastings** Nebraska, USA
110C1 **Hastings** NZ
108B2 **Hatfield** Aust
12B1 **Hatham Inlet** USA
85D3 **Häthras** India
73B5 **Ha Tinh** Viet
108B2 **Hattah** Aust
11C3 **Hatteras,C** USA
19C3 **Hattiesburg** USA
59B3 **Hatvan** Hung
99E2 **Haud** Region, Eth
39F7 **Haugesund** Nor
110C1 **Hauhungaroa Range** *Mts* NZ
13F1 **Hautain** *R* Can
110B1 **Hauraki G** NZ
111A3 **Hauroko,L** NZ
47C1 **Hausstock** *Mt* Switz
96B1 **Haut Atlas** *Mts* Mor
98B2 **Haute Kotto** Region, CAR
46C1 **Hautes Fagnes** *Mts* Belg
46B1 **Hautmont** Belg
96B1 **Hauts Plateaux** *Mts* Alg
90D3 **Hauzdar** Iran
18B1 **Havana** USA
Havana = Habana

87B3 Havankulam Sri Lanka
110C1 Havelock North NZ
43B4 Haverfordwest Wales
16D1 Haverhill USA
87B2 Häveri India
16C2 Haverstraw USA
59B3 Havlíčkův Brod Czech Republic
8C2 Havre France
16A3 Havre de Grace USA
7D4 Havre-St-Pierre Can
54C2 Havsa Turk
21C4 Hawaii i Hawaiian Is
21C4 Hawaii Volcanoes Nat Pk Hawaiian Is
111A2 Hawea,L NZ
110B1 Hawera NZ
42C2 Hawick Scot
111A2 Hawkdun Range Mts NZ
110C1 Hawke B NZ
109D2 Hawke,C Aust
108A2 Hawker Aust
76B1 Hawng Luk Myan
93D3 Hawr al Habbaniyah L Iraq
93E3 Hawr al Hammār L Iraq
21B2 Hawthorne USA
108B2 Hay Aust
5G3 Hay R Can
46D2 Hayange France
4B3 Haycock USA
6A1 Hayes R Can
6D2 Hayes Halvø Region Greenland
12E2 Hayes,Mt USA
5G3 Hay River Can
18A2 Haysville USA
22A2 Hayward California, USA
86B2 Hazārībāg India
46B1 Hazebrouck France
19B3 Hazelhurst USA
4G2 Hazel Str Can
5F4 Hazelton USA
13B3 Hazelton Mts Can
6C1 Hazen L Can
94B3 Hazeva Israel
16A3 Hazleton USA
108C3 Healesville Aust
12E2 Healy USA
104B6 Heard I Indian O
19A3 Hearne USA
10B2 Hearst USA
72C2 Hebei Province, China
109C1 Hebel Aust
72C2 Hebi China
72C2 Hebian China
7D4 Hebron Can
94B3 Hebron Israel
18A1 Hebron Nebraska, USA
5E4 Hecate Str Can
12H3 Heceta I USA
73B5 Hechi China
4G2 Hecla and Griper B Can
11C2 Hector,Mt NZ
38G6 Hede Sweden
39H6 Hedemora Sweden
20C1 He Devil Mt USA
56B2 Heerenveen Neth
46C1 Heerlen Neth
   Hefa = Haifa
73D3 Hefei China
73B4 Hefeng China
69F2 Hegang China
75B1 Hegura-jima I Japan
94B3 Heidan R Jordan
56B2 Heide Germany
101G1 Heidelberg Transvaal, S Africa
63E2 Heihe China
101G1 Heilbron S Africa
57B3 Heilbronn Germany
56C2 Heiligenstadt Germany
38K6 Heinola Fin

73B4 Hejiang China
6J3 Hekla Mt Iceland
76C1 Hekou Viet
73A5 Hekou Yaozou Zizhixian China
72B2 Helan China
72B2 Helan Shan Mt China
19B3 Helena Arkansas, USA
8D2 Helena Montana, USA
22D3 Helendale USA
71E3 Helen Reef I Pacific O
44B3 Helensburgh Scot
91B4 Helleh R Iran
51B2 Hellín Spain
20C1 Hells Canyon R USA
46D1 Hellweg Region, Germany
22B2 Helm USA
80E2 Helmand R Afghan
100A3 Helmeringhausen Namibia
46C1 Helmond Neth
44C2 Helmsdale Scot
74B2 Helong China
39G7 Helsingborg Sweden
   Helsingfors = Helsinki
56B1 Helsingør Den
38J6 Helsinki Fin
43B4 Helston Eng
92B4 Helwân Egypt
19A3 Hempstead USA
39H7 Hemse Sweden
72A3 Henan China
72C3 Henan Province, China
110B1 Hen and Chicken Is NZ
14A3 Henderson Kentucky, USA
9B3 Henderson Nevada, USA
19B3 Henderson Texas, USA
73E5 Heng-ch'un Taiwan
68B4 Hengduan Shan Mts China
56B2 Hengelo Neth
72B2 Hengshan China
72D2 Hengshui China
76D1 Hengxian China
73C4 Hengyang China
77A4 Henhoaha Nicobar Is
43D4 Henley-on-Thames Eng
56B2 Henlopen,C USA
78B4 Henrietta Maria,C Can
18A2 Henryetta USA
112C2 Henryk Arctowski Base Ant
6D3 Henry Kater Pen Can
68C2 Hentiyn Nuruu Mts Mongolia
76B2 Henzada Myan
73B5 Hepu China
80E2 Herat Afghan
5H4 Herbert Can
110C2 Herbertville NZ
46E1 Herborn Germany
26A4 Heredia Costa Rica
43C3 Hereford Eng
43C3 Hereford & Worcester County, Eng
46C1 Herentals Belg
47B1 Héricourt France
47C1 Herisau Switz
15D2 Herkimer USA
44E1 Herma Ness Pen Scot
109C2 Hermidale Aust
83B3 Hermitage NZ
   Hermon,Mt = Jebel ash Shaykh
24A2 Hermosillo Mexico
16A2 Herndon Pennsylvania, USA
22C2 Herndon California, USA

46D1 Herne Germany
56B1 Herning Den
90A2 Herowābad Iran
50A2 Herrera del Duque Spain
14C2 Hershey USA
43D4 Hertford County, Eng
94B2 Herzliya Israel
46C1 Hesbaye Region, Belg
46B1 Hesdin France
72B2 Heshui China
22D3 Hesperia USA
12H2 Hess R Can
57B2 Hessen State, Germ
12C2 Hetch Hetchy Res USA
42C2 Hexham Eng
73C5 He Xian China
73C5 Heyuan China
108B3 Heywood Aust
72D2 Heze China
77B3 Hialeah USA
10A2 Hibbing USA
110C1 Hicks Bay NZ
109C3 Hicks,Pt Aust
23B1 Hidalgo State, Mexico
24B2 Hidalgo del Parral Mexico
35B1 Hidrolândia Brazil
96A2 Hierro I Canary Is
75C1 Higashine Japan
74B4 Higashi-suidō Str Japan
20B2 High Desert USA
22B3 High Island USA
44B3 Highland Region, Scot
22D3 Highland USA
22C1 Highland Peak Mt USA
16B2 Highlands Falls USA
11B3 High Point USA
13D1 High Prairie Can
5C4 High River Can
17B2 High Springs USA
16B2 Hightstown USA
43D4 High Wycombe Eng
39J7 Hiiumaa I Estonia
80B3 Hijāz Region, S Arabia
75B2 Hikigawa Japan
75B1 Hikone Japan
110B1 Hikurangi NZ
12B2 Hildago Mexico
24B2 Hidalgo del Parral Mexico
56B2 Hildesheim Germany
27R3 Hillaby,Mt Barbados
56B1 Hillerød Den
14B3 Hillsboro Ohio, USA
20B1 Hillsboro Oregon, USA
19B3 Hillsboro Texas, USA
108C2 Hillston Aust
21C4 Hilo Hawaiian Is
44B3 Hillswick Scot
93C2 Hilvan Turk
56B2 Hilversum Neth
84D2 Himachal Pradesh State, India
82B3 Himalaya Mts Asia
85C4 Himatnagar India
74C4 Himeji Japan
74D3 Himi Japan
92C3 Hims Syria
12E2 Hinchinbrook Entrance USA
85D3 Hindan R India
84B1 Hindu Kush Mts Afghan
87B2 Hindupur India
13D1 Hines Creek Can
85D4 Hinganghat India
69E2 Hinggan Ling Upland China
85B3 Hingol R Pak
85D5 Hingoli India
38H5 Hinnøya I Nor
16C1 Hinsdale USA
13D2 Hinton Can
34B2 Hipolito Itrogoyen Arg

86A2 Hirakud Res India
92B2 Hirfanli Baraji Res Turk
87B2 Hirihar India
74E2 Hirosaki Japan
74C4 Hiroshima Japan
46C2 Hirson France
59B3 Hirşova Rom
56B1 Hirtshals Den
84D3 Hisār India
26C3 Hispaniola I Caribbean S
94C1 Hisyah Syria
93D3 Hit Iraq
73C4 Hitachi Japan
75C1 Hitachi-Ota Japan
43D4 Hitchin Eng
38F6 Hitra I Nor
75A2 Hiuchi-nada B Japan
75A2 Hiwasa Japan
56B1 Hjørring Den
76B1 Hka R Myan
97C4 Ho Ghana
76D1 Hoa Binh Viet
76D3 Hoa Da Viet
97C4 Hobart Aust
9C3 Hobbs USA
56B1 Hobro Den
13C2 Hobson L Can
96E3 Hobyo Somalia
76D1 Ho Chi Minh Viet
57C3 Hochkönig Mt Austria
54B1 Hódmező'hely Hung
59B3 Hodonín Czech Republic
74B2 Hoeryong N Korea
57C2 Hof Germany
38B2 Hofsjökull Mts Iceland
6B2 Höfn Iceland
96C2 Hoggar Upland Alg
46D1 Hohe Acht Mt Germany
72C1 Hohhot China
6J3 Höhn Iceland
68B3 Hoh Sai Hu L China
82C2 Hoh Xil Shan Mts China
99D2 Hoima Uganda
86C1 Hojai India
75A2 Hojo Japan
110B1 Hokianga Harbour B NZ
111B2 Hokitika NZ
74E2 Hokkaidō Japan
109C3 Holbrook Aust
9B3 Holbrook USA
19A2 Holdenville USA
87B2 Hole Narsipur India
27R3 Holetown Barbados
26B2 Holguín Cuba
111B2 Holitika NZ
12C2 Holitna R USA
59B3 Hollabrunn Austria
14A2 Holland USA
22B2 Hollister USA
19C3 Holly Springs USA
22C3 Hollywood California, USA
17B2 Hollywood Florida, USA
4G2 Holman Island Can
38H6 Holmsund Sweden
94B2 Holon Israel
56B1 Holstebro Den
6E3 Holsteinborg Greenland
14B2 Holt USA
18A2 Holton USA
12C2 Holy Cross USA
42B3 Holyhead Wales
42D2 Holy I Eng
43B3 Holy I Wales
16C1 Holyoke Massachusetts, USA
86A2 Homalin Myan
6D3 Home B Can
12D3 Homer Alaska, USA
19B3 Homer Louisiana, USA
111A2 Home Tunnel NZ
17B1 Homerville USA

Homestead

17B2 **Homestead** USA
17A1 **Homewood** USA
81B4 **Honnābad** India
101C3 **Homoine** Mozam
25D3 **Hondo** R Mexico
25D3 **Honduras** Republic, Cent America
25D3 **Honduras,G of** Honduras
39G6 **Henefoss** Nor
15C2 **Honesdale** USA
21A1 **Honey L** USA
76C1 **Hong** R Viet
76D1 **Hon Gai** Viet
73A4 **Honggou** China
73A4 **Hong Hu** L China
72B2 **Honghui** China
73C4 **Hongjiang** China
73C5 **Hong Kong** Colony, S E Asia
68D2 **Hongor** Mongolia
73B5 **Hongshui He** R China
72A3 **Hongyuan** China
72D3 **Hongze He** L China
107E1 **Honiara** Solomon Is
77C4 **Hon Khoai** I Camb
76D3 **Hon Lan** I Viet
38K6 **Honningsvåg** Nor
21C4 **Honolulu** Hawaiian Is
77C4 **Hon Panjang** I Viet
74D3 **Honshu** I Japan
20B1 **Hood,Mt** USA
20B1 **Hood River** USA
45C2 **Hook Head** C Irish Rep
12G3 **Hoonah** USA
12A2 **Hooper Bay** USA
101J1 **Hoopstad** S Africa
56A2 **Hoorn** Neth
9B3 **Hoover Dam** USA
12E2 **Hope** Alaska, USA
19B3 **Hope** Arkansas, USA
13C3 **Hope** Can
7D4 **Hopedale** Can
64D2 **Hopen** I Barents S
6D3 **Hopes Advance,C** Can
108B3 **Hopetoun** Aust
100B3 **Hopetown** S Africa
18C2 **Hopkinsville** USA
20B1 **Hoquiam** USA
93D1 **Horasan** Turk
99F1 **Hordiyo** Somalia
47C1 **Horgen** Switz
105H5 **Horizon Depth** Pacific O
91C4 **Hormuz,Str of** Oman/ Iran
59B3 **Horn** Austria
6H3 **Horn** C Iceland
38H5 **Hornavan** L Sweden
19B3 **Hornbeck** USA
20B2 **Hornbrook** USA
111B2 **Hornby** NZ
7B5 **Hornepayne** Can
4F3 **Horn Mts** Can
42D3 **Hornsea** Eng
72B1 **Horn Uul** Mt Mongolia
30E3 **Horqueta** Par
15C2 **Horseheads** USA
56C1 **Horsens** Den
20B1 **Horseshoe Bay** Can
108B3 **Horsham** Aust
43D4 **Horsham** Eng
39G7 **Horten** Nor
4F3 **Horton** R Can
76D2 **Hose Mts** Malay
85D4 **Hoshangābād** India
84D2 **Hoshiārpur** India
87B1 **Hospet** India
29C7 **Hoste** I Chile
82B2 **Hotan** China
19B3 **Hot Springs** Arkansas, USA
8C2 **Hot Springs** S. Dakota, USA
4G3 **Hottah** Can
46A2 **Houdan** France
72C2 **Houma** China
1984 **Houma** USA
16C2 **Housatonic** R USA
13B2 **Houston** Can

19C3 **Houston** Mississippi, USA
19A4 **Houston** Texas, USA
106A3 **Houtman** Is Aust
68B2 **Hovd** Mongolia
68C1 **Hövsgöl Nuur** L Mongolia
14A2 **Howard City** USA
12C1 **Howard P** USA
109C3 **Howe,C** Aust
101H1 **Howick** S Africa
44C2 **Hoy** I Scot
39F6 **Høyanger** Nor
59B2 **Hradec-Králové** Czech Republic
59B3 **Hranice** Czech Republic
59B3 **Hron** R Slovakia
73E5 **Hsin-chu** Taiwan
73E5 **Hsüeh Shan** Mt Taiwan
72B2 **Huachi** China
32B6 **Huacho** Peru
72C1 **Huade** China
72D3 **Huaibei** China
72D3 **Huaibin** China
72D3 **Huai He** R China
73C4 **Huaihua** China
72D3 **Huaiji** China
72D3 **Huainan** China
69E4 **Hua Hin** Taiwan
32B5 **Huallaga** R Peru
32B5 **Huallanca** Peru
32B5 **Huamachuco** Peru
100A2 **Huambo** Angola
32B6 **Huancabamba** Peru
32B6 **Huancavelica** Peru
32B6 **Huancayo** Peru
73D3 **Huangchuan** China
 Huang Hai = Yellow S
72D2 **Huang He** R China
72B2 **Huangling** China
76D2 **Huangliu** China
73C3 **Huangpi** China
73D4 **Huangshan** China
73C3 **Huangshi** China
34C3 **Huanguelén** Arg
73E4 **Huangyan** China
74B2 **Huanren** China
32B5 **Huánuco** Peru
30C2 **Huanuni** Bol
72B2 **Huan Xian** China
32B5 **Huaráz** Peru
32B6 **Huarmey** Peru
32B5 **Huascarán** Mt Peru
30B4 **Huasco** Chile
23B2 **Huatusco** Mexico
23B1 **Huauchinango** Mexico
23B2 **Huautla** Mexico
72C2 **Hua Xian** China
24B2 **Huayapan** R Mexico
73C3 **Hubei** Province, China
87B1 **Hubli** India
34C3 **Hucal** Arg
74B2 **Huch'ang** N Korea
42D3 **Huddersfield** Eng
39H6 **Hudiksvall** Sweden
17B2 **Hudson** Florida, USA
14B2 **Hudson** Michigan, USA
16C1 **Hudson** New York, USA
16C1 **Hudson** R USA
7B4 **Hudson B** Can
5H4 **Hudson Bay** Can
13C1 **Hudson's Hope** Can
6C3 **Hudson Str** Can
76D2 **Hue** Viet
23B1 **Huejutla** Mexico
50A2 **Huelva** Spain
23A2 **Hueramo** Mexico
51B2 **Huércal Overa** Spain
51B1 **Huesca** Spain
23B2 **Huexotla** Hist Site Mexico
107D3 **Hughenden** Aust
12D1 **Hughes** USA
86B2 **Hugli** R India
19A3 **Hugo** USA
73D4 **Hui'an** China

110C1 **Huiarau Range** Mts NZ
74B2 **Huich'ŏn** N Korea
74B2 **Huifa He** R China
32B3 **Huila** Mt Colombia
73D5 **Huilai** China
73A4 **Huili** China
74B2 **Huinan** China
34C2 **Huinca Renancó** Arg
25C3 **Huixtla** Mexico
73A4 **Huize** China
73C5 **Huizhou** China
23B2 **Hujuapan de Léon** Mexico
69F2 **Hulin** China
15C1 **Hull** Can
42D3 **Hull** Eng
58B1 **Hultsfred** Sweden
63D3 **Hulun Nur** L China
69E1 **Huma** China
33E5 **Humaitá** Brazil
100B4 **Humansdorp** S Africa
42D3 **Humber** R Eng
42D3 **Humberside** County, Eng
5H4 **Humboldt** Can
20C2 **Humboldt** R USA
20B2 **Humboldt B** USA
6D2 **Humboldt Gletscher** Gl Greenland
21B2 **Humboldt L** USA
108C1 **Humeburn** Aust
109C3 **Hume,L** Aust
100A2 **Humpata** Angola
22C2 **Humphreys** USA
38A1 **Húnaflói** B Iceland
73C4 **Hunan** Province, China
74C2 **Hunchun** China
13C2 **Hundred Mile House** Can
54B1 **Hunedoara** Rom
59B3 **Hungary** Republic, Europe
108B1 **Hungerford** Aust
74B3 **Hŭngnam** N Korea
74B2 **Hunjiang** China
46D2 **Hunsrück** Mts, Germany
109D2 **Hunter** R Aust
13B2 **Hunter I** Can
109C4 **Hunter Is** Aust
12D2 **Hunter,Mt** USA
14A3 **Huntingburg** USA
43D3 **Huntingdon** Eng
14A2 **Huntington** Indiana, USA
14B3 **Huntington** W Virginia, USA
22C4 **Huntington Beach** USA
22C2 **Huntington L** USA
110C1 **Huntly** NZ
44C3 **Huntly** Scot
12J2 **Hunt,Mt** Can
108A1 **Hunt Pen** Aust
17A1 **Huntsville** Alabama, USA
7C5 **Huntsville** Can
15C2 **Huntsville** Texas, USA
76D2 **Huong Khe** Viet
71F4 **Huon Peninsula** Pen PNG
109C4 **Huonville** Anst
14B1 **Hurd,C** Can
80B3 **Hurghada** Egypt
8D2 **Huron** S. Dakota, USA
14B1 **Huron,L** Can/USA
34A2 **Hurtado** Chile
111B2 **Hurunui** R NZ
38B1 **Husavík** Iceland
54C1 **Huşi** Rom
39G7 **Huskvarna** Sweden
12C1 **Huslia** USA
94B2 **Husn** Jordan
56B2 **Husum** Germany
109C1 **Hutton,Mt** Aust
72D2 **Hutuo He** R China
46C1 **Huy** Belg
72A2 **Huzhu** China
52C2 **Hvar** I Croatia
100B2 **Hwange** Zim

100B2 **Hwange Nat Pk** Zim
15D2 **Hyannis** USA
68B2 **Hyaryas Nuur** L Mongolia
5E4 **Hydaburg** Can
16C2 **Hyde Park** USA
81B3 **Hyderābād** India
85B3 **Hyderābād** Pak
49D3 **Hyères** France
12J2 **Hyland** R Can
8B2 **Hyndman Peak** Mt USA
38K6 **Hyrynsalmi** Fin
13D1 **Hythe** Can
74C4 **Hyuga** Japan
39J6 **Hyvikää** Fin

I

31C4 **Iaçu** Brazil
54C2 **Ialomiţa** R Rom
54C1 **Iaşi** Rom
97C4 **Ibadan** Nig
32B3 **Ibagué** Colombia
54B2 **Ibar** R Montenegro/ Serbia, Yugos
32B3 **Ibarra** Ecuador
35B1 **Ibiá** Brazil
30E4 **Ibicuí** R Brazil
34D2 **Ibicuy** Arg
51C2 **Ibiza** Spain
51C2 **Ibiza** I Spain
101D2 **Ibo** Mozam
31C4 **Ibotirama** Brazil
91C5 **'Ibri** Oman
32B6 **Ica** Peru
32D4 **Içá** R Brazil
32D3 **Icana** Brazil
38A1 **Iceland** Republic, N Atlantic O
13C2 **Ice Mt** Can
87A1 **Ichalkaranji** India
74E3 **Ichihara** Japan
75B1 **Ichinohe** Japan
74E3 **Ichinoseki** Japan
12F3 **Icy B** USA
4B2 **Icy C** USA
19B3 **Idabell** USA
8B2 **Idaho Falls** USA
20B2 **Idanha** USA
46D2 **Idar Oberstein** Germany
95A2 **Idehan Marzūg** Desert Libya
95A2 **Idehan Ubari** Desert Libya
96C2 **Idelès** Alg
68B2 **Iderlym Gol** R Mongolia
95C2 **Idfu** Egypt
55B3 **Idhi Oros** Mt Greece
55B3 **Idhra** I Greece
98B3 **Idiofa** Zaire
12C2 **Iditarod** R USA
92C2 **Idlib** Syria
39K7 **Idritsa** Russian Fed
100B4 **Idutywa** S Africa
55C3 **Ierápetra** Greece
46B1 **Ieper** Belg
63D2 **Iet Oktyobr'ya** Russian Fed
99D3 **Ifakara** Tanz
71F3 **Ifalik** I Pacific O
101D3 **Ifanadiana** Madag
97C3 **Ife** Nig
97C3 **Iferouane** Niger
78C2 **Igan** Malay
35B2 **Igaranava** Brazil
93E2 **Iğdir** Iran
39H6 **Iggesund** Sweden
34B2 **Iglesia** Arg
53A3 **Iglesias** Sardegna
6B3 **Igloolik** Can
1A2 **Ignace** Can
55B3 **Igoumenitsa** Greece
61H2 **Igra** Russian Fed
23B2 **Iguala** Mexico
35B2 **Iguape** Brazil
32A4 **Iguatama** Brazil
31D3 **Iguatu** Brazil
98A3 **Iguéla** Gabon
101D3 **Ihosy** Madag
74D3 **Iida** Japan
75B1 **Iide-san** Mt Japan
38K6 **Iisalmi** Fin

75A2 Iizuka Japan
97C4 Ijebu Ode Nig
56B2 IJsselmeer S Neth
55C3 Ikaría I Greece
74E2 Ikeda Japan
98C3 Ikela Zaïre
42F1 Ikhtiman Bulg
12D3 Ikolik,C USA
101D2 Ikopa R Madag
79B2 Ilagan Phil
90A3 Ilám Iran
47C1 Ilanz Switz
13F1 Ile à la Crosse Can
13F1 Ile à la Crosse,L Can
89G8 Ilebo Zaïre
96D1 Ile de Jerba I Tunisia
48B2 Ile de Noirmoutier I France
48B2 Ile de Ré I France
107F3 Ile des Pins I Nouvelle Calédonie
48A2 Ile d'Ouessant I France
48B2 Ile d'Yeu I France
61J3 Ilek R Russian Fed
107F2 Iles Bélep Nouvelle Calédonie
107E2 Iles Chesterfield Nouvelle Calédonie
43B4 Iles d'Hyères I France
92B1 Ilgaz Dağlari Mts Turk
101C3 Ilha Bazaruto I Mozam
33G3 Ilha De Maracá I Brazil
33G4 Ilha de Marajó I Brazil
35B2 Ilha de São Sebastião I Brazil
33G6 Ilha do Bananal Region Brazil
35C2 Ilha Grande I Brazil
35C2 Ilha Santo Amaro I Brazil
96A1 Ilhas Selvagens I Atlantic O
35A2 Ilha Solteira Dam Brazil
31D4 Ilhéus Brazil
12C3 Iliamna L USA
12D2 Iliamna V USA
79B4 Iligan Phil
63C2 Ilim R Russian Fed
63C2 Ilim Russian Fed
63G3 Il'inskiy Russian Fed
55B3 Iliodhrómia I Greece
79B4 Illana B Phil
34A2 Illapel Chile
34A2 Illapel R Chile
97C3 Illéla Niger
47D1 Iller R Germany
4C4 Illimani L USA
10A2 Illinois State, USA
18B2 Illinois R USA
96C3 Illizi Alg
30B2 Ilo Peru
79B3 Iloilo Phil
38L6 Ilomantsi Fin
97C4 Ilorin Nig
75B1 Imabari Japan
51B1 Imaichi Japan
60C1 Imatra Fin
30G4 Imbituba Brazil
99E2 Imi Eth
20C2 Imlay USA
47D1 Immenstadt Germany
52B2 Imola Italy
31B3 Imperatriz Brazil
52A2 Imperia Italy
98B2 Impfondo Congo
86C2 Imphal India
47C1 Imst Austria
12B1 Imuruk L USA
90A2 Ina Japan
76B2 In Afahleleh Well Alg
75B2 Inamba-jima I Japan
96C2 In Amenas Alg
38K5 Inari Fin
38K5 Inarijärvi L Fin

75C1 Inawashiro-ko L Japan
96C2 In Belbel Alg
60E5 Ince Burun Pt Turk
92B2 Incekum Burun Pt Turk
74B3 Inch'ŏn S Korea
96B2 In Dagouber Well Mali
35B1 Indaia R Brazil
38H6 Indals R Sweden
21B2 Independence USA
18A2 Independence Kansas, USA
18B2 Independence Missouri, USA
78A3 Inderagiri R Indon
61H4 Inderborskly Kazakhstan
83B3 India Federal Republic, Asia
14A2 Indiana State, USA
15C2 Indiana USA
104C6 Indian-Antarctic Ridge Indian O
14A3 Indianapolis USA
Indian Desert = Thar Desert
7J4 Indian Harbour Can
104B4 Indian O
18B1 Indianola Iowa, USA
19B3 Indianola Mississippi, USA
35B1 Indianópolis Brazil
76D2 Indo China Region, S E Asia
70C4 Indonesia Republic, S E Asia
85D4 Indore India
78B4 Indramayu Indon
48C2 Indre R France
84C2 Indus R Pak
92B2 Inebolu Turk
96C2 In Ebeggi Well Alg
96C2 In Ecker Alg
92A1 Inegöl Turk
96D2 In Ezzane Alg
97C3 Ingal Niger
14B2 Ingersoll Can
107D2 Ingham Aust
6D2 Inglefield Land Region Can
110B1 Inglewood NZ
109C1 Inglewood Queensland, Aust
22C4 Inglewood USA
108B3 Inglewood Victoria, Aust
38B2 Ingólfshöfði I Iceland
57C3 Ingolstadt Germany
86B2 Ingraj Bāzār India
96C3 In-Guezzam Well Alg
101C3 Inhambane Mozam
101C3 Inharrime Mozam
35B1 Inhumas Brazil
32D3 Inírida R Colombia
45A2 Inishbofin I Irish Rep
45A1 Inishkea I Irish Rep
45B2 Inishmaan I Irish Rep
45B2 Inishmore I Irish Rep
45B1 Inishmurray I Irish Rep
45C1 Inishowen District, Irish Rep
45A2 Inishshark I Irish Rep
45A2 Inishturk I Irish Rep
109C1 Injune Aust
12H3 Inklin Can
12H3 Inklin R Can
12C1 Inland L USA
47D1 Inn R Austria
108B1 Innamincka Aust
68C2 Inner Mongolia Autonomous Region, China
107D2 Innisfail Aust
12C2 Innoko R USA
57C3 Innsbruck Austria
98B3 Inongo Zaïre
58B2 Inowrocław Pol
96C2 In Salah Alg
47B1 Interlaken Switz

24C3 Intexpec Mexico
47C2 Intra Italy
78D1 Intu Indon
75C1 Inubo-saki C Japan
7C4 Inukjuak Can
4E3 Inuvik Can
4F3 Inuvik Region Can
44B3 Inveraray Scot
111A3 Invercargill NZ
44C3 Inverbervie Scot
13D2 Invermere Can
44A3 Inverness Scot
44C3 Inverurie Scot
108A2 Investigator Str Aust
68A1 Inya Russian Fed
21B2 Inyokern USA
98B3 Inza R Zaïre
55B3 Ioánnina Greece
18A2 Iola USA
44B3 Iona I Scot
100A2 Iôna Nat Pk Angola
20C1 Ione USA
Ionian Is = Ionioi Nisoi
55A3 Ionian S Italy/Greece
55B3 Ionioi Nisoi Is Greece
55C3 Ios I Greece
10A2 Iowa R USA
10A2 Iowa City USA
35B1 Ipameri Brazil
35C1 Ipanema Brazil
61F4 Ipatovo Russian Fed
32B3 Ipiales Colombia
77C5 Ipoh Malay
30F2 Iporá Brazil
55C2 Ipsala Turk
109D1 Ipswich Aust
43E3 Ipswich Eng
16D1 Ipswich USA
30B3 Iquique Chile
32C4 Iquitos Peru
55C3 Iráklion Greece
80D2 Iran Republic, S W Asia
91D4 Iranshahr Iran
23A1 Irapuato Mexico
93D3 Iraq Republic, S W Asia
95A2 Irã Wan Watercourse Libya
94F2 Irbid Jordan
61K2 Irbit Russian Fed
36C3 Ireland Republic, NW Europe
33F3 Ireng R Guyana
74B3 Iri S Korea
71E4 Irian Jaya Province, Indon
95B3 Iriba Chad
93D3 Iriga Phil
99D3 Iringa Tanz
69E4 Iriomote I Japan
33G5 Iriri R Brazil
42B3 Irish S Eng/Irish Rep
12D1 Irkillik R USA
63C2 Irkutsk Russian Fed
65J4 Irlysh R Kazakhstan
108A2 Iron Knob Aust
14A1 Iron Mountain USA
107D2 Iron Range Aust
14A1 Iron River USA
14B3 Ironton USA
14A2 Ironwood USA
10B2 Iroquois Falls Can
75B2 Iro-zaki C Japan
76A2 Irrawaddy,Mouths of the Myan
65H4 Irtysh R Russian Fed
51B1 Irun Spain
42B2 Irvine Scot
19A3 Irving USA
79B4 Isabela Phil
32J7 Isabela I Ecuador
4H2 Isachsen Can
4H2 Isachsen,C Can
6H3 Isafjördur Iceland
75A2 Isahaya Japan
98C2 Isangi Zaïre
47D1 Isar R Germany
44E1 Isbister Scot
47D1 Ischgl Austria
52B2 Ischia I Italy

75B2 Ise Japan
47D2 Iseo Italy
47D1 Iserlohn Germany
53B2 Isernia Italy
75B2 Ise-wan B Japan
69E4 Ishigaki I Japan
74E2 Ishikari R Japan
74E2 Ishikari-wan B Japan
69H4 Ishim Russian Fed
65H4 Ishim R Kazakhstan
74E3 Ishinomaki Japan
75C1 Ishioka Japan
84C1 Ishkashim Afghan
14A1 Ishpeming USA
61G3 Isil'kul Russian Fed
99D2 Isiolo Kenya
98C2 Isiro Zaïre
92C2 Iskenderun Turk
92C2 Iskenferun Körfezi B Turk
92B1 Iskilip Turk
65K4 Iskitim Russian Fed
54B2 Iskur R Bulg
12H3 Iskut R Can
23B2 Isla Mexico
34C3 Isla Bermejo I Arg
27E4 Isla Blanquilla Ven
32A2 Isla Coiba I Panama
9B4 Isla de Cedros I Mexico
29B4 Isla de Chiloé I Chile
25D2 Isla de Cozumel I Mexico
26C3 Isla de la Gonâve I
26A2 Isla de la Juventud I Cuba
34D2 Isla de las Lechiguanas I Arg
3K8 Isla del Coco I Costa Rica
25D3 Isla del Maíz I Caribbean S
23B1 Isla de Lobos I Mexico
29D6 Isla de los Estados I Arg
28E2 Isla de Marajó I Brazil
105L5 Isla de Pascua I Pacific O
26A4 Isla de Providencia I Caribbean S
26A4 Isla de San Andres I Caribbean S
30G4 Isla de Santa Catarina I Brazil
33G2 Isla du Diable I French Guiana
31E2 Isla Fernando de Noronha I Brazil
29C6 Isla Grande de Tierra del Fuego I Arg/Chile
27D4 Isla la Tortuga I Ven
84C2 Islamabad Pak
24A2 Isla Magdalena I Mexico
27E4 Isla Margarita Ven
34A3 Isla Mocha Chile
10A1 Island L Can
108A2 Island Lg Aust
110B1 Islands,B of NZ
32A4 Isla Puná I Ecuador
103D6 Isla San Ambrosia I Pacific O
103D6 Isla San Felix I Pacific O
24A2 Isla Santa Margarita I Mexico
34A3 Isla Santa Maria I Chile
51C2 Islas Baleares Is Spain
96A2 Islas Canarias Is Atlantic O
51C2 Islas Columbretes Is Spain
25D3 Islas de la Bahia Is Honduras
26A4 Islas del Maíz Is Caribbean S
33E1 Islas de Margarita Is Ven

Islas Diego Ramírez

29C7 **Islas Diego Ramirez** *Is* Chile
32J7 **Islas Galapagos** *Is* Pacific O
30H6 **Islas Juan Fernández** *Is* Chile
32D1 **Islas los Roques** *Is* Ven
   Islas Malvinas = Falkland Is
105L3 **Islas Revilla Gigedo** *Is* Pacific O
29C7 **Islas Wollaston** *Is* Chile
97A3 **Isla Tidra** *I* Maur
29B5 **Isla Weilington** *I* Chile
48C2 **Isle** *F* France
104B5 **Isle Amsterdam** *I* Indian O
43D4 **Isle of Wight** *I* Eng
10B2 **Isle Royale** *I* USA
104B5 **Isle St Paul** *I* Indian O
104A6 **Isles Crozet** *I* Indian O
105J4 **Isles la de la Société** Pacific O
105K5 **Isles Gambier** *Is* Pacific O
101D2 **Isles Glorieuses** *Is* Madag
104B6 **Isles Kerguelen** *Is* Indian O
105K4 **Isles Marquises** *Is* Pacific O
105J4 **Isles Tuamotu** *Is* Pacific O
105J5 **Isles Tubai** *Is* Pacific O
22B1 **Isleton** USA
92B3 **Ismâ'ilîya** Egypt
101D3 **Isoanala** Madag
101C2 **Isoka** Zambia
53B3 **Isola Egadi** *I* Italy
52B2 **Isola Ponziane** *I* Italy
53B3 **Isole Lipari** *Is* Italy
52C2 **Isoles Tremiti** *Is* Italy
75B1 **Isosaki** Japan
92B2 **Isparta** Turk
94B2 **Israel** Republic, S W Asia
51C2 **Isser** *R* Alg
48C2 **Issoire** France
49C2 **Issoudun** France
92A1 **Istanbul** Turk
55B3 **Istiáia** Greece
25C3 **Istmo de Tehuantepec** *Isthmus* Mexico
17B2 **Istokpoga,L** USA
52B1 **Istra** *Pen* Croatia
35B1 **Itaberai** Brazil
35C1 **Itabira** Brazil
35C2 **Itabirito** Brazil
33F4 **Itabuna** Brazil
33F4 **Itacoatiara** Brazil
32B2 **Itagui** Colombia
33F4 **Itaituba** Brazil
30C4 **Itajaí** Brazil
35B2 **Itajuba** Brazil
52B2 **Italy** Republic, Europe
35D1 **Itamaraju** Brazil
35C1 **Itamarandiba** Brazil
35C1 **Itambacuri** Brazil
35C1 **Itambé** *Mt* Brazil
86C1 **Itänagar** India
35B2 **Itanhaém** Brazil
35B2 **Itanhém** Brazil
35C1 **Itaobim** Brazil
35B2 **Itapecerica** Brazil
35C2 **Itaperuna** Brazil
31C5 **Itapetinga** Brazil
35B2 **Itapetininga** Brazil
35B2 **Itapeva** Brazil
33F4 **Itapicuru** Brazil
35B1 **Itapiranga** Brazil
30E4 **Itaqui** Brazil
35C1 **Itarantim** Brazil
35B2 **Itararé** Brazil
35B2 **Itararé** *R* Brazil
35C2 **Itaúna** Brazil

33E6 **Iténez** *R* Brazil/Bol
15C2 **Ithaca** USA
96C2 **Itanbiri** *R* Zaire
35C1 **Itinga** Brazil
6E3 **Itivdleq** Greenland
75B2 **Ito** Japan
74D3 **Toigawa** Japan
33E6 **Itonomas** *R* Bol
35B2 **Itu** Brazil
35B1 **Itumbiara** Brazil
35A1 **Iturama** Brazil
30C3 **Iturbe** Arg
35B1 **Iturutaba** Brazil
56B2 **Itzehoe** Germany
58D2 **Ivacevichi** Belarus
35A2 **Ivai** *R* Brazil
38K5 **Ivalo** Fin
54A2 **Ivangrad** Montenegro, Yugos
108J2 **Ivanhoe** Aust
59C3 **Ivano-Frankovsk** Ukraine
61F2 **Ivanovo** Russian Fed
65H3 **Ivdel'** Russian Fed
98B2 **Ivindo** *R* Gabon
101D3 **Ivohibe** Madag
101D2 **Ivongo Soanierana** Madag
52A1 **Ivrea** Italy
6C3 **Ivujivik** Can
74E3 **Iwaki** Japan
74C4 **Iwakuni** Japan
74E2 **Iwanai** Japan
69G4 **Iwo** Nig
23B1 **Ixmiquilpa** Mexico
23A2 **Ixtapa** Mexico
23A1 **Ixtlán** Mexico
75A2 **Iyo** Japan
75A2 **Iyo-nada** *B* Japan
65G4 **Izhevsk** Russian Fed
64G3 **Izhma** Russian Fed
91C5 **Izki** Oman
60C4 **Izmail** Ukraine
92A2 **Izmir** Turk
55C3 **Izmir Körfezi** *B* Turk
92A1 **Izmit** Turk
92A1 **Iznik** Turk
55C2 **Iznik Golü** *L* Turk
94C2 **Izra'** Syria
23B2 **Izúcar de Matamoros** Mexico
75B2 **Izumi-sano** Japan
75A1 **Izumo** Japan
74D4 **Izu-shotô** *Is* Japan

J

95B1 **Jabal al Akhdar** *Mts* Libya
94C2 **Jabal al 'Arab** Syria
95A2 **Jabal as Sawdâ** *Mts* Libya
91B5 **Jabal az Zannah** UAE
94C1 **Jabal Halîmah** Leb/Syria
83B3 **Jabalpur** India
59B2 **Jablonec nad Nisou** Czech Republic
31D3 **Jaboatão** Brazil
35B2 **Jaboticabal** Brazil
51B1 **Jaca** Spain
23B1 **Jacala** Mexico
33F5 **Jacareacanga** Brazil
35B2 **Jacareí** Brazil
30F3 **Jacarezinho** Brazil
29C2 **Jáchal** Arg
35C1 **Jacinto** Brazil
13F2 **Jackfish L** Can
109C1 **Jackson** Aust
22B1 **Jackson** California, USA
14B2 **Jackson** Michigan, USA
19B3 **Jackson** Mississippi, USA
18C2 **Jackson** Missouri, USA
14B3 **Jackson** Ohio, USA
11B3 **Jackson** Tennessee, USA
111B2 **Jackson,C** NZ
111A2 **Jackson Head** *Pt* NZ
19B3 **Jacksonville** Arkansas, USA

17B1 **Jacksonville** Florida, USA
18B2 **Jacksonville** Illinois, USA
17C1 **Jacksonville** N Carolina, USA
19A3 **Jacksonville** Texas, USA
17B1 **Jacksonville Beach** USA
26C3 **Jacmel** Haiti
84B3 **Jacobabad** Pak
31C4 **Jacobina** Brazil
23A2 **Jacona** Mexico
   Jadotville = Likasi
32B5 **Jaén** Peru
50B2 **Jaén** Spain
   Jaffa = Tel Aviv Yafo
108A3 **Jaffa,C** Aust
87B3 **Jaffna** Sri Lanka
86B2 **Jagannathganj Ghat** Bang
87C1 **Jagdalpur** India
91C4 **Jagin** *R* Iran
87B1 **Jagtial** India
29F2 **Jaguarão** *R* Brazil
35B2 **Jahrom** Iran
86D5 **Jäina** India
72A2 **Jainca** China
85C3 **Jaipur** India
90C2 **Jajarm** Iran
52C2 **Jajce** Bosnia-Herzegovina
78B4 **Jakarta** Indon
6E3 **Jakobshavn** Greenland
38J6 **Jakobstad** Fin
84B2 **Jalai-Kut** Afghan
84D2 **Jalandhar** India
23B2 **Jalapa** Mexico
35A2 **Jales** Brazil
86B1 **Jaleswar** Nepal
85B4 **Jalgaon** India
97D4 **Jalingo** Nig
51B1 **Jalón** *R* Spain
85C3 **Jalor** India
23A1 **Jalostotitlan** Mexico
86B1 **Jalpáiguri** India
23B1 **Jalpan** Mexico
95B2 **Jâlû Oasis** Libya
32A4 **Jama** Ecuador
26B3 **Jamaica** *I* Caribbean S
26B3 **Jamaica Chan** Caribbean S
86B2 **Jamalpur** Bang
78A3 **Jambi** Indon
85C4 **Jambussar** India
7B4 **James B** Can
5J5 **Jameston** USA
108D2 **Jamestown** Aust
8D2 **Jamestown** N. Dakota, USA
15C2 **Jamestown** New York, USA
16D2 **Jamestown** Rhode Island, USA
23B2 **Jamiltepec** Mexico
87B1 **Jamkhandi** India
84C2 **Jammu** India
84D2 **Jammu and Kashmir** State, India
85B4 **Jamnagar** India
84C3 **Jampur** Pak
38K6 **Jämsä** Fin
86B2 **Jamshedpur** India
86B1 **Janakpur** Nepal
35C1 **Janaúba** Brazil
90B3 **Jandaq** Iran
109D1 **Jandowae** Aust
1B1 **Jan Mayen** *I* Norwegian S
35C1 **Januária** Brazil
85D4 **Jaora** India
51 **Japan** Empire, E Asia
74C3 **Japan,S of** S E Asia
104F2 **Japan Trench** Pacific O
32D4 **Japurá** *R* Brazil
93C2 **Jarâbulus** Syria
35B1 **Jaraguá** Brazil

50B1 **Jarama** *R* Spain
94B2 **Jarash** Jordan
30E3 **Jardim** Brazil
51B2 **Jardin** *R* Spain
26B2 **Jardines de la Reina** *Is* Cuba
   Jargalant = Hovd
33G3 **Jari** *R* Brazil
86C1 **Jaria Jhanjail** Bang
46C2 **Jarny** France
58B2 **Jarocin** Pol
59C2 **Jaroslaw** Pol
38G6 **Järpen** Sweden
72A2 **Jartai** China
85C4 **Jasdan** India
97C4 **Jasikan** Ghana
84C3 **Jask** Iran
59C3 **Jaslo** Pol
29D6 **Jason Is** Falkland Is
87B2 **Jasper** Arkansas, USA
13D2 **Jasper** Can
17B1 **Jasper** Florida, USA
14A3 **Jasper** Indiana, USA
19B3 **Jasper** Texas, USA
13D2 **Jasper Nat Pk** Can
58B2 **Jastrowie** Pol
35A1 **Jataí** Brazil
51B2 **Játiva** Spain
35B2 **Jaú** Brazil
32B6 **Jauja** Peru
84A1 **Jaunpur** India
   Java = Jawa
87B2 **Javadi Hills** India
32C5 **Javari** = Yavari
70B4 **Java S** Indon
106A2 **Java Trench** Indon
78B4 **Jawa** *I* Indon
77D4 **Jayapura** Indon
32F7 **Jayrûd** Syria
96B2 **Jbel Ouarkziz** *Mts* Mor
96B1 **Jbel Sarhro** *Mt* Mor
19B4 **Jeanerette** USA
97C4 **Jebba** Nig
93D2 **Jebel 'Abd al 'Aziz** *Mt* Syria
95B3 **Jebel Abyad** Sudan
91C5 **Jebel Akhdar** *Mt* Oman
92C3 **Jebel al Lawz** *Mt* S Arabia
94B2 **Jebel ash Shaykh** *Mt* Syria
95C2 **Jebel Asoteriba** *Mt* Sudan
94B3 **Jebel Ed Dabab** *Mt* Jordan
92C3 **Jebel esh Sharqi** *Mt* Leb/Syria
94C3 **Jebel Ithriyat** *Mt* Jordan
91C5 **Jebel Ja'lan** *Mt* Oman
94B2 **Jebel Liban** *Mts* Leb
94B2 **Jebel Ma'lûlâ** *Mt* Syria
98C1 **Jebel Marra** *Mt* Sudan
94C3 **Jebel Mudeisisat** *Mt* Jordan
95C2 **Jebel Oda** *Mt* Sudan
94B3 **Jebel Qasr ed Deir** *Mt* Jordan
94B2 **Jebel Um ed Daraj** *Mt* Jordan
95B2 **Jebel Uweinat** *Mt* Sudan
42C2 **Jedburgh** Scot
   Jedda = Jiddah
59C2 **Jedrzejów** Pol
19B3 **Jefferson** Texas, USA
11A3 **Jefferson City** USA
8B3 **Jefferson,Mt** USA
60C2 **Jekabpils** Latvia
59B2 **Jelena Gora** Pol
60B2 **Jelgava** Latvia
78C4 **Jember** Indon
57C2 **Jena** Germany
78B2 **Jenaja** *I* Indon

47D1 Jenbach Austria
94B2 Jenin Israel
19B3 Jennings USA
59B2 Jenseniky Upland
Czech Republic
6F3 Jensen Nunatakker
Mt Greenland
6B3 Jens Munk I Can
108B3 Jeparit Aust
31D4 Jequié Brazil
35C1 Jequitaí R Brazil
31C5 Jequitinhonha Brazil
31C5 Jequitinhonha R
Brazil
50A2 Jerez de la Frontera
Spain
50A2 Jerez de los
Caballeros Spain
94B3 Jericho Israel
108C3 Jerilderie Aust
48B2 Jersey I UK
10C2 Jersey City USA
18B2 Jersey Shore USA
18B2 Jerseyville USA
92C3 Jerusalem Israel
109D3 Jervis B Aust
13C2 Jervis Inlet Sd Can
52B1 Jesenice Slovenia
86B2 Jessore Bang
11B3 Jesup USA
34C2 Jesus Maria Arg
62D2 Jewett City USA
54A2 Jezerce Mt Alb
58C2 Jezioro Mamry L Pol
58C2 Jezioro Śniardwy L
Pol
85C3 Jezzine Leb
85A2 Jhábua India
85D4 Jhálawar India
86A2 Jhársuguda India
85D3 Jhánsi India
84C2 Jhelum Pak
84C2 Jhelum R Pak
11C3 J H Kerr L USA
84D3 Jhunjhunūn India
69F2 Jiamusi China
74B2 Ji'an Jiangxi, China
74B2 Ji'an China
73D4 Jiande China
73D4 Jiang'an China
73D4 Jiangbiancun China
73A5 Jiangcheng China
73B3 Jiang Jiang R China
73C5 Jiangmen China
72D3 Jiangsu Province,
China
73C4 Jiangxi Province,
China
73A3 Jiangyou China
72D1 Jianping China
73A5 Jianshui China
73D4 Jian Xi R China
73D4 Jianyang China
73D4 Jiaonan China
72E2 Jiao Xian China
72E2 Jiaozhou Wan B
China
72C2 Jiaozuo China
73C3 Jiaxiang China
68B3 Jiayuguan China
81B3 Jiddah S Arabia
72D3 Jieshou China
72A3 Jiexiu China
72A3 Jigzhi China
59B3 Jihlava
Czech Republic
99E2 Jilib Somalia
69E2 Jilin China
51B1 Jiloca R Spain
99D2 Jima Eth
9C4 Jiménez Coahuila,
Mexico
72A3 Jinan China
84D3 Jind India
72D2 Jingbian China
73C4 Jingdezhen China
76C1 Jinghong China
73C3 Jingmen China
73B4 Jing Xiang China
73B4 Jing Xian China
72C2 Jining Nei Monggol,
China

72D2 Jining Shandong,
China
99D2 Jinja Uganda
76C1 Jinping China
73A4 Jinsha Jiang R
China
73C4 Jinshi China
72E2 Jin Xian China
72E1 Jinzhou China
33E5 Jiparaná R Brazil
32A4 Jipijapa Ecuador
23A2 Jiquilpan Mexico
91C4 Jiroft Iran
99E2 Jirriban Somalia
73B4 Jishou China
92C2 Jisr ash Shughūr
Syria
54B2 Jiu R Rom
73D4 Jiujiang China
73A4 Jiulong China
73D4 Jiulong Jiang R
China
69F2 Jixi China
94B3 Jiza Jordan
81C4 Jīzan S Arabia
97A3 Joal Sen
35C1 João Monlevade
Brazil
31E3 João Pessoa Brazil
35B1 João Pirheiro Brazil
38A2 Jocoli Arg
85C3 Jodhpur India
38K6 Joensuu Fin
46C2 Joeuf France
13D2 Joffre,Mt Can
86B1 Jogbani India
87A2 Jog Falls India
10B2 Johannesburg
S Africa
21B2 Johannesburg USA
6C2 Johan Pen Can
12D1 John R USA
20C2 John Day USA
20B1 John Day R USA
44C2 John O'Groats Scot
18A2 John Redmond Res
USA
11B3 Johnson City
Tennessee, USA
17B1 Johnston USA
27N2 Johnston Pt
St Vincent and the
Grenadines
77C5 Johor Bharu Malay
49C2 Joigny France
30G4 Joinville Brazil
61H3 Jok R Russian Fed
38H5 Jokkmokk Sweden
93E2 Jolfa Iran
10B2 Joliet USA
7C5 Joliette Can
79B4 Jolo Phil
79B4 Jolo I Phil
82D2 Joma Mt China
58C1 Jonava Lithuania
72A3 Jonê China
11A3 Jonesboro Arkansas,
USA
19B3 Jonesboro Louisiana,
USA
6B2 Jones Sd Can
58C1 Joniškis Lithuania
39J7 Jönköping Sweden
11A3 Joplin USA
92C3 Jordan Kingdom,
S W Asia
91B4 Jordan R Israel
20C2 Jordan Valley USA
86C1 Jorhāt India
38J5 Jörn Sweden
78C3 Jorong Indon
39F7 Jørpeland Nor
79B3 Jose Pañganiban Phil
106B2 Joseph Bonaparte G
Aust
64B3 Jotunheimen Mt Nor
94B2 Jouai'ya Leb
94B2 Jounié Leb
86C1 Jowai India
99E2 Jowhar Somalia
12H2 Joy,Mt Can

5F5 Juan de Fuca,Str of
Can/USA
101D2 Juan de Nova I
Mozam Chan
34D3 Juárez Arg
31D3 Juazeiro Brazil
31D3 Juazeiro do Norte
Brazil
99D2 Juba Sudan
99E2 Juba R Somalia
94B1 Jubail Leb
93D3 Jubbah S Arabia
96A2 Juby,C Mor
51B2 Jucar R Spain
23B2 Juchatengo Mexico
23A1 Juchipila R Mexico
23A1 Juchitán Mexico
57C3 Judenburg Austria
30A2 Juilaca Peru
73C4 Juiling Shan Hills
China
31C6 Juiz de Fora Brazil
30C3 Jujuy State, Arg
33F3 Julianatop Mt
Surinam
6F3 Julianehåb
Greenland
46D1 Jülich Germany
86A1 Jumla Nepal
94B3 Jum Suwwāna Mt
Jordan
85C4 Jūnāgadh India
72D2 Junan China
31B6 Jundiaí Brazil
5E4 Juneau USA
107D4 Junee Aust
22C2 June Lake USA
52A1 Jungfrau Mt Switz
16A2 Juniata R USA
30B2 Junín Arg
73A4 Junlian China
31B6 Juquiá Brazil
99C2 Jur R Sudan
42B2 Jura I Scot
49D2 Jura Mts France
43C4 Jura,Sound of Chan
Scot
94B3 Jurf ed Darāwish
Jordan
65K4 Jurga Russian Fed
60B2 Jūrmala Latvia
33F6 Juruena R Brazil
94C1 Jūsiyah Syria
34B2 Justo Daract Arg
32E4 Jutaí R Brazil
25D3 Juticalpa Honduras
Jutland = Jylland
90C3 Jūymand Iran
88K6 Juzur al Halaniyat Is
Oman
56B1 Jylland Pen Den
38K6 Jyväskylä Fin

K

82B2 K2 Mt China/India
90C2 Kaakhka
Turkmenistan
101H1 Kaapmuiden S Africa
71D4 Kabaena I Indon
97A4 Kabala Sierra Leone
99D3 Kabale Uganda
98C3 Kabalo Zaire
98C3 Kabambare Zaire
99D2 Kabarole Uganda
98C3 Kabinda Zaire
94A3 Kabir Kuh Mts Iran
100B2 Kabompo Zambia
100B2 Kabompo R Zambia
98C3 Kabongo Zaire
84B2 Kabul Afghan
85B4 Kachchh,G of India
61J2 Kachkanar
Russian Fed
63C2 Kachug Russian Fed
78B2 Kadan Myan
78B3 Kadapongan I Indon
85C4 Kadi India
108A2 Kadina Aust
92B2 Kadinhani Turk
87B2 Kadiri India
60E4 Kadiyevka Ukraine

100B2 Kadoma Zim
99C1 Kadugli Sudan
97C3 Kaduna Nig
97C3 Kaduna R Nig
97A3 Kaédi Maur
21C4 Kaena Pt Hawaiian Is
74B3 Kaesong N Korea
97C3 Kafanchan Nig
97A3 Kaffrine Sen
94C1 Kafrūn Bashūr Syria
100B2 Kafue Zambia
100B2 Kafue R Zambia
100B2 Kafue Nat Pk Zambia
74D3 Kaga Japan
65H6 Kagan Kazakhstan
93D1 Kağizman Turk
74C4 Kagoshima Japan
99D3 Kahama Tanz
84B3 Kahan Pak
78C3 Kahayan R Indon
98B3 Kahemba Zaire
46E1 Kahler Asten Mt
Germany
91C4 Kahnūj Iran
18B1 Kahoka USA
21C4 Kahoolawe I
Hawaiian Is
92C2 Kahramanmaraş
Turk
21C4 Kahuku Pt Hawaiian
Is
111B2 Kaiapoi NZ
33F2 Kaieteur Fall Guyana
72C3 Kaifeng China
110B1 Kaikohe NZ
111B2 Kaikoura NZ
111B2 Kaikoura Pen NZ
111B2 Kaikoura Range Mts
NZ
73B4 Kaili China
21C4 Kailua Hawaiian Is
21C4 Kaimana Indon
75B2 Kainan Japan
97C3 Kainji Res Nig
110B1 Kaipara Harbour B
NZ
73C5 Kaiping China
96D1 Kairouan Tunisia
22C2 Kaiser Peak Mt USA
46E2 Kaiserslautern
Germany
74B2 Kaishantun China
58D2 Kaisiadorys
Lithuania
110B1 Kaitaia NZ
111A3 Kaitangata NZ
84D3 Kaithal India
21C4 Kaiwi Chan Hawaiian
Is
73B3 Kai Xian China
73A5 Kaiyuan Liaoning,
China
74A2 Kaiyuan Yunnan,
China
12C2 Kaiyuh Mts USA
38K6 Kajaani Fin
84B2 Kajaki Afghan
99D3 Kajiado Kenya
99D1 Kajrān Afghan
99D1 Kaka Sudan
99D3 Kakamega Kenya
75A2 Kake Japan
12H3 Kake USA
12D3 Kakhonak USA
65E5 Kakhovskoye
Vodokhranilishche
Res Ukraine
91B4 Kākī Iran
87C1 Kākināda India
74C3 Kakogawa Japan
4D2 Kaktovik USA
75C1 Kakuda Japan
Kalaallit Nunaat =
Greenland
55B3 Kalabáka Greece
77C4 Kalabakan Malay
100B2 Kalabo Zambia
61F3 Kalach Russian Fed
86C2 Kaladan R Myan
21C4 Ka Lae C Hawaiian Is

100B3 Kalahari Desert Botswana
38J6 Kalajoki Fin
63D2 Kalakan Russian Fed
70A3 Kalakepen Indon
84C1 Kalam Pak
55B3 Kalámai Greece
10B2 Kalamazoo USA
84B3 Kalat Pak
92B1 Kaleik Turk
78D3 Kalembau I Indon
99C3 Kalémié Zaire
38L5 Kalevala Russian Fed
86C2 Kalewa Myan
12D2 Kalgin I USA
106B4 Kalgoorlie Aust
78B4 Kalianda Indon
79B3 Kalibo Phil
98C3 Kalima Zaire
78C3 Kalimantan Province, Indon
55C3 Kálimnos I Greece
86B1 Kálimpang India
100B3 Kaliningrad Russian Fed
60C3 Kalinkovichi Belarus
8B2 Kalispell USA
58B2 Kalisz Pol
99D3 Kaliua Tanz
38J5 Kalix R Sweden
100A3 Kalkfeld Namibia
94D3 Kalkrand Namibia
108A1 Kalkoopah R Aust
38K6 Kallavesi L Fin
55C3 Kallonís Kólpos B Greece
39H7 Kalmar Sweden
61G4 Kalmytskaya Respublika, Russian Fed
100B2 Kalomo Zambia
18B1 Kalona USA
13B2 Kalone Peak Mt Can
87A2 Kalpeni I India
85D3 Kálpi India
53A3 Kalaat Khasba Tunisia
12B2 Kalskag USA
12C2 Kaltag USA
60E3 Kaluga Russian Fed
39G7 Kalundborg Den
59C3 Kalush Ukraine
87B2 Kalyandurg India
60E2 Kalyazin Russian Fed
61H1 Kama R Russian Fed
74E3 Kamaishi Japan
84C2 Kamalia Pak
110C1 Kamanawa Mts NZ
100A2 Kamanjab Namibia
84D2 Kamat Mt India
87B3 Kamban India
61H2 Kambarka Russian Fed
97A4 Kambia Sierra Leone
59D3 Kamenets Podolskiy Ukraine
61F3 Kamenka Russian Fed
65K4 Kamen-na-Obi Russian Fed
61K2 Kamensk-Ural'skiy Russian Fed
5H3 Kamilukuak L Can
98C3 Kamina Zaire
7A3 Kaminak L Can
75C1 Kaminoyama Japan
5F4 Kamloops Can
93E1 Kamo Armenia
75C1 Kamogawa Japan
90D2 Kampala Uganda
77C5 Kampar Malay
78A2 Kampar R Indon
56B2 Kampen Neth
76B2 Kamphaeng Phet Thai
76C3 Kampot Camb
91D4 Kamsaptar Iran
61J2 Kamskoye Vodokhranilishche Res Russian Fed
85D4 Kámthi India
61G3 Kamyshin Russian Fed

61K2 Kamyshlov Russian Fed
7C4 Kanaaupscow R Can
98C3 Kananga Zaire
61G2 Kanash Russian Fed
75B1 Kanayama Japan
74D3 Kanazawa Japan
4C3 Kanbisha USA
87B2 Kānchipuram India
84B2 Kandahar Afghan
64E3 Kandalaksha Russian Fed
38L5 Kandalakshskaya Guba B Russian Fed
97C3 Kandi Benin
109C2 Kandos Aust
87C3 Kandy Sri Lanka
15C2 Kane USA
6C1 Kane Basin B Can
96B3 Kanem Desert Region Chad
97B3 Kangaba Mali
92C2 Kangal Turk
6E3 Kangâmiut Greenland
91B4 Kangān Iran
77C4 Kangar Malay
106C4 Kangaroo I Aust
6E3 Kangâtsiaq Greenland
90A3 Kangavar Iran
72C1 Kangbao China
82C3 Kangchenjunga Mt Nepal
73A4 Kangding China
6G3 Kangerdlugssuaq B Greenland
6G3 Kangerdlugssvatsaiq B Greenland
99D2 Kangetet Kenya
74B2 Kanggye N Korea
7D4 Kangiqsualujjuaq Can
7C2 Kangiqsujuaq Can
7C3 Kangirsuk Can
74B3 Kangnung S Korea
98B2 Kango Gabon
68B4 Kangto Mt China
72B3 Kang Xian China
77D4 Kanh Hung Viet
98C3 Kaniama Zaire
87B1 Kani Giri India
39J6 Kankaanpää Fin
14A2 Kankakee USA
14A2 Kankakee R USA
97B3 Kankan Guinea
86A2 Känker India
87B3 Kanniyakumari India
97C3 Kano Nig
74C4 Kanoya Japan
86A1 Kanpur India
9D3 Kansas State, USA
18A2 Kansas R USA
10A3 Kansas City USA
73D5 Kanshi China
63B2 Kansk Russian Fed
97C3 Kantchari Burkina
86B2 Kanthi India
12D2 Kantishna USA
12D2 Kantishna R USA
100B3 Kanye Botswana
68D4 Kao-hsiung Taiwan
100A2 Kaoka Veld Plain Namibia
97A3 Kaolack Sen
100B2 Kaoma Zambia
21C4 Kapaau Hawaiian Is
98C3 Kapanga Zaire
6F3 Kap Cort Adelaer C Greenland
6H3 Kap Dalton C Greenland
39H7 Kapellskär Sweden
6F3 Kap Farvel C Greenland
6G3 Kap Gustav Holm C Greenland
100B2 Kapiri Zambia
78C2 Kapit Malay
19B3 Kaplan USA
57C3 Kaplice Czech Republic
77B4 Kapoe Thai
99C3 Kapona Zaire

52C1 Kaposvár Hung
6C2 Kap Parry C Can
6H3 Kap Ravn C Greenland
78B3 Kapuas R Indon
108A2 Kapunda Aust
84D2 Kapurthala India
7B5 Kapuskasing Can
109D2 Kaputar Mt Aust
93E2 Kapydzhik Mt Armenia
6D2 Kap York C Greenland
92B1 Karabük Turk
54C2 Karacabey Turk
85B4 Karachi Pak
87A1 Karād India
60E5 Kara Daglari Mt Turk
54C5 Karadeniz Boğazi Sd Turk
68D1 Karaftit Russian Fed
65J5 Karaganda Kazakhstan
65J5 Karagayly Kazakhstan
87B2 Kāraikāl India
90B2 Karaj Iran
92C3 Karak Jordan
65J5 Kara Kalpakskaya Respublika, Uzbekistan
84D1 Karakax He R China
71D3 Karakelong I Indon
84D1 Karakoram Mts India
84D1 Karakoram P India/China
97A3 Karakoro R Maur/Sen
65G6 Karakumy Desert Russian Fed
94B3 Karama Jordan
92B2 Karaman Turk
65K5 Karamay China
111B2 Karamea NZ
111B2 Karamea Bight B NZ
85D4 Karanja India
92B2 Karapinar Turk
74A2 Kara S Russian Fed
100A3 Karasburg Namibia
38K5 Karasjok Nor
65J4 Karasuk Russian Fed
92C2 Karataş Turk
65H5 Kara Tau Mts Kazakhstan
76B3 Karathuri Myan
74B4 Karatsu Japan
91B4 Karāz Iran
93D3 Karbalā' Iraq
59C3 Karcag Hung
55B3 Kardhitsa Greece
64E3 Karel'skaya Respublika, Russian Fed
38J5 Karesvando Sweden
96B2 Karet Desert Region Maur
65K4 Kargasok Russian Fed
97D3 Kari Nig
100B2 Kariba Zim
100B2 Kariba L Zim/Zambia
100B2 Kariba Dam Zim/Zambia
95C3 Karima Sudan
78B3 Karimata I Indon
86C2 Karimganj Bang
87B1 Karimnagar India
99E1 Karin Somalia
39J6 Karis Fin
99C2 Karishimbe Mt Zaire
55B3 Káristos Greece
87A2 Kārkal India
71F4 Karkar I PNG
90A3 Karkheh R Iran
60D4 Karkinitskiy Zaliv B Ukraine
63B3 Karlik Shan Mt China
58B2 Karlino Pol
52C2 Karlobag Croatia
52C1 Karlovac Croatia
54B2 Karlovo Bulg
57C2 Karlovy Vary Czech Republic

39G7 Karlshamn Sweden
39H7 Karlskoga Sweden
39H7 Karlskrona Sweden
57B3 Karlsruhe Germany
39G7 Karlstad Sweden
12D3 Karluk USA
86C2 Karnafuli Res Bang
84D3 Karnal India
87A1 Karnataka State, India
54C2 Karnobat Bulg
100D2 Karoi Zim
99D3 Karonga Malawi
95C3 Karora Sudan
78D3 Karossa Indon
55C3 Kárpathos I Greece
6E2 Karrats Fjord Greenland
93D1 Kars Turk
65H4 Karsakpay Kazakhstan
58D1 Kärsava Latvia
80E2 Karshi Uzbekistan
38J6 Karstula Fin
54C2 Kartaba Leb
54C2 Kartal Turk
61K3 Kartaly Russian Fed
90A3 Kārūn R Iran
86A1 Karwa India
87A2 Kārwār India
82D1 Karymskoye Russian Fed
98B3 Kasai R Zaire
100C2 Kasaji Zaire
101C2 Kasama Zambia
99D3 Kasanga Tanz
87A2 Kasaragod India
5H3 Kasba L Can
100B2 Kasempa Zambia
100B2 Kasenga Zaire
99D2 Kasese Uganda
90B3 Kāshān Iran
12C2 Kashegelok USA
82B2 Kashi China
84D3 Kāshipur India
74D3 Kashiwazaki Japan
90C2 Kashmar Iran
86B3 Kashmir State, India
61F3 Kasimov Russian Fed
18C2 Kaskaskia R USA
38J6 Kaskinen Fin
61K2 Kasli Russian Fed
5G5 Kaslo Can
98C3 Kasonga Zaire
98B3 Kasongo-Lunda Zaire
55C3 Kásos I Greece
Kaspiyskiy = Lagan'
95C3 Kassala Sudan
56B2 Kassel Germany
96C1 Kasserine Tunisia
100A2 Kassinga Angola
92B1 Kastamonu Turk
55B3 Kastélli Greece
92A2 Kastellorizon I Greece
55B2 Kastoria Greece
55C3 Kástron Greece
54D3 Kasugai Japan
75A1 Kasumi Japan
101C2 Kasungu Malawi
84C2 Kasur Pak
100B2 Kataba Zambia
100B2 Katako-kombe Zaire
4D3 Katalla USA
63G2 Katangli Russian Fed
106A4 Katanning Aust
55B2 Katerini Greece
54E2 Kates Needle Mt Can/USA
82D3 Katha Myan
106C2 Katherine Aust
85C4 Kathiawar Pen Ind
86B1 Kathmandu Nepal
84D2 Kathua India
86B1 Katihar India
100A3 Katima Mulilo Namibia
4C4 Katmai,Mt USA
12D3 Katmai Nat Mon USA
86A2 Katni India
109D2 Katoomba Aust
59B2 Katowice Pol
39H7 Katrineholm Sweden

97C3 Katsina Nig
97C4 Katsina Ala Nig
75C1 Katsuta Japan
75C1 Katsuura Japan
75B1 Katsuy Japan
65H6 Kattakurgan Uzbekistan
39G7 Kattegat Str Den/ Sweden
21C4 Kauai I Hawaiian Is
21C4 Kauai Chan Hawaiian Is
21C4 Kaulakahi Chan Hawaiian Is
21C4 Kaunakaki Hawaiian Is
60B3 Kaunas Lithuania
97C3 Kaura Namoda Nig
38J5 Kautokeino Nor
55B2 Kavadarci Macedonia
55A2 Kavajë Alb
87B2 Kavali India
55A2 Kavála Greece
85B4 Kávda India
75B1 Kawagoe Japan
75B1 Kawaguchi Japan
110B1 Kawakawa NZ
97C3 Kawambwa Zambia
86A2 Kawardha India
15C2 Kawartha Lakes Can
74D3 Kawasaki Japan
110C1 Kawerau NZ
110B1 Kawhia NZ
97B3 Kaya Burkina
12F3 Kayak I USA
78D2 Kayan R Indon
87B3 Kayankulam India
97A3 Kayes Mali
92C2 Kayseri Turk
1B8 Kazach'ye Russian Fed
93E1 Kazakh Azerbaijan
65G5 Kazakhstan Republic, Asia
61G2 Kazan' Russian Fed
54C2 Kazanlük Bulg
69G4 Kazan Retto Is Japan
91B4 Kãzerün Iran
61H3 Kazhim Russian Fed
93E1 Kazi Magomed Azerbaijan
59C3 Kazincbarcika Hung
55B3 Kéa I Greece
21C4 Kealaikahiki Chan Hawaiian Is
8D2 Kearney USA
93C2 Keban Baraji Res Turk
97A3 Kébémer Sen
96C1 Kebili Tunisia
94C1 Kebir R Leb/Syria
38H5 Kebrekaise Mt Sweden
56C3 Kecskemét Hung
58C1 Kedainiai Lithuania
97B3 Kédougou Sen
12J2 Keele R Can
21J2 Keele Pk Mt Can
21B2 Keeler USA
15D2 Keene New Hampshire, USA
100A3 Keetmanshoop Namibia
18C1 Keewanee USA
63A3 Keewatin Region Can
63A3 Kefallinía I Greece
94B2 Kefar Sava Israel
97C4 Keffi Nig
38A2 Keflavík Iceland
5G4 Keg River Can
76B1 Kehsi Mansam Myan
108B3 Keith Aust
44C3 Keith Scot
4F3 Keith Arm B Can
6D3 Kekertuk Can
85D3 Kekri India
77C5 Kelang Malay
77C4 Kelantan R Malay
84B1 Kelif Turkmenistan
92C1 Kelkit R Turk
98B3 Kéllé Congo
4F2 Kellet,C Can

20C1 Kellogg USA
64D3 Kelloselka Fin
45C2 Kells Irish Rep
42J8 Kells Range Hills Scot
58C1 Kelme Lithuania
5G5 Kelowna Can
5F4 Kelsey Bay Can
42C2 Kelso Scot
20B1 Kelso USA
64E3 Kem' Russian Fed
38J6 Kem' R Russian Fed
97B3 Ke Macina Mali
13B2 Kemano Can
65K4 Kemerovo Russian Fed
38J5 Kemi Fin
38K5 Kemi R Fin
38K5 Kemijärvi Fin
46C1 Kempen Region, Belg
109D2 Kempsey Aust
57C3 Kempten Germany
12D2 Kenai USA
12D3 Kenai Mts USA
12D2 Kenai Pen USA
99D2 Kenamuke Swamp Sudan
42C2 Kendal Eng
109D2 Kendall Aust
71D4 Kendari Indon
78C3 Kendawangan Indon
86B2 Kendräpära India
20C1 Kendrick USA
97A4 Kenema Sierra Leone
98B3 Kenge Zaire
76B1 Kengtung Myan
83C4 Kenhardt S Africa
96B1 Kéniéba Mali
96B1 Kenitra Mor
45B3 Kenmare Irish Rep
45B3 Kenmare R Irish Rep
19B4 Kenner USA
18C2 Kennett USA
19B3 Kennett Square USA
20C1 Kennewick USA
5F4 Kenny Dam Can
7A5 Kenora Can
10B2 Kenosha USA
43E4 Kent County, Eng
5F4 Kent Washington, USA
14A2 Kentland USA
14B2 Kenton USA
4H3 Kent Pen Can
11B3 Kentucky State, USA
11B3 Kentucky L USA
19B3 Kentwood Louisiana, USA
14A2 Kentwood Michigan, USA
99D2 Kenya Republic, Africa
99D3 Kenya,Mt = Kirinyaga
18B1 Keokuk USA
86B2 Keonjhargarh India
71E4 Kepaluan Tanimbar Arch Indon
6H6 Keplavik Iceland
59B2 Kepno Pol
78B2 Kepulauan Anambas Arch Indon
71E4 Kepulauan Aru Arch Indon
78B2 Kepulauan Badas Is Indon
71E4 Kepulauan Banda Arch Indon
71D4 Kepulauan Banggai I Indon
71E4 Kepulauan Bunguran Seleten Arch Indon
71E4 Kepulauan Kai Arch Indon
71D4 Kepulauan Leti I Indon
78A3 Kepulauan Lingga Is Indon
70A4 Kepulauan Mentawi Arch Indon
78B2 Kepulauan Riau Arch Indon

78D4 Kepulauan Sabalana Arch Indon
71D3 Kepulauan Sangihe Arch Indon
71D4 Kepulauan Sula I Indon
71D3 Kepulauan Talaud Arch Indon
78B2 Kepulauan Tambelan Is Indon
71E4 Kepulauan Tanimbar I Indon
71D4 Kepulauan Togian I Indon
71D4 Kepulauan Tukambesi Is Indon
87B2 Kerala State, India
39K6 Kerava Fin
60E4 Kerch' Ukraine
71F4 Kerema PNG
20C1 Keremeps Can
95C3 Keren Eritrea
104B6 Kerguelen Ridge Indian O
99D3 Kericho Kenya
70B4 Kerinci Mt Indon
99D3 Kerio R Kenya
65G5 Kerki Turkmenistan
55A3 Kérkira Greece
55A3 Kérkira I Greece
91C3 Kerman Iran
22B2 Kerman USA
90A3 Kermãnshãh Iran
21B2 Kern R USA
13F2 Kerrobert Can
42C2 Kerry County, Irish Rep
17B1 Kershaw USA
78B3 Kertamulia Indon
71D4 Kerulen R Mongolia
96B2 Kerzaz Alg
55C2 Keşan Turk
74E3 Kesennuma Japan
38L5 Kesten 'ga Russian Fed
42C2 Keswick Eng
65K4 Ket R Russian Fed
97C4 Kéta Ghana
78C3 Ketapang Indon
5E4 Ketchikan USA
97C3 Ketia Niger
58C2 Kętrzyn Pol
43D3 Kettering Eng
14B3 Kettering USA
20C1 Kettle R Can
20C1 Kettle River Range Mts USA
7C3 Kettlestone B Can
90C3 Kevir-i Namak Salt Flat Iran
14A1 Kewaunee USA
14B1 Key Harbour Can
17B2 Key Largo USA
11B4 Key West USA
63C2 Kezhma Russian Fed
54A1 K'felghãza Hung
12J2 Kgun L USA
94C2 Khabab Syria
62H3 Khabarovsk Russian Fed
85B3 Khairpur Pak
85B3 Khairpur Region, Pak
100B3 Khakhea Botswana
55C3 Khálki I Greece
55B3 Khalkidhíki Pen Greece
55B3 Khalkís Greece
61G2 Khalturin Russian Fed
85D4 Khambhát,G of India
85D4 Khãmgaon India
76C2 Kham Keut Laos
85D4 Khammam India
90A2 Khamseh Mts Iran
76C2 Khan R Laos
84B1 Khanabad Afghan
93E3 Khãnaqin Iraq
85D4 Khandwa India
84C2 Khanewal Pak
94C3 Khan ez Zabib Jordan

77D4 Khanh Hung Viet
55B3 Khaniá Greece
84C3 Khanpur Pak
65H3 Khanty-Mansiysk Russian Fed
94B3 Khan Yunis Egypt
84D1 Khapalu India
68C2 Khapcheranga Russian Fed
61G4 Kharabali Russian Fed
86B2 Kharagpur India
84B3 Kharan Pak
90B3 Kharãnaq Iran
91B4 Khãrg Is Iran
95C2 Khârga Oasis Egypt
82C4 Khargon India
60E4 Khar'kov Ukraine
54C2 Kharmanli Bulg
61F2 Kharovsk Russian Fed
95C3 Khartoum Sudan
95C3 Khartoum North Sudan
74C2 Khasan Russian Fed
95C3 Khashm el Girba Sudan
86C1 Khasi-Jaintia Hills India
54C2 Khaskovo Bulg
1B9 Khatanga Russian Fed
76B3 Khawsa Myan
76C2 Khe Bo Viet
85C4 Khed Brahma India
51C2 Khemis Alg
96B1 Khenifra Mor
51D2 Kherrata Alg
60D4 Kherson Ukraine
63D3 Khilok Russian Fed
55C3 Khios Greece
55C3 Khíos I Greece
60C4 Khmel'nitskiy Ukraine
59C3 Khodorov Ukraine
84B1 Kholm Afghan
76D3 Khong Laos
91B4 Khonj Iran
69F2 Khor Russian Fed
91A3 Khorramãbad Iran
90C3 Khosf Iran
84B2 Khost Pak
60C4 Khotin Ukraine
12C2 Khotol Mt USA
60C3 Khoyniki Belarus
63F2 Khrebet Dzhugdzhur Mts Russian Fed
90C2 Khrebet Kopet Dag Mts Turkmenistan
64H3 Khrebet Pay-khoy Mts Russian Fed
82C1 Khrebet Tarbagatay Mts Kazakhstan
82A1 Khrebet Tukuringra Mts Russian Fed
82A1 Khudzhand Tajikistan
86B2 Khulna Bang
84D1 Khunjerab P China/ India
90B3 Khunsar Iran
91A4 Khurays S Arabia
86B2 Khurda India
84D3 Khurja India
84C2 Khushab Pak
94C2 Khushniyah Syria
59C3 Khust Ukraine
99C1 Khuwei Sudan
85B3 Khuzdar Pak
90B3 Khvãf Iran
61G3 Khvalynsk Russian Fed
90C3 Khvor Iran
93D2 Khvoy Iran
84C1 Khwaja Muhammad Mts Afghan
84C2 Khyber P Afghan/Pak

Kiambi

99C3 **Kiambi** Zaire
19A3 **Kiamichi** R USA
12B1 **Kiana** USA
98B3 **Kibangou** Congo
99D3 **Kibaya** Tanz
98C3 **Kibombo** Zaire
99D3 **Kibondo** Tanz
99D3 **Kibungu** Rwanda
55B2 **Kičevo** Macedonia
5G4 **Kicking Horse P** Can
91C2 **Kidal** Mali
43C3 **Kidderminster** Eng
97A3 **Kidira** Sen
110C1 **Kidnappers,C** NZ
56C2 **Kiel** Germany
59C2 **Kielce** Pol
56C2 **Kieler Bucht** B Germany
Kiev = Kiyev
80E2 **Kifab** Uzbekistan
97A3 **Kiffa** Maur
89H8 **Kigali** Rwanda
12A2 **Kigluaik Mts** USA
99C3 **Kigoma** Tanz
75B2 **Kii-sanchi** Mts Japan
74C4 **Kii-suido** B Japan
54B1 **Kikinda** Serbia, Yugos
55B3 **Kikládhes** Is Greece
71F4 **Kikori** PNG
98B3 **Kikwit** Zaire
21C4 **Kilauea Crater** Mt Hawaiian Is
4C3 **Kilbuck Mts** USA
74B2 **Kilchu** N Korea
109D1 **Kilcoy** Aust
45C2 **Kildare** County, Irish Rep
45C2 **Kildare** Irish Rep
19B3 **Kilgore** USA
99D3 **Kilimanjaro** Mt Tanz
99D3 **Kilindoni** Tanz
92C2 **Kilis** Turk
45B2 **Kilkee** Irish Rep
45C2 **Kilkenny** County, Irish Rep
45C2 **Kilkenny** Irish Rep
45B2 **Kilkieran B** Irish Rep
55B2 **Kilkis** Greece
45B1 **Killala B** Irish Rep
45B2 **Killaloe** Irish Rep
109D1 **Killarney** Aust
41B3 **Killarney** Irish Rep
19A3 **Killeen** USA
12D1 **Killik** R USA
44B3 **Killin** Scot
55B3 **Killini** Mt Greece
45B1 **Killybegs** Irish Rep
42B2 **Kilmarnock** Scot
61H2 **Kil'mez** Russian Fed
99D3 **Kilosa** Tanz
41B3 **Kilrush** Irish Rep
99C3 **Kilwa** Zaire
99D3 **Kilwa Kisiwani** Tanz
99D3 **Kilwa Kivinje** Tanz
108A2 **Kimba** Aust
12F2 **Kimball,Mt** USA
13D3 **Kimberley** Can
101F1 **Kimberley** S Africa
106B2 **Kimberley Plat** Aust
74B2 **Kimch'aek** N Korea
74B3 **Kimch'ŏn** S Korea
55B3 **Kími** Greece
60E2 **Kimry** Russian Fed
70C3 **Kinabalu** Mt Malay
78D1 **Kinabatangan** R Malay
14B2 **Kincardine** Can
13B1 **Kincolith** Can
19B3 **Kinder** USA
13F2 **Kindersley** Can
97A3 **Kindia** Guinea
98C3 **Kindu** Zaire
61H3 **Kinel'** Russian Fed
61F2 **Kineshma** Russian Fed
109D1 **Kingaroy** Aust
21A2 **King City** USA
5F4 **Kingcome Inlet** Can
7C4 **King George Is** Can
107D4 **King I** Aust
13B2 **King I** Can

106B2 **King Leopold Range** Mts Aust
9B3 **Kingman** USA
98C3 **Kingombe** Zaire
108A2 **Kingoonya** Aust
22C2 **Kingsburg** USA
21B2 **Kings Canyon Nat Pk** USA
108A3 **Kingscote** Aust
106B2 **King Sd** Aust
112C2 **King Sejong** Base Ant
14A1 **Kingsford** USA
17B1 **Kingsland** USA
43E3 **King's Lynn** Eng
16C2 **Kings Park** USA
8B2 **Kings Peak** Mt USA
107C4 **Kingston** Aust
7C5 **Kingston** Can
25E3 **Kingston** Jamaica
15D2 **Kingston** New York, USA
111A3 **Kingston** NZ
27E4 **Kingstown** St Vincent and the Grenadines
9D4 **Kingsville** USA
44B3 **Kingussie** Scot
4J3 **King William I** Can
100B4 **King William's Town** S Africa
98B3 **Kinkala** Congo
39G7 **Kinna** Sweden
44D3 **Kinnairds Head** Pt Scot
75B1 **Kinomoto** Japan
44C3 **Kinross** Scot
45B3 **Kinsale** Irish Rep
98B3 **Kinshasa** Zaire
78D3 **Kintap** Indon
42B2 **Kintyre** Pen Scot
13D1 **Kinuso** Can
99D2 **Kinyeti** Mt Sudan
55B3 **Kiparissía** Greece
55B3 **Kiparissiakós Kólpos** G Greece
15C1 **Kipawa,L** Can
99D3 **Kipili** Tanz
12B3 **Kipnuk** USA
45C2 **Kippure** Mt Irish Rep
100B2 **Kipushi** Zaire
63C2 **Kirensk** Russian Fed
Kirghizia = Kyrgyzstan
82B1 **Kirgizskiy Khrebet** Mts Kirghizia
98B3 **Kiri** Zaire
105G4 **Kiribati** Is Pacific O
92B2 **Kırıkkale** Turk
99D3 **Kirinyaga** Mt Kenya
60D2 **Kirishi** Russian Fed
85B3 **Kirithar Range** Mts Pak
55C3 **Kırkağaç** Turk
90A2 **Kūh Kirk Bulag Dāgh** Mt Iran
42C2 **Kirkby** Eng
44C3 **Kirkcaldy** Scot
42B2 **Kirkcudbright** Scot
38K5 **Kirkenes** Nor
7B5 **Kirkland Lake** Can
112A **Kirkpatrick,Mt** Ant
10A2 **Kirksville** USA
93D2 **Kirkūk** Iraq
44C2 **Kirkwall** Scot
18J2 **Kirkwood** USA
60D3 **Kirov** Russian Fed
61G2 **Kirov** Russian Fed
93D1 **Kirovakan** Armenia
61J2 **Kirovgrad** Russian Fed
60J4 **Kirovograd** Ukraine
61H2 **Kirs** Russian Fed
92B2 **Kirşehir** Turk
56C2 **Kiruna** Sweden
75B1 **Kiryū** Japan
98C2 **Kisangani** Zaire
75B1 **Kisarazu** Japan
86B1 **Kishanganj** India
85C3 **Kishangarh** India
60C4 **Kishinev** Moldova
75B2 **Kishiwada** Japan
99D3 **Kisii** Kenya
99D3 **Kisiju** Tanz

59B3 **Kiskunhalas** Hung
65F5 **Kislovodsk** Russian Fed
99E3 **Kismaayo** Somalia
75B1 **Kiso-sammyaku** Japan
97A4 **Kissidougou** Guinea
17B2 **Kissimmee,L** USA
99D3 **Kisumu** Kenya
59C3 **Kisvárda** Hung
97B3 **Kita** Mali
65H6 **Kitab** Uzbekistan
75C1 **Kitakata** Japan
74C4 **Kita-Kyūshū** Japan
99D2 **Kitale** Kenya
74E4 **Kitalo** I Japan
74E2 **Kitami** Japan
78B5 **Kitchener** Can
99D2 **Kitgum** Uganda
55B3 **Kíthira** I Greece
55B3 **Kíthnos** I Greece
94A1 **Kiti,C** Cyprus
4H2 **Kitikmeot** Region Can
5F4 **Kitimat** Can
38K5 **Kitnen** R Fin
75A2 **Kitsuki** Japan
15C2 **Kittanning** USA
38J5 **Kittilä** Fin
99D3 **Kitunda** Tanz
13B1 **Kitwanga** Can
100B2 **Kitwe** Zambia
57C3 **Kitzbühel** Austria
57C3 **Kitzbüheler Alpen** Mts Austria
57C3 **Kitzingen** Germany
98C3 **Kiumbi** Zaire
12B1 **Kivalina** USA
59D2 **Kivercy** Ukraine
99C3 **Kivu,L** Zaire/Rwanda
12B1 **Kiwalik** USA
61J2 **Kizel** Russian Fed
92C2 **Kizil** R Turk
80D2 **Kizyl-Arvat** Turkmenistan
90B2 **Kizyl-Atrek** Turkmenistan
57C2 **Kladno** Czech Republic
57C3 **Klagenfurt** Austria
60B2 **Klaipėda** Lithuania
20B2 **Klamath** R USA
20B2 **Klamath** USA
20B2 **Klamath Falls** USA
20B2 **Klamath Mts** USA
57C3 **Klatovy** Czech Republic
12H3 **Klawak** USA
94B1 **Kleiat** Leb
101G1 **Klerksdorp** S Africa
60E2 **Klin** Russian Fed
58B1 **Klintehamn** Sweden
60D3 **Klintsy** Russian Fed
54B2 **Ključ** Bosnia-Herzegovina
59B2 **Kłodzko** Pol
12G2 **Klondike** R Can/USA
12G2 **Klondike Plat** Can/USA
59B3 **Klosterneuburg** Austria
12G2 **Kluane** R Can
12G2 **Kluane L** Can
12G2 **Kluane Nat Pk** Can
59B2 **Kluczbork** Pol
12G3 **Klukwan** USA
12E2 **Klutina L** Can
12E2 **Knight I** USA
43C3 **Knighton** Wales
52C2 **Knin** Croatia
106A4 **Knob,C** Aust
46B1 **Knokke-Heist** Belg
112C9 **Knox Coast** Ant
11B3 **Knoxville** Tennessee, USA
6H3 **Knud Ramsussens Land** Region Greenland
78B3 **Koba** Indon
6F3 **Kobbermirebugt** Greenland
74D4 **Kobe** Japan

56C1 **København** Den
57C2 **Koblenz** Germany
60B3 **Kobrin** Russian Fed
71E4 **Kobroör** I Indon
12C1 **Kobuk** R USA
54B2 **Kočani** Macedonia
76C3 **Ko Chang** I Thai
86B1 **Koch Bihar** India
47D1 **Kochel** Germany
6C3 **Koch I** Can
Kochi = Cochin
74C4 **Kōchi** Japan
12D3 **Kodiak** USA
12D3 **Kodiak I** USA
87B2 **Kodiyakkari** India
99D2 **Kodok** Sudan
100A3 **Koes** Namibia
101G1 **Koffiefontein** S Africa
97B4 **Koforidua** Ghana
74D3 **Kofu** Japan
75B1 **Koga** Japan
39G7 **Køge** Den
84B2 **Koh-i-Baba** Mt Afghan
84B1 **Koh-i-Hisar** Mt Afghan
84B2 **Koh-i-Khurd** Mt Afghan
86C1 **Kohima** India
84B1 **Koh-i-Mazar** Mt Afghan
84B3 **Kohlu** Pak
60C2 **Kohtla Järve** Estoni
75B1 **Koide** Japan
77A4 **Koihoa** Is Nicobar Is
74B4 **Kŏje-do** I S Korea
65K5 **Kokchetav** Kazakhstan
39J6 **Kokemaki** L Fin
38K6 **Kokkola** Fin
107D1 **Kokoda** PNG
14A2 **Kokomo** USA
71E4 **Kokonau** Indon
65K5 **Kokpekty** Kazakhstan
7D4 **Koksoak** R Can
100B4 **Kokstad** S Africa
76C3 **Ko Kut** I Thai
38L5 **Kola** Russian Fed
77A4 **Kolaka** Indon
77B4 **Ko Lanta** I Thai
Kolān = Quilon
87B2 **Kolār** India
87B2 **Kolar Gold Fields** India
97A3 **Kolda** Sen
39F7 **Kolding** Den
87A1 **Kolhāpur** India
12C3 **Koliganek** USA
59B2 **Kolín** Czech Republi
57B2 **Köln** Germany
58B2 **Koło** Pol
58B2 **Kołobrzeg** Pol
97B3 **Kolokani** Mali
60C4 **Kolomna** Russian Fed
60C4 **Kolomyya** Ukraine
65K4 **Kolpashevo** Russian Fed
55B2 **Kólpos Merabéllou** Greece
55B2 **Kólpos Singitikós** G Greece
55B2 **Kólpos Strimonikós** G Greece
55B2 **Kólpos Toronaíos** G Greece
38L5 **Kol'skiy Poluostrov** Pen Russian Fed
38G6 **Kolvereid** Nor
100B2 **Kolwezi** Zaire
12F2 **Kolyma** R Russian Fed
54B2 **Kom** Mt Bulg/Serbi Yugos
79D2 **Koma** Eth
97D3 **Komaduga Gana** R Nig
59B3 **Komarno** Slovakia
101H1 **Komati** R S Africa
74D3 **Komatsu** Japan

75A2 Komatsushima
Japan
64G3 Komi Respublika,
Russian Fed
70C4 Komodo I Indon
71E4 Komoran I Indon
75B1 Komoro Japan
52C1 Komotini Greece
76D3 Kompong Cham
Camb
76D3 Kompong Chhnang
Mts Camb
77C3 Kompong Som Camb
76D3 Kompong Thom
Camb
76D3 Kompong Trabek
Camb
63F2 Komsomol's na
Amure Russian Fed
65H4 Konda R
Russian Fed
99D3 Kondoa Tanz
87B1 Kondukür India
6G3 Kong Christian IX
Land Region
Greenland
6F3 Kong Frederik VI Kyst
Mts Greenland
6F3 Kong Håkon VII Ant
64C2 Kong Karls Land Is
Barents S
78D2 Kongkemul Mt
Indon
98C3 Kongolo Zaïre
39F7 Kongsberg Den
39G6 Kongsvinger Nor
Königsberg =
Kaliningrad
58B2 Konin Pol
54A2 Konjic Bosnia-
Herzegovina
61D2 Konosha Russian Fed
75B1 Konosu Japan
60D3 Konotop Ukraine
59C2 Końskie Pol
72E2 Konstanz Germany
97C3 Kontagora Nig
76D3 Kontum Viet
92B2 Konya Turk
13D3 Kootenay R Can
85C5 Kopargaon India
39F7 Köpavogur Iceland
38A2 Kópavogur Iceland
52C1 Koper Slovenia
80D2 Kopet Dag Mts Iran/
Turkmenistan
61K2 Kopeysk Russian Fed
77C4 Ko Phangan I Thai
77C4 Ko Phuket I Thai
39H7 Köping Sweden
87B1 Koppal India
52C1 Koprivnica Croatia
85B4 Korangi Pak
52C1 Koraput India
86A2 Korba India
57B2 Korbach Germany
4B3 Korbuk R USA
55B2 Korçë I Croatia
52C1 Korčula I Croatia
72E2 Korea B China/Korea
74B4 Korea Str S Korea/
Japan
59D2 Korec Ukraine
92B1 Körğlu Tepesi Mt
Turk
97B4 Korhogo Ivory Coast
53C3 Kori Creek India
55B3 Korinthiakós Kólpos
G Greece
55B3 Kórinthos Greece
74E3 Kóriyama Japan
61K3 Korkino Russian Fed
92B2 Korkuteli Turk
82C1 Korla China
52C2 Kornat I Croatia
60D5 Köroğlu Tepesi Mt
Turk
99D3 Korogwe Tanz
108B3 Koroit Aust
71E3 Koror Palau Is,
Pacific O
59C3 Körös R Hung
60C3 Korosten Ukraine
95A3 Koro Toro Chad

12B3 Korovin I USA
69G2 Korsakov Russian Fed
39G7 Korsør Den
46B1 Kortrijk Belg
55C3 Kós I Greece
77C4 Ko Samui I Thai
58B2 Kościerzyna Pol
107D4 Kosciusko Mt Aust
12H3 Kosciusko I USA
74B4 Koshikijima-retto I
Japan
59C3 Košice Slovakia
74B3 Kosong N Korea
54A2 Kosovo Aut Republic,
Serbia, Yugos
54B2 Kosovska Mitrovica
Serbia, Yugos
97B4 Kossou L Ivory
Coast
101G1 Koster S Africa
99D1 Kosti Sudan
59D2 Kostopol' Ukraine
61F2 Kostroma
Russian Fed
56C2 Kostrzyn Pol
59H8 Koszalin Pol
85D3 Kota India
78A4 Kotaagung Indon
78B3 Kotabaharu Indon
78D3 Kotabaru Indon
77C4 Kota Bharu Malay
78A3 Kotabum Indon
84C2 Kot Addu Pak
78D1 Kota Kinabulu Malay
87C1 Kotapad India
99C2 Kotel'nich
Russian Fed
61F4 Kotel'nikovo
Russian Fed
39K6 Kotka Fin
64F3 Kotlas Russian Fed
12B2 Kotlik USA
54B2 Kotor Montenegro,
Yugos
60C4 Kotovsk Ukraine
85B3 Kotri Pak
87B1 Kottagudem India
87B3 Kottayam India
98C2 Kotto R CAR
87B2 Kottūru India
12B1 Kotzebue USA
4B3 Kotzebue Sd USA
97C3 Kouande Benin
98B2 Kouango CAR
97B3 Koudougou Burkina
98B3 Koulamoutou Gabon
97B3 Koulikoro Mali
97B3 Koupéla Burkina
33G2 Kourou French
Guiana
97B3 Kouroussa Guinea
98B1 Kousséri Cam
39K6 Kouvola Fin
38L5 Kovdor Russian Fed
Kovel' Ukraine
Kovno = Kaunas
61F2 Kovrov Russian Fed
61F3 Kovylkino
Russian Fed
60E1 Kovzha R
Russian Fed
77C4 Ko Way I Thai
73C5 Kowloon Hong Kong
84B2 Kowt-e-Ashrow
Afghan
92A2 Köyceğiz Turk
82L5 Koydor Russian Fed
87A1 Koyna Res India
128Z Koyuk USA
12B1 Koyuk R USA
12C2 Koyukuk R USA
12C1 Koyukuk R USA
92C2 Kozan Turk
55B2 Kozani Greece
Kozhikode = Calicut
61G2 Koz'modemyansk
Russian Fed
75B2 Kōzu-shima I Japan
39F7 Kragerø Nor
54B2 Kragujevac Serbia,
Yugos
77B3 Kra,Isthmus of Myan/
Malay
Krakatau = Rakata

94C1 Krak des Chevaliers
Hist Site Syria
Kraków = Cracow
54B2 Kraljevo Serbia,
Yugos
60E4 Kramatorsk Ukraine
38H6 Kramfors Sweden
52B1 Kranj Slovenia
61G1 Krasavino
Russian Fed
64G2 Krasino Russian Fed
61C3 Krasnik Pol
61G3 Krasnoarmeysk
Russian Fed
60E5 Krasnodar
Russian Fed
61J2 Krasnokamsk
Russian Fed
61J2 Krasnotur'insk
Russian Fed
61J2 Krasnoufimsk
Russian Fed
61J3 Krasnousol'-skiy
Russian Fed
65G3 Krasnovishersk
Russian Fed
65G5 Krasnovodsk
Turkmenistan
63B2 Krasnoyarsk
Russian Fed
59C2 Krasnystaw Pol
61J3 Krasnyy Kut
Russian Fed
60E4 Krasnyy Luch
Ukraine
61G4 Krasnyy Yar
Russian Fed
76D3 Kratie Camb
6E2 Kraulshavn
Greenland
56B2 Krefeld Germany
60D4 Kremenchug Ukraine
60D4 Kremenchugskoye
Vodokhranilische
Res Ukraine
59D2 Kremenets Ukraine
98A2 Kribi Cam
60D3 Krichev Belarus
61J4 Krimml Austria
87B3 Krishna R India
87A2 Krishnagiri India
87B2 Krishnanagar India
39F7 Kristiansand Nor
39G7 Kristianstad Sweden
64B3 Kristiansund Nor
38J6 Kristinehamn
Sweden
38J6 Kristiinankaupunki
Fin
55B3 Kriti I Greece
60D4 Krivoy Rog Ukraine
6G3 Krk I Croatia
6G3 Kronprins Frederik
Bjerge Mts
Greenland
39K7 Kronshtadt
Russian Fed
101G1 Kroonstad S Africa
65F5 Kropotkin
Russian Fed
101G1 Krugersdorp S Africa
78A4 Krui Indon
55A2 Kruje Alb
58D2 Krupki Belarus
54B2 Kruševac Serbia,
Yugos
12G3 Kruzof I USA
65E5 Krym Pen Ukraine
60E5 Krymsk Russian Fed
58B2 Krzyz Pol
96C1 Ksar El Boukhari Alg
96B1 Ksar el Kebir Mor
70A3 Kuala Malay
77C5 Kuala Dungun Malay
77C4 Kuala Kerai Malay
77C5 Kuala Kubu Baharu
Malay
77C5 Kuala Lipis Malay
77C5 Kuala Lumpur Malay
77C4 Kuala Trengganu
Malay
78D1 Kuamut Malay

74A2 Kuandian China
77C5 Kuantan Malay
93E1 Kuba Azerbaijan
71F4 Kubar PNG
78C2 Kuching Malay
70C3 Kudat Malay
78C4 Kudus Indon
61H2 Kudymkar
Russian Fed
57C3 Kufstein Austria
90C3 Kuh Duren Upland
Iran
90B3 Küh-e Bazmän Mt Iran
90B3 Küh-e Dinar Mt Iran
90C2 Küh-e Hazär Masjed
Mts Iran
91C4 Küh-e Jebäl Barez
Iran
90B3 Küh-e Karkas Mts
Iran
91C4 Küh-e Laleh Zar Mt
Iran
91C4 Küh-e Sahand Mt
Iran
91D4 Küh e Taftän Mt Iran
90A2 Kühhaye Sabalan
Mts Iran
90A3 Kühhä-ye Zägros Mts
Iran
38K6 Kuhmo Fin
90B3 Kühpäyeh Iran
90C3 Kühpäyeh Mt Iran
12C3 Kukaklek L USA
54B2 Kukës Alb
77C5 Kukup Malay
91C4 Kül R Iran
55C3 Kula Turk
61J4 Kulakshi Kazakhstan
99D2 Kulal,Mt Kenya
54B2 Kulata Bulg
60B2 Kuldiga Latvia
61H4 Kul'sary Kazakhstan
84D2 Kulu India
12C2 Kulu Turk
65J4 Kulunda Russian Fed
108B2 Kulwin Aust
61G5 Kuma R Russian Fed
75B1 Kumagaya Japan
78C3 Kumai Indon
74C4 Kumamoto Japan
75B2 Kumano Japan
54B2 Kumanovo
Macedonia
61G5 Kumara Russian Fed
97B4 Kumasi Ghana
65F5 Kumayri Armenia
98A2 Kumba Cam
87B2 Kumbakonam India
61J3 Kumertau
Russian Fed
74B3 Kümhwa S Korea
39H7 Kumla Sweden
87A2 Kumta India
82C1 Kümüx China
84C2 Kunar R Afghan
74D4 Kunda Estonia
87A2 Kundāpura India
85C4 Kunda India
84B1 Kunduz Afghan
89F9 Kunene R Angola
39G7 Kungsbacka Sweden
61J2 Kungur Russian Fed
76B1 Kunming Myan
82B2 Kunlun Shan Mts
China
73A4 Kunming China
74B3 Kunsan S Korea
38K6 Kuopio Fin
52C1 Kupa R Croatia/
Bosnia-Herzegovina
106B2 Kupang Indon
107D2 Kupiano PNG
12H3 Kupreanof I USA

Kupyansk

60E4 **Kupyansk** Ukraine
82C1 **Kuqa** China
75B1 **Kurabe** Japan
74C4 **Kurashiki** Japan
75A1 **Kurayoshi** Japan
54C2 **Kürdzhali** Bulg
74C4 **Kure** Japan
60B2 **Kuressaare** Estonia
63A1 **Kureyka** *R*
   Russian Fed
65H4 **Kurgan** Russian Fed
38J6 **Kurikka** Fin
   Kuril Is = Kuril'skoye
   Osrova
69H2 **Kuril'skiye Ostrova**
   Russian Fed
87B1 **Kurnool** India
75C1 **Kuroiso** Japan
11J82 **Kurow** NZ
109D2 **Kurri Kurri** Aust
60E3 **Kursk** Russian Fed
   Kurskiy Zaliv =
   Courland Lagoon
68A2 **Kuruktag** *R* China
100B3 **Kuruman** S Africa
74C4 **Kurume** Japan
87C3 **Kurunegala**
   Sri Lanka
65K5 **Kurunktag** *R* China
61J2 **Kusa** Russian Fed
55C3 **Kuşadasi Körfezi** *B*
   Turk
55C2 **Kus Golü** *L* Turk
74D4 **Kushimoto** Japan
74E2 **Kushiro** Japan
86B2 **Kushtia** Bang
61H3 **Kushum** *R*
   Kazakhstan
80E2 **Kushra** Afgan
65G4 **Kushva** Russian Fed
12B2 **Kuskokwim** *R* USA
12B3 **Kuskokwim B** *L* USA
12C2 **Kuskokwim Mts**
   USA
86A1 **Kusma** Nepal
74E2 **Kussharo-ko** *L*
   Japan
65H4 **Kustanay** Kazakhstan
92A2 **Kütahya** Turk
78D3 **Kutai** *R* Indon
59B3 **Kutina** Hrvatska
   Czech Republic
58B2 **Kutno** Pol
98B3 **Kutu** Zaire
98C1 **Kutubdia I** Bang
98C1 **Kutum** Sudan
7D4 **Kuujjuaq** Can
7C4 **Kuujjuarapik** Can
38K5 **Kuusamo** Fin
61J3 **Kuvandyk**
   Russian Fed
93E4 **Kuwait** Kuwait
80C3 **Kuwait** Sheikdom,
   S W Asia
75B1 **Kuwana** Japan
   Kuybyshev = Samara
65J4 **Kuybyshev**
   Russian Fed
61G3 **Kuybyshevskoye**
   Vodokhranilishche
   Res Russian Fed
63C2 **Kuytun** Russian Fed
60E5 **Kuzey Anadolu**
   Daglari *Mts* Turk
61G3 **Kuznetsk** Russian Fed
38J4 **Kvaenangen** *Sd* Nor
12C3 **Kvichak** USA
12C3 **Kvichak** *R* USA
12C3 **Kvichak B** USA
38G5 **Kvigtind** *Mt* Nor
38H5 **Kvikkjokk** Sweden
99D3 **Kwale** Kenya
74B3 **Kwangju** S Korea
98B3 **Kwango** *R* Zaire
100B3 **KwaZulu Natal**
   Province, S Africa
100B2 **Kwekwe** Zim
12B2 **Kwethluk** USA
12B2 **Kwethluk** *R* USA
58B2 **Kwidzyn** Pol
71E4 **Kwoka** *Mt* Indon
108C3 **Kyabram** Aust
76B2 **Kyaikkami** Myan
76B2 **Kyaikto** Myan

68C1 **Kyakhta** Russian Fed
108A2 **Kyancutta** Aust
76B1 **Kyaukme** Myan
76B1 **Kyauk-padaung**
   Myan
76A2 **Kyaukpyu** Myan
40B2 **Kyle of Lochalsh**
   Scot
46D1 **Kyll** *R* Germany
108B3 **Kyneton** Aust
99D2 **Kyoga** *L* Uganda
109D1 **Kyogle** Aust
74B3 **Kyŏngju** S Korea
74D3 **Kyoto** Japan
65J5 **Kyrgyzstan** Republic,
   Asia
65H4 **Kyshtym** Russian Fed
74C4 **Kyushu** *I* Japan
104E3 **Kyushu-Palau Ridge**
   Pacific O
54B2 **Kyustendil** Bulg
68B1 **Kyzyl** Russian Fed
65H5 **Kyzylkum** *Desert*
   Uzbekistan
65H5 **Kzyl Orda**
   Kazakhstan

L

99E2 **Laascaanood**
   Somalia
46E1 **Laasphe** Germany
99E1 **Laasqoray** Somalia
33E1 **La Asunción** Ven
96A2 **Lâayoune** Mor
23A1 **La Barca** Mexico
97A3 **Labé** Guinea
59D2 **Labe** *R*
   Czech Republic
15D1 **Labelle** Can
17B2 **La Belle** USA
12C3 **Laberge,L** Can
78D1 **Labi** Brunei
13E2 **la Biche,L** Can
61F5 **Labinsk** Russian Fed
94C1 **Laboué** Leb
34C2 **Laboulaye** Arg
7D4 **Labrador** *Region*
   Can
7D4 **Labrador City** Can
7E4 **Labrador S**
   Greenland/Can
33E5 **Lábrea** Brazil
78D1 **Labuan** Malay
78D1 **Labuan** *I* Malay
78A1 **Labuhan** Indon
76A2 **Labutta** Myan
65H3 **Labytnangi**
   Russian Fed
7C4 **Lac à l'eau Claire**
   Can
46B2 **La Capelle** France
34C2 **La Carlota** Arg
79B3 **La Carlota** Phil
12J1 **Lac Belot** *L* Can
7C4 **Lac Bienville** *L* Can
83B4 **Laccadive Is** India
47B2 **Lac d'Annecy** *L*
   France
4G3 **Lac de Gras** *L* Can
47B1 **Lac de Joux** *L* Switz
47B1 **Lac de Neuchâtel** *L*
   Switz
23A2 **Lac de Patzcuaro** *L*
   Mexico
23A2 **Lac de Sayula** *L*
   Mexico
4F3 **Lac des Bois** *L* Can
47B2 **Lac du Bourget** *L*
   France
25D3 **La Ceiba** Honduras
108A3 **Lacepede B** Aust
47B2 **La Châtre** France
47B1 **La-Chaux-de-Fonds**
   Switz
94B3 **Lachish** *Hist Site*
   Israel
107D4 **Lachlan** *R* Aust
32B2 **La Chorrera** Panama
15D1 **Lachute** Can
7D4 **Lac Joseph** *L* Can
15C2 **Lac la Biche** Can
4G3 **Lac la Martre** *L* Can
5H4 **Lac la Ronge** *L* Can

52A1 **Lac Léman** *L* Switz/
   France
10C1 **Lac Manouane** *L*
   Can
15D1 **Lac Megantic** Can
7C4 **Lac Mistassini** *L* Can
13E2 **Lacombe** Can
15D2 **Laconia** USA
50A1 **La Coruña** Spain
10A2 **La Crosse** USA
9C3 **La Cruces** USA
7A4 **Lac Seul** *L* Can
18B2 **La Cygne** USA
84D2 **Ladakh Range** India
85C3 **Ladnun** India
73B5 **Ladong** China
60D1 **Ladozhskoye Ozero** *L*
   Ukraine
6B2 **Lady Ann Str** Can
109C4 **Lady Barron** Aust
101G1 **Ladybrand** S Africa
13C3 **Ladysmith** Can
101G1 **Ladysmith** S Africa
71F4 **Lae** PNG
76C3 **Laem Ngop** Thai
56C1 **Laesø** *I* Den
10B2 **Lafayette** Indiana,
   USA
11A3 **Lafayette** Louisiana,
   USA
46B2 **La Fère** France
46B2 **La-Ferté-sous-Jouarre**
   France
97C4 **Lafia** Nig
97C4 **Lafiagi** Nig
48B2 **La Flèche** France
96C1 **La Galite** *I* Tunisia
56C1 **Lagan** *R* Sweden
31D4 **Lagarto** Brazil
96C1 **Laghouat** Alg
35C2 **Lagoa de Araruama**
   Brazil
29F2 **Lagoa dos Patos** *Lg*
   Brazil
32A4 **Lagoa Feia** Brazil
32B4 **Lago Agrio** Ecuador
35C1 **Lagoa Juparanã** *L*
   Brazil
29F2 **Lagoa mar Chiguita** *L*
   Arg
29F2 **Lagoa Mirim** *L*
   Brazil/Urug
29B6 **Lago Argentino** *L*
   Arg
29B5 **Lago Buenos Aires** *L*
   Arg
29C5 **Lago Cochrane** *L*
   Arg/Chile
29C5 **Lago Colhué Huapi** *L*
   Arg
24B2 **Lago de Chapala** *L*
   Mexico
32A2 **Lago de Chiriqui** *L*
   Panama
23A2 **Lago de Cuitzeo** *L*
   Mexico
29B3 **Lago de la Laja** *L*
   Chile
53A2 **Lago del Coghinas** *L*
   Sardegna
32C2 **Lago de Maracaibo** *L*
   Ven
25D3 **Lago de Nicaragua** *L*
   Nic
32A1 **Lago de Perlas** *L* Nic
52B2 **Lago di Bolsena** *L*
   Italy
52B2 **Lago di Bracciano** *L*
   Italy
52A1 **Lago di Como** *L* Italy
47C2 **Lago d'Idro** *L* Italy
52B1 **Lago di Garda** *L* Italy
47C2 **Lago di Lecco** *L* Italy
47C2 **Lago di Lugano** *L*
   Italy
47C2 **Lago d'Iseo** *L* Italy
47C2 **Lago d'Orta** *L* Italy
29B5 **Lago General Carrera**
   L Chile
52A1 **Lago Maggiore** *L*
   Italy
29C5 **Lago Musters** *L* Arg
48B3 **Lagon** France

29B4 **Lago Nahuel Haupi** *L*
   Arg
29B5 **Lago O'Higgins** *L*
   Chile
53A2 **Lago Omodeo** *L*
   Sardegna
30C2 **Lago Poopó** *L* Bol
29B4 **Lago Ranco** *L* Chile
32D6 **Lago Rogaguado** *L*
   Bol
97C4 **Lagos** Nig
50A2 **Lagos** Port
59B5 **Lago San Martin** *L*
   Arg/Chile
24B2 **Lagos de Moreno**
   Mexico
30C2 **Lago Titicaca** Bol/
   Peru
29B5 **Lago Viedma** *L* Arg
8B2 **La Grande** USA
106B2 **Lagrange** Aust
11B3 **La Grange** Georgia,
   USA
14A3 **La Grange** Kentucky,
   USA
19A4 **La Grange** Texas,
   USA
33E2 **La Gran Sabana** *Mts*
   Ven
47B2 **La Grave** France
48B3 **Lagroño** Spain
34A3 **Laguna Aluminé** *L*
   Arg
21B3 **Laguna Beach** USA
34C3 **Laguna Colorada**
   Grande *L* Arg
79B3 **Laguna de Bay** *Lg*
   Phil
25D3 **Laguna de Caratasca**
   Lg Honduras
25D4 **Laguna de Chiriqui** *L*
   Panama
25D3 **Laguna de Managua** *L*
   Nic
25D3 **Laguna de Nicaragua**
   L Nic
26A4 **Laguna de Perlas** *Lg*
   Nic
23B1 **Laguna de Pueblo**
   Viejo *L* Mexico
24C2 **Laguna de Tamiahua**
   Lg Mexico
25C5 **Laguna de Términos**
   Lg Mexico
23A1 **Laguna de Yuriria** *L*
   Mexico
23B1 **Laguna la Altamira**
   Mexico
24C2 **Laguna Madre** *Lg*
   Mexico
34C2 **Laguna Mar Chiquita**
   L Arg
29B4 **Laguna Nahuel Huapi**
   L Arg
34C2 **Laguna Paiva** Arg
29B4 **Laguna Ranco** Chile
9C4 **Laguna Seca** Mexico
23A2 **Laguna Tortugas** *L*
   Mexico
70C3 **Lahad Datu** Malay
78A3 **Lahat** Indon
38J6 **Lahia** Fin
90B2 **Lāhijān** Iran
46D1 **Lahn** *R* Germany
46D1 **Lahnstein** Germany
84C2 **Lahore** Pak
39K6 **Lahti** Fin
23A2 **La Huerta** Mexico
98B2 **Laï** Chad
73B5 **Laibin** China
76C1 **Lai Chau** Viet
100B4 **Laingsburg** S Africa
44B2 **Lairg** Scot
78A3 **Lais** Indon
79C4 **Lais** Phil
72E2 **Laiyang** China
72D2 **Laizhou Wan** *B*
   China
34A3 **Laja** *R* Chile
30F4 **Lajes** Brazil
22D4 **La Jolla** USA
9C3 **La Junta** USA
109C2 **Lake Cargelligo** Aust
11A3 **Lake Charles** USA

17B1 **Lake City** Florida, USA
17C1 **Lake City** S Carolina, USA
42C2 **Lake District** Region, Eng
22D4 **Lake Elsinore** USA
106C3 **Lake Eyre Basin** Aust
15C2 **Lakefield** Can
6D3 **Lake Harbour** Can
22C3 **Lake Hughes** USA
16B2 **Lakehurst** USA
19A4 **Lake Jackson** USA
13E2 **Lake la Biche** Can
17B2 **Lakeland** USA
7A5 **Lake of the Woods** Can
20B1 **Lake Oswego** USA
21A2 **Lakeport** USA
19B3 **Lake Providence** USA
111B2 **Lake Pukaki** NZ
109C3 **Lakes Entrance** Aust
22C2 **Lakeshore** USA
15C1 **Lake Stewart** Aust
15C1 **Lake Traverse** Can
8A2 **Lakeview** USA
20B1 **Lakeview Mt** Can
17B2 **Lake Village** USA
17B2 **Lake Wales** USA
22C4 **Lakewood** California, USA
16B2 **Lakewood** New Jersey, USA
14B2 **Lakewood** Ohio, USA
17B2 **Lake Worth** USA
111B2 **Lakhimpur** India
85B4 **Lakhpat** India
84C2 **Lakki** Pak
55B3 **Lakonikós Kólpos** G Greece
97B4 **Lakota** Ivory Coast
38K4 **Laksefjord** Inlet Nor
38K4 **Lakselv** Nor
34C2 **La Laguna** Arg
32A4 **La Libertad** Ecuador
34A2 **La Ligua** Chile
50A2 **La Linea** Spain
85D4 **Lalitpur** India
5H4 **La Loche** Can
13F1 **la Loche,L** Can
46C1 **La Louvière** Belg
26A4 **La Luz** Nic
7C5 **La Malbaie** Can
23B2 **La Malinche** Mt Mexico
50B2 **La Mancha** Region, Spain
9C3 **Lamar** Colorado, USA
18B2 **Lamar** Missouri, USA
19A4 **La Marque** USA
98B3 **Lambaréné** Gabon
32A5 **Lambayeque** Peru
112B10 **Lambert Gl** Ant
16B2 **Lambertville** USA
4F2 **Lamblon,C** Can
47C2 **Lambro** R Italy
14C1 **Lam Chi** R Thai
50A1 **Lamego** Port
47B2 **La Meije** Mt France
32B6 **La Merced** Peru
21B3 **La Mesa** USA
55B3 **Lamía** Greece
42C2 **Lammermuir Hills** Scot
39G7 **Lammhult** Sweden
79B3 **Lamon B** Phil
18B1 **Lamoni** USA
71F3 **Lamotrek** I Pacific O
43B3 **Lampeter** Wales
99E3 **Lamu** Kenya
47D1 **Lana** Italy
21C4 **Lanai** I Hawaiian Is
21C4 **Lanai City** Hawaiian Is
42C2 **Lanark** Scot
76B3 **Lanbi** I Myan
76C1 **Lancang** R China
42C3 **Lancashire** County, Eng
21B3 **Lancaster** California, USA

42C2 **Lancaster** Eng
18B1 **Lancaster** Mississippi, USA
15D2 **Lancaster** New Hampshire, USA
14B3 **Lancaster** Ohio, USA
16A2 **Lancaster** Pennsylvania, USA
17B1 **Lancaster** S Carolina, USA
6B2 **Lancaster Sd** Can
78B3 **Landak** R Indon
46E2 **Landan** Germany
57C3 **Landeck** Austria
8C2 **Lander** USA
34C2 **Landeta** Arg
57C3 **Landsberg** Germany
4F2 **Lands End C** Can
43B4 **Land's End C** Eng
57C3 **Landshut** Germany
39G7 **Landskrona** Sweden
17A1 **Lanett** USA
46E2 **Langenhagen** Germany
47B1 **Langenthal** Switz
42C2 **Langholm** Scot
38A2 **Langjökull** Mts Iceland
77B4 **Langkawi** I Malay
13C3 **Langley** Can
108C1 **Langlo** R Aust
47B1 **Langnau** Switz
49D2 **Langres** France
70A3 **langsa** Indon
68C2 **Lang Shan** Mts China
76D1 **Lang Son** Viet
48C3 **Languedoc** Region, France
29B3 **Lanin** Mt Arg
34A2 **Lanka,L** Phil
16B2 **Lansdale** USA
7B4 **Lansdowne House** Can
16B2 **Lansford** USA
10B2 **Lansing** USA
47B2 **Lanslebourg** France
96A2 **Lanzarote** I Canary Is
72A2 **Lanzhou** China
47B2 **Lanzo Torinese** Italy
79B2 **Laoag** Phil
76D1 **Lao Cai** Viet
72D1 **Laoha He** R China
45C2 **Laois** County, Irish Rep
46B2 **Laon** France
32B6 **La Oroya** Peru
76C2 **Laos** Republic, S E Asia
49C2 **Lapalisse** France
32B2 **La Palma** Panama
96A2 **La Palma** I Canary Is
34D3 **La Paragua** State, Arg
29E2 **La Paz** Arg
30B2 **La Paz** Arg
34D2 **La Paz** Bol
24A2 **La Paz** Mexico
69G2 **La Perouse Str** Japan/Russian Fed
23A1 **La Piedad** Mexico
21B3 **La Pine** USA
19B3 **Laplace** USA
23A2 **la Placita** Mexico
29E2 **La Plata** Arg
13F1 **La Plonge,L** Can
14A2 **La Porte** USA
39K6 **Lappeenranta** Fin
38H5 **Lappland** Region Sweden/Fin
34C2 **Laprida** Arg
1B8 **Laptev S** Russian Fed
38J6 **Lapua** Fin
79B3 **Lapu-Lapu** Phil
9B4 **La Purisima** Mexico
95B2 **Laqiya Arba'in** Well Sudan
30C3 **La Quiaca** Arg
52B2 **L'Aquila** Italy
91B4 **Lar** Iran
96B1 **Larache** Mor
8C2 **Laramie** USA

8C2 **Laramie Range** Mts USA
50B2 **Larca** Spain
9D4 **Laredo** USA
91B4 **Larestan** Region, Iran
46C1 **Largeau** = Faya
47B2 **L'Argentière** France
17B2 **Largo** USA
42B2 **Largs** Scot
90A2 **Läri** Iran
30C4 **La Rioja** Arg
30C4 **La Rioja** State, Arg
55B3 **Lárisa** Greece
85B3 **Larkana** Pak
92B3 **Larnaca** Cyprus
94A1 **Larnaca B** Cyprus
45C1 **Larne** N Ire
50A1 **La Robla** Spain
46C1 **La Roche-en-Ardenne** Belg
48B2 **La Rochelle** France
47B1 **La Roche-sur-Foron** France
48B2 **La Roche-sur-Yon** France
51B2 **La Roda** Spain
27D3 **La Romana** Dom Rep
5H4 **La Ronge** Can
5H4 **La Ronge,L** Can
39F7 **Larvik** Nor
65J3 **Laryak** Russian Fed
50B2 **La Sagra** Mt Spain
15D1 **La Salle** Can
18C1 **La Salle** USA
7C5 **La Sarre** Can
34C1 **Las Avispas** Arg
34A2 **Las Cabras** Chile
34A2 **Lascombe** Can
9C3 **Las Cruces** USA
26C3 **La Selle** Mt Haiti
72B2 **Lasengmia** China
34B1 **La Serena** Chile
28E3 **Las Flores** Arg
76B1 **Lashio** Myan
53C3 **La Sila** Mts Italy
90B2 **Läsjerd** Iran
34A3 **Las Lajas** Chile
50B2 **Las Marismas** Marshland Spain
96A2 **Las Palmas de Gran Canaria** Canary Is
47C2 **La Spezia** Italy
52A2 **Las Varillas** Arg
29C4 **Las Plumas** Arg
34C2 **Las Rosas** Arg
20B2 **Lassen Peak** Mt USA
20B2 **Lassen Volcanic Nat Pk** USA
23B2 **las Tinaj** Mexico
98B3 **Lastoursville** Gabon
52C2 **Lastovo** I Croatia
24B2 **Las Tres Marias** Is Mexico
34C2 **Las Varillas** Arg
9C3 **Las Vegas** USA
94B3 **Latakia = Al Lädhiqiyah**
53B2 **Latina** Italy
34C2 **La Toma** Arg
32D1 **La Tortuga** I Ven
79B2 **La Trinidad** Phil
109C4 **Latrobe** Aust
94B3 **Latrun** Israel
7C5 **La Tuque** Can
87B1 **Latur** India
58D2 **Latvia** Republic, Europe
107D5 **Launceston** Aust
43B4 **Launceston** Eng
25D3 **La Union** El Salvador
23A2 **La Union** Mexico
32B5 **La Unión** Peru
107D2 **Laura** Aust
15C3 **Laurel** Delaware, USA
16A3 **Laurel** Maryland, USA
11B3 **Laurel** Mississippi, USA
17B1 **Laurens** USA
52A1 **Laurino** Switz
91B4 **Lari** Iran
96B1 **Larache** Mor
8C2 **Laramie** USA
29B5 **Lautaro** Mt Chile

46D2 **Lauterecken** Germany
15D1 **Laval** Can
48B2 **Laval** France
22B2 **Laveaga Peak** Mt USA
47C2 **Laveno** Italy
31B6 **Lavras** Brazil
4A3 **Lavrentiya** Russian Fed
101H1 **Lavumisa** Swaziland
78D1 **Lawas** Malay
76B1 **Lawksawk** Myan
18A2 **Lawrence** Kansas, USA
15D2 **Lawrence** Massachusetts, USA
111A3 **Lawrence** NZ
14A3 **Lawrenceville** Illinois, USA
9D3 **Lawton** USA
91A5 **Layla** S Arabia
99D2 **Laylo** Sudan
23A2 **Lázaro Cárdenas** Mexico
99E1 **Laz Daua** Somalia
79B4 **Lazi** Phil
13F2 **Lead** USA
13F2 **Leader** Can
18A2 **Leavenworth** USA
58B2 **Leba** Pol
18B2 **Lebanon** Missouri, USA
20B2 **Lebanon** Oregon, USA
15C2 **Lebanon** Pennsylvania, USA
92C3 **Lebanon** Republic, S W Asia
101C3 **Lebombo** Mts Mozam/S Africa/Swaziland
58B2 **Lebork** Pol
47A2 **Le Bourg-d'Oisans** France
47B1 **Le Brassus** Switz
29B3 **Lebu** Chile
47B1 **Le Buet** Mt France
46B1 **Le Cateau** France
55A2 **Lecce** Italy
52A1 **Lecco** Italy
47D1 **Lech** R Austria
47D1 **Lechtaler Alpen** Mts Austria
49C2 **Le Creusot** France
43C3 **Ledbury** Eng
13E2 **Leduc** Can
16C1 **Lee** USA
45B3 **Lee** R Irish Rep
43C3 **Leeds** Eng
43C3 **Leek** Eng
56B2 **Leer** Germany
17B2 **Leesburg** Florida, USA
16A3 **Leesburg** Virginia, USA
19B3 **Leesville** USA
109C2 **Leeton** Aust
106H4 **Leeuwarden** Neth
22C2 **Leeuwin,C** Aust
26E3 **Leeward Is** Caribbean S
94A1 **Lefkara** Cyprus
79B3 **Legazpi** Phil
47D2 **Legnago** Italy
59B2 **Legnica** Pol
33F2 **Leguan Inlet** Guyana
32C4 **Leguizamo** Colombia
84D2 **Leh** India
48C2 **Le Havre** France
16B2 **Lehigh** USA
16B2 **Lehighton** USA
84C2 **Leiah** Pak
59B3 **Leibnitz** Austria
43D3 **Leicester** County, Eng
43D3 **Leicester** Eng
107C2 **Leichhardt** R Aust
56A2 **Leiden** Neth
54B3 **Leie** R Belg
106C4 **Leigh Creek** Aust
43D3 **Leighton Buzzard** Eng

56B2 **Leine** *R* Germany
45C2 **Leinster** Region,
Irish Rep
57C2 **Leipzig** Germany
50A2 **Leiria** Port
45B1 **Leirvik** Nor
45B1 **Leitrim** County,
Irish Rep
73C4 **Leiyang** China
73B5 **Leizhou Bandao** *Pen*
China
73C5 **Leizhou Wan** *B*
China
56A2 **Lek** *R* Neth
96C1 **Le Kef** Tunisia
19B3 **Leland** USA
54A2 **Lelija** *Mt* Bosnia-
Herzegovina
47B1 **Le Locle** France
48C2 **Le Mans** France
6D3 **Lemieux Is** Can
8C2 **Lemmon** USA
21B2 **Lemoore** USA
49C2 **Lempdes** France
86C2 **Lemro** *R* Myan
52C2 **Le Murge** Region,
Italy
63C2 **Lena** *R* Russian Fed
38L6 **Lendery** Russian Fed
73C4 **Lengshuijiang** China
**Leningrad = Sankt-
Peterburg**
112B7 **Leningradskaya** *Base*
Ant
61H3 **Leninogorsk**
Tatarskaya
Respublika,
Russian Fed
68A1 **Leninogorsk**
Kazakhstan
65K4 **Leninsk-Kuznetskiy**
Russian Fed
69F2 **Leninskoye**
Russian Fed
65F6 **Lenkoran'** Azerbaijan
46C1 **Lenne** *R* Germany
16C1 **Lenox** USA
46B1 **Lens** France
63D1 **Lensk** Russian Fed
53B3 **Lentini** Italy
76B3 **Lenya** *R* Myan
52B1 **Leoben** Austria
43C3 **Leominster** Eng
16D1 **Leominster** Eng
24B2 **León** Mexico
25D3 **León** Nic
50A1 **León** Region, Spain
50A1 **León** Spain
100A3 **Leonardville**
Namibia
106B3 **Leonora** Aust
35C2 **Leopoldina** Brazil
**Léopoldville =
Kinshasa**
60C3 **Lepel** Belarus
73D4 **Leping** China
49C2 **Le Puy-en-Velay**
France
98B2 **Léré** Chad
101G1 **Leribe** Lesotho
47C2 **Lerici** Italy
51C1 **Lérida** Spain
23A1 **Lerma** *R* Mexico
47D1 **Lermoos** Austria
55C3 **Léros** *I* Greece
44E1 **Lerwick** Scot
26C3 **Les Andelys** France
26C3 **Les Cayes** Haiti
47B2 **Les Écrins** *Mt* France
73A4 **Leshan** China
54B2 **Leskovac** Serbia,
Yugos
48B3 **Les Landes** Region,
France
101G1 **Leslie** S Africa
61H2 **Lesnoy** Russian Fed
63B2 **Lesosibirsk**
Russian Fed
101G1 **Lesotho** Kingdom,
S Africa
69F2 **Lesozavodsk**
Russian Fed
48B2 **Les Sables-d'Olonne**
France

112A **Lesser Antarctica**
Region, Ant
27D4 **Lesser Antilles** *Is*
Caribbean S
65F5 **Lesser Caucasus** *Mts*
Azerbaijan/Georgia
13E1 **Lesser Slave L** Can
55C3 **Lésvos** *I* Greece
58B2 **Leszno** Pol
86C2 **Letha Range** *Mts*
Myan
5G5 **Lethbridge** Can
33F3 **Lethem** Guyana
59D3 **Letichev** Ukraine
63D2 **Let Oktyabr'ya**
Russian Fed
78B2 **Letong** Indon
46A1 **Le Touquet-Paris-
Plage** France
76B2 **Letpadan** Myan
48C1 **Le Tréport** France
47B1 **Leuk** Switz
57A2 **Leuven** Belg
55B3 **Levádhia** Greece
38G6 **Levanger** Nor
47B2 **Levanna** *Mt* Italy
71D5 **Lévêque,C** Aust
46D1 **Leverkusen**
Germany
59B3 **Levice** Slovakia
47D1 **Levico** Italy
110C2 **Levin** NZ
7C5 **Levis** Can
15D2 **Levittown** USA
55B3 **Levká -ri** *Mt* Greece
55B3 **Levkás** Greece
55B3 **Levkás** *I* Greece
108B2 **Lévêque,C** Aust
54C2 **Levski** Bulg
43E4 **Lewes** Eng
40B2 **Lewis** *I* Scot
16A2 **Lewisburg** USA
111B2 **Lewis P** NZ
8B2 **Lewis Range** *Mts*
USA
8B2 **Lewiston** Idaho, USA
10C2 **Lewiston** Maine, USA
8C2 **Lewistown** Montana,
USA
15C2 **Lewistown**
Pennsylvania, USA
19B3 **Lewisville** USA
11B3 **Lexington** Kentucky,
USA
18B2 **Lexington** Missouri,
USA
15C3 **Lexington Park** USA
79C3 **Leyte G** Phil
82D3 **Lhasa** China
86B1 **Lhazê** China
70A3 **Lhokseumawe** Indon
86C1 **Lhozhag** China
68B4 **Lhunze** China
**Liancourt Rocks =
Tok-do**
79C4 **Lianga** Phil
72B3 **Liangdang** China
73C5 **Lianjiang** China
73C5 **Lian Xian** China
72D3 **Lianyungang** China
72B3 **Liaodong B∂ndao** *Pen*
China
72E1 **Liaodong Wan** *B*
China
72E1 **Liao He** *R* China
72E1 **Liaoning** Province,
China
72E1 **Liaoyang** China
72E1 **Liaoyuan** China
74B2 **Liaoyuang** China
4F3 **Liard** *R* Can
4F4 **Liard River** Can
46C2 **Liart** France
98B2 **Libenge** Zaire
9C3 **Liberal** USA
57C2 **Liberec**
Czech Republic
97A4 **Liberia** Republic,
Africa
18B2 **Liberty** Missouri,
USA

15D2 **Liberty** New York,
USA
19B3 **Liberty** Texas, USA
48B3 **Libourne** France
23B2 **Libres** Mexico
98A2 **Libreville** Gabon
95A2 **Libya** Republic,
Africa
95B2 **Libyan Desert** Libya
95B1 **Libyan Plat** Egypt
53B3 **Licata** Italy
43D3 **Lichfield** Eng
101C2 **Lichinga** Mozam
101G1 **Lichtenburg** S Africa
14B3 **Licking** *R* USA
22B2 **Lick Observatory**
USA
60C3 **Lida** Belarus
39G7 **Lidköping** Sweden
53B2 **Lido di Ostia** Italy
52A1 **Liechtenstein**
Principality, Europe
57B2 **Liège** Belg
58C1 **Lielupe** *R* Latvia
98C2 **Lienart** Zaire
57C3 **Lienz** Austria
60B2 **Liepāja** Latvia
46C1 **Lier** Belg
47B1 **Liestal** Switz
15C1 **Lièvre** *R* Can
57C3 **Liezen** Austria
45C1 **Liffey** *R* Irish Rep
107F3 **Lifu** *I* Nouvelle
Calédonie
109C1 **Lightning Ridge** Aust
46C2 **Ligny-en-Barrois**
France
101C2 **Ligonha** *R* Mozam
47C2 **Liguria** Region, Italy
52A2 **Ligurian** *S* Italy
21C4 **Lihue** Hawaiian Is
100B2 **Likasi** Zaire
49C1 **Lille** France
39G6 **Lillehammer** Nor
46B1 **Lillers** France
39G7 **Lillestrøm** Nor
13C2 **Lillooet** Can
13C2 **Lillooet** *R* Can
100B2 **Lilongwe** Malawi
79B4 **Liloy** Phil
54A2 **Lim** *R* Montenegro/
Serbia, Yugos
32B6 **Lima** Peru
50A1 **Lima** Spain
10B2 **Lima** USA
92B3 **Limassol** Cyprus
45C1 **Limavady** N Ire
34B3 **Limay** *R* Arg
98A2 **Limbe** Cam
101C2 **Limbe** Malawi
57B2 **Limburg** W Gem
31B6 **Limeira** Brazil
45B2 **Limerick** County,
Irish Rep
41B3 **Limerick** Irish Rep
56B1 **Limfjorden** *L* Den
106C2 **Limmen Bight** *B*
Aust
55C3 **Limnos** *I* Greece
31D3 **Limoeiro** Brazil
48C2 **Limoges** France
25D4 **Limón** Costa Rica
8C3 **Limon** USA
48C2 **Limousin** Region,
France
42D3 **Lincoln** County, Eng
42D3 **Lincoln** Eng
18C1 **Lincoln** Illinois, USA
8D2 **Lincoln** Nebraska,
USA
15D2 **Lincoln** New
Hampshire, USA
111B2 **Lincoln** NZ
80A **Lincoln** *S* Greenland

20B2 **Lincoln City** USA
14B2 **Lincoln Park** USA
52A2 **L'Incudina** *Mt* Corse
57B3 **Lindau** Germany
33F2 **Linden** Guyana
39F7 **Lindesnes** *C* Nor
99D3 **Lindi** Tanz
98C2 **Lindi** *R* Zaire
101G1 **Lindley** S Africa
55C3 **Líndos** Greece
15C2 **Lindsay** Can
105J3 **Line Is** Pacific O
72C2 **Linfen** China
76D2 **Lingao** China
79B2 **Lingayen** Phil
56B2 **Lingen** Germany
73C4 **Lingling** China
73B5 **Lingshan** China
72C2 **Lingshi** China
97A3 **Linguère** Sen
73E4 **Linhai** Rhejiang,
China
31D5 **Linhares** Brazil
72B1 **Linhe** China
74B2 **Linjiang** China
39H7 **Linköping** Sweden
72D2 **Linqing** China
35B2 **Lins** Brazil
72A2 **Lintao** China
47C1 **Linthal** Switz
68D2 **Linxi** China
72A2 **Linxia** China
57C3 **Linz** Austria
79B3 **Lipa** Phil
53B3 **Lipari** *I* Italy
61E3 **Lipetsk** Russian Fed
54B1 **Lipova** Rom
56B2 **Lippe** *R* Germany
46E1 **Lippstadt** Germany
99D2 **Lira** Uganda
98B3 **Liranga** Congo
98C2 **Lisala** Zaire
50A2 **Lisboa** Port
Lisbon = Lisboa
45C1 **Lisburn** N Ire
45C2 **Liscannor B** Irish Rep
73D4 **Lishui** China
73C4 **Li Shui** *R* China
60E4 **Lisichansk** Ukraine
48C2 **Lisieux** France
60E3 **Liski** Russian Fed
46B2 **L'Isle-Adam** France
47B1 **L'Isle-sur-le-Doubs**
France
107E3 **Lismore** Aust
45B2 **Listowel** Irish Rep
73B5 **Litang** China
94B2 **Litani** *R* Leb
33G3 **Litani** *R* Surinam
18C2 **Litchfield** USA
107E4 **Lithgow** Aust
60B2 **Lithuania** Republic,
Europe
16A2 **Lititz** USA
69F2 **Litovko** Russian Fed
19A3 **Little** *R* USA
11C4 **Little Abaco** *I*
The Bahamas
110C1 **Little Barrier I** NZ
13E2 **Little Bow** *R* Can
25D3 **Little Cayman** *I*
Caribbean S
16B3 **Little Egg Harbor** *B*
USA
26C2 **Little Inagua** *I*
Caribbean S
77A4 **Little Nicobar** *I*
Nicobar Is
11A3 **Little Rock** USA
22D3 **Littlerock** USA
13D2 **Little Smoky** Can
13D2 **Little Smoky** *R* Can
16A3 **Littlestown** USA
15D2 **Littleton** New
Hampshire, USA
74B2 **Liuhe** China
73B5 **Liuzhou** China
55B3 **Livanátais** Greece
58D1 **Līvāni** Latvia
12E1 **Livengood** USA
17B1 **Live Oak** USA
21A2 **Livermore** USA
7D5 **Liverpool** Can
42C3 **Liverpool** Eng

4E2 Liverpool B Can
42C3 Liverpool B Eng
6C2 Liverpool,C Can
109D2 Liverpool Range *Mts* Aust
8B2 Livingston Montana, USA
19B3 Livingston Texas, USA
44C4 Livingston UK
Livingstone = Maramba
19A3 Livingston,L USA
52C2 Livno Bosnia-Herzegovina
60E3 Livny Russian Fed
14B2 Livonia USA
52B2 Livorno Italy
99D3 Liwale Tanz
12E1 Ljubljana Slovenia
38G6 Ljungan *R* Sweden
39G7 Ljungby Sweden
39H6 Ljusdal Sweden
38H6 Ljusnan *R* Sweden
43C4 Llandeilo Wales
43C4 Llandovery Wales
43C3 Llandrindod Wells Wales
42C3 Llandudno Wales
43B4 Llanelli Wales
43C3 Llangollen Wales
9C3 Llano Estacado *Plat* USA
32C2 Llanos *Region*, Colombia/Ven
30D2 Llanos de Chiquitos *Region*, Bol
Lleida = Lérida
50A2 Llerena Spain
43B3 Lleyn *Pen* Wales
89E7 Llorin Nig
5H4 Lloydminster Can
30C3 Llullaillaco *Mt* Arg/Chile
30C3 Loa *R* Chile
49C2 Loan France
98B3 Loange *R* Zaire
108B3 Lobatse Botswana
98B2 Lobaye *R* CAR
34D3 Loberia Arg
100A2 Lobito Angola
34D3 Lobos Arg
47B2 Locano Italy
47C1 Locarno Switz
44B3 Loch Awe *L* Scot
44A3 Lochboisdale Scot
44A3 Loch Bracadale *Inlet* Scot
44B3 Loch Broom *Estuary* Scot
42B2 Loch Doon *L* Scot
44B3 Loch Earn *L* Scot
44B2 Loch Eriboll *Inlet* Scot
44B3 Loch Ericht *L* Scot
48C2 Loches France
44B3 Loch Etive *Inlet* Scot
44B3 Loch Ewe *Inlet* Scot
44B3 Loch Fyne *Inlet* Scot
44B3 Loch Hourn *Inlet* Scot
44B3 Lochinver Scot
44B3 Loch Katrine *L* Scot
44C3 Loch Leven *L* Scot
44B3 Loch Linnhe *Inlet* Scot
44B3 Loch Lochy *L* Scot
44B3 Loch Lomond *L* Scot
44B3 Loch Long *Inlet* Scot
44A3 Lochmaddy Scot
44B3 Loch Maree *L* Scot
44B3 Loch Morar *L* Scot
44B3 Lochnagar *Mt* Scot
44B3 Loch Ness *L* Scot
44B3 Loch Rannoch *L* Scot
44A2 Loch Roag *Inlet* Scot
44B3 Loch Sheil *L* Scot
44B2 Loch Shin *L* Scot
44A3 Loch Snizort *Inlet* Scot
44B3 Loch Sunart *Inlet* Scot
44B3 Loch Tay *L* Scot

44B3 Loch Torridon *Inlet* Scot
108A2 Lock Aust
42C2 Lockerbie Scot
15C2 Lock Haven USA
15C2 Lockport USA
76D3 Loc Ninh Viet
53C3 Locri Italy
94B3 Lod Israel
108B3 Loddon *R* Aust
60D1 Lodeynoye Pole Russian Fed
54A1 Lodhran Pak
21A2 Lodi USA
98C3 Lodja Zaire
47B1 Lods France
99D2 Lodwar Kenya
58B2 Łódź Pol
38G5 Lofoten *Is* Nor
8B2 Logan Utah, USA
4D3 Logan,Mt Can
14A2 Logansport Indiana, USA
19B3 Logansport Louisiana, USA
50B1 Logroño Spain
86A2 Lohardaga India
59B3 Lohja Fin
76B2 Loi Lan *Mt* Myan
39J6 Loimaa Fin
48C2 Loir *R* France
48C2 Loire *R* France
32B4 Loja Ecuador
50B2 Loja Spain
38K5 Lokan Tekojärvi *Res* Fin
46B1 Lokeren Belg
99D2 Lokitaung Kenya
58D1 Loknya Russian Fed
98C3 Lokolo *R* Zaire
98C3 Lokoro *R* Zaire
6D3 Loks Land *I* Can
56C2 Lolland *I* Den
54B2 Lom Bulg
98C3 Lomami *R* Zaire
97A4 Loma Mts Sierra Leone/Guinea
52C2 Lombardia *Region*, Italy
71D4 Lomblen *I* Indon
78D4 Lombok *I* Indon
97C4 Lomé Togo
98C3 Lomela Zaire
98C3 Lomela *R* Zaire
60C2 Lomonosov Russian Fed
47B1 Lomont *R* France
21A3 Lompoc USA
58C2 Łomza Pol
87A1 Lonāvale India
29B3 Loncoche Chile
7B5 London Can
43D4 London Eng
45C1 Londonderry N Ire
29B7 Londonderry,I Chile
108B2 Londonderry,C Aust
30C4 Londres Arg
30F3 Londrina Brazil
21B2 Lone Pine USA
11C4 Long I *The* Bahamas
71F4 Long I PNG
78C2 Long Akah Malay
47E1 Longarone Italy
34A3 Longaví *Mt* Chile
27H2 Long B Jamaica
17C1 Long B USA
9B3 Long Beach California, USA
15D2 Long Beach New York, USA
15D2 Long Branch USA
73D5 Longchuan China
20C2 Long Creek USA
109C4 Longford Aust
45C2 Longford County, Irish Rep
44D3 Longforgan Scot
72D1 Longhua China

7C4 Long I Can
10C2 Long I USA
16C2 Long Island Sd USA
7B4 Longlac Can
73B5 Longlin China
8C2 Longmont USA
78D2 Longnawan Indon
29B3 Longquimay Chile
107D3 Longreach Aust
72A2 Longshou Shan *Upland* China
42C2 Longtown Eng
15D1 Longueuil Can
34A3 Longuimay Chile
46C2 Longuyon France
11A3 Longview Texas, USA
8A2 Longview Washington, USA
46C2 Longwy France
72A3 Longxi China
77D3 Long Xuyen Viet
73D4 Longyan China
73D5 Longzhou China
47D2 Lonigo Italy
49D2 Lons-le-Saunier France
10B2 Lorain USA
84B2 Loralai Pak
90B3 Lordegān Iran
107E4 Lord Howe *I* Aust
105G5 Lord Howe Rise Pacific O
6A3 Lord Mayor B Can
9C3 Lordsburg USA
35B2 Lorena Brazil
47E2 Loreo Italy
23A1 Loreto Mexico
48B2 Lorient France
108B3 Lorne Aust
57B3 Lörrach Germany
49D2 Lorraine *Region* France
9C3 Los Alamos USA
34A2 Los Andes Chile
29B3 Los Angeles Chile
9B3 Los Angeles USA
21A2 Los Banos USA
34B2 Los Cerrillos Arg
21A2 Los Gatos USA
52B2 Lošinj *I* Croatia
29B3 Los Lagos Chile
24B2 Los Mochis Mexico
22B3 Los Olivos USA
34A3 Los Sauces Chile
44C3 Lossiemouth Scot
27E4 Los Testigos *Is* Ven
29B2 Los Vilos Chile
48C3 Lot *R* France
34A3 Lota Chile
42C2 Lothian *Region*, Scot
99D2 Lotikipi Plain Sudan/Kenya
98C3 Loto Zaire
47B1 Lötschberg Tunnel Switz
38K5 Lotta *R* Fin/Russian Fed
108B2 Loxton Aust
5F4 Loyd George,Mt Can
54A2 Loznica Serbia, Yugos
23A2 Los Reyes Mexico
65H3 Lozva *R* Russian Fed
100B2 Luacano Angola
98C3 Luachimo Angola
98C3 Lualaba *R* Zaire
100B2 Luampa Zambia
100B2 Luân Angola
73D3 Lu'an China
98B3 Luanda Angola
100A2 Luando *R* Angola
100B2 Luanginga *R* Angola
76C1 Luang Namtha Laos
76C2 Luang Prabang Laos
100B2 Luangue *R* Angola
100C2 Luangwa *R* Zambia
72D1 Luan He *R* China
72D1 Luanping China
100B2 Luanshya Zambia
100B2 Luapula *R* Zaire
50A1 Luarca Spain
98B3 Lubalo Angola
58D2 L'uban Belarus
79B3 Lubang Is Phil
100A2 Lubango Angola
9C3 Lubbock USA
56C2 Lübeck Germany
98B3 Lubefu *R* Zaire
98C3 Lubero *R* Zaire
98C3 Lubilash *R* Zaire
59C2 Lublin Pol
60D3 Lubny Ukraine
78C2 Lubok Antu Malay
98C3 Lubudi *R* Zaire
98C3 Lubudi Zaire

45C2 Lough Derravaragh *L*
4H2 Loughead I Can
45C2 Lough Ennell *L* Irish Rep
41B3 Lough Erne *L* N Ire
40B2 Lough Foyle *Estuary* N Ire/Irish Rep
40B3 Lough Neagh *L* N Ire
45C1 Lough Oughter *L* Irish Rep
45B2 Loughrea Irish Rep
45C2 Lough Ree *L* Irish Rep
45C2 Lough Sheelin *L* Irish Rep
42B2 Lough Strangford *L* Irish Rep
45C1 Lough Swilly *Estuary* Irish Rep
14B3 Louisa USA
70C3 Louisa Reef *I* S E Asia
12E1 Louise,L USA
107E2 Louisiade Arch Solomon Is
11A3 Louisiana State, USA
17B1 Louisville Georgia, USA
11B3 Louisville Kentucky, USA
38L5 Loukhi Russian Fed
48B3 Lourdes France
108C2 Louth Aust
45C2 Louth County, Irish Rep
42D3 Louth Eng
Louvain = Leuven
49C2 Louviers France
60D2 Lovat *R* Russian Fed
54B2 Lovech Bulg
21B1 Lovelock USA
52B1 Lovere Italy
9C3 Lovington USA
38L5 Lovozero Russian Fed
6B3 Low,C Can
10C2 Lowell Massachusetts, USA
20B2 Lowell Oregon, USA
16D1 Lowell USA
111B2 Lower Hutt NZ
43E3 Lowestoft Eng
58B2 Łowicz Pol

Lubuklinggau

78A3 Lubuklinggau Indon
33C8 Lubumbashi Zaire
98C3 Lubutu Zaire
79B3 Lucban Phil
52B2 Lucca Italy
42C8 Luce B Scot
19C3 Lucedale USA
79B3 Lucena Phil
59B3 Lucenec Slovakia
Lucerne = Luzern
73C5 Luchuan China
56C2 Luckenwalde Germany
101F1 Luckhoff S Africa
86A1 Lucknow India
100B2 Lucusse Angola
46D1 Lüdenscheid Germany
100A3 Lüderitz Namibia
11A2 Ludhiana India
14A2 Ludington USA
43C3 Ludlow Eng
54C2 Ludogorie Upland Bulg
17B1 Ludowici USA
54B1 Luduş Rom
39H6 Ludvika Sweden
57B3 Ludwigsburg Germany
57B3 Ludwigshafen Germany
56C2 Ludwigslust Germany
98C3 Luebo Zaire
98C3 Luema R Zaire
98C3 Luembe R Angola
100A2 Luena Angola
100B2 Luene R Angola
72B3 Lüeyang China
73D5 Lufeng China
11A3 Lufkin USA
60C2 Luga Russian Fed
60C2 Luga R Russian Fed
52A1 Lugano Switz
60E4 Lugansk Ukraine
101C2 Lugela Mozam
101C2 Lugenda R Mozam
50A1 Lugo Spain
54B1 Lugoj Rom
72A3 Luhuo China
98B3 Lui R Angola
100B2 Luiana Angola
100B2 Luiana R Angola
Luichow Peninsula = Leizhou Bandao
47C2 Luino Italy
98B2 Luionga R Zaire
72B2 Luipan Shan Upland China
100B2 Luishia Zaire
68B4 Luixi China
98C3 Luiza Zaire
34B2 Luján Arg
34D2 Luján Arg
73D3 Lujiang China
98B3 Lukenie R Zaire
64E4 Luki Russian Fed
98B3 Lukolela Zaire
58C2 Lukòw Pol
98C3 Lukuga R Zaire
100B2 Lukulu Zambia
38J5 Lulea Sweden
38J5 Luleå Sweden
54C2 Lüleburgaz Turk
72C2 Lüliang Shan Mts China
19A4 Luling USA
98C2 Lulonga R Zaire
Luluabourg = Kananga
100B2 Lumbala Kaquengue Angola
11C3 Lumberton USA
78D1 Lumbis Indon
86C1 Lumding India
100B2 Lumeje Angola
11A3 Lumsden NZ
39G7 Lund Sweden
101C2 Lundazi Zambia
43B4 Lundy I Eng
56C2 Lüneburg Germany
46D2 Luneville France
100B2 Lunga R Zambia
86C2 Lunglei India

100A2 Lungue Bungo R Angola
58D2 Luninec Belarus
98B3 Luobomo Congo
73B5 Luocheng China
72C3 Luoding China
72C3 Luohe R Henan, China
72B2 Luo He R Shaanxi, China
73C4 Luoxiao Shan Hills China
72C3 Luoyang China
98B3 Luozi Zaire
100B2 Lupane Zim
101C2 Lupilichi Mozam
Lu Qu = Tao He
30E4 Luque Par
45C1 Lurgan N Ire
100A2 Lurio R Mozam
90A3 Luristan Region, Iran
100B2 Lusaka Zambia
98C3 Lusambo Zaire
55A2 Lushnjë Alb
99D3 Lushoto Tanz
68B4 Lushui China
72E2 Lüshun China
43D4 Luton Eng
60C3 Lutsk Ukraine
99E2 Luuq Somalia
99C3 Luvua R Zaire
99D3 Luwegu R Tanz
100C2 Luwingu Zambia
71D4 Luwuk Indon
46D2 Luxembourg Grand Duchy, N W Europe
49D2 Luxembourg Lux
73A5 Luxi China
95C2 Luxor Egypt
61G1 Luza Russian Fed
61G1 Luza R Russian Fed
52A1 Luzern Switz
73B5 Luzhai China
73B4 Luzhi China
73B4 Luzhou China
35B1 Luziânia Brazil
79B2 Luzon I Phil
79B1 Luzon Str Phil
59C3 L'vov Ukraine
42C2 Lybster Scot
38H6 Lycksele Sweden
100B3 Lydenburg S Africa
8B3 Lyell,Mt USA
16A2 Lykens USA
43E4 Lyme B Eng
43C4 Lyme Regis Eng
11C3 Lynching R USA
108A2 Lyndhurst Aust
15D2 Lynn USA
12G3 Lynn Canal Sd USA
17A1 Lynn Haven USA
5H4 Lynn Lake Can
5H4 Lynx L Can
49C2 Lyon France
12G3 Lynn Canal Sd USA
17B1 Lyons Georgia, USA
106A3 Lyons R Aust
47B2 Lys R Italy
61J2 Lys'va Russian Fed
111B2 Lyttelton NZ
13C2 Lytton Can
22A1 Lytton USA
58D2 Lyubeshov Ukraine
60E2 Lyublino Russian Fed

M

76C1 Ma R Viet
94B2 Ma'agan Jordan
94B2 Ma'ad Tarshiha Israel
92C3 Ma'an Jordan
73D3 Ma'anshan China
94B2 Ma'arrat an Nu'mān Syria
46C1 Maas R Neth
94B2 Maaseik Belg
79B3 Maasin Phil
57B2 Maastricht Neth
101C3 Mabalane Mozam
33F3 Mabaruma Guyana
42E3 Mablethorpe Eng
101C3 Mabote Mozam
58C2 Mabrita Belarus

58D2 M'adel Belarus
35C2 Macaé Brazil
9D3 McAlester USA
9D4 McAllen USA
101C2 Macaloge Mozam
33G3 Macapá Brazil
35C1 Macarani Brazil
32B4 Macas Ecuador
31D3 Macaú Brazil
73C5 Macau Dependency, China
98C2 M'Bari R CAR
13C2 McBride Can
12F2 McCarthy USA
13A2 McCauley I Can
42C3 Macclesfield Eng
6B1 McClintock B Can
4H2 McClintock Chan Can
16A2 McClure USA
22B2 McClure,L USA
4G2 McClure Str Can
19B3 McComb USA
98C3 Macconde Moz
6C2 Macculloch,C Can
13C1 McCusker,Mt Can
4F4 McDame Can
20C2 McDermitt USA
13E2 Macdonald R Can
106C3 Macdonnell Ranges Mts Aust
50A1 Macedo de Cavaleiros Port
55B2 Macedonia Republic, Europe
31D3 Maceió Brazil
97B4 Macenta Guinea
52B2 Macerata Italy
100A2 Macfarlane,L Aust
19B3 McGehee USA
45B3 MacGillycuddys Reeks Mts Irish Rep
4C3 McGrath USA
35B2 Machado Brazil
101C3 Machaila Mozam
99D3 Machakos Kenya
32B4 Machala Ecuador
101C3 Machaze Mozam
87B1 Mācherla India
94B2 Machgharab Leb
87C1 Machilipatnam India
32C1 Machiques Ven
32C6 Machu-Picchu Hist Site Peru
101C3 Macia Mozam
107D3 MacIntyre R Aust
107D3 Mackay Aust
106B3 Mackay,L Aust
14C2 McKeesport USA
13C1 Mackenzie R Can
4E3 Mackenzie B Can
4G2 Mackenzie King I Can
4E3 Mackenzie Mts Can
14B1 Mackinac,Str of USA
14B1 Mackinaw City USA
12D2 McKinley,Mt USA
19A3 McKinney USA
6C2 Mackinson Inlet B Can
109D2 Macksville Aust
20B2 Mclaoughlin,Mt USA
109D1 Maclean Aust
100B4 Maclear S Africa
5G4 McLennan Can
13D2 McLeod R Can
4G3 McLeod B Can
106A3 McLeod,L Aust
13C1 McLeod Lake Can
4E3 Macmillan R Can
12H2 Macmillan P Can
20B1 McMinnville Oregon, USA
112B7 McMurdo Base Ant
13D2 McNaughton L Can
18B1 Macomb USA
53A2 Macomer Sardegna
101C2 Macomia Mozam
49C2 Mâcon France
11B3 Macon Georgia, USA
18B2 Macon Missouri, USA
100B2 Macondo Angola
18A2 McPherson USA

104F6 Macquarie Is Aust
109C2 Macquarie R Aust
109C4 Macquarie Harbour B Aust
109D2 Macquarie,L Aust
17B1 McRae USA
112B11 Mac. Robertson Land Region, Ant
45B3 Macroom Irish Rep
96C1 M'Sila Alg
4G3 McTavish Arm B Can
108A1 Macumba R Aust
47C2 Macunaga Italy
4J3 McVicar Arm B Can
59B3 M'yarovár Hung
94B3 Mādaba Jordan
95A3 Madadi Well Chad
89J10 Madagascar I Indian O
95A2 Madama Niger
71F4 Madang PNG
97C3 Madaoua Niger
96C2 Madaripur Bang
90B2 Madau Turkmenistan
15C1 Madawaska R Can
96A1 Madeira I Atlantic O
33E5 Madeira R Brazil
7D5 Madeleine, Isle de la Can
24B2 Madera Mexico
21A2 Madera USA
86B1 Madhubani India
86A2 Madhya Pradesh State, India
87B2 Madikeri India
98B3 Madimba Zaire
Madikéri Kayes Congo
98B3 Madingou Congo
86D2 Madison Indiana, USA
14A2 Madison Wisconsin, USA
18C2 Madisonville Kentucky, USA
19A3 Madisonville Texas, USA
78C4 Madiun Indon
99D2 Mado Gashi Kenya
47D1 Madonna Di Campiglio Italy
87C2 Madras India
20B2 Madras USA
29A6 Madre de Dios I Chile
32D6 Madre de Dios R Bol
50B1 Madrid Spain
50B2 Madridejos Spain
78C4 Madura I Indon
87B3 Madurai India
75B1 Maebashi Japan
76B3 Mae Khlong R Thai
77B4 Mae Nam Lunang R Thai
76C2 Mae Nam Mun R Thai
76B2 Mae Nam Ping R Thai
101D2 Maevatanana Madag
101G1 Mafeteng Lesotho
109C3 Maffra Aust
99D3 Mafia I Tanz
101G1 Mafikeng S Africa
30G4 Mafra Brazil
92C3 Mafraq Jordan
92C3 Magangué Colombia
34D3 Magdalena Arg
24A1 Magdalena Mexico
26C4 Magdalena R Colombia
78D1 Madmbang,Mt Malay
56C2 Magdeburg Germany
31C6 Mage Brazil
78C4 Magelang Indon
47C1 Maggia R Switz
92B4 Maghagha Egypt
45C1 Magherafelt N Ire
55A2 Maglie Italy
61J3 Magnitogorsk Russian Fed
19B3 Magnolia USA
101C2 Magoé Mozam

15D1 Magog Can
23B1 Magosal Mexico
13E2 Magrath Can
7A3 Maguse River Can
76B1 Magwe Myan
90A2 Mahābād Iran
Mahabharat Range Mts Nepal
87A1 Mahād India
85D4 Mahaba Hills India
101D2 Mahajanga Madag
100B3 Mahalapye Botswana
86A2 Mahānadī R India
101D2 Mahanoro Madag
16A2 Mahanoy City USA
87A1 Maharashtra State, India
86A2 Mahāsamund India
76C2 Maha Sarakham Thai
87A1 Mahavavy R Madag
87B1 Mahbubnagar India
96D1 Mahdia Tunisia
87B2 Mahe India
85D4 Mahekar India
101D2 Mahéli / Comoros
86A2 Mahendragarh India
99D3 Mahenge Tanz
85C4 Mahesāna India
110C1 Mahia Pen NZ
85D3 Mahoba India
51C2 Mahón Spain
12J1 Mahony L Can
96D1 Mahrès Tunisia
85C4 Mahuva India
32C1 Maicao Colombia
47B1 Maiche France
43E4 Maidstone Eng
86A2 Maiduguri Nig
76B3 Mail Kyun / Myan
84A1 Maimana Afghan
14B1 Main Chan Can
98B3 Mai-Ndombe L Zaire
10D2 Maine State, USA
48B2 Maine Region France
44C2 Mainland / Scot
85D3 Mainpuri India
46A2 Maintenon France
101D2 Maintirano Madag
57B2 Mainz Germany
97A4 Maio / Cape Verde
29C2 Maipó R Arg/Chile
34D3 Maipú Arg
32D1 Maiquetía Ven
47B2 Maira R Italy
86C1 Mairābāri India
86C2 Maiskhal I Bang
107E4 Maitland New South Wales, Aust
108A2 Maitland S Australia, Aust
112C12 Maitri Base Ant
74D2 Maizuru Japan
70C4 Majene Indon
30B2 Majes R Peru
99D2 Maji Eth
72D2 Majia He R China
Majunga = Mahajanga
70C4 Makale Indon
86B1 Makalu Mt China/Nepal
98B2 Makanza Zaire
52C2 Makarska Croatia
61F2 Makaryev Russian Fed
Makassar = Ujung Pandang
78D3 Makassar Str Indon
61H4 Makat Kazakhstan
97A4 Makeni Sierra Leone
60E4 Makeyevka Ukraine
100B3 Makgadikgadi Salt Pan Botswana
61G5 Makhachkala Russian Fed
99D3 Makindu Kenya
88H5 Makkah S Arabia
59C3 Makó Hungary
98B2 Makokou Gabon
110C1 Makorako,Mt NZ

98B2 Makoua Congo
85A3 Makrāna India
84A3 Makran Coast Range Mts Pak
96C1 Makthar Tunisia
93D2 Mākū Iran
98C3 Makumbi Zaire
74C4 Makurazaki Japan
97C4 Makurdi Nig
79B4 Malabang Phil
87A2 Malabar Coast India
89E7 Malabo Bioko
77C5 Malacca,Str of S E Asia
32C2 Málaga Colombia
50B2 Málaga Spain
101D3 Malaimbandy Madag
107F1 Malaita / Solomon Is
99D2 Malakal Sudan
84C2 Malakand Pak
78C4 Malang Indon
98B3 Malange Angola
97C3 Malanville Benin
39H7 Mälaren L Sweden
34B3 Malargüe Arg
12F3 Malaspina Gl USA
93C2 Malatya Turk
101C3 Malawi Republic, Africa
Malawi,L = Nyasa,L
79C4 Malaybalay Phil
90A3 Malāyer Iran
70B3 Malaysia Federation, S E Asia
93D2 Malazgirt Turk
58B2 Malbork Pol
56C2 Malchin Germany
18C2 Malden USA
83B5 Maldives Is Indian O
104B4 Maldive Ridge Indian O
29F2 Maldonado Urug
47D1 Male Italy
85C4 Malegaon India
59B3 Malé Karpaty Upland Slovakia
98B3 Malema Mozam
84B2 Mālestān Afghan
38H5 Malgomaj L Sweden
95B3 Malha Well Sudan
20C2 Malheur L USA
97B3 Mali Republic, Africa
78D1 Malinau Indon
99E3 Malindi Kenya
Malines = Mechelen
40B2 Malin Head Pt Irish Rep
86A2 Malkala Range Mts India
85D4 Malkāpur India
55C2 Malkara Turk
54C2 Malko Tŭrnovo Bulg
44B3 Mallaig Scot
95C2 Mallawi Egypt
47D1 Málles Venosta Italy
51C2 Mallorca I Spain
45B2 Mallow Irish Rep
38G6 Malm Nor
38J5 Malmberget Sweden
46D1 Malmédy Germany
43C4 Malmesbury Eng
100A4 Malmesbury S Africa
39G7 Malmö Sweden
61G2 Malmyzh Russian Fed
79B3 Malolos Phil
15D2 Malone USA
10G1 Maloti Mts Lesotho
38F6 Måløy Nor
28A2 Malpelo I Colombia
34A2 Malpo R Chile
85D3 Malpura India
54A2 Malta Montana, USA
53B3 Malta Chan Malta/ Italy
53B3 Malta I Medit S
100A3 Maltahöhe Namibia
42D2 Malton Eng
39G6 Malung Sweden
87A1 Malvan India
19B3 Malvern USA
85D4 Malwa Plat India

61G4 Malyy Uzen' R Kazakhstan
63D2 Mama Russian Fed
61H2 Mamadysh Russian Fed
99C2 Mambasa Zaire
71E4 Mamberamo R Indon
98B2 Mambéré R CAR
98A2 Mamfé Cam
33D6 Mamoré R Bol
97A3 Mamou Guinea
101D2 Mampikony Madag
97B4 Mampong Ghana
94B3 Mamshit Hist Site Israel
100B3 Mamuno Botswana
97B4 Man Ivory Coast
21C4 Mana Hawaiian Is
101D3 Manabo Madag
33E4 Manacapuru Brazil
51C2 Manacor Spain
71D3 Manado Indon
25D3 Managua Nic
101D3 Manakara Madag
101D3 Mananara Madag
101D3 Mananjary Madag
111A3 Manapouri NZ
111A3 Manapouri,L NZ
86C1 Manas Bhutan
82C1 Manas China
65K5 Manas He L China
82A1 Manaslu Mt Nepal
16B2 Manasquan USA
33F4 Manaus Brazil
92B2 Manavgat Turk
93C2 Manbij Syria
42B2 Man,Calf of / Eng
87B1 Mancheral India
15D2 Manchester Connecticut, USA
42C3 Manchester Eng
10C2 Manchester New Hampshire, USA
16A2 Manchester Pennsylvania, USA
69E2 Mand R Iran
99D3 Manda Tanz
35A2 Mandaguari Brazil
39F7 Mandal Nor
76B1 Mandalay Myan
68C2 Mandalgovi Mongolia
8C2 Mandan USA
14A2 Mandelona USA
99E2 Mandera Eth
26B3 Mandeville Jamaica
101D2 Mandimba Mozam
86A2 Mandla India
101D2 Mandritsara Madag
85D4 Mandsaur India
53C2 Manduria Italy
85B4 Māndvi India
87B2 Mandya India
42D3 Manfield Eng
53C2 Manfredonia Italy
35D1 Manga Desert Region Niger
110C1 Mangakino NZ
54C2 Mangalia Rom
98B1 Mangalmé Chad
87A2 Mangalore India
78B3 Manggar Indon
98B1 Mangoche Malawi
101D3 Mangoky R Madag
71D4 Mangole I Indon
85B4 Māngral India
63E2 Mangui China
31C6 Manhuaçu Brazil
87A1 Mania R Madag
101C2 Manica Mozam
7S Manicouagan R Can
91A4 Manīfah S Arabia
79B3 Manila Phil
109D2 Manilla Aust
97B3 Maninian Ivory Coast
85D4 Manipur State, India
86C2 Manipur R Myan
92A2 Manisa Turk

41C3 Man,Isle of Irish S
14A2 Manistee USA
14A1 Manistique USA
5H4 Manitoba Province, Can
5J4 Manitoba,L Can
13F2 Manito L Can
14A1 Manitou Is USA
7B5 Manitoulin I Can
15C1 Maniwaki Can
32B2 Manizales Colombia
101D3 Manja Madag
106A4 Manjimup Aust
81B1 Mānjra R India
10A2 Mankato USA
97B4 Mankono Ivory Coast
12D2 Manley Hot Springs USA
110B1 Manly NZ
85C4 Manmād India
78A3 Manna Indon
108A2 Mannahill Aust
87B3 Mannar Sri Lanka
87B3 Mannar,G of India
87B2 Mannārgudi India
57B3 Mannheim Germany
13D1 Manning Can
13D1 Mannville Can
17B1 Manning USA
71E4 Manokwari Indon
98C3 Manono Zaire
76B3 Manoron Myan
75B1 Mano-wan B Japan
74B2 Manp'o N Korea
86D3 Mānsa India
100B2 Mansa Zambia
6B3 Mansel I Can
19B2 Mansfield Arkansas, USA
108C3 Mansfield Aust
19B3 Mansfield Louisiana, USA
16D1 Mansfield Massachusetts, USA
10B2 Mansfield Ohio, USA
15C2 Mansfield Pennsylvania, USA
71E2 Mansyu Deep Pacific O
32A4 Manta Ecuador
79A4 Mantalingajan,Mt Phil
32B6 Mantaro R Peru
22B2 Manteca USA
48C2 Mantes France
52B1 Mantova Italy
38J6 Mänttä Fin
61F2 Manturovo Russian Fed
35A2 Manuel Ribas Brazil
79B4 Manukan Phil
110B1 Manukau NZ
71F4 Manus I Pacific O
50B2 Manzanares Spain
25E2 Manzanillo Cuba
24B3 Manzanillo Mexico
63D3 Manzhouli China
94C3 Manzil Jordan
101C3 Manzini Swaziland
98B1 Mao Chad
72A2 Maomao Shan Mt China
73C5 Maoming China
101C3 Mapai Mozam
78B3 Mapin I Phil
79A4 Mapin I Phil
5H5 Maple Creek Can
101H1 Maputo Mozam
101H1 Maputo R Mozam
Ma Qu = Huange He
72A3 Maqu China
86B1 Maquan He R China
98B3 Maquela do Zombo Angola
29C4 Maquinchao Arg
31B3 Marabá Brazil
32C1 Maracaibo Ven
32C2 Maracay Ven
95A2 Marādah Libya
97C3 Maradi Niger
90A2 Marāgheh Iran

Maralal

99D2 **Maralal** Kenya
107F1 **Maramasike** *I* / Solomon Is
100B2 **Maramba** Zambia
90A2 **Marand** Iran
31B2 **Maranhōa** State, Brazil
109C1 **Maranoa** *R* Aust
32B4 **Marañón** *R* Peru
7B5 **Marathon** Can
17B2 **Marathon** Florida, USA
78D2 **Maratua** *I* Indon
23A2 **Maravatio** Mexico
79B4 **Marawi** Phil
34B2 **Marayes** Arg
50B2 **Marbella** Spain
106A3 **Marble Bar** Aust
100B3 **Marblehall** S Africa
16D1 **Marblehead** USA
57B2 **Marburg** Germany
57B2 **Marche** Belg
50A2 **Marchean** Spain
46C1 **Marche-en-Famenne** Belg
32J7 **Marchena** *I* / Ecuador
17B2 **Marco** USA
34C2 **Marcos Juárez** Arg
12E2 **Marcus Baker,Mt** USA
15D2 **Marcy,Mt** USA
84C2 **Mardan** Pak
29E3 **Mar del Plata** Arg
93D2 **Mardin** Turk
99D1 **Mareb** *R* Eritrea/Eth
16B1 **Margaretville** USA
43E4 **Margate** Eng
54B1 **Marghita** Rom
109C4 **Maria I** Aust
104F3 **Mariana Is** Pacific O
13E1 **Mariana Lake** Can
104F3 **Marianas Trench** Pacific O
86C1 **Mariani** India
19B3 **Marianna** Arkansas, USA
17A1 **Marianna** Florida, USA
7G4 **Maria Van Diemen,C** NZ
59B3 **Mariazell** Austria
52C1 **Maribor** Slovenia
99C2 **Maridi** Sudan
112B5 **Marie Byrd Land** Region, Ant
27E3 **Marie Galante** *I* Caribbean S
39H6 **Mariehamn** Fin
16C1 **Marienbourg** Belg
33G2 **Marienburg** Surinam
100A3 **Mariental** Namibia
39G7 **Mariestad** Swed
17B1 **Marietta** Georgia, USA
14B3 **Marietta** Ohio, USA
19A3 **Marietta** Oklahoma, USA
27Q2 **Marigot** Dominica
60B3 **Marijampole** Lithuania
31B6 **Marilia** Brazil
98B3 **Marimba** Angola
79B3 **Marinduque** *I* Phil
10B2 **Marinette** USA
30F3 **Maringá** Brazil
98C2 **Maringa** *R* Zaire
18B2 **Marion** Arkansas, USA
18C2 **Marion** Illinois, USA
10B2 **Marion** Indiana, USA
10B2 **Marion** Ohio, USA
17C1 **Marion** S Carolina, USA
11B3 **Marion,L** USA
107E2 **Marion Reef** Aust
21B2 **Mariposa** USA
22B2 **Mariposa** *R* USA
22B2 **Mariposa Res** USA
60C5 **Marista** *R* Bulg
60E4 **Mariupol'** Ukraine
61G2 **Mariyskaya Respublika,** Russian Fed
94B2 **Marjayoun** Leb

58D2 **Marjina Gorki** Belarus
94B3 **Marka** Jordan
99E2 **Marka** Somalia
56C1 **Markaryd** Sweden
43C3 **Market Drayton** Eng
43D3 **Market Harborough** Eng
112A **Markham,Mt** Ant
22C1 **Markleeville** USA
16D1 **Marlboro** Massachusetts, USA
107D3 **Marlborough** Aust
46B2 **Marle** France
19A3 **Marlin** USA
48C3 **Marmande** France
55C2 **Marmara Adi** / Turk
92A1 **Marmara,S of** Turk
55C3 **Marmaris** Turk
14B3 **Marmet** USA
52B1 **Marmolada** *Mt* Italy
12D3 **Marmot B** USA
47A1 **Marmoutier** France
46B2 **Marne** Department, France
46B2 **Marne** *R* France
98B2 **Maro** Chad
101D2 **Maroantsetra** Madag
101C2 **Marondera** Zim
33G3 **Maroni** *R* French Guiana
109D1 **Maroochydore** Aust
98B1 **Maroua** Cam
101D2 **Marovoay** Madag
118A4 **Marquesas Keys** / USA
10B2 **Marquette** USA
46A1 **Marquise** France
109C2 **Marra** *R* Aust
96B1 **Marracuene** Mozam
96B1 **Marrakech** Mor
106C3 **Marree** Aust
19B4 **Marrero** USA
101C2 **Marromeu** Mozam
101C2 **Marrupa** Mozam
95C2 **Marsa Alam** Egypt
99D2 **Marsabit** Kenya
53B3 **Marsala** Italy
49D3 **Marseille** France
12B2 **Marshall** Alaska, USA
14A3 **Marshall** Illinois, USA
14B2 **Marshall** Michigan, USA
18B2 **Marshall** Missouri, USA
11A3 **Marshall** Texas, USA
105G3 **Marshall Is** Pacific O
18B2 **Marshfield** Missouri, USA
26B1 **Marsh Harbour** The Bahamas
19B4 **Marsh I** USA
12H2 **Marsh L** Can
76B2 **Martaban,G of** Myan
78C3 **Martapura** Indon
78C3 **Martapura** Indon
15D2 **Martha's Vineyard** *I* USA
49D2 **Martigny** Switz
59B3 **Martin** Slovakia
111C2 **Martinborough** NZ
34B3 **Martin de Loyola** Arg
23B1 **Martinez de la Torre** Mexico
27E4 **Martinique** *I* Caribbean S
17A1 **Martin,L** USA
15C3 **Martinsburg** USA
14B2 **Martins Ferry** USA
103G6 **Martin Vaz** *I* Atlantic O
49D3 **Martiques** France
110C2 **Marton** NZ
50B2 **Martos** Spain
78D1 **Marudi** Malay
84B2 **Maruf** Afghan
75A2 **Marugame** Japan
85C3 **Marwar** India
65H6 **Mary** Turkmenistan
107E3 **Maryborough** Queensland, Aust

108B3 **Maryborough** Victoria, Aust
5F4 **Mary Henry,Mt** Can
10C3 **Maryland** State, USA
42C2 **Maryport** Eng
21A2 **Marysville** California, USA
18A2 **Marysville** Kansas, USA
20B1 **Marysville** Washington, USA
10A2 **Maryville** Missouri, USA
18B1 **Maryville** Missouri, USA
95A2 **Marzuq** Libya
94B2 **Mas'adah** Syria
Masada = **Mezada**
94B2 **Mas'adah** Syria
99D3 **Masai Steppe** Tanz
99D3 **Masaka** Uganda
93E2 **Masally** Azerbaijan
74B3 **Masan** S Korea
101C2 **Masasi** Tanz
25D3 **Masaya** Nic
79B3 **Masbate** Phil
79B3 **Masbate** *I* Phil
96C1 **Mascara** Alg
23A1 **Mascota** Mexico
35D1 **Mascote** Brazil
101G1 **Maseru** Lesotho
66C3 **Mashad** Iran
90A2 **Mashhad** Iran
98B3 **Masi-Manimba** Zaire
99D2 **Masindi** Uganda
99C3 **Masisi** Zaire
90A3 **Masjed Soleyman** Iran
101E2 **Masoala** *C* Madag
10A2 **Mason City** USA
52B2 **Masqat** Oman
52B2 **Massa** Italy
10C2 **Massachusetts** State, USA
15D2 **Massachusetts B** USA
98B1 **Massakori** Chad
101C3 **Massangena** Mozam
15D2 Massawa = **Mits'iwa**
99B1 **Massena** USA
14B1 **Massey** Can
49C2 **Massif Central** *Mts* France
98B2 **Massif de l'Adamaoua** *Mts* Cam
26C3 **Massif de la Hotte** *Mts* Haiti
101D3 **Massif de l'Isalo** *Upland* Madag
98C2 **Massif des Bongo** *Upland* CAR
49D2 **Massif du Pelvoux** *Mts* France
101D2 **Massif du Tsaratanana** *Mt* Madag
14B2 **Massinga** Mozam
97B3 **Massina** Region, Mali
101C3 **Massinga** Mozam
101C3 **Massingir** Mozam
Massoukou = **Franceville**
61H4 **Masteksay** Kazakhstan
111C2 **Masterton** NZ
100C3 **Masvingo** Zim
92C2 **Masyaf** Syria
98B3 **Matadi** Zaire
25D3 **Matagalpa** Nic
7C4 **Matagami** Can
90A4 **Matagorda B** USA
110C1 **Matakana I** NZ
100A2 **Matala** Angola
97A3 **Matam** Sen
97C3 **Matameye** Niger
24C2 **Matamoros** Mexico
95B2 **Ma'tan as Sarra** *Well* Libya
7D5 **Matane** Can
25D2 **Matanzas** Cuba
34A2 **Mataquito** *R* Chile

87C3 **Matara** Sri Lanka
106A1 **Mataram** Indon
30B2 **Matarani** Peru
51C1 **Mataró** Spain
111A3 **Mataura** NZ
24B2 **Matehuala** Mexico
27L1 **Matelot** Trinidad
53C2 **Matera** Italy
59C3 **Mátészalka** Hung
83D3 **Mathura** India
79C4 **Mati** Phil
78D3 **Matisiri** *I* Indon
43D3 **Matlock** Eng
33F6 **Mato Grosso** Brazil
33F6 **Mato Grosso** State, Brazil
30E2 **Mato Grosso do Sul** State, Brazil
101H1 **Matola** Mozam
91C5 **Matrah** Oman
92A3 **Matrūh** Egypt
74C3 **Matsue** Japan
74E2 **Matsumae** Japan
74D3 **Matsumoto** Japan
74D4 **Matsusaka** Japan
74C4 **Matsuyama** Japan
7B5 **Mattagami** *R* Can
15C1 **Mattawa** Can
Matterhorn *Mt* Italy/Switz
26C2 **Matthew Town** The Bahamas
14C3 **Mattoon** USA
18C2 **Mattoon** USA
84B2 **Matun** Afghan
27L1 **Matura B** Trinidad
33E2 **Maturin** Ven
86A1 **Mau** India
101C2 **Maua** Mozam
49C1 **Maubeuge** France
108B2 **Maude** Aust
103J8 **Maud Seamount** Atlantic O
21C4 **Maui** / Hawaiian Is
34A3 **Maule** *R* Chile
14B2 **Maumee** USA
14B2 **Maumee** *R* USA
100B2 **Maun** Botswana
21C4 **Mauna Kea** *Mt* Hawaiian Is
21C4 **Mauna Loa** *Mt* Hawaiian Is
4F3 **Maunoir** *L* Can
4F3 **Maunoir,L** Can
48C2 **Mauriac** France
96A2 **Mauritania** Republic, Africa
100E3 **Mauritius** / Indian O
100B2 **Mavinga** Angola
86C2 **Mawlaik** Myan
Mawlamyine = **Moulmein**
112C10 **Mawson** *Base* Ant
78B3 **Maya** *I* Indon
63F2 **Maya** *R* Russian Fed
93D2 **Mayādīn** Syria
11C4 **Mayaguana** *I* The Bahamas
27D3 **Mayagüez** Puerto Rico
97C3 **Mayahi** Niger
98B3 **Mayama** Congo
90A2 **Mayamey** Iran
42B2 **Maybole** Scot
10C3 **May,C** USA
109C4 **Maydena** Aust
46D1 **Mayen** Germany
48B2 **Mayenne** France
13D2 **Mayerthorpe** Can
18C2 **Mayfield** USA
61E5 **Maykop** Russian Fed
84B2 **Maymaneh** Afghan
76B1 **Maymyo** Myan
4E3 **Mayo** Can
45B2 **Mayo** County, Irish Rep
16A3 **Mayo** USA
45B1 **Mayo,Mts of** Irish Rep
79B3 **Mayon** *Mt* Phil
51C2 **Mayor** *Mt* Spain
34C3 **Mayor Buratovich** Arg
110C1 **Mayor I** NZ

30D2 Mayor P Lagerenza Par
101D2 Mayotte / Indian O
27H2 May Pen Jamaica
16B3 May Point,C USA
47D1 Mayrhofen Austria
16B3 Mays Landing USA
14B3 Maysville USA
98B3 Mayumba Gabon
100B2 Mazabuka Zambia
84D1 Mazar China
94B3 Mazār Jordan
53B3 Mazara del Vallo Italy
84B1 Mazar-i-Sharif Afghan
24B2 Mazatlán Mexico
60B2 Mazeikiai Lithuania
94B3 Mazra Jordan
101C3 Mbabane Swaziland
98B3 Mbaiki CAR
99D2 Mbala Zambia
100B3 Mbalabala Zim
99D2 Mbale Uganda
98B2 Mbalmayo Cam
98B2 Mbam R Cam
101C2 Mbamba Bay USA
98B2 Mbandaka Zaïre
98B3 Mbanza Congo Angola
98B3 Mbanza-Ngungu Zaïre
99D3 Mbarara Uganda
98B2 Mbenza Congo
98B3 Mbère R Cam
99D3 Mbeya Tanz
98B3 Mbinda Congo
97A3 Mbout Maur
98B3 Mbuji-Mayi Zaïre
99D3 Mbulu Tanz
96B2 Mcherrah Region, Alg
101C2 Mchinji Malawi
8C5 Mdrak Viet
98B3 Mead,L USA
5H4 Meadow Lake Can
14B2 Meadville USA
7E4 Mealy Mts Can
109C1 Meandarra Aust
5G4 Meander River Can
45C2 Meath County, Irish Rep
49C2 Meaux France
16C1 Mechanicville USA
56A2 Mechelen Belg
96B1 Mecheria Alg
56C2 Mecklenburger Bucht B Germany
56C2 Mecklenburg-Vorpommern State Germany
56C2 Meconta Mozam
101C2 Mecuburi Mozam
101D2 Mecufi Mozam
101C2 Mecula Mozam
70A3 Medan Indon
34C3 Medanos Arg
34D2 Medanosa,Pt Arg
13E2 Medecine Hat Can
32B2 Medellín Colombia
96D1 Medenine Tunisia
8A2 Medford USA
54C2 Medgidia Rom
34B2 Media Agua Arg
20B1 Medias Rom
20E1 Medical Lake USA
5G5 Medicine Hat Can
35C1 Medina Brazil
80B3 Medina S Arabia
50B1 Medinaceli Spain
50B1 Medina del Campo Spain
50A1 Medina de Rio Seco Spain
86B2 Medinipur India
88E4 Mediterranean S Europe
13F2 Medley Can
61J3 Mednogorsk Russian Fed
86D1 Mêdog China
98B2 Medouneu Gabon
61F3 Medvedista R Russian Fed
64E3 Medvezh'yegorsk Russian Fed

106A3 Meekatharra Aust
84D3 Meerut India
99D2 Mēga Eth
55B3 Megalópolis Greece
55B3 Mégara Greece
86C1 Meghālaya State, India
86A2 Meghna R Bang
94B2 Megiddo Hist Site Israel
91B4 Mehran R Iran
90B3 Mehriz Iran
35B1 Meia Ponte R Brazil
98B2 Meiganga Cam
76B1 Meiktila Myan
47C1 Meiringen Switz
73A4 Meishan China
57C2 Meissen Germany
73D5 Mei Xian China
73D5 Meizhou China
30B3 Mejillones Chile
98B2 Mekambo Gabon
99D1 Mek'elê Eth
96B1 Meknès Mor
76D3 Mekong R Camb
77C5 Melaka Malay
104F4 Melanesia Region Pacific O
78C3 Melawi R Indon
107D4 Melbourne Aust
11B4 Melbourne USA
9C4 Melchor Muzquiz Mexico
61J3 Meleuz Russian Fed
98B1 Melfi Chad
5H4 Melfort Can
96B1 Melilla N W Africa
29B4 Melimoyu Mt Chile
34C2 Melincué Arg
34A2 Melipilla Chile
60E4 Melitopol' Ukraine
6D2 Melville Bugt B Greenland
99D2 Melka Guba Eth
101H1 Melmoth S Africa
34C2 Melo Arg
29F2 Melo Urug
22B2 Melones Res USA
12D1 Melozitna R USA
47C1 Mels Switz
43D3 Melton Mowbray Eng
49C2 Melun France
5H4 Melville Can
27Q2 Melville,C Dominica
4F3 Melville Hills Mts Can
106C2 Melville I Aust
4G2 Melville I Can
7E4 Melville,L Can
6B3 Melville Pen Can
45B1 Melvin,L Irish Rep
70B4 Memboro Indon
106A1 Memboro Indon
57C3 Memmingen Germany
11B3 Mempawah Indon
19B3 Memphis Tennessee, USA
99C2 Mena USA
43B3 Menai Str Wales
97C3 Ménaka Mali
92A2 Menasha USA
78C3 Mendawai R Indon
49C3 Mende France
99D2 Mendebo Mts Eth
43C4 Mendip Hills Upland Eng
20B2 Mendocino,C USA
105J2 Mendocino Seascarp Pacific O
22B2 Mendota California, USA
29C2 Mendoza Arg
29C3 Mendoza State, Arg
55C3 Menemen Belg
46B1 Menen Belg
72D3 Mengcheng China
78B3 Menggala Indon
76B1 Menghai China
73A5 Mengla China
76B1 Menglian China
73A5 Mengzi China
107D4 Menindee Aust

108B2 Menindee L Aust
108A3 Meningie Aust
14A1 Menominee USA
14A2 Menomonee Falls USA
100A2 Menongue Angola
51C1 Menorca / Spain
12F2 Mentasta Mts USA
78B3 Mentok Indon
18D2 Mentor USA
46B2 Ménu France
72A2 Menyuan China
61H2 Menzelinsk Russian Fed
56B2 Meppen Germany
78D2 Merah Indon
18B2 Meramec R USA
52B1 Merano Italy
71F4 Merauke Indon
22B2 Merced R USA
29B2 Mercedario Mt Chile
29C2 Mercedes Arg
29E2 Mercedes Buenos Aires, Arg
34C2 Mercedes Corrientes, Arg
29E2 Mercedes Urug
110C1 Mercury B NZ
110C1 Mercury Is NZ
4F2 Mercy B Can
5H4 Mercy,C Can
99E2 Meregh Somalia
76B3 Mergui Myan
99D2 Mergui Arch Myan
25D2 Mérida Mexico
50A2 Mérida Spain
32C2 Mérida Ven
11B3 Meridian USA
109C3 Merimbula Aust
108B2 Meringur Aust
99C3 Merowe Sudan
106A4 Merredin Aust
42B2 Merrick Mt Scot
14A2 Merrillville USA
13C2 Merritt Can
17B2 Merritt Island USA
109D2 Merriwa Aust
99E1 Mersa Fatma Eritrea
51B2 Mers el Kebir Alg
42C3 Mersey R Eng
42C3 Merseyside Metropolitan County, Eng
92B2 Mersin Turk
77C5 Mersing Malay
85C3 Merta India
43C4 Merthyr Tydfil Wales
50A2 Mertola Port
90D3 Meru Mt Tanz
60E5 Merzifon Turk
46D2 Merzig Germany
9C3 Mesa USA
99E1 Meschede Germany
93D1 Mescit Dağ Mt Turk
12C3 Meshik USA
99C2 Meshra'Er Req Sudan
47C1 Mesocco Switz
55B3 Mesolóngion Greece
19A3 Mesquite Texas, USA
101C2 Messalo R Mozam
53C3 Messina Italy
100B3 Messina S Africa
55B3 Messini Greece
55B3 Messiniakós Kólpos G Greece
54B2 Mesta R Bulg
52B1 Mestre Italy
32C3 Meta R Colombia
60D2 Meta R Russian Fed
32D2 Meta R Ven
6C3 Meta Incognito Pen Can
19B4 Metairie USA
20C1 Metaline Falls USA
30D4 Metán Arg
101C2 Metangula Mozam
53C2 Metaponto Italy
44C3 Methil Scot
16D1 Methuen USA
111B2 Methven NZ
12H3 Metlakatla USA

18C2 Metropolis USA
87B2 Mettur India
49D2 Metz France
70A3 Meulaboh Indon
46A2 Meulan France
46C2 Meuse Department, France
19A3 Meuse R France
19A3 Mexia USA
24A1 Mexicali Mexico
24B2 Mexico Federal Republic, Cent America
24C3 México Mexico
23A2 México State, Mexico
18B2 Mexico USA
24C2 México,G of Cent America
94B3 Mezada Hist Site Israel
23B2 Mezcala Mexico
64F3 Mezen' Russian Fed
64G2 Mezhdusharskiy, Ostrov / Russian Fed
85D4 Mhow India
23B2 Miahuatlán Mexico
11B4 Miami Florida, USA
18B2 Miami Oklahoma, USA
11B4 Miami Beach USA
90A2 Miandowāb Iran
101D2 Miandrivazo Madag
90A2 Mianeh Iran
84C2 Mianwali Pak
73A3 Mianyang China
73C3 Mianyang China
73A3 Mianzhu China
72E2 Miaodao Qundao Arch China
73B4 Miao Ling Upland China
61K3 Miass Russian Fed
59B3 Michalovce Slovakia
27D3 Miches Dom Rep
10B2 Michigan State, USA
14A2 Michigan City USA
10B2 Michigan,L USA
7B5 Michipicoten I Can
23A2 Michoacan State, Mexico
54C2 Michurin Bulg
61F3 Michurinsk Russian Fed
104F3 Micronesia Region Pacific O
78B2 Midai / Indon
102F4 Mid Atlantic Ridge Atlantic O
46B1 Middelburg Neth
20B2 Middle Alkali L USA
16D2 Middleboro USA
100B4 Middleburg Cape Province, S Africa
16A2 Middleburg Pennsylvania, USA
101G1 Middleburg Transvaal, S Africa
16B1 Middlebury USA
15D2 Middlebury USA
11B3 Middlesboro USA
42D2 Middlesbrough Eng
16C2 Middletown Connecticut, USA
16B3 Middletown Delaware, USA
15D2 Middletown New York, USA
14B3 Middletown Ohio, USA
16A2 Middletown Pennsylvania, USA
96B1 Midelt Mor
43C4 Mid Glamorgan County, Wales
104B4 Mid Indian Basin Indian O
104B4 Mid Indian Ridge Indian O
7C5 Midland Can
14B2 Midland Michigan, USA
9C3 Midland Texas, USA
101D3 Midongy Atsimo Madag

105G2 **Mid Pacific Mts** Pacific O
20C2 **Midvale** USA
105H2 **Midway Is** Pacific O
18A2 **Midwest City** USA
93D2 **Midyat** Turk
54B2 **Midžor** *Mt* Serbia, Yugos
59B2 **Mielec** Pol
54C1 **Miercurea-Ciuc** Rom
50A1 **Mieres** Spain
16A2 **Mifflintown** USA
75A2 **Mihara** Japan
72D1 **Mijun Shuiku** *Res* China
54B2 **Mikhaylovgrad** Bulg
61F3 **Mikhaylovka** Russian Fed
65J4 **Mikhaylovskiy** Russian Fed
38K6 **Mikkeli** Fin
55C3 **Mikonos** *I* Greece
59B3 **Mikulov** Czech Republic
99D3 **Mikumi** Tanz
74D3 **Mikuni-sammyaku** *Mts* Japan
75B2 **Mikura-jima** *I* Japan
32B4 **Milagro** Ecuador
Milan = **Milano**
51C2 **Milana** Alg
101C2 **Milange** Mozam
52A1 **Milano** Italy
92A2 **Milas** Turk
107D4 **Mildura** Aust
73A5 **Mile** China
93D3 **Mileh Tharthar** *L* Iraq
107E3 **Miles** Aust
8C2 **Miles City** USA
16C2 **Milford** Connecticut, USA
15C3 **Milford** Delaware, USA
15D2 **Milford** Massachusetts, USA
18A1 **Milford** Nebraska, USA
16B2 **Milford** Pennsylvania, USA
43B4 **Milford Haven** Wales
43B4 **Milford Haven** *Sd* Wales
18A2 **Milford L** USA
111A3 **Milford Sd** NZ
13E2 **Milk River** Can
49C3 **Millau** France
16C2 **Millbrook** USA
17B1 **Milledgeville** USA
12F2 **Miller,Mt** USA
61F4 **Millerovo** Russian Fed
16A2 **Millersburg** USA
107D5 **Millers Creek** Aust
16C1 **Millers Falls** USA
16C2 **Millerton** USA
22C2 **Millerton L** USA
108B3 **Millicent** Aust
109D1 **Millmerran** Aust
45B2 **Milltown Malbay** Irish Rep
22A2 **Mill Valley** USA
15D3 **Millville** USA
6H2 **Milne Land** *I* Greenland
21C4 **Milolii** Hawaiian Is
55A2 **Milos** *I* Greece
107D3 **Milparinka** Aust
16A2 **Milroy** USA
111A3 **Milton** NZ
16A2 **Milton** Pennsylvania, USA
10B2 **Milwaukee** USA
51C2 **Mina** *R* Alg
93E4 **Minā' al Ahmadī** Kuwait
91C4 **Mināb** Iran
74C4 **Minamata** Japan
78A2 **Minas** Indon
29E2 **Minas** Urug
31B5 **Minas Gerais** State, Brazil
35C1 **Minas Novas** Brazil
25C3 **Minatitlan** Mexico

76A1 **Minbu** Myan
76A1 **Minbya** Myan
34A2 **Mincha** Chile
44A3 **Minch,Little** *Sd* Scot
44A2 **Minch,North** *Sd* Scot
40B2 **Minch,The** *Sd* Scot
12D2 **Minchumina,L** USA
47D2 **Mincio** *R* Italy
79B4 **Mindanao** *I* Phil
19B3 **Minden** Louisiana, USA
56B2 **Minden** Germany
108B2 **Mindona L** Aust
71D3 **Mindoro** *I* Phil
79B3 **Mindoro Str** Phil
45C3 **Mine Hd** *C* Irish Rep
43C4 **Minehead** Eng
30F2 **Mineiros** Brazil
19A3 **Mineola** USA
23B1 **Mineral de Monte** Mexico
16A2 **Minersville** USA
108B2 **Mingary** Aust
72A2 **Minhe** China
87A3 **Minicoy** *I* India
73D4 **Min Jiang** *R* Fujian, China
73A4 **Min Jiang** *R* Sichuan, China
22C2 **Minkler** USA
108A2 **Minlaton** Aust
72A2 **Minle** China
97C4 **Minna** Nig
10A2 **Minneapolis** USA
5J4 **Minnedosa** Can
10A2 **Minnesota** State, USA
50A1 **Miño** *R* Spain
8C2 **Minot** USA
72A2 **Minqin** China
72A3 **Min Shan** *Upland* China
60C3 **Minsk** Belarus
58C2 **Mińsk Mazowiecki** Pol
12E2 **Minto** USA
4G2 **Minto Inlet** *B* Can
7C4 **Minto,L** Can
63B2 **Minusinsk**
72A3 **Min Xian** China
7E5 **Miquelon** Can
22D3 **Mirage L** USA
87A1 **Miraj** India
29E3 **Miramar** Arg
84B2 **Miram Shah** Pak
50B1 **Miranda de Ebro** Spain
47D2 **Mirandola** Italy
84B2 **Mir Bachchen Kūt** Afghan
78D1 **Miri** Malay
84A3 **Mirik,C** Maur
63A1 **Mirnoye** Russian Fed
63D1 **Mirnyy** Russian Fed
112C9 **Mirnyy** *Base* Ant
84C2 **Mirpur** Pak
85B3 **Mirpur Khas** Pak
55B3 **Mirtoan S** Greece
74B3 **Miryang** S Korea
86A1 **Mirzāpur** India
23B2 **Misantla** Mexico
84C1 **Misgar** Pak
14A2 **Mishawaka** USA
12B1 **Misheguk Mt** USA
75A2 **Mi-shima** *I* Japan
107E2 **Misima** *I* Solomon Is
30F4 **Misiones** State, Arg
59C3 **Miskolc** Hung
94C2 **Mismiyah** Syria
71E4 **Misoöl** *I* Indon
95A1 **Misrātah** Libya
7B5 **Missinaibi** *R* Can
20B1 **Mission City** Can
15C2 **Mississauga** Can
11A3 **Mississippi** State, USA
11A3 **Mississippi** *R* USA
19C3 **Mississippi Delta** USA
8B2 **Missoula** USA
96B1 **Missour** Mor
11A3 **Missouri** State, USA

10A2 **Missouri** *R* USA
10C1 **Mistassini,L** Can
30B2 **Misti** *Mt* Peru
109C1 **Mitchell** Aust
8D2 **Mitchell** *R* Aust
107D2 **Mitchell** *R* Aust
11B3 **Mitchell,Mt** USA
45B2 **Mitchelstown** Irish Rep
84C3 **Mithankot** Pak
55C3 **Mitilíni** Greece
23B2 **Mitla** Mexico
95C3 **Mits'iwa** Eritrea
32C3 **Mitu** Colombia
99C3 **Mitumbar Mts** Zaire
98C3 **Mitwaba** Zaire
98B2 **Mitzic** Gabon
75B1 **Miura** Japan
72C3 **Mi Xian** China
69B4 **Miyake** *I* Japan
75B2 **Miyake-jima** *I* Japan
69E4 **Miyako** *I* Japan
74C4 **Miyakonojō** Japan
74C4 **Miyazaki** Japan
75B1 **Miyazu** Japan
74C4 **Miyoshi** Japan
72D1 **Miyun** China
72D1 **Mizan Teferi** Eth
95A1 **Mizdah** Libya
45B3 **Mizen Hd** *C* Irish Rep
54C1 **Mizil** Rom
86C2 **Mizo Hills** India
86C2 **Mizoram** Union Territory, India
94B3 **Mizpe Ramon** Israel
112B11 **Mizuho** *Base* Ant
74E3 **Mizusawa** Japan
39H7 **Mjölby** Sweden
100B2 **Mkushi** Zambia
101H1 **Mkuzi** S Africa
57C2 **Mladá Boleslav** Czech Republic
58C2 **Mława** Pol
52C2 **Mljet** *I* Croatia
101D2 **Mmabatho** S Africa
84D2 **Mnadi** India
97A4 **Moa** *R* Sierra Leone
94B3 **Moab** Region, Jordan
9C3 **Moab** USA
98B3 **Moanda** Congo
98B3 **Moanda** Gabon
99C3 **Moba** Zaire
75C1 **Mobara** Japan
98C2 **Mobaye** CAR
98C2 **Mobayi** Zaire
10A3 **Moberly** USA
11B3 **Mobile** USA
11B3 **Mobile B** USA
8C2 **Mobridge** USA
101D2 **Moçambique** Mozam
76C1 **Moc Chau** Viet
100B3 **Mochudi** Botswana
101D2 **Mocimboa da Praia** Mozam
32B3 **Moco** Colombia
35B2 **Mococa** Brazil
34D2 **Mocoreta** *R* Arg
23B1 **Moctezuma** *R* Mexico
101C2 **Mocuba** Mozam
47B2 **Modane** France
101G1 **Modder** *R* S Africa
52B2 **Modena** Italy
46D2 **Moder** *R* France
8A3 **Modesto** USA
22B2 **Modesto** USA
53B3 **Modica** Italy
59B3 **Mödling** Austria
47C1 **Moesa** *R* Switz
42C2 **Moffat** Scot
84D2 **Moga** India
35B2 **Mogi das Cruzes** Brazil
60C3 **Mogilev** Belarus
60C4 **Mogilev Podolskiy** Ukraine
35B2 **Mogi-Mirim** Brazil
101D2 **Mogincual** Mozam
47E2 **Mogliano** Italy
34B2 **Mogna** Arg

68D1 **Mogocha** Russian Fed
65K4 **Mogochin** Russian Fed
50A2 **Moguer** Spain
110C1 **Mohaka** *R* NZ
86C2 **Mohanganj** Bang
15D2 **Mohawk** *R* USA
99D3 **Mohoro** Tanz
65J5 **Mointy** Kazakhstan
38G5 **Mo i Rana** Nor
48C3 **Moissac** France
21B2 **Mojave** USA
22D3 **Mojave** *R* USA
9B3 **Mojave Desert** USA
78C4 **Mojokerto** Indon
86B1 **Mokama** India
110B1 **Mokau** *R* NZ
22B1 **Mokelumne Aqueduct** USA
22B1 **Mokelumne Hill** USA
22B1 **Mokelumne North Fork** *R* USA
101G1 **Mokhotlong** Lesotho
96D1 **Moknine** Tunisia
86C1 **Mokokchung** India
98B1 **Mokolo** Cam
74B4 **Mokp'o** S Korea
61F3 **Moksha** *R* Russian Fed
23B1 **Molango** Mexico
55B3 **Moláoi** Greece
60C4 **Moldavia = Moldova**
38F6 **Molde** Nor
60C4 **Moldova** Republic, Europe
54B1 **Moldoveanu** *Mt* Rom
100B3 **Molepolole** Botswana
53C2 **Molfetta** Italy
34A3 **Molina** Chile
30B2 **Mollendo** Peru
60C3 **Molodechno** Belarus
112C11 **Molodezhnaya** *Base* Ant
21C4 **Molokai** *I* Hawaiian Is
61G2 **Moloma** *R* Russian Fed
109C2 **Molong** Aust
100B3 **Molopo** *R* Botswana
98B2 **Molounddu** Cam
8D1 **Molson L** Can
71D4 **Molucca S** Indon
71D4 **Moluccas** *Is* Indon
101C2 **Moma** Mozam
31C3 **Mombaca** Brazil
99D3 **Mombasa** Kenya
99C3 **Mompono** Zaire
56C2 **Mon** *I* Den
44A3 **Monach Is** Scot
49D3 **Monaco** Principality, Europe
44B3 **Monadhliath Mts** Scot
45C1 **Monaghan** County, Irish Rep
45C1 **Monaghan** Irish Rep
27D3 **Mona Pass** Caribbean S
13B2 **Monarch Mt** Can
5G4 **Monashee Mts** Can
41B3 **Monasterevin** Irish Rep
47B2 **Moncalieri** Italy
31B2 **Monção** Brazil
38L5 **Monchegorsk** Russian Fed
56B2 **Mönchen-gladbach** Germany
24B2 **Monclova** Mexico
7D5 **Moncton** Can
9C4 **Monctova** Mexico
50A1 **Mondego** *R* Port
52A2 **Mondovì** Italy
14C2 **Moneague** Jamaica
14C2 **Monessen** USA
18B2 **Monett** USA
52B1 **Monfalcone** Italy

50A1	Monforte de Lemos Spain
98C2	Monga Zaïre
98C2	Mongala *R* Zaïre
99D2	Mongalla Sudan
96D1	Mong Cai Viet
98B1	Mongo Chad
68B2	Mongolia Republic, Asia
100B2	Mongu Zambia
21B2	Monitor Range *Mts* USA
98C3	Monkoto Zaïre
43C4	Monmouth Eng
18B1	Monmouth USA
13C2	Monmouth,Mt Can
97C4	Mono *R* Togo
21B2	Mono L USA
53C2	Monopoli Italy
51B1	Monreal del Campo Spain
19B3	Monroe Louisiana, USA
14B2	Monroe Michigan, USA
18B2	Monroe Washington, USA
18B2	Monroe City USA
97A4	Monrovia Lib
20D3	Monrovia USA
56A2	Mons Belg
16C1	Monson USA
58B1	Mönsterås Sweden
101D2	Montagne d'Ambre *Mt* Madag
96C1	Montagnes des Ouled Nail *Mts* Alg
12E3	Montague I USA
49C3	Mont Aigoual *Mt* France
48B2	Montaigu France
53C3	Montalto *Mt* Italy
8B2	Montana State, USA
50A1	Montañas de León *Mts* Spain
48B2	Montargis France
48C3	Montauban France
15D2	Montauk USA
15D2	Montauk Pt *C* USA
49D2	Montbéliard France
52A1	Mont Blanc *Mt* France/Italy
49C2	Montceau les Mines France
51C1	Montceny *Mt* Spain
49D3	Mont Cinto *Mt* Corse
46C2	Montcornet France
48B3	Mont-de-Marsan France
47D2	Montdidier France
30D2	Monteagudo Bol
33G4	Monte Alegre Brazil
52B2	Monte Amiata *Mt* Italy
47D2	Monte Baldo *Mt* Italy
15C1	Montebello Can
106A3	Monte Bello Is Aust
47C2	Montebelluna Italy
49D3	Monte Carlo Monaco
35B1	Monte Carmelo Brazil
34D2	Monte Caseros Arg
52B2	Monte Cimone *Mt* Italy
52A2	Monte Cinto *Mt* Corse
34B2	Monte Coman Arg
52B2	Monte Corno *Mt* Italy
27C3	Montecristi Dom Rep
52B2	Montecristo *I* Italy
23A1	Monte Escobedo Mexico
53C2	Monte Gargano *Mt* Italy
26B3	Montego Bay Jamaica
47D2	Monte Grappa *Mt* Italy
47C2	Monte Lesima *Mt* Italy

49C3	Montélimar France
53B2	Monte Miletto *Mt* Italy
50A2	Montemo-o-Novo Port
26B5	Montená Colombia
54A2	Montenegro Republic, Yugos
31B3	Monte Pascoal *Mt* Brazil
34A2	Monte Patria Chile
53C3	Monte Pollino *Mt* Italy
101C2	Montepuez Mozam
8A3	Monterey California, USA
15C3	Monterey Virginia, USA
32B2	Monterey B USA
32B2	Montería Colombia
30D2	Montero Bol
47B2	Monte Rosa *Mt* Italy/Switz
24B2	Monterrey Mexico
31C5	Montes Claros Brazil
50B2	Montes de Toledo *Mts* Spain
29E2	Montevideo Urug
47B2	Monte Viso *Mt* Italy
27P2	Mont Gimie *Mt* St Lucia
11B3	Montgomery Alabama, USA
96C2	Mont Gréboun Niger
47B1	Montherme France
47B1	Monthey Switz
16B2	Monticello Arkansas, USA
16B2	Monticello New York, USA
9C3	Monticello Utah, USA
53A2	Monti del Gennargentu *Mt* Sardegna
47D2	Monti Lessini *Mts* Italy
53B3	Monti Nebrodi *Mts* Italy
7C5	Mont-Laurier Can
48C2	Montluçon France
7C5	Montmagny Can
46C2	Montmédy France
49C3	Mont Mézenc *Mt* France
46B2	Montmirail France
50B2	Montoro Spain
9D1	Mont Pelat *Mt* France
14B2	Montpelier Ohio, USA
10C2	Montpelier Vermont, USA
49C3	Montpellier France
7C5	Montréal Can
48C1	Montreuil France
52A1	Montreux Switz
48C2	Mont Risoux *Mt* France
8C3	Montrose Colorado, USA
40C2	Montrose Scot
48B2	Mont-St-Michel France
96B1	Monts des Ksour *Mts* Alg
51C3	Monts des Ouled Neil *Mts* Alg
51C2	Monts du Hodna *Mts* Alg
27E3	Montserrat *I* Caribbean S
10C1	Monts Otish *Mts* Can
12B1	Monument Mt USA
9B3	Monument V USA
98C2	Monveda Zaïre
76B1	Monywa Myan
52A1	Monza Italy
100B2	Monze Zambia
101H1	Mooi *R* S Africa
101G1	Mooi River S Africa

108B1	Moomba Aust
109D2	Moonbi Range *Mts* Aust
108B1	Moonda L Aust
109D1	Moonie Aust
109C1	Moonie *R* Aust
108A2	Moonta Aust
106A3	Moora Aust
106A3	Moore,L Aust
42C2	Moorfoot Hills Scot
8D2	Moorhead USA
22C3	Moorpark USA
7B4	Moose *R* Can
5H4	Moose Jaw Can
5H4	Moosomin Can
7B4	Moosonee Can
16D2	Moosup USA
101C2	Mopeia Mozam
97B3	Mopti Mali
30B2	Moquegua Peru
39G6	Mora Sweden
31D3	Morada Brazil
84D3	Morādābād India
35B1	Morada Nova de Minas *L* Brazil
101D2	Morafenobe Madag
101D2	Moramanga Madag
27A2	Morant Bay Jamaica
27J2	Morant Pt Jamaica
87B3	Moratuwa Sri Lanka
59B3	Morava *R* Austria/ Slovakia
54B2	Morava *R* Serbia, Yugos
90C2	Moraveh Tappeh Iran
40C2	Moray Firth *Estuary* Scot
47C1	Morbegno Italy
85C4	Morbi India
90D2	Mor Dağ *Mt* Turk
5J5	Morden Can
61F3	Mordovskaya Respublika, Russian Fed
42C2	Morecambe Eng
42C2	Morecambe B Eng
107D3	Moree Aust
14B3	Morehead USA
47C1	Mörel Switz
24B3	Morelia Mexico
23B2	Morelos State, Mexico
85D3	Morena India
5E4	Moresby I Can
109D1	Moreton I Aust
46B2	Moreuil France
47B1	Morez France
19B4	Morgan City USA
22B2	Morgan Hill USA
14C3	Morgantown USA
101C1	Morgenzon S Africa
47B1	Morges Switz
74C2	Mori Japan
27K1	Moriatio Tobago
13B2	Morice L Can
13E2	Morinville Can
74E3	Morioka Japan
109D2	Morisset Aust
63D1	Morkoka *R* Russian Fed
48B2	Morlaix France
27Q2	Morne Diablotin *Mt* Dominica
106C2	Mornington I Aust
85B3	Moro Pak
96B2	Morocco Kingdom, Africa
79B4	Moro G Phil
99D3	Morogoro Tanz
24C2	Moroleon Mexico
101D3	Morombe Madag
26B2	Morón Cuba
101D3	Morondava Madag
50A2	Moron de la Frontera Spain
101D2	Moroni Comoros
71D3	Morotai *I* Indon
99D2	Moroto Uganda
61F4	Morozovsk Russian Fed
42D2	Morpeth Eng
19B2	Morrilton USA
35B1	Morrinhos Brazil

110C1	Morrinsville NZ
16B2	Morristown New Jersey, USA
15C2	Morristown New York, USA
15C2	Morrisville Pennsylvania, USA
21A2	Morro Bay USA
23A2	Morro de Papanoa Mexico
23A2	Morro de Petatlán Mexico
101C2	Morrumbala Mozam
101C3	Morrumbene Mozam
61F3	Morshansk Russian Fed
47C2	Mortara Italy
34C2	Morteros Arg
33G6	Mortes *R* Mato Grosso, Brazil
35C1	Mortes *R* Minas Gerais, Brazil
108B3	Mortlake Aust
27L1	Moruga Trinidad
109D3	Moruya Aust
109C1	Morven Aust
44B3	Morvern *Pen* Scot
109C3	Morwell Aust
76B3	Moscos Is Myan
	Moscow = Moskva
20C1	Moscow Idaho, USA
56B2	Mosel *R* Germany
46D2	Moselle Department, France
46D2	Moselle *R* France
20C1	Moses Lake USA
111B3	Mosgiel NZ
99D3	Moshi Tanz
38G5	Mosjøen Nor
63G2	Moskal'vo Russian Fed
64E4	Moskva Russian Fed
35C1	Mosquito *R* Brazil
39G7	Moss Nor
98B3	Mossaka Congo
100B4	Mossel Bay S Africa
98B3	Mossendjo Congo
108B2	Mossgiel Aust
31D3	Mossoró Brazil
57C2	Most Czech Republic
96C1	Mostaganem Alg
54A2	Mostar Bosnia-Herzegovina
60C3	Mosty Belarus
	Mosul = Al Mawşil
39H7	Motala Sweden
42C2	Motherwell Scot
86A1	Motihãri India
51B2	Motilla del Palancar Spain
50B2	Motril Spain
111B2	Motueka NZ
111B2	Motueka *R* NZ
47B1	Moudon Switz
98B3	Mouila Gabon
108B2	Moulamein Aust
4G2	Mould Bay Can
49C2	Moulins France
76B2	Moulmein Myan
96B1	Moulouya *R* Mor
17B1	Moultrie USA
17C1	Moultrie,L USA
18C2	Mound City Illinois, USA
18B2	Mound City Missouri, USA
98B2	Moundou Chad
14B3	Moundsville USA
12J1	Mountain *R* Can
17A1	Mountain Brook USA
18B2	Mountain Grove USA
18B2	Mountain Home Arkansas, USA
22A2	Mountain View USA
12B2	Mountain Village USA
16A3	Mount Airy Maryland, USA
16A3	Mount Carmel USA
14A3	Mount Dutton Aust
108A2	Mount Eba Aust
108B3	Mount Gambier Aust
16B3	Mount Holly USA

Mount Holly Springs

16A2 Mount Holly Springs USA
108A2 Mount Hope Aust
106C3 Mount Isa Aust
108A2 Mount Lofty Range Mts Aust
12D2 Mount McKinley Nat Pk USA
108A3 Mount Magnet Aust
108B3 Mount Manara Aust
107E3 Mount Morgan Aust
19B3 Mount Pleasant Texas, USA
20B1 Mount Rainier Nat Pk USA
43B4 Mounts B Eng
20B2 Mount Shasta USA
11B3 Mount Vernon USA
19A3 Mount Vernon Kentucky, USA
20B1 Mount Vernon Washington, USA
45C1 Mourne Mts N Ire
98B1 Moussoro Chad
86B2 Mouths of the Ganga India/Bang
85B4 Mouths of the Indus Pak
77D4 Mouths of the Mekong Viet
97C4 Mouths of the Niger Nig
47B1 Moûtier Switz
47B2 Moûtiers France
96C2 Mouydîr Mts Alg
90D1 Mouyondzi Congo
46C2 Mouzon France
59B3 M'óvár Hung
23A1 Moyahua Mexico
99D2 Moyale Kenya
97A4 Moyamba Sierra Leone
96B1 Moyen Atlas Mts Mor
100B4 Moyeni Lesotho
99D2 Moyo Uganda
32B5 Moyobamba Peru
84D1 Moyu China
101C3 Mozambique Republic, Africa
101C3 Mozambique Chan Mozam/Madag
61H2 Mozhga Russian Fed
60C3 Mozyr' Belarus
99D3 Mpanda Tanz
101C2 Mpika Zambia
99D3 Mporokosa Zambia
100D Mposhi Zambia
99D3 Mpoulungu Zambia
99D3 Mpwapwa Tanz
60E3 Mtsensk Russian Fed
101H1 Mtubatuba S Africa
101D2 Mtwara Tanz
76C2 Muang Chainat Thai
76C2 Muang Chiang Rai Thai
76C2 Muang Kalasin Thai
76C2 Muang Khon Kaen Thai
76B2 Muang Lampang Thai
76B2 Muang Lamphun Thai
76C2 Muang Loei Thai
76C2 Muang Lom Sak Thai
76C2 Muang Nakhon Phanom Thai
76B2 Muang Nakhon Sawan Thai
76C2 Muang Nan Thai
76C2 Muang Phayao Thai
76C2 Muang Phetchabun Thai
76C2 Muang Phichit Thai
76C2 Muang Phitsanulok Thai
76C2 Muang Phrae Thai
76C2 Muang Roi Et Thai
76C2 Muang Sakon Nakhon Thai
76C3 Muang Samut Prakan Thai

76C2 Muang Uthai Thani Thai
76C2 Muang Yasothon Thai
77C5 Muar Malay
78C2 Muara Brunei
70B4 Muara Indon
78A3 Muaralakitan Indon
78A3 Muaratebo Indon
78A3 Muaratewah Indon
78A3 Muaremim Indon
76A2 Muaungmaya Myan
99D2 Mubende Uganda
100C2 Muchinga Mts Zambia
44A3 Muck I Scot
109C1 Muckadilla Aust
100B2 Muconda Angola
35D1 Mucuri Brazil
35C1 Mucuri R Brazil
100B2 Mucusso Angola
69E2 Mudanjiang China
100C2 Mudgee Aust
76B2 Mudon Myan
101C2 Mueda Mozam
107F3 Mueo Nouvelle Calédonie
100B2 Mufulira Zambia
73C4 Mufu Shan Hills China
Mugadishu = Muqdisho
93C4 Mughayra S Arabia
92A2 Muğla Turk
65G5 Mugodzhary Mts Kazakhstan
73A3 Muguaping China
93D3 Muhaywir Iraq
57C3 Mühldorf Germany
57C2 Mühlhausen Germany
38K6 Muhos Fin
77C4 Mui Bai Bung C Camb
45C2 Muine Bheag Irish Rep
100B2 Mujimbeji Zambia
59C3 Mukachevo Ukraine
78C2 Mukah Malay
69G4 Muko-jima I Japan
86A1 Muktinath Nepal
84B2 Mukur Afghan
18B2 Mulberry USA
12C2 Mulchatna R USA
34A3 Mulchén Chile
56C2 Mulde R Germany
71F5 Mulgrave I Aust
50B2 Mulhacén Mt Spain
46B1 Mülheim Germany
49D2 Mulhouse France
73A4 Muli China
44B3 Mull I Scot
87C3 Mullaitivu Sri Lanka
109C2 Mullaley Aust
108A3 Mullewa Aust
16B3 Mullica R USA
45C2 Mullingar Irish Rep
42B2 Mull of Kintyre Pt Scot
45C1 Mull of Oa C Scot
109D1 Mullumbimby Aust
100B2 Mulobezi Zambia
84C2 Multan Pak
Mumbai = Bombay
100B2 Mumbwa Zambia
61G4 Mumra Russian Fed
71D4 Muna I Indon
57C3 München Germany
14A2 Muncie USA
15C2 Muncy USA
56D1 Münden Germany
109D1 Mundubbera Aust
109C1 Mungallala Aust
109C1 Mungallala R Aust
99C2 Mungbere Zaire
86A2 Mungeli India
86B1 Munger India
109C1 Mungindi Aust
Munich = München
14A1 Munising USA
29B6 Muñoz Gomero,Pen Chile
45B2 Munster Region, Irish Rep

47C1 Münster Switz
56B2 Münster Germany
54B1 Muntii Apuseni Mts Rom
54B1 Muntii Călimanilor Mts Rom
54B1 Muntii Carpatii Meridionali Mts Rom
54B1 Muntii Rodnei Mts Rom
54B1 Muntii Zarandului Mts Rom
71R Munyati R Zim
93C2 Munzur Silsilesi Mts Turk
64D3 Muomio Fin
76C1 Muong Khoua Laos
76D3 Muong Man Viet
76C1 Muong Nong Laos
76C1 Muong Ou Neua Laos
76C1 Muong Sai Laos
76C1 Muong Sen Viet
76C1 Muong Sing Laos
76C1 Muong Son Laos
38J5 Muonio Fin
38J5 Muonio R Sweden/Fin
99E2 Muqdisho Somalia
52B1 Mur R Austria
74D3 Murakami Japan
29B5 Murallón Mt Arg/Chile
61G2 Murashi Russian Fed
93D2 Murat R Turk
53A3 Muravera Sardegna
75C1 Murayama Japan
90B3 Murcheh Khvort Iran
111B2 Murchison NZ
106A3 Murchison R Aust
51B2 Murcia Region, Spain
51B2 Murcia Spain
54B1 Mures R Rom
46E2 Murg R Germany
65H6 Murgab R Turkmenistan
84B2 Murgha Kibzai Pak
109D1 Murgon Aust
86B2 Muri India
53C1 Muriaé Brazil
98C3 Muriege Angola
64E3 Murmansk Russian Fed
61F2 Murom Russian Fed
74E2 Muroran Japan
50A1 Muros Spain
74C4 Muroto Japan
75A2 Muroto-zaki C Japan
22B1 Murphy Idaho, USA
22B1 Murphys USA
18C2 Murray Kentucky, USA
108B2 Murray R USA
13C2 Murray R Can
108A3 Murray Bridge Aust
71F4 Murray,L PNG
17B1 Murray,L USA
105J2 Murray Seacarp Pacific O
108B2 Murrumbidgee R Aust
109C2 Murrumburrah Aust
109D2 Murrurundi Aust
47B1 Murten Switz
108B3 Murtoa Aust
110C1 Murupara NZ
109D1 Murwillimbah Aust
93D2 Muş Turk
54B2 Musala Mt Bulg
74B2 Musan N Korea
91C4 Musandam Pen Oman
Muscat = Masqat
91C5 Muscat Region, Oman
106C3 Musgrave Range Mts Aust
98B3 Mushie Zaire
14A2 Muskegon USA
14A2 Muskegon R USA
14A2 Muskogee USA
15C2 Muskoka,L Can
95C3 Musmar Sudan

99D3 Musoma Tanz
8C2 Musselshell R USA
100A2 Mussende Angola
48C2 Mussidan France
55C2 Mustafa-Kemalpasa Turk
86A1 Mustang Nepal
109D2 Muswellbrook Aust
95B2 Mut Egypt
101C2 Mutarara Mozam
101C2 Mutare Zim
101C2 Mutoko Zim
101D2 Mutsamudu Comoros
100B2 Mutshatsha Zaire
74E2 Mutsu Japan
74E2 Mutsu-wan B Japan
45B2 Mutton I Irish Rep
72B2 Mu Us Shamo Desert China
98B3 Muxima Angola
63D2 Muya Russian Fed
38L6 Muyezerskiy Russian Fed
99D3 Muyinga Burundi
98C3 Muyumba Zaire
82A1 Muyun Kum Desert Kazakhstan
84C2 Muzaffarābād Pak
84C2 Muzaffargarh Pak
84D3 Muzaffarnagar India
86B1 Muzaffarpur India
64H3 Muzhi Russian Fed
82C2 Muztag Mt China
82B2 Muztagata Mt China
100C2 Mvuma Zim
99D3 Mwanza Tanz
98C3 Mwanza Zaire
98C3 Mweka Zaire
100C3 Mwenezi Zim
98C3 Mwene Ditu Zaire
100C3 Mwenga Zaire
99C3 Mwenga Zaire
100B2 Mwinilunga Zambia
83D4 Myanaung Myan
83D3 Myanmar Asia
86D2 Myingyan Myan
76B1 Myingyao Myan
76B3 Myinmoletkat Mt Myan
82D3 Myitkyina Myan
76B3 Myitta Myan
86C2 Mymensingh Bang
69F3 Myojin I Japan
38F6 Myrdalsjökur Ice Cap Iceland
17C1 Myrtle Beach USA
20B2 Myrtle Creek USA
39G7 Mysen Nor
56C2 Mysibor Pol
64F3 Mys Kanin Nos C Russian Fed
59B3 Myslenice Pol
69H1 Mys Lopatka C Russian Fed
87B2 Mysore India
60D5 Mys Sarych C Ukraine
16D2 Mystic USA
61H5 Mys Tyub-Karagan P Kazakhstan
63G2 Mys Yelizavety C Russian Fed
64H2 Mys Zhelaniya C Russian Fed
77D3 My Tho Viet
20B2 Myrtle Point USA
101C2 Mzimba Malawi
101C2 Mzuzú Malawi

N

21C4 Naalehu Hawaiian Is
39J6 Naantali Fin
45C2 Naas Irish Rep
75B2 Nabari Japan
61H2 Naberezhnye Chelny Russian Fed
12F2 Nabesna R USA
96D1 Nabeul Tunisia
94B2 Nablus Israel
101D2 Nacala Mozam
20B1 Naches USA
101C2 Nachingwea Tanz

19B3 Nacogdoches USA
76A3 Nacondam I
Indian O
24B1 Nacozari Mexico
50C4 Nadiad India
50B2 Nador Mor
90B3 Nadūshan Iran
59C3 Nadvornaya Ukraine
56C1 Naestved Den
75A2 Näfürah Libya
82D3 Naga Hills Myan
75A2 Nagahama Japan
82D3 Naga Hills Myan
86C1 Nagai Japan
86C1 Nāgāland State,
India
74D3 Nagano Japan
74D3 Nagaoka Japan
86C1 Nagaon India
87B2 Nagappattinam India
85C4 Nagar Parkar India
74B4 Nagasaki Japan
74D3 Nagashima Japan
75A2 Nagato Japan
85C3 Nāgaur India
87B3 Nāgercoil India
85B3 Nagha Kalat Pak
84D3 Nagina India
74D3 Nagoya Japan
85D4 Nāgpur India
82D2 Naggu China
59B3 Nagykanizsa Hung
59B3 Nagykörös Hung
69E4 Naha Japan
8A2 Nahaimo Can
84D2 Nāhan India
4F3 Nahanni Butte Can
94B2 Nahariya Israel
90A3 Nahāvand Iran
46D2 Nahe R Germany
72D2 Nahpu China
72E1 Naimen Qi China
7D4 Nain Can
90B3 Na'in Iran
84D3 Naini Tal India
44C3 Nairn Scot
86C1 Nairobi Kenya
90B3 Najafābād Iran
74C2 Najin N Korea
75A2 Nakama Japan
74E3 Nakaminato Japan
74D3 Nakamura Japan
75B1 Nakano Japan
75A1 Nakano-shima I
Japan
74C4 Nakatsu Japan
75B1 Nakatsu-gawa
Japan
95C3 Nak'fa Eritrea
93E2 Nakhichevan
Azerbaijan
92B4 Nakhl Egypt
74C2 Nakhodka
Russian Fed
76C3 Nakhon Pathom
Thai
76C3 Nakhon Ratchasima
Thai
77C4 Nakhon Si
Thammarat Thai
12H3 Nakina Can
7B4 Nakina Ontario, Can
12C3 Naknek USA
12C3 Naknek L USA
4C4 Nakrek USA
39G8 Nakskov Den
86C1 Nakuru Kenya
13D2 Nakusp Can
61F5 Nal'chik Russian Fed
87B1 Nalgonda India
87B1 Nallamala Range Mts
India
95A1 Nālūt Libya
101H1 Namaacha Mozam
65G6 Namak L Iran
90C3 Namakzar-e Shadad
Salt Flat Iran
65J5 Namangan
Uzbekistan
101C2 Namapa Mozam
100A4 Namaqualand
Region, S Africa
109D1 Nambour Aust
109D2 Nambucca Heads
Aust

77D4 Nam Can Viet
82D2 Nam Co L China
76D1 Nam Dinh Viet
101C2 Nametil Mozam
74B4 Namhae-do I S
Korea
100A2 Namib Desert
Namibia
100A2 Namibe Angola
100A3 Namibia Republic,
Africa
82D3 Namjagbarwa Feng
Mt China
71D4 Namlea Indon
109C2 Namoi R Aust
13D1 Nampa Can
20C2 Nampa USA
97B3 Nampala Mali
76C2 Nam Phong Thai
74B3 Namp'o N Korea
101C2 Nampula Mozam
38G6 Namsos Nor
76B1 Namton Myan
86D2 Namtu Myan
13B2 Namu Can
101C2 Namuno Mozam
46C1 Namur Belg
100A2 Namutoni Namibia
74B3 Namwŏn S Korea
13C3 Nanaimo Can
74B2 Nanan N Korea
109D1 Nanango Aust
74D3 Nanao Japan
75B1 Naruto-jima I
Japan
73B3 Nanbu China
73D4 Nanchang China
73B3 Nanchong China
49D2 Nancy France
87B1 Nānded India
109D2 Nandewar Range
Mts Aust
45C4 Nandurbar India
87B1 Nandyāl India
88B2 Nanga Eboko Cam
84C1 Nanga Parbat Mt
Pak
78C3 Nangapinoh Indon
78C3 Nangatayap Indon
74B2 Nangnim Sanmaek
Mts N Korea
86C1 Nang Xian China
67F3 Nangzhou China
87B2 Nanjangüd India
72D3 Nanjing China
Nanking = Nanjing
75A2 Nankoku Japan
73C4 Nan Ling Region,
China
76D1 Nanliu R China
73B5 Nanning China
73F5 Nanortalik
Greenland
73B3 Nanpan Jiang R
China
86A1 Nānpāra India
73C4 Nanping China
6A1 Nansen Sd Can
99D3 Nansio Tanz
48B2 Nantes France
13E2 Nanton Can
72C3 Nantong China
10C2 Nantucket I USA
35C1 Nanuque Brazil
72C3 Nanyang China
72D2 Nanyang Hu L China
99D2 Nanyuki Kenya
74D3 Naoetsu Japan
85B4 Naokot Pak
22A1 Napa USA
15C2 Napanee Can
65K4 Napas Russian Fed
6E3 Napassoq Greenland
76D2 Nape Laos
110C1 Napier NZ
Naples = Napoli
17B2 Naples Florida, USA
19B3 Naples Texas, USA
73B5 Napo China
32C4 Napo R Peru/
Ecuador
53B2 Napoli Italy
90A2 Naqadeh Iran

92C4 Naqb Ishtar Jordan
75B2 Nara Japan
97B3 Nara Mali
107D4 Naracoorte Aust
86B3 Narainpur India
87C1 Narasaraopet India
77C4 Narathiwat Thai
86C2 Narayanganj Bang
87B1 Nārāyenpet India
49C3 Narbonne France
84D2 Narendranagar India
6C2 Nares Str Can
58C2 Narew R Pol
75C1 Narew Japan
85C4 Narmada R India
84D3 Nārnaul India
60E2 Naro Fominsk
Russian Fed
99D3 Narok Kenya
84C2 Narowal Pak
107D4 Narrabri Aust
109C1 Narran L Aust
109C2 Narrandera Aust
106A4 Narrogin Aust
109C2 Narromine Aust
85D4 Narsimhapur India
87C1 Narsipatnam India
6F3 Narssalik Greenland
6F3 Narssaq Greenland
6F3 Narssarssuaq
Greenland
75C1 Narugo Japan
75B2 Naruto Japan
60C2 Narva Russian Fed
38H5 Narvik Nor
84D3 Narwāna India
64G2 Nar'yan Mar
Russian Fed
108B1 Narylico Aust
65J5 Naryn Kirghizia
97C4 Nasarawa Nig
103D5 Nasca Ridge
Pacific O
16D1 Nashua USA
19B3 Nashville Arkansas,
USA
11B3 Nashville Tennessee,
USA
54A1 Našice Croatia
85D4 Näsik India
99D2 Nasir Sudan
13B1 Nass R Can
26B1 Nassau
The Bahamas
16C1 Nassau USA
92C4 Nasser,L Egypt
39G7 Nässjö Sweden
7C4 Nastapoka Is Can
100B3 Nata Botswana
31D3 Natal Brazil
70A3 Natal Indon
90B3 Natanz Iran
7D4 Natashquan Can
7D4 Natashquan R Can
19B3 Natchez USA
19B3 Natchitoches USA
108C3 Nathalia Aust
Nathorsts Land
Region Greenland
13C1 Nation R Can
21B3 National City USA
75C1 Natori Japan
99D3 Natron L Tanz
106A4 Naturaliste,C Aust
47D1 Nauders Austria
56C2 Nauen Germany
16C2 Naugatuck USA
57C2 Naumburg Germany
94B3 Naur Jordan
105G4 Nauru I Pacific O
63C2 Naushki Russian Fed
23B1 Nautla Mexico
9C3 Navajo Res USA
Navalmoral de la
Mata Spain
29C7 Navarino I Chile
51B1 Navarra Province,
Spain
34D3 Navarro Arg
19A3 Navasota USA
19A3 Navasota R USA
50A1 Navia R Spain
34A2 Navidad Chile

85B4 Navlakhi India
60D3 Navlya Russian Fed
24B2 Navojoa Mexico
55B3 Návpaktos Greece
55B3 Návplion Greece
85C4 Navsari India
94C2 Nawá Syria
86B2 Nawāda India
85B3 Nawah Afghan
85B3 Nawabshah Pak
73B4 Naxi China
55C3 Náxos I Greece
23A1 Nayar Mexico
91B4 Nay Band Iran
74E2 Nayoro Japan
94B2 Nazareth Israel
48B2 Nazay France
32C6 Nazca Peru
92A2 Nazilli Turk
63A2 Nazimovo
Russian Fed
13C2 Nazko R Can
99D2 Nazret Eth
91C5 Nazwa Oman
65J4 Nazyayevsk
Russian Fed
98B3 Ndalatando Angola
98C2 Ndélé CAR
98B1 Ndendé Gabon
98B1 Ndjamena Chad
98B3 Ndjolé Gabon
100B2 Ndola Zambia
109C1 Neabul Aust
108A1 Neales R Aust
55B3 Neápolis Greece
43C4 Neath Wales
109C1 Nebine R Aust
65G6 Nebit Dag
Turkmenistan
8C2 Nebraska State, USA
18A1 Nebraska City USA
13C2 Nechako R Can
19A3 Neches R USA
34D3 Necochea Arg
86C1 Nédong China
9B3 Needles USA
14A2 Neenah USA
5J4 Neepawa Can
46C1 Neerpelt Belg
63D2 Neftelensk
Russian Fed
99D2 Negele Eth
94B3 Negev Desert Israel
60B4 Negolu Mt Rom
87B3 Negombo Sri Lanka
76A2 Negrais,C Myan
32A4 Negritos Peru
33E4 Negro R Amazonas,
Brazil
34D3 Negro R Arg
34D2 Negro R Urug
79B4 Negros I Phil
54C2 Negru Voda Rom
90D3 Nehbändän Iran
73B4 Neijiang China
72B1 Nei Monggol
Autonomous Region,
China
32B3 Neiva Colombia
99D2 Nejo Eth
99D2 Nek'emté Eth
60D2 Nelidovo
Russian Fed
87B2 Nellore India
69F2 Nel'ma Russian Fed
13D3 Nelson Can
111B2 Nelson NZ
7A4 Nelson R Can
108B3 Nelson,C Aust
13D3 Nelson I USA
97B3 Néma Maur
72A1 Nemagt Uul Mt
Mongolia
58C1 Nemen R Lithuania
54C1 Nemira Mt Rom
74F2 Nemuro Japan
63E3 Nen R China
41B3 Nenagh Irish Rep
12E2 Nenana USA
12E2 Nenana R USA
43D3 Nene R Eng
69E2 Nenjiang China
18A2 Neodesha USA

Neosho

18B2 **Neosho** USA
63C2 **Nepa** Russian Fed
82C3 **Nepal** Kingdom, Asia
86A1 **Nepalganj** Nepal
45B1 **Nephin** Mt Irish Rep
94B3 **Neqarot** R Israel
34A3 **Nequén** State, Arg
68D1 **Nerchinsk**
Russian Fed
52C2 **Neretva** R Bosnia-
Herzegovina/Croatia
71F2 **Nero Deep** Pacific O
38C1 **Neskaupstaður**
Iceland
46B2 **Nesle** France
7E5 **Nesleyville** Can
55B2 **Néstos** R Greece
94B2 **Netanya** Israel
16B2 **Netherton** Eng
Netherlands
Kingdom, Europe
3M7 **Netherlands Antilles**
Is Caribbean S
86C2 **Netrakona** Bang
6C3 **Nettilling L** Can
56C2 **Neubrandenburg**
Germany
47B1 **Neuchâtel** Switz
46C2 **Neufchâteau** Belg
48C2 **Neufchâtel** France
46A2 **Neufchâtel-en-Bray**
France
56B2 **Neumünster**
Germany
52C1 **Neunkirchen** Austria
46D2 **Neunkirchen**
Germany
34B3 **Neuquén** Arg
29B4 **Neuquén** State, Arg
34B3 **Neuquén** R Arg
56C2 **Neuruppin** Germany
46D1 **Neuss** Germany
46E2 **Neustadt** Germany
56C2 **Neustadt** Germany
46D1 **Neustrelitz** Germany
46D1 **Neuwied** Germany
8B3 **Nevada** State, USA
18B2 **Nevada** USA
34A3 **Nevada de Chillán**
Mts Arg/Chile
23A2 **Nevada de Collima**
Mexico
23B2 **Nevada de Toluca** Mt
Mexico
94B3 **Nevatim** Israel
60C2 **Nevel'** Russian Fed
49C2 **Nevers** France
109C2 **Nevertire** Aust
27E3 **Nevis** I Caribbean S
58D2 **Nevis** R Belarus/
Lithuania
92B2 **Nevşehir** Turk
61K2 **Nev'yansk**
Russian Fed
101C2 **Newala** Tanz
14A3 **New Albany** Indiana,
USA
19C3 **New Albany**
Mississippi, USA
33F2 **New Amsterdam**
Guyana
109C1 **New Angledool** Aust
15C3 **Newark** Delaware,
USA
10C2 **Newark** New Jersey,
USA
14B2 **Newark** Ohio, USA
43D3 **Newark-upon-Trent**
Eng
15D2 **New Bedford** USA
13B2 **New Bella Bella** Can
20B1 **Newberg** USA
11C3 **New Bern** USA
17B1 **Newberry** USA
26B2 **New Bight**
The Bahamas
14B3 **New Boston** USA
9D4 **New Braunfels** USA
16C2 **New Britain** USA
7D5 **New Brunswick**
Province, Can
16B2 **New Brunswick** USA
16B2 **Newburgh** USA
43D4 **Newbury** Eng

16D1 **Newburyport** USA
16C2 **New Canaan** USA
109D2 **Newcastle** Aust
14A3 **New Castle** Indiana,
USA
42B2 **Newcastle** N Ire
14B2 **New Castle**
Pennsylvania, USA
101C1 **Newcastle** S Africa
8C2 **Newcastle** Wyoming,
USA
42D2 **Newcastle upon Tyne**
Eng
106C2 **Newcastle Waters**
Aust
45B2 **Newcastle West**
Irish Rep
84D3 **New Delhi** India
109D2 **New England Range**
Mts Aust
12B3 **Newenham,C** USA
43D4 **New Forest,The** Eng
7D4 **Newfoundland**
Province, Can
7E5 **Newfoundland** I
Can
102F2 **Newfoundland Basin**
Atlantic O
18B2 **New Franklin** USA
42B2 **New Galloway** Scot
107E1 **New Georgia** I
Solomon Is
7D5 **New Glasgow** Can
71F4 **New Guinea** SE Asia
12D3 **Newhalen** USA
22C3 **Newhall** USA
10C2 **New Hampshire**
State, USA
101H1 **New Hanover** I
S Africa
43E4 **Newhaven** Eng
15D2 **New Haven** USA
13B1 **New Hazelton** Can
19B3 **New Iberia** USA
10C2 **New Jersey** State,
USA
7C5 **New Liskeard** Can
16C2 **New London** USA
106A3 **Newman** Aust
22B2 **Newman** USA
43E3 **Newmarket** Eng
45B2 **Newmarket** Irish Rep
15C3 **New Market** USA
9C3 **New Mexico** State,
USA
16C2 **New Milford**
Connecticut, USA
17B1 **Newnan** USA
109C4 **New Norfolk** Aust
11A3 **New Orleans** USA
16B2 **New Paltz** USA
14B2 **New Philadelphia**
USA
110B1 **New Plymouth** NZ
18B2 **Newport** Arkansas,
USA
43D4 **Newport** Eng
14B3 **Newport** Kentucky,
USA
20B2 **Newport** Oregon,
USA
16A2 **Newport**
Pennsylvania, USA
15D2 **Newport** Rhode
Island, USA
15D2 **Newport** Vermont,
USA
43C4 **Newport** Wales
20C1 **Newport**
Washington, USA
22D4 **Newport Beach** USA
11C3 **Newport News** USA
26B1 **New Providence** I
Caribbean S
43B4 **Newquay** Eng
6C3 **New Quebec Crater**
Can
45C2 **New Ross** Irish Rep
45C1 **Newry** N Ire
New Siberian Is =
**Novosibirskiye
Ostrova**
17B2 **New Smyrna Beach**
USA

107D4 **New South Wales**
State, Aust
12C3 **New Stuyahok** USA
18A2 **Newton** Kansas,
USA
16D1 **Newton**
Massachusetts, USA
19C3 **Newton** Mississippi,
USA
16B2 **Newton** New York,
USA
16C2 **New York** USA
43C4 **Newton Abbot** Eng
45C1 **Newton Stewart**
N Ire
42B2 **Newton Stewart**
Scot
43C3 **Newtown** Wales
42B2 **Newtownards** N Ire
42B2 **Newville** USA
5F5 **New Westminster**
Can
10C2 **New York** State, USA
10C2 **New York** USA
110 **New Zealand**
Dominion, SW
Pacific O
105G6 **New Zealand Plat**
Pacific O
61F2 **Neya** Russian Fed
91B4 **Neyriz** Iran
90C2 **Neyshābūr** Iran
60D3 **Nezhin** Russian Fed
98B3 **Ngabé** Congo
100B3 **Ngami** L Botswana
110C1 **Ngaruawahia** NZ
110C1 **Ngaruroro** R NZ
110C1 **Ngauruhoe,Mt** NZ
98B3 **Ngo** Congo
76D2 **Ngoc Linh** Mt Viet
98B2 **Ngoko** R Cam
88B3 **Ngoring Hu** L China
99D3 **Ngorongoro Crater**
Tanz
98B3 **N'Gounié** R Gabon
98B3 **Nguigmi** Niger
71E3 **Ngulu** I Pacific O
97D3 **Nguru** Nig
76D3 **Nha Trang** Viet
108B3 **Nhill** Aust
101H1 **Nhlangano**
Swaziland
76D2 **Nhommarath** Laos
106C2 **Nhulunbuy** Aust
97B3 **Niafounké** Mali
14A1 **Niagara** USA
15C2 **Niagara Falls** Can
15C2 **Niagara Falls** USA
70C3 **Niah** Malay
97B4 **Niakaramandougou**
Ivory Coast
97C3 **Niamey** Niger
99C2 **Niangara** Zaire
98 **Nia Nia** Zaire
70A3 **Nias** I Indon
25D3 **Nicaragua** Republic,
Cent America
53C3 **Nicastro** Italy
49D3 **Nice** France
26B1 **Nicholl's Town**
The Bahamas
83D5 **Nicobar Is** Indian O
92B2 **Nicosia** Cyprus
25D3 **Nicoya,Pen de**
Costa Rica
58C2 **Nidzica** Pol
46D2 **Niederbronn** France
56B2 **Niedersachsen** State,
Germany
99C3 **Niemba** Zaire
56B2 **Nienburg** Germany
97B3 **Niéri** R Germany
97B4 **Niete,Mt** Lib
33F2 **Nieuw Amsterdam**
Surinam
33F2 **Nieuw Nickerie**
Surinam
46B1 **Nieuwpoort** Belg
92B2 **Niğde** Turk
97C3 **Niger** Republic,
Africa
97C4 **Niger** R Nig
97C4 **Nigeria** Federal
Republic, Africa
55B2 **Nigrita** Greece

75C1 **Nihommatsu** Japan
74D3 **Niigata** Japan
74C4 **Niihama** Japan
75B2 **Nii-jima** I Japan
75A2 **Niimi** Japan
74D3 **Niitsu** Japan
94B3 **Nijil** Jordan
56B2 **Nijmegen** Neth
64E3 **Nikel'** Russian Fed
97C3 **Nikki** Benin
74D3 **Nikko** Japan
60D4 **Nikolayev** Ukraine
61G4 **Nikolayevsk**
Russian Fed
63G2 **Nikolayevsk-na-
Amure** Russian Fed
61G2 **Nikol'sk** Russian Fed
61G3 **Nikol'sk** Russian Fed
60D4 **Nikopol** Ukraine
92C1 **Niksar** Turk
91D4 **Nikshahr** Iran
54A2 **Nikšić** Montenegro,
Yugos
71D4 **Nila** I Indon
80B3 **Nile** R N E Africa
14A2 **Niles** USA
87B2 **Nilgiri Hills** India
85C4 **Nimach** India
49C3 **Nîmes** France
109C3 **Nimmitabel** Aust
99D2 **Nimule** Sudan
83B5 **Nine Degree Chan**
Indian O
104C4 **Ninety-East Ridge**
Indian O
109C3 **Ninety Mile Beach**
Aust
73D4 **Ningde** China
73D4 **Ningdu** China
68B3 **Ningjing Shan** Mts
China
76D1 **Ningming** China
73A4 **Ningnan** China
72B2 **Ningxia** Province,
China
72B2 **Ning Xian** China
73B5 **Ninh Binh** Vietnam
107D1 **Ninigo Is** PNG
12D2 **Ninilchik** USA
8D2 **Niobrara** R USA
98B3 **Nioki** Zaire
97B3 **Nioro du Sahel** Mali
48B2 **Niort** France
5H4 **Nipawin** Can
7B5 **Nipigon** Can
7B5 **Nipigon,L** Can
7B5 **Nipissing** R Can
14B1 **Nipissing,L** Can
87B1 **Nirmal** India
86B1 **Nirmali** India
54B2 **Niš** Serbia, Yugos
81C4 **Nisāb** Yemen
69F4 **Nishino-shima** I
Japan
75A1 **Nishino-shima** I
Japan
75A2 **Nishiwaki** Japan
12G2 **Nisling** R Can
12H2 **Nisutlin** R Can
7C4 **Nitchequon** Can
31C6 **Niterói** Brazil
42C2 **Nith** R Scot
59B3 **Nitra** Slovakia
14B3 **Nitro** USA
78C2 **Niut** Mt Malay
46C1 **Nivelles** Belg
49C2 **Nivernais** Region,
France
38L5 **Nivskiy** Russian Fed
87B1 **Nizāmābād** India
94B3 **Nizana** Hist Site
Israel
61J2 **Nizhniye Sergi**
Russian Fed
65F4 **Nizhniy Novgorod**
Russian Fed
61F3 **Nizhniy Lomov**
Russian Fed
65G4 **Nizhniy Tagil**
Russian Fed
63B1 **Nizhnyaya Tunguska**
R Russian Fed
93C2 **Nizip** Turk
100B2 **Njoko** R Zambia

99D3	Njombe Tanz
98B2	Nkambé Cam
101C2	Nkhata Bay Malawi
98B2	Nkongsamba Cam
97C3	N'Konni Niger
86C2	Noakhali Bang
12B1	Noatak USA
12C1	Noatak R USA
74C4	Nobeoka Japan
47D1	Noce R Italy
23A1	Nochistlán Mexico
23B2	Nochixtlán Mexico
19A3	Nocona USA
24A1	Nogales Sonora, Mexico
9B3	Nogales USA
23B2	Nogales Veracruz, Mexico
47D2	Nogara Italy
75A2	Nogata Japan
60E2	Noginsk Russian Fed
34D2	Nogoya Arg
34D2	Nogoyá R Arg
84C3	Nohar India
75B2	Nojima-zaki C Japan
98B2	Nola CAR
61G2	Nolinsk Russian Fed
16D2	Nomans Land I USA
12A2	Nome USA
46D2	Nomeny France
72B1	Nomgon Mongolia
5H3	Nonacho L Can
76C2	Nong Khai Thai
101H1	Nongoma S Africa
12B1	Noorvik USA
13B3	Nootka Sd Can
98B3	Noqui Angola
7C5	Noranda Can
6N5	Nord Department, France
64D2	Nordaustlandet I Barents S
13D2	Nordegg Can
38F6	Nordfjord Inlet Nor
39E8	Nordfriesische Is Germany
56C2	Nordhausen Germ
56B2	Nordrhein Westfalen Germ
38J4	Nordkapp C Nor
6E3	Norden Greenland
38H5	Nord Stronfjället Mt Sweden
1B9	Nordvik Russian Fed
45C2	Nore R Irish Rep
43E3	Norfolk County, Eng
8D2	Norfolk Nebraska, USA
11C3	Norfolk Virginia, USA
107F3	Norfolk I USA
18B2	Norfolk L USA
105G5	Norfolk Ridge Pacific O
1C10	Noril'sk Russian Fed
18C1	Normal USA
19A2	Norman USA
44B2	Normandie Region, France
107D2	Normanton Aust
12J1	Norman Wells Can
4B3	Norne USA
15C2	Norristown USA
39H7	Norrköping Sweden
39H6	Norrsundet Sweden
39H7	Norrtälje Sweden
106B4	Norseman Aust
63F2	Norsk Russian Fed
6F5	North S N W Europe
42D2	Northallerton Eng
106A4	Northam Aust
102E3	North American Basin Atlantic O
106A3	Northampton Aust
43D3	Northampton County, Eng
43D3	Northampton Eng
15D2	Northampton USA
4G3	North Arm B Can
17B1	North Augusta USA
6D4	North Aulatsvik I Can
13F2	North Battleford Can
7C5	North Bay Can
20B2	North Bend USA
44C3	North Berwick Scot
7D5	North,C Can
7G4	North C NZ
11B3	North Carolina State, USA
20B1	North Cascade Nat Pk USA
14B1	North Chan Can
42B2	North Chan Ire/Scot
8C2	North Dakota State, USA
43E4	North Downs Eng
14C2	North East Eng
102H2	North East Atlantic Basin Atlantic O
4B3	Northeast C USA
100B3	Northern Cape Province, S Africa
40B3	Northern Ireland UK
71F2	Northern Mariana Islands Pacific O
27L1	Northern Range Mts Trinidad
106C2	Northern Territory Aust
100B3	Northern Transvaal Province, S Africa
44C3	North Esk R Scot
16C1	Northfield Massachusetts, USA
110B1	North I NZ
74B3	North Korea Republic, S E Asia
	North Land = Severnaya Zemlya
19B3	North Little Rock USA
1B4	North Magnetic Pole Can
17B2	North Miami USA
17B2	North Miami Beach USA
8C2	North Platte USA
8C2	North Platte R USA
27R3	North Pt Barbados
14B1	North Pt USA
40B2	North Rona I Scot
44C2	North Ronaldsay I Scot
13F2	North Saskatchewan R Can
40D2	North Sea N W Europe
4D3	North Slope Region USA
109D1	North Stradbroke I Aust
110B1	North Taranaki Bight B NZ
44A3	North Truchas Peak Mt USA
44A3	North Uist I Scot
42C2	Northumberland County, Eng
107E3	Northumberland Is Aust
42C2	Northumberland Str Can
20B1	North Vancouver Can
43E3	North Walsham Eng
12F2	Northway USA
100B3	North West Province, S Africa
106A3	North West C Aust
84C2	North West Frontier Province, Pak
7D4	North West River Can
4F3	North West Territories Can
42C2	North York Moors Nat Pk Eng
12B2	Norton B USA
12B2	Norton Sd USA
112B1	Norvegia,C Ant
16C2	Norwalk Connecticut, USA
14B2	Norwalk Ohio, USA
39F6	Norway Kingdom, Europe
5J4	Norway House Can
6A2	Norwegian B Can
102H1	Norwegian Basin Norwegian S
64A3	Norwegian S N W Europe
16C2	Norwich Connecticut, USA
43E3	Norwich Eng
16D1	Norwood Massachusetts, USA
14B3	Norwood Ohio, USA
54C2	Nos Emine C Bulg
74D2	Noshiro Japan
54C2	Nos Kaliakra C Bulg
44E1	Noss I Scot
91D4	Nosratābād Iran
101D2	Nosy Barren I Madag
101D2	Nosy Bé I Madag
101E2	Nosy Boraha I Madag
101E2	Nosy Varika Madag
58B2	Noteć R Pol
53C3	Noto Italy
39F7	Notodden Nor
75B1	Noto-hantō Pen Japan
7E5	Notre Dams B Can
43D3	Nottingham County, Eng
43D3	Nottingham Eng
6C3	Nottingham I Can
6C3	Nottingham Island Can
96A2	Nouadhibou Maur
97A3	Nouakchott Maur
107F3	Nouméa Nouvelle Calédonie
98B3	Nouna Burkina
107F3	Nouvelle Calédonie I S W Pacific O
98B3	Nova Caipemba Angola
34A3	Nova Esperança Brazil
35C2	Nova Friburgo Brazil
100A2	Nova Gaia Angola
35B2	Nova Granada Brazil
35B2	Nova Horizonte Brazil
35C1	Nova Lima Brazil
	Nova Lisboa = Huambo
35A2	Nova Londrina Brazil
101C3	Nova Mambone Mozam
52A1	Novara Italy
7D5	Nova Scotia Province, Can
22A1	Novato USA
35C1	Nova Venécia Brazil
60D4	Novaya Kakhovka Ukraine
64G2	Novaya Zemlya I Barents S
54C2	Nova Zagora Bulg
31C2	Nove Russas Brazil
54A1	Nové Zámky Slovakia
60D2	Novgorod Russian Fed
47C2	Novi Ligure Italy
54B2	Novi Pazar Bulg
54B2	Novi Pazar Serbia, Yugos
54A1	Novi Sad Serbia, Yugos
61J3	Novoalekseyevka Kazakhstan
61F3	Novoanninskiy Russian Fed
61E4	Novocherkassk Russian Fed
60C3	Novograd Volynskiy Ukraine
60D2	Novogrudok Russian Fed
30F4	Novo Hamburgo Brazil
65H5	Novokazalinsk Kazakhstan
65K4	Novokuznetsk Russian Fed
112B12	Novolazarevskaya Base Ant
52C1	Novo Mesto Slovenia
60E3	Novomoskovsk Russian Fed
60E5	Novorossiysk Russian Fed
65K4	Novosibirsk Russian Fed
1B8	Novosibirskiye Ostrova I Russian Fed
61J3	Novotroitsk Russian Fed
61G3	Novo Uzensk Russian Fed
59C2	Novovolynsk Ukraine
61G2	Novo Vyatsk Russian Fed
60D3	Novozybkov Russian Fed
58C2	Novy Dwór Pol
61K2	Novyy Lyalya Russian Fed
61H5	Novyy Port Russian Fed
61H5	Novyy Uzen Kazakhstan
58B2	Nowa Sól Pol
18A2	Nowata USA
	Nowgong = Nagaon
12D2	Nowitna R USA
109D2	Nowra Aust
90B2	Now Shahr Iran
75A2	Nowshak Maur
59C3	Nowy Sącz Pol
12H3	Noyes I USA
46B2	Noyon France
97B4	Nsawam Ghana
97B4	Nsukka Nig
91D3	Nuba Mts Sudan
81B3	Nubian Desert Sudan
34A3	Nuble R Chile
9D4	Nueces R USA
5J3	Nueltin L Can
26A2	Nueva Gerona Cuba
34A3	Nueva Imperial Chile
9C4	Nueva Laredo Mexico
34D2	Nueva Palmira Urug
24B2	Nueva Rosita Mexico
26B2	Nuevitas Cuba
24B1	Nuevo Casas Grandes Mexico
24C2	Nuevo Laredo Mexico
99E2	Nugaal Region, Somalia
6E2	Nûgâtsiaq Greenland
6E2	Nugssuag Pen Greenland
6E2	Nûgussuaq I Greenland
108A2	Nukey Bluff Mt Aust
93D3	Nukhayb Iraq
65G5	Nukus Uzbekistan
12C2	Nulato USA
106B4	Nullarbor Plain Aust
97D4	Numan Nig
75B1	Numata Japan
98C2	Numatinna R Sudan
72D3	Numazu Japan
71E4	Numfoor I Indon
108C3	Numurkah Aust
12B2	Nunapitchuk USA
84D2	Nunkun Mt India
53A2	Nuoro Sardegna
91B3	Nurābād Iran
47C2	Nure R Italy
108A2	Nuriootpa Aust
84C1	Nuristan Upland Afghan
61J2	Nurlat Russian Fed
38K6	Nurmes Fin
57C2	Nürnberg Germany
93D2	Nusaybin Turk
12C3	Nushagak R USA
12C3	Nushagak B USA
12C3	Nushagak Pen USA
84B3	Nushki Pak
7D4	Nutak Can
12F2	Nutzotin Mts USA
6E3	Nuuk = Godthåb
86A1	Nuwakot Nepal
87C3	Nuwara-Eliya Sri Lanka
6C3	Nuyukjuak Can

Nyack

16C2 **Nyack** USA
99D2 **Nyahururu** Kenya
108B3 **Nyah West** Aust
4C3 **Nyai** USA
68B3 **Nyainqentanglha Sham** Mts China
99D3 **Nyakabindi** Tanz
98C1 **Nyala** Sudan
86B1 **Nyalam** China
98C2 **Nyamlell** Sudan
64F3 **Nyandoma** Russian Fed
100C2 **Nyanga** Zim
98B3 **Nyanga** R Gabon
101C2 **Nyasa L** Malawi/Mozam
Nyaunglebin Myan
61J2 **Nyazepetrovsk** Russian Fed
39G7 **Nyborg** Den
39H7 **Nybro** Sweden
64J3 **Nyda** Russian Fed
6D1 **Nyeboes Land** Region Can
99D3 **Nyeri** Kenya
101C2 **Nyimba** Zambia
82D3 **Nyingchi** China
99D3 **Nyiregyhaza** Hung
99D2 **Nyiru,Mt** Kenya
38J6 **Nykarleby** Fin
39F7 **Nykøbing** Den
39G8 **Nykøbing** Den
39H7 **Nyköping** Sweden
100B3 **Nylstroom** S Africa
109C2 **Nymagee** Aust
97D3 **Nynäshamn** Sweden
109C2 **Nyngan** Aust
47B1 **Nyon** Switz
98B2 **Nyong** R Cam
49D3 **Nyons** France
59J2 **Nysa** Pol
20C2 **Nyssa** USA
63D1 **Nyurba** Russian Fed
99D3 **Nzega** Tanz
97B4 **Nzérékore** Guinea
98B3 **N'zeto** Angola

O

6F3 **Oaggsimiut** Greenland
8C2 **Oahe Res** USA
21C4 **Oahu** I Hawaiian Is
108B2 **Oakbank** Aust
52C2 **Oakdale** USA
109D1 **Oakey** Aust
21A2 **Oakland** California, USA
20B2 **Oakland** Oregon, USA
14A3 **Oakland City** USA
14A2 **Oak Lawn** USA
22B2 **Oakley** California, USA
20B2 **Oakridge** USA
14C2 **Oakville** Can
111B3 **Oamaru** NZ
112B7 **Oates Land** Region, Ant
109C4 **Oatlands** Aust
23B2 **Oaxaca** Mexico
23B2 **Oaxaca** State, Mexico
65J3 **Ob'** R Russian Fed
75B1 **Obama** Japan
111A3 **Oban** NZ
44B3 **Oban** Scot
75C1 **Obanazawa** Japan
47D1 **Oberammergau** Germany
46D1 **Oberhausen** Germany
47D1 **Oberstdorf** Germany
71D4 **Obi** I Indon
33F4 **Obidos** Brazil
74E2 **Obihiro** Japan
98C2 **Obo** CAR
99E1 **Obock** Djibouti
58B2 **Oborniki** Pol
60E3 **Oboyan** Russian Fed
20B2 **O'Brien** USA
61H3 **Obshchiy Syrt** Mts Russian Fed
64J3 **Obskaya Guba** B Russian Fed

97B4 **Obuasi** Ghana
17B2 **Ocala** USA
32C2 **Ocana** Colombia
50B2 **Ocaño** Spain
12G3 **Ocean C** USA
15C3 **Ocean City** Maryland, USA
16B3 **Ocean City** New Jersey, USA
5F4 **Ocean Falls** Can
22D4 **Oceanside** USA
19C3 **Ocean Springs** USA
61H2 **Ocher** Russian Fed
44C3 **Ochil Hills** Scot
17B1 **Ochlockonee** R USA
27H1 **Ocho Rios** Jamaica
17B1 **Ocmulgee** R USA
17B1 **Oconee** R USA
14A2 **Oconto** USA
23A1 **Ocotlán** Jalisco, Mexico
23B2 **Ocotlán** Oaxaca, Mexico
97B4 **Oda** Ghana
75A1 **Oda** Japan
38B2 **Ódáðahraun** Region, Iceland
74E2 **Odate** Japan
74D3 **Odawara** Japan
39F6 **Odda** Nor
50A2 **Odemira** Port
55C3 **Odemis** Turk
101G1 **Odendaalsrus** S Africa
39G7 **Odense** Den
56C2 **Oder** R Pol/Germany
9C3 **Odessa** Texas, USA
60D4 **Odessa** Ukraine
20C1 **Odessa** Washington, USA
97B4 **Odienné** Ivory Coast
59B2 **Odra** R Pol
31C3 **Oeiras** Brazil
53C2 **Ofanto** R Italy
94B3 **Ofaqim** Israel
45C2 **Offaly** County, Irish Rep
49D1 **Offenbach** Germany
49D2 **Offenburg** Germany
99E2 **Ogaden** Region, Eth
74D3 **Ogaki** Japan
8C2 **Ogallala** USA
69G4 **Ogasawara Gunto** Is Japan
97C4 **Ogbomosho** Nig
8B2 **Ogden** Utah, USA
15C2 **Ogdensburg** USA
17B1 **Ogeechee** R USA
12G1 **Ogilvie** Can
4E3 **Ogilvie Mts** Can
17B1 **Oglethorpe,Mt** USA
47D1 **Oglio** R Italy
47B1 **Ognon** R France
97C4 **Ogoja** Nig
98A3 **Ogooué** R Gabon
58C1 **Ogre** Latvia
96B2 **Oguilet Khenachich** Well Mali
52C1 **Ogulin** Croatia
111A3 **Ohai** NZ
110C1 **Ohakune** NZ
96C2 **Ohanet** Alg
111A2 **Ohau,L** NZ
10B2 **Ohio** State, USA
14A3 **Ohio** R USA
100A2 **Ohopoho** Namibia
57C2 **Ohre** R Czech Republic
55B2 **Ohrid** Macedonia
55B2 **Ohridsko Jezero** L Macedonia/Alb
110B1 **Ohura** NZ
33G3 **Oiapoque** French Guiana
68B2 **Oijiaojing** China
14C2 **Oil City** USA
21B2 **Oildale** USA
46B2 **Oise** Department, France
49C2 **Oise** R France
74C4 **Oita** Japan
22C3 **Ojai** USA
24B2 **Ojinaga** Mexico

23B2 **Ojitlán** Mexico
75B1 **Ojiya** Japan
30C4 **Ojos del Salado** Mt Arg
23A1 **Ojzeloz** Mexico
60E3 **Oka** R Russian Fed
100A3 **Okahandja** Namibia
20C1 **Okanagan Falls** Can
13D2 **Okanagan L** Can
20C1 **Okanagan P** USA
20B1 **Okanogan Range** Mts Can/USA
84C2 **Okara** Pak
100A2 **Okavango** R Angola/Namibia
100B2 **Okavango Delta** Marsh Botswana
74D3 **Okaya** Japan
74C4 **Okayama** Japan
75B2 **Okazaki** Japan
17B2 **Okeechobee** USA
17B2 **Okeechobee,L** USA
17B1 **Okefenokee Swamp** USA
97C4 **Okene** Nig
87A3 **Okha** India
69G1 **Okha** Russian Fed
86B1 **Okhaldunga** Nepal
62J3 **Okhotsk,S of** Russian Fed
69E4 **Okinawa** I Japan
69E4 **Okinawa gunto** Arch Japan
74C3 **Oki-shoto** Is Japan
9D3 **Oklahoma** State, USA
18A2 **Oklahoma City** USA
18A2 **Okmulgee** USA
98B3 **Okondja** Gabon
98B3 **Okoyo** Congo
97C4 **Okpara** R Nig
61J4 **Oktyabr'sk** Kazakhstan
61H3 **Oktyabr'skiy** Russian Fed
74D2 **Okushiri-tó** I Japan
38A2 **Ólafsvik** Iceland
39H7 **Oland** I Sweden
108B2 **Olary** Aust
18B2 **Olathe** USA
29D3 **Olavarria** Arg
53A2 **Olbia** Sardegna
12G1 **Old Crow** Can
56B2 **Oldenburg** Niedersachsen, Germany
56C2 **Oldenburg** Schleswig-Holstein, Germany
15C2 **Old Forge** USA
42C3 **Oldham** Eng
12D3 **Old Harbor** USA
41B3 **Old Head of Kinsale** C Scot
16C2 **Old Lyme** USA
13E2 **Olds** Can
72D1 **Oldziyt** Mongolia
15C2 **Olean** USA
63E2 **Olekma** R
63D1 **Olekminsk** Russian Fed
38L5 **Olenegorsk** Russian Fed
58D2 **Olevsk** Ukraine
69F2 **Ol'ga** Russian Fed
100A3 **Olifants** R Namibia
55B2 **Ólimbos** Mt Greece
35B2 **Olimpia** Brazil
23B2 **Olinala** Mexico
31E3 **Olinda** Brazil
34C2 **Oliva** Arg
29C2 **Olivares** Mt Arg
35C2 **Oliveira** Brazil
13D3 **Oliver** Can
30C3 **Ollague** Chile
30C3 **Ollagüe** Mt Bol
18C2 **Olney** USA
68E1 **Olochi** Russian Fed
39G7 **Olofstrom** Sweden
98B3 **Olombo** Congo
59B3 **Olomouc** Czech Republic

60D1 **Olonets** Russian Fed
79B3 **Olongapo** Phil
48B3 **Oloron Ste Marie** France
68D1 **Olovyannaya** Russian Fed
46D1 **Olpe** Germany
58C2 **Olsztyn** Pol
54C2 **Olt** R Rom
47B1 **Olten** Switz
20B1 **Olympia** USA
20B1 **Olympic Nat Pk** USA
Olympus = **Ólimbos**
20B1 **Olympus,Mt** USA
65J4 **Om'** R Russian Fed
75B1 **Omachi** Japan
75B2 **Omae-zaki** C Japan
45C2 **Omagh** N Ire
18A1 **Omaha** USA
20C1 **Omak** USA
91C5 **Oman** Sultanate, Arabian Pen
91C4 **Oman,G of** UAE
98A3 **Omboué** Gabon
99D1 **Omdurman** Sudan
23B2 **Ometepec** Mexico
99H1 **Om Hajer** Eritrea
13B1 **Omineca** R Can
13B1 **Omineca Mts** Can
75B1 **Omiya** Japan
12A3 **Ommaney,C** USA
4H2 **Ommanney B** Can
99D2 **Omo** R Eth
65J4 **Omsk** Russian Fed
74B4 **Omura** Japan
74C4 **Omuta** Japan
61H2 **Omutninsk** Russian Fed
78D3 **Onang** Indon
14B1 **Onaping L** Can
100A2 **Oncocua** Angola
100A2 **Ondangua** Namibia
59C3 **Ondava** R Slovakia
68D2 **Ondörhaan** Molgolia
83B5 **One and Half Degree Chan** Indian O
64E3 **Onega** Russian Fed
64E3 **Onega** R Russian Fed
15C2 **Oneida L** USA
8D2 **O'Neill** USA
69H2 **Onekotan** I Russian Fed
98C3 **Onema** Zaire
15D2 **Oneonta** USA
54C1 **Onesti** Rom
64E3 **Onezhskoye Ozero** L Russian Fed
100A2 **Ongiva** Angola
74B3 **Ongjin** N Korea
72D1 **Ongniud Qi** China
87C1 **Ongole** India
13D3 **Onieda L** USA
101D3 **Onilahy** R Madag
97C4 **Onitsha** Nig
68C2 **Onjüül** Mongolia
75B1 **Ono** Japan
75B2 **Onohara-jima** I Japan
74C4 **Onomichi** Japan
106A3 **Onslow** Aust
17C1 **Onslow B** USA
75B1 **Ontake-san** Mt Japan
22D3 **Ontario** California, USA
20C2 **Ontario** Oregon, USA
7A4 **Ontario** Province, Can
15C2 **Ontario,L** Can/USA
51B2 **Onteniente** Spain
106C3 **Oodnadatta** Aust
106C4 **Ooldea** Aust
18A2 **Oologah L** USA
46B1 **Oostende** Belg
46B1 **Oosterschelde** Estuary Neth
87B2 **Ootacamund** India
14B2 **Ootsa L** Can
69H1 **Opala** Russian Fed
98C3 **Opala** Zaire
87C3 **Opanake** Sri Lanka
61G2 **Oparino** Russian Fed

59B3 Opava
  Czech Republic
17A1 Opelika USA
19B3 Opelousas USA
58D1 Ophir USA
58D1 Opochka
  Russian Fed
59B2 Opole Pol
  Oporto = Porto
110C1 Opotiki NZ
17A1 Opp USA
38F6 Oppdal Nor
110B1 Opunake NZ
54B1 Oradea Rom
88D3 Oraefajökull Mts
  Iceland
85D2 Orai India
96B1 Oran Alg
30D3 Orán Arg
109C2 Orange Aust
22D4 Orange California,
  USA
49C3 Orange France
19B3 Orange Texas, USA
100A3 Orange S Africa
17B1 Orangeburg USA
101G1 Orange Free State
  Province, S Africa
17B1 Orange Park USA
14B2 Orangeville Can
56C2 Oranienburg
  Germany
79C3 Oras Phil
54B1 Orăştie Rom
54B1 Oraviţa Rom
109C3 Orbost Aust
46B1 Orchies France
47B2 Orco R Italy
10B2 Ord R Aust
10B2 Ord,Mt Aust
93C1 Ordu Turk
39H7 Örebro Sweden
8A2 Oregon State, USA
18B2 Oregon USA
14B2 Oregon City USA
39H6 Öregrund Sweden
60E2 Orekhovo Zuyevo
  Russian Fed
60E3 Orel Russian Fed
61H3 Orenburg
  Russian Fed
34D3 Orense Arg
50A1 Orense Spain
56C1 Øresund Str Den/
  Sweden
111A3 Oreti R NZ
55C3 Orhaneli R Turk
68C2 Orhon Gol R
  Mongolia
23B2 Oriental Mexico
108B1 Oriente Arg
51B2 Orihuela Spain
15C2 Orillia Can
33E2 Orinoco R Ven
86A2 Orissa State, India
53A3 Oristano Sardegna
36K6 Orivesi L Fin
33F4 Oriximiná Brazil
23B2 Orizaba Mexico
35B1 Orizona Brazil
35B2 Orlândia Brazil
17B2 Orlando USA
48C2 Orléanais Region
  France
48C2 Orléans France
63B2 Orlik Russian Fed
82A3 Ormara Pak
79B3 Ormoc Phil
17B2 Ormond Beach
  USA
46C2 Ornain R France
47B1 Ornans France
48B2 Orne R France
38H6 Örnsköldsvik
  Sweden
32C3 Orocué Colombia
94B3 Oron Israel
79B4 Oroquieta Phil
59C3 Oroshaza Hung
21A2 Oroville California,
  USA

20C1 Oroville Washington,
  USA
47B1 Orsières Switz
65G4 Orsk Russian Fed
38F6 Ørsta Nor
48B3 Orthez France
50A1 Ortigueira Spain
47D1 Ortles Mts Italy
27L1 Ortoire R Trinidad
93E2 Orūmīyeh Iran
30C2 Oruro Bol
61J2 Osa Russian Fed
18B2 Osage R USA
75B1 Osaka Japan
26D2 Osa,Pen de Costa
  Rica
18C2 Osceola Arkansas,
  USA
18B1 Osceola Iowa, USA
20C2 Osgood Mts USA
15C2 Oshawa Can
75B2 O-shima I Japan
10B2 Oshkosh USA
97C4 Oshogbo Nig
7B5 Oshosh Nig
98B3 Oshwe Zaire
54A1 Osijek Croatia
65K5 Osinniki Russian Fed
58D2 Osipovichi Belarus
18B1 Oskaloosa USA
60A2 Oskarshamn
  Sweden
39G7 Oslo Nor
92C2 Osmaniye Turk
56B2 Osnabrück Germany
30F4 Osório Brazil
29B4 Osorno Chile
50B1 Osorno Spain
20C1 Osoyoos Can
13C1 Ospika R Can
17D5 Ossa,Mt Aust
16C2 Ossining USA
60D2 Ostashkov
  Russian Fed
  Ostend = Oostende
38G6 Østerdalen V Nor
38G6 Østersund Sweden
56B2 Ostfriesische Inseln
  Is Germany
39H6 Osthammar Sweden
53B2 Ostia Italy
47D2 Ostiglia Italy
59B3 Ostrava
  Czech Republic
58B2 Ostróda Pol
58B2 Ostroleka Pol
60C2 Ostrov Russian Fed
64J2 Ostrov Belyy I
  Russian Fed
64H1 Ostrov Greem Bell I
  Barents S
64F3 Ostrov Kolguyev I
  Russian Fed
74F2 Ostrov Kunashir I
  Russian Fed
64F2 Ostrov
  Mechdusharskiy I
  Russian Fed
90B2 Ostrov Ogurchinskiy
  I Turkmenistan
64G1 Ostrov Rudol'fa I
  Barents S
64G2 Ostrov Vaygach I
  Russian Fed
64F2 Ostrov Vrangelya I
  Russian Fed
58B2 Ostrów Wlkp. Pol
59C2 Ostrowiec Pol
58B2 Ostrów Mazowiecka
  Pol
50A2 Osuna Spain
15C2 Oswego USA
15C2 Oswego USA
43C3 Oswestry Eng
59B2 Oświęcim Pol
111B3 Otago Pen NZ
110C2 Otaki NZ
74E2 Otaru Japan
32B3 Otavalo Ecuador
100A2 Otavi Namibia
75C1 Otawara Japan
20C1 Othello USA
55B3 Óthris Mt Greece

16C1 Otis Massachusetts,
  USA
16B2 Otisville USA
100A3 Otjiwarongo
  Namibia
72B2 Otog Qi China
110C1 Otorohanga NZ
55A2 Otranto Italy
55A2 Otranto,Str of Chan
  Italy/Alb
14A2 Otsego USA
75B1 Otsu Japan
39F6 Otta Nor
39F7 Otta R Nor
15C1 Ottawa Can
18A2 Ottawa Kansas, USA
15C1 Ottawa R Can
7B4 Ottawa Is Can
7B4 Otter Rapids Can
6B1 Otto Fjord Can
101G1 Ottosdal S Africa
18B1 Ottumwa USA
46D2 Ottweiler Germany
97C4 Oturkpo Nig
32B5 Otusco Peru
108B3 Otway,C Aust
47D1 Otz Austria
47D1 Ötztal Mts Austria
76C1 Ou R Laos
19B3 Ouachita R USA
19B3 Ouachita,L USA
19B3 Ouachita Mts USA
96A2 Ouadane Maur
98C2 Ouadda CAR
98C1 Ouaddai Desert
  Region Chad
97B3 Ouagadougou
  Burkina
97B3 Ouahigouya Burkina
98C2 Ouaka CAR
97C3 Oualam Niger
96C2 Ouallen Alg
98C2 Ouanda Djallé CAR
98C2 Ouangate Region,
  Maur
96C1 Ouargla Alg
98C2 Ouarra R CAR
96B1 Ouarzazate Mor
51C2 Ouassel R Alg
97B4 Oubangui R Congo
46B1 Oudenaarde Belg
100B4 Oudtshoorn S Africa
51B2 Oued Tlélat Alg
96B1 Oued Zem Mor
98B2 Ouesso Congo
96B1 Ouezzane Mor
98B2 Ouham R Chad
97C4 Ouidah Benin
96B1 Oujda Mor
38J6 Oulainen Fin
38K5 Oulu Fin
38K6 Oulu R Fin
38K6 Oulujärvi L Fin
95B3 Oum Chalouba Chad
98B1 Oum Hadjer Chad
95B3 Oum Haouach
  Watercourse Chad
95B3 Ouniana Kébir
  Chad
46D1 Our R Germany
46B2 Ourcq R France
51B1 Ourense = Orense
31C3 Ouricuri Brazil
35B2 Ourinhos Brazil
31C5 Ouro Prêto Brazil
46C1 Ourthe R Belg
42D2 Ouse R Eng
43E3 Ouse R Eng
40B2 Outer Hebrides Is
  Scot
22C4 Outer Santa Barbara
  Chan USA
100A3 Outjo Namibia
38K6 Outokumpu Fin
108B3 Ouyen Aust
47C2 Ovada Italy
34A2 Ovalle Chile
100A2 Ovamboland Region,
  Namibia
61H5 Ova Tyuleni Is
  Kazakhstan
38J5 Övertorneå Sweden

50A1 Oviedo Spain
60C3 Ovruch Ukraine
63E2 Ovsyanka
  Russian Fed
111A3 Owaka NZ
75B2 Owase Japan
11B3 Owensboro USA
21B2 Owens L USA
14B2 Owen Sound Can
107D1 Owen Stanley Range
  Mts PNG
97H4 Owerri Nig
97C4 Owo Nig
14B2 Owosso USA
20C2 Owyhee R USA
20C2 Owyhee Mts USA
32B6 Oxapampa Peru
39H7 Oxelösund Sweden
43D4 Oxford County, Eng
43D4 Oxford Eng
16D1 Oxford
  Massachusetts, USA
19C3 Oxford Mississippi,
  USA
43E4 Ox Mts Irish Rep
22C3 Oxnard USA
74D3 Oyama Japan
18E2 Oyem Gabon
98B2 Oyem Gabon
44B3 Oykel R Scot
39F6 Øyre Nor
109C4 Oyster B Aust
79B4 Ozamiz Phil
17A1 Ozark USA
18B2 Ozark Plat USA
18C2 Ozarks,L of the USA
59C3 Ozd Hung
65K5 Ozero Alakol L
  Kazakhstan/
  Russian Fed
65H5 Ozero Balkhash L
  Kazakhstan
64E3 Ozero Baykal L
  Kazakhstan
65J4 Ozero Chany L
  Russian Fed
69F1 Ozero
  Chukchagirskoye
  Russian Fed
69F1 Ozero Evoron
  Russian Fed
  Ozero Chudskoye =
  Peipus,L
60D2 Ozero Il'men L
  Russian Fed
38L5 Ozero Imandra L
  Russian Fed
82B1 Ozero Issyk Kul' L
  Kirghizia
69F2 Ozero Khanka L
  China/Russian Fed
38L5 Ozero Kovdozero L
  Russian Fed
38L5 Ozero Kuyto L
  Russian Fed
38L5 Ozero Pyaozero L
  Russian Fed
65H4 Ozero Tengiz L
  Kazakhstan
38L5 Ozero Topozero L
  Russian Fed
65K5 Ozero Zaysan
  Kazakhstan
23B1 Ozuluama Mexico

P

100A4 Paarl S Africa
44A3 Pabbay I Scot
58B2 Pabianice Pol
86B2 Pabna Bang
58D2 Pabrade Lithuania
32B5 Pacasmayo Peru
23B1 Pachuca Mexico
105K6 Pacific-Antarctic
  Ridge Pacific O
22B2 Pacific Grove USA
78C4 Pacitan Indon
35C1 Pacui R Brazil
70B4 Padang Indon
56B2 Paderborn Germany
5J3 Padlei Can
86C2 Padma R Bang
47D2 Padova Italy
9D4 Padre I USA

Padstow

43B4 **Padstow** Eng
108B3 **Padthaway** Aust
14A3 **Paducah** Kentucky, USA
    Padua = Padova
11B3 **Paducah** USA
38L5 **Padunskoye More** L Russian Fed
74A3 **Paengnyŏng-do** I S Korea
110C1 **Paeroa** NZ
100C3 **Pafuri** Mozam
52B2 **Pag** I Croatia
14A3 **Pagadian** Phil
70B4 **Pagai Selatan** I Indon
70B4 **Pagai Utara** I Indon
71F2 **Pagan** I Pacific O
78D3 **Pagatan** Indon
55C3 **Pagondhas** Greece
110C2 **Pahiatua** NZ
21C4 **Pahoa** Hawaiian Is
17B2 **Pahokee** USA
39K6 **Päijänne** L Fin
21C4 **Pailolo Chan** Hawaiian Is
14B2 **Painesville** USA
9B3 **Painted Desert** USA
32A5 **Paita** Peru
38J5 **Pajala** Sweden
80E3 **Pakistan** Republic, Asia
76C2 **Pak Lay** Laos
86D2 **Pakokku** Myan
13E2 **Pakowki L** Can
52C1 **Pakrac** Croatia
54A1 **Paks** Hung
76C2 **Pak Sane** Laos
76D2 **Pakse** Laos
99D2 **Pakwach** Uganda
98B3 **Pala** Chad
52C2 **Palagruža** I Croatia
46B2 **Palaiseau** France
    Palakhat = Palghat
78C3 **Palangkaraya** Indon
87B1 **Palani** India
85C4 **Palanpur** India
100B3 **Palapye** Botswana
17B2 **Palatka** USA
54C3 **Palau** Is Pacific O
76B3 **Palaw** Myan
79A4 **Palawan** I Phil
79A4 **Palawan Pass** Phil
87B3 **Palayankottai** India
78A3 **Palembang** Indon
50B1 **Palencia** Spain
94A1 **Paleokhorio** Cyprus
53B3 **Palermo** Italy
19A3 **Palestine** USA
86C2 **Paletwa** Myan
87B2 **Pälghät** India
85C3 **Pali** India
85C4 **Palitana** India
87B3 **Palk Str** India/ Sri Lanka
61G3 **Pallasovka** Russian Fed
38J5 **Pallastunturi** Mt Fin
111B2 **Palliser B** NZ
111C2 **Palliser,C** NZ
101D2 **Palma** Mozam
51C2 **Palma de Mallorca** Spain
31D3 **Palmares** Brazil
26A5 **Palmar Sur** Costa Rica
31B4 **Palmas** Brazil
97B4 **Palmas,C** Lib
26B2 **Palma Soriano** Cuba
17B2 **Palm Bay** USA
17B2 **Palm Beach** USA
22C3 **Palmdale** USA
31D3 **Palmeira dos Indos** Brazil
12E2 **Palmer** USA
112C3 **Palmer** Base Ant
112C3 **Palmer Arch** Ant
112B3 **Palmer Land** Region Ant
111B3 **Palmerston** NZ
110C2 **Palmerston North** NZ
16B2 **Palmerton** USA
17B2 **Palmetto** USA
53C3 **Palmi** Italy
32B3 **Palmira** Colombia
107D2 **Palm Is** Aust
21B3 **Palm Springs** USA
18B2 **Palmyra** Missouri, USA
16A2 **Palmyra** Pennsylvania, USA
86B2 **Palmyras Pt** India
22A2 **Palo Alto** USA
78B2 **Paloh** Indon
99D1 **Paloich** Sudan
21B3 **Palomar Mt** USA
70D4 **Palopo** Indon
70C4 **Palu** Indon
93C2 **Palu** Turk
84D3 **Palwal** India
97C3 **Pama** Burkina
78B4 **Pamekasan** Indon
78B4 **Pameungpeuk** Indon
48C3 **Pamiers** France
82B2 **Pamir** Mts China
65J6 **Pamir** R Russian Fed
11C3 **Pamlico Sd** USA
9C3 **Pampa** USA
34B2 **Pampa de la Salinas** Salt pan Arg
34B3 **Pampa de la Varita** Plain Arg
32C2 **Pamplona** Colombia
50B1 **Pamplona** Spain
54B2 **Panagyurishte** Bulg
87A1 **Panaji** India
32B2 **Panamá** Panama
32A2 **Panama** Republic, Cent America
26B5 **Panama Canal** Panama
17A1 **Panama City** USA
21B2 **Panamint Range** Mts USA
21B2 **Panamint V** USA
47D2 **Panaro** R Italy
79B3 **Panay** I Phil
54B2 **Pancevo** Serbia, Yugos
79B3 **Pandan** Indon
81B1 **Pandharpur** India
108A1 **Pandie Pandie** Aust
58C1 **Panevėžys** Lithuania
65K5 **Panfilov** Kazakhstan
76B1 **Pang** R Myan
99D3 **Pangani** Tanz
99D3 **Pangani** R Tanz
98C3 **Pangi** Zaïre
78B3 **Pangkalpinang** Indon
6D3 **Pangnirtung** Can
76B1 **Pangtara** Myan
79B4 **Pangutaran Group** Is Phil
84D3 **Panipat** India
84B2 **Panjao** Afghan
74B3 **P'anmunjŏm** N Korea
86A2 **Panna** India
35A2 **Panorama** Brazil
53B3 **Pantelleria** I Medit S
23B1 **Pantepec** Mexico
23B1 **Pánuco** Mexico
23B1 **Pánuco** R Mexico
73A4 **Pan Xian** China
35C3 **Paola** Italy
14A3 **Paoli** USA
59B3 **Pápa** Hung
110B1 **Papakura** NZ
23B2 **Papaloapan** R Mexico
23B1 **Papantla** Mexico
44E1 **Papa Stour** I Scot
110B1 **Papatoetoe** NZ
44C2 **Papa Westray** I Scot
107D1 **Papua,G of** PNG
107D1 **Papua New Guinea** Republic, S E Asia
34A2 **Papudo** Chile
76B2 **Papun** Myan
33G4 **Pará** State, Brazil
31B2 **Pará** R Brazil
35B1 **Paraburdoo** Aust
32B6 **Paracas,Pen de** Peru
35B1 **Paracatu** Brazil
35B1 **Paracatu** R Brazil
108A2 **Parachilna** Aust
84C2 **Parachinar** Pak
54B2 **Paracin** Serbia, Yugos
35C1 **Pará de Minas** Brazil
21A2 **Paradise** California, USA
18B2 **Paragould** USA
33E6 **Paragua** R Bol
32E2 **Paragua** R Ven
30E2 **Paraguaí** R Brazil
30E4 **Paraguari** Par
30E3 **Paraguay** Republic, S America
30E3 **Paraguay** R Par
31D3 **Paraíba** State, Brazil
35B2 **Paraíba** R Brazil
35C2 **Paraíba do Sul** R Brazil
97C4 **Parakou** Benin
108A2 **Parakylia** Aust
87B3 **Paramakkudi** India
33F2 **Paramaribo** Surinam
69H1 **Paramushir** I Russian Fed
30F3 **Paraná** State, Brazil
34C2 **Paraná** Urug
30E2 **Paraná** R Arg
31B4 **Paraná** R Brazil
30G4 **Paranaguá** Brazil
35A1 **Paranaíba** Brazil
35A1 **Paranaíba** R Brazil
35A2 **Paranapanema** R Brazil
35A2 **Paranavaí** Brazil
79B4 **Parang** Phil
35C1 **Paraope** R Brazil
110B2 **Paraparaumu** NZ
87B1 **Parbhani** India
94B2 **Pardes Hanna** Israel
34D3 **Pardo** Arg
35D1 **Pardo** R Bahia, Brazil
35A2 **Pardo** R Mato Grosso do Sul, Brazil
35B1 **Pardo** R Minas Gerais, Brazil
35B2 **Pardo** R Sao Paulo, Brazil
59B2 **Pardubice** Czech Republic
69F4 **Parece Vela** Reef Pacific O
10C2 **Parent** Can
70C4 **Parepare** Indon
34C3 **Parera** Arg
70B4 **Pariaman** Indon
33E1 **Paria,Pen de** Ven
48C2 **Paris** France
14B3 **Paris** Kentucky, USA
19A3 **Paris** Texas, USA
14B3 **Parkersburg** USA
109C2 **Parkes** Aust
87B1 **Parli** India
47D2 **Parma** Italy
14B2 **Parma** USA
31C2 **Parnaíba** Brazil
31C2 **Parnaíba** R Brazil
55B3 **Párnon Óros** Mts Greece
60B2 **Pärnu** Estonia
86B1 **Paro** Bhutan
108B1 **Paroo** R Aust
108B2 **Paroo Channel** R Aust
55C3 **Páros** I Greece
47B2 **Parpaillon** Mts France
34A3 **Parral** Chile
109D2 **Parramatta** Aust
9C4 **Parras** Mexico
6B3 **Parry B** Can
4G2 **Parry Is** Can
7C5 **Parry Sd** Can
14B1 **Parry Sound** Can
57C3 **Parsberg** Germany
5F4 **Parsnip** R Can
18A2 **Parsons** Kansas, USA
14C3 **Parsons** West Virginia, USA
48B2 **Parthenay** France
53B3 **Partinico** Italy
74C2 **Partizansk** Russian Fed
33G4 **Paru** R Brazil
101G1 **Parys** S Africa
19A4 **Pasadena** Texas, USA
22C3 **Pasadena** California, USA
78D3 **Pasangkayu** Indon
76B2 **Pasawing** Myan
19C3 **Pascagoula** USA
54C1 **Pașcani** Rom
20C1 **Pasco** USA
54C1 **Pas-de-Calais** Department, France
39G8 **Pasewalk** Germany
91C4 **Pashú'īyeh** Iran
108B4 **Pasley,C** Aust
29E2 **Paso de los Toros** Urug
29B4 **Paso Limay** Arg
21A2 **Paso Robles** USA
45B3 **Passage West** Irish Rep
16B2 **Passaic** USA
57C3 **Passau** Germany
30E4 **Passo de los Libres** Arg
47D1 **Passo di Stelvio** Mt Italy
30F4 **Passo Fundo** Brazil
35B2 **Passos** Brazil
47B2 **Passy** France
32B4 **Pastaza** R Peru
34C3 **Pasteur** Arg
5H4 **Pas,The** Can
32B3 **Pasto** Colombia
12B2 **Pastol B** USA
47D2 **Pasubio** Mt Italy
58C1 **Pasvalys** Lithuania
85C4 **Pătan** India
86B1 **Patan** Nepal
108B3 **Patchewollock** Aust
111B2 **Patea** NZ
111B2 **Patea** R NZ
53B3 **Paterno** Italy
16B2 **Paterson** USA
111A3 **Paterson Inlet** B NZ
84D2 **Pathankot** India
    Pathein = Bassein
84D2 **Patiāla** India
32B6 **Pativilca** Peru
55C3 **Pátmos** I Greece
86B1 **Patna** India
93D2 **Patnos** Turk
63D2 **Patomskoye Nagor'ye** Upland Russian Fed
31D3 **Patos** Brazil
35B1 **Patos de Minas** Brazil
34B2 **Patquia** Arg
55B3 **Pátrai** Greece
35B1 **Patrocínio** Brazil
99E3 **Patta** I Kenya
78C4 **Pattallasang** Indon
77C4 **Pattani** Thai
22B2 **Patterson** California, USA
19B4 **Patterson** Louisiana, USA
12H2 **Patterson,Mt** Can
22C2 **Patterson Mt** USA
13B1 **Pattullo,Mt** Can
31D3 **Patu** Brazil
86C2 **Patuakhali** Bang
25D3 **Patuca** R Honduras
23A2 **Pátzcuaro** Mexico
48B2 **Pau** France
4F3 **Paulatuk** Can
31C3 **Paulistana** Brazil
101H1 **Paulpietersburg** S Africa
19A3 **Pauls Valley** USA
76B2 **Paungde** Myan
84D2 **Pauri** India
38H5 **Pauske** Nor
35C1 **Pavão** Brazil
47C2 **Pavia** Italy
65J4 **Pavlodar** Kazakhstan
61J2 **Pavlovka** Russian Fed

61F2 Pavlovo Russian Fed
61F3 Pavlovsk Russian Fed
78C3 Pawan R Indon
78A2 Pawtuska USA
16D2 Pawtucket USA
47B1 Payerne Switz
20C2 Payette USA
7C4 Payne,L Can
34D2 Paysandu Urug
46A2 Pays-de-Bray Region, France
54B2 Pazardzhik Bulg
13D1 Peace R Can
17B2 Peace R USA
13D1 Peace River Can
43D3 Peak District Nat Pk Eng
108A1 Peake R Aust
109C2 Peak Hill Aust
71E4 Peak Mandala Mt Indon
42D3 Peak,The Mt Eng
19B3 Pearl R USA
21C4 Pearl City Hawaiian Is
21C4 Pearl Harbor Hawaiian Is
4H2 Peary Chan Can
101C2 Pebane Mozam
54B2 Peć Serbia, Yugos
35C1 Pecanha Brazil
19B4 Pecan Island USA
38L5 Pechenga Russian Fed
61F1 Pechora R Russian Fed
64G3 Pechorskoye More S Russian Fed
53C3 Pecoraro Mt Italy
9C3 Pecos USA
9C3 Pecos R USA
59B3 Pécs Hung
108A1 Pedirka Aust
35C1 Pedra Azul Brazil
35B2 Pedregulho Brazil
26B3 Pedro Cays Is Caribbean S
30C3 Pedro de Valdivia Chile
30E3 Pedro Juan Caballero Par
30C4 Pedro Luro Arg
23B1 Pedro Mentova USA
87C3 Pedro,Pt Sri Lanka
108B2 Peebinga Aust
42C2 Peebles Scot
17C1 Pee Dee R USA
16C2 Peekskill USA
42B2 Peel Eng
12H1 Peel R Can
4J2 Peel Sd Can
108A1 Peera Peera Poolanna L
13E1 Peerless L Can
71E4 Peg Arfak Mt Indon
111B2 Pegasus B NZ
83D4 Pegu Myan
78A3 Pegunungan Barisan Mts Indon
78C2 Pegunungan Iran Mts Malay/Indon
71E4 Pegunungan Maoke Mts Indon
78D3 Pegunungan Meratus Mts Indon
78C2 Pegunungan Muller Mts Indon
78C3 Pegunungan Schwaner Mts Indon
78A3 Pegunungan Tigapuluh Mts Indon
76B2 Pegu Yoma Mts Myan
34C2 Pehuajó Arg
Péipsi Järve = Peipus,L
39K7 Peipus, Lake Estonia/ Russian Fed
35A2 Peixe R Sao Paulo, Brazil
72D3 Pei Xian China
78C3 Pekalongan Indon

77C5 Pekan Malay
78A2 Pekanbaru Indon
18C1 Pekin USA
Peking = Beijing
77C5 Pelabohan Kelang Malay
78C4 Pelau Pelau Kangean Is Indon
78C4 Pelau Pelau Karim'njawa Arch Indon
78D4 Pelau Pelau Postilyon Is Indon
54B1 Peleaga Mt Rom
63D2 Peleduy Russian Fed
14B2 Peleе I Can
71D4 Peleng I Indon
12G3 Pelican USA
69F1 Peliny Osipenko Russian Fed
34C3 Pellegrini Arg
38J5 Pello Fin
12H2 Pelly R Can
6A3 Pelly Bay Can
12H2 Pelly Crossing Can
12H2 Pelly Mts Can
30F5 Pelotas Brazil
30F4 Pelotas R Brazil
47B2 Pelvoux Region, France
78B4 Pemalang Indon
78B4 Pematang Indon
101D2 Pemba Mozam
99D3 Pemba I Tanz
13C2 Pemberton USA
71C4 Pemberton Aust
15C1 Pembroke Can
17B1 Pembroke USA
43B4 Pembroke Wales
34A3 Pemuco Chile
78D2 Penambo Range Mts Malay
35A2 Penápolis Brazil
50A2 Peñarroya Spain
51B1 Peñarroya Mt Spain
50A1 Peña Trevina Mt Spain
19C2 Pende R Chad
12J3 Pendelton,Mt Can
20C1 Pendleton USA
20C1 Pend Oreille R USA
31D4 Penedo Brazil
85D5 Penganga R India
73D5 P'eng-hu Lieh-tao Is Taiwan
72E2 Penglai China
73B4 Pengshui China
71E4 Pengunungan Maoke Mts Indon
26C4 Peninsula de la Guajiri Pen Colombia
27E4 Peninsula de Paria Pen Ven
77C5 Peninsular Malaysia Malay
10D2 Peninsula de Gaspé Pen Can
23A1 Penjamo Mexico
87B2 Penner R India
42C2 Pennine Chain Mts Eng
16B3 Penns Grove USA
10C2 Pennsylvania State, USA
15D3 Penny Highlands Mts Can
108B3 Penola Aust
106C4 Penong Aust
42C2 Penrith Eng
11B3 Pensacola USA
112A Pensacola Mts Ant
78D1 Pensiangan Malay
13D3 Penticton Can
44C2 Pentland Firth Chan Scot
42C2 Pentland Hills Scot
61G3 Penza Russian Fed
43B4 Penzance Eng
63E2 Penzhina R Russian Fed
78A3 Perabumulh Indon
77C5 Perak I Malay
78A2 Perawang Indon
32B3 Pereira Colombia

35A2 Pereira Barreto Brazil
61F4 Perelazovskiy Russian Fed
12D3 Perenosa B USA
34C2 Pergamino Arg
7C4 Peribonca R Can
48C2 Périgueux France
25E4 Perlas Arch de Is Panama
61J2 Perm' Russian Fed
Pernambuco = Recife
31D3 Pernambuco State, Brazil
108A2 Pernatty Lg Aust
54B2 Pernik Bulg
46B2 Péronne France
23B2 Perote Mexico
49C3 Perpignan France
22D4 Perris USA
17B1 Perry Florida, USA
17B1 Perry Georgia, USA
18A2 Perry Oklahoma, USA
4H3 Perry River Can
14B2 Perrysburg USA
12C3 Perryville Alaska, USA
18C2 Perryville Missouri, USA
106A4 Perth Aust
44C3 Perth Scot
16B2 Perth Amboy USA
32C6 Peru Republic, S America
18C1 Peru USA
103E5 Peru-Chile Trench Pacific O
52B2 Perugia Italy
52C2 Perušic Croatia
93D2 Pervari Turk
61F3 Pervomaysk Russian Fed
60D4 Pervomaysk Ukraine
61J2 Pervoural'sk Russian Fed
52B2 Pesaro Italy
22A2 Pescadero USA
Pescadores = P'eng-hu Lieh-tao
52B2 Pescara Italy
47D2 Peschiera Italy
84C2 Peshawar Pak
52B2 Peskopi Alb
14A1 Pestigo USA
60E2 Pestovo Russian Fed
94B2 Petah Tiqwa Israel
21A2 Petaluma USA
46C2 Pétange Lux
23A2 Petatlan Mexico
101C2 Petauke Zambia
108A2 Peterborough Aust
15C2 Peterborough Can
43D3 Peterborough Eng
44D3 Peterhead Scot
6D1 Petermann Gletscher Gl Greenland
106B3 Petermann Range Mts Aust
29B3 Peteroa Mt Arg/Chile
13F1 Peter Pond L Can
12H3 Petersburg Alaska, USA
85C4 Petlad India
23B2 Petalcingo Mexico
25D2 Peto Mexico
63D2 Petomskoye Nagor'ye Upland Russian Fed
34A2 Petorca Chile
34C3 Petoskey USA
31C3 Petrolina Brazil
65H4 Petropavlovsk Kazakhstan
35C2 Petrópolis Brazil
61G3 Petrovsk Russian Fed
68C1 Petrovsk Zabaykal'skiy Russian Fed
64E3 Petrozavodsk Russian Fed
101G1 Petrus S Africa
101G1 Petrusburg S Africa

1B7 Pevek Russian Fed
46D2 Pfälzer Wald Region, Germany
57B3 Pforzheim Germany
84D2 Phagwara India
85C3 Phalodi India
84D2 Phalsbourg France
87A1 Phaltan India
77B4 Phangnga Thai
76D3 Phan Rang Viet
76D3 Phan Thiet Viet
17A1 Phenix City USA
76B3 Phet Buri Thai
76D3 Phiafay Laos
19C3 Philadelphia Mississippi, USA
16B2 Philadelphia Pennsylvania, USA
Philippeville = Skikda
46C1 Philippeville France
71D2 Philippine S Pacific O
71D2 Philippines Republic, S E Asia
104E3 Philippine Trench Pacific O
15C2 Philipsburg Pennsylvania, USA
12E1 Philip Smith Mts USA
79B2 Philippine S Phil
6B1 Phillips B Can
16B2 Phillipsburg New Jersey, USA
6B2 Philpots Pen Can
76C3 Phnom Penh Camb
9B3 Phoenix Arizona, USA
16B2 Phoenixville USA
76C1 Phong Saly Laos
Phra Nakhon = Bangkok
76C2 Phu Bia Mt Laos
76C2 Phu Cuong Viet
77B4 Phuket Thai
86A2 Phulbani India
76C2 Phu Miang Mt Thai
76D2 Phu Set Mt Laos
76C1 Phu Tho Viet
77D4 Phu Vinh Viet
47C2 Piacenza Italy
109C2 Pian R Aust
52B2 Pianosa I Italy
52C2 Pianosa I Italy
58C2 Piaseczno Pol
54C1 Piatra-Neamt Rom
31C3 Piaui State, Brazil
47E2 Piave R Italy
99D2 Pibor R Sudan
99D2 Pibor Post Sudan
46B1 Picardie Region, France
19C3 Picayune USA
47B2 Pic de Rochebrune Mt France
34A2 Pichilemu Chile
34C3 Pichi Mahuida Arg
42D2 Pickering Eng
7A4 Pickle Lake Can
96A1 Pico I Açores
47C1 Pico Bernina Mt Switz
51B1 Pico de Anito Mt Spain
24B3 Pico del Infiernillo Mt Mexico
27C3 Pico Duarte Mt Dom Rep
31C3 Picos Brazil
50B1 Picos de Europa Mt Spain
109D2 Picton Can
111B2 Picton NZ
95A2 Pic Toussidé Mt Chad
35B2 Piedade Brazil
22C2 Piedra USA
24B2 Piedras Negras Mexico
38K6 Pieksämäki Fin
38K6 Pielinen L Fin
47B2 Piemonte Region, Italy

Pierre

8C2 Pierre USA
59B3 Piešťany Slovakia
101H1 Pietermaritzburg S Africa
100B3 Pietersburg S Africa
101H1 Piet Retief S Africa
60B4 Pietrosu Mt Rom
47E1 Pieve di Cadore Italy
13C2 Pigeon L Can
18B2 Piggott USA
34C3 Piguë Arg
7A4 Pikangikum L Can
8C3 Pikes Peak USA
100A4 Piketberg S Africa
6F3 Pikintaleq Greenland
82B2 Pik Kommunizma Mt Tajikistan
98B2 Pikounda Congo
82C1 Pik Pobedy Mt China/Kirghizia
34D3 Pila Arg
52B2 Pila Pol
30E4 Pilar Par
30D3 Pilcomayo R Arg/Par
84D3 Pilibhit India
59B2 Pilica R Pol
109C2 Pillar,C Aust
55B3 Pilos Greece
12C3 Pilot Point USA
12B2 Pilot Station USA
17C4 Pilottown USA
33F4 Pimenta Brazil
77C4 Pinang I Malay
26A2 Pinar del Rio Cuba
34B2 Pinas Arg
14C2 Pinckneyville USA
16D3 Pinconning USA
52B2 Pińczów Pol
16A2 Pine Grove USA
17B2 Pine Hills USA
17B2 Pine I USA
19B3 Pineland USA
17B2 Pinellas Park USA
5G3 Pine Point Can
47B2 Pinerolo Italy
19B3 Pines,Lo'the USA
17B2 Pineville USA
72C3 Pingdingshan China
73B5 Pingguo China
72B2 Pingliang China
72B2 Pinglu China
73D4 Pingtan Dao I China
73E5 P'ing tung Taiwan
72A3 Pingwu China
73B5 Pingxiang Guangxi, China
73C4 Pingxiang Jiangxi, China
31B2 Pinheiro Brazil
70A3 Pini I Indon
55B3 Piniós R Greece
106A4 Pinjarra Aust
13C1 Pink Mountain Can
100B3 Pinnaroo Aust
Pinos,I de, I = Isla de la Juventud
21A2 Pinos,Pt USA
23B2 Pinotepa Nacional Mexico
70C4 Pinrang Indon
60C3 Pinsk Belarus
32J7 Pinta I Ecuador
61G1 Pinyug Russian Fed
8B3 Pioche USA
52B2 Piombino Italy
6H3 Piórsá Iceland
59B2 Piotrków Trybunalski Pol
44E2 Piper Oilfield N Sea
21B2 Piper Peak USA
10C2 Pipmuacan Res Can
14B2 Piqua USA
35B1 Piracicuba Brazil
35B2 Piracicaba Brazil

35B2 Piraçununga Brazil
35B2 Piraí do Sul Brazil
55B3 Piraiévs Greece
35B2 Pirajuí Brazil
35A1 Piranhas Brazil
35C1 Pirapora Brazil
35B1 Pirenópolis Brazil
35B1 Pires do Rio Brazil
55B3 Pírgos Greece
Pirineos = Pyrénées
31C2 Piripiri Brazil
46D2 Pirmasens Germany
54B2 Pirot Serbia, Yugos
84C2 Pir Panjäl Range Mts Pak
71D4 Piru Indon
22C3 Piru Creek R USA
49E3 Pisa Italy
32B6 Pisco Peru
57C3 Písek Czech Republic
84B2 Pishin Pak
34C3 Pissis Mt Arg
49E3 Pistoia Italy
50B1 Pisuerga R Spain
20B2 Pit R USA
32B3 Pitalito Colombia
105K5 Pitcairn I Pacific O
38H5 Pite R Sweden
38J5 Piteå Sweden
54B2 Piteşti Rom
63B2 Pit Gorodok Russian Fed
38L6 Pitkyaranta Russian Fed
44C3 Pitlochry Scot
34A3 Pitrufquen Chile
13B2 Pitt I Can
22B1 Pittsburg California, USA
18B2 Pittsburg Kansas, USA
14C2 Pittsburgh USA
18B2 Pittsfield Illinois, USA
16C1 Pittsfield Massachusetts, USA
109D1 Pittsworth Aust
86A1 Piuthan Nepal
47D1 Pizzo Redorta Mt Italy
38B2 Þjórsá Iceland
32A5 Pjura Peru
7E5 Placentia B Can
22B1 Placerville USA
46B1 Plaine des Flandres Plain Belg/France
96C2 Plaine du Tidikelt Desert Region
9C3 Plainview Texas, USA
22B2 Planada USA
30F2 Planalto de Mato Grosso Plat Brazil
31D3 Planalto do Borborema Plat Brazil
32A1 Planalto do Mato Grosso Mts Brazil
19A3 Plano USA
17B2 Plantation USA
17B2 Plant City USA
50A1 Plasencia Spain
61K3 Plast Russian Fed
69F2 Plastun Russian Fed
96C2 Plateau du Tademait Alg
46D2 Plateau Lorrain Plat France
48C2 Plateaux de Limousin Plat France
51C2 Plateaux du Sersou Plat Alg
26C5 Plato Colombia
8C2 Platte R USA
15D2 Plattsburgh USA
18A1 Plattsmouth USA
57C2 Plauen Germany
60E3 Plavsk Russian Fed
23A2 Playa Azul Mexico
32A4 Playas Ecuador
23B2 Playa Vicente Mexico
50A1 Plaza de Moro Almanzor Mt Spain

22B2 Pleasanton California, USA
16B3 Pleasantville USA
14A3 Pleasure Ridge Park USA
76D3 Pleiku Viet
110C1 Plenty,B of NZ
58B2 Pleszew Pol
7C4 Pletipi,L Can
54B2 Pleven Bulg
54A2 Pljevlja Montenegro, Yugos
52C2 Ploče Croatia
52B2 Płock Pol
48B2 Ploërmel France
54C2 Ploieşti Rom
60B3 Płońsk Pol
54C2 Plovdiv Bulg
20C1 Plummer USA
12C2 Plummer,Mt USA
100B3 Plumtree Zim
22B1 Plymouth California, USA
43B4 Plymouth Eng
14A2 Plymouth Indiana, USA
16D2 Plymouth Massachusetts, USA
15C2 Plymouth Pennsylvania, USA
43B4 Plymouth Sd Eng
43C3 Plynlimon Mt Wales
57C3 Plzeň Czech Republic
58B2 Pniewy Pol
38K6 Pnyäselkä L Fin
97B3 Pô Burkina
47E2 Po R Italy
97C4 Pobé Benin
69G2 Pobedino Russian Fed
8B2 Pocatello USA
15C3 Pocomoke City USA
35B2 Pocos de Caldas Brazil
54A2 Podgorica Montenegro, Yugos
47D2 Po di Volano R Italy
63B1 Podkamennaya R Russian Fed
60E2 Podol'sk Russian Fed
59D3 Podol'skaya Vozvyshennost' Upland Ukraine
60D1 Podporozh'ye Russian Fed
61F1 Podyuga Russian Fed
100A3 Pofadder S Africa
74B3 P'ohang S Korea
112C9 Poinsett,C Ant
108C2 Point Aust
27E3 Pointe-à-Pitre Guadeloupe
48B2 Pointe de Barfleur Pt France
98B3 Pointe Noire Congo
98A2 Pointe Pongara Pt Gabon
108B3 Point Fairy Aust
27L1 Point Fortin Trinidad
4B3 Point Hope USA
4G3 Point L Can
12B1 Point Lay USA
16D2 Point Pleasant New Jersey, USA
14B3 Point Pleasant W Virginia, USA
47B2 Point St Bernard Mt France
48C2 Poitiers France
48B2 Poitou Region, France
46A2 Poix France
85C3 Pokaran India
109C1 Pokataroo Aust
61G3 Pokrovsk Russian Fed
63E1 Pokrovsk Russian Fed
58B2 Poland Republic, Europe
92B2 Polatli Turk
78D3 Polewali Indon
47A1 Poligny France
55B2 Políyiros Greece

87B2 Pollachi India
79B3 Pololo Is Phil
59D2 Polonnye Ukraine
58D1 Polotsk Russian Fed
60D4 Poltava Russian Fed
52C1 Polten Austria
64F3 Poluostrov Kanin Pen Russian Fed
61H5 Poluostrov Mangyshlak Pen Kazakhstan
38L5 Poluostrov Rybachiy Pen Russian Fed
64H2 Poluostrov Yamal Pen Russian Fed
38L5 Polyarnyy Murmansk, Russian Fed
1B8 Polyarnyy Yakutskaya, Russian Fed
105H3 Polynesia Region Pacific O
32B5 Pomabamba Peru
35C2 Pomba R Brazil
22D3 Pomona USA
18A2 Pomona Res USA
17B2 Pompano Beach USA
18B2 Pompton Lakes USA
18A2 Ponca City USA
27D3 Ponce Puerto Rico
17B2 Ponce de Leon B USA
87B2 Pondicherry India
6C2 Pond Inlet Can
50A1 Ponferrade Spain
98C2 Pongo R Sudan
101H1 Pongola R S Africa
86C2 Ponnaydoung Range Mts Myan
13E2 Ponoka Can
64F3 Ponoy Russian Fed
48B2 Pons France
35D1 Ponta da Baleia Pt Brazil
96A1 Ponta Delgada Açores
98B3 Ponta do Padrão Pt Angola
35C2 Ponta dos Búzios Pt Brazil
30F4 Ponta Grossa Brazil
35B2 Pontal Brazil
46D2 Pont-à-Mousson France
30E3 Ponta Pora Brazil
49D2 Pontarlier France
19B3 Pontchartrain,L USA
52B2 Pontedera Italy
52B2 Ponte Leccia Corse
50A1 Pontevedra Spain
18C1 Pontiac Illinois, USA
14B2 Pontiac Michigan, USA
78B3 Pontianak Indon
48B2 Pontivy France
46B2 Pontoise France
57C3 Pontotoc USA
43C4 Pontrypool Wales
43C4 Pontypridd Wales
43D4 Poole Eng
Poona = Pune
108B2 Pooncarie Aust
108B2 Poopelloe,L L Aust
12C2 Poorman USA
32B3 Popayán Colombia
46B1 Poperinge Belg
108B2 Popilta,L Aust
18B2 Poplar Bluff USA
19C3 Poplarville USA
107D1 Popndetta PNG
23B2 Popocatepetl Mt Mexico
98B3 Popokabaka Zaire
71F4 Popondetta PNG
54C2 Popovo Bulg
86B4 Porbandar India
13A2 Porcher I Can
12F1 Porcupine R Can/USA

52B1	Poreč Croatia
35A2	Porecatu Brazil
39J6	Pori Fin
111B2	Porirua NZ
38H5	Porjus Sweden
69G2	Poronaysk Russian Fed
47B1	Porrentruy Switz
38K4	Porsangen Inlet Nor
39F7	Porsgrunn Nor
45C1	Portadown N Ire
8D2	Portage la Prairie Can
13C3	Port Alberni Can
50A2	Portalegre Port
9C3	Portales USA
108B4	Port Alfred S Africa
13B2	Port Alice Can
13B2	Port Allen USA
20B1	Port Angeles USA
26B3	Port Antonio Jamaica
45C2	Portarlington Irish Rep
108A2	Port Arthur USA
108A2	Port Augusta Aust
26C3	Port-au-Prince Haiti
14B2	Port Austin USA
108B3	Port Campbell Aust
86B2	Port Canning India
7D5	Port Cartier Can
111A1	Port Chalmers NZ
17B2	Port Charlotte USA
16C2	Port Chester USA
15C2	Port Colborne Can
15C2	Port Credit Can
109C4	Port Davey B Aust
26C3	Port-de-Paix Haiti
77C5	Port Dickson Malay
100C4	Port Edward S Africa
35C1	Porteirinha Brazil
14B2	Port Elgin Can
100B4	Port Elizabeth S Africa
27N2	Porter Pt St Vincent and the Grenadines
21B2	Porterville USA
107D4	Port Fairy Aust
98A3	Port Gentil Gabon
19B3	Port Gibson USA
12D3	Port Graham USA
20B1	Port Hammond Can
89E7	Port Harcourt Nig
13B2	Port Hardy Can
7D5	Port Hawkesbury Can
106A3	Port Hedland Aust
	Port Heiden = Meshik
43B3	Porthmadog Wales
7E4	Port Hope Simpson Can
22C3	Port Hueneme USA
14B2	Port Huron USA
50A2	Portimão Port
109D2	Port Jackson B Aust
16C2	Port Jefferson USA
16B2	Port Jervis USA
109D2	Port Kembla Aust
14B2	Portland Indiana, USA
10C2	Portland Maine, USA
109C4	Portland New South Wales, Aust
20B1	Portland Oregon, USA
108B3	Portland Victoria, Aust
27H2	Portland Bight B Jamaica
43C4	Portland Bill Pt Eng
109C4	Portland,C Aust
13A1	Portland Canal Can/USA
110C1	Portland I NZ
27H2	Portland Pt Jamaica
45C2	Port Laoise Irish Rep
108A2	Port Lincoln Aust
97A4	Port Loko Sierra Leone
101E3	Port Louis Mauritius
108B3	Port MacDonnell Aust
13B2	Port McNeill Can

109D2	Port Macquarie Aust
12B3	Port Moller USA
107D1	Port Moresby PNG
100A3	Port Nolloth S Africa
16B3	Port Norris USA
89E7	Port Novo Benin
50A1	Porto Port
30F5	Pôrto Alegre Brazil
33F6	Pôrto Artur Brazil
30F3	Pôrto E Cunha Brazil
52B2	Portoferraio Italy
27E4	Port of Spain Trinidad
47D2	Portomaggiore Italy
97C4	Porto Novo Benin
20B1	Port Orchard USA
20B2	Port Orford USA
96A1	Porto Santo I Medeira
31D5	Pôrto Seguro Brazil
53A2	Porto Torres Sardegna
53A2	Porto Vecchio Corse
33E5	Pôrto Velho Brazil
111A3	Port Pegasus B NZ
108B3	Port Phillip B Aust
108A2	Port Pirie Aust
44A3	Portree Scot
20B1	Port Renfrew Can
27J2	Port Royal Jamaica
17B1	Port Royal Sd USA
45C1	Portrush N Ire
92B3	Port Saïd Egypt
17A2	Port St Joe USA
100B4	Port St Johns S Africa
7E4	Port Saunders Can
100C4	Port Shepstone S Africa
13A2	Port Simpson Can
27Q2	Portsmouth Dominica
11C3	Portsmouth Eng
14B3	Portsmouth Ohio, USA
11C3	Portsmouth Virginia, USA
109D2	Port Stephens B Aust
95C3	Port Sudan Sudan
19C3	Port Sulphur USA
38K5	Porttipahta Tekojärvi Res Fin
50A2	Portugal Republic, Europe
77C5	Port Weld Malay
32D6	Porvenir Bol
39K6	Porvoo Fin
30E4	Posadas Arg
50D2	Posadas Spain
47D1	Poschiavo Switz
6B2	Posheim Pen Can
90C3	Posht-e Badam Iran
71D4	Poso Indon
58D1	Postavy Belarus
14B2	Post Clinton USA
100B3	Postmasburg S Africa
52B1	Postojna Slovenia
74C2	Pos'yet Russian Fed
101G1	Potchetstroom S Africa
19B2	Poteau USA
53C2	Potenza Italy
100B3	Potgietersrus S Africa
89D4	Potiskum Nig
20C1	Potlatch USA
30C2	Potosi R USA
30C4	Potorillos Chile
56C2	Potsdam Germany
16B2	Pottstown USA
16B2	Pottsville USA
16C2	Poughkeepsie USA
35B2	Pouso Alegre Brazil
110C1	Poverty B NZ
61F3	Povorino Russian Fed
7C4	Povungnituk Can
8C2	Powder R USA
106C2	Powell Creek Aust

9B3	Powell,L USA
13C3	Powell River Can
8C2	Power R USA
43C3	Powys County, Wales
73D4	Poyang Hu L China
92B2	Pozantí Turk
23B1	Poza Rica Mexico
52B2	Poznań Pol
30E3	Pozo Colorado Par
53B2	Pozzuoli Italy
97B4	Pra R Ghana
76C3	Prachin Buri Thai
76B3	Prachuap Khiri Khan Thai
59B2	Praděd Mt Czech Republic
49C3	Pradelles France
35D1	Prado Brazil
	Prague = Praha
57C2	Praha Czech Republic
97A4	Praia Cape Verde
33E5	Prainha Brazil
18B2	Prairie Village USA
76C3	Prakhon Chai Thai
35B1	Prata Brazil
35B1	Prata R Brazil
	Prates = Dongsha Qundao
49E3	Prato Italy
16B1	Prattsville USA
17A1	Prattville USA
48B1	Prawle Pt Eng
78D4	Praya Indon
47D1	Predazzo Italy
63B2	Predivinsk Russian Fed
58C2	Pregolya R Russian Fed
76D3	Prek Kak Camb
56C2	Prenzlau Germany
76A2	Preparis I Myan
76A2	Preparis North Chan Myan
59B3	Přerov Czech Republic
23A2	Presa del Infiernillo Mexico
9B3	Prescott Arizona, USA
19B3	Prescott Arkansas, USA
15C2	Prescott Can
30D4	Presidencia Roque Sáenz Peña Arg
35A2	Presidente Epitácio Brazil
112C2	Presidente Frei Base Ant
23B2	Presidente Miguél Aleman L Mexico
35A2	Presidente Prudente Brazil
35A2	Presidente Venceslau Brazil
59B3	Prešov Slovakia
55B2	Prespansko Jezero L Macedonia, Yugos
10D2	Presque Isle USA
42C3	Preston Eng
8B2	Preston Idaho, USA
18B2	Preston Missouri, USA
42B2	Prestwick Scot
31B6	Prêto Brazil
35B1	Prêto R Brazil
101G1	Pretoria S Africa
55B3	Préveza Greece
76D3	Prey Veng Camb
8B3	Price USA
13B2	Price I Can
60D4	Prichernomorskaya Nizmennost' Lowland Ukraine
27M2	Prickly Pt Grenada
58C1	Priekule Lithuania
100B3	Prieska S Africa
20C1	Priest L USA
20C1	Priest River USA
55B2	Prilep Macedonia, Yugos
60D3	Priluki Ukraine
34C2	Primero R Arg

39K6	Primorsk Russian Fed
60E4	Primorsko-Akhtarsk Russian Fed
13F2	Primrose L Can
5H4	Prince Albert Can
4F2	Prince Albert,C Can
4G2	Prince Albert Pen Can
4G2	Prince Albert Sd Can
6C3	Prince Charles I Can
112B10	Prince Charles Mts Ant
7D5	Prince Edward I Can
13C2	Prince George Can
4H2	Prince Gustaf Adolp S Can
5E4	Prince of Wales I Can
71F5	Prince of Wales I Aust
4H2	Prince of Wales I Can
4G2	Prince of Wales Str Can
4F2	Prince Patrick I Can
6A2	Prince Regent Inlet Str Can
13A2	Prince Rupert Can
107D2	Princess Charlotte B Aust
13B2	Princess Royal I Can
27L1	Princes Town Trinidad
13C3	Princeton Can
18C2	Princeton Kentucky, USA
18B1	Princeton Missouri, USA
16B2	Princeton New Jersey, USA
4D3	Prince William USA
12E2	Prince William Sd USA
97C4	Principe I W Africa
20B2	Prineville USA
12E1	Pringle,Mt USA
6F3	Prins Christian Sund Sd Greenland
112B12	Prinsesse Astrid Kyst Region, Ant
112B12	Prinsesse Ragnhild Kyst Region, Ant
64B2	Prins Karls Forland I Barents S
25D3	Prinzapolca Nic
58D2	Pripet R Belarus
54B2	Pripyat' = Pripet
	Priština Serbia, Yugos
56C2	Pritzwalk Germany
61F3	Privolzhskaya Vozvyshennost' Upland Russian Fed
54B2	Prizren Serbia, Yugos
78C4	Probolinggo Indon
5G5	Procatello USA
87B2	Proddatūr India
25D2	Progreso Mexico
20B2	Project City USA
61F5	Prokhladnyy Russian Fed
61F4	Prokop'yevsk Russian Fed
61F4	Proletarskaya Russian Fed
64G2	Proliv Karskiye Vorota Str Can
	Prome = Pye
31D4	Propriá Brazil
20B2	Prospect Oregon, USA
107D3	Proserpine Aust
59B3	Prostějov Czech Republic
6E2	Prøven Greenland
49D3	Provence Region, France
16D2	Providence USA
15D2	Provincetown USA
49C2	Provins France
8B2	Provo USA

Provost

13E2 **Provost** Can
4D2 **Prudhoe Bay** USA
6D2 **Prudhoe Land**
Greenland
58C2 **Pruszkow** Pol
60C4 **Prut** R Romania/
Moldova
60C4 **Prutul** R Romania
52C3 **Pruzhany** Belarus
18A2 **Pryor** USA
59C3 **Przemys'l** Pol
55C3 **Psará** I Greece
60C2 **Pskov** Russian Fed
57B4 **Ptich** R Belarus
55B2 **Ptolemais** Greece
32C5 **Pucallpa** Peru
73D4 **Pucheng** China
34A3 **Pucón** Chile
38K5 **Pudasjärvi** Fin
87B2 **Pudukkottai** India
23B2 **Puebla** Mexico
23B2 **Puebla** State, Mexico
50A1 **Puebla de Sanabria**
Spain
50A1 **Puebla de Trives**
Spain
9C2 **Pueblo** USA
34B3 **Puelches** Arg
34B3 **Puelén** Arg
23A2 **Puenta Ixbapa**
Mexico
34B2 **Puente del Inca** Arg
32A5 **Puerta Aguja** Peru
30B2 **Puerta Coles** Peru
34B2 **Puerta de los Llanos**
Arg
31D3 **Puerta do Calcanhar**
Pt Brazil
32C1 **Puerta Gallinas**
Colombia
23B2 **Puerta Maldonado** Pt
Mexico
32A2 **Puerta Mariato**
Panama
29C5 **Puerta Médanosa** Pt
Arg
23A2 **Puerta Mongrove**
Mexico
25E4 **Puerta San Blas** Pt
Panama
23A2 **Puerta San Telmo**
Mexico
29B5 **Puerto Aisén** Chile
25D4 **Puerto Armuelles**
Panama
33F6 **Puerto Artur** Brazil
32B3 **Puerto Asis**
Colombia
32D2 **Puerto Ayacucho**
Ven
25D3 **Puerto Barrios**
Guatemala
32C2 **Puerto Berrio**
Colombia
32D1 **Puerto Cabello** Ven
25D3 **Puerto Cabezas** Nic
32D2 **Puerto Carreño**
Colombia
25D4 **Puerto Cortés** Costa
Rica
25D3 **Puerto Cortés**
Honduras
96A2 **Puerto del Rosario**
Canary Is
30F3 **Puerto E Cunha**
Brazil
32C1 **Puerto Fijo** Ven
31B3 **Puerto Franco** Brazil
32D6 **Puerto Heath** Bol
25D2 **Puerto Juarez**
Mexico
33E1 **Puerto la Cruz** Ven
50B2 **Puertollano** Spain
27C4 **Puerto Lopez**
Colombia
29D4 **Puerto Madryn** Arg
32D6 **Puerto Maldonado**
Peru
23B2 **Puerto Marquéz**
Mexico
29B4 **Puerto Montt** Chile
30E3 **Puerto Murtinho**
Brazil
29B6 **Puerto Natales** Chile

24A1 **Puerto Peñasco**
Mexico
29D4 **Puerto Pirámides**
Arg
27C3 **Puerto Plata** Dom
Rep
79A4 **Puerto Princesa** Phil
32B3 **Puerto Rico**
Colombia
27D3 **Puerto Rico** I
Caribbean S
27D3 **Puerto Rico Trench**
Caribbean S
23A2 **Puerto San Juan de
Lima** Mexico
33G4 **Puerto Santana**
Brazil
30E2 **Puerto Suárez** Bol
24B2 **Puerto Vallarta**
Mexico
29B4 **Puerto Varas** Chile
30D2 **Puerto Villarroel** Bol
61G3 **Pugachev**
Russian Fed
84C3 **Pugal** India
51C1 **Puigcerdá** Spain
111B2 **Pukaki,L** NZ
74B2 **Pukch'ŏng** N Korea
110B1 **Pukekohe** NZ
111B2 **Puketeraki Range**
Mts NZ
52B2 **Pula** Croatia
15C2 **Pulaski** New York,
USA
11E4 **Pulau Kolepom** I
Indon
70A4 **Pulau Pulau Batu** Is
Indon
58C2 **Pulawy** Pol
87C2 **Pulicat,L** India
84B1 **Pul-i-Khumri** Afghan
87B3 **Puliyangudi** India
20C1 **Pullman** USA
71E3 **Pulo Anna Merir** I
Pacific O
79B2 **Pulog,Mt** Phil
38L5 **Pulozero** Russian Fed
58C2 **Pultusk** Pol
30C4 **Puna de Atacama**
Arg
86B1 **Punakha** Bhutan
84C2 **Punch** Pak
87A1 **Pune** India
23A2 **Puneper** Mexico
98C3 **Puna** Zaire
34A2 **Punitaqui** Chile
84C2 **Punjab** Province, Pak
84D2 **Punjab** State, India
30B2 **Puno** Peru
24A2 **Punta Abreojos** Pt
Mexico
53C3 **Punta Alice** Pt Italy
34A1 **Punta Alta** Arg
29B6 **Punta Arenas** Chile
24A2 **Punta Baja** Pt
Mexico
34A2 **Punta Curaumilla** Pt
Chile
100A2 **Punta da Marca** Pt
Angola
101C3 **Punta da Barra Falsa**
Pt Mozam
29F2 **Punta del Este** Urug
24A2 **Punta Eugenia** Pt
Mexico
25D3 **Punta Gorda** Belize
17B2 **Punta Gorda** USA
34A3 **Punta Lavapié** Pt
Chile
34A2 **Punta Lengua de
Vaca** Pt Chile
53B2 **Punta Licosa** Pt Italy
34A1 **Punta Poroto** Pt
Chile
9B4 **Punta San Antonia** Pt
Chile
34A2 **Punta Topocalma**
Chile
73C4 **Puqi** China
64J3 **Pur** R Russian Fed
19A2 **Purcell** USA
12C1 **Purcell Mt** USA
13D2 **Purcell Mts** Can
34A3 **Purén** Chile

86B2 **Puri** India
87B1 **Pūrna** India
86B1 **Pūrnia** India
76C3 **Pursat** Camb
23A1 **Puruandro** Mexico
33E4 **Purus** R Brazil
19C3 **Purvis** USA
78B4 **Purwokerto** Indon
78C4 **Purworejo** Indon
85D5 **Pusad** India
74B3 **Pusan** S Korea
60D2 **Pushkin** Russian Fed
58D1 **Pustoshka**
Russian Fed
82D3 **Puta** Myan
34A2 **Putaendo** Chile
110C1 **Putaruru** NZ
72D3 **Putian** China
16D2 **Putnam** USA
87B3 **Puttalam** Sri Lanka
56C2 **Puttgarden** Germany
32B4 **Putumayo** R
Ecuador
78C2 **Putussibau** Indon
38K6 **Puulavesi** L Fin
20B1 **Puyallup** USA
49C2 **Puy de Sancy** Mt
France
111A3 **Puysegur Pt** NZ
99C3 **Pweto** Zaire
43B3 **Pwllheli** Wales
76B2 **Pyapon** Myan
61F5 **Pyatigorsk**
Russian Fed
83D4 **Pyè** Myan
74B3 **P'yŏngyang** N Korea
108B3 **Pyramid Hill** Aust
21B1 **Pyramid L** USA
111A2 **Pyramid,Mt** NZ
48B3 **Pyrénées** Mts France
76B2 **Pytalovo** Russian Fed
76B2 **Pyu** Myan

Q

94B2 **Qabatiya** Israel
94C3 **Qa'el Hafira** Mud
Flats Jordan
94C3 **Qa'el Jinz** Mud Flats
Jordan
68B3 **Qaidam Pendi** Salt
Flat China
94C2 **Qa Khanna** Salt
Marsh Jordan
99D1 **Qala'en Nahl** Sudan
84B2 **Qalat** Afghan
94C1 **Qal'at al Hisn** Syria
81C3 **Qal'at Bishah**
S Arabia
93E3 **Qal'at Sälih** Iraq
68B3 **Qamdo** China
99E1 **Qandala** Somalia
95B2 **Qara** Egypt
90A3 **Qare Shirin** Iran
91A4 **Qaryat al Ulyä**
S Arabia
94C3 **Qasr el Kharana**
Jordan
91D4 **Qasr-e-Qand** Iran
95B2 **Qasr Farafra** Egypt
94C2 **Qatana** Syria
91A4 **Qatar** Emirate,
Arabian Pen
94C3 **Qaträna** Jordan
95B2 **Qattâra Depression**
Egypt
90C3 **Qâyen** Iran
90A2 **Qazvin** Iran
95C2 **Qena** Egypt
90A2 **Qeydär** Iran
91B4 **Qeys** I Iran
94B3 **Qeziot** Israel
73B5 **Qian Jiang** R China
72E1 **Qian Shan** Upland
China
72E3 **Qidong** China
73B4 **Qijiang** China
84B2 **Qila Saifullah** Pak
72A2 **Qilian** China
68B3 **Qilian Shan** China
72B3 **Qin'an** China
72E2 **Qingdao** China
72A2 **Qinghai** Province,
China

68B3 **Qinghai Hu** L China
72D3 **Qingjiang** Jiangsu,
China
73D4 **Qingjiang** Jiangxi,
China
73B4 **Qing Jiang** R China
72C2 **Qingshuihe** China
72B2 **Qingshui He** R China
72B2 **Qingtonxia** China
72B2 **Qingyang** China
72A3 **Qingyuan** Liaoning,
China
73D4 **Qingyuan** Zhejiang,
China
82C2 **Qing Zang** Upland
China
72D2 **Qinhuangdao** China
72B3 **Qin Ling** Mts China
73B5 **Qinzhou** China
76E2 **Qionghai** China
73A3 **Qionglai Shan**
Upland China
76D1 **Qiongzhou Haixia** Str
China
69E2 **Qiqihar** China
94B2 **Qiryat Ata** Israel
94B3 **Qiryat Gat** Israel
94B2 **Qiryat Shemona**
Israel
94B2 **Qiryat Yam** Israel
94B2 **Qishon** R Israel
63A3 **Qitai** China
73C4 **Qiyang** China
72B1 **Qog Qi** China
90B2 **Qolleh-ye Damavand**
Mt Iran
90B3 **Qom** Iran
90B3 **Qomisheh** Iran
Qomolangma Feng =
Everest,Mt
94C1 **Qornet es Saouda** Mt
Leb
6E3 **Qôrnoq** Greenland
90A2 **Qorveh** Iran
91C4 **Qotbäbad** Iran
16C1 **Quabbin Res** USA
11A4 **Quakertown** USA
77C3 **Quam Phu Quoc** I
Viet
76D2 **Quang Ngai** Viet
76D2 **Quang Tri** Viet
77D4 **Quan Long** Viet
73D5 **Quanzhou** Fujian,
China
73C4 **Quanzhou** Guangxi,
China
5H4 **Qu' Appelle** R Can
91C5 **Quarayyät** Oman
13B2 **Quatsino Sd** Can
90C2 **Quchan** Iran
109C3 **Queanbeyan** Aust
15D1 **Québec** Can
7C4 **Quebec** Province,
Can
35B1 **Quebra-Anzol** R
Brazil
34D2 **Quebracho** Urug
30F4 **Quedas do Iguaçu**
Brazil/Arg
16A3 **Queen Anne** USA
13B2 **Queen Bess,Mt** Can
5E4 **Queen Charlotte** Is
Can
13B2 **Queen Charlotte Sd**
Can
13B2 **Queen Charlotte Str**
Can
4H1 **Queen Elizabeth Is**
Can
112B9 **Queen Mary Land**
Region, Ant
4H3 **Queen Maud G** Can
112A **Queen Maud Mts** Ant
16C2 **Queens** Borough,
New York, USA
108B3 **Queenscliff** Aust
107D3 **Queensland** State,
Aust
109C4 **Queenstown** Aust
111A3 **Queenstown** NZ
100B4 **Queenstown** S Africa
16A3 **Queenstown** USA
98B3 **Quela** Angola
101C2 **Quelimane** Mozam

34C3 Quemuquemú Arg
13C2 Quensel L Can
34D3 Quequén Arg
34D3 Quequén R Arg
23A1 Querétaro Mexico
23A1 Querétaro *State Mexico
13C2 Quesnel Can
64B2 Quetta Pak
25C3 Quezaltenango Guatemala
79B3 Quezon City Phil
100A2 Quibala Angola
32B2 Quibdó Colombia
48B2 Quiberon France
98B3 Quicama Nat Pk Angola
73A4 Quijing Chile
34A2 Quilima Chile
34C2 Quilino Arg
32C6 Quillabamba Peru
30C2 Quillacollo Bol
48C3 Quillan France
5H4 Quill L Can
5H4 Quill Lakes Can
34A2 Quillota Chile
108B1 Quilon India
10B3 Quilpie Aust
34A2 Quilpué Chile
98B3 Quimbele Angola
48B2 Quimper France
48B2 Quimperlé France
21A2 Quincy California, USA
10A3 Quincy Illinois, USA
16D1 Quincy Massachusetts, USA
34B2 Quines Arg
12B3 Quinhagak USA
76D3 Qui Nhon Viet
50B2 Quintanar de la Orden Spain
34A2 Quintero Chile
34C2 Quinto R Arg
34A3 Quiorine Chile
100A2 Quirima Angola
109D2 Quirindi Aust
101C3 Quissanga Mozam
101C3 Quissico Mozam
32B4 Quito Ecuador
31D2 Quixadá Brazil
108A2 Quorn Aust
4G3 Qurlurtuuk Can
95C2 Quseir Egypt
6E3 Qutdligssat Greenland
Quthing = Moyeni
73B3 Qu Xian Sichuan, China
73D4 Qu Xian Zhejiang, China
76D2 Quynh Luu Viet
72C2 Quzhou China
66C1 Qüzü China

R
38J6 Raahe Fin
44A3 Raasay I Scot
44A3 Raasay,Sound of Chan Scot
99F1 Raas Caseyr C Somalia
52B2 Rab I Croatia
78D4 Raba Indon
59B3 Rába R Hung
94B3 Rabba Jordan
80B3 Rabigh S Arabia
47B2 Racconigi Italy
7E5 Race,C C
34A2 Rachaya Leb
57C3 Rachel Mt Germany
76D3 Rach Gia Viet
14A2 Racine USA
59D3 Rădăuţi Rom
85C4 Radhanpur India
27L1 Radix,Pt Trinidad
58C2 Radom Pol
59B2 Radomsko Pol
58C1 Radviliskis Lithuania
4G3 Rae Can
86A1 Rãe Bareli India
6B3 Rae Isthmus Can

4G3 Rae L Can
110C1 Raetihi NZ
34C2 Rafaela Arg
94B3 Rafah Egypt
98C2 Rafai CAR
93D3 Rafhã Al Jumaymah S Arabia
91C3 Rafsanjãn Iran
98C2 Raga Sudan
27R3 Ragged Pt Barbados
53B3 Ragusa Italy
99D1 Rahad R Sudan
84C3 Rahimyar Khan Pak
90B3 Rãhjerd Iran
34D2 Raices Arg
86A2 Rãichur India
86A2 Rãigarh India
108B3 Rainbow Aust
17A1 Rainbow City USA
20B1 Rainier USA
20B1 Rainier,Mt USA
10A2 Rainy L Can
12D2 Rainy P USA
10A2 Rainy River Can
86A2 Raipur India
87C1 Rãjahmundry India
78C2 Rajang R Malay
87B1 Rãjapalaiyam India
85C3 Rãjasthan, State, India
84D3 Rãjgarh India
85C4 Rãjgarh State, India
85C4 Rãjkot India
86B2 Rãjmahãl Hills India
86A2 Raj Nãndgaon India
85C4 Rãjpipla India
86B2 Rãjshahi Bang
85D4 Rãjur India
111B2 Rakaia R NZ
78B4 Rakata I Indon
86C2 Raka Zangbo R China
59C3 Rakhov Ukraine
100B3 Rakops Botswana
58D2 Rakov Belarus
11C3 Raleigh USA
7A5 Ralny L Can
94B2 Rama Israel
94B3 Ramallah Israel
87B2 Rãmanãthapuram India
69G3 Ramapo Deep Pacific O
94B2 Ramat Gan Israel
46A2 Rambouillet France
86B2 Rãmgarh Bihar, India
85C3 Rãmgarh Rajosthan, India
90A3 Rãmhormoz Iran
94B3 Ramla Indon
91C5 Ramlat Al Wahibah Region, Oman
21B3 Ramona USA
84D3 Rãmpur India
85A3 Rãmpura India
90B2 Rãmsar Iran
42B2 Ramsey Eng
16B2 Ramsey USA
43B4 Ramsey I Wales
43E4 Ramsgate Eng
94C2 Ramtha Jordan
71F4 Ramu R PNG
34A2 Rancagua Chile
101G1 Randburg S Africa
39G7 Randers Den
101G1 Randfontein S Africa
15D2 Randolph Vermont, USA
111B3 Ranfurly NZ
86C2 Rangamati Bang
110C1 Rangiora NZ
111B2 Rangitata R NZ
110C1 Rangitikei R NZ
Rangoon = Yangon
86B1 Rangpur India
87B2 Rãnibennur India
94B3 Ranier,Mt Mt USA
86B2 Rãniganj India
109C2 Rankins Springs Aust
6A3 Ranklin Inlet Can

85B4 Rann of Kachchh Flood Area India
77B4 Ranong Thai
70A3 Rantauparapat Indon
18C1 Rantoul USA
49D3 Rapallo Italy
34A2 Rapel R Chile
6D3 Raper,C Can
8C2 Rapid City USA
15C3 Rapid River USA
15C3 Rappahannock R USA
47C1 Rapperswil Switz
16B2 Raritan B USA
95C2 Ras Abu Shagara C Sudan
93D2 Ra's al 'Ayn Syria
91C5 Ra's al Hadd C Oman
91C4 Ras al Kaimah UAE
91C4 Ras-al-Kuh C Iran
81D4 Ra's al Madrakah C Oman
91A4 Ra's az Zawr C S Arabia
95C2 Rãs Bãnas C Egypt
94A3 Ras Burún C Egypt
99D1 Ras Dashan Mt Eth
90A3 Ra's-e-Barkan Pt Iran
92A3 Rãs el Kenãyis Pt Egypt
81D4 Ra's Fartak C Yemen
95C2 Rãs Ghãrib Egypt
99D1 Rashad Sudan
94B3 Rashãdiya Jordan
92B3 Rashid Egypt
90A2 Rasht Iran
91C5 Ra's Jibish C Oman
99E1 Ras Khanzira C Somalia
84B3 Ras Koh Mt Pak
95C2 Rãs Muhammad C Egypt
96A2 Ras Nouadhibou C Maur
69H2 Rasshua I Russian Fed
61F3 Rasskazovo Russian Fed
91A4 Ra's Tanãqib C S Arabia
91B4 Ra's Tannúrah S Arabia
57B3 Rastatt Germany
Ras Uarc = Cabo Tres Forcas
99F1 Ras Xaafuun C Somalia
84B3 Ratangarh India
76B3 Rat Buri Thai
85D3 Rath India
57C2 Rathenow Germany
45B2 Rathkeale Irish Rep
45C1 Rathlin I N Ire
45B2 Rath Luirc Irish Rep
85D4 Ratlam India
87A1 Ratnãgiri India
87C3 Ratnapura Sri Lanka
58C2 Ratno Ukraine
47D1 Rattenberg Austria
39H6 Rättvik Sweden
22A2 Raul Soares Brazil
39J6 Rauma Fin
86A2 Raurkela India
90A3 Rãvãnsar Iran
90C3 Rãvar Iran
59C2 Rava Russkaya Ukraine
16C1 Ravena USA
52B2 Ravenna Italy
57B3 Ravensburg Germany
107D2 Ravenshoe Aust
42E2 Ravenspurn Oilfield N Sea
91A4 Rãvi R Pak
84C2 Rãwalpindi Pak
93D2 Rawãndúz Iraq
58B2 Rawicz Pol
106B4 Rawlinna Aust

8C2 Rawlins USA
29C4 Rawson Arg
78C3 Raya Mt Indon
87B2 Rãyadurg India
94C2 Rayak Leb
7E5 Ray,C Can
91C4 Rãyen Iran
22C2 Raymond California, USA
20B1 Raymond Washington, USA
109D2 Raymond Terrace Aust
12D1 Ray Mts USA
23B1 Rayon Mexico
90A2 Razan Iran
53B2 Razgrad Bulg
21C1 Razim L Rom
16B2 Reading Eng
16B2 Reading USA
4G3 Read Island Can
16C1 Readsboro USA
16C1 Real de Padre Arg
34C3 Realicó Arg
95B2 Rebiana Well Libya
95B2 Rebiana Sand Sea Libya
38L6 Reboly Russian Fed
106B4 Recherche,Arch of the Is Aust
31E3 Recife Brazil
107F2 Récifs D'Entrecasteaux Nouvelle Calédonie
46D1 Recklinghausen Germany
30E4 Reconquista Arg
19B3 Red R USA
77C4 Redang I Malay
16B2 Red Bank New Jersey, USA
21A1 Red Bluff USA
42D2 Redcar Eng
13E2 Redcliff Can
100D1 Redcliffe Aust
109B2 Red Cliffs Aust
13E2 Red Deer Can
13E2 Red Deer R Can
20B2 Redding USA
10A2 Red L USA
7A4 Red Lake Can
22D3 Redlands USA
16A3 Red Lion USA
20B2 Redmond USA
18A1 Red Oak USA
48B2 Redon France
22C4 Redondo Beach USA
13E2 Redoubt V USA
73B5 Red River Delta Vietnam
13E2 Red Sea Africa/ Arabian Pen
13E2 Redwater Can
22A2 Redwood City USA
14A2 Reed City USA
22C2 Reedley USA
20B2 Reedsport USA
111B2 Reefton NZ
93C2 Refahiye Turk
35D1 Regência Brazil
57C3 Regensburg Germany
96C2 Reggane Alg
53C3 Reggio di Calabria Italy
47D2 Reggio Nell'Emilia Italy
54B1 Reghin Rom
5H4 Regina Can
100A3 Rehoboth Namibia
15C3 Rehoboth Beach USA
94B3 Rehovot Israel
32D1 Reicito Ven
43D4 Reigate Eng
46C2 Reims France
5H4 Reindeer R Can
50B1 Reinosa Spain
16B2 Reisterstown USA
10G1 Reitz S Africa
44B3 Reliance Can
108A2 Remarkable,Mt Aust
78C4 Rembang Indon
91C4 Remeshk Iran

Remscheid

46D1 Remscheid Germany
18C2 Rend,L USA
56B2 Rendsburg Germany
15C1 Renfrew USA
78A3 Rengat Indon
34A2 Rengo Chile
59D3 Reni Ukraine
99D1 Renk Sudan
6H2 Renland Pen Greenland
108B2 Renmark Aust
107F2 Rennell I Solomon Is
48B2 Rennes France
21B2 Reno USA
47D2 Reno R Italy
15C2 Renovo USA
49C1 Rensselaer USA
20B1 Renton USA
70D4 Reo Indon
35B2 Represa de Furnas Dam Brazil
30E3 Represa Ilha Grande Dam Brazil
30E3 Represa Itaipu Dam Brazil
35A2 Represa Porto Primavera Dam Brazil
35B1 Represa Três Marias Dam Brazil
20C1 Republic USA
41B3 Republic of Ireland NW Europe
6B3 Repulse Bay Can
15C1 Réservoir Baskatong Res Can
10C1 Réservoir de la Grande 2 Res Can
10C1 Réservoir de la Grande 3 Res Can
7C4 Réservoir de la Grande 4 Res Can
7C5 Réservoir Cabonga Res Can
7D4 Réservoir Caniapiscau Res Can
7C5 Réservoir Gouin Res Can
10D1 Réservoir Manicouagan Res Can
90B2 Reshteh-ye Alborz Mts Iran
72A2 Reshui China
30E4 Resistencia Arg
54B1 Resita Rom
6A2 Resolute Can
111A3 Resolution I NZ
6D3 Resolution Island Can
101H1 Ressano Garcia Mozam
34B2 Retamito Arg
46C2 Rethel France
55B3 Réthimnon Greece
89K10 Reunion I Indian O
51C1 Reus Spain
47C1 Reuss R Switz
47D1 Reutte Austria
61K3 Revda Russian Fed
13D2 Revelstoke Can
24A3 Revillagigedo Is Mexico
12H3 Revillagigedo I USA
86A2 Rewa India
84D3 Rewari India
8B2 Rexburg USA
38A2 Reykjavik Iceland
24C2 Reynosa Mexico
48B2 Rezé France
58D1 Rezekne Latvia
61K2 Rezh Russian Fed
47C1 Rhätikon Mts Austria/Switz
94B1 Rhazir Republic, Leb
56B2 Rhein R W Europe
46E1 Rheine Germany
47B1 Rheinfelden Switz
49D2 Rheinland Pfalz Region, Germany
47C1 Rheinwaldhorn Mt Switz

Rhine = Rhein
16C2 Rhinebeck USA
10B2 Rhinelander USA
47C2 Rho Italy
15D2 Rhode Island State, USA
16D2 Rhode Island Sd USA
49C3 Rhodes = Ródhos
49C3 Rhône R France
43C3 Rhyl Wales
31D4 Riachão do Jacuipe Brazil
50A1 Ria de Arosa B Spain
50A1 Ria de Betanzos B Spain
50A1 Ria de Corcubion B Spain
50A1 Ria de Lage B Spain
50A1 Ria de Sta Marta B Spain
50A1 Ria de Vigo B Spain
84C2 Riäsi Pak
50A1 Ribadeo Spain
35A2 Ribas do Rio Pardo Brazil
101C2 Ribauè Mozam
42C3 Ribble R Eng
35B2 Ribeira Brazil
35B2 Ribeirão Prêto Brazil
32D6 Riberalta Bol
15C2 Rice L Can
10A2 Rice Lake USA
101H1 Richard's Bay S Africa
19A3 Richardson USA
12G1 Richardson Mts Can
8B3 Richfield USA
20C1 Richland USA
22A2 Richmond California, USA
101H1 Richmond Natal, S Africa
109D2 Richmond New South Wales, Aust
111B2 Richmond NZ
107D3 Richmond Queensland, Aust
10C3 Richmond Virginia, USA
111B2 Richmond Range Mts NZ
15C2 Rideau,L Can
17B1 Ridgeland USA
15C2 Ridgway USA
27D4 Riecito Ven
47D1 Rienza R Italy
57C2 Riesa Germany
29B6 Riesco I Chile
101F1 Riet R S Africa
52B2 Rieti Italy
50B2 Rif Mts Mor
58C1 Riga Latvia
60B2 Riga,G of Estonia/Latvia
90B3 Rīgan Iran
20C1 Riggins USA
7E4 Rigolet Can
39J6 Riihimaki Fin
52B1 Rijeka Croatia
13E2 Rimbey Can
39H7 Rimbo Sweden
52B2 Rimini Italy
54C1 Rîmnicu Sărat Rom
54B1 Rîmnicu Vîlcea Rom
10D2 Rimouski Can
23A1 Rincón de Romos Mexico
39F7 Ringkøbing Den
99D2 Rio Benito Eq Guinea
32D5 Rio Branco Brazil
24B1 Rio Bravo del Norte R Mexico/USA
32C1 Riochacha Colombia
35B2 Rio Claro Brazil
27L1 Rio Claro Trinidad
34C3 Rio Colorado Arg
34C2 Rio Cuarto Arg
31D4 Rio de Jacuipe Brazil
35C2 Rio de Janeiro Brazil
35C2 Rio de Janeiro State, Brazil
29E3 Rio de la Plata Est Arg/Urug

29C6 Rio Gallegos Arg
29C6 Rio Grande Arg
30F5 Rio Grande Brazil
26D4 Rio Grande R Nic
25D3 Rio Grande R Mexico/USA
24B2 Rio Grande Mexico/USA
23A1 Rio Grande de Santiago Mexico
31D3 Rio Grande do Norte State, Brazil
30F4 Rio Grande do Sul State, Brazil
103G6 Rio Grande Rise Atlantic O
26C4 Riohacha Colombia
49C2 Riom France
32B4 Riombamba Ecuador
30C2 Rio Mulatos Bol
29C3 Rio Negro State, Arg
30F4 Rio Pardo Brazil
34C2 Rio Tercero Arg
33E6 Rio Theodore Roosevelt R Brazil
29B6 Rio Turbio Arg
35A1 Rio Verde Brazil
23A1 Rio Verde Mexico
14B3 Ripley Ohio, USA
14B3 Ripley West Virginia, USA
42D2 Ripon Eng
22B2 Ripon USA
94B3 Rishon le Zion Israel
16A3 Rising Sun USA
39F7 Risør Nor
6E2 Ritenbenk Greenland
22C2 Ritter,Mt USA
20C1 Ritzville USA
34B2 Rivadavia Arg
34A1 Rivadavia Chile
34C3 Rivadavia Gonzalez Moreno Arg
47D2 Riva de Garda Italy
29C3 Rivera Arg
29E2 Rivera Urug
22B2 Riverbank USA
97B4 River Cess Lib
16C2 Riverhead USA
108B3 Riverina Aust
111A3 Riversdale NZ
22D4 Riverside USA
13B2 Rivers Inlet Can
111A3 Riverton NZ
8C2 Riverton USA
17A3 Riviera Beach USA
7C4 Rivière aux Feuilles R Can
7D4 Rivière de la Baleine R Can
7D4 Rivière du Petit Mécatina R Can
46C2 Rivigny-sur-Ornain France
93D1 Rize Turk
72D2 Rizhao China
Rizhskiy Zaliv = Riga,G of
39F7 Rjukan Nor
6B2 Roanes Pen Can
49C2 Roanne France
17A1 Roanoke Alabama, USA
11C3 Roanoke Virginia, USA
11C3 Roanoke R USA
45B3 Roaringwater B Irish Rep
38J6 Robertsfors Sweden
19B2 Robert S Kerr Res USA
97A4 Robertsport Lib
7C5 Roberval Can
30H6 Robinson Crusoe I Chile
108B2 Robinvale Aust
13D2 Robson,Mt Can
24A3 Roca Partida I Mexico
103G5 Rocas I Atlantic O
31E2 Rocas I Brazil
29F2 Rocha Urug
42C3 Rochdale Eng
48B2 Rochefort France
5G3 Rocher River Can

108B3 Rochester Aust
7C5 Rochester Can
43E4 Rochester Eng
10A2 Rochester Minnesota, USA
15D2 Rochester New Hampshire, USA
10C2 Rochester New York, USA
10B2 Rockford USA
11B3 Rock Hill USA
10A2 Rock Island USA
108B3 Rocklands Res Aust
17B2 Rockledge USA
8C2 Rock Springs Wyoming, USA
110B2 Rocks Pt NZ
109C3 Rock,The Aust
16C2 Rockville Connecticut, USA
14A3 Rockville Indiana, USA
16A3 Rockville Maryland, USA
14B1 Rocky Island L Can
13E2 Rocky Mountain House Can
8B1 Rocky Mts Can/USA
12B2 Rocky Pt USA
56C2 Rødbyhavn Den
34B2 Rodeo Arg
49C3 Rodez France
55C3 Ródhos Greece
55C3 Ródhos I Greece
52C2 Rodi Garganico Italy
54B2 Rodopi Planina Mts Bulg
106A3 Roebourne Aust
46C1 Roermond Neth
46B1 Roeselare Belg
6B3 Roes Welcome Sd Can
18B2 Rogers USA
14B1 Rogers City USA
20B2 Rogue R USA
85B3 Rohn Pak
84D3 Rohtak India
58C1 Roja Latvia
35A2 Rolândia Brazil
18B2 Rolla USA
109C1 Roma Aust
52B2 Roma Italy
47C2 Romagnano Italy
17C1 Romain,C USA
54C1 Roman Rom
103H5 Romanche Gap Atlantic O
71D4 Romang I Indon
60B4 Romania Republic, E Europe
17B2 Romano,C USA
49D2 Romans sur Isère France
79B3 Romblon Phil
Rome = Roma
17A1 Rome Georgia, USA
15C2 Rome New York, USA
46B2 Romilly-sur-Seine France
15C3 Romney USA
60D3 Romny Ukraine
56B1 Rømø I Den
47B1 Romont Switz
48C2 Romorantin France
50A2 Ronda Spain
33E6 Rondônia Brazil
24F6 Rondônia State, Brazil
30F2 Rondonópolis Brazil
73A4 Rong'an China
73B4 Rongchang China
72E2 Rongcheng China
73B4 Rongjiang China
73B4 Rong Jiang R China
76A1 Rongklang Range Mts Myan
39G7 Rønne Den
39H7 Ronneby Sweden
112B2 Ronne Ice Shelf Ant
46B1 Ronse Belg
46A1 Ronthieu Region, France
9C3 Roof Butte Mt USA

84D3 **Roorkee** India
46C1 **Roosendaal** Neth
112B6 **Roosevelt I** Ant
106C2 **Roper** R Aust
33E3 **Roraima** State, Brazil
33E3 **Roraima** Mt Ven
38G6 **Røros** Nor
47C1 **Rorschach** Switz
38G6 **Rørvik** Nor
27D2 **Rosalie** Dominica
22C3 **Rosamond L** USA
34C2 **Rosario** Arg
31C2 **Rosário** Brazil
34D2 **Rosario del Tala** Arg
42B2 **Roscoff** France
45B2 **Roscommon** County, Irish Rep
45B3 **Roscommon** Irish Rep
45C2 **Roscrea** Irish Rep
27E3 **Roseau** Dominica
109C4 **Rosebery** Aust
20B2 **Roseburg** USA
19A4 **Rosenberg** USA
57C3 **Rosenheim** Germany
13F2 **Rosetown** Can
54B2 **Roșiori de Vede** Rom
39G7 **Roskilde** Den
60D3 **Roslavl'** Russian Fed
61E2 **Roslyatino** Russian Fed
111B2 **Ross** NZ
12H2 **Ross** R Can
40B3 **Rossan** Pt Irish Rep
53D3 **Rossano** Italy
19C3 **Ross Barnet Res** USA
15C1 **Rosseau L** L Can
107E2 **Rossel I** Solomon Is
112A **Ross Ice Shelf** Ant
20B1 **Ross L** USA
13D3 **Rossland** Can
45C2 **Rosslare** Irish Rep
111C2 **Ross,Mt** NZ
97A3 **Rosso** Maur
43C4 **Ross-on-Wye** Eng
60E4 **Rossosh** Russian Fed
4E3 **Ross River** Can
112B6 **Ross S** Ant
91B4 **Rostāq** Iran
56C2 **Rostock** Germany
Rostov = Rostov-na-Donu
61E4 **Rostov-na-Donu** Russian Fed
17B1 **Roswell** Georgia, USA
9C3 **Roswell** New Mexico, USA
71F2 **Rota** Pacific O
56B2 **Rotenburg** Niedersachsen, Germany
46E1 **Rothaar-Geb** Region Germany
112C3 **Rothera** Base Ant
42D3 **Rotherham** Eng
42B2 **Rothesay** Scot
117B5 **Roti** I Indon
108C2 **Roto** Aust
111B2 **Rotoiti,L** NZ
111C2 **Rotorua** NZ
111C1 **Rotorua,L** NZ
56A2 **Rotterdam** Neth
46B1 **Roubaix** France
42B2 **Rouen** France
42E3 **Rough** Oilfield N Sea
Roulers = Roeselare
101E3 **Round I** Mauritius
109D2 **Round Mt** Aust
8C2 **Roundup** USA
44C2 **Rousay** I Scot
48C3 **Roussillon** Region, France
42B2 **Rouyn** Can
38K5 **Rovaniemi** Fin
47D2 **Rovereto** Italy
47D2 **Rovigo** Italy
52B1 **Rovinj** Croatia
59D2 **Rovno** Ukraine
90A2 **Row'ān** Iran
109C1 **Rowena** Aust
6C3 **Rowley I** Can
84D2 **Rowley Shoals** Aust

79A3 **Roxas** Palawan, Phil
79B3 **Roxas** Panay, Phil
11A3 **Roxburgh** NZ
45C2 **Royal Canal** Irish Rep
43D3 **Royal Leamington Spa** Eng
14B2 **Royal Oak** USA
43E4 **Royal Tunbridge Wells** Eng
48B2 **Royan** France
48B2 **Royan** France
43D3 **Royston** Eng
59C3 **Rozhnava** Slovakia
48B2 **Rozoy** France
61F3 **Rtishchevo** Russian Fed
99D3 **Ruaha Nat Pk** Tanz
110C1 **Ruahine Range** Mts NZ
110C1 **Ruapehu,Mt** NZ
65D3 **Rub al Khāli** Desert S Arabia
44A3 **Rubha Hunish** Scot
35A2 **Rubineia** Brazil
65K4 **Rubtsovsk** Russian Fed
12C2 **Ruby** USA
91C4 **Rūdān** Iran
69F2 **Rudnaya Pristan'** Russian Fed
54B2 **Rudoka Planina** Mt Macedonia
72E3 **Rudong** China
11E4 **Rudyard** USA
46A1 **Rue** France
48C2 **Ruffec** France
99D3 **Rufiji** R Tanz
34C2 **Rufino** Arg
97A3 **Rufisque** Sen
100B2 **Rufunsa** Zambia
43D3 **Rugby** Eng
39G8 **Rügen** I Germany
56B2 **Ruhr** R Germany
73D4 **Ruijin** China
54B2 **Rukwa** L Tanz
91A4 **Rum** I Scot
54A1 **Ruma** Serbia, Yugos
91A4 **Rumah** S Arabia
98C2 **Rumbek** Sudan
26C2 **Rum Cay** I Caribbean S
47A2 **Rumilly** France
106C2 **Rum Jungle** Aust
101C2 **Rumphi** Malawi
111B2 **Runanga** NZ
110C1 **Runaway,C** NZ
100C3 **Rundi** R Zim
100A2 **Rundu** Namibia
99D3 **Rungwa** Tanz
99D3 **Rungwa** R Tanz
99D3 **Rungwe** Mt Tanz
82C2 **Ruoqiang** China
72B2 **Ruo Shui** R China
54C1 **Rupea** Rom
7C4 **Rupert** R Can
46D1 **Rur** R Germany
32D6 **Rurrenabaque** Bol
101C2 **Rusape** Zim
54C2 **Ruse** Bulg
18B1 **Rushville** Illinois, USA
108B2 **Rushworth** Aust
19A3 **Rusk** USA
44A3 **Rusk** I Scot
110B1 **Russell** NZ
18B2 **Russellville** Arkansas, USA
18C2 **Russellville** Kentucky, USA
21A2 **Russian** R USA
62C3 **Russian Fed** Asia/Europe
93E1 **Rustavi** Georgia
101G1 **Rustenburg** S Africa
19B3 **Ruston** USA
99C3 **Rutana** Burundi
46E1 **Rüthen** Germany
23B2 **Rutla** Mexico
15D2 **Rutland** USA
84D2 **Rutog** China
Ruvu = Pangani

101D2 **Ruvuma** R Tanz/Mozam
99D2 **Ruwenzori Range** Mts Uganda/Zaire
101C2 **Ruya** R Zim
59B3 **Ružomberok** Slovakia
99C3 **Rwanda** Republic, Africa
60E3 **Ryazan'** Russian Fed
61F3 **Ryazhsk** Russian Fed
60E2 **Rybinsk** Russian Fed
60E2 **Rybinskoye Vodokhranilishche** Res Russian Fed
13D1 **Rycroft** Can
43E4 **Ryde** Eng
20C2 **Rye Patch Res** USA
60D3 **Ryl'sk** Russian Fed
61D4 **Ryn Peski** Desert Kazakhstan
74D3 **Ryōtsu** Japan
59D3 **Ryskany** Moldova
69E4 **Ryūkyū Retto** Arch Japan
59C2 **Rzeszów** Pol
61F2 **Rzhev** Russian Fed

S

91B3 **Sa'ādatābād** Iran
56C2 **Saale** R Germany
47B1 **Saanen** Switz
46D2 **Saar** R Germany
57B3 **Saarbrücken** Germany
46D2 **Saarburg** Germany
39J7 **Saaremaa** I Estonia
46D2 **Saarland** State, Germany
46D2 **Saarlouis** Germany
34C3 **Saavedra** Arg
54A2 **Šabac** Serbia, Yugos
51C1 **Sabadell** Spain
75B1 **Sabae** Japan
78D1 **Sabah** State, Malay
26C4 **Sabanalarga** Colombia
70A3 **Sabang** Indon
87C1 **Sabarī** R India
94B2 **Sabastiya** Israel
30C2 **Sabaya** Bol
93C3 **Sab'Bi'ār** Syria
94B3 **Sabha** Jordan
95A2 **Sabhā** Libya
24B2 **Sabinas** Mexico
24B2 **Sabinas Hidalgo** Mexico
19A3 **Sabine** R USA
19B4 **Sabine L** USA
91B5 **Sabkhat Matti** Salt Marsh UAE
94A3 **Sabkhet El Bardawil** Lg Egypt
79B3 **Sablayan** Phil
7D5 **Sable,C** Can
7D5 **Sable,I** Can
90C2 **Sabzevār** Iran
10A1 **Sachigo** R Can
56C2 **Sachsen** State, Germany
56C2 **Sachsen-Anhalt** State, Germany
4F2 **Sachs Harbour** Can
47B1 **Säckingen** Germany
22B1 **Sacramento** USA
22B1 **Sacramento** R USA
21A1 **Sacramento** V USA
9C3 **Sacramento Mts** USA
81C4 **Sa'dah** Yemen
54B2 **Sadanski** Bulg
50A2 **Sado** R Port
74D3 **Sado-shima** I Japan
85C3 **Sādri** India
Safad = Zefat
42C3 **Safed Koh** Mts Afghan
39G7 **Saffle** Sweden
92C3 **Safi** Jordan
96B1 **Safi** Mor

90A3 **Safidabeh** Iran
94C1 **Şāfītā** Syria
93E3 **Şafwān** Iraq
75A2 **Saga** Japan
76B1 **Sagaing** Myan
75B2 **Sagami-nada** B Japan
85D4 **Sāgar** India
16C2 **Sag Harbor** USA
14B2 **Saginaw** USA
14B2 **Saginaw B** USA
26B2 **Sagua de Tánamo** Cuba
26B2 **Sagua la Grande** Cuba
7C5 **Saguenay** R Can
51B2 **Sagunto** Spain
94C3 **Sahāb** Jordan
50A1 **Sahagún** Spain
96C2 **Sahara** Desert N Africa
84D3 **Saharanpur** India
84C2 **Sahiwal** Pak
93D3 **Şahrā al Hijārah** Desert Region Iraq
23A1 **Sahuayo** Mexico
107D1 **Saibai** I Aust
96C1 **Saïda** Alg
94B2 **Saïda** Leb
94C4 **Sa'īdabad** Iran
51B2 **Saidia** Mor
86B1 **Saidpur** India
84C2 **Saidu** India
75A1 **Saigo** Japan
Saigon = Ho Chi Minh
76C2 **Saiha** India
68D2 **Saihan Tal** China
75A2 **Saijo** Japan
74C4 **Saiki** Japan
42C2 **St Abb's Head** Pt Scot
43D4 **St Albans** Eng
15D2 **St Albans** Vermont, USA
14B3 **St Albans** West Virginia, USA
43C4 **St Albans Head** C Eng
13E1 **St Albert** Can
46B1 **St Amand-les-Eaux** France
48C2 **St Amand-Mont Rond** France
17A2 **St Andrew B** USA
44C3 **St Andrews** Scot
17B1 **St Andrew Sd** USA
27H1 **St Ann's Bay** Jamaica
7E4 **St Anthony** Can
108B3 **St Arnaud** Aust
17B2 **St Augustine** USA
43B4 **St Austell** Eng
46D2 **St-Avold** France
42C2 **St Bees Head** Pt Eng
47B2 **St-Bonnet** France
43B4 **St Brides B** Wales
48B2 **St-Brieuc** France
15C2 **St Catharines** Can
27M2 **St Catherine,Mt** Grenada
17B1 **St Catherines I** USA
43C4 **St Catherines Pt** Eng
49C2 **St Chamond** France
18B2 **St Charles** Missouri, USA
14B2 **St Clair** USA
14B2 **St Clair,L** Can/USA
14B2 **St Clair Shores** USA
49D2 **St Claud** France
10A2 **St Cloud** USA
47B1 **Ste Croix** Switz
27E3 **St Croix** I Caribbean S
43B3 **St Davids Head** Pt Wales
46B2 **St Denis** France
101E3 **St Denis** Réunion
46C2 **St Dizier** France
12F2 **St Elias,Mt** USA
12G3 **St Elias Mts** Can
48B2 **Saintes** France
49C2 **St Étienne** France
18B2 **St Francis** R USA
100B4 **St Francis,C** S Africa

St Gallen

47C1 **St Gallen** Switz
48C3 **St-Gaudens** France
109C1 **St George** Aust
17B1 **St George** South
  Carolina, USA
9B3 **St George** Utah,
  USA
17B2 **St George** Florida,
  USA
20B2 **St George,Pt** USA
15D1 **St-Georges** Can
27E4 **St George's**
  Grenada
45C3 **St George's Chan**
  Irish Rep/Wales
46A2 **St-Germain-en-Laye**
  France
47B2 **St-Gervais** France
47C1 **St Gotthard** P Switz
43B4 **St Govans Head** Pt
  Wales
22A1 **St Helena** /
103H5 **St Helena** /
  Atlantic O
100A4 **St Helena B** S Africa
17B1 **St Helena Sd** USA
109C4 **St Helens** Aust
42C3 **St Helens** Eng
20B1 **St Helens** USA
20B1 **St Helens,Mt** USA
48B2 **St Helier** Jersey
47B1 **St Hippolyte** France
46C1 **St-Hubert** Belg
7C5 **St-Hyacinthe** Can
14B1 **St Ignace** Can
43B4 **St Ives** Eng
18B2 **St James** Missouri,
  USA
5E4 **St James,C** Can
15D1 **St Jean** Can
48B2 **St Jean d'Angely**
  France
47B2 **St-Jean-de-**
  Maurienne France
10C2 **St Jean,L** Can
15D1 **St-Jérôme** Can
20C1 **St Joe** R USA
7D5 **Saint John** Can
7E5 **St John's** Can
14B2 **St Johns** Michigan,
  USA
17B2 **St Johns** R USA
15D2 **St Johnsbury** USA
15D1 **St-Joseph** Can
19B3 **St Joseph** Louisiana,
  USA
14A2 **St Joseph** Michigan,
  USA
18B2 **St Joseph** Missouri,
  USA
27L1 **St Joseph** Trinidad
14B2 **St Joseph** R Can
14B1 **St Joseph I** Can
7A4 **St Joseph,L** Can
47B1 **St Julien** France
48C2 **St-Junien** France
46B2 **St-Just-en-Chaussée**
  France
40B2 **St Kilda** / Scot
27E3 **St Kitts-Nevis** /s
  Caribbean S
47A1 **St-Laurent** France
7D5 **St Lawrence** R Can
7D5 **Saint Lawrence,G** of
  Can
4A3 **St Lawrence I** USA
48B2 **St Lawrence Seaway**
  Can/USA
48B2 **St Lô** France
97A3 **St Louis** Sen
11A3 **St Louis** USA
27E4 **St Lucia** /
  Caribbean S
101H1 **St Lucia,L** S Africa
44E1 **St Magnus** B Scot
48B2 **St Malo** France
20C1 **St Maries** USA
27E3 **St Martin** /
  Caribbean S
108A2 **St Mary Peak** Mt
  Aust
109C4 **St Marys** Aust
15C2 **St Marys** USA
17B1 **St Marys** R USA

46C2 **Ste-Menehould**
  France
12B2 **St Michael** USA
16A3 **St Michaels** USA
47B2 **St-Michel** France
46C2 **St-Mihiel** France
47C1 **St Moritz** Switz
48B2 **St-Nazaire** France
46C1 **St-Niklaas** Belg
46B1 **St-Omer** France
13E2 **St Paul** Can
10A2 **St Paul** Minnesota,
  USA
97A4 **St Paul** R Lib
17B2 **St Petersburg** USA
7E5 **St Pierre** Can
15D1 **St Pierre,L** Can
46B1 **St-Pol-Sur-Ternoise**
  France
59B3 **St Pölten** Austria
46B2 **St Quentin** France
49D3 **St Raphaël** France
101D2 **St Sébastien** C
  Madag
17B1 **St Simons I** USA
17B1 **St Stephen** USA
14B2 **St Thomas** Can
49D3 **St Tropez** France
46C1 **St Truiden** Belg
46A1 **St-Valéry-sur-Somme**
  France
27E4 **St Vincent and the**
  Grenadines /s
  Caribbean S
108A2 **St Vincent,G** Aust
46C1 **St-Vith** Germany
46D2 **St Wendel** Germany
71F2 **Saipan** / Pacific O
84B2 **Saiydabad** Afghan
30C2 **Sajama** Mt Bol
72A4 **Sakai** Japan
75A2 **Sakaidi** Japan
75A1 **Sakaiminato** Japan
93D4 **Sakâkah** S Arabia
15D1 **Sakami,L** Can
100B2 **Sakania** Zaïre
101D3 **Sakaraha** Madag
60D5 **Sakarya** R Turk
58C1 **Sakasleja** Latvia
74D3 **Sakata** Japan
97C4 **Saketé** Benin
69G1 **Sakhalin** /
  Russian Fed
69E4 **Sakishima gunto** /s
  Japan
97A4 **Sal** / Cape Verde
61F4 **Sal** R Russian Fed
39H7 **Sala** Sweden
34C2 **Saladillo** R Arg
34C2 **Saladillo** R Arg
34D3 **Salado** R
  Buenos Aires, Arg
34B1 **Salado** R Mendoza/
  San Luis, Arg
30D4 **Salado** R Sante Fe,
  Arg
97B4 **Salaga** Ghana
76C3 **Sala Hintoun** Camb
98B1 **Salal** Chad
81D4 **Salâlah** Oman
34A2 **Salamanca** Chile
24C1 **Salamanca** Mexico
50A1 **Salamanca** Spain
15C2 **Salamanca** USA
98B2 **Salamat** R Chad
71F4 **Salamaua** PNG
15C2 **Salamonica** USA
78D1 **Salang** Indon
38H5 **Salangen** Nor
30C3 **Salar de Arizaro** Arg
30C3 **Salar de Atacama**
  Salt Pan Chile
30C2 **Salar de Coipasa**
  Salt Pan Bol
30C3 **Salar de Uyuni**
  Salt Pan Bol
47C2 **Salasomaggiore**
  Italy
61J3 **Salavat** Russian Fed
70D4 **Salayar** Indon
105L5 **Sala y Gomez** /
  Pacific O
34C3 **Salazar** Arg
48C2 **Salbris** France

12E2 **Salcha** R USA
100A4 **Saldanha** S Africa
94C2 **Saldhad** Syria
34C3 **Saldungaray** Arg
58C1 **Saldus** Latvia
109C3 **Sale** Aust
18C2 **Salem** Illinois, USA
87B2 **Salem** India
16D1 **Salem**
  Massachusetts, USA
16B3 **Salem** New Jersey,
  USA
20B2 **Salem** Oregon, USA
78C4 **Salembu Besar** /
  Indon
39G6 **Salen** Sweden
53B2 **Salerno** Italy
42C3 **Salford** Eng
54A1 **Salgot** Hung
59B3 **Salgótarjan** Hung
31D3 **Saigueiro** Brazil
55C3 **Salihli** Turk
101C2 **Salima** Malawi
39K6 **Salimaa** L Fin
18A2 **Salina** Kansas, USA
53B3 **Salina** / Italy
23B2 **Salina Cruz** Mexico
30C3 **Salina de Arizato**
  Arg
34B3 **Salina Grande**
  Salt pan Arg
34B2 **Salina La Antigua**
  Salt pan Arg
25C1 **Salinas** Brazil
22B2 **Salinas** USA
22B2 **Salinas** R USA
34B3 **Salinas de Llancaneb**
  Salt Pan Arg
34B2 **Salinas Grandes** Salt
  Pan Arg
19B3 **Saline** R Arkansas,
  USA
27M2 **Salines,Pt** Grenada
31B2 **Salinópolis** Brazil
47A1 **Salins** France
15C3 **Salisbury** Harare**=**
  Salisbury = Harare
15C3 **Salisbury** Maryland,
  USA
6C3 **Salisbury I** Can
43D4 **Salisbury Plain** Eng
38K5 **Salla** Fin
47B2 **Sallanches** France
18B2 **Sallisaw** USA
6C3 **Salluit** Can
86A1 **Sallyana** Nepal
93D2 **Salmas** Iran
38L6 **Salmi** Russian Fed
20C1 **Salmon** Can
8B2 **Salmon** USA
13D2 **Salmon Arm** Can
8B2 **Salmon River Mts**
  USA
39J6 **Salo** Fin
47D2 **Salò** Italy
49D3 **Salon-de-Provence**
  France
Salonica =
  Salonica =
  Thessaloniki
54B1 **Salonta** Rom
38K6 **Salpausselka** Region,
  Fin
34B2 **Salsacate** Arg
61F4 **Sal'sk** Russian Fed
94B2 **Salt** Jordan
30C3 **Salta** Arg
30C3 **Salta** State, Arg
24B2 **Saltillo** México
8B2 **Salt Lake City** USA
34C2 **Salto** Arg
34D2 **Salto** Urug
32C3 **Salto Angostura**
  Waterfall Colombia
35D1 **Salto da Divisa** Brazil
33E2 **Salto del Angel**
  Waterfall Ven
30E3 **Salto del Guaira**
  Waterfall Brazil
32C4 **Salto Grande**
  Waterfall Colombia
84C2 **Salt Range** Mts Pak
27H2 **Salt River** Jamaica
17B1 **Saluda** USA
47B2 **Saluzzo** Italy

31D4 **Salvador** Brazil
19B4 **Salvador,L** USA
23A1 **Salvatierra** Mexico
91B5 **Salwah** Qatar
76B1 **Salween** R Myan
93E2 **Sal'yany** Azerbaijan
57C3 **Salzburg** Austria
56C2 **Salzgitter** Germany
56C2 **Salzwedel** Germany
68B1 **Samagaltay**
  Russian Fed
79B4 **Samales Group** /s
  Phil
27D3 **Samaná** Dom Rep
92C2 **Samandaǧi** Turk
84B1 **Samangan** Afghan
79C3 **Samar** / Phil
65G4 **Samara** Russian Fed
107E2 **Samarai** PNG
78D3 **Samarinda** Indon
80E2 **Samarkand**
  Uzbekistan
93D3 **Sâmarrâ'** Iraq
79B3 **Samar S** Phil
86A2 **Sambalpur** India
78B2 **Sambas** Indon
101D2 **Sambava** Madag
84D3 **Sambhal** India
78D3 **Samboja** Indon
59C3 **Sambor** Ukraine
46B1 **Sambre** R France
74B3 **Samch'ók** S Korea
99D3 **Same** Tanz
47C1 **Samedan** Switz
46A1 **Samer** France
100B2 **Samfya** Zambia
76C1 **Samka** Myan
55C2 **Sámos** / Greec
55C2 **Samothráki** / Greec
34C2 **Sampacho** Arg
78D3 **Sampaga** Indon
78D3 **Sampit** Indon
78C3 **Sampit** R Indon
19B3 **Sam Rayburn Res**
  USA
76C3 **Samrong** Camb
56C1 **Samsø** / Den
92C1 **Samsun** Turk
97B3 **San** Mali
76D3 **San** R Camb
81C4 **San'a'** Yemen
98B2 **Sanaga** R Cam
29C2 **San Agustin** Arg
79C4 **San Agustin,C** Phil
90A2 **Sanandaj** Iran
22B1 **San Andreas** USA
25C3 **San Andrés Tuxtla**
  Mexico
9C3 **San Angelo** USA
53A3 **San Antioco**
  Sardegna
53A3 **San Antioco** / Medit
  S
34A2 **San Antonio** Chile
9C3 **San Antonio** New
  Mexico, USA
79B2 **San Antonio** Phil
9D4 **San Antonio** R
  Texas, USA
51C2 **San Antonio Abad**
  Spain
25D2 **San Antonio,C** Cuba
26A2 **San Antonio de los**
  Banos Cuba
22D3 **San Antonio,Mt** USA
29C4 **San Antonio Oeste**
  Arg
34D3 **San Augustin** Arg
34B2 **San Augustin de**
  Valle Feril Arg
85D4 **Sanawad** India
23A1 **San Bartolo** Mexico
24A3 **San Benedicto** /
  Mexico
22B2 **San Benito** R USA
22B2 **San Benito Mt** USA
22D3 **San Bernardino** USA
34A2 **San Bernardo** Chile
17A2 **San Blas,C** USA
34A3 **San Carlos** Chile
32A1 **San Carlos** Nic
79B2 **San Carlos** Phil

29B4 San Carlos de Bariloche Arg
69E4 San-chung Taiwan
61G2 Sanchursk Russian Fed
34A3 San Clemente Chile
22D4 San Clemente I USA
21B3 San Clemente I USA
34C2 San Cristóbal Arg
25C3 San Cristóbal Mexico
23A1 San Cristóbal Ven
32J7 San Cristóbal / Ecuador
107F2 San Cristóbal / Solomon Is
25E2 Sancti Spiritus Cuba
78C3 Sandai Indon
70C3 Sandakan Malay
44C2 Sanday / Scot
9C3 Sanderson USA
13F1 Sandfly L Can
21B3 San Diego USA
92B2 Sandikli Turk
86A1 Sandila India
39F7 Sandnes Nor
38G5 Sandnessjøen Nor
98C3 Sandoa Zaïre
59C2 Sandomierz Pol
38D3 Sandoy Føroyar
20C1 Sandpoint USA
49D2 Sandski Italy
18A2 Sand Springs USA
106A3 Sandstone Aust
73C4 Sandu China
14B2 Sandusky USA
39H6 Sandviken Sweden
7A4 Sandy L Can
34C2 San Elcano Arg
9B3 San Felipe Baja Cal, Mexico
34A2 San Felipe Chile
23A1 San Felipe Guanajuato, Mexico
27D4 San Felipe Ven
51C1 San Feliu de Guixols Spain
33A5 San Felix / Pacific O
34A2 San Fernando Chile
79B2 San Fernando Phil
50A2 San Fernando Spain
27E4 San Fernando Trinidad
22C3 San Fernando USA
32D2 San Fernando Ven
17B2 Sanford Florida, USA
34C2 Sanford,Mt USA
34C2 San Francisco Arg
26A2 San Francisco Dom Rep
22A2 San Francisco USA
22A2 San Francisco B USA
24B2 San Francisco del Oro Mexico
23A1 San Francisco del Rincon Mexico
85C5 San Gabriel Mts USA
85C5 Sangamner India
18C2 Sangamon R USA
71F2 Sangan / Indon
22C2 Sanger USA
72C2 Sanggan He R China
78C2 Sanggau Indon
98B2 Sangha R Congo
98B3 Sangha Pak
76D2 Sanghkla Buri Thai
78D2 Sangkulirang Indon
87A1 Sāngli India
98B2 Sangmélima Cam
9B3 San Gorgonio Mt USA
9C3 Sangre de Cristo Mts USA
34A2 San Gregorio USA
22A2 San Gregorio USA
84D2 Sangrūr India
30E4 San Ignacio Arg
79B3 San Isidro Phil
32B2 San Jacinto Colombia
21B3 San Jacinto Peak Mt USA

34A3 San Javier Chile
34D2 San Javier Sante Fe, Arg
74D3 Sanjō / Japan
31C6 São João del Rei Brazil
22B2 San Joaquin R USA
22B2 San Joaquin Valley USA
32A1 San José Costa Rica
25C3 San José Guatemala
79B2 San Jose Luzon, Phil
79B3 San Jose Mindoro, Phil
22B2 San Jose USA
9B4 San José / Mexico
30D2 San José de Chiquitos Bol
34D2 San José de Feliciano Arg
34B2 San José de Jachal Arg
34C2 San José de la Dormida Arg
31B6 San José do Rio Prêto Brazil
24B2 San José del Cabo Mexico
34B2 San Juan Arg
27D3 San Juan Puerto Rico
34B2 San Juan State, Arg
27L1 San Juan Trinidad
32D2 San Juan Ven
26B2 San Juan Mt Cuba
8C3 San Juan Mts USA
34B2 San Juan R Arg
23B2 San Juan R Mexico
25D3 San Juan R Nic/ Costa Rica
23B2 San Juan Bautista Mexico
30E4 San Juan Bautista Par
22B2 San Juan Bautista USA
25D3 San Juan del Norte Nic
27D4 San Juan de los Cayos Ven
23A1 San Juan de loz Lagoz Mexico
23A1 San Juan del Rio Mexico
25D3 San Juan del Sur Nic
20B1 San Juan Is USA
23B2 San Juan Tepozcolula Mexico
29C5 San Julián Arg
34C2 San Justo Arg
60D2 Sankt-Peterburg Russian Fed
98C3 Sankuru R Zaïre
93C2 Sanlurfa Turk
32B3 San Lorenzo Ecuador
34C2 San Lorenzo Arg
22B2 San Lucas USA
34B2 San Luis Arg
34B2 San Luis State, Arg
23A1 San Luis de la Paz Mexico
21A2 San Luis Obispo USA
23A1 San Luis Potosi Mexico
22B2 San Luis Res USA
53A3 Sanluri Sardegna
33D2 San Maigualida Mts Ven
34D3 San Manuel Arg
34A2 San Marcos Chile
23B2 San Marcos Mexico
52B2 San Marino Republic, Europe
34B2 San Martin Mendoza, Arg
112C3 San Martin Base Ant
47D1 San Martino di Castroza Italy
23B2 San Martin Tuxmelucan Mexico
22A2 San Mateo USA
30E2 San Matias Bol
72C3 Sanmenxia China

25D3 San Miguel El Salvador
22B3 San Miguel / USA
23A1 San Miguel del Allende Mexico
34D3 San Miguel del Monte Arg
30C4 San Miguel de Tucuman Arg
73D4 Sanming China
9B3 San Nicolas / USA
34C2 San Nicolás de los Arroyos Arg
101G1 Sannieshof S Africa
97B4 Sanniquellie Lib
52B3 Sanok Pol
22D4 San Onofre USA
22D4 San Onofre Colombia
79B3 San Pablo Phil
21A2 San Pablo B USA
34D2 San Pedro Buenos Aires, Arg
97B4 San Pedro Ivory Coast
30D3 San Pedro Jujuy, Arg
30E3 San Pedro Par
22C4 San Pedro Chan USA
9C4 San Pedro de los Colonias Mexico
25D3 San Pedro Sula Honduras
53A3 San Pietro / Medit S
24A1 San Quintin Mexico
34B2 San Rafael Arg
22A2 San Rafael USA
34B2 San Rafael Mts USA
49D3 San Remo Italy
34C2 San Salvador Arg
26C2 San Salvador / Caribbean S
32J7 San Salvador / Ecuador
30D3 San Salvador de Jujuy Arg
97C3 Sansanné - Mango Togo
51B1 San Sebastian Spain
53C2 San Severo Italy
30C2 Santa Ana Bol
25C3 Santa Ana Guatemala
22D4 Santa Ana USA
22D4 Santa Ana USA
22C3 Santa Barbara Mexico
22C3 Santa Barbara USA
22C4 Santa Barbara USA
22B3 Santa Barbara Chan USA
22C4 Santa Catalina Res USA
22C4 Santa Catalina,G of USA
30F4 Santa Catarina State, Brazil
26B2 Santa Clara Cuba
22B2 Santa Clara USA
22C3 Santa Clara R USA
29C5 Santa Cruz Arg
30D2 Santa Cruz Bol
34A2 Santa Cruz Chile
79B3 Santa Cruz Phil
29B5 Santa Cruz State, Arg
22A2 Santa Cruz USA
22C4 Santa Cruz / USA
35D1 Santa Cruz Cabrália Brazil
22C3 Santa Cruz Chan USA
96A2 Santa Cruz de la Palma Canary Is
96A2 Santa Cruz del Sur Cuba
96A2 Santa Cruz de Tenerife Canary Is
100B2 Santa Cruz do Cuando Angola
35B2 Santa Cruz do Rio Pardo Brazil
22A2 Santa Cruz Mts USA
34D2 Santa Elena Arg

33E3 Santa Elena Ven
34C2 Santa Fe Arg
34C2 Santa Fe State, Arg
9C3 Santa Fe USA
35A1 Santa Helena de Goiás Brazil
73B3 Santai China
29B6 Santa Inés / Chile
34B3 Santa Isabel La Pampa, Arg
34C2 Santa Isabel Sante Fe, Arg
107E1 Santa Isabel / Solomon Is
21A2 Santa Lucia Ra USA
21A2 Santa Lucia Range Mts USA
97A4 Santa Luzia / Cape Verde
9B4 Santa Margarita / Mexico
22D4 Santa Margarita R USA
30F4 Santa Maria Brazil
26C4 Santa Maria Colombia
21A3 Santa Maria USA
96A1 Santa Maria / Açores
23B1 Santa Maria R Queretaro, Mexico
23A1 Santa Maria del Rio Mexico
32C1 Santa Marta Colombia
22C3 Santa Monica USA
22C4 Santa Monica B USA
29E2 Santana do Livramento Brazil
32C3 Santander Colombia
50B1 Santander Spain
51C2 Santañy Spain
22C3 Santa Paula USA
31C2 Santa Quitéria Brazil
33G4 Santarem Brazil
50A2 Santarém Port
22A1 Santa Rosa California, USA
25D3 Santa Rosa Honduras
34C3 Santa Rosa La Pampa, Arg
34B2 Santa Rosa Mendoza, Arg
34B2 Santa Rosa San Luis, Arg
22B3 Santa Rosa / USA
24A2 Santa Rosalia Mexico
20C2 Santa Rosa Range Mts USA
31D3 Santa Talhada Brazil
35C1 Santa Teresa Brazil
53A2 Santa Teresa di Gallura Sardegna
22B3 Santa Ynez R USA
22B3 Santa Ynez Mts USA
17C1 Santee R USA
47C2 Santhia Italy
34A2 Santiago Chile
27C3 Santiago Dom Rep
32A2 Santiago Panama
79B2 Santiago Phil
32B4 Santiago R Peru
50A1 Santiago de Compostela Spain
26B2 Santiago de Cuba Cuba
30D4 Santiago del Estero Arg
30D4 Santiago del Estero State, Arg
22C4 Santiago Peak Mt USA
31C5 Santo State, Brazil
35A2 Santo Anastácio Brazil
35A2 Santo Angelo Brazil
97A4 Santo Antão / Cape Verde
35A2 Santo Antonio da Platina Brazil
27D3 Santo Domingo Dom Rep

Santos

35B2 **Santos** Brazil
35C2 **Santos Dumont** Brazil
30E4 **Santo Tomé** Arg
29B5 **San Valentin** *Mt* Chile
34A2 **San Vicente** Chile
98B3 **Sanza Pomba** Angola
30E4 **São Borja** Brazil
35B2 **São Carlos** Brazil
33G5 **São Félix** Mato Grosso, Brazil
35C2 **São Fidélis** Brazil
35C1 **São Francisco** Brazil
31D3 **São Francisco** *R* Brazil
30G4 **São Francisco do Sul** Brazil
35B1 **São Gotardo** Brazil
99D3 **São Hill** Tanz
35C2 **São João da Barra** Brazil
35B2 **São João da Boa Vista** Brazil
35C1 **São João da Ponte** Brazil
35C2 **São João del Rei** Brazil
35B2 **São Joaquim da Barra** Brazil
96A1 **São Jorge** *I* Açores
35B2 **São José do Rio Prêto** Brazil
35B2 **São José dos Campos** Brazil
31C2 **São Luís** Brazil
35B1 **São Marcos** *R* Brazil
35C1 **São Maria do Suaçuí** Brazil
35D1 **São Mateus** Brazil
35C1 **São Mateus** *R* Brazil
96A1 **São Miguel** *I* Açores
49C2 **Saône** *R* France
97A4 **São Nicolau** *I* Cape Verde
35B2 **São Paulo** Brazil
35A2 **São Paulo** State, Brazil
31C3 **São Raimundo Nonato** Brazil
35B1 **São Romão** Brazil
35B2 **São Sebastia do Paraíso** Brazil
35A1 **São Simão** Goias, Brazil
35B2 **São Simão** Sao Paulo, Brazil
97A4 **São Tiago** *I* Cape Verde
97C4 **São Tomé** *I* W Africa
97C4 **São Tomé and Principe** Republic, W Africa
96B2 **Saoura** *Watercourse* Alg
35B2 **São Vicente** Brazil
97A4 **São Vicente** *I* Cape Verde
55C2 **Sápai** Greece
78D4 **Sape** Indon
97C4 **Sapele** Nig
74E2 **Sapporo** Japan
53C2 **Sapri** Italy
18A2 **Sapulpa** USA
90A2 **Saráb** Iran
54A2 **Sarajevo** Bosnia-Herzegovina
90D2 **Sarakhs** Iran
61J3 **Saraktash** Russian Fed
63A2 **Sarala** Russian Fed
15D2 **Saranac L** USA
15D2 **Saranac Lake** USA
55B3 **Sarandë** Alb
79C4 **Sarangani** *Is* Phil
61H2 **Saransk** Russian Fed
17B2 **Sarapul** Russian Fed
54C1 **Sarata** Ukraine
15D2 **Saratoga Springs** USA

78C2 **Saratok** Malay
61G3 **Saratov** Russian Fed
61G3 **Saratovskoye Vodokhranilishche** *Res* Russian Fed
67F4 **Sarawak** State, Malay
92A2 **Saraykoy** Turk
90C3 **Sarbisheh** Iran
47D1 **Sarca** *R* Italy
95A2 **Sardalas** Libya
90A2 **Sar Dasht** Iran
52A2 **Sardegna** *I* Medit S
Sardinia = Sardegna
38H5 **Sarektjåkkå** *Mt* Sweden
84C2 **Sargodha** Pak
98B2 **Sarh** Chad
90B2 **Sari** Iran
94B2 **Sarida** *R* Isreal
93D1 **Sarikamiş** Turk
10TD3 **Sarina** Aust
47B1 **Sarine** *R* Switz
84B1 **Sar-i-Pul** Afghan
95B2 **Sarir** Libya
95A2 **Sarir Tibesti** *Desert* Libya
74B3 **Sariwon** N Korea
48B2 **Sark** *I* UK
92C2 **Sarkişla** Turk
84B3 **Sarobi** Afghan
78A3 **Sarolangun** Indon
55B3 **Saronikós Kólpos** *G* Greece
47C2 **Saronno** Italy
55C2 **Saros Körfezi** *B* Turk
39G7 **Sarpsborg** Nor
42D2 **Sarralbe** France
46D2 **Sarrebourg** France
42D2 **Sarreguemines** France
46D2 **Sarre-Union** France
51B1 **Sarrion** Spain
85B3 **Sartanahu** Pak
53A2 **Sartène** Corse
48B2 **Sarthe** *R* France
61H4 **Sarykamys** Kazakhstan
65H5 **Sarysu** *R* Kazakhstan
86A2 **Sasarám** India
74B4 **Sasebo** Japan
5H4 **Saskatchewan** Province, Can
5H4 **Saskatchewan** *R* Can
13F2 **Saskatoon** Can
101G1 **Sasolburg** S Africa
61F3 **Sasovo** Russian Fed
97B4 **Sassandra** Ivory Coast
97B4 **Sassandra** *R* Ivory Coast
53A2 **Sassari** Sardegna
47D2 **Sassnitz** Germany
34C2 **Sastre** Arg
87A1 **Sátāra** India
4G2 **Satellite B** Can
78D4 **Satengar** *Is* Indon
39H6 **Säter** Sweden
17B1 **Satilla** *R* USA
61J2 **Satka** Russian Fed
84D2 **Satluj** *R* India
86A2 **Satna** India
85C4 **Sátpura Range** *Mts* India
54B1 **Satu Mare** Rom
34D2 **Sauce** Arg
39F7 **Sauda** Nor
80C3 **Saudi Arabia** Kingdom, Arabian Pen
46D2 **Sauer** *R* Germany/Lux
46D1 **Sauerland** Region, Germany
38B1 **Sauðárkrókur** Iceland

14A2 **Saugatuck** USA
16C1 **Saugerties** USA
13B2 **Saugstad,Mt** Can
7B5 **Sault Sainte Marie** Can
14B1 **Sault Ste Marie** Can
14B1 **Sault Ste Marie** Can
71E4 **Saumlaki** Indon
48B2 **Saumur** France
98C3 **Saurimo** Angola
27M2 **Sauteurs** Grenada
54A2 **Sava** *R* Serbia, Yugos
97C4 **Savalou** Benin
17B1 **Savannah** Georgia, USA
17B1 **Savannah** *R* USA
76C2 **Savannakhet** Laos
26B3 **Savanna la Mar** Jamaica
7A4 **Savant Lake** Can
76D2 **Savaranae** Laos
97C4 **Savé** Benin
101C3 **Save** *R* Mozam
90B3 **Săveh** Iran
46D2 **Saverne** France
47B2 **Savigliano** Italy
46B2 **Savigny** France
49D2 **Savoie** *Region* France
52A2 **Savona** Italy
38K6 **Savonlinna** Fin
4A3 **Savoonga** Fin
38K5 **Savukoski** Fin
71D4 **Savu S** Indon
76A1 **Saw** Myan
85D3 **Sawai Mādhopur** India
78A2 **Sawang** Indon
76B2 **Sawankhalok** Thai
75C1 **Sawara** Japan
12E1 **Sawtooth Mt** USA
106B2 **Sawu** *I* Indon
9C3 **Say** Niger
84B1 **Sayghan** Afghan
9185 **Sayhut** Yem
61G4 **Saykhin** Kazakhstan
68D2 **Saynshand** Mongolia
61H5 **Say-Utes** Kazakhstan
16C2 **Sayville** USA
13B2 **Sayward** Can
57C3 **Sázava** *R* Czech Republic
51C2 **Sbisseb** *R* Alg
42C2 **Scafell Pike** *Mt* Eng
44E1 **Scalloway** Scot
44C2 **Scapa Flow** *Sd* Scot
15C2 **Scarborough** Can
42D2 **Scarborough** Eng
27E4 **Scarborough** Tobago
44A2 **Scarp** *I* Scot
45B2 **Scarriff** Irish Rep
52A1 **Schaffhausen** Switz
57C3 **Scharding** Austria
46D1 **Scharteberg** *Mt* Germany
7D4 **Schefferville** Can
46D1 **Schelde** *R* Belg
10C2 **Schenectady** USA
47D2 **Schio** Italy
46D1 **Schleiden** Germany
56B2 **Schleswig** Germany
56B2 **Schleswig Holstein** State, Germany
16B1 **Schoharie** USA
71F4 **Schouten** *Is* PNG
7B5 **Schreiber** Can
21B2 **Schurz** USA
16A2 **Schuykill Haven** USA
16B2 **Schuylkill** *R* USA
57B3 **Schwabische Alb** *Upland* Germany
12C1 **Schwatka Mts** USA
57B3 **Schwarzwald** *Upland* Germany
47C1 **Schwatz** Austria
57C2 **Schweinfurt** Germany
101G1 **Schweizer Reneke** S Africa
56C2 **Schwerin** Germany
47C1 **Schwyz** Switz
53B3 **Sciacca** Italy

14B3 **Scioto** *R* USA
109D2 **Scone** Aust
6H2 **Scoresby Sd** Greenland
103F7 **Scotia Ridge** Atlantic O
103F7 **Scotia S** Atlantic O
44B3 **Scotland** Country, UK
112B7 **Scott Base** Ant
13B2 **Scott,C** Can
9C2 **Scott City** USA
112C6 **Scott I** Ant
6C2 **Scott Inlet** *B* Can
20B2 **Scott,Mt** USA
106B2 **Scott Reef** Timor S
8C2 **Scottsbluff** USA
17A1 **Scottsboro** USA
109C4 **Scottsdale** Aust
10C2 **Scranton** USA
47D1 **Scuol** Switz
Scutari = Shkodër
5J4 **Seal** *R* Can
108B3 **Sea Lake** Aust
18B2 **Searcy** USA
22B2 **Seaside** California, USA
20B1 **Seaside** Oregon, USA
16B3 **Seaside Park** USA
20B1 **Seattle** USA
22A1 **Sebastopol** USA
58D1 **Sebez** Russian Fed
17B2 **Sebring** USA
111A3 **Secretary I** NZ
15B2 **Sedalia** USA
46C2 **Sedan** France
111B2 **Seddonville** NZ
94B3 **Sede Boqer** Israel
94B3 **Sederot** Israel
97A3 **Sédhiou** Sen
94B3 **Sedom** Israel
100A3 **Seeheim** Namibia
111B2 **Sefton,Mt** NZ
77C5 **Segamat** Malay
97B3 **Segorbe** Spain
97B3 **Ségou** Mali
Ségou = Coco
50B1 **Segovia** Spain
51C1 **Segre** *R* Spain
96A2 **Séguéla** Ivory Coast
96A2 **Seguia el Hamra** *Watercourse* Mor
34C2 **Segundo** *R* Arg
50B2 **Seguntur** Indon
50B2 **Segura** *R* Spain
85B3 **Sehwan** Pak
46D2 **Seille** *R* France
38J6 **Seinäjoki** Fin
48C2 **Seine** *R* France
46B2 **Seine-et-Marne** Department, France
99D3 **Sekenke** Tanz
5H4 **Sek'ot'a** Eth
20B1 **Selah** USA
71E4 **Selaru** *I* Indon
78D4 **Selat Alas** *Str* Indon
78B3 **Selat Bangka** *Str* Indon
78A3 **Selat Berhala** *B* Indon
78D4 **Selat Dampier** *Str* Indon
78B3 **Selat Gaspar** *Str* Indon
78D4 **Selat Lombok** *Str* Indon
78D4 **Selat Sapo** *Str* Indon
78B4 **Selat Sunda** *Str* Indon
71D4 **Selat Wetar** *Chan* Indon
12B1 **Selawik** USA
12B1 **Selawik** *R* USA
12B1 **Selawik L** USA
42D3 **Selby** Eng
12D3 **Seldovia** USA
100B3 **Selebi Pikwe** Botswana
96H3 **Setfoss** Iceland
9B3 **Selima Oasis** Sudan
5J4 **Selkirk** Can
42C2 **Selkirk** Scot

13D2 **Selkirk Mts** Can
22C2 **Selma** California, USA
50B2 **Selouane** Mor
12H2 **Selous,Mt** Can
78B3 **Selta Karimata** Str Indon
32C5 **Selvas** Region, Brazil
107D3 **Selwyn** Aust
4E3 **Selwyn Mts** Can
78C4 **Semarang** Indon
61E2 **Semenov** Russian Fed
12C3 **Semidi Is** USA
60E3 **Semiluki** Russian Fed
19A2 **Seminole** Oklahoma, USA
17B1 **Seminole,L** USA
65K4 **Semipalatinsk** Kazakhstan
79B3 **Semirara Is** Phil
90B3 **Semirom** Iran
78C2 **Semitau** Indon
90B2 **Semnān** Iran
46C2 **Semois** R Belg
32B2 **Sempoala** Hist Site, Mexico
32D5 **Sena Madureira** Brazil
100B2 **Senanga** Zambia
19C3 **Senatobia** USA
74E3 **Sendai** Honshū, Japan
74C4 **Sendai** Kyūshū, Japan
85D4 **Sendwha** India
15C2 **Seneca Falls** USA
97A3 **Senegal** Republic, Africa
97A3 **Sénégal** R Maur Sen
101G1 **Senekal** S Africa
31D4 **Senhor do Bonfim** Brazil
52B2 **Senigallia** Italy
52C2 **Senj** Croatia
69E4 **Senkaku Gunto** Is Japan
46B2 **Senlis** France
99D1 **Sennar** Sudan
7C5 **Senneterre** Can
49C2 **Sens** France
54A1 **Senta** Serbia, Yugos
98C3 **Sentery** Zaïre
13C2 **Sentinel Peak** Mt Can
85D4 **Seoni** India
Seoul = Soul
110B2 **Separation Pt** NZ
76D2 **Sepone** Laos
7D4 **Sept-Iles** Can
95A2 **Séquédine** Niger
21B2 **Sequoia Nat Pk,** USA
71D4 **Seram** I Indon
71B4 **Serang** Indon
78B3 **Serasan** I Indon
54A2 **Serbia** Republic, Yugos
61F3 **Serdobsk** Russian Fed
77C5 **Seremban** Malay
99D3 **Serengeti Nat Pk** Tanz
100C2 **Serenje** Zambia
59D3 **Seret** R Ukraine
61G2 **Sergach** Russian Fed
65H3 **Sergino** Russian Fed
31D4 **Sergipe** State, Brazil
60E2 **Segiyev Posad** Russian Fed
78C2 **Seria** Brunei
78C2 **Serian** Malay
55B3 **Sérifos** I Greece
47C2 **Serio** R Italy
95B2 **Serir Calanscio** Desert Libya
46C2 **Sermaize-les-Bains** France
71H3 **Sermata** I Indon
61H3 **Sernovodsk** Russian Fed
65H4 **Serov** Russian Fed
100B3 **Serowe** Botswana
50A2 **Serpa** Port

60E3 **Serpukhov** Russian Fed
35B2 **Serra da Canastra** Mts Brazil
50A1 **Serra da Estrela** Mts Port
35B2 **Serra da Mantiqueira** Mts Brazil
35A1 **Serra da Mombuca** Brazil
35C1 **Serra do Cabral** Mt Brazil
33F5 **Serra do Cachimbo** Mts Brazil
35A1 **Serra do Caiapó** Mts Brazil
35A2 **Serra do Cantu** Mts Brazil
35C2 **Serra do Caparaó** Mts Brazil
31C5 **Serra do Chifre** Brazil
35C1 **Serra do Espinhaço** Mts Brazil
35B2 **Serra do Mar** Mts Brazil
35A2 **Serra do Mirante** Mts Brazil
33G3 **Serra do Navio** Brazil
35B2 **Serra do Paranapiacaba** Mts Brazil
33F6 **Serra dos Caiabis** Mts Brazil
35A2 **Serra dos Dourados** Brazil
33E6 **Serra dos Parecis** Mts Brazil
35B1 **Serra dos Pilões** Mts Brazil
35A1 **Serra Dourada** Brazil
33F6 **Serra Formosa** Brazil
55B2 **Sérrai** Greece
25D3 **Serrana Bank** I Caribbean S
51B1 **Serrana de Cuenca** Mts Spain
35A1 **Serranópolis** Brazil
33E3 **Serra Pacaraima** Mts Brazil/Ven
33E3 **Serra Parima** Mts Brazil
33G3 **Serra Tumucumaque** Brazil
46B2 **Serre** R France
34B2 **Serrezuela** Arg
31D4 **Serrinha** Brazil
6G3 **Serrmilik** Greenland
35C1 **Serro** Brazil
35A2 **Sertanópolis** Brazil
72A3 **Sertar** China
78C3 **Seruyan** R Indon
100A2 **Sesfontein** Namibia
100B2 **Sesheke** Zambia
37D4 **Sestri Levante** Italy
74D2 **Setana** Japan
49C3 **Sète** France
35C1 **Sete Lagoas** Brazil
96C1 **Sétif** Alg
75A2 **Seto Naikai** S Japan
96B1 **Settat** Mor
42C2 **Settle** Eng
5G4 **Settler** Can
50A2 **Sétubal** Port
93E1 **Sevan,Oz** L Armenia
60D5 **Sevastopol'** Ukraine
7B4 **Severn** R Can
43C3 **Severn** R Eng
59D3 **Severnaya Zemlya** I Russian Fed
63C2 **Severo-Baykalskoye** Russian Fed
60E4 **Severo Donets** Ukraine
64E3 **Severodvinsk** Russian Fed
64H3 **Severo Sos'va** R Russian Fed
8B3 **Sevier** R USA
8B3 **Sevier L** USA
50A2 **Sevilla** Spain

Seville = Sevilla
54C2 **Sevlievo** Bulg
97A4 **Sewa** R Sierra Leone
12E2 **Seward** Alaska, USA
18A1 **Seward** Nebraska, USA
12A1 **Seward Pen** USA
13D1 **Sexsmith** Can
89K8 **Seychelles** Is Indian O
38C1 **Seyðisfjörður** Iceland
92C2 **Seyhan** Turk
60E3 **Seym** R Russian Fed
108C3 **Seymour** Aust
16C2 **Seymour** Connecticut, USA
14A3 **Seymour** Indiana, USA
46B2 **Sézanne** France
96D1 **Sfax** Tunisia
54C1 **Sfîntu Gheorghe** Rom
56A2 **'s-Gravenhage** Neth
72B3 **Shaanxi** Province, China
98C3 **Shabunda** Zaïre
82B2 **Shache** China
112C9 **Shackleton Ice Shelf** Ant
85B3 **Shadadkot** Pak
91B3 **Shādhām** R Iran
43C4 **Shaftesbury** Eng
29G8 **Shag Rocks** Is South Georgia
90A3 **Shāhābād** Iran
94C2 **Shahbā** Syria
91C3 **Shahdap** Iran
86B2 **Shahdol** India
90A2 **Shāhīn Dezh** Iran
90C3 **Shāh Kūh** Iran
91C3 **Shahr-e Bābak** Iran
90B3 **Shahr Kord** Iran
87B1 **Shājābād** India
84D3 **Shājahānpur** India
85D4 **Shājapur** India
61F4 **Shakhty** Russian Fed
61G2 **Shakhun'ya** Russian Fed
97C4 **Shaki** Nig
12B2 **Shaktoolik** USA
91J2 **Shamary** Russian Fed
99D2 **Shambe** Sudan
16A2 **Shamokin** USA
16B1 **Shandaken** USA
72D2 **Shandong** Province, China
72C3 **Shangchuan Dao** I China
72C1 **Shangdu** China
73E3 **Shanghai** China
72C3 **Shangnan** China
100B2 **Shangombo** Zambia
73D4 **Shangrao** China
73B5 **Shangsi** China
72C3 **Shang Xian** China
41B3 **Shannon** R Irish Rep
72D3 **Shanqiu** China
74B2 **Shansonggang** China
63F2 **Shantarskiye Ostrova** I Russian Fed
73D5 **Shantou** China
72C2 **Shanxi** Province, China
72D3 **Shan Xian** China
73C5 **Shaoguan** China
73C4 **Shaoxing** China
73C4 **Shaoyang** China
44C2 **Shapinsay** I Scot
94C2 **Shaqqā** Syria
72A1 **Sharhulsan** Mongolia
94B2 **Sharon,Plain of** Israel
61G2 **Sharya** Russian Fed
99D2 **Shashemanē** Eth
73C3 **Shashi** China
20B2 **Shasta L** USA
20B2 **Shasta,Mt** USA

93E3 **Shatt al Gharrat** R Iraq
94B3 **Shaubak** Jordan
13F3 **Shaunavon** Can
22C2 **Shaver L** USA
16B2 **Shawangunk Mt** USA
15D1 **Shawinigan** Can
19A2 **Shawnee** Oklahoma, USA
73D4 **Sha Xian** China
106B3 **Shay Gap** Aust
94C2 **Shaykh Miskin** Syria
99E1 **Shaykh 'Uthmān** Yemen
60E3 **Shchekino** Russian Fed
60D3 **Shchors** Ukraine
65J4 **Shchuchinsk** Kazakhstan
99E2 **Shebele** R Eth
14A2 **Sheboygan** USA
98B2 **Shebshi Mts** Nig
12F1 **Sheenjek** R USA
43C4 **Sheep Haven** Estuary Irish Rep
43E3 **Sheerness** Eng
94B2 **Shefar'am** Israel
42D3 **Sheffield** Eng
84C2 **Shekhupura** Pak
13B1 **Shelagyote Peak** Mt Can
16C1 **Shelburne Falls** USA
8B2 **Shelby** Michigan, USA
8B2 **Shelby** Montana, USA
14A3 **Shelbyville** Indiana, USA
12H2 **Sheldon,Mt** Can
12D3 **Shelikof Str** USA
109D2 **Shellharbour** Aust
111A3 **Shelter Pt** NZ
20B1 **Shelton** USA
93E1 **Shemakha** Azerbaijan
18A1 **Shenandoah** USA
14C3 **Shenandoah** R USA
15C3 **Shenandoah Nat Pk** USA
97C4 **Shendam** Nig
95C2 **Shendi** Sudan
72C2 **Shenmu** China
72E1 **Shenyang** China
73C5 **Shenzhen** China
85D3 **Sheopur** India
59D2 **Shepetovka** Ukraine
108C3 **Shepparton** Aust
43C4 **Sherborne** Eng
97A4 **Sherbro** I Sierra Leone
15D1 **Sherbrooke** Can
85C3 **Shergarh** India
19B3 **Sheridan** Arkansas, USA
8C2 **Sheridan** Wyoming, USA
19A3 **Sherman** USA
56B2 **s-Hertogenbosch** Neth
12H3 **Sheslay** Can
40C1 **Shetland** Is Scot
93E1 **Shevchenko = Aktau**
91B4 **Sheyk Sho'eyb** I Iran
69H2 **Shiashkotan** I Russian Fed
84B1 **Shibarghan** Afghan
74D3 **Shibata** Japan
95C1 **Shibin el Kom** Egypt
75B1 **Shibukawa** Japan
72C2 **Shijiazhuang** China
84B3 **Shikarpur** Pak
67G3 **Shikoku** Japan
74C4 **Shikoku-sanchi** Mts Japan
86B1 **Shiliguri** India
61F3 **Shilka** Russian Fed
68D1 **Shilka** R Russian Fed
16B2 **Shillington** USA
86C1 **Shillong** India
61F3 **Shilovo** Russian Fed
75A2 **Shimabara** Japan

Shimada

75B2 **Shimada** Japan	54B1 **Sibiu** Rom	23B2 **Sierra de Zongolica** Mexico	49D2 **Simplon** *Mt* Switz
69E1 **Shimanovsk** Russian Fed	70A3 **Sibolga** Indon	34C2 **Sierra Grande** *Mts* Arg	47C1 **Simplon** *P* Switz
74D3 **Shimizu** Japan	86C1 **Sibsāgar** India	97A4 **Sierra Leone** Republic, Africa	4C2 **Simpson,C** USA
74D3 **Shimla** India	78C2 **Sibu** Malay	97A4 **Sierra Leone,C** Sierra Leone	106C3 **Simpson Desert** Aust
75B2 **Shimoda** Japan	79B4 **Sibuguay** *B* Phil	79B2 **Sierra Madre** Phil	6B3 **Simpson Pen** Can
87B2 **Shimoga** India	98B2 **Sibut** CAR	23A2 **Sierra Madre del Sur** *Mts* Mexico	39G7 **Simrishamn** Sweden
74C4 **Shimonoseki** Japan	79B3 **Sibuyan** *I* Phil	24B2 **Sierra Madre Occidental** *Mts* Mexico	69H2 **Simushir** *I* Russian Fed
75B1 **Shimano** *R* Japan	79B3 **Sibuyan S** Phil	24C2 **Sierra Madre Oriental** *Mts* Mexico	99E2 **Sina Dhaqa** Somalia
91C5 **Shinās** Oman	73A3 **Sichuan** Province, China	34B2 **Sierra Malanzan** *Mts* Arg	92B4 **Sinai** *Pen* Egypt
74D4 **Shingū** Japan	53B3 **Sicilia** *I Medit S*	9C4 **Sierra Mojada** Mexico	32B2 **Sincelejo** Colombia
75C1 **Shinjō** Japan	53B3 **Sicilian** *Chan* Italy/ Tunisia	50A2 **Sierra Morena** *Mts* Spain	17B1 **Sinclair,L** USA
74D3 **Shinminato** Japan	**Sicily** = **Sicilia**	50B2 **Sierra Nevada** *Mts* Spain	85D3 **Sind** *R* India
94C1 **Shinshar** Syria	32C6 **Sicuani** Peru	21A2 **Sierra Nevada** *Mts* USA	85D3 **Sind** Region, Pak
99D3 **Shinyanga** Tanz	85C4 **Siddhapur** India	32C1 **Sierra Nevada de Santa Marta** *Mts* Colombia	55C3 **Sindirği** Turk
74E3 **Shiogama** Japan	87B1 **Siddipet** India		86B2 **Sindri** India
75B2 **Shiono-misaki** *C* Japan	86A2 **Sidhi** India	34B2 **Sierra Pié de Palo** *Mts* Arg	50A2 **Sines** Port
73A5 **Shiping** China	44C3 **Sidlaw Hills** Scot	47B1 **Sierre** Switz	99D1 **Singa** Sudan
16A2 **Shippensburg** USA	112B5 **Sidley,Mt** Ant	55B3 **Sifnos** *I* Greece	77C5 **Singapore** Republic, S E Asia
72B3 **Shiquan** China	20B1 **Sidney** Can	59C3 **Sighetu Marmaţiei** Rom	
75C1 **Shirakawa** Japan	8C2 **Sidney** Nebraska, USA	54B1 **Sighişoara** Rom	77C5 **Singapore,Str of** S E Asia
75B1 **Shirane-san** *Mt* Japan		38B1 **Siglufjörđur** Iceland	78D4 **Singaraja** Indon
	15C2 **Sidney** New York, USA	50B1 **Sigüenza** Spain	99D3 **Singida** Tanz
75B1 **Shirani-san** *Mt* Japan	14B2 **Sidney** Ohio, USA	97B3 **Siguiri** Guinea	78B2 **Singkawang** Indon
91B4 **Shiraz** Iran	17B1 **Sidney Lanier,L** USA	**Sihanoukville** = **Kompong Som**	109D2 **Singleton** Aust
90B3 **Shir Kūh** Iran	**Sidon** = **Säida**		76B1 **Singu** Myan
75B1 **Shirotori** Japan	58C2 **Siedlce** Pol	85E4 **Sihora** India	53A2 **Siniscola** Sardegna
90C2 **Shirvan** Iran	46D1 **Sieg** *R* Germany	93D2 **Siirt** Turk	93D2 **Sinjār** Iraq
12A1 **Shishmaref** USA	46D1 **Siegburg** Germany	68B3 **Sikai Hu** *L* China	84B2 **Sinkai Hills** *Mts* Afghan
12A1 **Shishmaref Inlet** USA	46D1 **Siegen** Germany	85D3 **Sikar** India	95C3 **Sinkat** Sudan
	76C3 **Siem Reap** Camb	84B2 **Sikaram** *Mt* Afghan	82C1 **Sinkiang** Autonomous Region, China
4B3 **Shishmaret** USA	52B2 **Siena** Italy	97B3 **Sikasso** Mali	
72B2 **Shitanjing** China	58B2 **Sierpc** Pol	18C2 **Sikeston** USA	33G2 **Sinnamary** French Guiana
14A3 **Shively** USA	23B2 **Sierra Andrés Tuxtla** Mexico	55C3 **Síkinos** *I* Greece	92C1 **Sinop** Turk
85D3 **Shivpuri** India		55B3 **Sikionía** Greece	54B1 **Sîntana** Rom
94B3 **Shivta** *Hist Site* Israel	34B3 **Sierra Auca Mahuida** *Mts* Arg	86B1 **Sikkim** State, India	78C2 **Sintang** Indon
101C2 **Shiwa Ngandu** Zambia	9C3 **Sierra Blanca** USA	50A1 **Sil** *R* Spain	50A2 **Sintra** Port
72C3 **Shiyan** China	51B1 **Sierra de Albarracin** *Mts* Spain	47D1 **Silandro** Italy	32B2 **Sinú** *R* Colombia
72B2 **Shizuishan** China		23A1 **Silao** Mexico	74A2 **Sinŭiju** N Korea
75B1 **Shizuoka** Japan	50B2 **Sierra de Alcaraz** *Mts* Spain	79B3 **Silay** Phil	59B3 **Siófok** Hung
54C2 **Shkodër** Alb	34B2 **Sierra de Cordoba** *Mts* Arg	86C2 **Silchar** India	47B1 **Sion** Switz
109D2 **Shoalhaven** *R* Aust		96C2 **Silet** Alg	8D2 **Sioux City** USA
75A2 **Shobara** Japan	50A1 **Sierra de Gredos** *Mts* Spain	86A1 **Silgarhi** Nepal	8D2 **Sioux Falls** USA
87B2 **Shoranūr** India	50A2 **Sierra de Guadalupe** *Mts* Spain	92B2 **Silifke** Turk	10A2 **Sioux Lookout** Can
21B2 **Shoshone** *Mts* USA		82C2 **Siling Co** *L* China	79B4 **Sipalay** Phil
60D3 **Shostka** Ukraine	50B1 **Sierra de Guadarrama** *Mts* Spain	54C2 **Silistra** Bulg	27L1 **Siparia** Trinidad
19B3 **Shreveport** USA	51B1 **Sierra de Guara** *Mts* Spain	39F7 **Silkeborg** Den	69E2 **Siping** China
43C3 **Shrewsbury** Eng	51B1 **Sierra de Gudar** *Mts* Spain	47E1 **Sillian** Austria	112B3 **Siple** *Base* Ant
43C3 **Shropshire** County, Eng	23B2 **Sierra de Juárez** Mexico	18B2 **Siloam Springs** USA	112B5 **Siple I** Ant
72E1 **Shuanglia** China	34C3 **Sierra de la Ventana** *Mts* Arg	19B3 **Silsbee** USA	79B3 **Sipocot** Phil
69F2 **Shuangyashan** China		93A2 **Şiltou** *Well* Chad	70A4 **Sipora** Indon
61J4 **Shubar-Kuduk** Kazakhstan	51C1 **Sierra del Codi** *Mts* Spain	58C1 **Silute** Lithuania	79B4 **Siquijor** *I* Phil
72D2 **Shu He** *R* China	34B2 **Sierra del Morro** *Mt* Arg	93D2 **Silvan** Turk	87B2 **Sira** India
73A4 **Shuicheng** China	34B3 **Sierra del Nevado** *Mts* Arg	35B1 **Silvania** Brazil	53C3 **Siracusa** Italy
84C3 **Shujaabad** Pak	24B2 **Sierra de los Alamitos** *Mts* Mexico	85C4 **Silvassa** India	86B2 **Sirajganj** Bang
85D4 **Shujālpur** India		21B2 **Silver City** Nevada, USA	13C2 **Sir Alexander,Mt** Can
68B2 **Shule He** China	50B2 **Sierra de los Filabres** Spain	9C3 **Silver City** New Mexico, USA	91B5 **Sir Bani Yās** *I* UAE
54C2 **Shumen** Bulg	23A1 **Sierra de los Huicholes** Mexico	20B2 **Silver Lake** USA	106C2 **Sir Edward Pellew Group** *Is* Aust
61G2 **Shumerlya** Russian Fed	23B2 **Sierra de Miahuatlán** Mexico	16A3 **Silver Spring** USA	
73D4 **Shuncheng** China	23A1 **Sierra de Morones** *Mts* Mexico	13B2 **Silverthrone Mt** Can	54C1 **Siret** *R* Rom
12C1 **Shungnak** USA		108B2 **Silverton** Aust	12J2 **Sir James McBrien,Mt** Can
72C2 **Shuo Xian** China	50A2 **Sierra de Ronda** *Mts* Spain	47C1 **Silvretta** *Mts* Austria/Switz	87B2 **Sir Kālahasti** India
90A3 **Shūr Gaz** Iran	34B2 **Sierra de San Luis** *Mts* Arg	78C2 **Simanggang** Malay	13D2 **Sir Laurier,Mt** Can
100B2 **Shurugwi** Zim	50B2 **Sierra de Segura** *Mts* Spain	76C1 **Simao** China	85C4 **Sirohi** India
13D2 **Shushan L** Can	50B1 **Sierra de Urbion** *Mts* Spain	90A3 **Simareh** *R* Iran	87B1 **Sironcha** India
61F2 **Shuya** Russian Fed	34B2 **Sierra de Uspallata** *Mts* Arg	75C3 **Simav** Turk	85D4 **Sironj** India
12D3 **Shuyak I** USA	34B2 **Sierra de Valle Fértil** *Mts* Arg	55C3 **Simav** *R* Turk	55B3 **Síros** *I* Greece
82D3 **Shwebo** Myan		61G3 **Simbirsk** Russian Fed	91B4 **Sirri** *I* Iran
76B2 **Shwegyin** Myan		15C2 **Simcoe,L** Can	84D3 **Sirsa** India
84A2 **Siah Koh** *Mts* Afghan		70A3 **Simeulue** *I* Indon	13D2 **Sir Sandford,Mt** Can
84C2 **Sialkot** Pak		60D5 **Simferopol'** Ukraine	87A2 **Sirsi** India
Sian = **Xi'an**		55C3 **Simi** *I* Greece	95A1 **Sirte Desert** Libya
79C4 **Siarao** *I* Phil		46D1 **Simmern** Germany	95A1 **Sirte,G of** Libya
79B4 **Siaton** Phil		13B2 **Simoon Sound** Can	52C1 **Sisak** Croatia
58C1 **Siauliai** Lithuania			76C2 **Sissone** France
65G4 **Sibay** Russian Fed			90D3 **Sistan** Region, Iran/ Afghan
101H1 **Sibayi** *L* S Africa			49D3 **Sisteron** France
52C2 **Šibenik** Croatia			63B2 **Sistig Khem** Russian Fed
70A4 **Siberut** *I* Indon			86A1 **Sitapur** India
84B3 **Sibi** Pak			55C3 **Sitia** Greece
68C1 **Sibirskoye** Russian Fed			4E4 **Sitka** USA
98B3 **Sibiti** Congo			12D3 **Sitkalidak I** USA
99D3 **Sibiti** *R* Tanz			12D3 **Sitkinak I** USA

76B2 **Sittang** *R* Myan
46C1 **Sittard** Neth
86C2 **Sittwe** Myan
78C4 **Situbondo** Indon
92C2 **Sivas** Turk
92D2 **Siverek** Turk
92B2 **Sivrihisar** Turk
95B2 **Siwa** Egypt
86A1 **Siwalik Range** *Mts* India
72D3 **Siyang** China
56C1 **Sjaelland** *I* Den
39J7 **Skagen** Den
39F7 **Skagerrak** *Str* Nor/Den
20B1 **Skagit** *R* USA
20B1 **Skagit** *R* USA
4E4 **Skagway** USA
39G7 **Skara** Sweden
59C2 **Skarzysko-Kamlenna** Pol
5F4 **Skeena** *R* Can
13B1 **Skeena Mts** Can
4D3 **Skeenjek** *R* USA
42E3 **Skegness** Eng
39H5 **Skelleftе** *R* Sweden
38J6 **Skellefteå** Sweden
55B3 **Skiathos** *I* Greece
45B3 **Skibbereen** Irish Rep
5K4 **Skidegate** Can
58C2 **Skiemiewice** Pol
39F7 **Skien** Nor
96C1 **Skikda** Alg
74C4 **Skikoku** *I* Japan
42D3 **Skipton** Eng
55B3 **Skiros** *I* Greece
39F7 **Skive** Den
56B1 **Skjern** Den
6F3 **Skjoldungen** Greenland
14A2 **Skokie** USA
55B3 **Skópelos** *I* Greece
55B2 **Skopje** Macedonia
39G7 **Skövde** Sweden
63E2 **Skovorodino** Russian Fed
4C3 **Skwentna** USA
58B2 **Skwierzyna** Pol
40B2 **Skye** *I* Scot
39G7 **Slagelse** Den
45C2 **Slaney** *R* Irish Rep
54B2 **Slatina** Rom
78C4 **Slaung** Indon
5G3 **Slave** *R* Can
13E1 **Slave Lake** Can
65J4 **Slavgorod** Russian Fed
59D2 **Slavuta** Ukraine
60E4 **Slavyansk** Ukraine
44B3 **Sleat,Sound of** *Chan* Scot
12C2 **Sleetmute** USA
45C2 **Sleeve Bloom** *Mts* Irish Rep
19C3 **Slidell** USA
16B2 **Slide Mt** USA
45B1 **Sligo** County, Irish Rep
41B3 **Sligo** Irish Rep
41B3 **Sligo B** Irish Rep
54C2 **Sliven** Bulg
54C2 **Slobozia** Rom
13D3 **Slocan** Can
52B1 **Slonim** Belarus
43D4 **Slough** Eng
22B2 **Slough** *R* USA
59B3 **Slovakia** Republic, Europe
52B1 **Slovenia** Republic, Europe
52B1 **Slubice** Pol
59D2 **Sluch'** *R* Ukraine
58B2 **Słupsk** Pol
52B2 **Slutsk** Belarus
58D2 **Slutsk** *R* Belarus
41A3 **Slyne Head** *Pt* Irish Rep
63C2 **Slyudyanka** Russian Fed
7D4 **Smallwood Res** Can
52B3 **Smederevo** Serbia, Yugos

54B2 **Smederevska Palanka** Serbia, Yugos
60D4 **Smela** Ukraine
15C2 **Smethport** USA
13E1 **Smith** Can
4F3 **Smith Arm** *B* Can
13B2 **Smithers** Can
7C3 **Smith I** Can
13B2 **Smith Sd** Can
15C2 **Smiths Falls** Can
109C4 **Smithton** Aust
13D1 **Smoky** *R* Can
109D2 **Smoky C** Aust
13E2 **Smoky Lake** Can
38F6 **Smøla** *I* Nor
60D3 **Smolensk** Russian Fed
55B2 **Smólikas** *Mt* Greece
54B2 **Smolyan** Bulg
58D2 **Smorgon'** Belarus
16B3 **Smyrna** Delaware, USA
17B1 **Smyrna** Georgia, USA
42B2 **Snaefell** *Mt* Eng
38B2 **Snafell** *Mt* Iceland
8B2 **Snake** *R* USA
8B2 **Snake River Canyon** USA
56B2 **Sneek** Neth
45B3 **Sneem** Irish Rep
22B2 **Snelling** USA
59B2 **Snězka** *Mt* Pol/Czech Republic
38F6 **Snøhetta** *Mt* Nor
20B1 **Snohomish** USA
20B1 **Snoqualmie** *R* USA
76D3 **Snoul** Camb
43B3 **Snowdon** *Mt* Wales
43B3 **Snowdonia Nat Pk** Wales
4G3 **Snowdrift** Can
5H4 **Snow Lake** Can
108A2 **Snowtown** Aust
109C3 **Snowy Mts** Aust
9C3 **Snyder** USA
78A4 **Soan-kundo** *I* S Korea
99D2 **Sobat** *R* Sudan
31C2 **Sobral** Brazil
58C2 **Sochaczew** Pol
61E5 **Sochi** Russian Fed
9C3 **Socorro** USA
24A3 **Socorro** *I* Mexico
34A2 **Socos** Chile
81D4 **Socotra** *I* Yemen
38K5 **Sodankylä** *I* Fin
39H6 **Soderhamn** Sweden
39H7 **Södertälje** Sweden
99C1 **Sodiri** Sudan
99D2 **Sodo** Eth
46E1 **Soest** Germany
101C2 **Sofala** Mozam
Sofia = **Sofiya**
54C2 **Sofiya** Bulg
69G4 **Sofu Gan** / Japan
32C2 **Sogamoso** Colombia
39F6 **Sognefjorden** *Inlet* Nor
98D2 **Sog Xian** China
95C2 **Sohâg** Egypt
84D3 **Sohipat** India
46B1 **Soignies** Belg
46B2 **Soissons** France
85C3 **Sojat** India
74A3 **Söjoson-man** *B* N Korea
92A2 **Söke** Turk
97C4 **Sokodé** Togo
68E2 **Sokol** Russian Fed
97B3 **Sokolo** Mali
6H3 **Sokongens Øy** / Greenland
99D1 **Sokota** Eth
97C3 **Sokoto** Nig
97C3 **Sokoto** *R* Nig
111A2 **Solander I** NZ
79B2 **Solano** Phil
87B1 **Solapur** India
47D1 **Solbad Hall** Austria
47D1 **Sölden** Austria
12D2 **Soldotna** USA
26C4 **Soledad** Colombia

43D4 **Solent** *Sd* Eng
46B1 **Solesmes** France
58D2 **Soligorsk** Belarus
61J2 **Solikamsk** Russian Fed
32C4 **Solimões** *R* Peru
46D1 **Solingen** Germany
38H6 **Sollefteå** Sweden
61H3 **Sol'lletsk** Russian Fed
70B4 **Solok** Indon
105G4 **Solomon** *Is* Pacific O
47B1 **Solothurn** Switz
39F8 **Soltau** Germany
22B3 **Solvang** USA
42C2 **Solway Firth** *Estuary* Eng/Scot
100B2 **Solwezi** Zambia
75C1 **Sōma** Japan
55C3 **Soma** Turk
81C5 **Somalia** Republic, E Africa
54A1 **Sombor** Serbia, Yugos
107D2 **Somerset East**, USA
43C4 **Somerset** County, Eng
16D2 **Somerset** Massachusetts, USA
15C2 **Somerset** Pennsylvania, USA
100B4 **Somerset East** S Africa
16B3 **Somerset I** Can
16B3 **Somers Point** USA
16D2 **Somerville** USA
19A3 **Somerville** USA
54B1 **Somes** *R* Rom
46B2 **Somme** Department, France
46B2 **Somme** *R* France
46C2 **Sommesous** France
86A2 **Son** *R* India
74A3 **Sonch'ŏn** N Korea
39F8 **Sønderborg** Den
6E3 **Søndre Strømfjord** Greenland
47C1 **Sondrio** Italy
76D3 **Song Ba** *R* Viet
76D3 **Song Cau** Viet
101C2 **Songea** Tanz
73E3 **Songjiang** China
77C4 **Songkhla** Thai
74B3 **Songnim** N Korea
76D3 **Song Pahang** *R* Malay
72A3 **Songpan** China
72C1 **Sonid Youqi** China
76C1 **Son La** Viet
85B3 **Sonmiani** Pak
85B3 **Sonmiani Bay** Pak
22A1 **Sonoma** USA
22B2 **Sonora** California, USA
24A2 **Sonora** *R* Mexico
9B3 **Sonoran Desert** USA
22C1 **Sonora P** USA
25D3 **Sonsonate** El Salvador
71F2 **Sonsorol** *I* Pacific O
10B2 **Soo Canals** Can/USA
13C3 **Sooke** Can
58B2 **Sopot** Pol
59B3 **Sopron** Hung
22B2 **Soquel** USA
53C3 **Sora** Italy
94B3 **Sored** *R* Israel
15D1 **Sorel** Can
109C4 **Sorell** Aust
92C2 **Sorgun** Turk
50B1 **Soria** Spain
38J5 **Sørkjosen** Nor
64C2 **Sørksop** *R* Barents S
61H4 **Sor Mertvyy Kultuk** *Plain* Kazakhstan
35B2 **Sorocaba** Brazil
61H3 **Sorochinsk** Russian Fed
71E3 **Soroi** *I* Pacific O
60C4 **Soroki** Moldova
71E4 **Sorong** Indon
71E4 **Sorong** Province, Indon
99D2 **Soroti** Uganda

38J4 **Sørøya** *I* Nor
53B2 **Sorrento** Italy
38K5 **Sorsatunturi** *Mt* Fin
38H5 **Sorsele** Sweden
79B3 **Sorsogon** Phil
38L6 **Sortavala** Russian Fed
74B3 **Sŏsan** S Korea
59B2 **Sosnowiec** Pol
65H4 **Sos'va** Russian Fed
98B2 **Souanké** Congo
97B4 **Soubré** Ivory Coast
16B2 **Souderton** USA
27P2 **Soufrière** St Lucia
27N2 **Soufrière** *Mt* St Vincent and the Grenadines
48C3 **Souillac** France
96C1 **Souk Ahras** Alg
74B3 **Soul** S Korea
51C2 **Soummam** *R* Alg
Sour = **Tyr**
101G1 **Sources,Mt aux** Lesotho
31D3 **Sousa** Brazil
96D1 **Sousse** Tunisia
100B4 **South Africa** Republic, Africa
16B2 **South Amboy** USA
14B2 **Southampton** Can
43D4 **Southampton** Eng
16C2 **Southampton** USA
6B3 **Southampton I** Can
28F6 **South Atlantic O**
7D4 **South Aulatsivik I** Can
106C3 **South Australia** State, Aust
104E5 **South Australian Basin** Indian O
19C3 **Southaven** USA
17B2 **South Bay** USA
14B1 **South Baymouth** Can
14A2 **South Bend** Indiana, USA
20B1 **South Bend** Washington, USA
16D1 **Southbridge** USA
5J4 **South Cape** = Ka Lae
11B3 **South Carolina** State, USA
70C2 **South China S** S E Asia
8C2 **South Dakota** State, USA
16C1 **South Deerfield** USA
43D4 **South Downs** Eng
109C4 **South East C** Aust
111A2 **Southen Alps** *Mts* NZ
5H4 **Southend** Can
43E4 **Southend-on-Sea** Eng
111A2 **Southern Alps** *Mts* NZ
106A4 **Southern Cross** Aust
5J4 **Southern Indian L** Can
27H2 **Southfield** Jamaica
105G5 **South Fiji Basin** Pacific O
12D2 **South Fork** *R* Alaska, USA
22B1 **South Fork** *R* California, USA
28F8 **South Georgia I** S Atlantic O
43C4 **South Glamorgan** County, Wales
14A2 **South Haven** USA
5J3 **South Henik L** Can
104F3 **South Honshu Ridge** Pacific O
111A2 **South I** NZ
16C2 **Southington** USA
74B3 **South Korea** Republic, S E Asia
21A2 **South Lake Tahoe** USA
112C8 **South Magnetic Pole** Ant
17B2 **South Miami** USA
16A3 **South Mt** USA

South Nahanni

4F3	South Nahanni *R* Can	100B4	Springfontein *S* Africa
26G1	South Negril Pt Jamaica	101G1	Springs *S* Africa
103F8	South Orkney *Is* Atlantic O	41D3	Spurn Head *Pt* Eng
8C2	South Platte *R* USA	13C3	Squamish Can
80E	South Pole Ant	60E3	Sredne-Russkaya Vozvyshennost *Upland* Russian Fed
42C3	Southport Eng	63B1	Sredne Sibirskoye Ploskogorye *Tableland* Russian Fed
27R3	South Pt Barbados		
16B2	South River USA		
44C2	South Ronaldsay *I* Scot	61J2	Sredniy Ural *Mts* Russian Fed
103C7	South Sandwich Trench Atlantic O	76D3	Srepok *R* Camb
22A2	South San Francisco USA	68D1	Sretensk Russian Fed
5H4	South Saskatchewan *R* Can	76C3	Sre Umbell Camb
42D2	South Shields Eng	83C5	Sri Lanka Republic, *S* Asia
110B1	South Taranaki Bight *B* NZ	84C2	Srinagar India
44A3	South Uist *I* Scot	87A1	Srivardhan India
	South West Africa = Namibia	58B2	Środa Wlk. Pol
107D5	South West C Aust	30H6	Sta Clara *I* Chile
105J5	South West Pacific Basin Pacific O	32J7	Sta Cruz *I* Ecuador
103D5	South West Peru Ridge Pacific O	62D2	Stade Germany
		44A3	Staffa *I* Scot
43D3	South Yorkshire County, Eng	43C3	Stafford County, Eng
		43C3	Stafford Eng
58C1	Sovetsk Russian Fed	16C2	Stafford Springs USA
61G2	Sovetsk Russian Fed		Stalingrad = Volgograd
101G1	Soweto *S* Africa		
98B3	Soyo Congo Angola	6A1	Stallworthy,C Can
60D3	Sozh *R* Belarus	59C2	Stakowa Wola Pol
46C1	Spa Belg	32J7	Sta Maria *I* Ecuador
50A1	Spain Kingdom, SW Europe	16C2	Stamford Connecticut, USA
43D3	Spalding Eng	16B1	Stamford New York, USA
14B1	Spanish *R* Can	100A3	Stampriet Namibia
26B3	Spanish Town Jamaica	101G1	Standerton *S* Africa
21B2	Sparks USA	14B2	Standish USA
11B3	Spartanburg USA	101H1	Stanger *S* Africa
55B3	Sparti Greece	22B2	Stanislaus *R* USA
69F2	Spassk Dal'niy Russian Fed	54B2	Stanke Dimitrov Bulg
27F3	Speightstown Barbados	109C4	Stanley Aust
		29E6	Stanley Falkland Is
12E2	Spenard USA	87B2	Stanley Res India
14A3	Spencer Indiana, USA		Stanleyville = Kisangani
8D2	Spencer Iowa, USA	25D3	Stann Creek Belize
106A3	Spencer Bay Can	63E2	Stanovoy Khrebet *Mts* Russian Fed
108A2	Spencer,C Aust		
108A2	Spencer G Aust	47C1	Stans Switz
6C3	Spencer I Can	109D1	Stanthorpe Aust
111B2	Spenser Mts NZ	59C2	Starachowice Pol
45B2	Sperrin *Mts* N Ire	54B2	Stara Planina *Mts* Bulg
44C3	Spey *R* Scot		
57B3	Speyer Germany	60D2	Staraya Russa Russian Fed
27K1	Speyside Tobago	54C2	Stara Zagora Bulg
47B1	Spiez Switz	58B2	Stargard Szczeciński Pol
12F1	Spike Mt USA		
20C1	Spirit Lake USA	19C3	Starkville USA
5G4	Spirit River Can	57C3	Starnberg Germany
	Spitsbergen = Svalbard	58B2	Starogard Gdański Pol
64C2	Spitsbergen *I* Barents S	59D3	Starokonstantinov Ukraine
57C3	Spittal Austria	43C4	Start Pt Eng
38F6	Spjelkavik Nor	60E3	Staryy Oskol Russian Fed
52C2	Split Croatia		
47C1	Splügen Switz	15C2	State College USA
20C1	Spokane USA	16B2	Staten I USA
55C3	Sporádhes *Is* Greece	17B1	Statesboro USA
20C2	Spray USA	15C3	Staunton USA
56C2	Spree *R* Germany	39F7	Stavanger Nor
100A3	Springbok *S* Africa	54B2	Stavelot Belg
18B2	Springdale USA	61F4	Stavropol' Russian Fed
10B3	Springfield Illinois, USA		
10C2	Springfield Massachusetts, USA	108B3	Stawell Aust
		59B2	Stawno Pol
18B2	Springfield Missouri, USA	20B2	Stayton USA
		12B2	Stebbins USA
14B3	Springfield Ohio, USA	12F2	Steele,Mt USA
20B2	Springfield Oregon, USA	16A2	Steelton USA
		20C2	Steens Mt USA
15D2	Springfield Vermont, USA	6E2	Steenstrups Gletscher *Gl* Greenland
		4H2	Stefansson I Can
		101H1	Stegi Swaziland
47D1	Steinach Austria	53C3	Stroboli *I* Italy
8D2	Steinbach Can	6E3	Strømfjord Greenland
38G6	Steinkjer Nor	44C2	Stromness Scot
13C2	Stein Mt USA	18A1	Stromsburg USA
23B2	Stemaco Mexico	38H6	Stromsund Sweden
46C2	Stenay France	38G6	Ströms Vattudal *L* Sweden
56C2	Stendal Germany		
110B2	Stephens,C NZ	44C2	Stronsay *I* Scot
108B2	Stephens Creek Aust	43C4	Stroud Eng
14A1	Stephenson USA	16B2	Stroudsburg USA
12H3	Stephens Pass USA	43B3	Struma *R* Bulg
7E5	Stephenville Can	43B3	Strumble Head *Pt* Wales
100B4	Sterkstroom *S* Africa		
8C2	Sterling Colorado, USA	55B2	Strumica Macedonia
		59C3	Stryy Ukraine
14B2	Sterling Heights USA	59C3	Stryy *R* Ukraine
61J3	Sterlitamak Russian Fed	108B1	Strzelecki Creek *R* Aust
13E2	Stettler Can		
14B2	Steubenville USA	17B2	Stuart Florida, USA
4D3	Stevens Village USA	22J3	Stuart *R* Can
13B1	Stewart Can	12B2	Stuart I USA
21B2	Stewart *I* USA	13C2	Stuart L Can
12G2	Stewart *R* Can	47D1	Stubaier Alpen *Mts* Austria
12G2	Stewart Crossing Can		
111A3	Stewart I NZ	76D3	Stung Sen Camb
107F1	Stewart Is Solomon Is	76D3	Stung Treng Camb
4E3	Stewart River Can	52A2	Stura *R* Italy
16A3	Stewartstown USA	112C7	Sturge I Ant
101G1	Steyn *S* Africa	14C1	Sturgeon Bay USA
57C3	Steyr Austria	14C1	Sturgeon Falls Can
12G3	Stika USA	18C2	Sturgis Kentucky, USA
12H3	Stikine *R* Can		
12H3	Stikine Ranges *Mts* Can	14A2	Sturgis Michigan, USA
		106B2	Sturt Creek *R* Aust
18A2	Stillwater Oklahoma, USA	108B1	Sturt Desert Aust
		100B4	Stutterheim *S* Africa
21B2	Stillwater Range *Mts* USA	1983	Stuttgart USA
		57B3	Stuttgart Germany
108A2	Stirling Aust	38A1	Stykkishólmur Iceland
44C3	Stirling Scot		
16C1	Stockbridge USA	59D2	Styr' *R* Ukraine
59B3	Stockerau Austria	35C1	Suapui Grande *R* Brazil
39H7	Stockholm Sweden	34C2	Suardi Arg
42C3	Stockport Eng	78B2	Subi *I* Indon
22B2	Stockton California, USA	54A1	Subotica Serbia, Yugos
42D2	Stockton Eng	60C4	Suceava Rom
18B2	Stockton L USA	45C2	Suck *R* Irish Rep
43C3	Stoke-on-Trent Eng	30C2	Sucre Bol
38A2	Stokkseyri Iceland	35A1	Sucuriú *R* Brazil
38G5	Stokmarknes Nor	98C1	Sudan Republic, Africa
39K8	Stolbtsy Belarus		
58D2	Stolin Belarus	14B1	Sudbury Can
16B2	Stone Harbor USA	43E3	Sudbury Eng
44C3	Stonehaven Scot	99C2	Sudd *Swamp* Sudan
19A3	Stonewall USA	33F2	Suddie Guyana
12D2	Stony *R* USA	98B2	Sue *R* Sudan
38H5	Storavan *L* Sweden	4H2	Suerdrup Is Can
38C5	Støren Nor	92B4	Suez Egypt
109C4	Storm B Aust	92B3	Suez Canal Egypt
44A2	Stornoway Scot	92B4	Suez,G of Egypt
59D3	Storozhinets Ukraine	16B2	Suffern USA
		43E3	Suffolk County, Eng
16C2	Storrs USA	109D2	Sugarloaf Pt Aust
38G6	Storsjön *L* Sweden	91C5	Suhār Oman
38H5	Storuman Sweden	68C1	Sühbaatar Mongolia
10E3	Stoughton USA	84B3	Sui Pak
45C1	Strabane N Ire	72C2	Suide China
109C4	Strahan Aust	69E2	Suihua China
56C2	Stralsund Germany	73B4	Suining China
38D7	Stranda Nor	46C2	Suippes France
42B2	Stranraer Scot	41B3	Suir *R* Irish Rep
49D2	Strasbourg France	73C3	Sui Xian China
15C3	Strasburg USA	72E1	Suizhong China
14B2	Stratford Can	85C3	Sujangarh India
16C2	Stratford Connecticut, USA	78B4	Sukabumi Indon
		78C3	Sukadana Borneo, Indon
110B1	Stratford NZ		
43D3	Stratford-on-Avon Eng	78B4	Sukadana Sumatra, Indon
108A3	Strathalbyn Aust	74E3	Sukagawa Japan
42B2	Strathclyde Region, Scot	78C3	Sukaraya Indon
		60E3	Sukhinichi Russian Fed
13E2	Strathmore Can		
18C1	Streator USA	61F2	Sukhona *R* Russian Fed
47C2	Stresa Italy		
53C3	Stretto de Messina *Str* Italy/Sicily	61F5	Sukhumi Georgia
		6E3	Sukkertoppen Greenland
38D3	Streymoy Føroyar		

6E3 Sukkertoppen *L* Greenland
38L6 Sukkozero Russian Fed
85B3 Sukkur Pak
87C1 Sukma India
95A2 Süknah Libya
100A3 Sukses Namibia
75A2 Sukumo Japan
13C1 Sukunka *R* Can
60E3 Sula *R* Russian Fed
84B3 Sulaiman Range *Mts* Pak
70C4 Sulawesi *I* Indon
54C1 Sulina Rom
38H5 Sulitjelma Nor
32A4 Sullana Peru
13B2 Sullivan USA
13B2 Sullivan Bay Can
13E2 Sullivan L Can
52B2 Sulmona Italy
19B3 Sulphur Louisiana, USA
19A3 Sulphur Oklahoma, USA
19A3 Sulphur Springs USA
86A1 Sultanpur India
79E4 Sulu Arch Phil
70C3 Sulu S Philip
30D4 Sumampa Arg
70B4 Sumatera *I* Indon
70C4 Sumba *I* Indon
78D4 Sumbawa Indon
78D4 Sumbawa Besar Indon
99D3 Sumbawanga Tanz
100A2 Sumbe Angola
44E2 Sumburgh Head *Pt* Scot
78C4 Sumenep Indon
69G3 Sumisu *I* Japan
13D3 Summerland Can
5F4 Summit Lake Can
21B2 Summit Mt USA
11B2 Sumner,L NZ
75A2 Sumoto Japan
17B1 Sumter USA
60D3 Sumy Ukraine
16A2 Sunbury USA
34C2 Sunchales Arg
74B3 Sunch'ang S Korea
74B4 Sunch'ŏn S Korea
86A2 Sundargarh India
86B2 Sunderbans *Swamp* India
42D2 Sunderland Eng
13E2 Sundre Can
15C1 Sundridge Can
38H6 Sundsvall Sweden
38C3 Suduroy Ferovar
78D3 Sungaianyar Indon
78A3 Sungaisalak Indon
20C1 Sunnyside USA
21A2 Sunnyvale USA
63D1 Suntar Russian Fed
97B4 Sunyani Ghana
75A2 Suō-nada *B* Japan
38K6 Suonejoki Fin
86B1 Supaul India
18A1 Superior Nebraska, USA
10A2 Superior Wisconsin, USA
10B2 Superior,L Can/USA
76C3 Suphan Buri Thai
93D2 Süphan Dağ Turk
71C4 Supiori *I* Indon
93E3 Suq ash Suyukh Iraq
72D3 Suqian China
Suquta = Socotra
91C5 Sūr Oman
61G3 Sura *R* Russian Fed
78C4 Surabaya Indon
75B2 Suraga-wan *B* Japan
78C4 Surakarta Indon
109C1 Surat Aust
85C4 Surat India
84C3 Süratgarh India
77B4 Surat Thani Thai
85C4 Surendranagar India
16B3 Surf City USA
64J3 Surgut Russian Fed
87B1 Suriāpet India
90D2 Sürich Switz

79C4 Surigao Phil
76C3 Surin Thai
33F3 Surinam Republic, S America
43D4 Surrey County, Eng
47C1 Sursee Switz
95A1 Surt Libya
38A2 Surtsey *I* Iceland
78A3 Surutangan Indon
47B2 Susa Italy
75A2 Susa Japan
21A1 Susanville USA
47D1 Süsch Switz
12E2 Susitna *R* USA
16A3 Susquehanna *R* USA
16B2 Sussex USA
43D4 Sussex West Eng
13B1 Sustut Peak *Mt* Can
100B4 Sutherland S Africa
84C2 Sutlej *R* Pak
21A2 Sutter Creek USA
14B3 Sutton USA
12C3 Sutwik *I* USA
74D3 Suwa Japan
58C2 Suwałki Pol
17B2 Suwannee *R* USA
94B2 Suweilih Jordan
74B3 Suwŏn S Korea
72D3 Su Xian China
73E3 Suzhou China
74D3 Suzu Japan
75B2 Suzuka Japan
75B1 Suzu-misaki *C* Japan
64C2 Svalbard *Is* Barents S
59C3 Svalyava Ukraine
38G5 Svartisen *Mt* Nor
76D3 Svay Rieng Camb
38G6 Sveg Sweden
39G7 Svendborg Den
Sverdlovsk = Yekaterinburg
6A1 Sverdrup Chan Can
57C2 Svetlaya Russian Fed
58C2 Svetlogorsk Russian Fed
39K6 Svetlograd Russian Fed
54B2 Svetozarevo Serbia, Yugos
54C2 Svilengrad Bulg
58D2 Svir' *R* Belarus
59B3 Svitavy Czech Republic
57C2 Svobodny Russian Fed
38G5 Svolvær Nor
107E3 Swain Reefs Aust
17B1 Swainsboro USA
100A3 Swakopmund Namibia
43C4 Swale *R* Eng
70C3 Swallow Reef *I* S E Asia
87B2 Swamihalli India
25D3 Swan *I* Honduras
43D4 Swanage Eng
108B3 Swan Hill Aust
13D2 Swan Hills Can
13D2 Swan Hills *Mts* Can
26A3 Swan *I* Caribbean S
5H4 Swan River Can
43C4 Swansea S Wales
43C4 Swansea *B* Wales
101G1 Swartruggens S Africa
Swatow = Shantou
101H1 Swaziland Kingdom, S Africa
39G7 Sweden Kingdom, N Europe
20B2 Sweet Home USA
9C3 Sweetwater USA
100B4 Swellendam S Africa
59B2 Świdnica Pol
58B2 Świdwin Pol
58B2 Świebodzin Pol
58B2 Świecie Pol
5H4 Swift Current Can
43D4 Swindon Eng
45B2 Swinford Irish Rep

56C2 Świnoujście Pol
49D2 Switzerland Federal Republic, Europe
45C2 Swords Irish Rep
109D2 Sydney Aust
7D5 Sydney Can
74G3 Syktyvkar Russian Fed
17A1 Sylacauga USA
38G6 Sylarna *Mt* Sweden
86C2 Sylhet Bang
56B1 Sylt *I* Germany
14B2 Sylvania USA
112C11 Syowa *Base* Ant
Syracuse = Siracusa
15C2 Syracuse USA
65H5 Syr Darya *R* Kazakhstan
93C2 Syria Republic, S W Asia

61J2 Sysert' Russian Fed
61G3 Syzran' Russian Fed
56C2 Szczecin Pol
58B2 Szczecinek Pol
58C2 Szczytno Pol
59C3 Szeged Hung
59B3 Székesfehérvár Hung
59B3 Szekszard Hung
59B3 Szolnok Hung
59B3 Szombathely Hung
58B2 Szprotawa Pol

T

90C3 Tabas Iran
23A1 Tabasco Mexico
32D4 Tabatinga Brazil
96B2 Tabelbala Alg
76C3 Tabeng Camb
13E2 Taber Can
79B3 Tablas *I* Phil
100A4 Table Mt S Africa
12F1 Table Mt USA
18B2 Table Rock Res USA
78B3 Taboali Indon
57C3 Tábor Czech Republic
99D3 Tabora Tanz
97B4 Tabou Ivory Coast
90A2 Tabriz Iran
92C4 Tabūk S Arabia
23A2 Tacámbaro Mexico
82C1 Tacheng China
79C3 Tacloban Phil
30B2 Tacna Peru
8A2 Tacoma USA
99E1 Tadjoura Djibouti
87B2 Tādpatri India
74B3 Taebaek Sanmaek *Mts* S Korea
74B3 Taegu S Korea
74B4 Taehŭksan *I* S Korea
74B3 Taejŏn S Korea
51B1 Tafalla Spain
96C2 Tafasaset *Watercourse* Alg
43C4 Taff *R* Wales
94B3 Tafila Jordan
60E4 Taganrog Ukraine
97A3 Tagant Region, Maur
79B4 Tagbilaran Phil
96B2 Taguenout Hagguerete *Well* Maur
107E2 Tagula *I* Solomon Is
79C4 Tagum Phil
Tagus = Tejo
96C2 Tahat *Mt* Alg
105J4 Tahiti *I* Pacific O
18A2 Tahlequah USA
21A2 Tahoe,L USA
97C3 Tahoua Niger
71D3 Tahuna Indon
72D2 Tai'an China
72B3 Taibai Shan *Mt* China
72D1 Taibus Qi China
73E5 T'ai-chung Taiwan
111B3 Taieri *R* NZ
72C2 Taihang Shan China
110C1 Taihape NZ
72E3 Tai Hu *L* China
108A3 Tailem Bend Aust
44B3 Tain Scot

73E5 T'ai-nan Taiwan
35C1 Taioheae Pacific O
73E5 T'ai pei Taiwan
77C5 Taiping Malay
75C1 Taira Japan
78A3 Tais Indon
75A1 Taisha Japan
29B5 Taitao,Pen de Chile
75C1 T'ai-tung Taiwan
38K5 Taivalkoski Fin
69E4 Taiwan Republic, China
Taiwan Haixia = Formosa Str
72C2 Taiyuan China
72D3 Taizhou China
81C4 Ta'izz Yemen
82A2 Tajikistan Republic, Asia
50B1 Tajo *R* Spain
76B2 Tak Thai
74D3 Takada Japan
75A2 Takahashi Japan
110B2 Takaka NZ
74C4 Takamatsu Japan
74D3 Takaoka Japan
110B1 Takapuna NZ
74D3 Takasaki Japan
74D3 Takayama Japan
75B1 Takefu Japan
70C3 Takengon Indon
74D3 Takeo Japan
75A2 Takeo Japan
Take-shima = Tok-do
90A2 Takestan Iran
75A2 Taketa Japan
4G3 Takijvak *L* Can
99D1 Takkaze *R* Eritrea/Eth
13B1 Takla *L* Can
13B1 Takla Landing Can
12B2 Takslesluk *L* USA
12H2 Taku Arm *R* Can
23A1 Tala Mexico
59B3 Talabanya Hung
84C2 Talagang Pak
34A2 Talagante Chile
87B3 Talaimannar Sri Lanka
97C3 Talak *Desert* Region, Niger
78A3 Talangbetutu Indon
32A4 Talara Peru
50B2 Talavera de la Reina Spain
34A3 Talca Chile
34A3 Talcahuano Chile
86B2 Tälcher India
82B1 Taldy Kurgan Kazakhstan
78D4 Taliabu *I* Indon
84B1 Taligan Afghan
99D2 Tali Post Sudan
78D4 Taliwang Indon
12E2 Talkeetna USA
12E2 Talkeetna Mts USA
17A1 Talladega USA
93D2 Tall 'Afar Iraq
17B1 Tallahassee USA
94C1 Tall Bisah Syria
60B2 Tallinn Estonia
94C1 Tall Kalakh Syria
19B3 Tallulah USA
60D4 Tal'noye Ukraine
58C2 Talpaki Russian Fed
30B4 Taltal Chile
109C1 Talwood Aust
78D3 Tamabo Range *Mts* Malay
97B4 Tamale Ghana
96C2 Tamanrasset Alg
96C2 Tamanrasset *Watercourse* Alg
19B3 Tamaqua USA
Tamatave = Toamasina
23A2 Tamazula Jalisco, Mexico
23B1 Tamazulápan Mexico
23B1 Tamazunchale Mexico
97A3 Tambacounda Sen
61F3 Tambov Russian Fed
50A1 Tambre *R* Spain
98C2 Tambura Sudan

Tamchaket

97A3	Tamchaket Maur
50A1	Tamega R Port
23B1	Tamiahua Mexico
87B2	Tamil Nadu State, India
76D2	Tam Ky Viet
17B2	Tampa USA
17B2	Tampa B USA
39J6	Tampere Fin
23B1	Tampico Mexico
68D2	Tamsagbulag Mongolia
86C2	Tamu Myan
23B1	Tamuis Mexico
109D2	Tamworth Aust
43D3	Tamworth Eng
38K4	Tana Nor
99D1	Tana L Eth
89C3	Tana R Kenya
38K5	Tana R Nor/Fin
75B2	Tanabe Japan
38M4	Tanafjord Inlet Nor
78D3	Tanahgrogot Indon
71E4	Tanahmerah Indon
12D1	Tanana USA
12E2	Tanana R USA
	Tananarive = Antananarivo
47C2	Tanaro R Italy
74B2	Tanch'on N Korea
34D3	Tandil Arg
78B2	Tandjung Datu Pt Indon
71E4	Tandjung d'Urville C Indon
78D3	Tandjung Layar C Indon
78B3	Tandjung Lumut C Indon
78D2	Tandjung Mangkalihat C Indon
78C3	Tandjung Sambar C Indon
78C2	Tandjung Sirik C Malay
71E4	Tandjung Vals C Indon
85B3	Tando Adam Pak
85B3	Tando Muhammad Khan Pak
108B2	Tanduo L Aust
87B1	Tandur India
110C1	Taneatua NZ
76B2	Taner Range Mts Myan/Thai
96B2	Tanezrouft Desert Region Alg
91C4	Tang Iran
99D3	Tanga Tanz
60E4	Tanganrog Russian Fed
99C3	Tanganyika,L Tanz/Zaire
96B1	Tanger Mor
82C2	Tanggula Shan Mts China
	Tangier = Tanger
78A2	Tangjungpinang Indon
82C2	Tangra Yumco L China
72D2	Tangshan China
79B4	Tangub Phil
63C2	Tanguy Russian Fed
	Tanintharyi =
79B4	Tanjay Phil
101D3	Tanjona Ankaboa C Madag
101D2	Tanjona Babaomby C Madag
101D2	Tanjona Vilanandro C Madag
101D3	Tanjona Vohimena C Madag
78C4	Tanjong Bugel C Indon
78B4	Tanjong Cangkuang C Indon
78C3	Tanjong Puting C Indon
78C3	Tanjong Selatan C Indon
78D3	Tanjung Indon
70A3	Tanjungbalai Indon
78A3	Tanjung Jabung Pt Indon
78B3	Tanjungpandan Indon
78B4	Tanjung Priok Indon
78D2	Tanjungredeb Indon
78D2	Tanjungselor Indon
84C2	Tank Pak
68B1	Tannu Ola Mts Russian Fed
97B4	Tano R Ghana
97C3	Tanout Niger
23B1	Tanquian Mexico
73E4	Tan-shui Taiwan
86A1	Tansing Nepal
95C1	Tanta Egypt
96A2	Tan-Tan Mor
4B3	Tanunak USA
99D3	Tanzania Republic, Africa
72A3	Tao He R China
72B2	Taole China
96B1	Taourirt Mor
60C2	Tapa Estonia
25C3	Tapachula Mexico
33F4	Tapajos R Brazil
34C3	Tapalquen Arg
70B4	Tapan Indon
111A3	Tapanui NZ
32D5	Tapauá R Brazil
85D4	Tapi R India
86B1	Taplejung Nepal
111B2	Tapuaenuku Mt NZ
35B2	Tapuaritinga Brazil
79B4	Tapul Group Is Phil
33E4	Tapurucuara Brazil
109D1	Tara Aust
65J4	Tara Russian Fed
65J4	Tara R Russian Fed
54A2	Tara R Bosnia-Herzegovina/Montenegro, Yugos
97D4	Taraba R Nig
30D2	Tarabuco Bol
	Tarabulus = Tripoli
50B1	Taracon Spain
110C1	Taradale NZ
108B1	Tarakan, Mt NZ
44A3	Taransay I Scot
53C2	Taranto Italy
32B5	Tarapoto Peru
49C2	Tarare France
110C2	Tararua Range Mts NZ
96C2	Tarat Alg
110C1	Tarawera NZ
51B1	Tarazona Spain
44C3	Tarbat Ness Pen Scot
84C2	Tarbela Res Pak
42B2	Tarbert Strathclyde, Scot
44A3	Tarbert Western Isles, Scot
48C3	Tarbes France
106C4	Tarcoola Aust
109C2	Tarcoon Aust
109D2	Taree Aust
96A2	Tarfaya Mor
91B5	Tarif UAE
30D3	Tarija Bol
87B2	Tarikere India
81C4	Tarim Yemen
99D3	Tarime Tanz
82C1	Tarim He R China
82C2	Tarim Pendi Basin China
84B2	Tarin Kut Afghan
18A1	Tarkio USA
79B2	Tarlac Phil
32B6	Tarma Peru
49D2	Tarn R France
59C2	Tarnobrzeg Pol
59C3	Tarnow Pol
107D3	Taroom Aust
51C1	Tarragona Spain
109C4	Tarraleah Aust
51C1	Tarrasa Spain
16C2	Tarrytown USA
92B2	Tarsus Turk
44D2	Tartan Oilfield N Sea
47D2	Tartaro R Italy
60C2	Tartu Estonia
92C3	Tartūs Syria
35C1	Tarumirim Brazil
70A3	Tarutung Indon
52B1	Tarvisio Italy
80D1	Tashauz Turkmenistan
86C1	Tashigang Bhutan
82A1	Tashkent Uzbekistan
65K4	Tashtagol Russian Fed
63A2	Tashtyp Russian Fed
78B4	Tasikmalaya Indon
94B2	Tasil Syria
6E2	Tasiussaq Greenland
95A3	Tasker Well Niger
110B2	Tasman B NZ
107D5	Tasmania I Aust
111B2	Tasman Mts NZ
109C4	Tasman Pen Aust
107E4	Tasman S NZ/Aust
92C1	Taşova Turk
96C2	Tassili du Hoggar Desert Region, Alg
96C2	Tassili N'jjer Desert Region, Alg
96B2	Tata Mor
96D1	Tataouine Tunisia
65J4	Tatarsk Russian Fed
69G2	Tatarskiy Proliv Str Russian Fed
61G2	Tatarstan Russian Fed
75B1	Tateyama Japan
5G3	Tathlina L Can
12E2	Tatitlek USA
13C2	Tatla Lake Can
59B3	Tatry Mts Pol/Slovakia
75A2	Tatsuno Japan
85B4	Tatta Pak
35B2	Tatui Brazil
32B2	Tatvan Turk
31C3	Taua Brazil
35B2	Taubaté Brazil
110C1	Taumarunui NZ
101F1	Taung S Africa
76B2	Taungdwingyi Myan
76B1	Taung-gyi Myan
76A2	Taungup Myan
84C2	Taunsa Pak
43C4	Taunton Eng
16D2	Taunton USA
46E1	Taunus Region, Germany
110C1	Taupo NZ
110C1	Taupo,L NZ
58C1	Taurage Lithuania
110C1	Tauranga NZ
110C1	Tauranga Harbour B NZ
110B1	Tauroa Pt NZ
7A3	Tavani Can
7A3	Tavani Can
65H4	Tavda R Russian Fed
43B4	Tavistock Eng
76B3	Tavoy Myan
76B3	Tavoy Pt Myan
92A2	Tavsanli Turk
111B2	Tawa NZ
19A3	Tawakoni,L USA
14B2	Tawas City USA
70C3	Tawau Malay
98C1	Taweisha Sudan
79B4	Tawitawi I Phil
79B4	Tawitawi Group Is Phil
23B2	Taxco Mexico
23B2	Taxcoco Mexico
44C3	Tay R Scot
78C3	Tayan Indon
12B1	Taylor Alaska, USA
13C1	Taylor Can
14B2	Taylor Michigan, USA
19A3	Taylor Texas, USA
18C2	Taylorville USA
80B3	Taymā' S Arabia
63B1	Taymura R
76D3	Tay Ninh Viet
63B2	Tayshet Russian Fed
68B2	Tayshir Mongolia
44C3	Tayside Region, Scot
79A3	Taytay Phil
90D3	Tayyebāt Iran
96B1	Taza Mor
95B2	Tazirbu Libya
12E2	Tazlina L USA
64J3	Tazovskiy Russian Fed
65F5	Tbilisi Georgia
98B3	Tchibanga Gabon
95A2	Tchigai,Plat du Niger
97C3	Tchin Tabaradene Niger
98B2	Tcholliré Cam
58B2	Tczew Pol
111A3	Te Anau NZ
111A3	Te Anau,L NZ
110C1	Te Aroha NZ
110C1	Te Awamutu NZ
96C1	Tébessa Alg
23A2	Teboman Mexico
23A2	Tecaíltlán Mexico
23A2	Tecate Mexico
61K2	Techa R Russian Fed
23A1	Tecolotlán Mexico
23A2	Tecpan Mexico
54C1	Tecuci Rom
18A1	Tecumseh USA
80E2	Tedzhen Turkmenistan
65H6	Tedzhen R Turkmenistan
42D2	Tees R Eng
33E4	Tefé Brazil
78B4	Teginmeng Indon
25D3	Tegucigalpa Honduras
21B3	Tehachapi Mts USA
21B2	Tehachapi P USA
4J3	Tehek L Can
90B2	Tehrān Iran
23B2	Tehuacán Mexico
23B2	Tehuantepec Mexico
23B2	Tehuitzingo Mexico
43B3	Teifi R Wales
50A2	Tejo R Port
23A2	Tejupilco Mexico
111B2	Tekapo,L NZ
82B1	Tekeli Kazakhstan
92A1	Tekirdağ Turk
55C2	Tekir Dağlari Mts
86C2	Teknaf Bang
110C1	Te Kuiti NZ
25D3	Tela Honduras
94B2	Tel Aviv Yafo Israel
34B3	Telén Arg
21B2	Telescope Peak Mt USA
33F5	Teles Pires R Brazil
47D1	Telfs Austria
63A2	Teli Russian Fed
94B3	Tell el Meise Mt Jordan
12A1	Teller USA
87B2	Tellicherry India
77C5	Telok Anson Malay
78D2	Télok Darvel Malay
71E4	Télok Flamingo B Indon
78C3	Télok Kumai B Indon
78B4	Télok Pelabuanratu B Indon
78D4	Télok Saleh B Indon
78C3	Télok Sampit B Indon
78B3	Télok Sukadona B Indon
23B2	Teloloapán Mexico
64G3	Tel'pos-iz Mt Russian Fed
58C1	Telšiai Lithuania
78C3	Telukbatang Indon
71E4	Teluk Berau B Indon
78B4	Telukbetung Indon
70D4	Teluk Bone B Indon
71E4	Teluk Cendrawasih B Indon
78D3	Teluk Mandar B Indon
71D4	Teluk Tolo B Indon
70D3	Teluk Tomini B Indon

71D3 Téluk Weda B Indon
14B1 Temagami,L Can
23B2 Temascal Mexico
78A3 Tembesi R Indon
78A3 Tembilahan Indon
27E5 Tembladar Ven
77C5 Temerloh Malay
65G5 Temir Kazakhstan
65J4 Temirtau Kazakhstan
77C5 Temiscaming Can
109C2 Temora Aust
9B3 Tempe USA
19A3 Temple USA
45C2 Templemore Irish Rep
23B1 Tempoal Mexico
34A3 Temuco Chile
111B2 Temuka NZ
32B4 Tena Ecuador
87C1 Tenali India
23B2 Tenancingo Mexico
76B3 Tenasserim Myan
78C3 Tewah Indon
43A4 Tenby Wales
99E1 Tendaho Eth
83D5 Ten Degree Chan
  Indian O
98B1 Ténéré Desert
  Region Niger
96A2 Tenerife I Canary Is
76B1 Teng R Myan
78D3 Tenggarong Indon
72A2 Tengger Shamo
  Desert China
112C2 Teniente Jubany
  Base Ant
112C2 Teniente Rodolfo
  Marsh Martin Base
  Ant
87B3 Tenkāsi India
100B2 Tenke Zaire
97B3 Tenkodogo Burkina
106C2 Tennant Creek Aust
11B3 Tennessee State,
  USA
18C2 Tennessee R USA
34A2 Teno Chile
78D1 Tenom Malay
25C3 Tenosique Mexico
109D1 Tenterfield Aust
17B2 Ten Thousand Is
  USA
23A1 Teocaltiche Mexico
35C1 Teófilo Otôni Brazil
23B2 Teotihiucan Hist Site,
  Mexico
23B2 Tepatitlan Mexico
23A1 Tepatitlan Mexico
24B2 Tepehuanes Mexico
23B2 Tepeji Mexico
23A1 Tepic Mexico
57C2 Teplice
  Czech Republic
110C1 Te Puke NZ
23A1 Tequila Mexico
23B2 Tequistepec Mexico
51C1 Ter R Spain
97C3 Téra Niger
52B2 Teradomari Japan
52B2 Teramo Italy
96A1 Terceira I Açores
59D3 Terebovlya Ukraine
35C2 Teresina Brazil
35C2 Teresópolis Brazil
92C1 Terme Turk
80E2 Termez Uzbekistan
52B2 Termoli Italy
78D1 Ternate Indon
52B2 Terni Italy
59D3 Ternopil Ukraine
13B2 Terrace Italy
53B2 Terracina Italy
112C8 Terre Adélie Region,
  Ant
19B4 Terre Bonne B USA
14A3 Terre Haute USA
19A3 Terrell USA
56B2 Terschelling I Neth
51B1 Teruel Spain
4C2 Teshekpuk L USA
4C2 Teshekpuk L USA
74E2 Teshio R Japan
68B2 Tesiyn Gol Mts
  Mongolia

12H2 Teslin Can
12H3 Teslin R Can
12H2 Teslin L Can
63B3 Teslyn Gol R
  Mongolia
96C2 Tessalit Mali
97C3 Tessaoua Niger
101C2 Tete Mozam
23A2 Tetela Mexico
96B1 Tetouan Mor
61D2 Tetyushi
  Russian Fed
30D3 Teuco R Arg
23A1 Teotl de Gonzalez
  Ortega Mexico
71D4 Teun I Indon
52B2 Tevere R Italy
42C2 Teviot R Scot
65J4 Tevriz Russian Fed
111A3 Te Waewae B NZ
78C3 Tewah Indon
109D1 Tewantin Aust
72A3 Têwo China
19B3 Texarkana USA
19B3 Texarkana,L USA
109D1 Texas Aust
19A3 Texas State, USA
19B4 Texas City USA
56A2 Texel I Neth
19A3 Texoma,L USA
101G1 Teyateyaneng
  Lesotho
23B2 Teziutlán Mexico
86C1 Tezpur India
76C1 Tha Laos
101G1 Thabana Ntlenyana
  Mt Lesotho
101G1 Thaba Putsoa Mt
  Lesotho
76B3 Thagyettaw Myan
76D1 Thai Binh Viet
76C2 Thailand Kingdom,
  S E Asia
76C3 Thailand,G of Thai
76A2 Thai Nguyen Viet
76C2 Thakhek Laos
84C2 Thai Pak
77C4 Thale Luang L Thai
109C1 Thallon Aust
13B1 Thames NZ
43E4 Thames R Eng
110C2 Thames NZ
76D2 Thanh Hoah Viet
87B2 Thanjavur India
76C3 Thanlwin = Salween
85C3 Thar Desert India
108B1 Thargomindah Aust
55B2 Thásos I Greece
76B2 Thaton Myan
76B2 Thayetmyo Myan
5F5 The Dalles USA
91B4 The Gulf S W Asia
4H3 Thelon R Can
107E3 Theodore Aust
9B3 Theodore Roosevelt L
  USA
55B2 Thermaïkós Kólpos
  G Greece
8C2 Thermopolis USA
4F2 Thesiger B Can
14B1 Thessalon Can
55B2 Thessaloníki Greece
43E3 Thetford Eng
15D1 Thetford Mines Can
101G1 Theunissen S Africa
19B4 Thibodaux USA
5J4 Thicket Portage Can
8D2 Thief River Falls
  USA
20B2 Thielsen,Mt USA
49C2 Thiers France
97A3 Thiès Sen
99D3 Thika Kenya
86B1 Thimphu Bhutan
49D2 Thionville France
55C3 Thíra I Greece
42D2 Thirsk Eng
  Thiruvananthapuram
  = Trivandrum
39F7 Thisted Den
55B3 Thívai Greece
48C2 Thiviers France
17B1 Thomaston Georgia,
  USA
45C2 Thomastown
  Irish Rep

17B1 Thomasville Georgia,
  USA
6A2 Thom Bay Can
5J4 Thompson Can
18B1 Thompson R USA
4G3 Thompson Landing
  Can
13C2 Thompson R Can
16C2 Thompsonville USA
17B1 Thomson USA
107D3 Thomson R Aust
76C3 Thon Buri Thai
76B2 Thongwa Myan
46B1 Thonon-les-Bains
  France
42C2 Thornhill Scot
48B2 Thouars France
15C2 Thousand Is Can/
  USA
13E2 Three Hills Can
7G4 Three Kings Is NZ
76B2 Three Pagodas P
  Thai
14A2 Three Rivers
  Michigan, USA
20B2 Three Sisters Mt
  USA
  Thrissur = Trichūr
6D2 Thule Greenland
47B1 Thun Switz
18D2 Thunder Bay Can
47B1 Thuner See L Switz
77B4 Thung Song Thai
47C1 Thur R Switz
57C2 Thüringen State,
  Germany
57C2 Thüringer Wald
  Upland Germany
45C2 Thurles Irish Rep
71F5 Thursday I Aust
44C2 Thurso Scot
112B4 Thurston I Ant
47C1 Thusis Switz
108B1 Thylungra Aust
86A1 Tiandong China
73B5 Tian'e China
73B5 Tianjin China
72D2 Tianjin China
73B5 Tianlin China
82C1 Tian Shan Mts C
  Asia
72B3 Tianshui China
72A3 Tianzhu China
96C1 Tiaret Alg
94B2 Tiberias Israel
94B2 Tiberias,L Israel
  Tiber,R = Tevere,R
95A2 Tibesti Mountain
  Region Chad
82C2 Tibet Autonomous
  Region, China
108B1 Tibooburra Aust
86A1 Tibrikot Nepal
24A2 Tiburón I Mexico
97B3 Tichitt Maur
96A2 Tichla Maur
74C2 Ticino R Italy/Switz
15D2 Ticonderoga USA
25D2 Ticul Mexico
97A3 Tidjikja Maur
47C1 Tiefencastel Switz
74A2 Tieling China
46B1 Tielt Belg
46C1 Tienen Belg
65J5 Tien Shan Mts
  China/Kirghizia
72D2 Tientsin China
39H6 Tierp Sweden
23B2 Tierra Blanca Mexico
23B2 Tierra Colorada
  Mexico
29C6 Tierra del Fuego
  Territory, Arg
28C8 Tierra del Fuego I
  Arg/Chile
35B2 Tietê Brazil
35A2 Tietê R Brazil
14B2 Tiffin USA
17B1 Tifton USA
32B4 Tigre R Peru
33E2 Tigre R Ven
93E3 Tigris R Iraq
23B1 Tihuatlán Mexico
21B3 Tijuana Mexico

85D4 Tikamgarh India
60D2 Tikhin Russian Fed
61F4 Tikhoretsk
  Russian Fed
93D3 Tikrit Iraq
1B8 Tiksi Russian Fed
46C1 Tilburg Neth
43E4 Tilbury Eng
30C3 Tilcara Arg
10C1 Tilcha Aust
76A1 Tilin Myan
97C3 Tillabéri Niger
2081 Tillamook USA
97C3 Tillia Niger
55C3 Tílos I Greece
108B2 Tilpa Aust
32B3 Tiluá Colombia
64G3 Timanskiy Kryazh
  Mts Russian Fed
111B2 Timaru NZ
60E4 Timashevsk
  Russian Fed
55B3 Timbákion Greece
19B4 Timbalier B USA
97B3 Timbédra Maur
  Timbuktu =
  Tombouctou
97B3 Timétrine Monts Mts
  Mali
97C3 Timia Niger
27J3 Timis R Rom
54B1 Timisoara Rom
10B2 Timmins Can
106B1 Timor I Indon
106B2 Timor S Aust/Indon
74C4 Timote Arg
27D5 Tinaco Ven
87B2 Tindivanam India
90A2 Tindouf Alg
96B2 Tinfouchy Alg
96C2 Tin Fouye Alg
6F3 Tingmiarmiut
  Greenland
32B5 Tingo Maria Peru
97B3 Tingrela Ivory Coast
86B1 Tingri China
71F2 Tinian Pacific O
55C3 Tínos I Greece
43B4 Tintagel Head Pt
  Eng
96C2 Tin Tarabine
  Watercourse Alg
108B3 Tintinara Aust
96C2 Tin Zaouaten Alg
22C2 Tioga P USA
77C5 Tioman I Malay
47D1 Tione Italy
45C2 Tipperary County,
  Irish Rep
41B3 Tipperary Irish Rep
18B2 Tipton Missouri, USA
87B2 Tiptur India
23A2 Tiquicheo Mexico
55A2 Tiranë Alb
77B3 Tirano Italy
60C4 Tiraspol Moldova
87B2 Tirchchirāppalli
  India
55C3 Tire Turk
93C1 Tirebolu Turk
44A3 Tiree I Scot
54C2 Tîrgovişte Rom
54B1 Tirgu Jiu Rom
54B1 Tirgu Mures Rom
84C1 Tirich Mir Mt Pak
96A2 Tiris Region, Mor
61J3 Tirlyanskiy
  Russian Fed
54B1 Tirnăveni Rom
55B3 Tírnavos Greece
85D4 Tirodi India
47D1 Tirol Province,
  Austria
53A2 Tirso R Sardegna
87B3 Tiruchchendūr India
87B3 Tirunelveli India
87B2 Tirupati India
87B2 Tiruppattūr India
87B2 Tiruppur India
87B2 Tiruvannamalai
  India
19A3 Tishomingo USA

Tisīyah

94C2	Tisīyah Syria
59C3	Tisza R Hung
86A2	Titlagarh India
58C2	Titov Veles Macedonia
98C2	Titule Zaire
17B2	Titusville USA
43C4	Tiverton Eng
52B2	Tivoli Italy
23B2	Tixtla Mexico
99E2	Tiyeglow Somalia
23B2	Tizayuca Mexico
25D2	Tizimín Mexico
96C1	Tizi Ouzou Alg
96B2	Tiznit Mor
23A1	Tizpan el Alto Mexico
23B2	Tlacolula Mexico
23B2	Tlacotalpan Mexico
23B2	Tlalchapa Mexico
23B2	Tlalnepantla Mexico
23B2	Tlalpan Mexico
23A1	Tlaltenango Mexico
23B2	Tlancualpican Mexico
23B2	Tlapa Mexico
23B2	Tlapacoyan Mexico
23A1	Tlaquepaque Mexico
23B2	Tlaxcala Mexico
23B2	Tlaxcala State, Mexico
23B2	Tlaxiaco Mexico
96B1	Tlemcen Alg
101D2	Toamasina Madag
34C3	Toay Arg
75B2	Toba Japan
84B2	Toba and Kakar Ranges Mts Pak
27E4	Tobago /
13C2	Toba Inlet Sd Can
71D3	Tobelo Indon
14B1	Tobermory Can
44A3	Tobermory Scot
71E3	Tobi / Pacific O
21B1	Tobin,Mt USA
65H4	Tobol R Kazakhstan
70D4	Toboli Indon
65H4	Tobol'sk Russian Fed
	Tobruk = Tubruq
31B2	Tocantins R Brazil
31B3	Tocantins State, Brazil
17B1	Toccoa USA
47C1	Toce R Italy
30B3	Tocopilla Chile
30C3	Tocorpuri Mt Chile
26C3	Tocuyo R Ven
85D3	Toda India
47C1	Tödi Mt Switz
75A1	Todong S Korea
9B4	Todos Santos Mexico
13E2	Tofield Can
13B3	Tofino Can
12B3	Togiak USA
12B3	Togiak B USA
97C4	Togo Republic, Africa
72C1	Togtoh China
12F2	Tok USA
74E2	Tokachi R Japan
75B1	Tokamachi Japan
95C3	Tokar Sudan
69E4	Tokara Retto Arch Japan
92C1	Tokat Turk
74B3	Tökchök-kundo Arch S Korea
65J5	Tokmak Kirghizia
110C1	Tokomaru Bay NZ
75A1	Tok-to / S Korea
12H3	Toku R Can/USA
78C3	Tokung Indon
69E4	Tokuno / Japan
74C4	Tokushima Japan
75A2	Tokuyama Japan
74D3	Tōkyō Japan
110C1	Tolaga Bay NZ
101D3	Tôlanaro Madag
30F3	Toledo Brazil
50B2	Toledo Spain
14B2	Toledo USA
19B3	Toledo Bend Res USA
101D3	Toliara Madag
23B1	Toliman Mexico
32B3	Tolina Mt Colombia
51B1	Tolosa Spain
29B3	Toltén Chile
23B2	Toluca Mexico
61G3	Tol'yatti Russian Fed
74E2	Tomakomai Japan
78D1	Tomani Malay
58C2	Tomaszow Mazowiecka Pol
11B3	Tombigbee R USA
98B3	Tomboco Angola
35C2	Tombos Brazil
97B3	Tombouctou Mali
100A2	Tomboua Angola
34A3	Tomé Chile
50B2	Tomelloso Spain
50A2	Tomer Port
106B3	Tomkinson Range Mts Aust
63E2	Tommot Russian Fed
55B2	Tomorrit Mt Alb
65K4	Tomsk Russian Fed
16B3	Toms River USA
25C2	Tonalá Mexico
20C1	Tonasket USA
15C2	Tonawanda USA
105H4	Tonga / Pacific O
101H1	Tongaat S Africa
73D3	Tongcheng China
72B2	Tongchuan China
72A2	Tongde China
46C1	Tongeren Belg
76D2	Tonggu Jiao / China
73A5	Tonghai China
74B2	Tonghua China
74B3	Tongjosŏn-man N Korea
76D1	Tongkin,G of China/ Viet
72E1	Tonglia China
73D3	Tongling China
108B2	Tongo Aust
34A2	Tongoy Chile
73B4	Tongren Guizhou, China
72A2	Tongren Qinghai, China
86C1	Tongsa Bhutan
76B1	Tongta Myan
68B3	Tongtian He R China
44B2	Tongue Scot
72D2	Tong Xian China
72B2	Tongxin China
73A4	Tongzi China
9C4	Tonichi Mexico
99C2	Tonj Sudan
85D3	Tonk India
18A2	Tonkawa USA
76C3	Tonle Sap L Camb
21B2	Tonopah USA
12E2	Tonsina USA
8B2	Tooele USA
109D1	Toogoolawah Aust
108B1	Toompine Aust
109D1	Toowoomba Aust
22C1	Topaz L USA
18A2	Topeka USA
9C4	Topolobampo Mexico
20B1	Toppenish USA
99D2	Tor Eth
55C3	Torbalí Turk
90C2	Torbat-e-Heydariyeh Iran
90C2	Torbat-e Jam Iran
12D2	Torbert,Mt USA
50A1	Tordesillas Spain
56C2	Torgau Germany
46B1	Torhout Belg
69G3	Tori / Japan
47D2	Torino Italy
99D2	Torit Sudan
35A1	Torixoreu Brazil
50A1	Tormes R Spain
13E2	Tornado Mt Can
38J5	Torne L Sweden
38H5	Torneträsk Sweden
7D4	Torngat Mts Can
38J5	Tornio Fin
34C3	Tornquist Arg
15C2	Toronto USA
60D2	Toropets Russian Fed
99D2	Tororo Uganda
92B2	Toros Dağları Mts Turk
43C4	Torquay Eng
22C4	Torrance USA
50A2	Torrão Port
51C1	Torreblanca Spain
53B2	Torre del Greco Italy
50B1	Torrelavega Spain
50B2	Torremolinos Spain
108A2	Torrens,L Aust
24B2	Torreón Mexico
47B2	Torre Pellice Italy
107D2	Torres Str Aust
50A2	Torres Vedras Port
16C2	Torrington Connecticut, USA
8C2	Torrington Wyoming, USA
9C4	Torrón Mexico
38D3	Tórshavn Føroyar
47C2	Tortona Italy
51C1	Tortosa Spain
90D2	Torūd Iran
58B2	Toruń Pol
40B2	Tory / Irish Rep
60D2	Torzhok Russian Fed
75A2	Tosa Japan
74C4	Tosa-shimizu Japan
74C4	Tosa-wan B Japan
75B2	To-shima / Japan
	Toshkent = Tashkent
60D2	Tosno Russian Fed
75A2	Tosu Japan
92B1	Tosya Turk
61F1	Tot'ma Russian Fed
43C4	Totnes Eng
33F2	Totness Surinam
23B2	Totolapan Mexico
51B2	Totona Spain
109C2	Tottenham Aust
74C3	Tottori Japan
97B4	Touba Ivory Coast
97A3	Touba Sen
96B1	Toubkal Mt Mor
97B3	Tougan Burkina
96C1	Touggourt Alg
97A3	Tougué Guinea
46C2	Toul France
49D3	Toulon France
48C3	Toulouse France
97B4	Toumodi Ivory Coast
76B2	Toungoo Myan
46B1	Tourcoing France
96A2	Tourine Maur
48B1	Tournai Belg
49C2	Tours France
74E2	Towada Japan
74E2	Towada-ko L Japan
15C2	Towanda USA
107D2	Townsville Aust
16A3	Towson USA
43C4	Towy R Wales
74D3	Toyama Japan
75B1	Toyama-wan B Japan
75B2	Toyohashi Japan
75B2	Toyonaka Japan
75A1	Toyooka Japan
74D3	Toyota Japan
96C1	Tozeur Tunisia
46D2	Traben-Trarbach Germany
93C1	Trabzon Turk
22B2	Tracy California, USA
34A3	Traiguén Chile
13D3	Trail Can
41B3	Tralee Irish Rep
45B2	Tralee B Irish Rep
45C2	Tramore Irish Rep
39G7	Tranås Sweden
77B4	Trang Thai
71E4	Trangan / Indon
109C2	Trangie Aust
12E2	Transalaskan Pipeline USA
	Transylvanian Alps = Munţii Carpaţii Meridionali
53B2	Trapani Italy
109C3	Traralgon Aust
97A3	Trarza Region, Maur
76C3	Trat Thai
108B2	Traveller's L Aust
56C2	Travemünde Germany
14A2	Traverse City USA
12C1	Traverse Peak Mt USA
111B2	Travers,Mt NZ
47C2	Trebbia R Italy
59B3	Třebíč Czech Republic
54A2	Trebinje Bosnia-Herzegovina
57C3	Trebon Czech Republic
29F2	Treinta y Tres Urug
29C4	Trelew Arg
39G7	Trelleborg Sweden
43B3	Tremadog B Wales
15D1	Tremblant,Mt Can
13C2	Trembleur,L Can
16A2	Tremont USA
59B3	Trenčín Slovakia
34C3	Trenque Lauquén Arg
43D3	Trent R Eng
47D1	Trentino Region, Italy
47D1	Trento Italy
15C2	Trenton Can
18B1	Trenton Missouri, USA
16B2	Trenton New Jersey, USA
7E5	Trepassey Can
34C3	Tres Arroyos Arg
35B2	Tres Corações Brazil
30F3	Três Lagoas Brazil
34C3	Tres Lomas Arg
22B2	Tres Pinos USA
35C2	Três Rios Brazil
47C2	Treviglio Italy
47C2	Treviso Italy
47C2	Trezzo Italy
87B2	Trichur India
108C2	Trida Aust
46D2	Trier Germany
52B1	Trieste Italy
45C2	Trim Irish Rep
87C3	Trincomalee Sri Lanka
33E6	Trinidad Bol
29E2	Trinidad Urug
9C3	Trinidad USA
34C3	Trinidad / Arg
27E4	Trinidad / Caribbean S
103G6	Trinidade / Atlantic O
27E4	Trinidad & Tobago Republic Caribbean S
19A3	Trinity USA
9D3	Trinity R USA
7E5	Trinity B Can
12D3	Trinity Is USA
17A1	Trion USA
94B1	Tripoli Leb
95A1	Tripoli Libya
55B3	Tripolis Greece
86C2	Tripura State, India
103H6	Tristan da Cunha Is Atlantic O
87B3	Trivandrum India
59B3	Trnava Slovakia
107D1	Trobriand Is PNG
15D1	Trois-Rivières Can
65H4	Troitsk Russian Fed
39G7	Trollhättan Sweden
38F6	Trollheimen Mt Nor
89K9	Tromelin / Indian O
38H5	Tromsø Nor
38G6	Trondheim Nor
38G6	Trondheimfjord Inlet Nor
42B2	Troon Scot
102J3	Tropic of Cancer
103J6	Tropic of Capricorn
96B2	Troudenni Mali
7A4	Trout L Ontario, Can
17A1	Troy Alabama, USA
16C1	Troy New York, USA
14B2	Troy Ohio, USA
54B2	Troyan Bulg
49C2	Troyes France

91B5 Trucial Coast Region, UAE
21A2 Truckee *R* USA
25D3 Trujillo Honduras
32B5 Trujillo Peru
50A2 Trujillo Spain
32C2 Trujillo Ven
109C2 Trundle Aust
7D5 Truro Can
43B4 Truro Eng
68B2 Tsagaan Nuur *L* Mongolia
68B1 Tsagan-Tologoy Russian Fed
101D2 Tsaratanana Madag
83B3 Tsau Botswana
99D3 Tsavo Kenya
99D3 Tsavo Nat Pk Kenya
65J4 Tselinograd Kazakhstan
100A3 Tses Namibia
68C2 Tsetserleg Mongolia
97C1 Tsévié Togo
100B3 Tshabong Botswana
100B3 Tshane Botswana
98B3 Tshela Zaïre
98C3 Tshibala Zaïre
98C3 Tshikapa Zaïre
98C3 Tshuapa *R* Zaïre
101D3 Tsihombe Madag
61F4 Tsimlyanskoye Vodokhranilishche *Res* Russian Fed
101D2 Tsiroanomandidy Madag
13B2 Tsitsutl Peak *Mt* Can
58D2 Tsna *R* Belarus
72B1 Tsogt Ovoo Mongolia
68C2 Tsomog Mongolia
75B2 Tsu Japan
75B1 Tsubata Japan
75A2 Tsuchiura Japan
74E2 Tsugaru-kaikyō *Str* Japan
50A1 Tua *R* Port
45B2 Tuam Irish Rep
60E5 Tuapse Russian Fed
111A3 Tuatapere NZ
30G4 Tubarão Brazil
94B2 Tubas Israel
79A4 Tubbataha Reefs *Is* Phil
57B3 Tübingen Germany
95B1 Tubruq Libya
98B3 Tuckerton USA
98B3 Tucson USA
29E2 Tucumán State, Arg
34B2 Tucunuco Arg
32C2 Tucupita Ven
51B1 Tudela Spain
93C3 Tudmur Syria
101H1 Tugela *R* S Africa
109D2 Tuggerah *L* Aust
12D3 Tugidak *I* USA
79B2 Tuguegarao Phil
63F2 Tugur Russian Fed
72D2 Tuhai He *R* China
4E3 Tuktoyaktuk Can
58E1 Tukums Latvia
99D3 Tukuyu Tanz
84B1 Tukzar Afghan
60E3 Tula Russian Fed
23B1 Tulancingo Mexico
78A3 Tulangbawang *R* Indon
32B3 Tulcán Colombia
60C5 Tulcea Rom
59J1 Tul'chin Ukr
94B2 Tulkarm Israel
48C2 Tulle France
19B3 Tullos USA
45C2 Tullow Irish Rep
18A2 Tulsa USA

93C3 Tulūl ash Shāmīyah *Desert Region* Syria/ S Arabia
63C2 Tulun Russian Fed
78C4 Tulungagung Indon
32B3 Tumaco Colombia
109C3 Tumbarumba Aust
32A4 Tumbes Ecuador
108A2 Tumby Bay Aust
74B2 Tumen China
87B2 Tumkūr India
77C4 Tumpat Malay
85D4 Tumsar India
97B3 Tumu Ghana
109C3 Tumut Aust
109C3 Tumut *R* Aust
27L1 Tunapuna Trinidad
93C2 Tunceli Turk
99D3 Tunduma Zambia
101C2 Tunduru Tanz
54C2 Tundzha *R* Bulg
87B1 Tungabhadra *R* India
68D4 Tung-Chiang Taiwan
38B2 Tungnafellsjökull *Mts* Iceland
12J2 Tungsten Can
63B1 Tunguska *R* Russian Fed
87C1 Tuni India
96D1 Tunis Tunisia
88E4 Tunisia Republic, N Africa
32C2 Tunja Colombia
12B2 Tuntutuliak USA
34B2 Tunuyán Arg
34B2 Tunuyán *R* Arg
22C2 Tuolumne Meadows USA
31B6 Tupã Brazil
35B1 Tupaciguara Brazil
15D2 Tupelo USA
34B2 Tupungato Arg
29C2 Tupungato *Mt* Arg
86C1 Tura India
63C1 Tura Russian Fed
64E3 Tura *R* Russian Fed
90C2 Turān Iran
63B2 Turan Russian Fed
93A1 Turayf S Arabia
80E3 Turbat Pak
32B2 Turbo Colombia
54B1 Turda Rom
63A3 Turfan Depression China
65H4 Turgay Kazakhstan
63B3 Turgen Uul *Mt* Mongolia
54C2 Turgovishte Bulg
92A2 Turgutlu Turk
92C1 Turhal Turk
37K7 Türi Estonia
51B2 Turia *R* Spain
31H6 Turin = Torino
61K2 Turinsk Russian Fed
69F2 Turiy Rog Russian Fed
99D2 Turkana,L Kenya/Eth
82A1 Turkestan Region, C Asia
65H5 Turkestan Kazakhstan
92C2 Turkey Republic, W Asia
80D1 Turkmenistan Republic, Asia
90B2 Turkmenskiy Zaliv *B* Turkmenistan
27C2 Turks Is Caribbean S
39J6 Turku Fin
99D2 Turkwel *R* Kenya
22B2 Turlock USA
22B2 Turlock L USA
110C2 Turnagain,C NZ
25D3 Turneffe I Belize
16C1 Turners Falls USA
44C4 Turnhout Belg
13F1 Turnor L Can
54B2 Turnu Măgurele Rom
63A3 Turpan China
26B2 Turquino *Mt* Cuba
80E1 Turtkul' Uzbekistan

18A2 Turtle Creek Res USA
13F2 Turtle L Can
63A1 Turukhansk Russian Fed
68C1 Turuntayevo Russian Fed
35A1 Turvo *R* Goias, Brazil
35B2 Turvo *R* São Paulo, Brazil
58C2 Tur'ya *R* Ukraine
19D1 Tuscaloosa USA
18C2 Tuscola USA
87B3 Tusharik Iran
Tutera = Tudela
80C1 Tuticorin India
54C2 Tutrakan Bulg
57B3 Tuttlingen Germany
68C2 Tuul Gol *R* Mongolia
105G4 Tuvalu *Is* Pacific O
63B2 Tuvinskaya Respublika, Russian Fed
23A2 Tuxpan Jalisco, Mexico
24B2 Tuxpan Nayarit, Mexico
23B1 Tuxpan Veracruz, Mexico
23B2 Tuxtepec Mexico
25C3 Tuxtla Gutiérrez Mexico
50A1 Túy Spain
76D3 Tuy Hoa Viet
92B2 Tuz Gölü *Salt L* Turk
93D3 Tuz Khurmātū Iraq
54A2 Tuzla Bosnia-Herzegovina
60E2 Tver' Russian Fed
42B2 Tweed *R* Eng/Scot
109D1 Tweed Heads Aust
42C2 Tweedsmuir Hills Aust
7E5 Twillingate Can
8B2 Twin Falls USA
111B2 Twins,The *Mt* NZ
14A2 Two Rivers USA
63E2 Tygda Russian Fed
19A3 Tyler USA
65K3 Tym *R* Russian Fed
69G1 Tymovskoye Russian Fed
42E2 Tyne *R* Eng
42D2 Tyne and Wear Metropolitan County, Eng
42D2 Tynemouth Eng
38G6 Tynset Nor
12D3 Tyonek USA
94B2 Tyr Leb
Tyre = Tyr
45C1 Tyrone County, N Ire
108B3 Tyrrell,L Aust
53B3 Tyrrhenian S Italy
Tyumen'
94B2 Tyumen' Russian Fed
41B3 Tywyn Wales
55B3 Tzoumérka *Mt* Greece

U

99E2 Uarscieh Somalia
31C5 Ubá Brazil
35C1 Ubai Brazil
98B3 Ubangi *R* CAR
87B2 Ubaye *R* France
75A2 Ube Japan
50B2 Ubeda Spain
6E2 Ubekendt Ejland *I* Greenland
35B1 Uberaba Brazil
35B1 Uberlândia Brazil
76C2 Ubon Ratchathani Thai
58D2 Ubort *R* Belarus
98C3 Ubundi Zaïre
32C5 Ucayali *R* Peru
84C3 Uch Pak
63F2 Uchar *R* Russian Fed
74E2 Uchiura-wan *B* Japan
63B2 Uda *R* Russian Fed
85C4 Udaipur India
86B1 Udaipur Garhi Nepal

34D3 Udaquoila Arg
39G7 Uddevalla Sweden
38H5 Uddjaur *L* Sweden
87B1 Udgir India
84D2 Udhampur India
61H2 Udmurtskaya Respublika,
76C2 Udon Thani Thai
63F2 Udskaya Guba *B* Russian Fed
87A2 Udupi India
76B2 Ueda Japan
99C2 Uele *R* Zaïre
56C2 Uelzen Germany
98C2 Uere *R* Zaïre
61J3 Ufa Russian Fed
61J2 Ufa *R* Russian Fed
100A3 Ugab *R* Namibia
99D3 Ugalla *R* Tanz
12D3 Ugak B USA
99D2 Uganda Republic, Africa
12C3 Ugashik B USA
12C3 Ugashik L USA
47B2 Ugine France
69G2 Uglegorsk Russian Fed
60E2 Uglich Russian Fed
60E3 Ugra *R* Russian Fed
44A3 Uig Scot
98B3 Uige Angola
61H4 Ural Kazakhstan
8B2 Uinta Mts USA
100B4 Uitenhage S Africa
59C3 Ujfehértó Hung
75B2 Uji Japan
99C3 Ujiji Tanz
30D3 Ujina Chile
78A4 Ujung Pandang Indon
99D3 Ukerewe *I* Tanz
86C1 Ukhrul India
21A2 Ukiah California, USA
20B1 Ukiah Oregon, USA
58C1 Ukmerge Lithuania
60C4 Ukraine Republic, Europe
68B2 Ulaanbaatar Mongolia
68B2 Ulaangom Mongolia
72C1 Ulaan Uul Mongolia
72B1 Ulangar Hu *L* China
68C1 Ulan Ude Russian Fed
68B3 Ulan Ul Hu *L* China
34B2 Ulapes Arg
74B3 Ulchin S Korea
54A2 Ulcinj Montenegro, Yugos
68B2 Uldz Mongolia
68B2 Uliastay Mongolia
58C1 Ulladulla Aust
44B3 Ullapool Scot
38H5 Ullsfjorden *Inlet* Nor
42C2 Ullswater *L* Eng
74C3 Ullung-do *I* S Korea
57C3 Ulm Germany
108A1 Uloowaranie,L Aust
74B3 Ulsan S Korea
45C1 Ulster Region, N Ire
65K5 Ulungur He *R* China
65K5 Ulungur Hu *L* China
44A3 Ulva *I* Scot
42C2 Ulverston Eng
109C4 Ulverstone Aust
63G2 Ulya *R* Russian Fed
60D4 Uman Ukraine
6E2 Umanak Greenland
86A2 Umaria India
85B3 Umarkot Pak
108A1 Umaroona,L Aust
20C1 Umatilla USA
38L5 Umba Russian Fed
99D3 Umba *R* Tanz
64D3 Umeå Sweden
38J6 Umeälven Sweden
101H1 Umfolozi *R* S Africa
4C3 Umiat USA
85C4 Umm al Qaiwain UAE

Umm as Samīm

91C5 Umm as Samim *Salt Marsh* Oman
99C1 Umm Bell Sudan
98C1 Umm Keddada Sudan
99D1 Umm Ruwaba Sudan
91B5 Umm Sa'id Qatar
20B2 Umpqua *R* USA
85D4 Umred India
100B4 Umtata S Africa
35A2 Umuarama Brazil
52C1 Una *R* Bosnia-Herzegovina/Croatia
35B1 Unaí Brazil
12B2 Unalakleet USA
80C3 Unayzah S Arabia
16C2 Uncasville USA
101G1 Underberg S Africa
60D3 Unecha Russian Fed
94B3 Uneisa Jordan
7D4 Ungava B Can
30F4 União de Vitória Brazil
34B3 Unión Arg
18B2 Union Missouri, USA
17B1 Union S Carolina, USA
14C2 Union City Pennsylvania, USA
17A1 Union Springs USA
15C2 Uniontown USA
91B5 United Arab Emirates Arabian Pen
36C3 United Kingdom Kingdom, W Europe
2H4 United States of America
6B1 United States Range Mts Can
13F2 Unity Can
20C2 Unity USA
46D1 Unna Germany
86A1 Unnão India
44E1 Unst *I* Scot
13A1 Unuk *R* USA
92C1 Unye Turk
61F2 Unzha *R* Russian Fed
33E2 Upata Ven
98C3 Upemba Nat Pk Zaire
6E2 Upernavik Greenland
22D3 Upland USA
100B3 Uplington S Africa
13D2 Upper Arlington USA
13D2 Upper Arrow L Can
111C2 Upper Hutt NZ
20B2 Upper Klamath L USA
20B2 Upper L USA
45C1 Upper Lough Erne *L* N Ire
27L1 Upper Manzanilla Trinidad
39H7 Uppsala Sweden
72B1 Ural Qianqi China
91A4 Urairah S Arabia
61H3 Ural *R* Kazakhstan
61H3 Uralla Aust
65G4 Uralskiy Khrebet *Mts* Russian Fed
5H4 Uranium City Can
75B1 Urawa Japan
18C1 Urbana Illinois, USA
14B2 Urbana Ohio, USA
52B2 Urbino Italy
54B2 Uroševac Serbia, Yugos
31B4 Uruaçu Brazil
23A2 Uruapan Mexico
30E4 Uruguaiana Brazil
29E2 Uruguay Republic, S America
29E2 Uruguay *R* Urug
82C1 Urümqi China
69H2 Urup *I* Russian Fed
84B2 Uruzgan Afghan
61F3 Uryupinsk Russian Fed

61H2 Urzhum Russian Fed
54C2 Urziceni Rom
82C1 Usa China
75A2 Usa Japan
64G3 Usa *R* Russian Fed
92A2 Uşak Turk
100A3 Usakos Namibia
99D3 Ushashi Tanz
75A2 Ush Tobe Kazakhstan
29C6 Ushuaia Arg
63E2 Ushumun Russian Fed
43C4 Usk *R* Wales
92A1 Üsküdar Turk
63C2 Usolye Sibirskoye Russian Fed
34B2 Uspallata Arg
69F2 Ussuriysk Russian Fed
47C1 Uster Switz
53B3 Ustica *I* Italy
57C2 Ústí nad Labem Czech Republic
65J4 Ust'Ishim Russian Fed
58B2 Ustka Pol
65K5 Ust'-Kamenogorsk Kazakhstan
65J4 Ust Karabula Russian Fed
61J2 Ust'Katav Russian Fed
63C2 Ust'-Kut Russian Fed
61E4 Ust Labinsk Russian Fed
63F1 Ust Maya Russian Fed
1C8 Ust'Nera Russian Fed
63E2 Ust'Nyukzha Russian Fed
63C2 Ust'Ordynskiy Russian Fed
64G3 Ust'Tsil'ma Russian Fed
63F2 Ust'Umal'ta Russian Fed
65G5 Ustyurt Plateau *Plat* Kazakhstan
75A2 Usuki Japan
25C3 Usumacinta *R* Guatemala/Mexico
101H1 Usutu *R* Swaziland
8B3 Utah State, USA
8B2 Utah L USA
58D1 Utena Russian Fed
85B3 Uthal Pak
10C2 Utica USA
51B2 Utiel Spain
13D1 Utikuma L Can
56B2 Utrecht Neth
101H1 Utrecht S Africa
50A2 Utrera Spain
38K5 Utsjoki Fin
74D3 Utsunomiya Japan
76C2 Uttaradit Thai
86A1 Uttar Pradesh State, India
65H4 Uval Russian Fed
107F3 Uvéa *I* Nouvelle Calédonie
99D3 Uvinza Tanz
99C3 Uvira Zaire
6E2 Uvkusigssat Greenland
39J6 Uusikaupunki Fin
68B1 Uvs Nuur *L* China
74C4 Uwajima Japan
72B2 Uxin Qi China
63B2 Uyar Russian Fed
30C3 Uyuni Bol
80E1 Uzbekistan Republic, Asia
48C2 Uzerche France
57C3 Uzhgorod Ukraine
54A2 Užice Serbia, Yugos
60E3 Uzlovaya Russian Fed
92A1 Uzunköprü Turk

V

101F1 Vaal *R* S Africa
101G1 Vaal Dam *Res* S Africa

100B3 Vaalwater S Africa
38J6 Vaasa Fin
59B3 Vác Hung
53A3 Vacaria *R* Minas Gerais, Brazil
21A2 Vacaville USA
85C4 Vadodara India
38K4 Vadsø Nor
47C1 Vaduz Leichtenstein
38D3 Vágar Føroyar
29E3 Va Gesell Arg
59B3 Vah *R* Slovakia
87B2 Vaigai *R* India
65K3 Vakh *R* Russian Fed
60B4 Vâlcea Rom
29C4 Valcheta Arg
47D2 Valdagno Italy
60D2 Valday Russian Fed
60D2 Valdayskaya Vozvyshennost' *Upland* Russian Fed
32D2 Val de la Pascua Ven
50B2 Valdepeñas Spain
12E2 Valdez USA
29B3 Valdivia Chile
46B2 Val d'Oise *Department* France
17B1 Valdosta USA
20C2 Vale USA
13D2 Valemount Can
31D4 Valença Bahia, Brazil
35C2 Valença Rio de Janeiro, Brazil
49C3 Valence France
51B2 Valencia Region, Spain
51B2 Valencia Spain
32D1 Valencia Ven
45A3 Valencia / Irish Rep
50A2 Valencia de Alcantara Spain
46B1 Valenciennes France
47C2 Valenza Italy
32C2 Valera Ven
39K7 Valga Estonia
54A2 Valjevo Serbia, Yugos
Valka = Valga
39J6 Valkeakoski Fin
25D2 Valladolid Mexico
50B1 Valladolid Spain
47B2 Valle d'Aosta Region, Italy
27D5 Valle de la Pascua Ven
23A1 Valle de Santiago Ven
47B2 Valle d'Isère France
32C1 Valledupar Colombia
97C3 Vallée de l'Azaouak *V* Niger
97C3 Vallée Tilemsi *V* Mali
30D2 Valle Grande Bol
22A1 Vallejo USA
30B4 Vallenar Chile
53B3 Valletta Malta
8D2 Valley City USA
15D1 Valleyfield Can
13D1 Valleyview Can
47E2 Valli di Comacchio *Lg* Italy
51C1 Valls Spain
39J6 Valmiera Latvia
35A2 Valparaíso Brazil
34A2 Valparaíso Chile
23A1 Valparaiso Mexico
101G1 Vals *R* S Africa
85C4 Valsād India
60E3 Valuyki Russian Fed
50A2 Valverde del Camino Spain
38J6 Vammala Fin
93D2 Van Turk
63C1 Vanavara Russian Fed
18B2 Van Buren Arkansas, USA
13C3 Vancouver USA
20B1 Vancouver Can
5F5 Vancouver I Can

12G2 Vancouver,Mt Can
18C2 Vandalia Illinois, USA
14B3 Vandalia Ohio, USA
13C2 Vanderhoof Can
106C2 Van Diemen G *Gulf* Aust
39G7 Vänern *L* Sweden
39C7 Vänersborg Sweden
101D3 Vangaindrano Madag
92A1 Van Gölü *Salt L* Turk
76C2 Vang Vieng Laos
9C3 Van Horn USA
15C1 Vanier Can
1C6 Vankarem USA
38H6 Vännäs Sweden
48B2 Vannes France
47B2 Vanoise *Mts* France
100A4 Vanrhynsdorp S Africa
6B3 Vansittart I Can
105G4 Vanuatu *Is* Pacific O
14B3 Van Wert USA
47C2 Varallo Italy
90B2 Varamin Iran
86A1 Vārānasi India
38K4 Varangerfjord *Inlet* Nor
38K4 Varangerhalvøya *Pe* Nor
52C1 Varazdin Croatia
39G7 Varberg Sweden
39F7 Värde Den
38L4 Vardø Nor
52C2 Varéna Lithuania
47C2 Varenna Italy
47C2 Varese Italy
35B2 Varginha Brazil
38K6 Varkaus Fin
54C2 Varna Bulg
39G7 Värnamo Sweden
17B1 Varnville USA
35C1 Várzea da Palma Brazil
47C2 Varzi Italy
50B1 Vascongadas Region, Spain
60D3 Vasil'kov Ukraine
14B2 Vassar USA
39H7 Västerås Sweden
39H7 Västervik Sweden
52B2 Vasto Italy
65J4 Vasyugan *R* Russian Fed
38B2 Vatnajökull *Mts* Iceland
38A1 Vatneyri Iceland
54C1 Vatra Dornei Rom
39F7 Vättern *L* Sweden
9C3 Vaughn USA
32B3 Vaupés *R* Colombia
13E2 Vauxhall Can
87C3 Vavuniya Sri Lanka
39G7 Vaxjö Sweden
64G2 Vaygach, Ostrov *I* Russian Fed
23A1 Vedia Arg
38G5 Vega *I* Nor
13E2 Vegreville Can
34A2 Vejer de la Frontera Spain
39F7 Vejle Den
54C2 Velebit *Mts* Croatia
52C1 Velenje Slovenia
35C1 Velhas *R* Brazil
39K7 Velikaya *R* Russian Fed
60D2 Velikiye Luki Russian Fed
61G1 Velikiy Ustyug Russian Fed
54C2 Veliko Tŭrnovo Bulg
97A3 Vélingara Sen
38J7 Vellore India
61F1 Vel'sk Russian Fed
87B2 Vembanad L India
34C2 Venado Tuerto Arg
35B2 Veneslau Braz Braz
49C2 Vendôme France
12E1 Venetie USA
47D2 Veneto Region, Italy

47E2 Venezia Italy
32D2 Venezuela Republic, S America
87A1 Vengurla India
12C3 Veniaminof V USA
Venice = Venezia
52B2 Venkatagiri India
56B2 Venlo Neth
58C1 Venta R Latvia
101G1 Ventersburg S Africa
58C1 Ventspils Latvia
32D3 Ventuari R Ven
22C3 Ventura USA
60D1 Vepsovskaya Vozvyshennost' Upland Russian Fed
30D4 Vera Arg
51B2 Vera Spain
23B1 Veracruz Mexico
23B1 Veracruz State, Mexico
85C4 Veräval India
47C2 Verbania Italy
47C2 Vercelli Italy
35A1 Verde R Goias, Brazil
23A1 Verde R Jalisco, Mexico
23B2 Verde R Mato Grosso do Sul, Brazil
23B2 Verde R Oaxaca, Mexico
Verde,C = Cap Vert
35C1 Verde Grande R Brazil
34C3 Verde,Pen Arg
49D3 Verdon R France
46C2 Verdun France
101G1 Vereeniging S Africa
61H2 Vereshchagino Russian Fed
97A3 Verga,C Guinea
34D2 Vergara Arg
50A1 Verin Spain
63D2 Verkh Angara R Russian Fed
Verkhneural'sk Russian Fed
63E1 Verkhnevilyuysk Russian Fed
1C8 Verkhoyansk Russian Fed
35A1 Vermelho R Brazil
13E2 Vermilion Can
10C2 Vermont State, USA
22B2 Vernalis USA
13D2 Vernon Can
46A2 Vernon France
30D3 Vernon USA
17B2 Vero Beach USA
54B2 Veroia Greece
47D2 Verolanuova Italy
47D2 Verona Italy
46B2 Versailles France
101H1 Verulam S Africa
46C1 Vervins Belg
46B2 Vervins France
46C2 Vesle R France
49D2 Vesoul France
38G5 Vesterålen Is Nor
38G5 Vestfjorden Inlet Nor
Iceland
Vestmannaeyjar Iceland
53B2 Vesuvio Mt Italy
59B3 Veszprém Hung
39H7 Vetlanda Sweden
61F2 Vetluga R Russian Fed
46B1 Veurne Belg
47B1 Vevey Switz
47A2 Vexin Region, France
47A2 Veynes France
50A1 Viana do Castelo Port
Viangchan = Vientiane
49E3 Viareggio Italy
39F7 Viborg Den
53C3 Vibo Valentia Italy
Vic = Vich
112C2 Vicecomodoro Marambio Base Ant
52B1 Vicenza Italy
51C1 Vich Spain
32D3 Vichada R Colombia

61F2 Vichuga Russian Fed
49C2 Vichy France
19B3 Vicksburg USA
35C2 Vicosa Brazil
106C4 Victor Harbour Aust
34C2 Victoria Arg
13C3 Victoria Can
34A3 Victoria Chile
108B3 Victoria State, Aust
9D4 Victoria USA
106C2 Victoria R Aust
26B2 Victoria de las Tunas Cuba
100B2 Victoria Falls Zambia/Zim
4G2 Victoria I Can
108B2 Victoria,L Aust
99D3 Victoria,L C Africa
34A3 Victoria Land Region, Ant
86C2 Victoria,Mt Myan
99D2 Victoria Nile R Uganda
111B2 Victoria Range Mts NZ
106C2 Victoria River Downs Aust
4H3 Victoria Str Can
15D1 Victoriaville Can
108A4 Victoria West S Africa
34B3 Victorica Arg
21B3 Victorville USA
34C2 Vicuña Chile
34C2 Vicuña Mackenna Arg
17B1 Vidalia USA
54C2 Videle Rom
54C2 Vidin Bulg
85D4 Vidisha India
58D1 Vidzy Belarus
29D4 Viedma Arg
26A4 Viejo Costa Rica
Vielha = Viella
51C1 Viella Spain
Vienna = Wien
18C2 Vienna Illinois, USA
14B3 Vienna W Virginia, USA
49C2 Vienne France
48C2 Vienne R France
76C2 Vientiane Laos
47C1 Vierwaldstätter See L Switz
48C2 Vierzon France
53C2 Vieste Italy
70B2 Vietnam Republic, S E Asia
76D1 Vietri Viet
27P2 Vieux Fort St Lucia
79B2 Vigan Phil
47D2 Vigevano Italy
51A1 Vigo Spain
87C1 Vijayawäda India
55A2 Vijosé R Alb
38B2 Vik Iceland
54B2 Vikhren Mt Bulg
13E2 Viking Can
38G6 Vikna I Nor
101C2 Vila Maganja Mozam
101C2 Vila Machado Mozam
101C3 Vilculos Mozam
Vilanova la Geltrú = Villanueva-y-Geltrú
50A1 Vila Real Port
101C2 Vila Vasco da Gama Mozam
35C2 Vila Velha Brazil
58D2 Vileyka Belarus
33E6 Vilhena Brazil
60C2 Viljandi Estonia
101G1 Viljoenskroon S Africa
9C3 Villa Ahumada Mexico
34B2 Villa Atuel Arg
50A1 Villaba Spain
23A2 Villa Carranza Mexico

52B1 Villach Austria
34B2 Villa Colon Arg
34C2 Villa Constitución Arg
34C1 Villa de Maria Arg
23A1 Villa de Reyes Mexico
34B2 Villa Dolores Arg
47D2 Villafranca di Verona Italy
34C2 Villa General Mitre Arg
34B2 Villa General Roca Arg
34C2 Villaguay Arg
25C3 Villahermosa Mexico
23A1 Villa Hidalgo Mexico
34C2 Villa Huidobro Arg
34C3 Villa Iris Arg
34C2 Villa Maria Arg
30C2 Villa Montes Bol
23A1 Villanueva Mexico
50A1 Villa Nova de Gaia Port
50A2 Villanueva de la Serena Spain
51C1 Villanueva-y-Geltrú Spain
34B3 Villa Regina Arg
51B2 Villarreal Spain
34B3 Villarrica Chile
30E4 Villarrica Par
50B2 Villarrobledo Spain
34D2 Villa San José Arg
34C2 Villa Valeria Arg
32C3 Villavicencio Colombia
49C2 Villefranche France
7C5 Ville-Marie Can
51B2 Villena Spain
46B2 Villeneuve-St-Georges France
48C3 Villeneuve-sur-Lot France
19B3 Ville Platte USA
46B2 Villers-Cotterêts France
49C2 Villeurbanne France
101G1 Villiers S Africa
87B2 Villupuram India
58D2 Vilnius Lithuania
63D1 Vilyuy R Russian Fed
63E1 Vilyuysk Russian Fed
34A2 Viña del Mar Chile
51C1 Vinaroz Spain
14A3 Vincennes USA
38H5 Vindel R Sweden
85D4 Vindhya Range Mts India
16B3 Vineland USA
16D2 Vineyard Haven USA
76D2 Vinh Viet
76D3 Vinh Cam Ranh B Viet
77D4 Vinh Loi Viet
77D3 Vinh Long Viet
18A2 Vinita USA
54A1 Vinkovci Croatia
60C4 Vinnitsa Ukraine
112B3 Vinson Massif Upland Ant
100A3 Vioolsdrift S Africa
47D1 Vipiteno Italy
100A2 Virei Angola
35C1 Virgem da Lapa Brazil
101G1 Virginia S Africa
10C3 Virginia State, USA
10A2 Virginia USA
21B2 Virginia City USA
27E3 Virgin Is Caribbean S
52C1 Virovitica Croatia
46C2 Virton Belg
87B3 Virudunagar India
52C2 Vis I Croatia
21B2 Visalia USA
79B3 Visayan S Phil
39H7 Visby Sweden
4H2 Viscount Melville Sd Can

54A2 Višegrad Bosnia-Herzegovina
50A1 Viseu Port
83C4 Vishakhapatnam India
47B1 Visp Switz
49C1 Vissingen Neth
21B3 Vista USA
Vistula = Wisla
57C3 Vitavia R Czech Republic
87A1 Vite India
60D2 Vitebsk Belarus
52B2 Viterbo Italy
50A1 Vitigudino Spain
63D2 Vitim R Russian Fed
31C6 Vitória Brazil
31C4 Vitória da Conquista Brazil
48B2 Vitré France
46C2 Vitry-le-Francois France
38J5 Vittangi Sweden
53B3 Vittoria Italy
47E2 Vittorio Veneto Italy
69H2 Vityaz Depth Pacific O
50A1 Vivero Spain
63B1 Vivi R Russian Fed
34D3 Vivorata Arg
63C2 Vizhne-Angarsk Russian Fed
83C4 Vizianagaram India
54B1 Vladeasa Mt Rom
61F5 Vladikavkaz Russian Fed
65F4 Vladimir Russian Fed
59C2 Vladimir Volynskiy Ukraine
74C2 Vladivostok Russian Fed
56A2 Vlieland I Neth
46B1 Vlissingen Neth
55A2 Vlorë Alb
57C3 Vöcklabruck Austria
76D3 Voeune Sai Camb
47C2 Voghera Italy
101D2 Vohibinany Madag
101E2 Vohimarina Madag
99D2 Voi Kenya
97B4 Voinjama Lib
49D2 Voiron France
54A1 Vojvodina Aut Republic Serbia, Yugos
26A5 Volcán Baru Mt Panama
23B2 Volcán Citlaltepetl Mt Mexico
30C3 Volcán Lullaillaco Mt Chile
34A3 Volcán Copahue Mt Chile
34A3 Volcáno Domuyo Mt Arg
Volcano Is = Kazan Retto
29B3 Volcáno Lanin Mt Arg
Volcán Ollagüe Mt Chile
34A3 Volcáno Llaima Mt Chile
34B2 Volcáno Maipo Mt Arg
34A3 Volcáno Peteroa Mt Chile
34B3 Volcáno Tromen V Arg
23B2 Volcán Paracutin Mt Mexico
32B3 Volcán Puracé Mt Colombia
34A3 Volcán Tinguiririca Mt Arg/Chile
61J2 Volchansk Russian Fed
61G4 Volga R Russian Fed
61F4 Volgodonsk Russian Fed

Volgograd

61F4 **Volgograd**
Russian Fed
61G3 **Volgogradskoye Vodokhranilishche** *Res Russian Fed*
60D2 **Volkhov** Russian Fed
60D2 **Volkhov** *R*
Russian Fed
58C2 **Volkovysk** Belarus
101G1 **Volksrust** S Africa
61F2 **Vologda** Russian Fed
48B2 **Volognes** France
55B3 **Volos** Greece
61G3 **Vol'sk** Russian Fed
22B2 **Volta** R
97B3 **Volta Blanche** R
Burkina
97B4 **Volta,L** Ghana
97B3 **Volta Noire** R
Burkina
35C2 **Volta Redonda** Brazil
97B3 **Volta Rouge** R
Burkina
61F4 **Volzhskiy**
Russian Fed
12D2 **Von Frank Mt** USA
6J3 **Vopnafjörður** Iceland
47C1 **Voralberg** Province,
Austria
47C1 **Vorder Rhein** R
Switz
56C1 **Vordingborg** Den
64H3 **Vorkuta** Russian Fed
39G6 **Vorma** R Nor
60E3 **Voronezh**
Russian Fed
38M5 **Voron'ya** R
Russian Fed
39K7 **Võru** Estonia
49D2 **Vosges** Mt France
39F6 **Voss** Nor
63B2 **Vostochnyy Sayan**
Mts Russian Fed
112B9 **Vostok** Base Ant
61H2 **Votkinsk**
Russian Fed
46C2 **Vouziers** France
60D4 **Voznesensk** Ukraine
54B2 **Vranje** Serbia, Yugos
54B2 **Vratsa** Bulg
54A1 **Vrbas** Serbia, Yugos
52C2 **Vrbas** R Serbia,
Yugos
52B1 **Vrbovsko** Bosnia-
Herzegovina
101G1 **Vrede** S Africa
33F2 **Vreed en Hoop**
Guyana
54B1 **Vršac** Serbia, Yugos
52C2 **Vrtoče** Bosnia-
Herzegovina
100B3 **Vryburg** S Africa
101H1 **Vryheid** S Africa
54A1 **Vukovar** Croatia
13E2 **Vulcan** Can
53B3 **Vulcano** I Italy
7D3 **Vung Tau** Viet
38J5 **Vuollerim** Sweden
38L6 **Vyartsilya**
Russian Fed
61H2 **Vyatka** R
Russian Fed
69F2 **Vyazemskiy**
Russian Fed
60D2 **Vyaz'ma** Russian Fed
61F2 **Vyazniki** Russian Fed
60C1 **Vyborg** Russian Fed
64G3 **Vym'** R Russian Fed
43C3 **Vyrnwy** R Wales
60D2 **Vyshiy Volochek**
Russian Fed
59B3 **Vyškov**
Czech Republic
60E1 **Vytegra** Russian Fed

W

97B3 **Wa** Ghana
13E1 **Wabasca** Can
5G4 **Wabasca** R Can
13E1 **Wabasca L** Can
14A2 **Wabash** USA
14A3 **Wabash** R USA
5J4 **Wabowden** Can
7D4 **Wabush** Can

17B2 **Waccassasa B** USA
16D1 **Wachusett Res** USA
19A3 **Waco** USA
85B3 **Wad** Pak
95A2 **Waddān** Libya
5F4 **Waddington,Mt** Can
93E4 **Wadi al Batin**
Watercourse Iraq
93D3 **Wadi al Ghudaf**
Watercourse Iraq
94C2 **Wadi al Harir** V Syria
93D3 **Wadi al Mirah**
Watercourse Iraq/
S Arabia
93D3 **Wadi al Ubayyid**
Watercourse Iraq
93D3 **Wadi Ar'ar**
Watercourse
S Arabia
91A5 **Wadi as Hsabā'**
Watercourse
S Arabia
92C3 **Wadi as Sirhān** V
Jordan/S Arabia
94C2 **Wadi az Zaydi** V
Syria
94C3 **Wadi edh Dhab'i** V
Egypt
94A3 **Wadi el 'Arish** V
Egypt
94C3 **Wadi el Ghadaf** V
Jordan
94B3 **Wadi el Hasa** V
Jordan
94C3 **Wadi el Janab** V
Jordan
94B3 **Wadi el Jeib** V
Israel/Jordan
95B3 **Wadi el Milk**
Watercourse Sudan
92A3 **Wadi el Natrun**
Watercourse Egypt
94B3 **Wadi es Sir** Jordan
94B3 **Wadi Fidan** V
Jordan
94B3 **Wadi Hareidin** V
Egypt
93D3 **Wadi Hawrän** R Iraq
95B3 **Wadi Howa**
Watercourse Sudan
98C1 **Wadi Ibra**
Watercourse Sudan
94C2 **Wadi Luhfi**
Watercourse Jordan
94B3 **Wadi Mujib** V
Jordan
94B3 **Wadi Qītaiya** V
Egypt
80B3 **Wadi Sha'it**
Watercourse Egypt
99D1 **Wad Medani** Sudan
93E4 **Wafra** Kuwait
6B3 **Wager B** Can
6A3 **Wager Bay** Can
109C3 **Wagga Wagga** Aust
106A4 **Wagin** Aust
95A2 **Wāha** Libya
21C4 **Wahaiwa** Hawaiian Is
18A1 **Wahoo** USA
8D2 **Wahpeton** USA
87A1 **Wai** India
111B2 **Waiau** NZ
111A3 **Waiau** R NZ
111B2 **Waiau** R NZ
110C1 **Waihi** NZ
110C1 **Waikaremoana,L** NZ
110C1 **Waikato** R NZ
108A2 **Waikerie** Aust
111B3 **Waikouaiti** NZ
21C4 **Wailuku** Hawaiian Is
111B2 **Waimakariri** R NZ
111B2 **Waimate** NZ
21C4 **Waimea** Hawaiian Is
106B1 **Waingapu** Indon
13E2 **Wainwright** Can
4B2 **Wainwright** USA
111B2 **Waipara** NZ
110C2 **Waipukurau** NZ
111C2 **Wairarapa,L** NZ
111B2 **Wairoa** NZ
110C1 **Wairoa** R NZ
110C1 **Wairoa** R NZ
111B2 **Waitaki** R NZ

110B1 **Waitara** NZ
110C1 **Waitomo** NZ
110B1 **Waiuku** NZ
75B1 **Wajima** Japan
99E2 **Wajir** Kenya
75B1 **Wakasa-wan** B
Japan
111A3 **Wakatipu,L** NZ
74D4 **Wakayama** Japan
42D3 **Wakefield** Eng
27H1 **Wakefield** Jamaica
16D1 **Wakefield** Rhode
Island, USA
76B2 **Wakema** Myan
69G2 **Wakkanai** Japan
108C3 **Wakool** R Aust
59B2 **Wałbrzych** Pol
109D2 **Walcha** Aust
58B2 **Walcz** Pol
46D1 **Waldbröl** Germany
16B2 **Walden** USA
43C3 **Wales** Country, UK
12A1 **Wales** USA
6B3 **Wales I** Can
109C2 **Walgett** Aust
112B4 **Walgreen Coast**
Region, Ant
99C3 **Walikale** Zaire
21B2 **Walker** L USA
21B2 **Walkerton** Can
8B2 **Wallace** USA
108A2 **Wallaroo** Aust
109C3 **Walla Walla** Aust
20C1 **Walla Walla** USA
16C2 **Wallingford** USA
105H4 **Wallis and Futuna** Is
Pacific O
20C1 **Wallowa** USA
20C1 **Wallowa Mts** Mts
USA
109C1 **Wallumbilla** Aust
18B2 **Walnut Ridge** USA
110C1 **Walouru** NZ
43D3 **Walsall** Eng
9C3 **Walsenburg** USA
9C3 **Walsenburgh** USA
17B1 **Walterboro** USA
17A1 **Walter F George Res**
USA
16D1 **Waltham** USA
100A3 **Walvis Bay** Namibia
103J6 **Walvis Ridge**
Atlantic O
97C4 **Wamba** Nig
99C3 **Wamba** R Zaire
18A2 **Wamego** USA
84B2 **Wana** Pak
108B1 **Wanaaring** Aust
111A2 **Wanaka** NZ
111A2 **Wanaka,L** NZ
14B1 **Wanapitei L** Can
109C1 **Wandoan** Aust
108B3 **Wangaella** Aust
110C1 **Wanganui** NZ
110C1 **Wanganui** R NZ
109C3 **Wangaratta** Aust
99E2 **Wanle Weyne**
Somalia
76E2 **Wanning** China
87B1 **Wanparti** India
73B3 **Wanxian** China
73B3 **Wanyuan** China
13D2 **Wapiti** R Can
18B2 **Wappapello,L** USA
16C2 **Wappingers Falls**
USA
87B1 **Warangal** India
109C4 **Waratah** Aust
109C3 **Waratah B** Aust
108C3 **Warburton** Aust
108A1 **Warburton** R Aust
109C1 **Ward** R Aust
101G1 **Warden** S Africa
99E2 **Warder** Eth
85D4 **Wardha** India
111A3 **Ware** Can
16C1 **Ware** USA
16D2 **Wareham** USA
109D1 **Warialda** Aust
76C2 **Warin Chamrap**
Thai
100B3 **Warmbad** S Africa
16B2 **Warminster** USA
21B2 **Warm Springs** USA

56C2 **Warnemünde**
Germany
20B2 **Warner Mts** USA
17B1 **Warner Robins** USA
108B3 **Warracknabeal** Aust
108A1 **Warrandirinna,L** Aust
107D3 **Warrego** R Aust
19B3 **Warren** Arkansas,
USA
109C2 **Warren** Aust
16D2 **Warren**
Massachusetts, USA
12B2 **Warren** Ohio, USA
15C2 **Warren**
Pennsylvania, USA
45C1 **Warrenpoint** N Ire
18B2 **Warrensburg** USA
101F1 **Warrenton** S Africa
15C3 **Warrenton** USA
97C4 **Warri** Nig
42C3 **Warrington** Eng
108B3 **Warrnambool** Aust
Warsaw = Warszawa
58C2 **Warszawa** Pol
57B2 **Warta** R Pol
109D1 **Warwick** Aust
43D3 **Warwick** County,
Eng
43D3 **Warwick** Eng
16B2 **Warwick** New York,
USA
16D2 **Warwick** Rhode
Island, USA
8B3 **Wasatch Range** Mts
USA
101H1 **Wasbank** S Africa
21B2 **Wasco** USA
4H2 **Washburn L** Can
85D4 **Washim** India
10C3 **Washington** District
of Columbia, USA
14A3 **Washington** Georgia
USA
14A3 **Washington** Indiana,
USA
18B2 **Washington**
Missouri, USA
16B2 **Washington** New
Jersey, USA
15C2 **Washington**
Pennsylvania, USA
8A2 **Washington** State,
USA
14B3 **Washington Court
House** USA
6D1 **Washington Land**
Can
15D2 **Washington,Mt** USA
43E3 **Wash,The** Eng
85A3 **Washuk** Pak
12E2 **Wasilla** USA
7C4 **Waskaganish** Can
26A4 **Waspán** Nic
70D4 **Watampone** Indon
16C2 **Waterbury** USA
45C2 **Waterford** County,
Irish Rep
41B3 **Waterford** Irish Rep
45C2 **Waterford Harbour**
Irish Rep
46C1 **Waterloo** Belg
10A2 **Waterloo** Can
15C2 **Watertown** New
York, USA
101H1 **Waterval-Boven**
S Africa
10D2 **Waterville** Maine,
USA
14E1 **Werviliet** USA
5G4 **Waterways** Can
43D4 **Watford** Eng
15C2 **Watkins Glen** USA
8C1 **Watrous** Can
99C2 **Watsa** Zaire
12J2 **Watson Lake** Can
22B2 **Watsonville** USA
71E4 **Wau** PNG
99C2 **Wau** Sudan
78S **Waua** Can
109D2 **Wauchope** Aust
17B2 **Wauchula** USA
14A2 **Waukegan** USA
10B2 **Wausau** USA

Wingham

14A2 **Wauwatosa** USA
106C2 **Wave Hill** Aust
43E3 **Waveney** R Eng
1483 **Waverly** Ohio, USA
46C1 **Wavre** Belg
10B2 **Wawa** Can
95A2 **Wāw Al Kabīr** Libya
95A2 **Wāw an Nāmūs** Well Libya
22C3 **Wawona** USA
19A3 **Waxahachie** USA
17B1 **Waycross** USA
17B1 **Waynesboro** Georgia, USA
19C3 **Waynesboro** Mississippi, USA
16C3 **Waynesboro** Pennsylvania, USA
15C3 **Waynesboro** Virginia, USA
18B2 **Waynesville** Missouri, USA
84B2 **Wazi Khwa** Afghan
43E4 **Weald,The** Upland Eng
42C2 **Wear** R Eng
19A3 **Weatherford** Texas, USA
20B2 **Weaverville** USA
14B1 **Webbwood** Can
16D1 **Webster** USA
18B2 **Webster Groves** USA
29D6 **Weddell I** Falkland Is
11C2 **Weddell S** Ant
13C2 **Wedge Mt** Can
20B2 **Weed** USA
01H1 **Weenen** S Africa
109C2 **Wee Waa** Aust
72D1 **Weichang** China
57C3 **Weiden** Germany
72D2 **Weifang** China
72E2 **Weihai** China
72C2 **Wei He** R Henan, China
72C2 **Wei He** R Shaanxi, China
109C1 **Weilmoringle** Aust
73A4 **Weining** China
107D2 **Weipa** Aust
14B2 **Weirton** USA
72D3 **Weishan Hu** L China
57C2 **Weissenfels** Germ
17A1 **Weiss L** USA
101G1 **Welkom** S Africa
7C1 **Welland** Can
43D3 **Welland** R Eng
106C2 **Wellesley Is** Aust
12G2 **Wellesley L** Can
109C2 **Wellingborough** Eng
18A2 **Wellington** Kansas, USA
111B2 **Wellington** NZ
6A2 **Wellington Chan** Can
13C2 **Wells** Can
43C4 **Wells** Eng
110B1 **Wellsford** NZ
106B3 **Wells,L** Aust
15C3 **Wels** Austria
43C3 **Welshpool** Wales
13D1 **Wembley** Can
7C4 **Wemindji** Can
20B1 **Wenatchee** USA
20C1 **Wenatchee** R USA
97B4 **Wenchi** Ghana
72E2 **Wenden** China
73E4 **Wenling** China
32J7 **Wenman** I Ecuador
73A5 **Wenshan** China
73A4 **Wenxian** China
72A3 **Wen Xian** China
73E4 **Wenzhou** China
73C4 **Wenzhu** China
01G1 **Wepener** S Africa
12E1 **Werneke Mts** Can
72C2 **Werra** R Germany
109C2 **Werris Creek** Aust
56E2 **Wesel** Germany
56E2 **Weser** R Germany
106C2 **Wessel Is** Aust
14A2 **West Allis** USA

104C4 **West Australian Basin** Indian O
104C5 **West Australian Ridge** Indian O
19C3 **West B** USA
86B2 **West Bengal** State, India
43D3 **West Bromwich** Eng
16B3 **West Chester** USA
46D1 **Westerburg** Germ
56B2 **Westerland** Germany
16D2 **Westerly** USA
106A3 **Western Australia** State, Aust
100A4 **Western Cape** Province, S Africa
87A1 **Western Ghats** Mts India
44A3 **Western Isles** Scot
96A2 **Western Sahara** Region, Mor
105H4 **Western Samoa** Is Pacific O
46B1 **Westerschelde** Estuary Neth
46D1 **Westerwald** Region, Germany
49D1 **Westfalen** Region, Germany
29D6 **West Falkland** I Falkland Is
16C1 **Westfield** Massachusetts, USA
15C2 **Westfield** New York, USA
18C2 **West Frankfort** USA
109C1 **Westgate** Aust
43C4 **West Glamorgan** County, Wales
102E3 **West Indies** Is Caribbean S
13E2 **Westlock** Can
14B2 **West Lorne** Can
45C2 **Westmeath** County, Irish Rep
18B2 **West Memphis** USA
43D3 **West Midlands** County, Eng
17B1 **Westminster** Eng
15D1 **Westminster** Maryland, USA
17B1 **Westminster** S Carolina, USA
100B3 **West Nicholson** Zim
78D1 **West Malay** Malay
14B3 **Weston** USA
43C4 **Weston-super-Mare** Eng
17B2 **West Palm Beach** USA
18B2 **West Plains** USA
22B1 **West Point** California, USA
19C3 **West Point** Mississippi, USA
16C2 **West Point** New York, USA
12F2 **West Point** Mt USA
45B2 **Westport** Irish Rep
111B2 **Westport** NZ
44C2 **Westray** I Scot
13C2 **West Road** R Can
42E3 **West Sole** Oilfield N Sea
11B3 **West Virginia** State, USA
22C1 **West Walker** R USA
109C2 **West Wyalong** Aust
42D3 **West Yorkshire** County, Eng
71D4 **Wetar** I Indon
13E2 **Wetaskiwin** Can
99D3 **Wete** Tanz
46E1 **Wetzlar** Germany
Wevok = Cape Lisburne
71F4 **Wewak** PNG
19A2 **Wewoka** USA
45C2 **Wexford** County, Irish Rep
45C2 **Wexford** Irish Rep
5H5 **Weyburn** Can
43C4 **Weymouth** Eng
16D1 **Weymouth** USA

110C1 **Whakatane** NZ
110C1 **Whakatane** R NZ
44E1 **Whalsay** I Scot
110B1 **Whangarei** NZ
42D3 **Wharfe** R Eng
19A4 **Wharton** USA
111B2 **Whataroa** NZ
16A3 **Wheaton** Maryland, USA
8B3 **Wheeler Peak** Mt Nevada, USA
9C3 **Wheeler Peak** Mt New Mexico, USA
14B2 **Wheeling** USA
13C3 **Whistler** Can
15C2 **Whitby** Can
42D2 **Whitby** Eng
18B2 **White** R Arkansas, USA
12E2 **White** R Can
14A3 **White** R Indiana, USA
8C2 **White** R S Dakota, USA
7E4 **White B** Can
108B2 **White Cliffs** Aust
40C2 **White Coomb** Mt Scot
13D2 **Whitecourt** Can
14A1 **Whitefish Pt** USA
7D4 **Whitegull L** Can
15D2 **Whitehall** New York, USA
16B2 **Whitehall** Pennsylvania, USA
42C2 **Whitehaven** Eng
12G2 **Whitehorse** Can
110C1 **White I** NZ
19B4 **White L** USA
47A3 **Whitemark** Aust
21B2 **White Mountain Peak** Mt USA
12E1 **White Mts** Alaska, USA
15D2 **White Mts** New Hampshire, USA
99D1 **White Nile** R Sudan
16C2 **White Plains** USA
7B5 **White River** Can
15D2 **White River Junction** USA
White S = Beloye More
13B2 **Whitesail L** Can
20B1 **White Salmon** USA
17C1 **Whiteville** USA
97B4 **White Volta** R Ghana
13B2 **Whitianga** NZ
17B1 **Whitmire** USA
21B2 **Whitney,Mt** USA
12E2 **Whittier** Alaska, USA
22C4 **Whittier** California, USA
5H3 **Wholdia L** Can
108A2 **Whyalla** Aust
14B2 **Wiarton** Can
18A2 **Wichita** USA
9D3 **Wichita Falls** USA
44C2 **Wick** Scot
45C2 **Wicklow** County, Irish Rep
45C2 **Wicklow** Irish Rep
45C2 **Wicklow Mts** Irish Rep
109C1 **Widgeegoara** R Aust
46E1 **Wied** R Germany
59B2 **Wielun** Pol
59B3 **Wien** Austria
59B3 **Wiener Neustadt** Austria
58C2 **Wieprz** R Pol
46E1 **Wiesbaden** Germany
42C3 **Wigan** Eng
42B2 **Wiggins** USA
42C3 **Wigtown** Scot
42B2 **Wigtown B** Scot
47C1 **Wil** Switz
108B2 **Wilcannia** Aust
21B2 **Wildcat Peak** Mt USA
47B1 **Wildhorn** Mt Switz
13E2 **Wild Horse** Can

47D1 **Wildspitze** Mt Austria
17B2 **Wildwood** Florida, USA
16B3 **Wildwood** New Jersey, USA
101G1 **Wilge** R S Africa
56B2 **Wilhelmshaven** Germany
15C2 **Wilkes-Barre** USA
112B8 **Wilkes Land** Ant
13F2 **Wilkie** Can
20B2 **Willamette** R USA
108B2 **Willandra** R Aust
20B1 **Willapa B** USA
9C3 **Willcox** USA
27D4 **Willemstad** Curaçao
108A1 **William Creek** Aust
108B3 **William,Mt** Aust
21A2 **Williams** California, USA
13C2 **Williams Lake** Can
15C2 **Williamsport** USA
14B3 **Williamstown** Massachusetts, USA
14B3 **Williamstown** W Virginia, USA
16B2 **Willimantic** USA
16B2 **Willingboro** USA
13D2 **Willingdon,Mt** Can
107E2 **Willis Group** Is Aust
17B2 **Williston** Florida, USA
100B4 **Williston** S Africa
13C1 **Williston L** Can
8D2 **Willmar** USA
108A3 **Willoughby,C** Aust
13C2 **Willow** R Can
20B2 **Willow Ranch** USA
18A2 **Willow Springs** USA
108A2 **Wilmington** Aust
16B3 **Wilmington** Delaware, USA
17C1 **Wilmington** N Carolina, USA
7A5 **Wilna** USA
11C3 **Wilson** USA
108B1 **Wilson** R Aust
6B3 **Wilson,C** Can
22C3 **Wilson,Mt** USA
20B1 **Wilson,Mt** Oregon, USA
109C3 **Wilsons Promontory** Pen Aust
43D4 **Wiltshire** County, Eng
46C2 **Wiltz** Lux
106B3 **Wiluna** Aust
14A2 **Winamac** USA
101G1 **Winburg** S Africa
16C1 **Winchendon** USA
15C1 **Winchester** Can
43D4 **Winchester** Eng
16C1 **Winchester** New Hampshire, USA
15C3 **Winchester** Virginia, USA
42C2 **Windermere** Eng
100A3 **Windhoek** Namibia
107D3 **Windorah** Aust
8C2 **Wind River Range** Mts USA
109D2 **Windsor** Aust
109D2 **Windsor** Connecticut, USA
43D4 **Windsor** Eng
7D5 **Windsor** Nova Scotia, Can
14B2 **Windsor** Ontario, Can
15D1 **Windsor** Quebec, Can
17B1 **Windsor Forest** USA
16C2 **Windsor Locks** USA
27E4 **Windward Is** Caribbean S
26C3 **Windward Pass** Caribbean S
13E1 **Winefred L** Can
18A2 **Winfield** Kansas, USA
109D2 **Wingham** Aust

Winifreda

34C3 Winifreda Arg
7B4 Winisk R Can
7B4 Winisk L Can
7682 Winkana Myan
20B1 Winlock USA
97B4 Winneba Ghana
14A2 Winnebago,L USA
20C2 Winnemucca USA
5J4 Winnipeg Can
5J4 Winnipeg,L Can
5J4 Winnipegosis Can
4J4 Winnipegosis,L Can
15D2 Winnipesaukee,L USA
10A2 Winona Minnesota, USA
19C3 Winona Mississippi, USA
15D2 Winooski USA
9B3 Winslow USA
16C2 Winsted USA
11B3 Winston-Salem USA
46E1 Winterberg Germany
17B2 Winter Garden USA
17B2 Winter Park USA
22B1 Winters USA
47C1 Winterthur Switz
107D3 Winton Aust
111A3 Winton NZ
43E3 Wisbech Eng
10B2 Wisconsin State, USA
7B5 Wisconsin Rapids USA
12D1 Wiseman USA
58B2 Wisla R Pol
56C2 Wismar Germany
33F2 Witagron Surinam
10101 Witbank S Africa
9D3 Witchita Falls USA
43D3 Witham R Eng
42E3 Withernsea Eng
97C4 Witney Eng
46D1 Witten Germany
56C2 Wittenberg Germany
106A3 Wittenoom Aust
46D1 Wittlich Germany
58B2 Wladyslawowo Pol
58B2 Wloclawek Pol
58C2 Wlodawa Pol
109C3 Wodonga Aust
47C1 Wohlen Switz
71E4 Wokam Indon
43D4 Woking Eng
71F3 Woleai I Pacific O
20B2 Wolf Creek USA
8C2 Wolf Point USA
57C3 Wolfsberg Austria
56C2 Wolfsburg Germany
5H4 Wollaston L Can
5H4 Wollaston Lake Can
4G3 Wollaston Pen Can
109D2 Wollongong Aust
101G1 Wolmaransstad S Africa
59B2 Wolow Pol
108B3 Wolseley Aust
43C3 Wolverhampton Eng
16A2 Womelsdorf USA
12F1 Wood,house USA
21A2 Woodland California, USA
20B1 Woodland Washington, USA
107E1 Woodlark I PNG
106C4 Woodmera Aust
106C3 Woodroffe,Mt Aust
14B2 Woodstock Ontario, Can

16B3 Woodstown USA
110C2 Woodville NZ
19B3 Woodville USA
10842 Woomera Aust
15D2 Woonsocket USA
14B2 Wooster USA
43C3 Worcester Eng
100A4 Worcester S Africa
16D1 Worcester USA
47E1 Wörgl Austria
42C2 Workington Eng
8C2 Worland USA
46E2 Worms Germany
43B4 Worms Head Pt Wales
43D4 Worthing Eng
8D2 Worthington USA
71D4 Wowoni I Indon
12H3 Wrangell USA
12H3 Wrangell I USA
12F2 Wrangell Mts USA
40B2 Wrath,C Scot
43C3 Wrexham Wales
17B1 Wrightsville USA
22D3 Wrightwood USA
4F3 Wrigley Can
59B2 Wroclaw Pol
58B2 Wrzesnia Pol
69E2 Wuchang China
76E1 Wuchuan China
72E2 Wuda China
72C2 Wuding He R China
72A3 Wudu China
73C4 Wugang China
72E2 Wuhai China
72C3 Wuhan China
73D3 Wuhu China
73D5 Wuhua China
84D2 Wujiang China
72B1 Wujia He R China
73B4 Wu Jiang R China
97C4 Wukari Nig
73B4 Wuling Shan Mts China
97D4 Wum Cam
73A4 Wumeng Shan Upland China
46D1 Wuppertal Germany
72B2 Wuqi China
72D2 Wuqing China
57B3 Würzburg Germany
57C2 Wurzen Germany
72C2 Wutai Shan Mt China
71F4 Wuvulu I Pacific O
72A2 Wuwei China
73D3 Wuxi China
73E3 Wuxing China
72C2 Wuyang China
73D4 Wuyi Shan Mts China
72B1 Wuyuan China
76D2 Wuzhi Shan Mts China
72B2 Wuzhong China
73C5 Wuzhou China
14B2 Wyandotte USA
109C1 Wyandra Aust
43C4 Wye R Eng
43C4 Wylye R Eng
43E3 Wymondham Eng
106B2 Wyndham Aust
18B2 Wynne USA
4G2 Wynniatt B Can
8C2 Wyoming State, USA
14A2 Wyoming USA
109D2 Wyong Aust

73B4 Xianfeng China
73C3 Xiangfan China
73C4 Xiang Jiang R China
73C4 Xiangtan Province, China
73C4 Xianning China
72B3 Xianyang China
72E3 Xiao Shui R China
73D4 Xiapu China
73A4 Xichang China
23B1 Xicotepec Mexico
76C2 Xieng Khouang Laos
73B4 Xifeng China
86B1 Xigazê China
72A1 Xi He R China
72B2 Xiji China
73C5 Xi Jiang R China
72E1 Xiliao He R China
73B5 Xilin China
23B1 Xilitla Mexico
73C4 Xinfeng China
72C1 Xinghe China
73D5 Xingning China
73B4 Xingren China
72C2 Xingtai China
33G4 Xingu R Brazil
72B2 Xingxingxia China
73A4 Xingyi China
72A2 Xining China
72E2 Xinjin Liaoning, China
73A3 Xinjin Sichuan, China
72D2 Xinwen China
72E2 Xin Xian China
72C2 Xinxiang China
73C3 Xinyang China
73C5 Xinyi Guangdong, China
72D3 Xinyi Jiangsu, China
72D3 Xi Ujimqin Qi China
74A2 Xiuyan China
23B2 Xochimilco Mexico
73B3 Xuancheng China
73B3 Xuanhan China
72D1 Xuanhua China
73A4 Xuanwei China
73A4 Xuddur Somalia
99E2 Xuddur Somalia
72A2 Xunhua China
73C5 Xun Jiang R China
69E2 Xunke China
73C5 Xunwu China
73C4 Xupu China
76E1 Xuwen China
73B4 Xuyong China
72D3 Xuzhou China

Y

73A4 Ya'an China
108B3 Yaapeet Aust
98B2 Yabassi Cam
68C1 Yablonovyy Khrebet Mts Russian Fed
94C2 Yabrūd Syria
20B2 Yachats USA
30D3 Yacuiba Bol
87B1 Yādgīr India
95A2 Yafran Libya
23A1 Yahualica Mexico
98C2 Yahuma Zaire
75B1 Yaita Japan
75B2 Yaizu Japan
73A4 Yajiang China
20B1 Yakima USA
20B1 Yakima R USA
97B3 Yako Burkina
98C2 Yakoma Zaire
74E2 Yakumo Japan
12G3 Yakutat USA
12G3 Yakutat B USA
63E1 Yakutsk Russian Fed
77C4 Yala Thai
23B2 Yalalag Mexico
98C2 Yalinga CAR
109C3 Yallourn Aust
68B3 Yalong R China
73A4 Yalong Jiang R China
54C2 Yalova Turk
60D5 Yalta Ukraine
74B2 Yalu Jiang R China
74D3 Yamagata Japan
74C4 Yamaguchi Japan

68D1 Yamarovka Russian Fed
109D1 Yamba New S Wales, Aust
108B2 Yamba S Australia, Aust
99C2 Yambio Sudan
54C2 Yambol Bulg
71E4 Yamdena I Indon
Yam Kinneret = Tiberias,L
108B1 Yamma Yamma,L Aust
97B4 Yamoussoukro Ivor Coast
85D3 Yamuna R India
86C1 Yamzho Yumco L China
63F1 Yana R Russian Fed
108B3 Yanac Aust
75A2 Yanagawa Japan
87C1 Yanam India
72B2 Yan'an China
80B3 Yanbu'al Bahr S Arabia
108B2 Yancannia Aust
72E3 Yancheng China
72D2 Yanchi China
108B1 Yandama R Aust
98C2 Yangambi Zaire
72C1 Yang He R China
73C5 Yangjiang China
76B2 Yangon Myan
73C3 Yangquan China
73C4 Yangshan China
73C3 Yangtze Gorges China
72E3 Yangtze,Mouths of the China
72D3 Yangzhou China
73B4 Yanhe China
74B2 Yanji China
108C3 Yanko R Aust
8D2 Yankton USA
68A2 Yangqi China
72D1 Yan Shan Hills China
108B1 Yantabulla Aust
72E2 Yantai China
72D2 Yanzhou China
98B2 Yaoundé Cam
71E4 Yapen I Pacific O
71E3 Yap Is Pacific O
71E2 Yaqui R Mexico
61G2 Yaransk Russian Fed
32C3 Yari R Colombia
74D3 Yariga-dake Mt Japan
82B2 Yarkant He R China
86C1 Yarlung Zangbo Jiang R China
7D5 Yarmouth Can
94B2 Yarmūk R Syria/Jordan
61E2 Yaroslavl' Russian Fed
94B2 Yarqon R Israel
31B2 Yarram Aust
109C3 Yarrawonga Aust
60D2 Yartsevo Russian Fed
63B1 Yartsevo Russian Fed
32B2 Yarumal Colombia
97C3 Yashi Nig
97C4 Yashikera Nig
61F4 Yashkul' Russian Fed
84C1 Yasin Pak
59C3 Yasinya Ukraine
109C2 Yass Aust
109C2 Yass R Aust
75A1 Yasugi Japan
18A2 Yates Center USA
74C4 Yatolema Zaire
74C4 Yatsushiro Japan
84B3 Yatta Israel
32C4 Yavari Peru
85D4 Yavatmāl India
74C4 Yavoatmai India
76D2 Ya Xian China
90B3 Yazd Iran
90B3 Yazd-e Khvāst Iran
19B3 Yazoo R USA

X

84D1 Xaidulla China
72D1 Xai Moron He R China
101C3 Xai Xai Mozam
23B2 Xaltinguis Mexico
100A2 Xangongo Angola
46D1 Xanten Germany
55B3 Xanthi Greece
100B3 Xau,L Botswana
14B3 Xenia USA
72A2 Xiahe China
73D5 Xiamen China
72B3 Xi'an China

19B3 Yazoo City USA
76B2 Ye Myan
59D3 Yedintsy Moldova
108A2 Yeelanna Aust
60E3 Yefremov
 Russian Fed
61F4 Yegorlyk R
 Russian Fed
90C2 Yei Sudan
65H4 Yekaterinburg
 Russian Fed
60E3 Yelets Russian Fed
44E1 Yell I Scot
87B1 Yellandu India
 Yellow = Huang He
8B1 Yellowhead P Can
4G3 Yellowknife Can
5G4 Yellowmead P Can
109C2 Yellow Mt Aust
69E3 Yellow Sea China/
 Korea
8C2 Yellowstone R USA
8C2 Yellowstone L USA
6B1 Yelverton B Can
97C3 Yelwa Nig
81C4 Yemen Republic,
 Arabian Pen
76C1 Yen Bai Viet
97B3 Yendi Ghana
76B2 Yengan Myan
63B2 Yeniseysk
 Russian Fed
63B1 Yeniseyskiy Kryazh
 Ridge Russian Fed
64J2 Yeniseyskiy Zal B
 Russian Fed
12D2 Yentna R USA
43C4 Yeo R Eng
109C2 Yeoval Aust
43C4 Yeovil Eng
63C1 Yerbogachen
 Russian Fed
75F4 Yerevan Armenia
21B2 Yerington USA
21B3 Yermo USA
69E1 Yerofey-Pavlovich
 Russian Fed
94B3 Yeroham Israel
61G3 Yershov Russian Fed
 Yerushalayim =
 Jerusalem
92C1 Yesil R Turk
94B2 Yesud Hama'ala
 Israel
109D1 Yetman Aust
82B6 Yetti Maur
93E1 Yevlakh Azerbaijan
60D4 Yevpatoriya
 Ukraine
69E2 Ye Xian China
64D2 Yeysk Russian Fed
55B2 Yiannitsá Greece
73A4 Yibin China
73C3 Yichang China
69E2 Yichun China
73C3 Yijun China
54C2 Yildiz Dağları Upland
 Turk
92C2 Yildizeli Turk
73A5 Yiliang China
72B2 Yinchuan China
72D3 Ying He R China
73D3 Yingkou China
73D3 Yingshan Hubei,
 China
73B3 Yingshan Sichuan,
 China
73D4 Yingtan China
82C1 Yining China
72B3 Yin Shan Upland
 China
99D2 Yirga Alem Eth
90D2 Yirol Sudan
62D3 Yirshi China
73B5 Yishan China
63D3 Yishui China
55B3 Yíthion Greece
38J6 Yivieska Fin
73C4 Yiyang China
38K5 Yli-Kitka L Fin
38J5 Yllornio Sweden
19A4 Yoakum USA
23B2 Yogope Mexico
78C4 Yogyakarta Indon

13D2 Yoho Nat Pk Can
98B2 Yokadouma Can
75B2 Yokkaichi Japan
75B1 Yokohama Japan
75B1 Yokosuka Japan
74C3 Yonago Japan
74E3 Yonezawa Japan
73D4 Yong'an China
72C3 Yongchang China
74B3 Yóngch'on S Korea
73C4 Yongchuan China
72A2 Yongdeng China
73D5 Yongding He R
74B3 Yôngdôk S Korea
74B3 Yônghúng N Korea
74B3 Yongju S Korea
72B2 Yongning China
16C2 Yonkers USA
49C2 Yonne R France
42D3 York Eng
18A1 York Nebraska, USA
16A3 York Pennsylvania,
 USA
107D2 York,C Aust
108A3 Yorke Pen Aust
108A3 Yorketown Aust
7A4 York Factory Can
41C3 Yorkshire Moors
 Moorland Eng
42D2 Yorkshire Wolds
 Upland Eng
5H4 Yorkton Can
22B2 Yosemite L USA
22C1 Yosemite Nat Pk
 USA
75A2 Yoshii R Japan
75A2 Yoshino R Japan
62C2 Yoshkar Ola
 Russian Fed
74B4 Yôsu S Korea
41B3 Youghal Irish Rep
45C3 Youghal Harb
 Irish Rep
73B5 You Jiang R China
109C2 Young Aust
34D2 Young Arg
111A2 Young Range Mts
 NZ
13E2 Youngstown Can
14B2 Youngstown Ohio,
 USA
22A1 Yountville USA
73B4 Youyang China
92B2 Yozgat Turk
20B2 Yreka USA
39G7 Ystad Sweden
43C3 Ystwyth R Wales
44C3 Ythan R Scot
73C4 Yuan Jiang R
 Hunan, China
73A5 Yuan Jiang R
 Yunnan, China
73A4 Yuanmu China
72C2 Yuanping China
21A2 Yuba City USA
74E2 Yúbari Japan
25D3 Yucatan Pen Mexico
25D2 Yucatan Chan
 Mexico/Cuba
72C2 Yuci China
63F2 Yudoma R
 Russian Fed
73D4 Yudu China
73A4 Yuexi China
73C4 Yueyang China
54A2 Yugoslavia
 Republic, Europe
73B5 Yu Jiang R China
12C2 Yukon R Can/USA
4E3 Yukon Territory Can
76E1 Yulin Guangdong,
 China
73C5 Yulin Guangxi, China
72B2 Yulin Shaanxi, China
9B3 Yuma USA
72B2 Yumen China
72A2 Yunan China
74A3 Yuncheng China
73C5 Yunkai Dashan Hills
 China
108A2 Yunta Aust
72C3 Yunxi China

72C3 Yun Xian China
73B3 Yunyang China
32B5 Yurimaguas Peru
73E5 Yu Shan Mt Taiwan
38L6 Yushkozero
 Russian Fed
72D2 Yushu Tibet, China
73A5 Yuxi China
74F2 Yuzhno-Kuril'sk
 Russian Fed
69G2 Yuzhno-Sakhalinsk
 Russian Fed
61J3 Yuzh Ural Mts
 Russian Fed
46A2 Yvelines Department,
 France
47B1 Yverdon Switz

Z

56A2 Zaandam Neth
93D2 Zãb al Babir R Iraq
93D2 Zãb as Saghir R Iraq
68D2 Zabaykal'sk
 Russian Fed
93B2 Zabreh
 Czech Republic
59B2 Zabrze Pol
23A2 Zacapu Mexico
24B2 Zacatecas Mexico
23B2 Zacatepec Morelos,
 Mexico
23B2 Zacatepec Oaxaca,
 Mexico
23B2 Zacatlan Mexico
23A1 Zacoalco Mexico
23B1 Zacualtipam Mexico
52C2 Zadar Croatia
76B3 Zadetkyi I Myan
50A2 Zafra Spain
96C1 Zagazig Egypt
96B1 Zagora Mor
52C1 Zagreb Croatia
91D4 Zãhedãn Iran
94B2 Zahle Leb
51C2 Zahrez Chergui
 Marshland Alg
61H2 Zainsk Russian Fed
98C3 Zaire Republic, Africa
98B3 Zaire R Zaire/Congo
54B2 Zaječar Yugos
62E2 Zakamensk
 Russian Fed
93D2 Zakho Iraq
55B3 Zákinthos I Greece
59B3 Zakopane Pol
59B3 Zalaegerszeg Hung
54B1 Zalãu Rom
95A2 Zaltan Libya
89H9 Zambesi R Mozam
100B2 Zambezi Zambia
100B2 Zambezi R Zambia
100B2 Zambia Republic,
 Africa
79B4 Zamboanga Phil
79B4 Zamboanga Pen
 Phil
58C2 Zambrów Pol
32B4 Zamora Ecuador
24B2 Zamora Mexico
50A1 Zamora Spain
59C2 Zamosć Pol
72A3 Zamtang China
98B3 Zanaga Congo
52B2 Záncara R Spain
84D2 Zanda China
14B3 Zanesville USA
84D3 Zangla India
72A1 Zanjan Iran
34B2 Zanjitas Arg
99D3 Zanzibar Tanz
99D3 Zanzibar I Tanz
96C3 Zaouatallaz Alg

72D3 Zaozhuang China
93D2 Zap R Turk
39K7 Zapadnaja Dvina R
65H3 Zapadno-Sibirskaya
 Nizmennost'
 Lowland Russian Fed
63B2 Zapadnyy Sayan Mts
 Russian Fed
34A3 Zapala Arg
60E4 Zaporozh'ye Ukraine
93C2 Zara Turk
23A1 Zaragoza Mexico
50B1 Zaragoza Spain
90B2 Zarand Iran
90C3 Zarand Iran
80E2 Zaranj Afghan
33D2 Zarara Ven
58D1 Zarasai Lithuania
34D2 Zárate Arg
90B3 Zard Kuh Mt Iran
12H3 Zaremba I USA
82B3 Zarghun Shahr
 Afghan
84B2 Zargun Mt Pak
97C3 Zaria Nig
92C3 Zarqa Jordan
94B2 Zarqa R Jordan
32B4 Zaruma Ecuador
58B2 Zary Pol
96D1 Zarzis Tunisia
84D2 Zãskãr Mts India
84D2 Zãskãr R India
94C2 Zatara R Jordan
 Zatoka Gdanska =
 Gdansk,G of
69E1 Zavitinsk
 Russian Fed
59B2 Zawiercie Pol
63C2 Zayarsk Russian Fed
65K5 Zaysan Kazakhstan
82D3 Zayü China
68B4 Zayü Mt China
46B1 Zeebrugge Belg
94B3 Zeelim Israel
101G1 Zeerust S Africa
94B2 Zefat Israel
94C3 Zegueren
 Watercourse Mali
99E1 Zeila Somalia
57C2 Zeitz Germany
72A2 Zekog China
61G2 Zelenodol'sk
 Russian Fed
39K6 Zelenogorsk
 Russian Fed
47D1 Zell Austria
47B1 Zermatt Switz
69F2 Zeya Russian Fed
63A2 Zeya Res
 Russian Fed
50A1 Zézere R Port
94B3 Zghorta Leb
72D1 Zgierz Pol
72D1 Zhangjiakou China
73D4 Zhangping China
72D2 Zhangwei He R
 China
72E1 Zhangwu China
72A2 Zhangye China
73D5 Zhangzhou China
73C5 Zhanjiang China
73A4 Zhanyi China
73C5 Zhaoqing China
73A4 Zhaotong China
73A4 Zhaoyang Hu L
 China
61J4 Zharkamys
 Russian Fed
63E1 Zhatay Russian Fed
73D4 Zhejiang Province,
 China
67F3 Zhengou China

Zyyi

72C3 **Zhengzhou** China
72D3 **Zhenjiang** China
73A4 **Zhenxiong** China
73B4 **Zhenyuan** China
61F3 **Zherdevka**
    Russian Fed
73C3 **Zhicheng** China
68C1 **Zhigalovo**
    Russian Fed
73B4 **Zhijin** China
58D2 **Zhitkovichi** Belarus
60C3 **Zhitomir** Ukraine
60D3 **Zhlobin** Belarus
60C4 **Zhmerinka** Ukraine
84B2 **Zhob** Pak
58D2 **Zhodino** Latvia
72B2 **Zhongning** China
112C10 **Zhongshan** Base
    Ant
73C5 **Zhongshan** China
72B2 **Zhongwei** China
68B4 **Zhougdian** China
73E3 **Zhoushan Quandao**
    Arch China
72E2 **Zhuanghe** China
72A3 **Zhugqu** China
73C3 **Zhushan** China

73C4 **Zhuzhou** China
72D2 **Zibo** China
106C3 **Ziel,Mt** Aust
58B2 **Zielona Góra** Pol
76A1 **Zigaing** Myan
73A4 **Zigong** China
97A3 **Ziguinchor** Sen
23A2 **Zihuatanejo** Mexico
94B2 **Zikhron Ya'aqov**
    Israel
59B3 **Zilina** Slovakia
95A2 **Zillah** Libya
47D1 **Ziller** R Austria
47D1 **Zillertaler Alpen** Mts
    Austria
58D1 **Zilupe** Russian Fed
63C2 **Zima** Russian Fed
23B1 **Zimapan** Mexico
23B2 **Zimatlan** Mexico
100B2 **Zimbabwe** Republic,
    Africa
94B3 **Zin** R Israel
23B2 **Zinacatepec** Mexico
23A2 **Zinapécuaro** Mexico
97C3 **Zinder** Niger
73C4 **Zi Shui** China
23A2 **Zitácuaro** Mexico

57C2 **Zittau** Germany
72D2 **Ziya He** R China
72A3 **Ziyang** China
61J2 **Zlatoust**
    Russian Fed
59B3 **Zlin** Czech Republic
65K4 **Zmeinogorsk**
    Russian Fed
58B2 **Znin** Pol
59B3 **Znoimo**
    Czech Republic
100B3 **Zoekmekaar**
    S Africa
47B1 **Zofinger** Switz
72A3 **Zoigê** China
59D3 **Zolochev** Ukraine
101C2 **Zomba** Malawi
98B2 **Zongo** Zaire
92B1 **Zonguldak** Turk
97B4 **Zorzor** Lib
96A2 **Zouerate** Maur
54B1 **Zrenjanin** Serbia,
    Yugos
47C1 **Zug** Switz
47D1 **Zugspitze** Mt
    Germany
50A2 **Zujar** R Spain

100C2 **Zumbo** Mozam
23B2 **Zumpango** Mexico
97C4 **Zungeru** Nig
73B4 **Zunyi** China
76D1 **Zuo** R China
73B5 **Zuo Jiang** R China
47C1 **Zürich** Switz
47C1 **Zürichsee** L Switz
95A1 **Zuwárah** Libya
95A2 **Zuwaylah** Libya
61H2 **Zuyevka**
    Russian Fed
100B4 **Zvishavane** Zim
59B3 **Zvolen** Slovakia
54A2 **Zvornik** Bosnia-
    Herzegovina
97B4 **Zwedru** Lib
46D2 **Zweibrücken**
    Germany
47B1 **Zweisimmen** Switz
57C2 **Zwickau** Germany
56B2 **Zwolle** Neth
58C2 **Zyrardów** Pol
65K5 **Zyryanovsk**
    Kazakhstan
59B3 **Żywiec** Pol
94A1 **Zyyi** Cyprus